Encyclopedia
Macintosh

Encyclopedia
Macintosh®

Craig Danuloff

Deke McClelland

San Francisco · Paris · Düsseldorf · Soest

Acquisitions Editor: Dianne King
Editor: Eric Stone
Book Designer: Ingrid Owen
Technical Art: Deke McClelland
Typesetter: Publishing Resources Inc.
Proofreader: Edith Rex
Indexer: Julie Kawabata
Cover Designer: Thomas Ingalls + Associates
Cover Photographer: Michael Lamotte

Library of Congress Card Number: 89-63176
ISBN: 0-89588-628-6
Manufactured in the United States of America
10 9 8 7 6

Early one morning in March or April of 1984 I found myself having breakfast with a group of people I didn't know. The strange thing about this, beyond the fact that I was awake at that time of day, was that the breakfast was part of the interview process for a computer-store sales job. The group around me was the current staff of "sales representatives," and the meal was supposed to allow them to size me up.

I was feeling quite confident as we began. After all, I had my own IBM PC, knew WordStar, Lotus 1-2-3, and dBASE II, and was generally the cocky sort. I soon noticed, however, that none of these people seemed to care much about the PC or its software, and that the words *Apple*, *Lisa*, and *Macintosh* were getting tossed around quite a bit. As the conversation continued, I became aware of the fact that everyone except me was wearing an Apple pin, carrying an Apple pen, or writing on an Apple notepad. There were other jobs, I told myself. And besides, the more time I spent with this group, the more I felt like a Moonie who didn't like flowers.

When I was hired, the manager told me it was because they needed someone who would sell their IBM PCs and not push everyone into a Macintosh. For about 18 months I was the odd man out at that store, constantly engaging in good-natured arguments with my coworkers about the virtues of the PC versus the Mac.

Needless to say, I eventually was won over. Today I've got my own Apple pen, and probably scare others away when I start talking about the Mac.

This book is dedicated to the runny eggs I ate in March or April of 1984.

Craig M. Danuloff

Just coffee for me, thanks.

D. H. McClelland, II

Acknowledgments

For our involvement in this project we thank Dianne King at Sybex and Bill Gladstone at Waterside Productions. Both showed great faith at the outset of this project, and endurance as it has developed.

A number of people at Sybex worked very hard on the production of this book. In particular, our sincere thanks to Eric Stone for editing and reediting our endless changes and additions, and keeping the goals of the project in focus. This book is significantly improved as a result of his hard work. We also thank Edith Rex and the other Sybex proofreaders (and the many red pens that gave their lives).

At Publishing Resources Inc., we thank Tom Midgley and Ian Thompson for their research assistance and technical support, Scott Harmon for his Linotronic skills, and Susan Janow for keeping the whole thing moving ahead smoothly.

John Duane provided programming and design services for the HyperCard stack version of this book. Thanks, Duke.

A great number of software companies and their representatives provided us with evaluation software, technical information, and technical support. These include Sara Charf and Mike Poole at Microsoft, Renée Matthews at Claris, Carl Jamison at Aldus, Larry Davis at Alsoft, Jim Von Ehr at Altsys, Rick Barron at Affinity Microsystems, Lavon Collins and Julie Hurd at Adobe Systems, Zoe Roizen at T/Maker, Tracy Owens and Martha Keaveny at Ashton-Tate, Sue Nail at CE Software, Stuart Henigson at Silicon Beach, Nichole Noland at Electronic Arts, and Matthew Smith at Preferred Publishers.

1, 2, 3, 4, 5, 6, 8, 8, 9: R.D., S.R., J.G., A.E., and J.M.

Deepest gratitude to Elizabeth Pheasant for countless lunches, pots of coffee, lots of love, and everything else that goes with a perfect marriage. Every book I write is dedicated to you.

Special thanks to each of the following for their technical reviews and assistance:

Loftus E. Becker, Jr.

Scott Converse

Ed Glascow

Sandy Greenberg

Micheal Kimble

Clayton Klayburner

Mel Potter

David Ramsey

Contents

Section Two
Applications

Section Three
Hardware

Section Four
Resources

Section Five
Glossary

Introduction

en·cy′·clo·pe′·di·a

a book or set of books containing articles on various topics, usually in alphabetical arrangement, covering all branches of knowledge or, less commonly, all aspects of one single subject

— Random House Dictionary of the English Language

It's amazing how much influence a single word can have. When this book was in its earliest stages, we knew that we wanted to present the most comprehensive collection of information about the Macintosh ever assembled, but we were having some trouble deciding on the very best way to accomplish this task. When the word *encyclopedia* became associated with the project, everything suddenly fell into place.

Of course, the prospect of sitting down to write an encyclopedia is a little daunting. Fortunately, we did not have to start entirely from scratch, because so much information about the Macintosh was available for use in our research. In fact, most people would agree that the problem with information about the Macintosh hasn't been its scarcity, but its organization. It has been nearly impossible to quickly find the exact information you need, although almost anyone will tell you, "I've seen that somewhere."

The best Macintosh information has been scattered across hundreds of magazines, newsletters, technical manuals, and books, a few HyperCard stacks, thousands of on-line messages, and the brains of a relatively small number of Mac enthusiasts. So to create *Encyclopedia Macintosh*, we scoured every conceivable Macintosh-related information source, talked with all the Mac experts we could find, and dusted off our own bag of tips and tricks. Then we clarified and organized all of this information, and packed the explanations, tips, and product reviews we thought Mac users should know about into this book.

Three kinds of Mac users were kept in mind throughout this process: the one who just wants to get some work done (and is not yet a "Cult of Macintosh" member), the aspiring "power-user" (who has had the interest but not the time or information resources), and the full-fledged Mac maniac (who loves the Mac and wants to know everything about it). As a result, you'll find that we have included enough introductory information to allow the occasional user to reap the full benefit of all this information; provided explanations of how and why things work, and discussions of vital utilities, that will allow almost anyone to attain true power-user status; and sprinkled it all with little-known-facts and never-before-available listings so that even the most well informed Mac users will find themselves clearing a little shelf space within arm's reach of their Mac.

What You Need to Know

To get the most benefit from *Encyclopedia Macintosh*, you need only be comfortable with the basic operation of your Mac. If you know how to start your Mac up and run your software, you should have enough grounding to make use of all the information we present. If you are sort of a Macintosh beginner, you may want to read through the introductory text in each entry before going back to read the tips, product reviews, and Quick References. You may also want to make frequent use of the cross-references we've included, and the Glossary in Section 5.

If you are comfortable on the Mac, we think you'll find all the detail each entry in this book includes very informative. Feel free to jump around the entries or even between sections—this book was not written with any linear pathway in mind. Most often you'll probably use it as a reference or a problem-solving tool, searching for specific answers to the questions or problems you encounter while using your Mac. You should find both the Contents and the Index helpful for quickly locating specific information.

How This Book Is Organized

This book is arranged very much like a real encyclopedia, except instead of having different volumes, we use *sections* as our major divisions. Our five sections are System Software & Utilities, Applications, Hardware, Resources, and Glossary. Each section is divided into alphabetically ordered *entries,* ranging from 3 to 30 pages apiece. Each entry provides complete explanations, tips, product reviews, and in some cases convenient Quick Reference charts.

Within most entries you will find liberal cross-references to related information in other entries or even other sections. To help you in navigating the various sections and entries, we've included the section name in the upper-left corner of left-hand pages, as well as the current entry name in the upper-right corner of right-hand pages. A listing of all entries in the book is included in the Table of Contents. A complete index is at the back of the book.

Here's what you will find in each of the five sections:

Section 1: System Software & Utilities. In this section we examine every aspect of the software and utilities that help you control your Macintosh, organize your disks and files, and work more productively in your software applications. Any software that is not designed to create or modify data, but rather to manage your hardware and other software applications, or to provide a utility function, is covered in this section.

Included here are introductory explanations, extensive tip listings, and reviews of important software utilities. Much of the software reviewed in this section is noncommercial software—it is not sold through normal software-distribution channels but instead is distributed through user groups and on-line services—falling into the public-domain, shareware, and freeware categories. These software packages are not normally reviewed in the popular Macintosh press, but offer tremendous features that you may want to take advantage of.

Section 2: Applications. This section is dedicated to the major Macintosh software categories: word processors, spreadsheets, painting software, drawing software, page-composition software, and HyperCard. For each of these we introduce the basic concepts that make software in this category useful, and the features that distinguish the available packages from one another. We then look directly at each of the major software packages in each category, providing tip lists and Quick References containing extensive keyboard charts and menu maps. For software applications that you are already using, this one-stop-shopping assembly of information will allow you to file away a whole stack of software manuals, and have quick access to the kind of reference information you need on a daily basis. For software you are not using, our complete coverage enables you to get a good idea of the features and interface each package offers, so you can make a more informed buying decision.

Section 3: Hardware. In this section a wide range of hardware-related topics are covered. We look at add-on products and peripherals, compare the various Macintosh models to help you decide on upgrading or new purchases, document many types of do-it-yourself maintenance and upgrades (including RAM installation), and provide technical specifications for various ports on your Macintosh. Additionally, this section includes a number of simple explanations of how parts of your computer and peripheral devices operate; this will help you to use your machine more productively and to troubleshoot problems more successfully.

Section 4: Resources. Although we have tried to include all the information you'll ever need here in *Encyclopedia Macintosh*, this section directs you to hundreds of other information sources, just in case. You'll find a complete list of Macintosh books, magazines, and bulletin boards, information about user groups, and vendor and product information for every product mentioned anywhere in *Encyclopedia Macintosh*.

Section 5: Glossary. Like any glossary, this section is designed to help you understand terms and phrases you encounter in *Encyclopedia Macintosh* or in other Macintosh-related information sources.

About Our Tips

Almost every entry in the System Software & Utilities and Applications sections includes tip lists. In an effort to make these lists most useful to you, we have arranged our tips in a logical order: beginning tips first, then intermediate tips, and finally advanced tips. Of course, deciding whether a particular tip is beginning, intermediate, or advanced is somewhat subjective, so you shouldn't take these ratings too strictly. Their purpose is to allow advanced users to skip over tips they probably already know, and to inform less experienced users which tips may be slightly more advanced. Our classifications are based on both the technical level of the tip itself, and its obscurity.

The rating of a tip can be discerned from the kind of symbol that precedes it. Hollow diamonds precede beginning tips, semihollow diamonds precede intermediate tips, and solid diamonds precede advanced tips, like this:

◇   This is a beginning tip, as indicated by the hollow diamond.

◈   This is an intermediate tip, as indicated by the semihollow diamond.

◆   This is an advanced tip, as indicated by the solid diamond.

About Our Product Reviews

The System Software & Utilities and Applications sections also include reviews of a wide number of software products. These reviews are not thorough product analyses or comparisons, but rather are designed to alert you to the existence and best features of many impressive products. Vendor information and pricing for each product mentioned anywhere in this book are included in Section 4.

Although you'll find an extensive array of software presented in this format, these lists are not totally comprehensive. It would have been impossible for us to cover every application and utility in existence, especially in the noncommercial software categories. If you run across software that is similar to some we've discussed, you might find it helpful to compare its features with those we have presented. If you think you've found something really useful, please let us know about it.

In the System Software & Utilities section, each product is accompanied by several icons that we use to call out extensive memory requirements, report the commercial or noncommercial status of the product, rate exceptionally good or bad products, and indicate color compatibility. In the Applications section, these icons are replaced with a list of the file formats supported by each particular application. The following icons are used in the System Software & Utilities section:

Two megabytes of RAM required
The software needs a minimum of 2 or 4 megabytes of RAM, respectively.

Public-domain software
The software is in the public domain. This software is available without charge, and can be used or modified in any way; the author has given up

all rights to it. Note that much of what is often called public-domain software is really freeware. The terminology isn't completely universal, although it is becoming so, and many older products were called public-domain when their authors meant them to be freeware. We have classified software as freeware unless it is specifically designated as public-domain by its author.

Freeware

There is no charge for the software, but the developer retains its copyright. This means you can obtain and use this software without any cost, and freely distribute it, as long as you do not modify it.

Shareware

Shareware software is available without charge, but only so that you can try it out. If you decide that you want to keep the product and continue to use it, you must mail the software author a registration fee. This registration process entitles you to continue using the product, and in some cases you get a new version and documentation, bonus utilities, or even additional software.

Commercial software

You can buy commercial software from the vendor or their dealers.

Thumbs up

This icon indicates that we like this software, because it either provides very useful features or represents a good value.

Thumbs down

This software we don't like. Usually our reasons for this are explained in the accompanying review.

Color-compatible

A program preceded by this icon supports or takes advantage of color. Not every program that runs in color gets this icon, only those whose support of color is more than incidental.

About Our Quick References

Another feature of the Applications section is Quick References, which are included for all major software applications. Quick References contain toolbox descriptions, menu maps, and keyboard-equivalent charts. Keyboard charts include alphabetical listings of every keyboard equivalent the application supports. Legends to the symbols used to represent the special keys on your Mac keyboard are included on the left-hand page of each keyboard-equivalent chart.

Conventions

To make your reading easier, we have followed a number of typographic and symbolic conventions throughout this book:

- Literal menu names, command names, button text, and key names are set in SMALL CAPS.

- The names of options found inside dialog boxes are listed "in quotes."

- Words that are included in our Glossary in Section 5 are **bold**. Note, however, that not every occurrence of a glossary word has been bold-faced, so whenever you encounter a word whose definition you are not sure of, you should check the Glossary.

- The symbols below have been used in Quick Reference lists to represent keys on the Macintosh keyboard. These are commonly accepted symbols for these keys, appearing in the menus and dialog boxes of many of the most popular software applications.

⌘ **Command or Apple key**
Available on all keyboards, twice on extended keyboards.

⇧ **Shift key**
Available twice on all keyboards.

⌥ **Option or alt key**
Available on all keyboards, twice on extended keyboards.

⌃ **Control key**
Available on standard SE keyboards and later, twice on extended keyboards.

⇥ **Tab key**
Available on all keyboards.

↩ **Return key**
Available on all keyboards.

⌃ **Enter key**
Available on Mac Plus keyboards and later.

⌫ **Delete or backspace key**
Available on all keyboards.

⌦ **Forward delete (del) key**
Available on extended keyboards only.

⎋ **Escape (esc) key**
Available on standard SE keyboards and later.

⎵ **Space bar**
Available on all keyboards.

⌨ **Keypad key**
This symbol precedes characters that must be accessed from the keypad, available on Mac Plus keyboards and later.

↑← **Arrow keys**
→↓ Available on Mac Plus keyboards and later.

F1 **Function keys**
Available on extended keyboards only.

• Many Macintosh software operations involve operating your mouse on its own or while pressing a key. The symbols used to denote mouse actions are shown below.

⬉ **Click**
Clicking involves moving an on-screen cursor over an icon or other screen image and quickly pressing and releasing the mouse button. Clicking is employed most often to select or activate an icon, element, or tool.

⬉⬉ **Double-click**
This action involves quickly pressing and releasing the mouse button twice in rapid succession. Some application operations call for triple clicking, quadruple clicking, and so on.

Drag
When you drag with a mouse, you press and hold the mouse button, move the mouse to a different location, and then release. Dragging is a common technique for moving icons and for drawing.

Option-click
Option-clicking involves pressing the option key while clicking with your mouse. Generally, the key is pressed before clicking and released after the click is completed. Variations include shift-clicking, shift-option-clicking, option-dragging, and so on.

The Suggestion Box

The information that is included in this edition of *Encyclopedia Macintosh* has been culled from a very wide range of sources in the Macintosh community. Because we intend to keep this book up to date with periodic revisions, we invite you to let us know about any tips, tricks, or products that you feel should be included in future editions of *Encyclopedia Macintosh,* or to send us comments about this edition. We can be reached by mail at Publishing Resources Inc., 1750-1 30th Street #602, Boulder, CO, 80301; on CompuServe at 76566,1722; on the Connect Information Service (MacNet) at PUBRES; or on AppleLink at PUBRES.

Section One

System Software & Utilities

Chooser

Apple's Chooser desk accessory is used primarily to select the printer driver that will be used when the PAGE SETUP or PRINT command is chosen. The Chooser is also used by AppleShare and other networking products to select file-server volumes and network zones. Devices that appear in the Chooser have a file type of either PRER or RDEV. See the Printer Drivers entry later in this section for more information about specific drivers.

In the Chooser's "User name" option box, you enter a name that will identify your Mac on an AppleTalk network. This name appears in the PRINT STATUS dialog box, is seen by other network users in their PRINT STATUS dialog boxes when you are printing, and is used by some other network software and utilities. Note that under AppleShare, your user name is not necessarily the name used to register your station on the network, although you may want to make these two the same in order to minimize confusion.

The "AppleTalk" option, with its "On" and "Off" radio buttons, must be set "On" when AppleTalk cabling is connected to your Mac and you will be using any network devices or communicating via the AppleTalk network. It should be set "Off" when no AppleTalk cabling is connected to your Mac.

Under MultiFinder, the Chooser's "Background printing" option provides **print spooling** for all PostScript printing; this allows you to continue working as your documents are printed. The "Background printing" option is dimmed (unavailable) when you are not using MultiFinder, or when the Backgrounder file is not in your System folder. See the MultiFinder entry later in this section for complete details.

Chooser Tips

◇ **Enable Chooser drivers by placing them in the System folder**. Each time the Chooser is opened, it looks through the System folder, presenting in its left window the icons of all valid printer and network drivers found in the System folder.

◇ **Disable Chooser drivers by removing them from the System folder**. The Chooser cannot access drivers from any other location, so you may keep unused drivers elsewhere on your drive or diskette. You can even keep these drivers in a folder inside the System folder; they will not be available to the Chooser.

◇ **The name of the Chooser's programmer appears when you click on the Chooser version number**.

◇ **Use the LaserWriter driver to prepare files for PostScript printing even when no LaserWriter is attached to your Mac.** Adding a Laser-Writer driver to your System folder allows you to prepare files for output on any PostScript printer, even if you don't have a PostScript printer attached to your Macintosh. This process is fully explained in the Printer Drivers entry later in this section.

Clipboard

The ability to cut and paste text or graphics either within or between applications has always been a cornerstone of Macintosh software. Regardless of the software you are using, the ever-present EDIT menu almost certainly contains the CUT (⌘-X), COPY (⌘-C), and PASTE (⌘-V) commands. The CLEAR command is also common, allowing you to delete the current selection without transferring it to the Clipboard, thus maintaining the current Clipboard contents.

Virtually any element in any application offering the CUT and COPY commands can be transferred to the Clipboard. However, elements in nonstandard formats (any format other than TEXT, PICT, and MPNT) can only be pasted within or between applications supporting those formats. The TEXT, PICT, and MPNT formats can be considered standard formats since almost every Macintosh application accepts them. When the contents of the Clipboard are pasted into the Scrapbook, the format(s) contained in the element are listed in the lower-right corner of the Scrapbook window.

Clipboard Tips

◇ **Clipboard contents are lost when the Mac is shut down.** If your Mac crashes, or if it is shut down or restarted, information on the Clipboard is lost; you can no longer paste the last cut or copied object when the computer is restarted. Several utilities are available to save the contents of your Clipboard to the Clipboard file in your System folder in the event of a System crash, thereby eliminating the possibility of losing Clipboard data.

◇ **You can transfer Clipboard objects to the Scrapbook for long-term storage.** Since the Clipboard content is replaced as soon as another object is cut or copied, and since Clipboard contents are lost on crash or shutdown, you should save objects that have been moved to the Clipboard to a more permanent location, such as the Scrapbook or another file, if you do not wish to lose them.

◇ **The Clipboard is not cleared when an application is quit.** The last cut or copied object remains on the Clipboard as long as your Mac is running. This allows you to cut or copy an object from one application, launch another application, and then paste the Clipboard contents in the new application. Using this method, you can transfer objects between many applications that do not have compatible file formats as long as their Clipboard formats are compatible. When using this method of transfer, you should always use the COPY command rather than the CUT command to avoid the possibility of data loss due to a System crash.

◇ **Clipboard contents will usually (but not always) remain when you switch between applications in MultiFinder.** Some applications unexpectedly get an empty Clipboard when you switch to them under MultiFinder. Returning to the previous application will regain the Clipboard content, which you can then transfer via the Scrapbook.

◇ **Larger Clipboard contents may be saved to disk.** If the contents of the Clipboard cannot fit in those sections of RAM allocated to the Clipboard, the Clipboard data may be written to disk. Some applications always save their Clipboard contents to disk. The Clipboard size at which the Clipboard is automatically saved to disk is dependent upon the application that you are using. On a Macintosh with 1 megabyte of RAM, the Clipboard may contain up to 400K before saving to disk. Using disk space expands the theoretical limit of the Clipboard to the size of your hard drive. When quitting an application you may occasionally see the SAVE LARGE CLIPBOARD TO DISK? dialog box. If you may need the Clipboard contents later, click the YES button.

◇ **You can delete the Clipboard file at any time**. Deleting the Clipboard file from your System folder may cause you to lose the current contents of the Clipboard, but will have no other effect. A new Clipboard file will be created when it is needed.

◇ **The ⌫ key deletes selected objects without disturbing the current Clipboard contents**. To remove an object without transferring it to the Clipboard, select the object(s) and then use the BACKSPACE key or CLEAR command. This will delete the selected object without transferring it to the Clipboard. By not moving the deleted object to the Clipboard, you avoid deleting the current Clipboard contents, which you may want to use again.

◆ **Minimizing the Clipboard's content will conserve memory**. Since the Clipboard content is usually kept in RAM, some memory is freed by replacing a large Clipboard object with a small one. (A single character would be the smallest object possible.) Depending on how the application stores its "Undo" data, you may also free additional RAM by copying a small object twice—once for the Clipboard and once for the Undo.

Clipboard Utilities

⊞ MultiClip

MultiClip is a DA/init that provides a superset of the Clipboard's functions and also has the features of an enhanced Scrapbook. Each time you cut or copy an object to MultiClip, the previous MultiClip objects are not replaced; instead, a new Clipboard frame containing the new object is added. Clipboard frames can hold objects in text, MacPaint, and PICT formats. You can then select any Clipboard frame to paste, or paste Clipboard frames in the same order as they were created or in the reverse order that they were created. A set of Clipboard frames can be saved to disk as a MultiClip file, or as a Scrapbook file; individual frames can be saved as independent graphic or text files. MultiClip can also convert existing Scrapbook files into a set of Clipboard frames.

MultiClip is a tremendous advance over Apple's Clipboard/Scrapbook system. Beyond its basic features, we like the fact that it provides a high degree of user customization, allows you to edit the text in text frames, and allows you to select subsections of graphic frames. If you do a lot of cutting and pasting, or manipulating of Scrapbook objects, you'll love MultiClip.

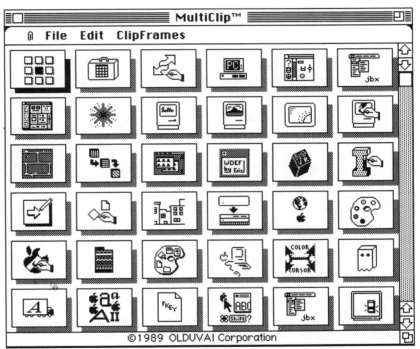

MultiClip is a Clipboard/Scrapbook replacement that can hold many different objects and allows you to easily paste any of them into your documents.

The Clipper
This handy DA allows you to quickly and accurately scale and trim the current Clipboard contents. Objects can be scaled to fit a certain size, to an exact measurement, or to a specific percentage of their original size. When used in MultiFinder or along with a painting or drawing DA, The Clipper becomes indispensable for importing your graphics into word-processing or page-composition applications.

ClipShare   ⬚⬚

This utility from Olduvai (which remains "vaporware" as this review is written) will allow you to send a Clipboard file via AppleTalk to any other network user. According to Olduvai, you may send the Clipboard to another user's Clipboard, or add it to their Scrapbook file. This is essentially a little E-Mail system just for Clipboard and Scrapbook data.

The value of ClipShare will depend upon how smoothly it is integrated into general Macintosh operation. If it takes as much effort to share your Clipboard as to E-mail a file or to simply transfer the Clipboard file via SneakerNet—the networking system whereby you carry a disk from one location to another—then who needs it? We suggest that you get some personal recommendations or check out magazine reviews before buying this product.

DeskPaint, Canvas, McSink, MocWrite   ⬚⬚, ⬚⬚, ⬚⬚, ⬚⬚

A number of desk accessories allow you to quickly edit graphics or text that are on the Clipboard. Some of these use the Clipboard contents by default, while others require you to paste the Clipboard elements before editing them.

Clipboard Magician   ⬚⬚

This rather rough DA/init, written by an Apple engineer, can convert data on the Clipboard between file and data formats, and add the data to existing files. Clipboard Magician includes manipulations for items in text, PICT, and MacPaint format, plus file information, data fork data, and resource fork resources. For example, after a PICT graphic has been transferred to the Clipboard, it can be transformed into an ICON, SICN, or CURS resource, added to the data or resource fork of any file, printed, or dumped in hex format. Each type of data has its own list of available manipulations.

Included with Clipboard Magician is information that allows programmers to create and add new manipulations. Because Clipboard Magician is rather technically oriented, it is not for everyone; but as a demonstration of powerful data manipulation implemented in a very simple manner, it is a very impressive utility.

Connectivity

In the "good old days," the problem of connecting Macintosh and PC computers together, or sharing data between these computers, did not exist, because Macintosh users wanted nothing to do with anyone who used a PC, and vice versa. Today, due to the Mac's successful penetration of the business market, it is common and accepted for PCs and Macs to exchange data, share peripheral devices, and even share applications.

To share data between a Mac and a PC, two things must happen: The file must be *transferred* and the data must be *converted*. File transfer is the physical movement of the file from Mac to PC or PC to Mac. Data conversion changes the **file format** of your data so that it can be used in your destination software. Some file-transfer utilities also provide data conversion—combining transfer and conversion into a single step—while others require that conversion be performed separately. Some files do not need to be converted, because they are already in a format that can be used on the other machine. Examples of files that do not need to be converted include text (ASCII) files, which can be used on both PCs and Macs; files from applications running in both environments, whose file formats have been specifically designed to run on both machines (like PageMaker); and files that can be converted as they are saved, such as in Excel, which can save files in the Lotus .WKS format.

File Transfer Utilities

File transfer can be accomplished in four different ways: cable connections, local area networks, DOS-compatible disk drives attached to the Mac (or Mac-compatible drives attached to the PC), and telecommunications. The method that is best for you depends on the amount of data you need to transfer, how often you will have to transfer data, and the type of file-format conversion you require. Cable connections or local area networks are the best choice if your file-transfer needs are heavy and you have both a Macintosh and a PC in the same location. DOS-compatible disk drives allow you to transfer files without having a DOS computer, and telecommunications are best suited for occasional or long-distance file transfer.

Cable Connections

Cable connections are the least expensive method of transferring files between Macs and PCs, involving a simple cable connection and software that runs simultaneously on both computers. Of course, this method assumes that the machines are located very near to each other—within just a few feet. Five programs—MacLink Plus, LapLink Mac, xFer, QuickShare, and MacChuck—support this type of file transfer.

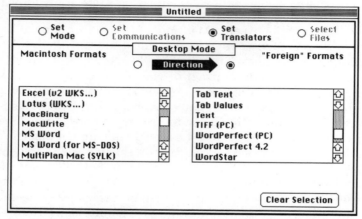

MacLink Plus supports the conversion of text files between most popular PC and Mac formats.

Many telecommunications packages can also transfer data between Mac and PC when they are linked via a serial connection. Of course, both telecommunications packages must support a common file-transfer format, and must specifically support serial communications.

 MacLink Plus, LapLink Mac, xFer, QuickShare, MacChuck   ⑤⑤
Each of these programs consists of software running simultaneously on a PC and a Macintosh that are physically connected. MacLink Plus, LapLink Mac, MacChuck, and xFer use a serial connection and support file transfer at speeds of up to 57000 baud. QuickShare uses a SCSI connection and can therefore increase the speed of data transfers by 150 times, although it does require that an add-on board (which is included with the software) be installed in the PC.

MacLink Plus, LapLink Mac, QuickShare, and xFer offer a wide range of popular data conversions during the file-transfer process. MacChuck provides no data conversion inherently, so you must use AFE or an equivalent to convert the transferred data files, if necessary.

Local Area Networks

Most of the **local area networks** (LANs) that support both Macs and PCs allow files to be transferred easily. Most LANs, however, do not offer inherent data conversion, so an external utility like Apple File Exchange must be used when file conversion is necessary. Using TOPS, for example, you can transfer files by simply mounting a disk or volume from one machine on the other, and then copying the file to or from that volume.

Compatible Disk Drives

Adding a DOS-compatible disk drive to the Macintosh, or a Macintosh-compatible disk drive to the PC, makes file transfer as easy as copying files from one disk to another. Apple's SuperDrive, included in the SE, SE/30, IIx, and IIcx, can read and write 3.5" PC disks in either 720K or 1.44MB format. Under System Software 6.0, Apple File Exchange must be used to transfer data to and from PC disks in the SuperDrive, but System 7.0 is rumored to allow PC disks to mount on the Finder desktop so that files can simply be drag-copied (although data conversion will still need to be performed separately, when required). An init called DOS Mounter, available from Dayna Communications, allows PC disks to mount on the Finder desktop using System Software 6.0.

Kennect Technology and PLI each offer external floppy drives with features similar to the Apple SuperDrive. Kennect's DRIVE 2.4 supports all available Macintosh, ProDOS, and PC formats, plus a proprietary format that can store 2.4 megabytes of data on a high-density floppy disk. PLI's TurboFloppy supports both Macintosh and PC formats. The main advantage of these drives is that they can be added to any existing Macintosh, and that they are priced lower than the Apple SuperDrive upgrade. Their only drawback is that they cannot mount PC disks on the Finder desktop.

DaynaFile is a disk drive that connects to any Mac with a SCSI port. It can be configured with a 1.2MB 5.25" PC drive, a 360K 5.25" PC drive, or a 1.44MB/720K 3.5" PC drive. Because the 360K and 1.2MB drives are separate—unlike the real PC, 1.2 megabyte Dayna drives cannot read 360K disks—and the DaynaFile cabinet only holds two drives, you cannot support all four PC disk formats (360K, 720K, 1.2MB, and 1.44MB) with a single DaynaFile. Included with the DaynaFile is a special version of MacLink Plus that provides extensive file-format conversion. PC disks inserted into a drive on the DaynaFile mount on the Finder desktop, so you can transfer files to and from these disks by drag-copying. DaynaFile is an excellent solution to PC/Mac data-transfer problems.

Apple also sells a 5.25" PC disk drive, but it can read only 360K PC disks. Unless you are sure that is the only format of drive you will ever need to read, we advise you against buying this product.

Two different drives that allow PCs to read Macintosh disks are available: MatchMaker from MicroSolutions, and Central Point Software's Deluxe Option Board. MatchMaker is an add-on board for the PC that allows an external Mac drive to be connected to the PC. The Deluxe Option Board uses the 3.5" drives already in your PC.

Telecommunications

Another way to transfer data between the Mac and a PC is to send the data over the phone lines (via modem) directly to the other computer, or to upload the data to a bulletin board and then have the other computer download it.

Transferring data via modem directly from the Mac to a PC, or vice versa, requires that the two telecommunications packages support a common transfer format, but this should not be a problem, because virtually any two packages will have some common formats. Once a connection has been established between the two computers and their telecommunications packages, data is transferred when the sender selects their software's SEND FILE command (or equivalent), and the receiver simultaneously selects their RECEIVE FILE command (or equivalent).

Many people find it easier to transfer their data to a bulletin board because uploading to and downloading from these services is usually far less complicated than establishing a connection and transferring files via a direct modem connection. Any file uploaded to a bulletin board by a Mac or PC can be downloaded by the other, but remember that this process accomplishes data transfer only; in most cases data conversion will have to be performed either before or after the transfer.

Data Conversion Utilities

 Apple File Exchange
Apple File Exchange (AFE) is a data-conversion program included with
the System Software; unfortunately, it is provided without any of the translators that would really make it useful. (Translators are the plug-in modules that direct the actual conversion from one format to another.) A few
translators can be found in the public domain, but the only way to obtain
a wide variety of translators is to purchase the MacLink Plus Translators.

 MacLink Plus Translators
These translators add the ability to convert files between all of the most
popular Macintosh formats (such as MacWrite, Microsoft Word, and text)
and the most popular PC file formats (including WordPerfect, WordStar,
Microsoft Word, and text)

Running Programs

There are several different ways to run DOS-based applications on a Macintosh. The first involves add-on *PC coprocessor boards,* hardware products
that provide your Mac with a PC-compatible coprocessor. PC coprocessor
boards are discussed in the Accelerators and Coprocessors entry in Section 3. Another method relies on software emulation to allow PC software
to run on the Mac. You can also connect your PC to your Mac, and control
programs that are running on the remote PC right from the Mac keyboard.

 SoftPC
When SoftPC was announced, most people did not believe that a software
product was going to allow them to run PC applications on any 68020 (or
68030) Macintosh. But SoftPC has proven its claims, allowing virtually any
application that runs on a PC/XT in either monochrome or CGA mode to
run on the Macintosh. SoftPC requires at least 2 megabytes of RAM (4 megabytes is preferred), and needs about 2 megabytes of hard-drive space for its
application files. (You will also want available hard-drive space to allow
SoftPC to create a PC disk drive on your Mac.)

Running SoftPC produces a window with the familiar DOS C> prompt, and
from that point it is operated just like a PC. Data can be accessed from your
Macintosh drives, from a remote PC floppy drive, from any PC hard-drive

volumes mounted via TOPS, or from a DaynaFile connected to your Macintosh. Software applications run at about the speed of an XT. SoftPC is a very good solution if you have a few PC programs that you like to run occasionally, or if you have one or two frequently used programs and would rather not keep a real PC around. SoftPC is MultiFinder-compatible, and allows you to transfer data to and from the application running in the SoftPC window using the Clipboard.

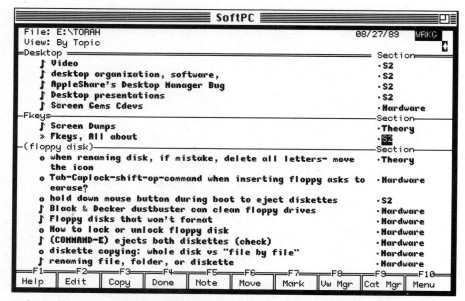

SoftPC allows any PC software to run on the Mac. Shown here is Lotus Agenda running in a SoftPC window on a Mac II.

 MacChuck

If you have a PC and would like to be able to run PC applications in a window on your Mac, MacChuck is for you. This amazing program puts your PC screen in a window on your Mac, and lets you control the PC from your Mac keyboard. You can connect your PC and Mac with the serial cable that accompanies MacChuck, or you can rely on your existing Apple-Talk connection if you are also using TOPS or AppleShare PC.

The best thing about MacChuck is its speed; the PC software is actually running on the PC, and so it runs just as fast as it always does. While your PC cannot be used for another purpose while being used with MacChuck, the PC's own keyboard and monitor remain functional. In fact you may want to just use MacChuck to monitor operations that are being run and controlled on the PC.

MacChuck provides utilities for transferring files from the Mac to the PC or from the PC to the Mac, and allows you to copy and paste text between the PC window and the Mac. MacChuck will run under MultiFinder, and uses only 160K of RAM to do so. We are very impressed with MacChuck, and think that if you already have a PC you will find that the speed and simplicity of MacChuck make it a better choice than SoftPC.

Control Panel

The Macintosh Control Panel, which is an Apple-supplied desk accessory, has always allowed Mac users to specify their preferences for basic Macintosh functions. Originally, the Control Panel only offered access to preferences regarding the System file and Finder: the ability to set the time and alarm clock, sound level, keyboard response rate, speed of insertion-point flashing, desktop pattern, and in later versions, the RAM cache. But since System file 4.0, any developer has been able to offer user-controlled features via the Control Panel. Software that takes advantage of this opportunity is known as a Control Device or cdev, and has the file type cdev.

In most cases, the cdev format is used when software provides relatively simple features and therefore does not require the more elaborate interface provided by a complete application or desk accessory. Inits offering system-level enhancements are a common example. Many peripherals, such as monitors and drawing tablets, also provide their software control in the Control Panel.

Control Panel Tips

◇ **Enable cdevs by placing them in the System folder.** Each time the Control Panel is opened, it looks through the System folder and displays the icons of all files with the cdev file type. Some cdevs, however, include init resources that require your Macintosh to be restarted before they will function properly. This is especially true of cdevs that control a hardware device. If a newly added cdev is not functioning properly, try rebooting the Mac. Similarly, changes made to the options of cdev/inits may not take effect until the Mac is restarted.

◇ **Disable cdevs by removing them from the System folder.** The Control Panel cannot access cdevs from any folder other than the one containing the System file and Finder. This allows you to keep unused cdevs anywhere else on your drive or diskette. You may even keep cdevs in a folder inside the System folder; they will not be available to the Control Panel.

◆ **Rearrange the order in which cdevs appear in the Control Panel by renaming them.** Cdevs are listed alphabetically in the Control Panel (with the exception of the General cdev, which usually appears at the top of the listing), so renaming them changes the order in which they appear. Use symbols and numbers in the cdev names to force specific cdevs to the top or bottom. To rename some of the Apple cdevs (such as General and Keyboard), you must first duplicate them and then rename the duplicates. (You can then trash the original files.) A cdev named Control-1, reviewed below, allows you to modify the alphabetization of cdevs as listed in the Control Panel.

◇ **Click the Control Panel's version number to see the names of the Control Panel's programmers.**

◇ **Cdevs list "Control Panel Document" in the TYPE column of the By Name, By Date, By Size, or By Kind windows at the Finder.**

◇ **Certain cdevs only appear in your Control Panel if you have the hardware to support them.** For example, the Sound, Color, and Monitors cdevs will not appear in the Control Panel of a Mac Plus or SE, even if they are in the System folder. The Startup Device cdev appears on SE, SE/30, and Mac II models, but not on the Mac Plus. Apple's Installer application does not install extraneous cdevs in your System folder, but if you updated system by simply dragging files from the System Software disks, your System folder may very well have unneeded cdevs, which you may remove (though they don't harm anything by being there).

◇ **Reset the parameter RAM (PRAM) on any Mac II or SE via the Control Panel**. Holding down SHIFT-COMMAND-OPTION while choosing the CONTROL PANEL command from the APPLE menu brings up the ZAP PRAM dialog box, which allows you to confirm or cancel reinitialization of your Mac's parameter RAM. MultiFinder must be turned off before this can be done, because the Control Panel cannot be accessed when the SHIFT key is pressed in MultiFinder. See the RAM entry in Section 4 for more information on the PRAM.

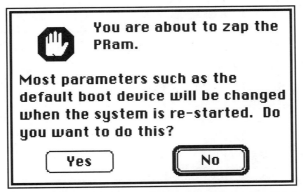

The ZAP PRAM dialog can be accessed from the Control Panel.

Cdev Utilities

 Control-1, DA menuz   ⑤⑤, ❧①⑤⑩
Control-1 allows you to select any cdev to automatically be at the top of the Control Panel's cdev list, regardless of the alphabetization. DA menuz adds a hierarchical menu to your Control Panel DA, allowing you to open the Control Panel directly to any cdev. See the Desk Accessories entry for more information about DA menuz.

 cdev shrinker   ⑤⑩
One drawback of using lots of cdevs is that the scrolling list in your Control Panel gets extremely long because the Control Panel displays the icon

for each cdev. The cdev shrinker eliminates this problem by eliminating the icons from the Control Panel scrolling list, leaving only the cdev names. This allows over 20 cdev names to appear in the listing before you need to scroll.

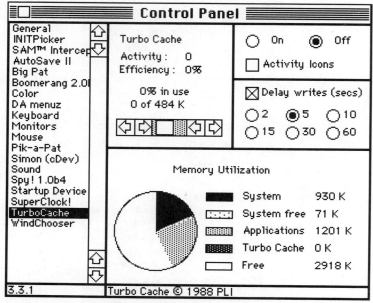

With the cdev Shrinker installed, your Control Panel displays the names of all cdevs being used instead of their icons.

Customization

It is often said that the Macintosh has a personality. If this is true, then each Macintosh user certainly has one as well. One manifestation of this is the tremendous amount of customization that Mac users perform.

You can customize your Mac in a number of ways. The applications, utilities, fonts, DA's, sounds, inits, and Fkeys you choose define one aspect of your Mac's personality, and your arrangement of files and folders adds another. Here we are going to look at several specific changes you can make to the way your Mac presents itself. Most of this customization is not difficult because it is made possible by the modular and extensible nature of Apple's System Software; this design allows Apple to easily upgrade and customize the Mac itself—localizing the Macintosh for different markets and fixing System Software bugs—but it is more commonly used by third-party Mac programmers and end-users who want to add features or change the way existing features are implemented.

Customizing Startup Screens

Normally, your Macintosh greets you with the familiar WELCOME TO MACINTOSH dialog box each time the machine is turned on or restarted. You can change this greeting either by modifying the message itself, or by replacing the dialog box entirely.

It used to be easy to modify the *Welcome to Macintosh* message with a utility called BootEdit, but unfortunately this utility hasn't been compatible with the last few versions of the System Software and ROMs. You can still change this message, however; search for the phrase *Welcome to Macintosh* in the System file's **resource fork** using one of the disk editors described in the Disks and Drives entry later in this section, and then replace this phrase with one of your own. Be careful not to exceed the 20 characters of the original message; doing so may damage other data in the resource and make it impossible to start your Mac using the altered System file. It would be a good idea to try your modification out on a floppy startup disk before implementing it on your hard drive.

You can replace the WELCOME TO MACINTOSH dialog box entirely with any bit-mapped image by converting the image into startup-screen format, naming it StartupScreen, and putting it in your System folder. Documents in MacPaint format can be converted into startup-screen format using one of several utilities, and many graphics applications now include startup-screen format as a standard file-format option. Utilities that can convert MacPaint images into startup-screen format include Widgets and Screen Maker, but these utilities only allow you to define startup screens the size of original 7-inch Mac monitors. On larger monitors these StartupScreen files will be centered on your display.

Some graphic applications can save files directly into startup-screen format. Applications offering startup-screen format include MacPaint 2.0, SuperPaint, NuPaint, and PixelPaint. Each of these allows you to create startup screens up to 12 inches wide, and provides you with control over how the image will be centered on your monitor.

Color startup screens can be used on color-equipped Macintoshes. If your color graphics software cannot save in startup-screen format you can transfer any color image into the StartupScreen file using ResEdit. To do this, first paste the color image you want to use into the Scrapbook. Open ResEdit, open the Scrapbook file, open the PICT resource, and then copy the color image. Now open an existing StartupScreen file, open its PICT resource, and select the PASTE command. Now use ResEdit's GET INFO command to give your color graphic an ID number of 0, and change the existing PICT=0 resources to use another ID number. Save these changes to the StartupScreen file, and your color ID=0 PICT resource is now your startup screen.

Startup Screen Utilities

Widgets, ScreenMaker
Each of these utilities allows you to select any MacPaint-format file and convert it into startup-screen format. Name this converted file *StartupScreen* and place it into your System folder and it will be displayed at startup.

Dawn
Looking at the same startup screen day after day, even if it is one you have customized, can become a little boring. Dawn (formerly ScreenMaster) allows you to configure up to ten different startup screens, one of which is then displayed each time you boot your Macintosh.

MacWelcome
When set as the startup application, MacWelcome displays a large dialog box containing a message of up to 100 lines for the user to read. This is designed for environments in which different people will be using the Macintosh and you want to give them initial instructions of some kind. MacWelcome allows you to specify another application to be launched after the message has been run, so you do not entirely waste your startup application on MacWelcome itself. It is MultiFinder-compatible.

Customizing the Desktop Pattern

As you probably know, the simplest way to customize your desktop pattern is to simply use the "Desktop pattern" option in the General cdev accessed in the Control Panel. Using ResEdit, you can edit these choices permanently by modifying the PAT# resources. You can also use files in MacPaint format as your desktop pattern by using one of the utility programs described below.

You can display any graphic file on your desktop by using DeskScene, ColorDesk, or Backdrop.

Desktop Pattern Utilities

 DeskScene   ⒻⓌ

This old utility (circa 1986, written by original Finder programmer Bruce Horn) still operates with System Software 6.0, allowing you to permanently or temporarily (until reboot) install any MacPaint file as your desktop pattern. It also provides a command to remove an installed desktop image, returning your original desktop pattern.

ColorDesk

Paul Mercer's ColorDesk is an init/cdev that allows you to select a single color image for use as your desktop. The cdev provides complete control over the configuration, including the ability to stretch or compress the image to fit on your desktop, to select which screen the desktop should be placed on (if you have more than one monitor attached), and to temporarily remove the desktop graphic.

 Backdrop

When the Backdrop init has been installed, MacPaint-format documents kept in a folder named *Screens* that is in your System folder are used as desktop patterns. If more than one file is in the Screens folder, one will be selected at random each time your Mac is started up. An accompanying DA allows you to select an image to be your desktop graphic immediately, or play an on-screen slide show of all available images. Backdrop is incompatible with Mac II's and the SE/30.

 Big Pat, Pik-a-Pat

Big Pat allows you create background patterns by drawing in 2×2, 4×4, 8×8, 16×16, or 32×32 pixel grids, as opposed to the 8×8 pixel grid provided by the General cdev. Using the different grid sizes allows you to create much more elaborate background patterns. Pik-a-Pat is a companion product that allows you to save patterns created in Big Pat, and then switch among the patterns you have saved.

Customizing Window Displays

Each time the Finder places icons in a window, lists file names and creators, or performs virtually any other manipulation of the screen display, its actions are controlled by variables stored in the Finder's LAYO resource. These variables control how far each icon is offset from the others, how many characters of a file name fit in the file-name column, and other such attributes.

By editing the Finder's LAYO=128 resource, you can change the way the Finder displays windows and icons on the Finder desktop. You can edit the LAYO resource using ResEdit (which is fully described in the Resources entry later in this section), or you can use a utility called Layout, described below, which simplifies this process tremendously.

Some of the more important LAYO options that you might want to change are "Icon Horz. spacing," which specifies how many pixels apart file icons are placed (setting a larger number will move icons farther apart, thereby eliminating file-name overlap); "Icon Vert. spacing," which controls the leading, in pixels, for all file-name lists (reducing this number will fit more file names into a window); "Icon Vert. phase," which specifies how icons line up next to each other (0 lines up all icons on the same line, while a higher number like 15 will offset them slightly, eliminating file-name overlap); and "Skip trash warnings," which when set to 0 will allow you to delete System files (type ZSYS) or applications (type APPL) without responding to the ARE YOU SURE YOU WANT TO DELETE? dialog box.

LAYO ID = 128 from Finder	
Font ID	3
Font Size	9
Screen Hdr Hgt	20
Icon Horz. spacing	64
Icon Vert. spacing	64
Icon Vert. phase	0
Sm. Icon Horz.	96
Sm. Icon Vert.	20

Values in the Finder's LAYO resource, which can be modified with ResEdit or Layout, determine how windows and icons are displayed at the Finder desktop.

Layout

Layout is a utility that lets you edit the Finder's LAYO resource without resorting to the brute-force methods required by ResEdit. Layout makes it easy to change icon spacing, column widths in text views, and the font and size of the icon titles. Additionally, you can toggle on or off the warnings received when you drag items to the trash, the ability to see a folder's parent directory by double-clicking on the title bar, and the zoom effect usually used when windows are opened and closed. This is an excellent utility. On color Macs, you can also change the coloration of icons, and the colors that appear in your COLOR menu.

MainWDEF, AltWDEF, NEVR
These inits give your Mac windows the look of the new NeXT computer. They are more beneficial as a change of pace than any real improvement. Of the three, AltWDEF has the most features, allowing you to open any window with an unmodified window graphic, when desired.

Name	Size	Kind	Last Modified	
! Agenda Session	6K	Navigator 2.1 doc...	Thu, Jun 1, 1989	7:05 PM
! Mac Session	10K	Navigator 2.1 doc...	Tue, Jun 27, 1989	2:02 AM
Cserve FAX instructions	7K	Word 4.0 document	Thu, Apr 13, 1989	6:23 PM
Mac Files Session	30K	Navigator 2.1 doc...	Thu, Jun 22, 1989	2:00 AM
PageMaker Confer Txt	35K	document	Fri, Mar 3, 1989	6:46 PM
PC Magnet	15K	document	Tue, Apr 11, 1989	6:14 PM
Résumé	5K	Word 4.0 document	Tue, Jun 20, 1989	4:26 PM
Stuffit Search!	8K	document	Thu, May 18, 1989	2:11 AM

This is how a Finder window looks when you use the MainWDEF init and Scroll2. MainWDEF provides the new window look, and Scroll2 adds the additional direction arrows at each end of the scroll bars.

Scroll2
Scroll2 adds an extra scroll arrow to each end of all scroll bars on the Macintosh so that you can scroll in either direction without having to move your mouse all the way to the other end of the scroll bar. Although it takes some getting used to, this is ultimately a must-have accessory. After a few days with Scroll2 you will miss it the instant you sit down at someone else's Mac. Scroll2 is installed into your System file with the Installer application, and it can be removed with the Installer application (thereby restoring the original scroll arrows). We have used Scroll2 with dozens of Macintosh applications without experiencing any troublesome incompatibilities. (It will not work with MacWrite II, but does not interfere with MacWrite's operation.)

Customizing Menus

Ever wish there were a keyboard equivalent for the Finder's SHUT DOWN command? Or that the EMPTY TRASH command read "Take out the garbage"? Well, like many other Macintosh features, menu commands can be customized fairly easily. There used to be several utility programs that made menu customization especially simple, but none of these have been updated to work with recent System Software. Menu commands must now be edited using ResEdit, but menu editing is one of the most straightforward ResEdit tasks. With ResEdit you can add keyboard equivalents to menu commands, change command names, and even alter the type style used to display the commands in virtually every menu on the Mac. The Resources entry, later in this section, includes complete instructions on using ResEdit.

Some applications, such as those from Microsoft, may not use MENU resources. This is because their developers created their own menu system rather than relying on the Menu Manager routines from the Mac's ROM. (Microsoft Word 4.0, however, offers an unprecedented level of control over the menus from the COMMANDS… command, as explained in the Word entry in Section 2.)

Before editing MENU resources for the purpose of adding keyboard equivalents, you should consider the use of a macro program, which allows you to easily select any keyboard equivalent to invoke any command. See the Macros entry later in this section for complete details on the use of macros. Also, while changing command names and their appearance may be fun, it does tend to degrade the Mac's standard user interface and so should be performed sparingly.

Menu Editing with ResEdit

An introduction to the use of ResEdit is included in the Resources entry later in this section. If you are unfamiliar with ResEdit, read that entry before editing any menus as described here.

Menus are kept in MENU resources. Double-click on the MENU resource to open it. The dialog box you will see depends on the version of ResEdit you are using. Versions older than 1.3 will present a standard ResEdit dialog, in which you can change a command name by altering the text in the "menuItem" option box, add an icon to the command line by entering an icon ID number in the Icon# option box, change or add a keyboard equivalent by changing the key shown in the "key equiv" option box, and change any type-style attributes from 0 (off) to 1 (on) using the radio buttons next to the attribute name. ResEdit version 1.3 or later has a new MENU dialog, which makes it easier to edit the menu, allows you to specify colors for each menu command, and shows you the effects of your edits in the upper-right corner of your screen. Close the resource by clicking the Close box in the menu title, and then close the open application in the same way. A dialog box will appear, asking you if you want to save your changes. If you do, your edited menu will appear as soon as the application is run.

MENU ID = 3 from MORE™ U1.1	
height	0
procID	0
filler	0
enableFlgs	$FFFF6EDF
title	Edit
*****	
menuItem	Undo
icon#	0
key equiv	Z
mark Char	

In versions of ResEdit prior to 1.3, the MENU resource was presented in list format just like all other resources.

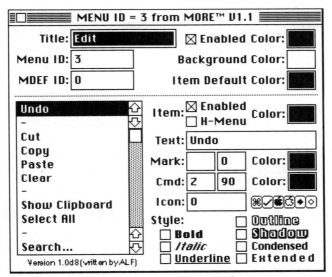

The MENU resource window in ResEdit 1.3 has been improved to make menu editing easier, and to allow menu colors to be specified.

Customizing Icons

All Macintosh icons are maintained as small bit-mapped drawings stored in the ICON, ICN#, or SICN resources in Mac applications. By editing these icons—which is as easy as editing any other bit-mapped graphic—using ResEdit or a specialized icon editor, you can change the appearance of virtually any icon appearing on your Mac. We recommend that you restrain yourself from performing too many icon modifications, and of course, changes should always be made to copies of your software.

Icon Editing with ResEdit

An introduction to the use of ResEdit is included in the Resources entry later in this section. If you are unfamiliar with ResEdit, read that entry before editing any menus as described here.

A palette of icons will appear when the ICON, ICN#, or SICN resources are opened. These are all the icons available. Double-click on any of these miniature icons and a much larger editing window will appear. If you have opened an ICN# resource, on the left side of the new window is the icon, which you can edit by simply clicking bits on and off. On the right side is the icon mask, which provides the background on which the icon sits. Usually the icon mask is used to provide a plain white background—this is accomplished with a solid black icon mask—although this is not required. The lower portion of the window shows the icon in actual size, and is updated as you edit so you can monitor your results. ICON resources provide only a large icon, since ICON-type icons have no masks.

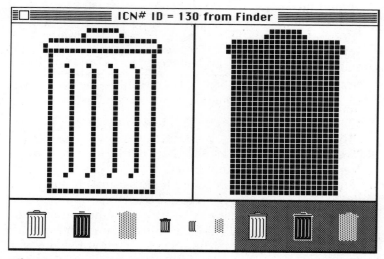

When icons are opened in ResEdit they appear as editable bit-mapped graphics.

To add a completely new icon, select the NEW command from the FILE menu while the ICON, ICN#, or SICN palette is open and selected. You can also copy (or cut, which you probably don't want to do) an icon from one application and paste it into another. Icons are selected for use by their ID number, and occasionally by their name. You can change an icon's ID number and name by selecting the icon and choosing the GET INFO command (⌘-I) from the FILE menu. To substitute a new icon for an old one, create or paste in a new icon, rename and renumber it so that it is exactly the same as the one you want it to replace, and then remove the old icon's name and number. (You don't have to delete it.) Renaming or renumbering it could accidentally cause a conflict with another existing icon.

Icon Editors

A few years ago a large number of icon-editing utilities were available, but very few have been updated to completely work under recent versions of the System Software. (It seems that Macintosh hackers have found better things to work on than lowly old icons.) A few good generic icon editors still exist, however, and some new specialized ones have appeared recently.

Icon Designer, Easy Icon
These utilities let you edit the icons contained in most Mac applications while avoiding the more intimidating technical aspects of ResEdit. Both allow you to open any application and easily scroll through all of the application's ICON resource icons. You can edit the icons you wish; several special effects are available, such as inverting the icon and nudging the icon one pixel at a time in either direction.

Small Icon Editor
This utility is specifically designed to allow you to edit SICN resources, and is one of the best icon editors we have seen. Small Icon Editor has many features that make SICN icon editing easier, as well as a pleasant design and an intuitive interface.

Earth
This init replaces the boring old ￼ icon at the top of your APPLE menu with a constantly rotating globe. Editing Earth's SICN resource allows you to edit the globes, replacing them with any series of images that you want constantly appearing at the top of your APPLE menu. The Small Icon Editor utility described earlier is perfect for this task. If you add multiple SICN resources to the Earth file, the one using ID number 128 will be used.

bootDiskIcon
Because the icons used by hard drives are not kept in System file resources, they are usually impossible to edit. The bootDiskIcon init, however, does allow you to assign a new icon to your startup disk (but not to any other disks or volumes). The default icon is a Mac II, but this icon may be edited in ResEdit.

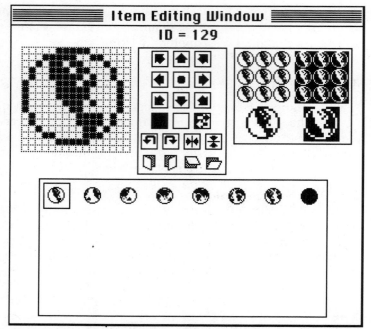

Using the Small Icon Editor you can edit or replace the globes that Earth displays in place of the ⬛ *icon at the top of your* APPLE *menu.*

Facade

Facade is an init with which you can assign new icons to your hard drive, network volumes, volume partitions, and floppy disks. Facade does require the use of ResEdit, but that shouldn't discourage you. Used creatively, this is one of the best customizations you can make to your Macintosh. Facade includes about ten icons, but you can easily edit any of these or add your own new ones.

To use Facade, launch ResEdit and open the Facade application. Open the ICN# resources, and find, create, or paste in an icon you want to use for one of your disks or volumes. Select the icon, choose the GET INFO... command (⌘-I) from the FILE menu, and then name the icon with the exact name of the disk or volume that will display the icon; this icon will then be substituted for the disk or volume's normal icon. In addition to your hard drive and volume partitions, you might want to create a unique icon for disks named Untitled.

```
┌─────────────────────────────────────────────────┐
│ ▤▢▬▬▬▬   Info for ICN# 256 from Façade  ▬▬▬▬▬    │
├─────────────────────────────────────────────────┤
│  Type:    ICN#           Size:   256            │
│                                                 │
│  Name:   ┃CMD's II                        ┃    │
│  ID:     ┌─────────┐                            │
│          │ 256     │      Owner type            │
│          └─────────┘    ┌──────────┬──┐         │
│     Owner ID:  ┌────────┐│ DRVR     │⇧ │         │
│                │        ││ WDEF     │  │         │
│     Sub ID:    └────────┘│ MDEF     │⇩ │         │
│                          └──────────┴──┘         │
│  Attributes:                                    │
│  ☐ System Heap    ☐ Locked        ☐ Preload    │
│  ☒ Purgeable      ☐ Protected                   │
└─────────────────────────────────────────────────┘
```

To set one of Facade's icons to replace your hard-drive icon, give the ICN#
resource the same name as your hard drive.

Customizing Dialog Boxes

Macintosh dialog boxes are composed of windows, text, icons, buttons, and
options. They are put together in a remarkably modular fashion, and you
can therefore significantly modify any dialog box using ResEdit. Our warning again: Don't modify too many dialog boxes. Most of the message and
button text is well-written, and conveys its information clearly and
concisely; any changes you make could confuse others who try to use your
Macintosh. We do, however, think that some dialog-box editing is useful
(and fun). In particular, many dialog boxes become much clearer when their
button text is made more explicit. For example, we like to change the button text in "Delete this file?" dialog boxes to "Delete" rather than "Yes,"
and many other buttons to "No!" or "Abort!" rather than "Cancel." We also
like to change "Drive" buttons to "Drive>" to convey a sense of motion,
and other "Yes" buttons to "Do it."

Dialog-Box Editing in ResEdit

An introduction to the use of ResEdit is included in the Resources entry later in this section. If you are unfamiliar with ResEdit, read that entry before editing any menus as described here.

Dialog boxes and their elements are stored in four different resources: ALRT, DITL, DLOG, and STR#. The ALRT and DLOG resources contain bit-mapped images of the dialog boxes, but double-clicking on one of these dialogs allows you to edit its message, button text, and size. DITL resources present only their text and buttons for editing, and STR# resources are lists of strings used in other dialog boxes.

To edit any of these resources in ResEdit, open the application whose dialog boxes you wish to edit, double-click on the ALRT, DITL, DLOG, or STR# resources, double-click on one of the specific ID numbers listed, and then edit away. To alter the text of a button, double-click on the button to enter the button-editing dialog.

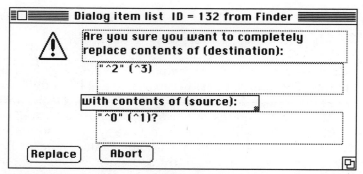

In this DITL resource, double-clicking on the text message or the buttons allows you to edit this text.

```
┌─────────────────────────────────────────────────────┐
│ ▤□▤▤▤▤▤▤ STR#  ID = 7168 from Finder ▤▤▤▤▤▤ │
├─────────────────────────────────────────────────┬───┤
│ numStrings    6                                 │ ⇧ │
│     *****                                       │   │
│   The string    ┌─────────────────────────────┐ │   │
│                 │ Finder:                     │ │   │
│     *****        └─────────────────────────────┘ │   │
│   The string    ┌─────────────────────────────┐ │   │
│                 │ System:                     │ │   │
│     *****        └─────────────────────────────┘ │   │
│   The string    ┌─────────────────────────────┐ │   │
│                 │ Elvis, Steve, Pete & Bruce  │ │   │
│     *****        └─────────────────────────────┘ │   │
│   The string    ┌─────────────────────────────┐ │   │
│                 │ ©Apple Computer, Inc. 1983-88│ │   │
│     *****        └─────────────────────────────┘ │ ⇩ │
└─────────────────────────────────────────────────┴───┘
```

STR# resources include many text strings that are used by other dialog boxes. This resource contains the text used by the ABOUT THE FINDER dialog box.

```
┌───────────────────────────────────────────────────────┐
│ ▤□▤▤▤▤ About the Macintosh™ Finder ▤▤▤▤ │
├───────────────────────────────────────────────────────┤
│  Finder :   6.1          Elvis, Steve, Pete & Bruce   │
│  System:   6.0.2         ©Apple Computer, Inc. 1983-88 │
│                                                         │
│  Total Memory :   5,120K                                │
│ ─────────────────────────────────────────────────────  │
│  📄 Finder       4,516K  ▓░░░░░░░░░░░░░░░░░░░░░░░        │
│  📄 System         604K  ▓▓▓                            │
│                                                         │
│                                                         │
└───────────────────────────────────────────────────────┘
```

The *ABOUT THE FINDER* dialog box reflects the modifications made to the STR# resource in ResEdit. (None of the Finder's programmers were named Elvis.)

Customizing Color

Although color is now an important part of many Macintosh applications, the System Software's support of color remains quite modest. The utilities below, however, make it possible for your System Software to take full advantage of your Mac's color abilities.

Color

Apple's Color cdev sets the color used for selected files and folders at the Finder. This feature is also provided, along with many others, by the Kolor cdev, which therefore supplants the need for Color.

Kolor

This is a replacement for Apple's Color cdev, allowing you to specify the color attributes of menus, scroll bars, and other screen elements. If you have a color monitor, or if you use gray values on your monochrome display, you definitely want to use this cdev. Interestingly, this cdev was written at Apple Computer, which retains its copyright. Option-clicking the Kolor icon in the Control Panel will reset all colors to their defaults.

Finder Colors

This utility allows you to easily edit the color definitions of the edit colors presented in the Finder's COLOR menu. Running the application brings up a listing of the colors, and double-clicking on any color accesses the APPLE COLOR WHEEL dialog box, which allows you to define the color to any shade supported on your Macintosh.

Color Finder, Icon Colorizer

These inits, with the help of ResEdit, CIcon Edit, and ResCicn, allow you to create and display colored icons on your Finder desktop. (Each pixel in the icon can be a different color.) Basically, these inits work like the Facade init described earlier; a new icon is created or modified and inserted in the Color Finder or Icon Colorizer ICN# resource, and then it is given the same name and ID number of the icon that you want it to replace. In addition to creating or editing the icon and renaming it, however, you must also color the icon, which is done using CIcon Edit or ResCicn.

Color Cursor

When this init is in the System folder of a color Mac, the arrow cursor becomes striped in the colors of the Apple logo. Very fashionable.

De-Customizing

Anonymity

Ever make a typing mistake while personalizing a new application? Anonymity is a utility that removes the personalization that is so often added to commercial software applications. Some applications will again ask you to enter your name and company information after Anonymity has been run, but other software will remain permanently depersonalized.

Painting the Mac

Steven Jobs, cofounder of Apple Computer, has been compared with Henry Ford as an entrepreneurial pioneer for many reasons, including the fact that he once made a remark similar to one for which Mr. Ford was famous: "Any color you want, as long as it's beige," said Mr. Jobs. Of course, when Apple learned that corporate America preferred platinum (read "gray") to beige, the switch was made.

A few years ago, a company called Aesthetics offered to repaint your Mac any color, or in one of several custom airbrushed effects. They did a very good job of it—painting the Mac, keyboard, and mouse for about $300. Unfortunately, the company is now defunct, so unless you are the really adventurous type, we hope you like platinum.

Desk Accessories

The desk accessories that accompanied the original Macintosh offered a variety of functions. Some, like NotePad, Calculator, and Puzzle, remained close to the "desk accessory" metaphor, while others, including Scrapbook, Control Panel, and Key Caps, offered functions specific to the Macintosh computer. It didn't take long, however, for Macintosh programmers to launch an avalanche of public-domain, shareware, and commercial desk accessories, addressing every possible area of utilities, System Software enhancements, entertainment, and even complete applications.

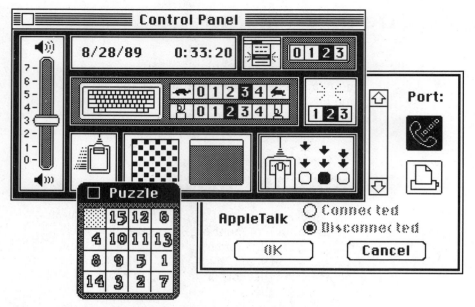

Some of the original Macintosh desk accessories, including the Control Panel, Chooser, and Puzzle.

But this flood of desk accessories uncovered a rather problematic limitation: The original System Software only supported 15 desk accessories. And because adding or deleting DA's was relatively difficult as well as time-consuming, the best way to work with a variety of DA's was to create several startup disks, each with a different set of DA's. When Macintosh hard drives were introduced, the process was altered so that different System files, each with different sets of installed DA's, were kept on disks and transferred to the hard disk when needed.

Overall, the 15 DA limit put quite a damper on the DA explosion. It took about 18 months from the January 1984 Macintosh introduction before the first solutions to the DA limit appeared. By mid-1987 a number of solutions were available, some better than others, but none ideal. A special version of Apple's Font/DA Mover called Font/DA Mover+ upped the limit from 15 to 18, and DA Installer+ from Dreams of the Phoenix allowed about 36 DA's to be installed.

Smashing the DA Limit

The concept of running desk accessories from their suitcases—without installing them—was first presented by Lofty Becker's Other... desk accessory. With Other... installed, you can access any desk accessory stored on disk in a standard DA suitcase. DA's accessed using Other... are added to your APPLE menu, where they remain until you reboot your Macintosh. Several utilities now offer the ability to run DA's from their suitcases, including DA Key Fkey (which in its most recent version is a replacement for Other...), DA Sampler, FONT-DA-FKEY sampler, Double Apple, Suitcase, Font/DA Juggler, and MasterJuggler. DA Sampler and FONT-DA-FKEY sampler have the limitation of an inability to open suitcases containing more than one DA, and the fact that they only allow access to one DA at a time. These utilities are, however, all free or inexpensive, and offer a great solution to the DA limit, especially for those who do not need the font-related features found in the commercial applications (which are described below) that offer this feature.

Suitcase is the init that really ended the problem of the DA limit for most Mac users. Suitcase offered elegance, simplicity, and a total annihilation of the DA limit. With Suitcase, hundreds of DA's could be loaded into the APPLE menu, and then accessed directly from the APPLE menu. Suitcase can open up to ten different DA suitcases, each of which may contain many DA's. Another advantage Suitcase offers over the DA runners described above is the ability to reattach DA suitcases each time the Mac is rebooted.

Font/DA Juggler leapfrogged Suitcase in features, and a features war has ensued, with Suitcase II and MasterJuggler being the current incarnations. In the Utilities Summary entry later in this section we will compare these two products directly, but for now we will just say that if you use your Macintosh, you should own one of these products.

Desk Accessories in the Present and Future

As Apple's System Software has been upgraded over the past few years, rumors of the death of desk accessories have circulated. With the advent of MultiFinder, you can access any application without quitting another (a feat once provided only by DA's), and so desk accessories have become obsolete—or so the theory goes. This theory doesn't take into account, however, the reality that many desk accessories provide functions not duplicated by traditional applications. Also, MultiFinder requires more RAM than many Macintosh users possess, and is therefore not yet a universal solution. Apple has confirmed that DA's will still be supported in System Software 7.0, so the rumored demise is now delayed, for a while at least. Chances are excellent, in any case, that whenever Apple stops supporting DA's, some new utility will resurrect them almost immediately.

The Font/DA Mover

⚑ **Font/DA Mover**   ⌘⌘

Apple's Font/DA Mover can add and delete DA's from any suitcase or System file, and allows you to create new DA suitcases. It is always important to use the most current version of this utility; version 3.8 is the version included along with System Software 6.0. The version number of the Font/DA Mover appears in the Font/DA Mover menu bar.

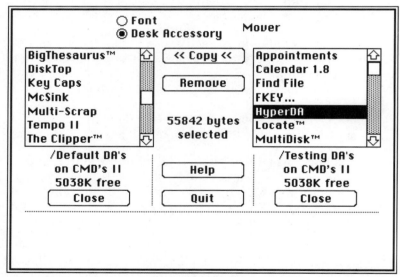

Two DA suitcases are open in this Font/DA Mover, and a DA is selected on the right.

Font/DA Mover Instructions

The Font/DA Mover's window is divided into three sections. The right and left sections are identical, each providing a scrolling file list that displays the contents of open System files and suitcases, and an OPEN/CLOSE button used to open and close System files and suitcases. The middle section provides a COPY button, which transfers DA's from one suitcase or System file to another; a REMOVE button, which deletes selected DA's from their current location; a HELP button, which displays help screens; and a QUIT button, which closes the Font/DA Mover, returning you to the Finder.

- **To add a desk accessory to your current System file.** Open the Font/ DA Mover by clicking on the Font/DA Mover icon. This will launch the Font/DA Mover and open your current System file in the file listing on the left. Since the "Fonts" option is selected by default, click the "Desk accessories" option near the top of the Font/DA Mover. The setting of this option determines whether you are moving fonts or DA's.

  Click the OPEN button below the right file listing and use the Standard File dialog to open the suitcase file containing the DA you wish to add. Each of the desk accessories in this suitcase will now appear in the right-hand file listing. Select the DA you wish to install; the COPY button now reads <<COPY indicating that the selected file will be copied from the right window into the left. Click this button and the DA is copied. The name of the DA will now appear in the left window; it has been installed in your System file.

  To add additional desk accessories, repeat this installation process. Click the CLOSE button under the right scrolling list and it will again become an OPEN button. When finished, click the QUIT button to exit the Font/DA Mover.

- **To delete a desk accessory from your current System file.** Open the Font/DA Mover by clicking on its icon. This will launch the Font/DA Mover application and open your current System file in the file listing on the left. Since the "Fonts" option is selected by default, click the "Desk accessories" option near the top of the Font/DA Mover. The setting of this option determines whether you are moving fonts or DA's. Select the DA you wish to delete from the DA list and click the REMOVE button. When finished, click the QUIT button.

- **To move a desk accessory from a System file into a suitcase.** Open the Font/DA Mover by clicking on its icon. This will launch the Font/DA Mover application and open your current System file in the file listing on the left. Since the "Fonts" option is selected by default, click the "Desk accessories" option near the top of the Font/DA

Mover. The setting of this option determines whether you are moving fonts or DA's.

If you wish to move the System file DA into an existing suitcase, click the OPEN button below the right file listing and use the Standard File dialog to open the correct suitcase file. If you wish to move the System file DA to a new suitcase, click the OPEN button below the right file listing, click the NEW button, and name and save your new DA suitcase. Select the DA you wish to copy from the System file in the right-hand file listing; the COPY button now reads COPY>> indicating that the selected file will be copied from the left window into the right. Click this COPY button and the DA will be copied. Its name appears in the right-hand window when it has been copied successfully.

To move additional desk accessories, repeat this process. Click the CLOSE button under the right scrolling list and it will again become an OPEN button. When finished, click the QUIT button to exit the Font/DA Mover.

- **To move a desk accessory from one suitcase to another.** Open the Font/DA Mover by clicking on its icon. This will launch the Font/DA Mover application and open your current System file in the file listing on the left. Since the "Fonts" option is selected by default, click the "Desk accessories" option near the top of the Font/DA Mover. The setting of this option determines whether you are moving fonts or DA's.

Click the OPEN button below the right file listing and use the Standard File dialog to open the suitcase file containing the DA you wish to move. Each of the desk accessories in this suitcase will now appear in the right-hand file listing. If you wish to move the DA into an existing suitcase, click the CLOSE button below the left-hand listing, and then click the OPEN button below the left-hand listing. Use the Standard File dialog to open the correct suitcase file. If you wish to move the System file DA to a new suitcase, click the CLOSE button below the left-hand listing, click the OPEN button below the left-hand listing, click the NEW button, and name and save your new DA suitcase.

Select the DA you wish to copy from the right-hand file listing; the COPY button now reads <<COPY indicating that the selected file will be copied from the suitcase displayed in the right-hand window into the suitcase displayed in the left-hand window. Click this COPY button and the DA will be copied. Its name appears in the right-hand window, indicating that it has been successfully copied. If you wish

to delete this DA from the source suitcase, select its name in the right scrolling list and click the REMOVE button.

To move additional desk accessories, repeat this process. When finished, click the QUIT button to exit the Font/DA Mover.

Font/DA Mover Tips

◇ **Hold down the ⌥ key while the Font/DA Mover is launching to open to DA's.** Normally, the Font/DA Mover opens with the "Font" option selected and the current fonts in the active System file displayed. Pressing the OPTION key as the Font/DA Mover is launching causes the "Desk accessories" option to be selected and the DA's in the active System file to be displayed. You can also open to the DA listing by double-clicking a DA suitcase at the Finder.

◇ **Launch the Font/DA Mover by double-clicking any font or DA suitcase from the Finder.** This will launch the Font/DA Mover and open the suitcase. The active System file will not be opened automatically.

◇ **Hold down the ⇧ key to select multiple fonts or DA's.** Pressing down the SHIFT key while selecting fonts or DA's in a scrolling window allows you to select any number of items to be copied or deleted together. You may drag upward or downward to select a series of items, or shift-click to select nonadjacent items.

◇ **The Font/DA Mover does not support desk accessories**. There is no APPLE menu while the Font/DA Mover is running, so you cannot run DA's while using it; we think this is very ironic. Also, although the Font/DA Mover runs in MultiFinder, it must be the foreground application; in order to access any other application or the Finder, you must quit the Font/DA Mover.

◆ **Hold down the ⌥ key while clicking the CLOSE button to eject the disk as the suitcase is closed**. If you are not using MultiFinder, this will eject and dismount the disk. In MultiFinder, the disk will be ejected but not dismounted. (A dimmed icon for the disk will remain on the Finder desktop.)

◆ **Hold down the ⌥ key while clicking the QUIT button to eject both disks before exiting the Font/DA Mover.** Both disks will only be ejected, however, if a suitcase file on each of them was open when the QUIT button was pressed.

◆ **DA's can be added directly to any application.** By installing desk accessories directly into the applications in which you will use them, you avoid excessively long DA menus, and you ensure that you will never select that DA accidentally in another application. You also, however, introduce the possibility of conflicts between a DA installed in an application and one installed normally, although we have not found this to be a problem (and we use lots of DA's). For example, the Word Finder DA that Microsoft provides along with Word will be used almost exclusively along with Word, and QuickBDownload will only be used along with your telecommunications package.

Installing a DA into an application is just like installing a DA into a suitcase or System file, except that you press the OPTION key while clicking the OPEN button in the Font/DA mover. This presents the same Standard File dialog box as usual, but instead of listing only DA suitcases and System files, it now lists every file that includes a resource fork. Locate the application into which you want to install the DA, and open it by either double-clicking on its name in the scrolling file list or selecting it and again clicking the OPEN button. Copy the DA into the application, as described above. The DA will appear only when the application into which it was installed is running.

◆ **Hold down the** ⬆ **key while clicking on any DA to display size information about the DA.** If you hold down the OPTION key and select any DA, a breakdown of the DA size will appear in the lower-left corner of the Font/DA Mover.

◆ **The Font/DA Mover will become obsolete under System Software 7.0.** Reportedly, when using System Software 7.0 you will install fonts and DA's by simply dragging them into the System folder. The Font/DA Mover application will no longer be used.

Desk Accessory Utilities

 Suitcase II   🖐§§

The introduction of Suitcase was a milestone in the maturity of the Macintosh. Suitcase added so much power to the Mac, in such a "Mac-like" fashion, that it became the biggest overnight sensation that the Mac software market has ever seen. Within weeks of Suitcase's commercial introduction, every Macintosh publication and legions of users were saying the same thing: If you use the Macintosh, you need Suitcase.

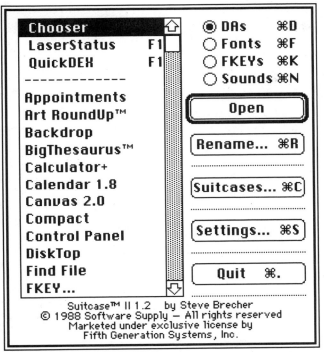

The Suitcase II main dialog box lists all DA's currently available and allows you to open other DA suitcases.

What Suitcase offers is the ability to quickly and easily add and remove fonts and desk accessories to and from the System file. But unlike Apple's Font/DA Mover, which physically transfers fonts and DA's when installing or removing them, Suitcase works by "tricking" the System file into thinking it had added or removed these items. Suitcase actually accesses fonts and DA's right from their suitcases, although fonts and DA's accessed via Suitcase act just as if they have been physically installed; DA's appear in the APPLE menu, with the list scrolling off the bottom of your display if it gets too long.

Suitcase II, the current version of Suitcase, adds a number of significant improvements over its predecessor. Most importantly, Suitcase II remembers which font and DA suitcases you have opened and automatically reopens them each time you start your Macintosh, regardless of where they are located (unless you open a particular font or DA set specifically for one-time use). Suitcase II also adds the ability to rename and reorder DA's as they appear in the APPLE menu, and supports Fkeys in addition to fonts and DA's. The only thing we don't like about Suitcase II is its interface, which uses too many layers of dialog boxes. See the Fkeys, Fonts, and Sounds entries for more information about Suitcase II.

Font/DA Juggler, MasterJuggler

Not long after the introduction of Suitcase, Alsoft's Font/DA Juggler was released, offering all of Suitcase's abilities, a cleaner user interface, plus plus the ability to automatically remount multiple suitcases at startup. Suitcase was later upgraded to Suitcase II, and Alsoft then released another competing product called MasterJuggler.

MasterJuggler's main dialog box lists the DA suitcases that are currently open and those that can be opened.

Font/DA Juggler offers the direct use of fonts and DA's right out of their suitcases, just like Suitcase. Also like Suitcase, it automatically reopens fonts and DA's at startup, allows you to quickly preview fonts, and offers font compression. MasterJuggler offers everything Font/DA Juggler does, and adds support for sounds and Fkeys, application launching and Multi-Finder window management. See the Fkeys, Fonts, and Sounds entries for more information about Font/DA Juggler and MasterJuggler.

DAs Key, Other..., FONT-FKEY-DA Sampler   ⑤Ⓦ, ⑤Ⓦ, ⑤Ⓦ

While not as sophisticated or powerful as Suitcase or MasterJuggler, these utilities do allow you to access DA's right from their suitcases. If you want to be able to access several DA's and then use them repeatedly before re-starting your Mac, then DAs Key is best for you. (DAs Key version 2.01 replaces Other...) We think that even Suitcase and MasterJuggler users would find DAs Key useful for accessing DA's that are rarely used and not worth keeping permanently under your Apple menu.

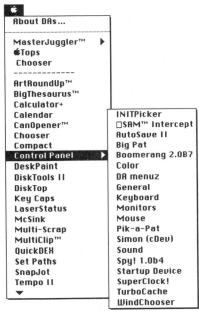

DA menuz adds a hierarchical pop-up menu to the Control Panel and all DA's that use menus.

DA menuz   ☝ⒻⓌ

This init adds several interesting features to your Mac. First, DA menuz (formerly HierDA) allows your desk accessories to present hierarchical menus right in the Apple menu. These hierarchical menus allow you to choose a DA and your first command from that DA at the same time, thereby saving yourself a step and perhaps a little time. This works well for some DA's, and not so well for others, but it works great for Apple's Control Panel, which when used with DA menuz allows you to directly select the cdev that you wish to access—the Control Panel is brought up with the selected cdev at the top of the scrolling list, already selected. This is a really convenient feature, and makes DA menuz worth having. You can configure DA menuz to add hierarchical menus to all DA's or just to the Control Panel.

DA menuz also provides a pop-up menu bar that gives you access to all menus in the current menu bar, including the Apple menu, and hierarchically, all commands in each of those menus. This ability, described below as provided by several other utilities, makes it easier to select commands and DA's on larger monitors, and is well-implemented in DA menuz.

A pop-up menu bar provides access to the menu bar anywhere your cursor is positioned.

Popit!, Pop-up, PopWMenu   SW, SW, FW

Each of these inits adds the ability to "pop up" your complete menu bar, including the Apple menu, at any location on the screen. Each menu hierarchically presents all of its commands, including the Apple menu, which presents all of your DA's. This is useful on larger screens when the trip to the menu bar may be a long one, although in any case it is a feature that takes some getting used to and some time to remember to use. To pop up the menu bar, some combination of a pressed key and the held-down mouse button is used.

Font/DA Utility

This utility, which Alsoft includs along with Font/DA Juggler and Master-Juggler, allows you to rename or renumber desk accessories. ID-number conflicts are generally not very troublesome for DA's because either the Font/DA Mover or the utility you are using to attach DA's takes care of number conflicts automatically, but in some cases the ability to easily renumber DA's is beneficial.

Desk Accessory Tips

◇ **Keep a backup set of your DA's on a floppy disk**. System files and hard disks can both go bad, and finding and reinstalling your DA's can be quite a time-consuming process. Therefore, it is an excellent idea to maintain one floppy disk with a single suitcase containing all of your regular DA's. This makes rebuilding your System file a snap. Even if you use Suitcase or Font/DA Juggler, keeping all your DA's in one place is still a timesaving idea.

◇ **Assign macro keys to each of your favorite DA's**. No matter how good you are with a mouse, a quick keystroke is often the best way to select a frequently used desk accessory. If you have an Apple extended keyboard, assigning DA's to function keys F5 through F15 is one good method of accessing your DA's. See the Macros entry later in this section for more macro-related tips.

◆ **ID conflicts among DA's are resolved automatically by most DA utilities**. When DA's are added to the System file with the Font/DA Mover, ID conflicts are corrected. When DA's are accessed via Suitcase, Font/DA Juggler, and MasterJuggler, conflicts are automatically handled by these utilities. Even Other... and DAs Key will alert you to ID conflicts and offer to correct them. If you do want to renumber DA's manually, Font/DA Utility and an old utility called DA Installer allow you to do this.

◆ **DA's can be renamed with Suitcase II, ResEdit, or Font/DA Utility**. Because DA's are listed alphabetically in the APPLE menu, renaming them allows you to force certain DA's to the top or bottom of your DA list. Suitcase II offers the simplest DA renaming, and also allows you to force certain DA's to the top of the list without renaming them.

If you use a lot of DA's, rather than using special characters to rename DA's you might just add a space before the name of each of your favorite DA's, thus forcing them to the top of the DA list. If you then rename a small unused DA, like the Alarm Clock, as "---------------", you can get an effect like this:

◆ **To use DA's under MultiFinder, the DA Handler file must be in your System folder**. If the DA Handler file is missing, all you will get is a beep when you try to access any DA. If you do not have enough RAM left under MultiFinder to run the DA you have selected, your Mac will also beep and not run the DA. DA Handler servers as the "homebase" for the DA while it is running under MultiFinder, allowing it to be available to many different applications and not be affected when an application is quit or launched. If DA Handler is missing, you can, however, launch DA's by holding down the OPTION key while selecting them, thereby making them available in only one application, as described below.

◆ **Press the ⬚ key while choosing a DA in MultiFinder to make the DA available in only one application**. As described above, under Multi-Finder, DA's are normally run with the DA Handler so that they are unaffected by the activities of any particular application. Holding down the OPTION key while choosing a DA instructs it to attach to the current application and not use the DA Handler. The effect of this is that if the application is quit the DA will be quit too, and that whenever the DA is selected the application to which it is attached will become the foreground application.

Desktop File

The Desktop file is a normal Macintosh file, maintained by the Finder for its own use. The Desktop file stores information about all of the other Macintosh files stored on that disk or, if the disk has a Finder, all files that the Finder comes in contact with. Specifically, the Desktop file holds icons and information from the BNDL resource of applications whose "Bundle" bit was set, the GET INFO... comments from all of these files, and information about the position of the file on the desktop. The Desktop file also keeps track of all open folder and volume windows and their positions.

You may not have noticed the Desktop file because the Finder stores it as an invisible file, meaning that it doesn't appear on the Finder desktop or in any windows. It is stored this way so users don't delete it accidentally (since they would probably not recognize it and assume it to be unnecessary). Many disk and file utilities do display invisible files in their listings, and you can see the Desktop file using any of these.

The Desktop file is created automatically the first time a disk mounts on the Finder desktop—not during the process of disk initialization—and it is updated each time files or folders on the disk are altered. The Desktop file is accessed each time a disk first appears on the Finder desktop, and again each time the Finder returns to its desktop. At this time, the information about the "look" of the disk (the placement of its icons and windows) is read from the Desktop file.

Desktop File: A Death Knell

The Desktop file was designed as part of the Macintosh System Software before Macintoshes used hard drives, before the HFS filing system, and therefore before large numbers of files where ever in use by the Macintosh. The widespread use of larger hard drives and HFS has put fantastic strains on the Desktop file, making it very slow and the source of many problems, which become more and more apparent as hard drives grow.

System Software 7.0 will replace the Desktop file with a new file called the Desktop Manager, which provides similar features but has been optimized to work with large storage devices. Interestingly, the AppleShare file server already uses the Desktop Manager file, and does not use a Desktop File.

It is actually possible to use the Desktop Manager file under System Software 6.0 by simply dragging it into your System folder. This may provide improved desktop performance—faster screen redraws when returning to the Finder—especially when using hard disks larger than 40 megabytes, but it is not officially recommended by Apple and may lead to some problems with software that relies on the Desktop file.

Desktop File Tips

◇ **A damaged Desktop file can cause a variety of problems.** Because the Desktop file plays such an important role in the operation of the Finder and other System Software—even some utilities and applications access it for information—a damaged Desktop file can cause a variety of serious problems. Most commonly, disks, drives, or volumes with damaged Desktop files will cause either the DISK HAS MINOR PROBLEMS dialog box, or the more serious DISK IS DAMAGED dialog box, to appear.

Fortunately, correcting problems with a Desktop file is relatively easy. The Desktop file can be rebuilt (as described below), and you can usually mount disks or volumes without accessing the Desktop file, so even if the file is damaged beyond repair the data on the disk should be recoverable. If you do encounter either the DISK HAS MINOR PROBLEMS or DISK IS DAMAGED dialog box, click the EJECT button and attempt to rebuild the desktop as described below. If this fails, back up the files as explained below and then repair or initialize the disk.

◇ **To rebuild the Desktop file, hold down the ⌘ and ⌥ keys while a disk is mounting**. Normally, the Desktop file that is created when a disk or volume is first used is continually updated but never completely recreated. Holding down the COMMAND and OPTION keys while any disk, drive, or volume mounts at the Finder desktop (usually when you first insert it) instructs the Finder to completely recreate the Desktop file on that disk, drive, or volume. When you do this a dialog box will appear, asking you to confirm that you want the Desktop file rebuilt. Upon your confirmation, a brand new Desktop file is created.

This takes some time as the Finder must scan every file on the disk, rereading all of the relevant information.

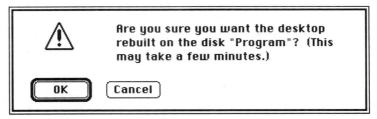

This dialog box appears when you press the COMMAND *and* OPTION *keys while a disk is mounted. Clicking the OK button will cause the Desktop file to be rebuilt.*

❖ **Rebuilding the Desktop file causes some information to be lost, but speeds up your Mac's operation**. When the Desktop file is rebuilt, new information is read from each file on the disk. This causes information about files no longer on the disk to be lost—you don't need this information anyway—and it causes all windows on the disk to be closed and files that were on the desktop to be returned to the disk. Additionally, the Get Info... comments are lost. This new, trimmer Desktop file, however, will be read more quickly, and each time you return to the Finder desktop it will appear more rapidly. When your Mac begins to appear sluggish upon returning to the Finder desktop, rebuild your Desktop file.

◆ **A file utility that displays invisible files can usually delete a damaged Desktop file**. Another way to correct problems stemming from a damaged Desktop file, especially when rebuilding the Desktop file is ineffective or impossible, is to delete the Desktop file entirely and allow a new one to be created when the disk is next mounted. To delete the Desktop file you will need a utility that allows you to display and delete invisible files, like MacTools, Symantec Tools, DiskTop, or Disk-Tools. Attempting to delete the Desktop file while at the Finder, or from a mounted disk while in MultiFinder, will result in the FILE IS BUSY Alert dialog box, and the Desktop file will not be deleted.

◆ **You can access files without accessing the Desktop file**. Anytime a disk is mounted but has not been displayed on the Finder desktop, the Desktop file has not been accessed. This allows you to access files on the disk with any application or desk accessory that can access files. When a floppy disk is damaged and its Desktop file cannot be rebuilt or repaired, insert the disk while any other application is running—you must not be using MultiFinder—and then use a DA like DiskTop or DiskTools to copy the files from the damaged disk onto a good disk or onto your hard drive. You can now reformat the floppy disk and, if it formats successfully, copy your files back onto it. See the Disks and Drives entry later in this section for more information about recovering files from damaged disks.

◆ **The Desktop file cannot be created or updated on locked volumes**. Like any other file, the Desktop file cannot be modified when it is on a locked volume. For this reason, any changes made to the placement of files, folders, or windows will not be remembered when performed on a locked disk. Of course, you cannot add new files to a locked disk anyway. Locked volumes that do not contain a Desktop file cannot be mounted at the Finder or in MultiFinder (although they can be used when not at the Finder or in MultiFinder).

◆ **The Can't create Desktop file Alert dialog.** Occasionally, when you try to rebuild the Desktop file, or after you delete a Desktop file, the Can't create Desktop file Alert dialog will appear. This may occur if there is not enough disk space to hold the Desktop file, if you have a damaged disk, or if the disk just needs a fresh start. In this case, back up the files from the disk, and then reformat the disk and recopy the files to it. If the disk can be formatted properly, it is safe to use.

◆ **The Disk too full - Changes not recorded Alert dialog**. When ejecting (dismounting) a disk, you may see the Disk too full - Changes not recorded Alert. This means that the updated Desktop file, which has been in RAM, cannot be written back to the disk because not enough space is available. Usually this will only mean that any changes to windows and file positions made while the disk was used will not be remembered; your disk is fine and can still be used, although this problem will persist until you free up a little space (20K or so).

◆ **Compact the Desktop file using Disk Express**. Another way to purge unused information from the Desktop file is by using the "Compact Desktop" option in Disk Express. This removes unused information and improves Finder performance, but does not cause the loss of any window information, Get Info... comments, or files on the desktop. See the Files entry later in this section for more information about Disk Express.

Dialog Boxes

Although Macintosh dialog boxes come in all shapes and sizes, there are only two basic types: those that request information from the user, and those that convey information to the user. Dialog boxes that convey information to you are called Alert dialog boxes. These usually include only an OK button with which you acknowledge that the presented information has been received. Dialog boxes that request information do so by presenting options. The basic types of options are radio buttons, check boxes, option boxes, pop-up menus, scrolling file lists, and buttons.

- **Radio buttons.** The round option buttons found in dialog boxes are called radio buttons because, like the buttons that select radio stations on your car radio, when one is selected the others are "deselected." In other words, radio buttons are mutually exclusive; one and only one radio button in a set can be selected at once.

- **Check boxes.** The square option boxes can be selected or deselected in any combination within their group.

- **Option boxes**. These are the small boxes into which data is entered from the keyboard. When the cursor is positioned over an option box it changes from an arrow to an insertion point. Clicking the mouse button at this time sets the cursor in that box so that data may be entered. Once inside an option box, you can use the BACKSPACE key and the arrow keys to position the cursor.

- **Pop-up menus.** Pop-up menus are just like menus that appear from the menu bar, except that they pop up inside of dialog boxes. Pop-up menus are usually marked in dialog boxes by a drop-shadow box containing the current option setting. Microsoft has improved on this display by adding a downward-pointing arrow to the side of its pop-up menus in Word 4.0; these arrows make the items much more readily identifiable as pop-up menus. We hope that other developers follow Microsoft's lead (in this one area) and make these arrows the standard symbol of pop-up menus in dialog boxes.

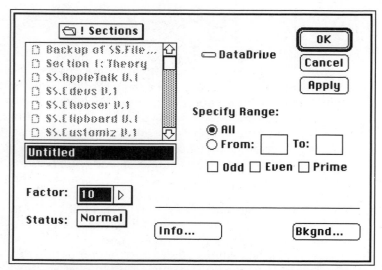

This fictional dialog box contains radio buttons, check boxes, option boxes, a scrolling file list, and buttons.

- **Scrolling file listing**. Dialog boxes that you use to open or save files include a scrolling file listing. This list displays the names of either all files, or all files of certain types, available in the current directory of the current drive. Above the scrolling list is the folder bar (or directory menu), which names the current directory. This folder bar turns into a pop-up menu whenever the current directory is a folder. Selecting this pop-up menu allows you to quickly move up or down the folder hierarchy. The name of the current drive, volume, or folder appears along with its icon (a folder, hard drive, or floppy disk) to the right of the scrolling file list. Clicking on the drive name will move the file-listing display up one level if a folder is currently displayed.

- **Buttons**. Buttons can execute an action or, if followed by ellipsis points, open another dialog box. Buttons circled with a heavy border are default buttons, and can be invoked with the RETURN or ENTER key.

Standard File Dialog Boxes

Many dialog boxes are provided to applications and utilities by the System file. These "community property" dialog boxes provide a common user interface for all Mac software, and save software developers effort by providing them with dialog boxes that will be needed by most applications. (Every application will need OPEN, SAVE, and PRINT dialog boxes, so why should that effort be duplicated for every new Mac application?) Applications can use dialog boxes from the System file as is, or they can modify them slightly to suit their particular needs.

The two most commonly used dialog boxes are called the Standard File Open dialog (SF open or SF get) and the Standard File Save dialog (SF save or SF put). The SF get dialog box, which is commonly used as an OPEN dialog box, is used to select files from disks. It provides a scrolling file listing, an OPEN button, a CANCEL button, and a DRIVE button. The SF put dialog, which is commonly used as a SAVE dialog box, is used to save files to disk, includes a scrolling file listing, a file-name option box, and DRIVE, SAVE, and CANCEL buttons.

Standard File Dialog Box Tricks

◇   **The ↑ and ↓ keys scroll through the files and folders in a scrolling list.**

◇   **Double-clicking on a folder opens the folder.** This is the equivalent of pressing COMMAND-↓ while the folder is selected.

◇   **Double-clicking on a file name opens the file.** This is the equivalent of clicking the OPEN button while the file name is selected.

◇   **Pressing the ➡︎ key is the equivalent of pressing the DRIVE button.**

◇   **⌘-E is the equivalent of pressing the EJECT button.**

◇   **⌘-D is the equivalent of pressing the DRIVE button.**

◇   **Clicking on the drive name and icon closes the current folder.** This is the equivalent of dragging down one level with the directory menu, or pressing COMMAND-↑.

◇   ⌘-↓ **opens the currently selected folder**. The folder must be high-
    lighted when COMMAND-↓ is pressed. This is the equivalent of
    double-clicking on the selected folder. There is no effect if a folder is
    not selected.

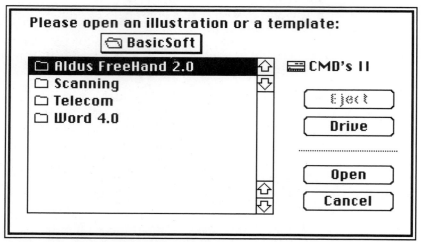

*Although Standard File dialog boxes may be slightly modified by each
application, they are all essentially the same, containing a scrolling file
list, and* EJECT, DRIVE, OPEN *(or* SAVE*), and* CANCEL *buttons.*

◇   ⌘-↑ **closes the currently selected folder**. This is the equivalent of
    dragging down one level with the directory menu in dialog boxes with
    scrolling file listings. There is no effect if the current directory is not
    a folder.

◇   **Typing the first letter or letters of a file name jumps down the scroll-
    ing list.** Rather than scrolling a long file listing, enter the first letter or
    letters of a file name and the list will automatically scroll to the first
    file starting with the character(s) entered, or the closest available file
    name. The more letters you type, the more specific the search.

    The length of the delay that distinguishes one multiple-letter search
    from several single-letter searches is determined by the "Key Repeat
    Rate" option set in the Keyboard cdev.

Universal Dialog Box Tips

◇ **A button enclosed in a heavy border is usually the default button**. Pressing the RETURN or ENTER key is the equivalent of clicking the default button in most cases.

◇ **The ↵ or ⤶ key can be pressed instead of clicking the OK button**. Pressing the RETURN or ENTER key can substitute for clicking the OK button in most dialog boxes—even some where the OK button is not enclosed in a heavy border.

◇ **⌘-Period is the equivalent of clicking the CANCEL button.** This shortcut works in most dialog boxes. As suggested in the Macros entry later in this section, creating a macro to assign COMMAND-PERIOD to any CANCEL button makes this shortcut universal.

◇ **Clicking on an option name is the equivalent of clicking its radio button or check box**. Clicking anywhere on the option name following a radio button or check box is the same as clicking the button or box itself; the option will become selected if it was deselected, and deselected if it was already selected.

◇ **➔| moves between option boxes**. In dialog boxes where more than one option box appears, you can press the TAB key to move from one option box to the next. Holding down the SHIFT key while pressing the TAB key moves you to the previous option box.

Microsoft Dialog Box Tips

◆ **The first letter of check-box and radio-button options toggles the option on and off**. This only works in dialog boxes without any text-entry option boxes.

◆ **⌘-First letter of any button name is the equivalent of clicking the button.** Of course, if more than one button starts with the same letter, this will only work for one of them.

◆ **⌘-First letter of pop-up menu option displays the menu**. You can then use ↑ and ↓ keys to scroll the pop-up menu options COMMAND-PERIOD hides the pop-up menu.

Dialog Box Utilities

 Boomerang   🖐️ⒻⓌ

Because the Standard File dialog box is used so commonly, a number of utilities have appeared, adding new features to this dialog box. Boomerang is the most recent of these, and by far the most ambitious. Boomerang adds a pop-up menu to Standard File dialog boxes. You access the pop-up menu by pressing and holding down the mouse button on the Boomerang icon. The pop-up menu presents four commands—FOLDER, FILE, DISK, and OPTION— each of which has its own hierarchical menu.

The FOLDER menu presents the feature that is at the heart of Boomerang: a list of the folders you use commonly. Selecting a folder from this list makes that folder the one currently displayed in the dialog box's scrolling file list, thereby saving you the effort of locating the folder with the DRIVE button and folder bar. Folder names can be permanently installed in this list, and Boomerang can automatically add the names of folders you use.

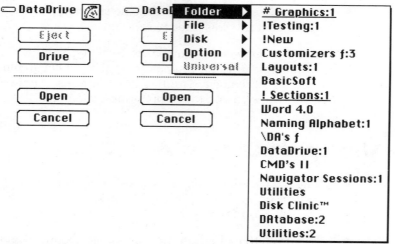

Boomerang adds this pop-up menu to all Standard File dialog boxes. On the left you can see the Boomerang icon as it appears in all Standard File dialog boxes before being pressed.

The FILE menu works just like the FOLDER menu, but lists commonly used files instead of folders. Selecting a file from the FILE menu causes the file's folder to be displayed in the scrolling file list, and the file itself to be selected. The DISK menu lists each disk, drive, or volume currently mounted, and the amount of free space each contains. Selecting a disk displays the root directory of that volume in the scrolling file list. The OPTION menu offers a few utility features such as the ability to create new folders, purge the FOLDER and FILE menu lists, and search for a specific file name.

In addition to these features, Boomerang also automatically selects the files and folders you have used most recently when manually navigating your drives and folders. Boomerang is one of the best utilities we've seen, and one that no frequent user should be without.

 ### SFVol ⓢⓦ

Boomerang has several predecessors, each of which provides one or two of Boomerang's many features. SFVol adds the ability to move directly to any volume, create a new folder, and display the amount of free space available on a drive. Before Boomerang, this was an indispensable utility. SFVol was written by Raymond Lau, who is now finishing a new Standard File dialog utility that will likely be quite impressive.

 ### SFScroll, Rebound ⓢⓦ, ⓕⓦ

These two inits also provide features included in Boomerang. SFScroll, written by Andy Hertzfeld, is the init that first introduced the concept of "memory" for scrolling lists. Normally, each time you open a dialog box that has a scrolling file listing, the top of the list is shown and no item in the list is selected. This is unfortunate because more often than not when opening a dialog box for the second time (or third or fourth) you will want to choose either the same file you did the last time, or a file directly above or below the one you chose the last time. If the file or files you are using are at the bottom of the scrolling file listing, you must scroll down to them each time you enter the dialog box.

SFScroll enabled the scrolling list in the current directory to remember what was selected the last time you accessed it. Rebound added the ability to remember the folder or file last selected on any drive or in any folder. Rebound made SFScroll obsolete, and Boomerang has made Rebound obsolete. But if you don't have Boomerang, Rebound is recommended.

⌧ DataDrive

CMD's II
DataDrive
New Folder... ⌘N
Free Space... ⌘F
About...

*This pop-up menu is presented when you click on the drive icon in any Standard
File dialog box when SFVol is in your System folder.*

 Dialog Keys   ⌐⌐

The Dialog Keys init, which is included along with DiskTop, adds a sort of
generic keyboard equivalent to dialog-box options. With Dialog Keys
installed, pressing COMMAND-SPACEBAR when in any dialog box will cause one
of the buttons or options in the dialog box to begin blinking. At this point,
you can press COMMAND-SPACEBAR again to select the flashing command,
COMMAND-TAB to move to the next button or option, or SHIFT-COMMAND-TAB to
move backwards. You can redefine these keystrokes using the QuickAccess
utility, which is also included.

Dialog Box Macros

Some of the macro programs available for the Mac provide special utilities
for working with buttons, check boxes, and radio buttons in dialog boxes.
QuicKeys has a special type of macro specifically for assigning keystrokes
to buttons; the "Buttons" option lets you enter the text that will be in the
button (e.g, *Cancel*) and then define a keystroke to press that button anytime it appears. A common use of this would be to assign COMMAND-PERIOD
to click the CANCEL button, thus making what is now an occasional shortcut
into a universal one. Or you may wish to assign ⌘-N to all No buttons, and
⌘-Y to all YES buttons. Tempo also recognizes button clicks in a way that
allows them to be defined universally.

Another use for macros in dialog boxes is to specify options. Tempo is
especially well suited to this task because its "smart options" can tell if a
radio button or check box is already checked or not. Since these options
toggle on and off, it is important that the macro not just blindly click the
option on; that could force the opposite setting from what you intended.
This is especially useful in an application such as PageMaker, where the
PRINT dialog box has sub–dialog boxes with various options. We have created

a Tempo macro that chooses the PRINT… command, makes sure the correct APD file is selected, changes four of the options in the POSTSCRIPT OPTIONS dialog box, and executes the print job. This eliminates eight mouse clicks each time we print a PageMaker file! Due to the complexities of working with dialog boxes, QuicKeys, AutoMac, and MacroMaker are not very useful in these cases. See the Macros, Emelda entry later in this section for more details.

Disks and Drives

Initializing and Formatting Disks

All Macintosh floppy disks and hard disk drives store data in concentric rings known as tracks, which are further divided into slices known as sectors. When these disks are manufactured, neither tracks nor sectors exist; the disk is just a smooth magnetic surface. Tracks and sectors are defined when the disk is **formatted** by a computer.

Unfortunately, the term *formatting* is one that has been butchered by computer users (and manufacturers and the press). This problem is exacerbated by the fact that there are two different types of formatting: **low-level formatting** and **high-level formatting**. In the Macintosh community these two processes are regularly described using any one of three terms: initializing, erasing, and formatting. In the best possible world, low-level formatting would be called *formatting*, high-level formatting would be called *initializing*, and erasing would be left to pencils. In our own attempt to improve the planet, we will use the terms thusly.

Low-level formatting defines the tracks and sectors on a disk. This process also verifies that each sector of the disk is capable of holding data. When a hard disk is formatted, any sectors that fail this verification are noted so they are never used. Apple has decided that if a floppy disk has any bad sectors it is rejected by the Finder—you receive the FORMAT FAILED dialog box—and cannot be used. Low-level formatting destroys any data on the disk so that data recovery or "undeletion" becomes impossible.

Initializing (high-level formatting) is the process of clearing the disk directory and file-allocation table. It does not actually change any file data on the disk (only data in the directory). Floppy disks are formatted and initialized in one action. So whether the process is called erasing, formatting, or initializing, floppy disks are always low-level formatted. This is true of the Finder's ERASE... command or an INITIALIZE button in a dialog box; each completely rewrites every sector on a floppy disk. Data can never be retrieved from an erased, formatted, or initialized floppy disk.

On hard drives, formatting and initializing are separate activities, although your hard-disk formatting software may not offer them as separate options. Choosing the ERASE command from the Finder, or clicking the INITIALIZE button in the THIS DISK IS DAMAGED Alert dialog, causes the hard drive to be initialized but not formatted. This is why data can usually be recovered when a hard drive has been initialized; the data still exists even though the directory maps to the data are gone. In order to low-level reformat a hard drive, you must use a special utility that specifically issues the low-level SCSI formatting commands. Several of these utilities are reviewed here.

HFS and MFS

During the formatting process, the Macintosh installs a file system, either the **Hierarchical Filing System (HFS)** or the **Macintosh Filing System (MFS)**. In the MFS system, folders are simply optical illusions that only the Finder believes; every file on a Macintosh disk is really at the same level, just as if no folders existed. When you work with MFS disks, the OPEN and SAVE dialog boxes list every file on a disk. You never have to go into a folder or come out of one to see any files; all files on the disk are listed in one long list, and it is impossible to have two files with the same name, even if they are in different folders.

With HFS, folders actually separate files, and this separation is recognized not only by the Finder but by every Macintosh application and dialog box. HFS makes it much easier to organize files than it was under the MFS system. HFS was developed when Macintosh hard drives were first introduced, because only with the storage capacity of a hard drive do the limitations of MFS become apparent. Imagine if every OPEN dialog box presented a single list of every file on your entire hard drive!

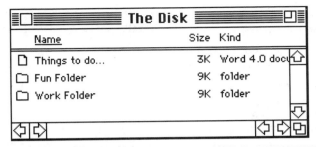

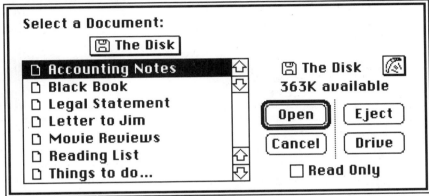

Even though most of the files in this MFS disk are in folders, they all appear together in the OPEN dialog box. On an HFS disk, the folders would be seen in the OPEN dialog box.

Floppy-Disk Formatting Utilities

Each time a disk is inserted into a Mac disk drive, the ROM-level mounting software checks that the disk has been formatted. If it hasn't, or if the mounting software thinks it hasn't (because the disk is damaged in some way), the THIS DISK IS DAMAGED—EJECT OR INITIALIZE dialog box appears, asking you if you want to eject the disk or initialize it as either a single-sided (400K) or double-sided (800K) disk (or as a high-density 1.44MB disk if using a high-density disk drive and diskette). If you want to format the disk, click the INITIALIZE button and the disk will be formatted and verified. If the disk was not previously named, you will also be prompted to name it. If this dialog box appears and you want to attempt to retrieve the data on the disk, click the EJECT button. See "Floppy-Disk Mounting/Dismounting/Ejecting Tips" later in this entry for more information.

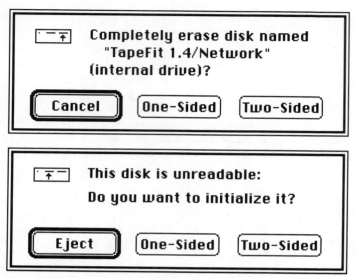

Two different dialog boxes allow you to initialize a floppy disk.

Initializing diskettes at the Finder is a fine way to initialize one or two disks, but it is so slow and requires so much dialog-box interaction that if you were formatting an entire box of disks you might hope for a better way. Thankfully, a number of excellent formatting programs are ready to help. Also, most disk-duplicating utilities format disks automatically as part of the duplication process, so there is no need to format disks that will be used in duplication.

    Eraser, Fast Formatter, Formatter Deluxe, Mass Init
Each of these programs can format 800K disks almost as fast as you can insert them into your disk drives because you set formatting options only once instead of responding to dialog-box inquiries for each disk. These utilities allow you to use two drives to initialize disks (if you have two drives), and most provide a warning if you try to format a disk that has already been formatted, although you can disable this feature if you wish. Some also allow you to skip the disk-verification process, thereby speeding up the process even more (but adding a small amount of risk to the use of the disks).

Eraser offers the most features of any of these programs, including the ability to detect non-Macintosh disks (previously formatted PC or Lisa disks) and to verify disks after formatting. As of this writing, only Beyond's Fast Formatter has been upgraded to support HDFD 1.44MB drives.

```
═══════════════════════ Eraser ═══════════════════════

   Name Disks: Untitled                  ☐ Serial # [        ]

   ┄┄┄┄┄┄┄┄┄┄┄┄┄┄┄┄┄┄┄┄┄┄┄┄┄┄┄┄┄┄┄┄┄┄┄┄┄┄┄┄┄┄┄┄┄┄┄┄┄┄┄

              One-sided  Two-sided   Blank   Non-Mac
     Prompt       ⊠          ⊠         ☐        ☐
     Eject        ○          ○         ○        ◉
     Erase        ◉          ◉         ◉        ○
     Certify      ○          ○

   ┄┄┄┄┄┄┄┄┄┄┄┄┄┄┄┄┄┄┄┄┄┄┄┄┄┄┄┄┄┄┄┄┄┄┄┄┄┄┄┄┄┄┄┄┄┄┄┄┄┄┄
       ☐ Erase One Side Only      ⊠ Certify After Erasing
   ┄┄┄┄┄┄┄┄┄┄┄┄┄┄┄┄┄┄┄┄┄┄┄┄┄┄┄┄┄┄┄┄┄┄┄┄┄┄┄┄┄┄┄┄┄┄┄┄┄┄┄
    [HEY!]   Insert a disk into any drive.
```

The Eraser utility allows you to quickly format many floppy disks.

Floppy Disk Tips

❖ **HFS and MFS disks can be distinguished by the presence or absence of the HFS pixel.** You can tell if a drive or disk is formatted as HFS or MFS by looking for the "HFS pixel" in the upper-left corner of any window from the drive or disk. If this pixel is on, the drive or volume uses the HFS; if it is off, the drive or volume uses the MFS.

❖ **Single-sided disks are formatted using MFS by default.** To format a single-sided disk as an HFS disk, press and hold the OPTION key while clicking the ONE-SIDED button in the COMPLETELY ERASE DISK? dialog box. You must keep the OPTION key depressed until the format is complete.

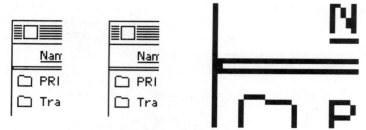

The HFS pixel can be seen in the left window between the two horizontal lines just above the folder icon. In the center window it is not present. An enlargement of the pixel is presented at right.

◇   **Double-sided disks are formatted using HFS by default.**

◇   **Single-sided disks can be formatted as double-sided (400K as 800K).** The only difference between single-sided disks and double-sided disks is that double-sided disks have been certified by the manufacturer on both sides and single-sided disks have only been certified on one side. Single-sided disks have exactly the same magnetic coating on both of their sides, but the manufacturer didn't bother testing the second side. The coating is applied to the second side so that the disk doesn't warp as it would if only coated on one side.

Understanding this, you can decide for yourself if you want to buy single-sided disks, which are somewhat cheaper, and format them double-sided. The arguments for and against this practice can be summed up this way:

For: As long as a floppy disk is formatted and verified properly as double-sided, it will probably work fine for its entire life. The Macintosh verification procedure is very stringent, rejecting a disk if a single sector fails to be verified. Why spend extra money?

Against: The small amount of money saved by using single-sided disks may not even make up the cost of recovering or reconstructing the data you lose the first time this method fails you. The additional cost of double-sided disks is insignificant in comparison with the value of your data.

Our opinion? Both points are well-taken, however we buy only double-sided disks, valuing our data more than a few cents per disk. Also, remember that if you do use single-sided disks you will have some failure rate, and those disks that fail will have to be used as single-sided. It has also been suggested that manufacturers sell double-sided disks that fail verification on their second side as single-sided disks, so your chance of a verification failure may be slightly higher than you might expect.

It is very important not to reformat single-sided disks that have been used in single-sided (400K) disk drives as double-sided (800K) disks. Even if these disks are verified properly, they should not be used as double-sided disks. This is because single-sided disk drives had a pad that rubbed against the unused side of the disks, providing pressure so the head on the other side of the disk could read accurately; this inevitably affected the surface of that side of the disk.

◆　**Single-sided and double-sided disks should not be formatted as high-density disks (400/800K as 1.44MB)**. With a slight mechanical modification it is possible to format single-sided disks and double-sided disks as high-density, but the difference between high-density disks and all other disks is substantial and should compel you not to modify 400/800K disks so that they can be formatted as 1.44MB disks. A unique thin recording surface on high-density diskettes supports the recording method used to squeeze 1.44MB on the disk. Because they don't have this recording surface, 400/800K disks make unreliable 1.44MB disks.

You may be wondering how you can even try to format a 400/800K disk as a 1.44MB disk. After all, high-density disk drives recognize 1.44MB disks by the unique hole in the disk itself, don't they? Yes they do, and so would-be money savers actually drill holes in their 400/800K disks. There are people doing this, and swearing that it works reliably, but we strongly advise against it.

◆　**High-density disks can be formatted as single-sided or double-sided disks (1.44MB as 400/800K)**. This too is unwise, however, primarily because a high-density disk formatted in either single-sided or double-sided format will be unusable in a high-density disk drive; the drive will sense that it is a high-density diskette (because of the special hole) and ask to format it, not recognizing that it is already being used as a single-sided or double-sided disk. Also, once a high-density disk has been formatted as either single-sided or double-sided, in cannot be reformatted as a high-density disk—the formatting of a single-sided or double-sided disk is too strong to be overwritten by the formatting of a high-density disk drive in high-density mode.

◆ **PC 3.5" double-sided floppy disks can be formatted as single-sided or double-sided Macintosh disks, and PC high-density disks can be formatted in Macintosh high-density format**. There is no difference between Macintosh and PC 3.5" floppy disks. Of course, for the reasons we've just listed, only a high-density 3.5" disk should be formatted as high-density (1.44MB). All other PC 3.5" disks are double-sided (intended for PC 720K disk drives) and can therefore be used safely as single-sided (400K) or double-sided (800K) Macintosh disks.

◆ **Recovering data from a formatted floppy disk**. There is no way to recover data from a floppy disk after it has been formatted. Sorry. Specific files that have been deleted (if the disk has not been formatted) can be recovered, as explained later in this entry.

◆ **Disks that won't format**. There are two kinds of diskettes that won't format: those that fail the Finder's formatting routines, and those that are ejected before the Finder even tries to format them. In the first case, two options are available. If a diskette fails to format as a double-sided disk, chances are good that it will format as a single-sided disk. Alternatively, another formatting utility may be able to format and verify the disk. It's hard to say why this is, but Apple appears to have set very high standards for Finder-formatted disks. If a suspect disk does format using a formatting utility, you might want to format and verify it again, or try to format it at the Finder, to confirm its quality. We would, however, recommend using any suspect disks as single-sided disks (assuming they pass single-sided verification), remembering our "data is more valuable than the disk" premise from a few paragraphs ago.

Disks that the Finder ejects before attempting to format them pose a more difficult problem. The best solution is to try another formatting utility, and if that is successful, again try to format the disk at the Finder. A trickier method is to "fool" your disk drive into thinking that a floppy has been inserted (although this is very difficult), and then when the DISK IS DAMAGED, INITIALIZE OR EJECT? dialog box appears, insert your bad disk and click the INITIALIZE button.

Hard-Disk Formatting Utilities

Formatting and initializing a hard drive is a much more complex process than that used to prepare a floppy disk. This is true because hard drives are complicated hardware products that vary from device to device—as opposed to floppy drives, which are all Sony drives—and because they connect to the Macintosh via the SCSI port, which is controlled by a complex set of SCSI commands. Each unique hardware configuration may require slightly different commands than the next to properly format and initialize the drive.

Also, there are two hard-drive formatting parameters that must be set according to the interaction between the computer's CPU and the hard drive. These are the hard drive's **sector interleave factor** and the SCSI data transfer loops. A drive's interleave factor determines how the sectors on each track of the hard disk are numbered, and consequently the speed with which the drive is able to read and write data. In most cases, Mac Plus computers will use an interleave factor of 3, Mac SE computers use an interleave of 2, and Mac II, IIx, IIcx, and SE/30 computers use an interleave of 1. See the Disk Drives entry in Section 3 for a complete explanation of interleave.

Data transfer loops are the method by which the CPU transfers data to and from the SCSI bus. Many hard drives support only two different transfer loops, but some, including La Cié's SilverLining hard-drive formatting software, offer several others. In most cases, you cannot manually select the data transfer loops—again SilverLining is the exception—but rather they are set automatically by the formatting software. See the Disk-Drive entry in Section 3 for a complete explanation of data transfer loops.

Fortunately, most hard-drive vendors include formatting software with their drives, and many even preformat the drive so it is ready to run as soon as it is installed. Over the past few years, the quality of most hard-drive formatting utilities has improved tremendously. Early formatting packages offered the user very little control, even less feedback, and minimal ability to function in less-than-optimal situations. Today, many packages offer an excellent range of user control over formatting options, complete feedback on the progress of drive formatting, documentation of errors encountered, and the ability to correct many problems that formerly would have meant sending your drive back to the manufacturer.

If your new hard drive does arrive preformatted and you are not sure that the interleave has been set properly, you might want to consider reformatting it. Even if you bought it from a local dealer (rather than by mail order), the interleave could be set improperly. Also, you might want to give your drive a "fresh start" when adding your System Software, applications, and utilities, especially if your drive arrived filled with software that you want to remove, thereby leaving your drive immediately fragmented.

 SilverLining, UniMac   ⁂⊞⊞, ⊞⊞

These two products seem to work on a great number of hard drives, and are often provided by resellers who buy their hard drives directly from OEM suppliers rather than traditional Macintosh hard-drive vendors. Of these two, SilverLining is undoubtedly the better product, offering a wider range of drive-testing and utility features, direct control over both drive interleave and data transfer loops, and complete support for resizable SCSI partitions with security.

Mounting and Dismounting Disks

Mounting and **dismounting** are the terms that describe the logical connection made between storage devices and the Macintosh. When a volume is mounted, its icon appears at the Finder desktop, and thereafter all Standard File dialog boxes, as well as any file-management DA's and utilities, can access the volume. When a volume has been dismounted, its icon no longer appears on the Finder desktop and it cannot be accessed by any software. Some storage devices, such as floppy disks, can be **ejected**, (physically disconnected) from the Macintosh without being dismounted (logically disconnected) from the Macintosh.

Mounting, Dismounting, and Ejecting Floppy Disks

When a floppy disk is inserted into one of the Mac's disk drives, software in ROM checks to see if the disk has been formatted, and if so, it reads the disk's directory information into RAM. The disk icon is then displayed on the desktop, indicating that the disk has been mounted. If the disk is not formatted, the THIS DISK IS UNREADABLE dialog box appears, asking you if you want to format the disk or eject it. If the disk has been formatted but has some problem, either the DISK NEEDS MINOR REPAIRS dialog box or the THIS DISK IS DAMAGED dialog box will appear. In the first case, you should allow the minor repairs, as these are almost always successful. In the second case, you should click the Eⁿᵉᶜᵀ button and attempt to retrieve your data as explained below, or your data will be irretrievably lost.

Floppy disks and other removable media can be ejected without being dismounted. When you select a floppy disk and choose the Eⁿᵉᶜᵀ command in the FILE menu, or eject the disk via keyboard equivalents, the disk is ejected but the dimmed icon of the disk remains on the desktop because the disk is still mounted. Dimmed disk icons reflect the fact that the disk is physically ejected but logically attached.

To eject and dismount a floppy disk, drag the disk icon to the trash can. This does not remove any of the data from the disk, but instead causes the Macintosh to remove the disk directory from RAM and eject and dismount the floppy disk. Dragging the disk icon to the trash can will eject the disk without dismounting it if any files on the disk are still in use; the dimmed disk icon will remain on the desktop. Most Eⁿᵉᶜᵀ buttons in dialog boxes do not dismount disks; they only eject them. DiskTop allows you to dismount disks by dragging them to the trash shown at the top DiskTop level.

Floppy-Disk Mounting/Dismounting/Ejecting Tips

◇ **Eject a selected disk using the FILE menu's Eⁿᵉᶜᵀ command (⌘-E).** Choosing the Eⁿᵉᶜᵀ command in the FILE menu (⌘-E) will eject the currently selected floppy disk. (The disk itself may be selected, or any file or folder on the disk.) This command will never dismount the disk; it will only eject it. Drag the disk icon to the trash to eject and dismount the disk.

◇ **Disks can be ejected with ⌘-⌥-1, ⌘-⌥-2, or ⌘-⌥-3.** At almost any time, pressing COMMAND-OPTION-1 will eject the inside floppy disk (right/bottom), pressing COMMAND-OPTION-2 will eject the external floppy disk (left/top), and pressing COMMAND-OPTION-3 will eject the external floppy disk on machines with two internal floppy drives. These commands eject the disk, but do not dismount it.

◇ **Drag a disk into the trash can to eject and dismount it.** When a disk icon is dragged into the trash can, the disk is always ejected, but it is dismounted only when no files on the disk are in use. You can tell if a disk has been successfully dismounted if its icon disappears. If the disk remains displayed as a dimmed icon, it has not been dismounted, and you will probably be asked to insert the disk sometime before you shut down. To dismount this disk, reinsert it, close any files in use or quit the active applications on the disk, and then drag the disk icon to the trash again.

◇ **Disks are automatically ejected and dismounted when either the Shut-down or Restart command is chosen.**

❖ **Hold the mouse button down during startup to eject inserted disks.** Holding down the mouse button just as a Macintosh starts to boot will eject all inserted floppies. (It also dismounts them since they were never really mounted.) If this does not work, your floppy drive is probably dead or not connected properly. Turn off the power for a minute or two and try again. See the "Disks that won't come out" tip below for more information.

❖ **The trash is emptied when a disk is dismounted, but not when it is ejected.** When a disk is ejected (without being dismounted), the trash is not emptied. Actions that would empty the trash while the disk is ejected will cause the Mac to prompt you to reinsert the disk. When a disk is dismounted, the trash is always emptied.

❖ **Ejecting disks manually.** All Macintosh floppy-disk drives still support manual disk ejection: Insert a straightened paper clip into the small hole to the right of the drive and push in. Your paper clip should only travel about ¼ inch before reaching the ejection lever; if your clip goes in farther, you have missed the lever. Only a small amount of force should be required to eject the disk. Don't force it. If you cannot eject the disk this way, something might be caught and you could cause further damage by trying too hard. See the next tip for more help. If this does eject the disk (and your Mac is turned on), the disk will not be dismounted.

"Jumbo" paper clips work much better than standard-guage clips, making better contact with the eject lever and withstanding the force applied during ejection without bending. By the way, keeping a pre-straightened heavy-guage paper clip around your Mac is definitely one subtle sign of a power-user. A few years ago someone actually sold a small folded piece of cardboard that said "Macintosh Power-User's Tool" on the outside and contained a straightened paper clip!

◆ **The THIS DISK IS DAMAGED dialog box.** After a floppy disk has been inserted, the THIS DISK IS DAMAGED dialog box may appear, offering you an INITIALIZE button and an EJECT button. Clicking the INITIALIZE button will permanently erase the disk; therefore you should click the EJECT button unless you do not want to attempt to save the data. The following steps should be taken to attempt data recovery:

1. If possible, try the disk in another disk drive. Disk drives can get out of alignment over time, and fail to read disks that they have written earlier or disk written on other disk drives. If your disk mounts properly on another drive, you should have your floppy drive aligned.

The THIS DISK IS DAMAGED *dialog box appears when the Mac finds something wrong with an inserted disk.*

2. Attempt to rebuild the Desktop file by holding down the COMMAND and OPTION keys when inserting the disk. If a dialog box appears asking you to confirm the rebuilding of the Desktop file, click the YES button and your disk may then mount normally. However, this will usually not work, and you will again see the THIS DISK IS DAMAGED dialog box. See the Desktop File entry earlier in this section for more information.

3. Attempt to repair the disk using Apple's Disk First Aid (from your System Software disks). To do this, run the Disk First Aid application (you should not be in MultiFinder), insert the disk, click the DRIVE button until the disk's name appears, click the OPEN button, and then click the REPAIR button. A message will appear stating either that the "Repair was successful," in which case you can quit Disk First Aid and your disk will probably mount at the Finder desktop normally, or that the "Disk failed to verify."

4. Use Symantec Utilities or MacTools to attempt to repair the disk or retrieve the data. These utilities can recover data from almost any damaged floppy disk if they are used before the disk is initialized.

◆ **The PLEASE INSERT DISK: *DISKNAME* dialog box**. Your Mac will often ask you for a disk that has been ejected but not dismounted, even if you are performing tasks that have no apparent relation to the ejected disk. This happens because the disk's directory information is kept in RAM until it is dismounted, and the Mac occasionally attempts to perform some housekeeping tasks on all mounted disks. This is why you should dismount floppy disks, not just eject them, when not using them.

If the disk is available, insert it, and then dismount it as soon as possible to avoid being asked for it again. If, however, the disk is unavailable—perhaps it has been taken away or is being used by another Macintosh—press COMMAND-PERIOD and you may be able to persuade the Mac to get by without this disk. You may see this dialog box several times; just keep responding with COMMAND-PERIOD. The only way to ensure that the Mac permanently forgets the disk is to reboot.

The PLEASE INSERT DISK: Dialog box appears when the Mac needs a disk that has been ejected but not dismounted.

Occasionally when you insert a disk that the Mac has asked for, it will act as if you have inserted the wrong disk, ejecting the disk and then immediately asking for it again. This usually happens because the disk has been modified by another Macintosh since being used in your Mac. All you can do in this case is try the COMMAND-PERIOD method just described.

◆ **Disks that won't come out.** There are a number of reasons why floppy disks occasionally cannot be ejected properly. If a disk has been inserted but the Mac acts as if it was not inserted—the disk icon does not appear on the desktop and it cannot be found in any dialog boxes with the DRIVE button—the disk cannot be ejected via the EJECT command but can usually be ejected using one of the keyboard ejection commands (⌘-⬏-1, ⌘-⬏-2, or ⌘-⬏-3), because these commands invoke a mechanical ejection in the disk drives.

If even the keyboard commands do not work, try to manually eject the disk (as described in the previous tip). If this works, then the Mac is not "seeing" the disk drive. First try to reboot; this will usually correct the problem. If the drive is still not operational, shut down the Mac, wait a few minutes before restarting it, and then try the drive again. If the drive remains nonfunctional, either the drive is dead, its cable has gone bad, or the cable is not connected properly. If you are comfortable with opening your Mac, do so and check that the drive cable is secure. If not, or if this does not solve the problem, it's time to visit your Mac repair shop. More information about opening your Mac and working with its disk drives is presented in the Disks and Drives entry in Section 3.

If the disk is physically stuck, which is usually due to a peeling disk label or a bent drive shutter, proceed slowly. What you don't want to do is bend the drive heads, as this will almost certainly ruin your disk drive. Try to eject the disk manually, but don't apply too much force—it should never require brute strength to eject a floppy disk. If the disk comes out partially before getting stuck, bring it out and reinsert it a few times, hoping that it will shake itself clear. If the disk remains stuck, you will probably have to take it to your dealer.

◆ **The yellow disk insert.** If Apple ships the Mac with these things, it's probably a good idea to use them when you transport your Mac, right? Wrong. In fact, the Sony drive mechanisms in the Mac automatically keep their heads apart whenever a disk is not inserted, so this insert is superfluous, but harmless. Interestingly, Apple charges its Authorized Service Centers with an "improper packaging" fee for any Mac returned to Apple without the inserts (but it also charges this fee if the Styrofoam is missing).

Hard Drives

Storage devices connected to the Macintosh via the SCSI port have very different mounting and dismounting behavior than floppy disks. Most SCSI hard drives automatically mount during startup. Most hard-drive partitions can be set to mount automatically, if desired, or you can use DA's to control their mounting. SCSI devices that use removable media act more like floppy drives, automatically mounting volumes as they are inserted.

When your hard drive has problems mounting, instead of the smiling little Mac giving way to the "Welcome to Macintosh" dialog box, you see a big flashing question mark inside a floppy-disk icon. As you may remember from your pre–hard disk days, this symbol is the Mac's way of telling you that it is all ready to go, but is in need of a boot disk.

"I don't use a boot disk," you say. "I've got a hard disk." Well, at the moment the Macintosh does not agree. As explained in Section 4, after the Mac runs a self test it goes looking for a floppy disk or hard drive with boot blocks and a copy of the System and Finder files. If for some reason the System file, Finder, or boot blocks go bad, or if mechanical components of your hard drive are not working properly, then the Mac is unable to boot up from the hard drive. And you are left staring at a flashing question mark.

You may react to this with horror (if you understand the gravity of the situation). But wait: The chances are good that one of three things is true:

• There is nothing wrong with your hard drive.

• Your hard drive has a minor problem with the System, Finder, or boot blocks that is easily corrected.

• Your data can be saved, but after saving your data you will have to reformat your hard drive.

In fact, about 80 percent of the time that hard drives fail it is not *necessary* that any data be lost. However, this is true only if you proceed very carefully as soon as you realize that a problem has occured. Data is probably *actually* lost between 50 and 70 percent of the time hard drives fail, with the variance occurring because the wrong move is made immediately after failure occurs.

In order to attempt to save your data and resurrect your hard drive, take the following steps,

- **Restart the Macintosh and all devices**. Turn off all devices and then turn them all back on again. The order in which they are switched on doesn't matter, as long as it's about the same time.

- **Check the SCSI connections**. With all devices including the Macintosh turned off, check that all cables are connected securely. Connecting or disconnecting SCSI cables while devices are turned on may "hang the SCSI bus," permanently damaging your hard drive or Macintosh.

- **Be sure each SCSI device has a unique SCSI ID number**. Conflicting SCSI ID's can cause the entire system to lock up, or just cause a single device to not operate properly. Be aware of the SCSI ID of each device; you will have to check the manual for each SCSI peripheral to determine how its SCSI ID is determined. (It may be either set via a hardware switch or software-controlled.) We recommend writing the SCSI ID number on the back of each of your SCSI devices when you first configure it, so that later you can quickly determine its ID.

  After you have checked the SCSI connection, SCSI termination, and SCSI ID numbers, turn on your Mac and all SCSI devices and see if the system boots properly. Each SCSI device connected to your Macintosh must be turned on or none of the devices will operate properly. If just one SCSI device is turned off, your hard drive may act as if it is turned off and not boot up your Mac.

- **Zap the PRAM**. Sometimes a hard drive will not mount when the parameter RAM data has been destroyed or jumbled. Zap the PRAM by holding down the shift, option, and command keys while choosing the Control Panel DA from the APPLE menu. You cannot do this while running MultiFinder.

- **Boot from a floppy disk**. If your drive is still not booting, restart your Macintosh and insert any valid startup disk (any floppy disk containing a System file and Finder) in the internal disk drive. After the Mac boots from this floppy disk, your hard drive may mount (appear) on the Finder desktop. In this case your hard disk itself is usually not damaged, but either the boot blocks or the System file is damaged.

If the THIS DISK IS DAMAGED, INITIALIZE OR EJECT Alert dialog box appears, click the EJECT button, unless you want to minimize or eliminate your chances of retrieving the data from the drive.

- **Try some mounting utilities**. If your drive does not mount when your Mac is booted from a floppy disk, you will have to try mounting the drive with some mounting utility software. Several utilities are available for the express purpose of mounting hard drives, and mounting is a "side effect" of several other utilities. Try any or all of the utilities listed later in this entry. As soon as your drive is mounted, continue with the steps documented below.

- **Drives that crash when mounting**. If your hard drive crashes when it attempts to mount on the desktop, try rebuilding its Desktop file. (Hold down the COMMAND and OPTION keys when it is mounting.) If this does not work, try mounting the drive using one of the mounting utilities just described while not at the Finder and not running MultiFinder. You should then be able to access the drive's files using a utility like DiskTop. At this time you should copy all important files to another drive or a floppy disk.

- **Retrieve your valuable data the first time the drive mounts**. Before attempting any repairs, or doing anything else, you should copy your most valuable data from the drive onto floppy disks (or another hard drive, if one is mounted) the first time the drive mounts. You may damage the drive further during repairs, or never be so lucky as to have it mount again, so take advantage of your first opportunity.

- **Attempt repairs with Disk First Aid**. The Disk First Aid utility included as part of Apple's System Software should be used as your first effort to repair the disk. Run the Disk First Aid application from your floppy drive and click the DRIVE button until the name of the damaged disk appears at the top of the dialog box. The disk name may appear as "Disk with bad name," but it will also give you a SCSI ID number so you can confirm that it is the drive in question. Click the OPEN button, select the REPAIR AUTOMATICALLY command from the OPTIONS menu, and then click the REPAIR button. Disk First Aid will then tell you either that it has completed repairs, or that it is unable to repair the disk. If Disk First Aid claims to have completed repairs, restart your Macintosh and see if your drive boots properly.

- **Repair the boot blocks and reinstall the System file**. If Disk First Aid did not correct your drive's problem, reboot again from a floppy disk and then delete the System file from your hard drive (moving all of its fonts and DA's to a separate file first) and run the Installer application from your Apple System Software's System Tools disk. This will copy a fresh System file onto your hard drive and rewrite the drive's boot blocks.

- **Rebuild the Desktop file on the damaged disks**. Normally if the Desktop file was the problem you would get the THIS DISK NEEDS MINOR RE-PAIRS Alert dialog and not the DISK IS DAMAGED Alert dialog, but this can work in some cases. Hold down the COMMAND and OPTION keys while inserting the disk. A dialog box should appear, asking you if you want to rebuild the Desktop on the disk. Click the OK button. If the DISK IS DAMAGED dialog box appears instead, again click the CANCEL button and try the repair methods listed below.

   If you get an error message saying that the Desktop file cannot be rebuilt, you can probably retrieve your data by inserting the disk while any application except the Finder is running (while not running MultiFinder) and copying files off the disk using any utility or DA that allows you access to the disk's files, such as DiskTools.

- **Initialize and save with SUM or PC Tools**. Both the Symantec Utilities and PC Tools can recover files from an initialized hard drive. While both perform much better and with higher recovery rates when they have been installed before the initialization, both may be able to recover data even after a drive has been entirely initialized.

- **Reinitialize or reformat the drive**. When all is lost, reformat your drive, reinstall its drivers, and start over. Good thing you back up so frequently—right?

Like floppy disks, most SCSI devices are dismounted when dragged into the trash can. Obviously, nonremovable media will not be physically ejected when dismounted, and in most cases even removable media (such as tape cartridges) must be ejected manually—but this should only be done after the volume has been dismounted. Volumes that will not dismount via the trash can may contain files that are still open, or may have to be dismounted using special utility software. As mentioned, MountEm has the ability to dismount SCSI devices.

Mounting Utilities

MountEm

The MountEm Fkey is very good at mounting SCSI drives. Like other Fkeys, it can be installed in your System file, or accessed via utilities like Suitcase II or MasterJuggler. You can also use MountEm to dismount drives, by holding down the CAPS LOCK key when invoking MountEm. See the Fkeys entry later in this section for more information about using Fkeys.

SCSI Tools

SCSI Tools is a cdev that shows the current status of each SCSI ID (mounted or not mounted) and includes a MOUNT button that attempts to mount all attached devices. We have never had very much luck with this utility, but others report good results from it; it probably depends upon the particular SCSI devices you are using.

Disk First Aid

Although not primarily a mounting utility, Disk First Aid must try to mount all devices when it is launched, because we've been able to mount otherwise unmountable drives with it several times. Just launch Disk First Aid, choose the OPEN... command from the FILE menu, click the DRIVE button a few times—until you see your drive's name appear—and then quit. If the drive was mounted it will appear at the Finder desktop.

SCSI Evaluator, SilverLining, UniMac

Like Disk First Aid, most hard-drive formatting and SCSI utilities mount available hard drives automatically or include mounting commands. These include SCSI Evaluator, SilverLining, and UniMac. In SCSI Evaluator, use the ID SEARCH button in the GET DRIVE GEOMETRY dialog box.

Naming Disks

◇ **Use the COPY and PASTE commands for quick disk renaming**. After duplicating a disk, select the source disk and choose the COPY command from the EDIT menu (⌘-C), and then select the destination disk and choose the PASTE command (⌘-V). The new disk is now named the same as the original.

◇ **Consider the effect of renaming files and folders**. Besides the obvious effect, renaming a file or folder will cause backup software to treat it as a changed file—in the case of folders, all subfiles and folders

will be considered "new"—and other software that depends on the
file name, such as macro utilities and launchers, will no longer recognize the file.

◆   **Use an "illegal" name to correct an accidental renaming.** If you begin
to change the name of a file you didn't want to rename, delete the
file's name completely or give it the same name as an existing file.
Neither will be allowed by the Finder, and the original name will be
restored.

Defragmenting Disks

Imagine trying to read a book if the words in each sentence were spread
randomly across all of the book's pages, with each word followed by directions to the next. Do you think this would slow down your reading speed?
Well, this is essentially what you are asking your hard drive to do when
you allow it to remain **fragmented**.

As explained in the Disk Drives entry in Section 3, both floppy disks and
hard drives store the data from one file in a number of different sectors on
a disk, which may be spread across any number of **tracks** on the various
drive **platters**. Files are assigned to **sectors** by software from the Mac's ROM,
which uses the information from the disk's directory entries to determine
the available sectors on a disk. When you first start to use a disk, virtually
every sector is available for use; as files are added they are written to contiguous sectors. This continues until you begin to delete files from your
disk, or rewrite existing files as they change or grow.

*This figure shows the location of one file on a hard drive. Notice that the file is
fragmented, as indicated by the three broken dashes; it is not written in consecutive sectors, which would appear as a single, solid line.*

When you delete a file, the sectors it used become available for another file. When another file needs to be written, the file manager uses these sectors, but if the entire file won't fit in the space left by the previously deleted file, the remainder of the new file is written to sectors elsewhere on the disk. As you continue to use your disk, adding, deleting, and rewriting files, it becomes less and less common for a file to be assigned to contiguous sectors.

In order to read or write a file in contiguous sectors, the disk head must be positioned over the track containing those sectors, and then it must wait while the disk's rotation brings the desired sectors underneath the read/write heads. The Mac can then read or write the file without repositioning the heads—unless not enough sectors are available in the track, in which case the next track is used so the read/write heads do not have to move very far.

This file is not fragmented; it is written in sequential sectors.

In order to read or write a file in discontiguous sectors, the disk head must move to each different track the file uses, and each time wait for the desired sectors to spin underneath the heads. This excess motion wears on the mechanical portions of the disk drive, and obviously slows down the process of reading or writing the file. File fragmentation is inevitable as long as we save, delete, and edit files on our disks. It is, however, possible to defragment your files, moving them around so that each is positioned in consecutive sectors. Three utility programs are available to help you defragment your disks; unfortunately, only one of them really performs the task they all claim.

Disk Express

Alsoft's Disk Express is the original Macintosh disk defragmenter, and it remains the only true defragmenter for the Macintosh. Disk Express performs true disk defragmenting by completely rearranging your disk so that every file written in contiguous sectors and all unused sectors are placed at the end of the disk. When Disk Express is finished, your drive is organized exactly as it would have been if you started with a blank disk and copied all of your files to the disk one at a time. Since all of the blank space on your disk is now sequential, newly created files will automatically be written to sequential sectors. As an added measure of prevention, Disk Express offers a "Prioritize" option that puts all system-related files and applications at the start of your defragmented disk. This prevents future fragmentation, since these files are the least likely to be deleted or to change in size. The amount of time it takes to defragment your drive depends on the amount of free space available and the size of the drive. Typically, defragmenting a 20Mb hard drive takes about 20 to 30 minutes.

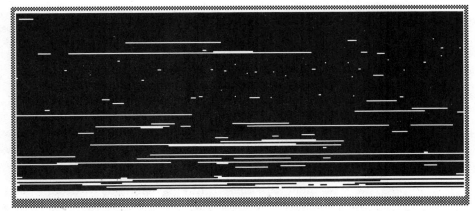

This drive is badly fragmented. Although 2.1Mb of free space remains, the largest group of sequential sectors is only 307k.

Disk Express also offers a "Quick Defragment" option, which moves all fragmented files into consecutive sectors, if possible, without rearranging all the files on the disk so that the unused sectors are at the end. This type of defragmentation is much faster than the full defragmentation performed by Disk Express's normal operation (taking only 5 or 10 minutes), but is useful only as a short-term improvement for your drive, and eventually leads to more fragmentation than it cures.

After the drive has been defragmented, all of its free space (indicated by the white space) is at the end of the drive.

Disk Express can also reduce the size of your Desktop file, eliminating icons and other information for software no longer being used, analyzing the hard drive's surface, and erasing the free space on your drive to prevent the unscrupulous from reading or extracting data from these sectors. All in all, Disk Express is an outstanding utility package and should be in the disk box of every hard-disk user.

HD TuneUp, Optimizer, TurboOptimizer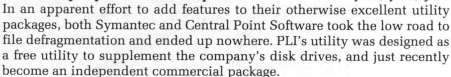
In an apparent effort to add features to their otherwise excellent utility packages, both Symantec and Central Point Software took the low road to file defragmentation and ended up nowhere. PLI's utility was designed as a free utility to supplement the company's disk drives, and just recently become an independent commercial package.

The problem with these utilities is that while, with some notable exceptions, they do move existing files into contiguous sectors, thus appearing to accomplish the goal of defragmentation, they leave the remaining free disk space scattered randomly across the disk. This only serves to accelerate the future fragmentation of the drive! Also, since these packages do not move all files in their defragmentation process, any large files for which they cannot locate a large enough group of contiguous sectors are not defragmented. So the files that most urgently need to be defragmented remain fragmented.

Use of these packages offers a temporary improvement over a fragmented drive, but unless they are used very frequently—every day or every few days—they are literally more trouble than they are worth. Running them, however, only takes a few minutes. If used to maintain a drive that has been defragmented with Disk Express, they would be of some value in delaying the requirement for another full defragmentation, but since Disk Express itself offers this type of option with its "Quick Defragment," you wouldn't want to buy these utilities for this purpose. Reportedly, however, SUM II will enhance HD TuneUp to provide true disk defragmenting.

Disk Optimization Tips

◇   **Back up your drive before defragmenting it**. If your computer loses power or experiences unexpected problems during defragmenting with Disk Express, data loss is almost assured. With the "file defragmenters" this would be much less likely, but still possible. (You would probably only lose the file being defragmented at the time of the interruption.) It is therefore wise to back up all data on any drives before defragmenting them. Of course, backing up is usually a wise idea, but it isn't always done. We've been using Disk Express often for the past two years, and have never experienced any data loss nor heard of anyone who has.

◆   **After formatting a hard drive, add system-related files and applications first**. With a little foresight you can minimize the amount of fragmentation that will occur on your drive. This is even more important if you will not be using Disk Express but will be using one of the file defragmenters instead. You do this by adding files to a newly formatted hard drive in an intelligent order, adding all those files that are very unlikely to change first, so that they are written in contiguous sections at the start of the drive, and leaving your ever-changing data files for the outer sections of the drive.

After formatting a drive, first add your most often used applications and utilities. Then add your System folder and all of its associated files. Use the Installer application if you want—see the System Software entry later in this section for details—or just copy the required System Software files and all other cdevs, inits, and print drivers you need. Use the Font/DA Mover to delete all unneeded fonts and DA's, and then add those you want to keep directly in the System file (as opposed to using Suitcase or Font/DA Juggler). If you are really compulsive you can then copy your System file to disk, remove the copy on your hard drive, defragment your drive, and then copy it back, thus eliminating any fragmenting that the Font/DA Mover operations caused; but this is not too important. Finally, add the rest of your applications and utilities. You will now have an essentially defragmented drive, and all your data files will be written to the contiguous sectors remaining on the drive.

Duplicating Disks

Producing a single copy of a Macintosh disk is as easy as dragging one disk icon onto another at the Finder. Doing so makes an exact copy of the source disk onto the destination disk; each sector of the disk is duplicated exactly, and **file fragmentation** is not reduced. This ensures that all files, including invisible files and those whose icons have been dragged to the desktop, will be copied properly. You should use this drag-copy method when duplicating application software from master disks.

You can duplicate a disk and cause the new copy to be defragmented by opening the source disk, selecting all of its files (using the SELECT ALL command, shift-clicking, or marqueeing), and dragging these files onto a blank formatted disk. Be aware, however, that any files whose icons have been dragged onto the desktop will not be copied in this manner unless you move them back into the disk. Also, this method will not copy invisible files unless it is done using a utility that displays invisible files, such as DiskTop.

To produce multiple copies of a single disk, or to copy disks that are either copy-protected or damaged in some way, a disk-duplicating utility is needed. A number of fine disk-duplicating programs are available independently, and others are included along with popular Macintosh utility packages. Always duplicate damaged disks before attempting file recovery, so that you can try again if your early recovery efforts fail and exacerbate the situation. Features to look for in a disk duplicator include copy speed, media formatting and verification, copy verification, serialization, and user-protection features.

A variety of software/hardware packages provide in-house commercial quantity duplication. These range in price from $1,500 to $11,000. These devices can format, duplicate, apply disk labels, and serialize disks. Many commercial businesses also provide disk duplication at rates as low as $1.20 per disk including the disk itself, duplication, and custom printed labels.

Mass Duplicators

Disk Dup+

Disk Dup+ is a very old shareware program that offers a simpler interface than its commercial rivals, without the loss of any basic features. It also offers one outstanding feature that neither of its commercial rivals does: the ability to write to both of the floppy drives on a two-drive Macintosh. This saves considerable time, especially if you want to get some other work done while only occasionally monitoring the duplication process. Disk Dup+ simply reads a source disk into RAM and then copies it onto as many disks as you care to insert. You can read a new master disk at any time, and elect to format every disk or only those that are previously unformatted.

```
┌──────────────────────────────────────────────────────────┐
│   ░░░    Disk Duplication                         v1.1   │
│   ░░░    ─────────────────────────────────────────────   │
│          [  New Master  ]              [   Quit   ]      │
│   ──────────────────────────────────────────────────────│
│   Volume Name:  none                          (type)    │
│                                                          │
│   Copies made:  0                   Status:             │
│                                                          │
│        Copy?   ⊠ Write        ⊠ Verify                  │
│      Initialize?  ○ Always      ◉ As necessary          │
│        ⊠ Warn before writing over valid data.           │
└──────────────────────────────────────────────────────────┘

┌──────────────────────────────────────────────────────────┐
│          Insert MASTER disk for reading.                 │
└──────────────────────────────────────────────────────────┘
```

The Disk Dup+ utility reads your master disk into RAM, and then writes the data back onto as many disks as you insert.

FastCopy, QuickCopy

Both the Symantec Utilities and PC Tools utility packages include stand-alone disk-duplicating software. Each allows you to create as many copies as needed, but with QuickCopy you must accomplish this by repeatedly inserting disks and clicking the WRITE DISK button, whereas in FastCopy you specify the number of copies required before beginning the duplication process and then simply insert the disks. Both of these programs offer you the option of formatting destination disks before writing to them, and both are MultiFinder-compatible (although you must reset the "Application memory size" option in the GET INFO dialog box to 1000K in order to avoid disk swapping).

FastCopy includes an extremely powerful track editor that allows you to correct a variety of disk errors in order to recover files. Some of the same capabilities are provided by the Symantec Tools program accompanying QuickCopy, but FastCopy makes these features somewhat easier to use. Overall, FastCopy also presents a better interface and more user feedback during the copying process, making it the preferred copier. Ironically, the old MacZap Copy on which QuickCopy is based had an interface similar to FastCopy's, but it has been lost somewhere in the process of becoming part of the Symantec Utilities (although the rest of the package had its interface improved dramatically).

Duplicating Copy-Protected Disks

Although copy protection is predominantly a thing of the past, Copy II Mac is still available to duplicate a disk that the above programs won't handle. Traditionally, Copy II Mac has been upgraded very frequently, and can copy almost anything.

 Copy II Mac   ✌︎⌽⌽
Copy II Mac was a vital tool back in the days of copy protection, performing bit-copies that could duplicate virtually any disk regardless of its protection scheme. Since protected disks are so rare today, and the disk duplicators described above offer so many features (including Central Point Software's own FastCopy), Copy II Mac is hardly ever needed. Its excellent track record, however, makes it the choice if you ever do encounter a disk that the other duplicators will not copy correctly.

Partitioning Hard Disks

As fully discussed in the Files entry later in this section, partitioning your hard drive into several different volumes is a good way of improving the organization of any large hard disk. Partitions allow you to separate files on a more dramatic scale than possible using only folders, and you can access partitions via the DRIVE button so you spend less time clicking through folders. Also, in some cases extra security features are available to files kept in a volume partition.

Creating partitions is relatively easy, and can be done using a variety of software applications and utilities. The differences between good partitioning software and bad relate to the effect the partitions have on your drive's performance, the security features offered, the ease with which partitions can be changed, and the compatibility of the partition with applications and utilities such as disk defragmenters, backup software, and hard-drive repair utilities.

There are two classes of partitioning software. The first, which we will call **SCSI partitions**, are created by hard-drive formatting utilities using low-level SCSI commands; the drive is aware of the partitions. **File System partitions**, on the other hand, are created by a partitioning utility after a drive has been formatted. They are created and maintained above the Macintosh file system; each partition is stored as a single large file on the drive, and all management of the illusory volume and its files is generated by the partitioning software, which modifies the File System Manager routines provided by the System Software. File System partitions are therefore theoretically more dangerous, although most have proven very reliable.

The biggest potential problem is that, since the File System partition is simply one large file as far as the drive is concerned, its information is kept as a single entry in the drive's directory. If this entry, or the directory as a whole, is damaged, all files in the partition are damaged as well. If more than one partition exists, a damaged directory would affect all of these partitions at once. With SCSI partitions, on the other hand, a separate directory is maintained for each partition on the drive, and each file on each partition has its own information within these directories. It is therefore much less likely for more than one partition to be damaged, and if a partition is damaged all of the files on that partition are not necessarily damaged. Also, some security utilities cannot provide full protection to File System partitions. See the Security entry later in this section for more information.

Partitioning Software

 SilverLining
SilverLining provides SCSI partitioning as part of its hard-drive formatting features. SilverLining partitions are unique among SCSI partitions in that they can be dynamically resized. When a partition is resized, the entire partition is automatically moved, if necessary, so that it occupies contiguous

sectors. Other files or partitions will even be moved to ensure this defragmentation. You can set each partition to mount automatically on startup, or use the Volume Mounter DA to mount them manually. Password protection is also available for each partition.

 MultiDisk, HD Partition, Hard Disk Partition

 Three different utilities, each of which operates with an init and a desk accessory, are available to create File System partitions. Alsoft's MultiDisk is the best of these, offering partitions that can be resized (if defined as resizable when they are created), password-protected, automatically mounted at startup, and encrypted. HD Partition, which is included as part of the Symantec Utilities package, offers fewer features than MultiDisk; most notably, its partitions cannot be resized, and password-protected partitions cannot mount automatically. FWB's Hard Disk Partition provides password protection, automatic partition mounting, and the ability to write-protect a partition so that its data is not changed accidentally. It does not, however, support partition resizing.

 Apple HD SC Setup

Although Apple's HD SC Setup software does offer a partitioning option, it can only be used to partition your drive between the Mac operating system and Apple's A/UX Unix operating system. It cannot create multiple Macintosh partitions.

Backing Up Hard Disks

Most of the tips and tricks you find in this book will save you a few seconds here and there. But here's one that can save you hours or days: Back up your hard drive regularly. Undoubtedly you've been told that before; but for most people, the effort and expense of initiating a backup program just doesn't sink in until they've lived through a disaster or two. (No, we're not saints ourselves—we've lived through a number of hard-drive crashes that resulted in tremendous amounts of lost work.)

Hard drives can be backed up either to large removable media (like tapes, cartridges, or high-capacity floppies) or to standard floppy disks. Using a removable-media mass storage system like a tape backup, cartridge, or high-capacity floppy drive, you can back up as much as 44 megabytes of data in 5 to 45 minutes. (Larger storage systems are also available.) These systems currently cost between $1000 and $2000 plus $20 to $150 per tape, cartridge, or disk.

Backing up your drives with a removable-media system is so fast and easy that you are much more likely to back up regularly if you have one of these systems than if you have to endure backup with ordinary floppies. Cartridge systems are the best value in removable media, and because they offer access times that rival traditional hard disks (usually around 25 ms), these drives can be used not only for creating backups but also for primary disk storage. (You can use them just like a regular hard disk when you're not using them to create backups.) One removable-media unit can support any number of Macs, either by actually being connected to each different Mac in order to back it up, or by using back up software that allows you to back up hard drives over AppleTalk.

Backing up a hard drive to floppies requires lots of disks, and you must participate actively in the entire backup (while the removable-media systems can run unattended). For these reasons, your backup software is somewhat more important when backing up to floppies than when backing up to tape or cartridge; the faster the backup procedure and the fewer disks it takes, the better. We recommend you consider investing in one of the better backup utilities if you are going to back up to floppies. Your time and the cost of backup disks will certainly make up for it.

Backup Strategies

No matter what media or software you use to perform your backups, here are a few tips you'll want to keep in mind.

◇ **Back up regularly**. Yes, we said this before, but it's worth repeating. If you use your Mac every day, you should back up your data files at least once a week. Nondata files, such as applications and utilities, are usually easier to replace if lost from your hard drive, and so you can probably get away with only backing them up when they change significantly—perhaps every two or three months.

◆ **Rotate between three sets of backup media**. It is almost as unwise to rely on a single backup copy of your data as it is to rely on your hard drive never going down. The safest method is to use three different sets of backup disks (or tapes or cartridges), using Set 1 for your first backup, Set 2 for your second, Set 3 for your third, Set 1 for your fourth, and so on. This not only provides you with protection should one of your backup sets go bad (or be destroyed), but it also allows you to have older copies of files available should you ever realize that you need them.

◆ **Keep one of your backup sets at another location**. It requires some effort to take a set home and then bring it back later, but in the event of fire or theft, a backup sitting next to your computer doesn't do a whole lot of good.

◆ **Do your own "personal backup" of important files**. Even if you have a well-implemented backup strategy, we advise that you take the time to copy important files to another hard drive, or to floppies, after you have done a lot of work on them. For example, while we use a tape backup system at our office, every day after working on this book we copied the one or two files that were changed and took them home. It wasn't worth running the tape for just one or two files, but there was too much work to be left exposed. The five minutes it takes to format a floppy disk and copy your files is a worthy way to end a day of work.

Backup Utilities

Macintosh backup utilities support either the **mirror-image backup strategy** or the **incremental backup strategy** (also known as **archival backup**). In the mirror-image backup strategy, your backup data always contains an exact copy of the files on your hard disk; older versions of files are deleted from the backup disks as the new ones are added. When the incremental backup strategy is used, files are never deleted from your backup disks, but instead all new or updated files are added to the backup disks each time the backup is performed.

The benefit of a mirror-image backup strategy is that the disk space or number of disks required for your backup grows very slowly, if at all. The drawback of this system is that older versions of your files are not available after your data has been backed up. The benefit of incremental backup is that every different version of every file you have ever had on your drive remains available to you. The problem is that a tremendous amount of disk space or a tremendous number of disks will be required to hold all these backup files.

Before the introduction of Retrospect, we used only mirror-image backup programs, because the incremental-backup packages did not offer the kind of features that made the time and space required by this backup strategy reasonable. And since we alternate between two or three backup sets, the redundancy provided by incremental backup was not one of our requirements. We have now turned to Retrospect for all our backup needs, although if we were using floppy disks as backup media—we use a tape drive—we would probably stick with Redux.

 HD Backup

Apple's HD Backup, included on your System Software disks, is a rather clumsy incremental-backup program that consumes more disks and requires more of your time and effort than any other backup program available. The biggest problem with HD Backup is that its incremental backups are always measured from the first time you backed up your hard disk, not from the last time. This forces you to repeatedly back up files that have not been altered since they were last backed up, wasting both time and disk space. HD Backup cannot back up to tape or to removable cartridges. A version of this program is also sold by PBI Software, but it is only slightly better than Apple's version and still not recommended.

 Retrospect

Retrospect is the newest and by far the most sophisticated backup software available. Retrospect provides incremental backup with a very wide range of options, and has been designed to support virtually any tape drive, removable cartridge unit, and optical disk, as well as floppy-disk backup. File backup and restoration is controlled by *archive catalogs*, which list every file currently in the archive. Unlike most other packages that keep such files on the backup media, Retrospect keeps its archive catalogs on your hard disk, so you can quickly and easily examine the list of archived files and the files that have been changed on your hard drive.

Retrospect provides you with full control over which files are added to the archive, and supports the encryption and compression of archived files. Files can be restored from archives individually or en masse, and a number of unique options are provided for handling cases where a file being restored already exists on the destination volume; Retrospect can be instructed to keep the existing file, overwrite the existing file, rename the conflicting file, prompt you for a decision, or put the file in a different folder.

Retrospect includes a scripting language that you can use to customize complex backup instructions, and has the ability to automatically launch backups that are scheduled on the Retrospect calendar. Retrospect is MultiFinder-compatible, supports network backups of TOPS and Apple-Share volumes, and maintains AppleShare privileges.

```
▤▭    ════════════ Archiving ════════════ ▤▤
  ┌────┐ ┌────┐ ┌────┐ ┌────┐  ┌──────────┐ ┌──────────┐  ┌──────────┐
  │ ▭  │ │ ▯  │ │ 🔍 │ │ ✓  │  │  Find... │ │ Choose...│  │   Next   │
  └────┘ └────┘ └────┘ └────┘  └──────────┘ └──────────┘  └──────────┘
  Source Archive Browse Execute
  DataDrive:                                              0 files, 0 K
  ┌──────────────────────────────────────────────────────────────┐
  │       ⬆   🗀 DataDrive                                      ⬆  │
  │       ◆ 🗋 CPSDeleteInfo              1 K      document     ⬇  │
  │     ✓ 🗋 DataDrive Archive          87 K                      │
  │     ✓ 🗋 Desktop                    60 K                      │
  │       ◆ 🗋 Desktop DB               16 K                      │
  │       ◆ 🗋 Desktop DF               10 K                      │
  │       ◆ 🗋 Empower™ Prep             2 K                      │
  │       ◆ 🗋 GuardianDelData          14 K                      │
  │       ◆ 🗋 GuardianSavData         153 K                      │
  │     ✓ 🗋 SS&U Icons ClipFile         0 K                      │
  │       🗋 Treetop                     1 K                      │
  │       ◆ 🗋 XTreeDeletes              1 K        text          │
  │         🗀 !Testing                                           │
  │           🗋 Clipboard Magician 0.5 11 K                      │
  │           🗋 DAtabase DA           138 K                      │
  │          🖎 DAtabase Personalizer  39 K     application      │
  │           🗋 MacUser Minifinders  195 K  (DAtabase Builder)   │
  │         🗀 Encyclo Mac                                        │
  │       ◆ 🗋 EM – Entry List           6 K                   ⬆  │
  │       ◆ 🗋 Fax trans, ingrid sybex layouts  3 K              │
  │       ◆ 🗋 Product DataBase         12 K                      │
  │   ⬆   ◆ 🗋 Thank you letter          3 K                   ⬇  │
  │   ⬇   ◆ 🗋 Vendor DataBase           9 K                      │
  └──────────────────────────────────────────────────────────────┘
```

Each time you backup a drive with Retrospect a listing of the drive's files is pre-sented. Files preceded by a check mark will be backed up, files preceded by a diamond have not changed since the last back up, and files without a mark have been manually excempted from the backup.

 Redux

Redux is a powerful mirror-image backup program that can be used with floppy disks, some tape units, and removable cartridges. Like Retrospect, Redux works by presenting a graphical file directory and allowing you to select individual files to be included in the backup. You can determine which files will be included in the backup based on their names, modification dates, locations, or file types. Redux also provides a scripting language, which automatically remembers your backup preferences and can be customized to handle specific backup requirements.

 DiskFit, Network DiskFit

Until the recent introduction of Redux and Retrospect, DiskFit was the undisputed champion of backup software. While not offering an overabundance of features, DiskFit does get the job done without the kind of silly compromises that characterize most of the other early backup programs. In comparison with Redux and Retrospect (which incidentally is written by DiskFit's authors), DiskFit's biggest drawback is that it does not allow you to include or exclude specific files from the backup. It is, however, one of the few programs that copies files in Finder format. (You can insert its backup disks at any time and just drag-copy files from them back to your hard disk). The network version of DiskFit supports both TOPS and Apple-Share (**you can back up remote volumes via AppleTalk**), and it properly maintains all AppleShare privileges.

Error Codes

You will encounter three types of error codes on your Macintosh. The first type greets you at startup, sometimes along with the Sad Mac icon. The second type is a System Software–level error that can appear at any time while you are using your Mac. And the third type is a ROM error generated and presented by specific applications or by the Finder. In some cases, knowing what these error codes mean can allow you to take corrective measures. In other cases, especially when dealing with System errors, the actual problem may be the result of a combination of factors, and the error code alone may not allow you to prevent the error from reoccurring.

Startup Errors

One of the first things that your Macintosh does after being turned on is run a series of internal diagnostics that verify the well-being of the ROM, RAM, and other internal components. These tests are executed very quickly, and when they are successfully passed your Mac begins to look for a startup disk. When one of these tests fails, the Sad Mac icon usually appears on your screen, and below it the error code describing the self-test failure. On the Mac II's and the SE/30, an unfamiliar startup chord is played when a test failure occurs.

Sad Mac Error Codes on the Mac Plus

On the Mac Plus, the first characters of the error code indicate whether a software or hardware failure has occurred. If the first two characters of the error code are *OF,* some kind of software error has occurred. Any other characters in the first two positions indicate a hardware failure. If the first two characters are *OF*, the next four numbers specify exactly where the failure was found, as listed:

0001	Bus Error
0002	Address Error
0003	Illegal Instruction
0004	Zero Divide
0005	Check Instruction
0006	TrapV Instruction
0007	Privilege Violation
0008	Trace
0009	Trap Error (Line 1010)
000A	Trap Error (Line 1111)
000B	Exception Error
000C	Core Routine Error
000D	Interrupt Error
000E	I/O Error
000F	Segment Loader Error
0010	Floating Error
0011	0018 Pack Errors
0019	Out of Memory
001A	Launch Error
001C	Stack Heap Crash
0064	Damaged System File
0065	Damaged Finder

If the first two characters are *01*, a ROM error has occurred, and the last four digits have no significance. If the first two characters are *02* to *05*, some type of RAM error has occurred, and the last four digits pinpoint the RAM chip that is causing the error. Converting these last four digits from hexadecimal to decimal provides you with the chip number that has failed. The following tables shows the last four digits of the Sad Mac error code as they specify RAM chips on the Mac Plus:

Column:	5	6	7	8	9	10	11	12
Row F	0001	0002	0004	0008	0010	0020	0040	0080
Row G	0100	0200	0400	0800	1000	2000	4000	8000

Sad Mac Error Codes on the Mac SE

On the Mac SE, two rows of eight-digit numbers appear below the Sad Mac icon. When these error codes indicate a SIMM chip failure, the error codes listed here are used. Sometimes these codes are unreadable, and sometimes the Mac restarts itself after flashing the codes briefly. In these cases, SIMMs 3 and 4 are probably at fault and should be replaced. Note that the SIMM indicated by the code depends on whether your SE logic board uses a solder-type resistor or a jumper-type resistor. Soldred resistors are found primarily in older SE's (pre-1989), while jumper resistors are found in all newer models. See the Computers entry in Section 3 for more information about the differences between these two types of logic boards, and for information about replacing SIMMs. In the tables below, *X* indicates that any number may occupy the position.

Solder-type SE Sad Mac Error Codes

SIMM #1	SIMM #2	SIMM #3	SIMM #4
0000000E	0000000E	00000004	00000004
000000xx	0000xx00	000000xx	0000xx00
0000000E	0000000E	00000004	00000004
00xx00xx	xx00xx00	00xx00xx	xx00xx00
00000002	00000002	00000005	00000005
000000xx	0000xx00	000000xx	0000xx00
00000002	00000002	00000005	00000005
00xx00xx	xx00xx00	00xx00xx	xx00xx00
00000003	00000003		
000000xx	0000xx00		
00000003	00000003		
00xx00xx	xx00xx00		

Jumper-type SE Sad Mac Error Codes

SIMM #1	SIMM #2	SIMM #3	SIMM #4
00000004	00000004	0000000E	0000000E
000000xx	0000xx00	000000xx	0000xx00
00000004	00000004	0000000E	0000000E
00xx00xx	xx00xx00	00xx00xx	xx00xx00
00000005	00000005	00000002	00000002
000000xx	0000xx00	000000xx	0000xx00
00000005	00000005	00000002	00000002
00xx00xx	xx00xx00	00xx00xx	xx00xx00
		00000003	00000003
		000000xx	0000xx00
		00000003	00000003
		00xx00xx	xx00xx00

Mac II, IIx, IIcx Error Tones

In the Mac II family and in the SE/30, sounds are used instead of error codes to specify failures during the power-on test. During a normal startup, the startup chord is played when the Mac is first powered on. If you hear a second chord or series of notes, a failure has occurred. This second chord or series of notes is then followed by a third sound, which is also a series of notes. The second sound made is the one specifying the failure.

If the second sound is a short harsh chord, a hardware failure has been detected. A long, medium-pitched chord indicates that RAM Bank 1 contains at least one faulty SIMM, and a long, high-pitched chord indicates that RAM Bank 2 contains at least one faulty SIMM. A utility called the Diagnostic Sound Sampler has been created by Apple to play these chords so you can familiarize yourself with them and the differences between them, but unfortunately this software is only available to Authorized Apple Service Technicians.

System Error Codes

These error codes appear in the BOMB dialog box, accompanied by the FINDER and RESTART buttons. The FINDER and RESTART buttons will sometimes be available, although often they are dimmed and unavailable. The reason for this is that either the Mac's memory was too messed up to allow them to operate, or the program currently operating did not provide for handling this type of error.

Some System errors are the result of distinct bugs in the program you are using, although the interaction between your inits, DA's, and applications is more likely the cause. If you begin to notice an increased number of System errors, try removing any new inits you are using, or even try working without any inits for a while to see if the problem clears up. Chances are very good that init incompatibility has something to do with your problem.

The next most common cause of System errors is a lack of available RAM. While the System Software and most applications can work in situations where RAM is tight, they almost always perform with fewer errors when given a little "breathing room." If your Mac has more than 2 megabytes of RAM, increasing the size of your System heap (as documented in the RAM entry in Section 3), and increasing the amount of RAM allocated to each application used under MultiFinder (as documented in the MultiFinder entry later in this section), will almost certainly reduce the frequency with which you encounter System errors.

Good programs can catch some System errors when they occur and correct the situation internally. Some programs bomb more than others not only because they cause more system errors, but also because they don't handle errors as efficiently when they occur. You will rarely see these errors when working in MultiFinder, because MultiFinder usually traps System errors and exits the application. When this happens you will see MultiFinder's APPLICATION HAS QUIT UNEXPECTEDLY dialog box. While this will cause you to lose your work in one application, any other applications that you are using will be unaffected.

The list below explains the System error codes that you are most likely to encounter.

ID-01: This error will only appear on Mac II's (and Lisas). It is a bus error involving an invalid memory reference.

ID-02: This is an address error; a request has been made for a memory address that does not exist.

ID-03: This is an illegal-instruction error; the CPU received an instruction it could not handle.

ID-04: This appears when the Mac is told to divide by zero.

ID-05: This error appears when a Check Register Against Bounds instruction failed, usually due to a number beyond the acceptable range.

ID-06: This error indicates a failed Trap On Overflow instruction. It usually occurs when a number in RAM grows faster than the space provided for it.

ID-07: This error appears when the Mac tries to run in an illegal mode. The Mac Plus and SE, for example, must always run in Supervisor mode.

ID-08: This is a trace error relating to the 68000 debugger.

ID-09: This is also a type of illegal-instruction error, indicating that the 1010 trap dispatcher has failed.

ID-10: Another illegal-instruction error, this indicates that the 1111 trap dispatcher has failed.

ID-11: This is the miscellaneous exception error covering any 68000 exception other than those handled by the above error codes.

ID-12: An illegal trap number was called, usually resulting from debugging code being run when the debugger is not present.

ID-13: Some hardware device has requested an interrupt vector table that was unavailable.

ID-14: This is an I/O system error resulting from a File Manager or Device Manager problem.

ID-15: An attempt to read a segment of code into RAM has failed.

ID-16: The floating-point bit halt was set.

ID-17 to ID-24: The System Software has requested a resource package that is unavailable. This may occur if you are trying to run a version of the System Software incompatible with the Mac's ROMs.

ID-25: This is a memory error suggesting that the requested memory is not available.

ID-26: This Segment Loader error occurs when a CODE 0 resource cannot be read into memory. It usually indicates a damaged application or file.

ID-27: This is an MFS file-map error indicating that the file map and disk blocks do not correspond.

ID-28: The software controlling the application stack has run into the System heap. It usually indicates that not enough memory is available.

ID-30: This error should bring up the PLEASE INSERT THE DISK dialog box, and should never appear as an error code.

ID-41: The Finder cannot be found on disk.

ROM Error Codes

Error codes that result from an application's use of ROM do not usually result in the BOMB dialog box, and in most cases are caught by the application that is running and presented to you as Alert dialogs. In these cases you will not see the error code itself, but will instead be presented with some explanation of what has happened. When you use some utility programs, or when an error code that your current application is not designed to handle is generated, you may see these error codes themselves in the Alert dialog:

-33: File directory full
-34: Disk full
-35: Requested volume does not exist
-36: I/0 error
-37: Bad name
-38: Attempt to access a file that was not open
-39: End-of-file error
-41: Memory full
-42: Too many files open
-43: File not found
-44: Tried to write to locked disk
-45: Tried to write to locked file
-46: Volume is locked
-47: File is busy
-48: Duplicate file name found
-49: File already open
-53: Volume has been ejected
-55: Volume already mounted
-56: Tried to mount a disk that doesn't exist
-57: Disk not a Macintosh disk
-59: Error during renaming
-60: Disk master directory block damaged
-61: Tried to write to a read-only file
-64 to -66: Font Manager errors
-91 to -99: AppleTalk errors
-100 to -101: Scrap Manager errors
-108 to -117: Storage allocation errors
-120 to -123: HFS errors
-192 to -199: Resource Manager errors
-200 to -206: Sound Manager errors
-290 to -351: Startup Manager errors
-1024 to -1029: AppleTalk errors
-1096 to -1105: AppleTalk errors
-3101 to -3109: AppleTalk errors
-4096 to -4101: Print Manager errors
-5000 to -5302: Apple Filing Protocol errors
-8132 to -8160: LaserWriter driver errors

Error Code Utilities

 SysErrors
This DA provides a listing of most of the error codes. Very little information is provided about each code, so this is most useful as a programmer's reference.

Resurrection: After the Crash

Okay, you've crashed. You're staring at the bomb, cursing your failure to save recently, and wondering what to do. If the BOMB dialog has a CONTINUE button, try pressing it. This may return you to the Finder; your unsaved work will be lost, but you won't have to reboot. This dialog box also has a RESTART button, which is usually dimmed but which, when available, saves you the trouble of reaching for the programmer's switch or the power button. A number of inits, Fkeys, and utility programs claim to increase your chances of being able to exit from the BOMB dialog box to the Finder without restarting, but none of these has been very reliable. Also, even when you can return to the Finder after a BOMB dialog, chances are very high that your Mac is in an unstable state, and you are best advised to restart your Mac using the Finder's RESTART command. This will reinitialize memory, reload your inits, and reduce the likelihood of another System crash.

The Programmer's Switch

Included with every Macintosh is a little plastic gizmo called the **programmer's switch** that when properly installed (there's always a catch) allows you to gracefully reboot your Mac when it has crashed beyond hope, or to access the built-in **debugger**. Although access to the debugger is really only useful to programmers and heavy hackers, the ability to gracefully restart the Macintosh is one that every Mac user needs; so everyone should install the programmer's switch.

Installing this switch can be a little tricky. Too bad Apple can't afford one more robot and just install these things before slipping the Macs into their boxes. The programmer's switch is installed a little differently on each Mac: On a Mac 128, 512, 512e, Plus, SE, and SE/30, the switch is installed on the left side of the Mac, in the grooves at the bottom near the back of the computer. On the Mac II and IIx it fits in the ridges at the back of the right side of the Mac, and on the IIcx it is installed on the front of the computer.

There are two buttons on the programmer's switch, the Reset button and the Interrupt button. You press the Reset button to restart your Mac when it crashes—all those times you now reach for the power switch. A restart with the Reset button is much kinder to your Mac than a power-switch restart. This is because the power supply is not turned off and then on, so the strain of the initial jolt of electricity is avoided.

If you ever do have to reboot your Mac with the power switch (when you crash so hard that the programmer's switch will not operate), turn the Mac off and wait five seconds or so before turning it back on. This allows the system to stabilize after the power is turned off, and to react naturally when it is turned back on. "Flipping" the switch off and then immediately on again will restart the machine, but this is sort of a self-imposed power surge that could damage your hardware.

Humor in the Guise of Adversity

 Bomber

Try running this application on a friend's Mac when they have stepped away for a minute or two. After launching, Bomber puts a realistic-looking BOMB dialog box on the screen with an available RESTART button, so when your friend returns they think something has crashed their Mac while they were away. The fun begins when your friend attempts to click the RESTART button. The button runs away! As the mouse pointer gets near the button, it moves, dodging to the left and right. It's a button that cannot be pushed.

When you stop laughing, you can wander over to your friend's Mac, grab the mouse, and click the dimmed RESUME button. This will quit Bomber gracefully. Of course, you could take a crueler approach and just wait for your friend to give up and restart their Mac using the programmer's switch or the power switch. Then you can wait till they walk away again....

 Files

File Names

There are only two basic rules for naming Macintosh files: File names can be no more than 32 characters long, and the colon (:) cannot be used in the file name. The 32-character limit is of dubious practical use, however, because the Finder and most dialog boxes have difficulty displaying file names longer than 22 characters. Still, this is vastly superior to the 8 characters allowed on other computer systems, and you can almost always descriptively name files in 20 characters or so.

The reason the colon is prohibited is that the Macintosh uses it internally to keep track of the folder and drive in which a file is kept. For example, a file named *workfile* in a folder called *Data* on a disk named *January 1989* is listed as *Data:January 1989:workfile* in the disk directory. Duplicate file names are not allowed on MFS disks, or within one HFS folder. (You can, however, use duplicate files names if the files are in different folders on the same HFS disk.)

File Naming Tips

Given this level of freedom in file naming, some people give their files long descriptive names, others use their own personal shorthand, and others have invented various standard codes that add all kinds of information to the file name. When devising your own file-naming strategy, keep in mind that the more obvious and descriptive the file name chosen, the easier it will be to locate and identify the file later on.

If your files are shared with others, descriptive file naming becomes even more important. We recommend creating a list of the file-naming conventions that are going to be used in your work group, and distributing them to each Mac user involved.

❖ **Put the unique portion of the file name first when projects have their own folders**. If you keep all of the files from a single project in their own folder, put the unique part of each file name first and the common part last, so you can benefit from the alphabetization of file names in Standard File dialog boxes and in Finder windows. For example, if working on articles for the May newsletter, use names like *Inter-*

view, *May News* and *Editorial, May News* rather than *May News, Editorial* and *May News, Dorran-Interview.* For files that are kept in a folder of mixed projects, however, common elements should be used in the first part of the file name so that all files from a single project appear together.

May Newsletter
Name
☐ Article 1, May-News
☐ Article 2, May-News
☐ Client Mailing List
☐ Editorial, May-News
☐ Interview, May-News
☐ MastHead, May-News
☐ Pub info, May-News

Misc. Projects
Name
☐ Cover Letter – North
☐ Cover Letter – East
☐ Cover Letter – South
☐ Cover Letter – West
☐ Payroll – July '89
☐ Payroll – June '89
☐ Proposal – Smith
☐ Proposal – Waters

Left: The common parts of file names are written first to separate them by project. Right: Common parts of the file names are written last, since the folder is entirely dedicated to one project.

◇ **Add application codes to the ends of file names.** If you keep data files from several different applications in a single folder, it is often helpful to be able to tell the application from the file name. Try adding a code to the end of the file name; for example, .I for Illustrator, .P for PageMaker, .W for Word, and .X for Excel.

◇ **Add version numbers to the ends of file names.** Working on the most current version of a file is obviously vital. When you work in a group, or when you save frequent backup copies of files, version numbers are a necessity. You may prefer not to use version numbers because the Mac tracks the last time a file was modified; the problem is that this time and date stamp can be updated by an action as simple as opening the file, so the most recently dated file may not contain the most current data. Few things are more disheartening than to find you have just spent an hour "sprucing up" an outdated copy of a document.

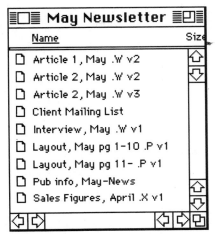

Adding application codes and version numbers to file names makes them more informative.

- **Add the date to file names for easy reference.** This information may be useful even though the Macintosh keeps track of the creation and modification dates, since these are not visible in most dialog boxes and Finder views, and since they can be updated accidentally, easily resulting in a date more recent than the actual one. Examples of files that would warrant a date in their name include such time-related items as payroll spreadsheets, telecommunication records, and correspondence sent to frequently contacted parties.

Special Characters in File Names

File and folder names are listed alphabetically in dialog boxes and Finder windows. By taking advantage of the way the Mac alphabetizes special characters and adding these characters to your file names, you can force certain files to specific positions in file listings. The table below documents the order in which special characters are alphabetized by the Macintosh, and provides the key combinations needed to access these characters while working in the Geneva or Chicago font (the standards used at the Finder and in dialog boxes).

□ (space bar)	□ . (.)	□ œ (Op-Q)	□ ¶ (Op-7)	□ º (Op-9)
□ ! (Sh-1)	□ / (/)	□ w (W)	□ ß (Op-S)	□ º (Op-0)
□ " (Op-[)	□ = (=)	□ z (Z)	□ ® (Op-R)	□ Ω (Op-Z)
□ " (Op-])	□ ? (Sh-/)	□ [([)	□ © (Op-C)	□ ¿ (Sh-Op-/)
□ # (Sh-3)	□ @ (Sh-2)	□] (])	□ ™ (Op-2)	□ ¡ (Op-1)
□ $ (Sh-4)	□ å (Op-A)	□ ^ (Sh-6)	□ ≠ (Op-=)	□ ¬ (Op-L)
□ % (Sh-5)	□ A (Sh-A)	□ ` (`)	□ ∞ (Op-5)	□ √ (Op-V)
□ & (Sh-7)	□ æ (Op-')	□ { (Sh-[)	□ ≤ (Op-,)	□ ƒ (Op-F)
□ ' (Op-])	□ B (Sh-B)	□ } (Sh-])	□ ≥ (Op-x)	□ ≈ (Op-X)
□ ' (Sh-Op-])	□ c (c)	□ ~ (Sh-`)	□ ¥ (Op-Y)	□ ∆ (Op-J)
□ ((Sh-9)	□ ç (Op-c)	□ † (Op-T)	□ µ (Op-M)	□ ... (Op-;)
□) (Sh-0)	□ E (Sh-E)	□ ¢ (Op-4)	□ ∂ (Op-D)	□ – (O--)
□ * (Sh-8)	□ f (f)	□ £ (Op-3)	□ Σ (Op-W)	□ — (Sh-Op--)
□ + (Sh-=)	□ G (SH-G)	□ § (Op-6)	□ π (Op-P)	□ ÷ (Op-/)
□ - (-)	□ ø (Op-O)	□ • (Op-8)	□ ∫ (Op-B)	

This listing, read vertically, shows the alphabetization of special characters and the key combinations that produce them.

File Organization

File organization involves the way you store your files on your hard disk, your floppy disks, and all your backup media (tapes, cartridges, etc.). In determining how to arrange and store files, keep these three goals in mind:

- The organization should be as logical as possible, so that if you don't know where a particular file is, you can easily determine its location.

- Files should be kept in relatively small groups, so that you don't have to scroll through long file listings.

- The hierarchy should remain simple enough that files can be accessed quickly and with minimal effort.

Of course, most of the files you use on a regular basis are kept on your hard drive. Most people use floppy disks to hold backup copies of their master application disks, utilities, files in transit, and, if no tape or cartridge medium is available, their archival and hard-disk backup files. If you have a tape backup unit or a removable cartridge drive, you probably use that for backing up your hard drive and archiving older data files.

Organizing Your Hard Drive

You organize a Mac hard drive by separating its files into folders and volumes. Most Mac users treat their hard drive as one large volume, and create many folders to group and arrange their files. Each folder on the Macintosh can contain either files or other folders, or both files and folders. As explained in the Disks and Drives entry earlier in this section, hard drives can be divided into several volume partitions using partitioning utilities or some hard-drive formatting programs. The benefit of using volume partitions is that each is recognized discretely by the Mac. You can mount or dismount them entirely, you can access them with the DRIVE button rather than searching nested folders, and they can provide security features not generally available for folders. See the Finder entry later in this section for more information about folders, and the Disks and Drives entry earlier in this section for a complete discussion of partitions.

Using folders and volumes, there are three popular ways to organize files on hard drives: application-based organization, project-based organization, and lack-of organization. The goals of a hard-drive organizational scheme are the same as those for our entire filing system:

- The organization should be as logical as possible, so that you can quickly and easily determine the location of any particular file.

- Files should be kept in relatively small groups, so that you don't have to scroll through long file listings.

- The hierarchy should not be too deep, so that files can be accessed quickly and with minimal effort.

File organization based on applications puts each major application in its own folder, and all files created by that application in the same folder or in subfolders. An example of this is shown in the next figure. In this case, all word-processing files are kept in the Word 4 folder, and all numeric files are kept in the Excel folder (some in a subfolder called February Payroll).

While this system may initially appear logical, in practice it turns out to be quite inefficient if (like most people) you tend to work on various parts of a single project rather than do all of your work in one application and then move on to another. Also, because application files are spread throughout folders containing data files, it is difficult to back up the data files without also backing up the large application files. In the project-based system, all applications are stored together in a single folder (perhaps with some subfolders for applications using more than one ancillary file), and all data files are stored in various project folders and subfolders. This system is generally preferred because it more accurately reflects the way most people work, and simplifies the procedure of backing up your data.

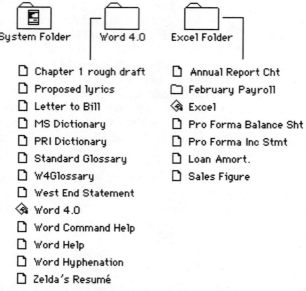

System Folder   Word 4.0   Excel Folder

☐ Chapter 1 rough draft ☐ Annual Report Cht
☐ Proposed lyrics   🗀 February Payroll
☐ Letter to Bill   ◈ Excel
☐ MS Dictionary   ☐ Pro Forma Balance Sht
☐ PRI Dictionary   ☐ Pro Forma Inc Stmt
☐ Standard Glossary   ☐ Loan Amort.
☐ W4Glossary   ☐ Sales Figure
☐ West End Statement
◈ Word 4.0
☐ Word Command Help
☐ Word Help
☐ Word Hyphenation
☐ Zelda's Resumé

Keeping files in folders with the applications that created them seems logical, but it can cause many problems.

Both of these organizations have merit, but ultimately your own comfort with a system is the most important factor. Some combination of these two systems, with a few exceptions along the way, is probably the most common arrangement. The Mac's filing system is so flexible that you can always change the way your files are organized (unlike certain C> prompt-based computers we know of), and most users go through a variety of organizational methods over time.

It is also important to point out that the utilities you use can dramatically affect the way your files are organized. If you use an application- and document-launching utility, for example, the placement of your applications can be based on purely organizational concerns because your need to access these files directly via the Finder is virtually eliminated. The use of volume-partitioning software would also alter the arrangement of your files and folders dramatically. An alternative file organization using volume partitions is shown later in this entry.

System Folder	Letters	Payroll	Utilities	BasicSoft

▫ Apple Legal Info	▫ Addison, 89 Payroll	◈ CanOpener™	▫ Aldus FreeHand 2.0
▫ Hoskins Regrets	▫ Bonus Calculator	▫ Dictionaries	◈ Excel
▫ MacUser Puzzle Solution	▫ Jackson, 89 Payroll	◈ Disk First Aid	▫ Home
▫ Miller Class List	▫ Keller, 89 Payroll	◈ Eraser	◈ HyperCard
▫ Rosenthal Confirmation	▫ Mitsky, 89 Payroll	◈ Font/DA Mover	◈ MacChuck 1.50
▫ Upgrade Request (Aldus)	▫ Payroll Summary '89	◈ HeapFixer™	◈ MORE™ V1.1
	▫ Tax Tables	◈ Retrospect	◈ PageMaker 3.02
	▫ Walsh, 89 Payroll	◈ Sentinel	
	▫ Watson, 89 Payroll	◈ StuffIt 1.5.1	

Keeping data files in separate folders according to their use, and grouping applications and utilities in their own folders, is the most common method of hard drive organization.

File Organization Tips

◇ **Use a System folder**. Your Finder and System file must be in the same folder, which is traditionally named *System folder*, although there are no real requirements as to how this folder is named. In fact, the System file and Finder do not even have to be in any folder; they could just be left in the root of your hard drive (not inside any folders), although this would lead to an intolerable mess.

The System folder must hold all cdevs, inits, and printer or network drivers (type PRER or RDEV) that you intend to use. Inits not in the System folder will not load during startup, cdevs not in the System folder cannot be seen by the Control Panel, and drivers not in the System folder cannot be used by the Chooser. Many applications create various temporary file and preferences files that are automatically added to your System folder and cannot be moved. Usually these are named in a way that allows you to identify the application that created them; if you do need to move or delete these files, you should consult the application's user manual to see if any problems will arise. Some applications, like PageMaker, allow their ancillary files to be kept in a subfolder of the System folder, allowing for a somewhat more organized System folder.

◇ **Don't keep printer fonts in the System folder**. Most manufacturers of PostScript fonts recommend that you keep printer fonts in your System folder. This causes your System folder to become very cluttered and to grow very large. In most cases, there are alternative places to store your printer fonts while still retaining access to them. If you use Suitcase II or MasterJuggler, keep your printer fonts in the same folder as your screen fonts and desk accessories. (Suitcase II and Master-Juggler automatically download printer fonts if they are kept in the same folder as at least one DA or screen font accessed by either of these programs.)

If you don't use Suitcase II or MasterJuggler, the shareware desk accessory Set Paths is for you. Set Paths allows you to specify any folder on any mounted volume as the one containing your printer fonts, and all applications can then access them. A commercial product called FontShare does nothing more than Set Paths but costs $295. (Set Paths asks only a $15 shareware contribution.) If your Mac is not connected to a network file server, you might want to keep your printer fonts in a Printer Fonts folder that is kept in your Utilities folder when using Set Paths.

If your Mac is connected to a network, fonts should be centrally stored on the file server and accessed using Set Paths from the file server's Printer Fonts folder or published Printer Fonts volume. This makes it unnecessary for every user to keep copies of all the printer fonts on their hard drive. Since most applications (with PageMaker 3.0 being one notable exception) will download printer fonts from the root directory of any mounted volume. TOPS or MacServe users don't even need to use SetPaths if they keep printer fonts in the root of a volume (not in any folder) that can be mounted by any network user.

◇ **Organization of applications**. Most users we know keep all of their software applications together in a single Applications folder with subfolders for applications containing several associated files (like MS Word). If you do not use a launching utility and want to avoid subfolders, keep everything in the applications folder, and use the VIEW BY KIND command so that the applications are grouped together and ordered alphabetically.

Some exceptions to this rule may be warranted. For example, certain specialty applications, used rarely or only with one group of data files, may be better kept with their data. For example, accounting software that works with one set of data files may be kept in a folder with its data rather than along with the other applications.

◆ **Organization of utilities.** As with applications, keeping utilities together in a Utilities folder with subfolders for utility groups (Font Utils folder) as needed seems to be the best practice. Utilities are separated from applications (although they are both executable programs) so that neither folder contains too many files, and because in practice, applications and utilities are used at distinctly different times for distinctly different purposes.

BasicSoft	Utilities
Name	**Name**
☐ Aldus FreeHand 2.0	☐ Disk Clinic™
◈ Excel	◈ Disk First Aid
☐ Excel Folder	◈ DiskQuick 2.10
☐ FileMaker Help	◈ Easy Icon v1.5
◈ FileMaker II	◈ Eraser
☐ Home	◈ FastCopy
◈ HyperCard	◈ Font/DA Mover
◈ MORE™ V1.1	◈ Font/DA Utility™
▓ PageMaker 3.02	☐ Fonts/DA's
☐ Resume MORE	◈ HeapFixer™
☐ Scanning	◈ ResEdit 1.3d1
☐ Telecom	☐ Retro.Help
☐ Word 4.0	◈ Retrospect
	◈ SAM Virus Clinic™

Keeping all applications in one folder, perhaps with subfolders, and all utilities in one folder, perhaps with subfolders, is usually the best strategy.

◆ **Organizing fonts and DA's when using Suitcase or Font/DA Juggler.** Since your fonts and DA's are not loaded into your System file, keep all fonts and DA's in a Fonts/DA's folder, perhaps as a subfolder of the Utilities folder or of the System folder. (We prefer keeping them in the Utilities folder.) If you use lots of fonts or DA's, you may want to split these up even further into a Fonts folder and a DA's folder.

Downloadable PostScript fonts should be kept in the same folder as your screen fonts if you are using Suitcase II or MasterJuggler, or in their own folder otherwise.

◇ **Name folders with the character ƒ instead of the word** *folder*. The ƒ character is produced with OPTION-F. We think this is more visually distinctive than the word *folder*, and helps in navigating at the Finder and in dialog boxes. This is really a personal preference, but one worth considering.

◇ **Don't nest too many folders**. While the ability to keep a folder inside another folder is the cornerstone of the HFS filing system, nesting folders too many layers deep (folders inside of folders inside of folders) is generally unwise because of the number of steps required to access the deepest levels. Most of your folder nesting should not get more than three or four levels deep, and your worst nesting situation should not go beyond five or six levels.

◇ **Mix files and folders in a folder if appropriate**. Some have advised that the contents of any folder should be either all folders or all files. While this rule may be great theoretically, it is too rigid for practical use, and we find that many situations warrant a collection of files and folders together.

◇ **Try to keep very few files in the root of your hard drive**. Files on a drive but not in any folders are in the drive's **root directory**. Generally, a drive's root directory should contain only folders—not any files. A benefit of this practice is that any files that do appear at the root are easy to identify as "to be filed."

◇ **Maintain a "Pre-Trash" folder**. If you have enough drive space and you're worried about throwing away files by mistake, create a folder named something like Pre-Trash and keep it in your root directory or even on the desktop next to the trash can. Discard files into this folder instead of the actual trash, and then empty this folder periodically or when you need the drive space. This allows you to review the files again before you actually trash them, retrieving those you decide you still need, or just leaving them in the Pre-Trash folder a little longer until you're sure they are useless.

◇ **Files and folders on the desktop**. Keeping frequently used files and folders right on the Finder desktop provides quick access to them at the expense of desktop clutter. We tend to keep a few of our most frequently accessed folders (System folder, Applications folder, Utilities folder, and primary data folders) on the desktop, but no application or data files.

If you ever want to return a file or folder on the desktop to the drive and folder it came from, select the file or folder and choose the PUT AWAY command from the Finder's FILE menu.

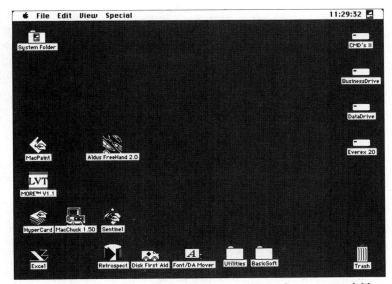

Many people keep their most frequently used applications and files on the Finder desktop for easy access.

◆ **HFS limits on number of folders and files.** As a practical limit, an HFS volume can support 65,536 files and folders. The theoretical limit is roughly 4.3 billion, but the way directory entries are stored causes this to be unattainable. Also, while theoretically HFS would support 65,535 files in a single folder, the numbering scheme used by the file directory places a practical limit of 32,767 files in a single folder. A single file can be up to 2 gigabytes.

Volume Partition Tips

If you decide to create hard-drive partitions to organize your files, as discussed in the Disks and Drive entry earlier in this section, the following tips are worth considering:

◇ **Create one volume partition for System Software, applications, and utilities.** Generally speaking, the files in your System folder, plus your applications, utilities, fonts, and DA's, do not change very often. Keeping all these files on their own volume allows you to defragment and back up this volume once, and then not have to worry about defragmenting or backing up the volume again for a long time. If you are using File System partitioning software, this volume should not be a partition, but the hard drive itself. And by keeping most of your application files together, you make defragmenting and backing up your data volumes faster and easier. This volume should be set as your startup volume with the Startup Device cdev.

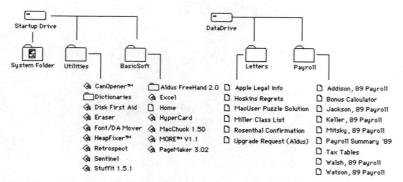

In this method of file organization, volume partitions are used to separate applications from data files. The Startup Drive volume contains the System folder, applications, utilities, and other nonchanging files, and the DataDrive volume contains all data files. Several different data-only volumes could be used if there were major classifications of data files.

◇ **Partition data files into major classifications**. While you do not want to create too many partitions, any group of data files that consumes over 20 percent of your hard drive should be considered a candidate for its own partition. In creating multiple partitions, there is a trade-off between the benefits of separate volumes and the desktop clutter and mounting headaches of separate volumes, so it is usually a good idea to partition in moderation. Partitions are especially appropriate for groups of data files that need special security, since most volume partitions can be set to require a password, and for groups of data that are not always used and can therefore be left unmounted, and out of the way, some of the time.

◆ **Keep a floppy startup disk with your volume mounting software handy**. In case your hard drive ever has trouble mounting, you don't want your only copy of your volume mounting software to be on the broken drive.

Organizing Files on Floppy Disks

Running a Macintosh on floppy disks alone is a true challenge. A minimally equipped System folder currently requires more than 800K, so trying to fit a System folder, application software, and data files on two 800K disks borders on the impossible. Of course, many floppy-based systems access hard disks over AppleTalk, which alleviates the problem to some degree by providing access to applications and data files over the network.

Creating a startup disk with the System file, Finder, and associated files on an 800K disk requires careful scrutiny of every file vying for disk space. Keep the following tips in mind:

◇ **Use only the required System Software files**. Create a new startup disk with the Installer application, using the Minimum Script from the Utilities 1 disk. You can then delete most of the System Software files, with the exception of the System file and Finder. You should delete MultiFinder, Backgrounder, Print Monitor, and DA Handler if you will not be using MultiFinder.

You should probably leave at least the General cdev, but many of the others (Mouse, Keyboard, Sound, Startup Device, Monitors, Key Layout, Easy Access, etc.) can go. Each of these cdevs sets variables stored in PRAM, which will not need to be altered often. Create a second startup disk containing all of these files and use that one when you need to alter any of the settings these cdevs control. (The settings are not lost when the Mac is shut down or rebooted.) Leave only the printer drivers you absolutely need, and put the Laser Prep file on a separate disk if you are using the LaserWriter driver. The Mac will prompt you for the disk containing the Laser Prep file when it is needed. See the System Software entry later in this section for more information about each of the System Software files.

◇ **Delete unneeded fonts, and larger sizes of all fonts**. Fonts take up a considerable amount of room in your System file. Using the Font/DA Mover, delete all fonts you will not be using, and remove the larger point sizes of the fonts you will be using frequently. (Larger-sized screen fonts take up much more space than smaller sizes.) You will be able to use the font at any size, even if you only leave one small point size in the System file. Font sizes that are loaded in the System file look better on screen, and print better to dot-matrix printers, but have no effect on PostScript (LaserWriter) output. If your Mac will be attached to a network hard disk, you may be able to access fonts from it, as described below.

◇ **Delete all unneeded DA's**. At the extreme, you can delete all DA's except one. (The Alarm Clock is usually the smallest, so leave that one.) If your Mac will be attached to a network hard disk, you may be able to access DA's from it, as described below.

◆ **Use inits sparingly**. Although there are many great inits available, some are too large to be used on a floppy-disk system. Many are only a few kilobytes, however, and can be used even on a floppy disk system.

◆ **Consider utilities that allow you to access fonts and DA's selectively or remotely**. Although the popular font/DA attachment utilities take up a good amount of disk space themselves, they do allow you to leverage that space by accessing lots of fonts, DA's, and Fkeys on another disk drive or from a network hard drive. The older version of Suitcase (1.2) is much smaller than Suitcase II and still works effectively (although it may be hard to locate), and Alsoft's Font/DA Juggler is smaller than their MasterJuggler program. Better still are the DA Key and similar utilities which take up only a few kilobytes of disk space. See the Fonts and Desk Accessories entries in this section for more information about these utilities.

Finding Files

Even with a good filing strategy, chances are high that you will occasionally forget the location or name of certain files. Fortunately, a number of utilities are available to quickly search your disks and drives in an attempt to locate your "missing" files. Most of these utilities allow you to search for files by file name, type, creator, or date last modified, and a few even let you search the file's content for specific words or phrases.

File Finding Utilities

 Find File   ⑤⑤

Apple's Find File DA lacks many of the advanced features that its commercial competitors offer, but adequately addresses the file-searching needs of most Macintosh users. Find File cannot launch a file once it is found, but it does display the file's location when the file is selected, or move it to the Finder desktop if requested. And it's hard to argue with free.

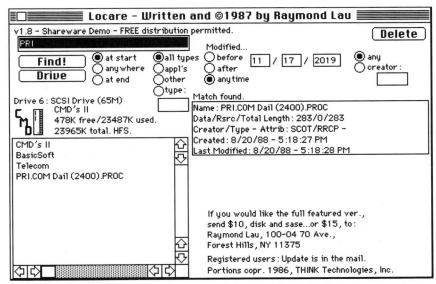

Locare is an Fkey file locator that performs quickly and offers a range of file-search options.

Locare

This file-finding Fkey is the most convenient way to find files by name, modification date, or creator. Written by Stuffit programmer Raymond Lau, Locare appears almost instantly when you press its Fkey combination, and then quickly finds the first file to meet your search criteria. A graphic display of the file's location is shown, as are the file's type, creator, modification date, and size. Clicking the FIND button again locates the next file matching your criteria. A DELETE button is provided so that you can delete any found file.

 FindSwell

An init/cdev called FindSwell also offers file-searching features, but is unique in that it appears as a new button in all Standard File dialog boxes, rather than as a DA. This is useful because you often need to find a file in order to open it. FindSwell offers only searches on file names, although you can limit your search by location and/or file type.

 Locate

The Locate DA from Central Point Software, included as part of the PC Tools Deluxe-Macintosh Version package, has the ability to search files by name, and to search through the data in files from Microsoft Word, Write, MacWrite, PageMaker, HyperCard, and several other file types. Locate can launch a file once it is found or move the file to the Finder desktop. One irritating feature of Locate is that you have to select a command from its menu or invoke a keyboard equivalent in order to see the path (location) of the file; clicking or double-clicking on the folder is not adequate. Also, while you can designate a specific search path, limiting the search to one drive or a certain folder only, the path is not remembered and must be reset each time you access the DA.

 FIND Commands in DiskTop, DiskTools

DiskTop and DiskTools, in addition to their other virtues, offer file-search features. Both can find files by name, type, creator, creation date, modification date, or file size. Files found are clearly listed, and selecting one of the found files graphically displays its location. Once found, a file can be launched, copied, moved, or deleted using the other DA commands. The worst thing about using these DA's as file locaters is that they are rather large, so they take longer to load than DA's dedicated to finding files. DiskTop 4.0, however, will correct this problem by listing its FIND command as a separate command in the APPLE menu.

GOfer

GOfer is a DA that allows you to search for files by their content, rather than by name or file attributes. Before searching, you use the WHAT, WHERE, and HOW buttons to specify what to search for, where to search, and how to search. GOfer's WHAT dialog box allows you to specify sophisticated search criteria using boolean logic. For example, you can search for all documents containing the word *accounting* or *taxes* within six lines of the word *audit* or *IRS*. The WHERE dialog box lets you select volumes or folders to search, and the HOW dialog box is used to specify whether GOfer will show each file as it is found, write all matching occurrences to a text file, pause to allow you to examine the matching occurrence, or quickly find all files with at least one matching occurrence. (These choices are not mutually exclusive.)

GOfer searches files relatively quickly, especially considering that no pre-processing of files is required. You must, however, be aware of the types of files that GOfer supports, as only these files are searched. Currently GOfer can search FullWrite, HyperCard, MacWrite, Excel, Word, Write, Works, More, PageMaker, Ready, Set, Go!, TeachText, ThinkTank, and WordPerfect files, in addition to plain text files. Because GOfer depends on the format these files produce, software updates that change an application's file format make GOfer unable to search the files until GOfer itself is updated.

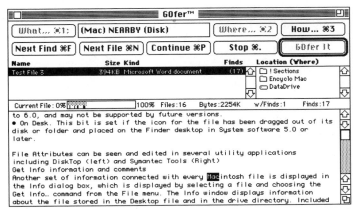

GOfer's main dialog displays the current search result, and provides the WHAT..., WHERE..., and HOW... buttons that are used to access additional dialog boxes.

CanOpener

CanOpener searches for a specific word or phrase in the files on any drive or folder, providing a list of all files that contain the word or phrase, and allowing you to look at the actual occurrence. This feature has only a fraction of the power offered by GOfer, although it can search every file on your disk, not just those in approved file formats.

File Cataloging Utilities

As your collection of floppy disks, tapes, cartridges, and hard-drive volumes grows, so too will the difficulty of keeping track of all the files spread across them. File cataloging utilities read the directory information from your disks and then provide a list of all your files, which you can bring up on screen and search or print. These utilities help to find the most recent copy of a particular file, eliminate duplicate files that are wasting disk space, and allow you to save a significant amount of time that is now spent searching.

 DiskQuick (Disk Librarian)

 DiskQuick a commercial version of a shareware program called Disk Librarian. DiskQuick reads the file information from any floppy disk or hard drive in just a few seconds, and presents two windows containing the information from all disks and drives you have cataloged. One is a DISKS window, which lists each separate floppy disk, hard-drive volume, tape or cartridge that has been cataloged. For each, you can see the space available on the drive, the date it was last modified, and the name, size, date modified, creator, and type of each file on the disk. The DOCUMENTS window presents a list of all documents on all cataloged disks, along with their file information and the name of the disk or drive they are on. Each window can be sorted by file name, date modified, size, free space, capacity, or date cataloged. You can optionally exclude invisible files, system files, Get Info comments, and file type and creator information. DISK or DOCUMENT windows can be printed, in your choice of font and type size.

 Disk Ranger

Disk Ranger provides all the disk cataloging features of DiskQuick, plus disk formatting, file and disk defragmenting, file encryption, and disk-label printing. DiskRanger reads disk information faster than DiskQuick does, and its file and folder sorts are almost instantaneous. Disk Ranger's FILTER dialog box lets you eliminate many specific file types, including System files, Finders, invisible files, desktop files, desk-accessory files, fonts, applications, or files with any two file types you specify. We have used DiskQuick for several years, but Disk Ranger's speed and feature list have convinced us that it's time for a change.

```
┌─────────────────────────────── Disks ───────────────────────────────┐
│                                                                      │
│ U.20-Inits *3                                                        │
│   space free on disk=355K  capacity=785K                             │
│   disk last modified on Wed, May 31, 1989 (as of Wed, May 31, 1989)  │
│        63K    Dawn™             Tue, May 30, 1989   4:57 PM (Daw3,xdev)│
│        22K    POWERmenus        Wed, May 31, 1989   3:32 PM (PWRm,xdev)│
│         5K    Aesthete          Sat, Feb 25, 1989   8:03 PM (œsth,INIT)│
│        17K    AutoSave II       Wed, May 31, 1989   9:36 PM (ASav,cdev)│
│        16K    Boomerang INIT    Wed, May 3, 1989   10:58 AM (bMRN,INIT)│
│         3K    CacheControl (cDev) Tue, Apr 11, 1989 8:00 PM (CaCR,xdev)│
│         3K    ClockAdjust ??    Sun, May 14, 1989  11:21 PM (RyTm,xdev)│
│        54K    ColorDesk (cdev)  Wed, Nov 30, 1988  11:48 AM (CDsk,xdev)│
│        21K    DA menuz cdev     Mon, May 22, 1989  11:27 PM (jbx!,cdev)│
│        59K    Empower™2.0.5     Wed, May 31, 1989   3:11 PM (Empw,xdev)│
│         2K    Enchanted Menus 88 Sat, Dec 24, 1988  5:46 PM (HOHO,INIT)│
│        86K    Fish!             Wed, May 24, 1989   2:06 AM (EdF!,xdev)│
│        24K    GuardDog! INIT    Fri, May 12, 1989  10:42 PM (WOOF,xdev)│
│        11K    Screener™ (cDev)  Mon, May 15, 1989   7:33 PM (sccv,cdev)│
│        22K    Turbo Cache       Wed, May 24, 1989   4:01 PM (TcP1,xdev)│
│        14K    Windows INIT      Mon, Dec 26, 1988   6:10 PM (JLWW,xdev)│
│ U10 - FKEYS *1                                                       │
│   space free on disk=239K  capacity=761K                             │
│   disk last modified on Wed, May 31, 1989 (as of Wed, May 31, 1989)  │
│   Folder : FKEY APPLICATIONS                                         │
│   space used in folder=326K  12 documents in folder.                 │
│       145K    FKEY Documentation  Sat, Jun 20, 1987  2:45 PM (MSWD,WDBN)│
│        22K    FKEY File Installer Wed, Dec 10, 1986  5:44 PM (FFKY,APPL)│
│        18K    FKEY Installer      Sun, Dec 8, 1985   1:38 AM (QD15,APPL)│
│        15K    FKEY Installer Manual Sat, Oct 4, 1986 9:10 PM (WORD,WDBN)│
│        13K    FKEY Installer Notes Tue, May 23, 2000 3:35 AM (MACA,WORD)│
└──────────────────────────────────────────────────────────────────────┘
```

This DISKS window from DiskQuick, displays information about all the files and folders on the cataloged floppy disks.

File Compression

"Disk space... the final frontier" read a button handed out at a recent trade show. Indeed, for many of us information does expand to fill our available storage space regardless of how much we make available. As a result, we are occasionally faced with the reality that the "Disk is full," and are forced to do some impromptu cleaning. One way to avoid having to delete files or transfer them to another storage medium (floppy or tape) is by compressing infrequently used files so that they take up less space on your hard disk when they are not being used. Although compressed files cannot be used until they are decompressed, savings of 50 percent are average for many types of data files.

File compression is quick and easy, and a side benefit is that it allows you to combine a number of files and folders into a single file icon. Almost all files to be sent by modem should be compressed and combined (when appropriate), since their smaller size will save transmission time (and therefore money) and it is much easier to send one file than several. Of course, files compressed for transmission or other transfer must be decompressed before they are used. This is why compression standards are important; if everyone involved uses the same compression utility, no one ever receives a file that they do not have the proper software to decompress. A number of other utility programs offer file compression, but these should only be used for in-house files, as only those formats discussed below are universally accepted as standards.

Stuffit

Stuffit is the currently undisputed king of the compression hill. Stuffit has been around for several years as a shareware program, and has been continually upgraded and improved by its author, Raymond Lau.

Stuffit creates files called Stuffit archives, which contain the compressed and (optionally) encrypted files. A new archive is created using the NEW... command from Stuffit's FILE menu. Once the archive is created, you can add files to it one at a time, add an entire folder or disk, or select any group of files to be added at once. Files in folders can maintain their HFS structure—they will stay in their folders when unstuffed—or folders can be stuffed as a single file. Stuffit can be instructed to delete the source files once they have been stuffed, or to leave them alone. Comments can be added to any file in the archive, or to the archive itself. By convention, Stuffit archives are named with the extension .SIT, allowing anyone who might receive the file to know that the file is in Stuffit format.

You can extract files from Stuffit archives using the Stuffit application itself, the Unstuffit DA, or the UnStuffit application; or, a file can be set up to extract itself when double-clicked if it is stuffed with the AutoStuff shell. Stuffit can also unpack files compressed with Packit II or III.

A new commercial version of Stuffit, called Stuffit Deluxe, is soon to be released by Aladdin Systems. This new version will allow multiple archives to be opened at once, and will feature a new compression algorithm called Better, and improved archive-management tools.

```
≣□≣▬▬▬▬▬≣ Old Backs/SIT ≣▬▬▬▬≣
File Name              Type Crea    Size %Saved
Backup of SS.Disks & Driv  WDBN MSWD    60928 45%  ⬆
Backup of SS.Files V.1     WDBN MSWD    98304 37%  ⬇
Backup of SS.Fkeys V.1     WDBN MSWD    19456 41%
Backup of SS.Inits         WDBN MSWD     7680 44%
Backup of SS.Screen Saver  WDBN MSWD     4096 48%
Backup of SS.Security V.1  WDBN MSWD     3072 55%
Backup of SS.Sound V.1     WDBN MSWD    13824 31%
Backup of SS.StartupDisk   WDBN MSWD     4096 49%
Backup of SS.Time V.1      WDBN MSWD     4608 41%
Backup of SS.Utilities     WDBN MSWD     4096 48%
Backup of System Soft & U  WDBN MSWD   283648 44%
Backup of TS. Section 1;   WDBN MSWD    95744 53%
Backup of UM V.1           WDBN MSWD    97280 46%
Backup of UM V.2           WDBN MSWD   129024 51%
Backup of Utils § 01       WDBN MSWD    33792 42%
Copy of Backup of SS&U F-  WDBN MSWD   173056 40%
Deep Backup #4             WDBN MSWD   250880 39%
Backup of SS&U F-Z         WDBN MSWD   373760 40%  ⬆
Backup of SS&U A-D         WDBN MSWD   325632 44%  ⬇
About EM...                WDBN MSWD     6144 42%
━━━━━━━━━━━━━━━━━━━━━━━━━━━━━━━━━━━━━━━━━━━
29 items,  1261k archive, 2160k decompressed.
 [Add] [Multiple] [Extract] [Delete] [Rename] [Info] [Comm...]
DataDrive:1561k free.
```

An open Stuffit archive displays all of its files and their sizes.

 Packit
Before Stuffit took over Macintosh file compression, a program called Packit was commonly used. Since Stuffit's arrival, Packit has not been updated, and .PIT files (compressed files created with Packit) have all but disappeared from commercial telecommunications services in favor of Stuffit's .SIT files. Stuffit can unpack .PIT files, so even if you do come across a Packit file, Stuffit can handle the task.

Arc.pop

On PC-compatible systems, the .ARC format is the standard in file compression. This utility allows Mac users to decompress files that have been compressed on the PC and stored in .ARC format.

File Copying Tips

◇ **Hold down the ⇧ key to select additional files without deselecting the previous selection.** Shift-clicking makes it possible to select multiple files in any one window in the Finder (or on the desktop), and in many scrolling file lists. Shift-clicking on a file that is already selected deselects that file. To drag-copy a group of files, keep the SHIFT key depressed, press and hold down the mouse button when selecting the last file to be added to the group, and then drag the files to the desired destination.

◇ **Warning: A lack of warning.** When you copy any file or folder to a new location, an Alert box will warn you if files or folders are being replaced. You are not, however, warned of any files being replaced inside of folders that are being replaced; the Alert dialog only mentions the folder itself, not its contents. When copying a folder, be sure you want to replace all of the files inside the folder.

◇ **Copying and moving files with desk accessories.** Many desk accessories, such as DiskTop and DiskTools, can also copy files. These DA's allow you to specify whether you want a file to be copied or moved, and of course they allow you to perform these operations without quitting the current application.

◇ **Duplicating all files on a disk.** There are two ways to copy all of the files on a disk to another disk from the Finder. You can either drag one disk icon on top of the other, or select all the files and folders on the source disk and drag them to the destination disk.

The difference is that dragging one disk icon onto another causes the previous content of the destination disk to be erased, and an exact copy of the source disk to be made; every sector of the disk is duplicated from the source onto the destination. This leaves files fragmented as they were originally, but guarantees that the disks are identical after the copy. This type of disk copying also verifies the copy, providing greater assurance of copy quality.

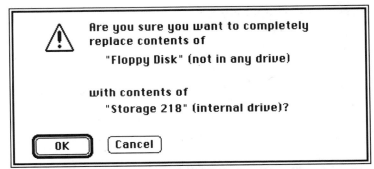

Dragging the icon of one floppy disk on top of the icon of another floppy disk causes the files on the source disk to replace those on the destination disk.

Selecting all files on a disk and dragging them to a destination disk does not erase the destination disk, so that disk must have enough free space to hold the copied files. If not, an Alert box is presented and the copy is canceled. This drag-copying method does eliminate file fragmentation to whatever extent possible based on the space available on the destination disk, but the copied files are not verified. Also, any files from the source disk that have been dragged onto the Finder desktop are not copied, because they were not selected when the drag-copy was executed.

◆ **Hold down the ⌥ key to copy files between folders on a disk**. Dragging files or folders between disks or volumes copies them; the original remains in place and the duplicate is placed at the destination. But dragging files between folders on a single drive (or volume) *moves* them to the destination, removing them from the source location. To copy (duplicate) files when moving them between folders on a volume, hold down the OPTION key when dragging them. This causes the original file to remain at the source location and a copy to be placed at the destination.

Copying oversized files

Files that are too large to fit onto floppy disks can either be compressed or be split into pieces. (File compression was discussed earlier in this entry.) A number of utilities, several of which are described here, offer the ability to split large files into smaller pieces.

HD Backup, Stuffit ⑤⑤, ◈①⑤⑩

Apple's HD Backup (included with the Apple System Software) and Stuffit (described in detail earlier in this entry) allow you to break large files into segments and then later recombine the files. HD Backup does not allow you to specify the segment names or sizes, and can only move files onto blank disks. (Any existing data on the disks used will be lost.) Stuffit, on the other hand, allows the user to select any segment size up to 3200K, name the files, save the segmented files on any volume, and use any disk or volume without losing its current data.

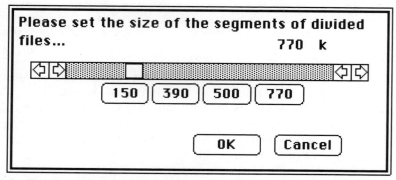

Stuffit can break large files into segments of any size, usually so that they can be transported via floppy disk and later recombined into a single file.

 Slicer, Splitt ⑤⑩, ⑤⑩

These two rather old utilities were designed to cut files into small pieces so that they could be used with DA text editors, which at one time could only handle very small files. They still serve this function, if it is needed, but they cannot be used to archive very large files to floppy disks.

 Disk Imager ◈①Ⓕ⑩

This utility is very interesting, and could be quite useful in certain circumstances. Disk Imager copies a floppy disk to a disk file, which can be telecommunicated and then returned to a floppy disk (using Disk Imager). This allows you to send the data from a damaged disk to someone via modem, and have them work on your damaged disk without ever having it!

Deleting Files

You can delete a Macintosh file by dragging it to the trash can on the Finder desktop, or by using a utility that provides a deletion command. When files are placed in the trash can they remain there, available for retrieval, until the trash is "emptied"; this occurs when the EMPTY TRASH command is chosen from the Finder's SPECIAL menu, or when one of several other events that empty the trash can occurs. (These are listed below.)

When the trash is emptied, the space that the file occupied on its disk becomes available for use by any other new file that is saved, but the actual file data is not removed from the disk. Most utilities that offer a deletion command delete files without first holding them for retrieval, but like the trash can most do not actually remove the data from the disk. Data from a deleted file remains on the disk until the areas of the disk that held the file are used to store another file, or until you specifically run a utility that erases the file from disk or erases all parts of your disk that are not holding any current files. Until then, a deleted file can usually be recovered (as documented later in this entry).

File Deletion Tips

◇ **When is the trash emptied?** The trash is emptied when the EMPTY TRASH, SHUT DOWN, or RESTART command is selected, when an application is run, or when the disk from which a file was trashed has a file copied onto it or is ejected or dismounted. When items are in the trash, the trash can bulges. When the trash has been emptied, the trash can returns to its normal size.

The Mac's trash can bulges when it contains files, and returns to normal after it has been emptied. At right are trash cans that have been customized with ResEdit.

◇ **Avoiding accidental deletion**. If you are not too tight for disk space, create a folder named "Pre-Trash" and put files in that folder instead of putting them in the trash. Then you can check this folder periodically and either retrieve the files or actually put them in the trash can.

◇ **Deleting locked, in-use, and System files**. Delete these files by holding down the OPTION key while dragging them into the trash can. Holding down the OPTION key also allows you to delete System files (type ZSYS) or applications (type APPL) without encountering the ARE YOU SURE YOU WANT TO DELETE? dialog box.

◆ **Deleting temporary files**. Do not delete temporary files unless you are sure that your application is finished with them. This is especially true when working in MultiFinder or when trying to free space on a disk with a DA that allows file deletion. If you delete a temporary file that an application is using, you may be unable to save your current document.

File Deletion Utilities

The only way to really delete a file is to have all areas on the disk where the file was stored written over, preferably with all 0's or a random set of 0's and 1's. These utilities do just that, thereby providing excellent security for your deleted files; they cannot be recovered in any way once they are deleted and the sectors have been rewritten.

 Complete Delete, FileZero, FileZero INIT 🖱PD, 🖱SW
Complete Delete and File Zero are simple utilities that allow you to select any file from a Standard File dialog box and delete that file entirely—resetting the sectors on the disk that hold the file to all zeros so the file data cannot be retrieved in any way. File Zero INIT modifies your System Software so that all files deleted on the Mac, including temporary files automatically deleted by software applications, are entirely removed.

 DiskExpress, Optimize 🖱$$, $$
Both of these defragmenting utilities offer the option of writing random strings of 0's and 1's to all unused areas of your disks. You can choose to have the unused areas overwritten once or three times (just in case).

After selecting a file for deletion, Complete Delete asks you to confirm that the file you are deleting will be impossible to recover.

Undeleting Files

Files deleted via the trash can or most DELETE buttons and commands still exist on disk, although they no longer appear at the Finder or in any directory listings. The utilities listed here can scan the disk and retrieve a deleted file as long as none of the disk sectors containing the file have been rewritten.

Symantec Utilities
Symantec Utilities for Macintosh (SUM) offers the most comprehensive set of undeletion utilities available for the Macintosh. SUM can recover files from both hard disks and floppy disks, and includes several different methods of file recovery, enabling it to handle all types of lost files—those deleted accidentally, those lost due to disk failure, and even those from hard-drive volumes that have been formatted or initialized.

If you purchase SUM before you lose or delete any files, and install and use it properly, you will be able to recover virtually any lost or deleted file, as long as the hard disk can still be accessed. Even if you don't purchase SUM until after you've lost or deleted a file, or improperly install the Guardian and Shield features, your chances of recovering files are excellent. We have used SUM to rescue files many times, and have never been disappointed.

PC Tools Deluxe for the Macintosh
Like SUM, PC Tools Deluxe offers a variety of different methods of file recovery, the best of which operate only if you've installed the PC Tools recovery features before the file loss or deletion. But the other ones provide

a good chance for data recovery even if it's "too late." The PC Tools Deluxe manual provides more technical details than does the SUM manual; advanced users may find this helpful.

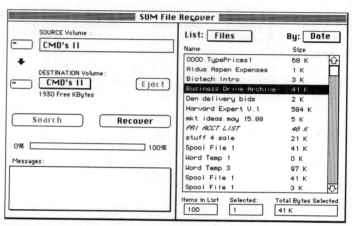

SUM Disk Clinic presents a list of recently deleted files, and indicates which of these may be undeleted.

 CanOpener   ⅃⅄⅁⅂

When a file is recovered but unusable from its original application, CanOpener can almost certainly recover the text and graphic data from the file. CanOpener opens any file, regardless of its format, and displays a list of the elements it found in the file. Selecting an element and clicking the VIEW button displays the text or graphic, which you can then export to a new file. CanOpener comes as both an application and a DA, having exactly the same features.

Printing Files from the Finder

Did you know that if you want to print a file, you can simply select the file icon at the Finder and choose the PRINT command from the File menu? This feature has been in the Mac Finder since version 1.0, but it doesn't get noticed much anymore. After the PRINT command is chosen, the required application will be opened (assuming it is available, of course) and the PRINT command will be executed. Depending upon the PRINT dialog box used by the application, it may or may not wait for you to enter print specifications and for the OK button to be clicked. After the PRINT command has been executed, the application is quit, and you are returned to the Finder.

Selecting multiple files from several different applications and choosing the Finder's PRINT command will cause each file to be printed in succession. Again, however, the PRINT dialog box of any application may require that its OK button be clicked (or the ENTER key pressed), so you generally cannot leave the Mac alone to do this work.

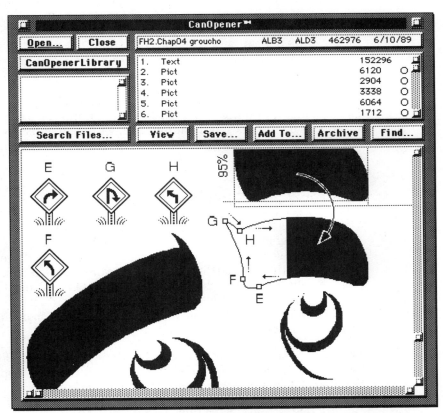

CanOpener allows you to view any text or graphic element in any file. This is an open PageMaker file, with one graphic being viewed.

Files: A Technical Look

Technically, Macintosh files are divided into two parts: the **data fork** and the **resource fork**. While it is generally unnecessary to understand this distinction in order to use your Macintosh and work with its files, it does come in handy when you want to retrieve data from a file that is damaged or to manipulate the file in any advanced way. Basically, the data fork holds what we would think of as traditional data (text, numbers, formatting commands), and the resource fork holds Macintosh resources, which are program elements. A file does not need to have both a resource fork and a data fork; it can have one or the other, or both. Many applications contain only resource forks, and many user-created files contain only data forks. Sporks are spoons and forks combined as a single utensil for use on camping trips.

Information about each file is maintained in the disk directory of each disk or volume that the file is copied to. This information includes the file's creation data, its last modification date, various details about its size and storage location on the disk, the file type, the file creator, and a list of file attributes.

File Type and File Creator

When a file is first created, its creator and type are specified by the application or programmer that is creating it. The **file creator** is a four-letter code identifying the specific application that created the file. Creator codes are registered with Apple so that no two applications assign their files the same creator code. The creator is used by the Finder (and various Finder replacements) to associate the file with its application. This is how the file is given an icon, and why it is possible to launch an application by double-clicking on a file that the application created.

The **file type** is a four-letter code identifying the **file format** used to save the file. File types enable applications to limit the files displayed in their Standard File dialog boxes to those files that the application can work with. For example, the OPEN dialog box in Microsoft Word allows you to select any file with a creator of TEXT, WDBN, WORD, or MW2S, because those file types represent the file formats that Word can work with. Files with other file types cannot be selected because Word cannot use them. File types are also registered with Apple.

Many applications let you save their files in a variety of popular file formats, at which time the file type is set according to the file format used. Saving a SuperPaint file in MacPaint format, with the MPNT file type, allows any utility capable of opening MacPaint files to have access to the graphic. Folders do not have file types or file creators. The file type and file creator can be seen and modified in many file manipulating DA's and utilities, such as DiskTop, DiskTools, and SetFileKey. In DiskTop you can always see the file type and creator of any file, and you can sort the file list by file type or creator by clicking on the Type or Creator column heading.

The Symantec Tools, as well as other utilities, allow you to quickly see technical information about any file.

Why would you want to modify these attributes? For one of two reasons: First, if an application assigns the file type or creator to a file incorrectly, or if these attributes are lost when a file is damaged in some way, you might need to correct them manually. Second, by modifying the file type you alter the set of applications that can open that file (or at least try to open it). For example, suppose someone sends you a file from Microsoft Word, but you don't have a copy of Word around. In order to read the data from the file you could simply change its file type from WDBN to TEXT; then any text editor or word processor could open the file and read it. Of course, most or all of the formatting would be lost, because the formatting commands that Word stored in the file would be meaningless to these other text editors. But the basic information the file contains would be available to you. Changing bit-mapped graphic images to the MPNT (MacPaint) file type is also common.

```
File:        4th Qtr '86 Wages Total
Size:        2938 bytes. 3K on disk.
Where:       BusinessDrive
Created:     Monday, May 8, 1989, 2:10 PM
Modified:    Monday, May 8, 1989, 2:10 PM

      Type  XLBN                Creator  XCEL
  ☐ Locked      ☐ Invisible    ☐ Bundle      ☐ Changed
  ☐ Bozo        ☐ Busy         ☐ System      ☒ Inited
      Change                         Cancel
```

The SetFileKey Fkey is one of many utilities that allows you to see and edit a file's type, creator, and other attributes.

File Attributes

Fifteen "file attributes" are maintained for each Macintosh file, each set as either on or off. Because the status of these attributes is used primarily by the Finder, Apple's official name for them is **Finder Flags**.

Generally speaking, these attributes are set and manipulated by application software or by the Finder itself, and are not intended to be manipulated by the user. However, understanding them can be useful because, like the file types and file creators, they can be set incorrectly by applications, and you can occasionally solve a strange problem by simply correcting an attribute setting. These attributes can be viewed and edited with a number of utilities, including DiskTop, DiskTools, Symantec Tools, FileStar, FileMaster, and many others.

Here is a brief explanation of each file attribute.

- **Locked**. When this attribute is set, a file cannot be placed in the Finder's trash can unless the OPTION key is held down, and cannot be deleted by some (but not all) other file-deletion utilities. In the case of data files, setting this bit makes it impossible for applications to update them, guaranteeing that they won't be updated or changed inadvertently by you or intentionally by those who shouldn't be changing them. The Locked attribute can be set in the Finder's GET INFO dialog box (where it is called a LOCK option), and in the other file-attribute editors.

  Setting this attribute can also make a data file into a template, since some applications, like Microsoft Word, allow you to change locked files but make you save them with a new name using the SAVE AS command.

- **Invisible**. When this attribute is set, the file will not appear at the Finder desktop or in most Standard File dialog boxes. A variety of files, including the Finder's own Desktop file, are kept invisible, usually so that the user doesn't delete them (either accidentally or on purpose).

- **Bundle**. This attribute tells the Finder that this file contains information that should be read into the Desktop file. It should be set for all application files (file type APPL).

- **System**. Files with this attribute set are part of Apple's System Software. The System file, Finder, and Clipboard file are examples. Files that have this bit set usually use the Macintosh icon, and they present a special warning when dragged into the trash can (unless the OPTION key is held down).

- **NoCopy** (formerly the Bozo bit). If this attribute is set with System Software earlier than 5.0, the file cannot be drag-copied onto another disk. This crude form of copy protection was phased out when Apple decided that copy protection was a dirty word. Isn't it an interesting sign of maturity that Apple is embarrassed to have a bit named Bozo?

- **Busy**. This attribute is temporarily set whenever the file is being used. In the case of an open data file, for example, this attribute prevents you from deleting the file accidentally.

- **Changed**. This attribute is set when a file or folder has been updated. It is used by backup utilities.

- **Inited**. This attribute is set by the Finder after it has seen a file. When this attribute is set, the Finder knows it doesn't have to read information from the BNDL resource again.

- **Cached**. This attribute probably was intended to inform the System Software about the suitability of a program for caching, but is not supported by any System Software up to 6.0, and may not be supported by future versions.

File attributes can be seen and edited in several utility applications, including DiskTop and Symantec Tools.

- **Shared**. With this attribute set, certain application files can be launched simultaneously on multiple machines (assuming that they are served on a network, of course). Some applications have this bit set inherently, while on others you must set it manually. While not all Mac applications can be multilaunched, many can, including MacWrite II, Excel, and PageMaker. See the Launchers entry later in this section for more information.

- **Always SwitchLaunch**. Some applications work best if the disk that they are on becomes the startup disk. Examples include Apple's Installer and Disk Express. Since System 5.0, you cannot switch-launch to an older version of the Finder, so disks containing applications with this bit set should always use the latest version of the System file and Finder. See the Launchers entry later in this section for more details.

- **Never SwitchLaunch**. This attribute would theoretically prevent a manual switch-launch when an application was launched, but it is not supported by any System Software up to 6.0, and may not be supported by future versions.

- **On Desk**. This bit is set if the icon for the file has been dragged out of its disk or folder and placed on the Finder desktop in System Software 5.0 or later.

Get Info Information and Get Info Comments

Another set of information connected with every Macintosh file is displayed in the GET INFO dialog box, which appears when you select a file and choose the GET INFO... command from the FILE menu. The GET INFO window displays file information stored in the Desktop file and in the drive directory. Included in the dialog is a small text-entry area used for comments about the file. A **Get Info comment** can hold more text than appears in the box, but you must use the arrow keys to scroll down to additional text, if it is available.

This Get Info comment is often used by software developers to write notes about files. Ideally, this would be a place where you could write yourself notes about your files. The problem is that this information is stored in the Desktop file, which is rebuilt occasionally (as discussed in the Desktop file entry earlier in this section), deleting all information in the Get Info comment. When System 7.0 replaces the Desktop file, this GET INFO dialog will, we hope, be replaced with a more functional tool.

System Software 6.0 added one improvement to the Get Info comments: Files that have a **creator signature string** have this information placed in the Get Info comment automatically whenever the Desktop file is first created or rebuilt. Many newer application files take advantage of this feature to provide Get Info comments that are not lost each time the Desktop file is rebuilt.

Editing the Data Fork

The data fork of a Macintosh data file holds the file's most important information—the text or graphics that the file contains. A number of utilities allow you to examine the data fork, and edit its contents. The most common use for data fork editing is the recovery of data from a file that can no longer be accessed by the software that created it (or any other software or utilities). Another common use is to change data that cannot be changed more directly. For example, someone we know once entered a check date outside of the current fiscal year into an accounting module, making it impossible to post the check to another module. The check could not be deleted, and the date could not be changed. Editing the date in the file's data fork solved the problem. Of course, all data fork editing should be done on backup copies of files.

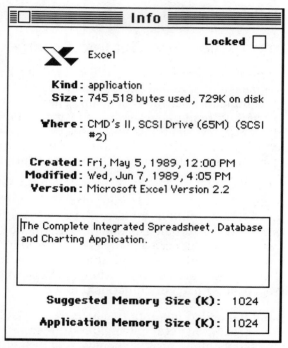

The INFO *dialog box displays some basic information about a file, and some file comments. Obviously, there are no rules against lies and exaggeration in the* GET INFO *comment boxes.*

 MacTools

After being launched, MacTools displays a Finder-like window for each currently mounted volume; this window includes every file, folder, and invisible file on that volume. The current status of the file's Invisible, Locked, and NoCopy attributes is shown, and you can edit these attributes by simply clicking their check boxes on or off. Selecting any file allows you to verify, rename, copy, delete, or edit the file. File editing is available for file-directory information, resource forks, or data forks. Fork editing displays both hex and ASCII sector information, and allows full editing. You can move through a file block by block, or directly locate any specific block number. However, there is no way to search for any specific data within the file.

 Symantec Tools

One of the core programs in the Symantec Utilities, Symantec Tools provides comprehensive file-editing capabilities. Files are selected for editing from a Standard File dialog box, and either fork of the selected file can be displayed. The FILE ATTRIBUTES command allows you to edit the file's type, creator, or attributes, and clicking the FILE MAP button will show you which sectors on the disk the file occupies. You can also view, but not edit, file-directory information, and you can search through a file for any particular hex or ASCII string value.

```
Edit File : SS.AppleTalk V.2
Data Fork                In Folder:                        ○ File Info
NumSectors: 21           Current Sector: 3                 ○ File Map
Size: 10752              Offset: 0                          ● Hex Edit
00000690   2063 6F6E 6E65 6374 6F72 7320 6174 2070   connectors at p
000006A0   7269 6365 7320 6173 206C 6F77 2061 7420   rices as low at
000006B0   2433 3020 7065 7220 6E6F 6465 2028 636F   $30 per node (co
000006C0   6D70 6172 6564 2077 6974 6820 2437 3520   mpared with $75
000006D0   6672 6F6D 2041 7070 6C65 292E 204F 7572   from Apple). Our
000006E0   2065 7870 6572 6965 6E63 6520 6861 7320    experience has
000006F0   6265 656E 2074 6861 7420 7468 6573 6520   been that these
00000700   D250 686F 6E65 4E45 542D 636F 6D70 6174   "PhoneNET-compat
00000710   6962 6C65 D320 7072 6F64 7563 7473 2077   ible" products w
00000720   6F72 6B20 7065 7266 6563 746C 792C 2061   ork perfectly, a
00000730   6E64 2077 6520 6861 7665 206E 6576 6572   nd we have never
00000740   2068 6561 7264 2072 6570 6F72 7473 206F    heard reports o
00000750   6620 616E 7920 7072 6F62 6C65 6D73 2077   f any problems w
00000760   6974 6820 616E 7920 6272 616E 6473 206F   ith any brands o
00000770   6620 4170 706C 6554 616C 6B20 636F 6E6E   f AppleTalk conn
00000780   6563 746F 7273 2C20 736F 2067 6F20 6168   ectors, so go ah
00000790   6561 6420 616E 6420 6275 7920 7468 6520   ead and buy the
000007A0   6368 6561 7065 7374 2062 7261 6E64 2079   cheapest brand y
000007B0   6F75 2063 616E 2066 696E 642E 2028 5765   ou can find. (We
000007C0   2075 7365 2043 4F4D 5055 4E45 542C 2046    use COMPUNET, F
000007D0   6172 616C 6C6F 6E20 616E 6420 4170 706C   arallon and Appl
000007E0   6520 636F 6E6E 6563 746F 7273 2E29 200D   e connectors.) .
000007F0   4170 706C 6554 616C 6B20 6578 7465 6E74   AppleTalk extent
```

The data fork editing window in Symantec Tools displays data in both hexadecimal and ASCII format, either of which may be edited.

 Fedit Plus

Fedit was one of the first file editors available for the Macintosh, but due to a poor shareware response—lots of people used it, but very few registered and paid their shareware fees—Fedit has not been maintained. Many of the features in Fedit Plus, which dates back to 1986, still function properly, but others do not. Of particular importance is the fact that while Fedit Plus is one of the few utilities to include a WRITE BOOT BLOCKS command, the boot blocks Fedit writes are invalid for System Software 6.0 or later. (If you have a damaged disk and think that rewriting the boot blocks will fix it, you should run Apple's Installer from System Software 6.0 or later, which will write the correct boot blocks.)

 MacSnoop   &1⑤Ⓦ

MacSnoop was written by Art Shummer specifically to address the void left by the loss of Fedit. MacSnoop can read and write any block of a file's resource or data fork, edit file attributes, display volume attributes, and rename or delete files.

 # Finder

As part of the Macintosh System Software, the **Finder** is usually not thought of as an application, but except for a few special privileges that it enjoys, the Finder is very much like other Macintosh applications. Instead of offering word-processing or database functions, however, the Finder provides disk and file management and application-launching abilities. The Finder is automatically run each time your Macintosh is turned on (unless another application has been selected to run at startup in the SET STARTUP... command). The Finder is also run automatically when any other application is quit, although there are ways to alter this as well.

MultiFinder, a special version of the Finder, offers all of the Finder's features, plus the ability to manage multiple open applications simultaneously. See the MultiFinder entry later in this section for complete details on MultiFinder's special features. Since MultiFinder is a superset of the Finder, most of the discussions in this section do apply to MultiFinder.

The Finder Desktop

The on-screen display shown when the Finder is running is known as the desktop. (We refer to it as the Finder desktop in this book to distinguish it from the Desktop file.) The Finder desktop includes a menu bar, icons for each mounted disk or volume, and a trash can. Disks and volumes may have open windows, files, or folders that also appear on the Finder desktop.

Because the Finder and its desktop are your gateway to applications, and because it is still used for most disk and file management (even with all of the fancy disk- and file-management utilities now available), maintaining an organized Finder desktop is a subtle but important aspect of using the Macintosh. Many of the issues surrounding desktop organization are discussed in other entries in this section, but before proceeding let's look at basic some ideas about organizing your Finder desktop. This discussion supplements the broader discussion of file organization presented in the Files entry earlier in this section.

The Finder automatically arranges the icons for all inserted disks and mounted drive volumes horizontally down the right edge of the desktop, and places the trash can in the lower-right corner. You may, however, position any files or folders anywhere on the desktop, and any folders may be opened into windows displaying folder contents. (Of course, all levels of nested folders may also be positioned on the desktop and/or opened.) The benefit of keeping frequently used files or folders on the desktop is that they can be accessed without the effort required to open the disk (and possibly the folders) within which they usually are located. The drawback of keeping files or folders on your desktop is the clutter it might create.

While this is certainly a matter of personal preference, we tend to keep a few folders on our desktop, including the System folder, the folder containing most of our applications, the folder containing our utility files, and a few folders for projects we work on frequently. We do not keep any applications or data files on our desktop, although this would be a more reasonable alternative if we used very large monitors. Also, we do not tend to keep any windows open on our desktop all the time, although some may be open for a few hours or so when we are using the files from a certain folder or disk frequently.

Windows

Whenever you work in the Finder, your open disks, volumes, and folders are displayed in **windows**, which are constantly being opened and manipulated. As more and more windows appear on the desktop, clutter becomes inevitable.

You can change the size and placement of any open window on the desktop by dragging the window's title bar, or clicking its Size box, Zoom box, or Close box. Many of these common actions are perfect macro assignments if you are using a macro utility. (See the Macros entry for more details.) The default size and placement of each window (where a window appears the first time you open a new disk or a new folder), and the placement of text columns and icons, are specified in the LAYO resource in the Finder file. Editing this resource (as discussed in the Customization entry) allows you to specify the size and placement of all new windows.

Window Management Tips

A few window-management tips are listed below. These are tips that no Mac user should be without, because they are helpful almost every time the Mac is used.

◇ **Open windows temporarily by pressing the ⌥ key.** If the OPTION key is pressed when a window is opened—when the disk icon or folder icon is double-clicked—the Desktop file is not notified that the window has been opened. This means that the window will not remain open when the Finder desktop is redrawn after you quit an application or restart the Mac.

   You can use the feature selectively when searching for a specific folder that is nested several layers deep. Open the first few windows with the OPTION key held down, and then open your final window without it. This will leave your final window open when the desktop is redrawn, but all the preceding ones closed.

◇ **Close every open window by holding down the ⌥ key and clicking the Close box in any open window.** This will close all open windows on the Finder desktop in rapid succession.

◇ **Close every open window by holding down the ⌥ key when quitting any application.** This is particularly useful when you've opened lots of windows to find a particular file. If you forgot to hold down the OPTION key while creating this mess, just remember to do it when returning to the desktop; no matter how messy you left the desktop, everything will be put away. Unfortunately, this does not work when using MultiFinder.

◆ **Move windows without selecting them by ⌘-dragging the menu bar.** This trick, which works in most applications offering windows, lets you move a nonselected window so you can see more of it, or so it hides less of another background window.

Desktop File
Versus the Finder's Desktop

The Desktop file is an invisible file, created and maintained by the Finder on every disk ever mounted and displayed on the desktop (except those mounted while full or locked). The Desktop file holds icons for all applications and data files associated with a particular drive or volume, and information about the location of each file, folder, and window on the desktop. If the Desktop file ever becomes damaged, the Finder will not be able to mount the disk and display it at the Finder. When the Desktop file becomes too large, the speed at which the Finder can redraw its desktop is slowed. The cure for either a damaged Desktop file or one that has grown large and slow is to rebuild the Desktop file. You can do this by holding down the COMMAND and OPTION keys as the disk is inserted, as a hard drive mounts, or as the desktop is redrawn after an application is quit. (This last method, rebuilding the Desktop file when quitting an application, cannot be done when running under MultiFinder.) See the Desktop File entry earlier in this section for more information.

Finder Commands

While most of the Finder's commands are intuitive and well-known, two of the Finder's menu commands are well worth discussing: RESTART and SHUT DOWN. These commands, obviously, are designed to initiate a "soft" reboot of your Macintosh and to prepare your Mac to be switched off, respectively. Whenever you need to reboot your Mac, it is important to use the RESTART command, as opposed to just flipping the power switch off and then on again. This is because the RESTART command allows the Mac to correctly dismount all mounted drives, updating their Desktop files and directories, and to prepare the hardware for the restart.

The same is true of the SHUT DOWN command; unless your Mac crashes and you are forced to turn off your Mac with the power switch, you should use the Finder's SHUT DOWN command. In addition to performing all the disk-dismounting operations of the RESTART command, the SHUT DOWN command performs any shutdown routines that have been installed in your System Software by utility software or inits. This is especially important if you use security or disk-recovery utilities.

Finder Utilities/Replacements

While the Finder's graphical system of disk management and application launching is largely responsible for the overall success of the Macintosh, the Finder is not always the most convenient way of managing disks and files. Several companies have attempted to build a better mouse trap—no pun intended—in terms of graphical disk- and file-management systems for the Macintosh. Other utilities provide the Finder's functions as a DA or Fkey, allowing access to these features when the Finder is unavailable.

MacTree Plus

None of the Finder's biggest file- or disk-management problems are solved by MacTree Plus. You cannot copy or move files from multiple directories, files must be placed in the MacTree Plus trash can to be deleted (and the trash can is often hidden from view by other windows), there is no fast way to copy files from one nested folder to another (other than opening the correct windows and moving and sizing them appropriately), and you can only get a good look at a complex hard disk by using several windows.

Worse yet, MacTree Plus's trash can empties the trash instantly—you cannot open the trash can and retrieve files—and although you can select folders from multiple levels and drag them to another drive, only the folders from the highest level are copied; you are given no warning that only some of the files you think you copied were actually copied. MacTree Plus does have a few very nice features, like letting you view the data inside some file types, and allowing you to see a list of all files on your drive as if they were not in folders, but in no way do these features make up for the mess you must endure in order to use them.

XTreeMac

After our experience with MacTree Plus, we didn't expect to like XTree-Mac very much; it is ostensibly a very similar product. But to our surprise we love XTreeMac! XtreeMac allows you to manage your drives and files more easily than you could at the Finder desktop. We find its graphic displays attractive and easy to negotiate, its combination of icon buttons, menu commands, and keyboard equivalents intelligent, and its unique Deskpad tremendous.

The Deskpad is a "holding area" where you can put files and folders from different drives. (The files and folders are not actually moved from their disk locations; the Deskpad icons simply represent the original files). Once on the Deskpad, files can be copied or moved as a group (regardless of the fact that they may have come from different drives and folders). Or you can just assemble on the Deskpad a group of files that you are working with and want to differentiate from the other files on your drives.

You do not have to copy files by first dragging them to the desktop; you can also copy (or move) a file by dragging its icon. When a file icon from one drive is dragged onto one of the disk icons at the top of the XTreeMac window, that drive's tree structure appears, and you can then drag the file directly into any folder. XTreeMac's menus allow you to filter the files that are displayed in the tree, hiding all invisible files, for example; there is also a full-featured FIND command, a configurable menu for launching applications and documents, and a file-undelete feature that allows you to retrieve files after they have been emptied out of the trash.

XTreeMac is a winner. If you have a hard drive full of files and folders, and especially if you use multiple hard drives or have your hard drive partitioned into volumes, XTreeMac deserves serious consideration.

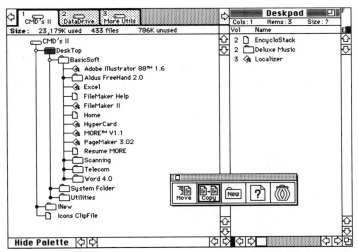

XTreeMac displays a graphic listing of the files and folders on your hard drive. The Deskpad window can hold copies of any files from any mounted volume, which you can then easily move or copy to another location.

DiskTop, DiskTools

Before MultiFinder was available, DA's and Fkeys that allowed you to perform simple tasks that could otherwise only be accomplished at the Finder were probably the biggest improvement to Mac productivity to appear. If you are still not working with MultiFinder, and even if you are, a utility that can quickly copy or delete a file without forcing you to exit your current application saves a tremendous amount of time and allows you to get back to your work quickly and with minimal distraction.

DiskTop					

	Copy	Move		HFS		▭ DataDrive
	Delete	Rename		20328K Used 89%		Eject
	Find	Sizes		2537K Free 11%	▭ DataDrive	Drive

▭ **Name**	Type	Creator	Data	Resource	Modified
▯ CPSDeleteInfo	????	MTLS	1K		6/27/89
▭ Deluxe Music	4 files/folders		---	---	7/30/89
▯ Desktop	FNDR	ERIK		49K	7/26/89
▯ Desktop DB	BTFL	DMGR	16K		7/30/89
▯ Desktop DF	DTFL	DMGR	10K		7/30/89
▯ Empower™ Prep	Empw	Empw		2K	7/2/89
▭ Encyclo Mac	13 files/folders		---	---	7/30/89
▯ GuardianDelData	GLON	INIT	14K		7/30/89
▯ GuardianSavData	GLOS	INIT	136K		7/24/89
▯ Icons ClipFile	MDOC	Kbel			7/30/89
▭ Navigator Sessions	25 files/folders		---	---	7/27/89
▭ Other Books	11 files/folders		---	---	7/25/89

The DiskTop DA provides you with the ability to perform most Finder file and drive manipulations without leaving the current application. Every Mac user should have DiskTop or one of its equivalents.

The most significant of the early utilities to provide Finder features was DiskTop. Version 1.2 is a shareware utility, but the enhanced DiskTop version 3.0 is now a commercial product. DiskTop allows you to do virtually everything that you can do from the Finder: copy, move, delete, and rename files, get file information, find files, and create new folders. DiskTop presents a graphic display of your files and folders, including file name, size, creator, and type. DiskTop's menu can be configured with any applications you want to be able to launch, and you can also launch any application or document by simply double-clicking on its icon. DiskTools is extremely similar to DiskTop, and could easily be considered a software clone; command for command it matches DiskTop's features, although we find its icon-based display somewhat less pleasing.

 DeskZap, File Minder, FileMaster, FileStar, Disk-File 🖳, 🅿️🅾️, 🖳, 🖳, 🖳
DeskZap, File Minder, FileMaster, and FileStar are smaller and therefore somewhat faster DA's than DiskTop and DiskTools, offering most of their features, without the graphic file-directory displays. Since all of these programs are either public-domain or shareware, they are a good way to go if you would rather save some money on a Finder utility, and can't find DiskTop 1.2 (which is still available in its shareware format). Disk-File is an older Fkey that can delete and rename files, set file attributes, and duplicate single-sided or double-sided disks, but it does not offer a file-copying feature.

Fkeys

For some reason, Fkeys have never gotten much respect as a Macintosh utility format. Fkeys are small utility programs that were originally intended to be executed with COMMAND-OPTION-NUMBER keystroke sequences, where NUMBER is any number on the keyboard between 0 and 9. (Numbers on the keypad can only be used if a special utility is installed.) Almost from the start, however, there have been ways to execute Fkeys from menus or from almost any assignable keyboard command. Apple has included four Fkeys in the System Software since its very first release, and during their heyday in 1985 and 1986, hundreds of Fkeys, mostly public-domain, freeware, or shareware, were produced and distributed.

Fkeys were popular in the Mac's first few years for two reasons: They offered a way to add functions to the Macintosh without using up any of the then precious DA slots, and for certain utility functions their direct keyboard invocation seemed more appropriate than a dedicated application or even a desk accessory. But there were some problems with Fkeys.

Problem #1: When Fkeys first appeared, a surprisingly ferocious debate existed in the Macintosh community between those who believed that only pure "point-and-click" software should be developed for the Mac and those who knew better. Of course, at this time the lines between the PC users and the Macintosh users were more clearly drawn than they are today, and neither side was above name-calling. To the Mac purists, any software requiring use of the keyboard stunk of "PC regression" and diluted the mouse-converted race.

Problem #2: Fkeys were never really legitimized by Apple or any other major Macintosh software vendor, and so to some degree they remained the province of Mac fanatics. Even though many excellent Fkeys and Fkey utilities became available, the use of Fkeys always retained a very "hacker-ish" feel that was never overcome by the masses of Mac users.

Problem #3: Just as Fkeys were gaining momentum and improving their quality and quantity, their raison d'être was eliminated when Suitcase broke the DA limit once and for all. Soon after, inits and cdevs, two more popular formats for small utilities, became popular, offering easier use and keyboard execution without the constraint of COMMAND-OPTION-NUMBER.

Many Fkeys still exist, however, and a good number are perfectly functional even with System 6.02 and MultiFinder. Many of the functions provided by these Fkeys are now available in newer cdevs, DA's, and inits, but a few Fkeys still offer unique abilities and may suit your needs perfectly. And the Fkey format is supported by Suitcase II, MasterJuggler, and QuicKeys, so if you have any of these popular utilities, using Fkeys is easier than ever.

Apple's Fkeys

Apple's original Fkeys haven't changed since the introduction of the original Macintosh 128k.

- ⌘-⇧-1: **Eject the disk in the internal (right) disk drive**. This sequence ejects the disk in the disk drive, but does not dismount it. Because this forces the drive's eject mechanism to operate without regard to the system software, this often works when other ejection methods will not. Also, this method can eject a disk that the Mac won't admit is inserted (i.e., that does not appear at the Finder desktop).

- ⌘-⇧-2: **Eject the disk in the external (left) disk drive**. This works just like COMMAND-SHIFT-1, but for the other drive.

- ⌘-⇧-0: **Eject the disk in third disk drive, if available**. This works just like COMMAND-SHIFT-1, but for external drives connected to Macs with two internal floppies.

- **⌘-⇧-3: Save a copy of the current display as a MacPaint file.** Each time this key combination is pressed, the Mac creates a new MacPaint file containing a **screen dump**, or picture, of the current display on your Macintosh screen. The new file is named Screen#, where # is set sequentially from 0 to 9—the first time you invoke the Fkey, Screen0 is created, the next time, Screen1 is created, and so on—and is placed in the current folder. After ten different screen dumps (Screen0 through Screen9) are saved in one folder, this feature will not function until you change the current folder or move or rename the files.

  Unfortunately, this Fkey has never been updated; it cannot create screen dumps while menus are selected, and it cannot handle today's larger Macintosh displays. If you try to create a screen dump when a menu is selected, it is not executed until the menu is released. Several commercial utility programs provide much-improved screen-dump abilities. See the System Software entry later in this section for details.

- **⌘-⇧-4: Print the current screen to ImageWriter.** If you have an ImageWriter connected to your Mac, pressing this key combination will print your current screen display to the ImageWriter. This Fkey does not, however, print the current screen on any PostScript printer.

Fkey Utilities

Fkey/Sound Installer, Fkey Manager, Fkey Installer
These three programs operate much like Apple's Font/DA Mover, allowing you to copy Fkeys from their suitcases into other suitcases or into System files. They also enable you to reset the number that is used in the key combination that invokes the Fkey. Fkey Manager is a rather old utility that still operates perfectly under System Software 6.0 and MultiFinder. Fkey/Sound Installer is provided by Alsoft along with MasterJuggler and Font/DA Juggler. Fkey Installer is another old utility that is incompatible with MultiFinder, but still operates fine otherwise.

Suitcase II, MasterJuggler, QuicKeys
Each of these utilities allows you to access and use Fkeys. Suitcase II and MasterJuggler let you mount Fkeys directly from Fkey suitcases, and then run them from the utility's own menu. These utilities handle all Fkey numbering conflicts automatically, so virtually any number of Fkeys can be used. QuicKeys allows you to run Fkeys that have been installed in the

System file (but not those attached via Suitcase or MasterJuggler), or to assign keyboard equivalents to these Fkeys.

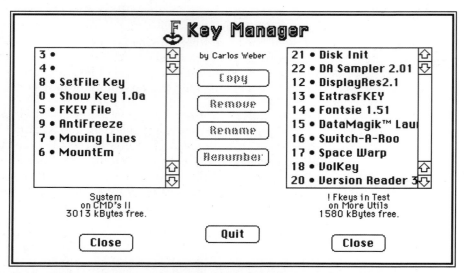

Carlos Weber's Fkey Manager has long been the favorite Fkey utility.

 FKey... DA, Fkey Sampler, FONT-FKEY-DA Sampler
These utilities let you run Fkeys directly from their suitcase, much like Suitcase II and MasterJuggler, although they are somewhat less convenient to use. Of the three, the Fkey... DA is our favorite.

 Show Key, Fkey View
One obvious problem with Fkeys is that it is easy to forget which ones you have installed and which COMMAND-OPTIONS-NUMBER combination is used to execute them (if applicable). Show Key and Fkey View are Fkeys that display a list of the Fkeys installed in your System file, and their associated keyboard-equivalent numbers. They do not list Fkeys accessed via Master-Juggler or Suitcase, although each of these utilities provides an Fkey list.

 # Fonts

It is the best of times. It is the worst of times. That's one way to describe the current situation in Macintosh fonts. While the range and quality of type-faces available for the Macintosh and its high-resolution PostScript print-ers has expanded phenomenally, so has the complexity of the Macintosh font world. And it looks as if things are going to get worse, possibly much worse, before they get any better.

The Good News: Thousands of Fonts

New York, Chicago, Geneva, Monaco, and Venice. To someone who has never used a Macintosh, this probably sounds like the itinerary for an exotic vacation. To a Mac user, it's just a trip to the FONT menu. These five fonts, included with every Mac since the first, give Mac users a freedom of ex-pression that computers before the Mac (except the Lisa, of course) had never provided. Within months after the Mac's introduction, Mac users could choose among several hundred different typefaces.

With the introduction of the LaserWriter and the many high-resolution output devices that followed it, the importance of Macintosh fonts intensi-fied; professional-quality communication demands professional-quality type. These printers also need a different kind of font than those used when output is made only to dot-matrix printers such as the ImageWriter. These new fonts called **laser fonts**, or **PostScript fonts**. Laser fonts are different from other fonts (often called **ImageWriter fonts** or **bit-mapped fonts**) in that they consist of two parts, a **screen font** that determines the on-screen appearance of the typeface, and a **printer font** that provides the PostScript printer with exact mathematical definitions of each character in the font. These printer fonts are used by the LaserWriter (or other PostScript printer) when the font is being printed.

Since bit-mapped fonts do not include the printer-font component, they cannot be output at high quality on PostScript printers. This has caused a lot of confusion; Mac users often prepare their documents in bit-mapped fonts and mistakenly expect to get high-quality output when they print them on a LaserWriter.

Berkeley

Boca Raton

Cape Canaveral

Carmel

Dallas

Detroit

FRANKFURT

Geneva

Hollywood

Las Vegas

London

Malibu

Monterey

New York

Sydney

Tokyo

Non-laser fonts are printed at a constant resolution regardless of your output device. To minimize confusion, vendors often name their non-laser fonts after famous cities.

Avant Garde Gothic Demibold

Bodoni Poster

Bookman Light Italic

Brush Script

Cooper Black Italic

Eurostile Demibold Oblique

Friz Quadrata Bold

Garamond Light Italic

Glypha

Goudy Bold Italic

Helvetica

Korinna Kursiv Regular

Palatino Roman

Peignot Demibold

Souvenir Demibold

Times Bold Italic

Univers Condensed Light

University Roman

Zapf Chancery Medium Italic

The typefaces above—displayed in 18-point type size—represent a very brief sampling of the thousands of laser fonts available to the Mac.

Apple's laser fonts, Courier, Helvetica, Times, and the often overlooked but extremely useful Symbol, are included with each copy of the System Software. Each of these fonts is available in several different type styles, including plain (sometimes called *roman* in the case of serifed fonts), italic (or oblique, if the face appears only slanted rather than cursive), bold, and bold-italic (or bold-oblique), except for Symbol, for which no style variations are available.

Adobe Systems, inventor of PostScript, was the early leader in the distribution of PostScript typefaces, but today a number of the world's oldest and largest typeface manufacturers—International Typeface Corporation (ITC), American Type Founders (Kingsley ATF), AGFA Compugraphic, Letraset, and Linotype—as well as many smaller firms, are selling their type libraries in PostScript format for use on the Macintosh.

There are several differences between the PostScript fonts available from different vendors. The first is the origin of the design used for the fonts. Most of Adobe's fonts are licensed implementations of traditional type designs. This means that Adobe's Galliard, for example, will match the Galliard type used by traditional typesetters as far as the shape of each character in the font. (Other differences, in aspects of the font such as its kerning pairs, may exist.) Many vendors do not license their font designs, but instead simply copy a licensed font. Usually these vendors assign their fonts a name very similar to the licensed font that is being copied (Option is a copy of Optima, Mechanical is a copy of Machine, etc.) Depending on your "type sophistication" you may or may not want to avoid using non-licensed fonts. (There is nothing illegal about nonlicensed fonts, they are just not approved by the owner of the original font's copyright.)

Another difference between PostScript fonts from various vendors is the actual PostScript language instructions the fonts uses to tell the PostScript printer how to render characters. Adobe Systems, with their obvious inside knowledge of the Adobe PostScript interpreter used in most PostScript printers, has given their fonts *hints* that help the font print clearly at smaller type sizes on low resolution devices (less than 10-point type on a 300 dot-per-inch printer). Other vendors have had to do without these hints, develop their own, or license Adobe's hinting technology. Thus far, the only font vendors that have licensed Adobe's hinting technology are Monotype, Agfa Compugraphic, and Varityper. Kingsley/ATF has developed its own hinting technology, and all other font vendors are not using any hinting at all.

Complexity, Compatibility, and Conflict

While the proliferation of PostScript fonts has generally been good news for Mac users, some significant problems have arisen. These problems are the result of the fact that the Mac's System Software was unprepared for the font explosion, and that the business interests of the manufacturers and vendors in the font market have generally triumphed over the interests of Mac users. In many ways, fonts have been victims of their own success.

The first problem fonts had was that apparently no one at Apple had considered the possibility of a font explosion. The System file and early Mac software wasn't designed to use more than a handful of different fonts. As a result, using a wide variety of fonts on early Macs meant either constantly adding and deleting fonts with the Font/DA Mover, or keeping multiple startup disks configured with different font combinations. And even if you could add lots of fonts to the System file, early Mac applications didn't offer scrolling font menus, so it was impossible to access more than ten or so fonts in most applications.

By the time System file 4.2 was released, many software applications offered their font choices in dialog boxes using scrolling font lists, and Apple had added the ability for font menus to scroll if they became too long for the Mac screen to display. Up to 128 fonts could now be used comfortably. But then the LaserWriter and laser fonts were introduced, and a new kind of font problem became apparent: Fonts are kept track of by the System file and by applications according to an ID number, and only 128 of these ID numbers were available.

Each font manufacturer assigns their fonts an ID number when the font is created, but the limited number of ID's available forced different vendors to assign their fonts conflicting ID numbers, and some vendors' libraries eventually grew so large that they were even forced to assign duplicate ID numbers to their own fonts. When fonts are installed with the Font/DA Mover the ID number of a font is changed if it conflicts with that of an existing font, and so fonts were often used with a different ID number than that originally set by the font manufacturer. This wasn't a problem until you tried to print a document on a Macintosh other than the one on which it was created. If any fonts used in the document had a different ID number on the Mac that created the file than they had on the Mac printing the file, incorrect fonts appeared in the printout.

Eventually, Apple solved the font-ID problem by introducing a new font-numbering scheme that supported 16,000 different font numbers. But this enhancement didn't appear until System Software 6.0. And since all of the screen fonts being used must be specifically upgraded to take advantage of this new numbering scheme, and some application software must be upgraded to correctly use these new fonts, the font-ID problem is disappearing slowly. For more technical information on the font-ID problem, see "Fonts: A Technical Look," later in this entry.

With the font-ID problem waning, Apple must have thought that it was time to throw a new wrench in the soup, so they decided to announce their plans to minimize their corporate support for PostScript printers and Post-Script laser fonts, and release a new competing type of fonts called **outline fonts**. Outline fonts, which will appear along with System Software 7.0, will offer the quality of PostScript on properly equipped output devices, and better on-screen font display. But users will have to contend with another major change in the accepted font standards (one that will not be without a fight as the PostScript world struggles to maintain its prominence) and inevitable confusion over which fonts can be printed on which printers. (Outline fonts, which will be available from Apple and other vendors, will only be printable on specially designed printers. PostScript fonts will continue to be required for use on the hundreds of thousands of existing PostScript output devices.)

If you create and print your documents at a single location, most of the more recent font problems may not affect you. If you use a service bureau to output your files, or send them to another department or branch of your company for review or output, you probably have already encountered the font ID issue. In this case, changing over to NFNT versions of all your screen fonts is probably a good idea, and will likely minimize or eliminate your ID conflicts.

Fonts: A Technical Look

It would be nice if understanding fonts on the Macintosh were easy, but unfortunately it isn't. Fonts perform a complex task involving the Mac's System Software, the application creating the document, and the output devices on which your documents will be printed; using fonts sometimes means understanding how fonts interact with each of these. Here we will examine the interaction of fonts with the System file, your applications, and printers, and we'll describe some utility software that can help you manage your fonts.

Screen Fonts

The fonts that you see in your FONT menu and move around with the Font/DA Mover are called *screen fonts*. A screen font is exactly what its name implies: a version of a font created especially to be viewed on screen. A screen font is the bit-mapped graphic drawn at a resolution of 72 dots-per-inch, just like an image created in MacPaint. Although it varies from manufacturer to manufacturer, most typefaces include five sizes for each screen font: 10-point, 12-point, 14-point, 18-point, and 24-point. A screen font may also be available in different styles. For example, Times includes Times, I Times Italic, B Times Bold, and BI Times BoldItalic. Obviously, you can use and display screen fonts in sizes and styles other than those provided by the manufacturer. When you ask the Mac to display a font size or style that is not available the Mac creates a mathematical simulation using the information from the nearest font that is available. This is why font sizes and styles that are actually available look better on screen than those you don't.

For bit-mapped fonts, the screen font constitutes the entire font. When you print a document that contains bit-mapped fonts, the same information that is used by the screen to display the font is sent to the printer, and basically you get the same quality as seen on screen—usually 72 dots per inch (which looks very jagged when printed). When you print a bit-mapped font that has been used in a size or style that was not really available, the printer has to mathematically calculate the font's appearance just like the screen did; and so bit-mapped fonts will look much worse when printed in these sizes and styles.

PostScript laser fonts, on the other hand, have matching printer-font files that provide the printer with the specialized information it needs to print the font's characters much more accurately than they were displayed on screen. Because of the way these printer fonts work, they can render the font perfectly, regardless of whether or not the screen font corresponding to the size and style of the font used was installed. If you try to print a PostScript font when the corresponding printer font is unavailable (not already downloaded to the printer's memory or available to be downloaded), the Mac reverts to the same method used to print bit-mapped fonts, and you will get jagged results that you'll probably find very unacceptable.

FONT, FOND, and NFNT

The System file, and most applications, keep track of screen fonts by their ID number. Until System Software 6.0, Mac fonts used two resources to manage and contain fonts. The FOND resources contained information describing a font family, and pointers to the specific location of each font that is available. These fonts were actually stored in FONT resources, which held the bit-mapped image of each character. Because of the way FONT ID numbers were selected, only 128 different fonts could be correctly handled. (Technically 256 fonts could be stored, but Apple reserved the first 128 for their own use.) Each font was given a FONT ID number by its manufacturer, but when the Font/DA Mover adds the font to your System file it changes the numbers as needed to avoid any ID number conflicts. (If you use Suitcase II or MasterJuggler to open two suitcases that have fonts using the same FONT ID number, you may encounter a font conflict that will confuse your software and prevent you from printing the fonts correctly.)

System 6.0 added support for a new font resource called NFNT (New Font Numbering Table) that can be used in place of the FONT resource. NFNT resources support a much wider range of ID numbers (16,000), and offer enhanced support for the stylized screen fonts available for most font families. To take advantage of NFNTs, you must either add NFNT resources to your older fonts—you can do this using one of several utilities, including Font/DA Utility (included with MasterJuggler) and Font Harmony (included with Suitcase II)—or get newer versions of the screen fonts that have had NFNT resources added to them by their manufacturers.

Even NFNT numbers can theoretically conflict, although Apple is registering NFNT numbers so that font vendors will each choose unique numbers when they create new versions of their screen fonts. Adobe Systems has recently released new NFNT-supporting versions of its entire screen-font library. These new screen fonts are being widely distributed through Post-Script service bureaus and on-line services. When using fonts with NFNT resources, you must use Font/DA Mover version 3.8 or later. Earlier versions didn't support the NFNT resource.

Apple is also encouraging application developers to write their applications so that they recognize fonts by name and not by ID number. Some applications, like PageMaker, XPress, and Ready,Set,Go!, already work this way, reducing but not eliminating the problems that font ID numbers cause. Most applications, however, currently rely on ID numbers (either FOND or NFNT), so eliminating ID conflicts remains vital.

Standard Apple Character Set (1 of 5)

The following pages contain ASCII code numbers and keyboard locations for every character available in the standard typeface keyboard configuration as defined by Apple. Most typefaces use this configuration, including all alpha-numeric typefaces available from Adobe. Fonts from smaller vendors, such as Casady-Greene and Altsys, frequently employ custom keyboard configurations. In such a case, you will have to consult the KeyCaps DA to locate an unusual character or use the chart provided with the font.

Throughout this chart, ⇧ represents the SHIFT key, ⌥ represents OPTION, and ⊔ represents the space bar. Other keys are represented by the letter, number, or punctuation that appears on the key. All key combinations should be pressed simultaneously. Key combinations separated by a comma are pressed sequentially. The phrase *no key* indicates a character that is not available from the keyboard, but that is included in the font. Depending on your software, these characters may be accessed in some other manner. Microsoft Word, for example, allows you to create a character by pressing COMMAND-OPTION-Q, entering the character's ASCII code number, and pressing RETURN.

All characters are listed in order of their ASCII numbers (ranging from 32 to 255). If no character appears at an ASCII location, then no character exists for that code number.

ASCII Numbers and Keyboard Locations

032		Space, standard	⊔	045	-	Hyphen	-
033	!	Exclamation point	⇧1	046	.	Period	.
034	"	Quotation mark, straight (Ditto)	⇧'	047	/	Slash (Virgule)	/
035	#	Number	⇧3	048	0	Zero	0
036	$	Dollar	⇧4	049	1	One	1
037	%	Percent	⇧5	050	2	Two	2
038	&	Ampersand	⇧7	051	3	Three	3
039	'	Apostrophe, straight	'	052	4	Four	4
040	(	Parenthesis, open	⇧9	053	5	Five	5
041	)	Parenthesis, close	⇧0	054	6	Six	6
042	*	Asterisk, superscripted	⇧8	055	7	Seven	7
043	+	Plus	⇧=	056	8	Eight	8
044	,	Comma	,	057	9	Nine	9

Standard Apple Character Set (2 of 5)

ASCII Numbers and Keyboard Locations (Cont.)

058	:	Colon	⇧;
059	;	Semicolon	;
060	<	Less than	⇧,
061	=	Equal	=
062	>	Greater than	⇧.
063	?	Question mark	⇧/
064	@	At	⇧2
065	**A**	A, capital	⇧A
066	**B**	B, capital	⇧B
067	**C**	C, capital	⇧C
068	**D**	D, capital	⇧D
069	**E**	E, capital	⇧E
070	**F**	F, capital	⇧F
071	**G**	G, capital	⇧G
072	**H**	H, capital	⇧H
073	**I**	I, capital	⇧I
074	**J**	J, capital	⇧J
075	**K**	K, capital	⇧K
076	**L**	L, capital	⇧L
077	**M**	M, capital	⇧M
078	**N**	N, capital	⇧N
079	**O**	O, capital	⇧O
080	**P**	P, capital	⇧P
081	**Q**	Q, capital	⇧Q
082	**R**	R, capital	⇧R
083	**S**	S, capital	⇧S
084	**T**	T, capital	⇧T
085	**U**	U, capital	⇧U
086	**V**	V, capital	⇧V
087	**W**	W, capital	⇧W
088	**X**	X, capital	⇧X
089	**Y**	Y, capital	⇧Y
090	**Z**	Z, capital	⇧Z
091	[	Bracket, left	[
092	\	Backslash	\
093	]	Bracket, right	]
094	^	Caret	⍨I, ⬓
095	_	Underscore	⇧-
096	`	Grave accent	~
097	**a**	a, lowercase	A
098	**b**	b, lowercase	B
099	**c**	c, lowercase	C
100	**d**	d, lowercase	D
101	**e**	e, lowercase	E
102	**f**	f, lowercase	F
103	**g**	g, lowercase	G
104	**h**	h, lowercase	H
105	**i**	i, lowercase	I
106	**j**	j, lowercase	J
107	**k**	k, lowercase	K

Standard Apple Character Set (3 of 5)

ASCII Numbers and Keyboard Locations (Cont.)

108	**l**	l, lowercase	L
109	**m**	m, lowercase	M
110	**n**	n, lowercase	N
111	**o**	o, lowercase	O
112	**p**	p, lowercase	P
113	**q**	q, lowercase	Q
114	**r**	r, lowercase	R
115	**s**	s, lowercase	S
116	**t**	t, lowercase	T
117	**u**	u, lowercase	U
118	**v**	v, lowercase	V
119	**w**	w, lowercase	W
120	**x**	x, lowercase	X
121	**y**	y, lowercase	Y
122	**z**	z, lowercase	Z
123	{	Brace, left	⇧[
124	|	Bar	⇧\
125	}	Brace, right	⇧]
126	~	Tilde mark (Similar) .... ⇧~ *or* ⌥N, ⎯	
127		.... *no key*	
128	**Ä**	A, capital ʷ/diaeresis .... ⌥U, ⇧A	
129	**Å**	A, capital ʷ/ring .... ⇧⌥A	
130	**Ç**	C, capital ʷ/cedilla .... ⇧⌥C	
131	**É**	E, capital ʷ/acute .... ⌥E, ⇧E	
132	**Ñ**	N, capital ʷ/tilde .... ⌥N, ⇧N	

133	**Ö**	O, capital ʷ/diaeresis .... ⌥U, ⇧O	
134	**Ü**	U, capital ʷ/diaeresis .... ⌥U, ⇧U	
135	**á**	a, lowercase ʷ/acute .... ⌥E, A	
136	**à**	a, lowercase ʷ/grave .... ⌥~, A	
137	**â**	a, lowercase ʷ/circumflex .... ⌥I, A	
138	**ä**	a, lowercase ʷ/diaeresis .... ⌥U, A	
139	**ã**	a, lowercase ʷ/tilde .... ⌥N, A	
140	**å**	a, lowercase ʷ/ring .... ⌥A	
141	**ç**	c, lowercase ʷ/cedilla .... ⌥C	
142	**é**	e, lowercase ʷ/acute .... ⌥E, E	
143	**è**	e, lowercase ʷ/grave .... ⌥~, E	
144	**ê**	e, lowercase ʷ/circumflex .... ⌥I, E	
145	**ë**	e, lowercase ʷ/diaeresis .... ⌥U, E	
146	**í**	i, lowercase ʷ/acute .... ⌥E, I	
147	**ì**	i, lowercase ʷ/grave .... ⌥~, I	
148	**î**	i, lowercase ʷ/circumflex .... ⌥I, I	
149	**ï**	i, lowercase ʷ/diaeresis .... ⌥U, I	
150	**ñ**	n, lowercase ʷ/tilde .... ⌥N, N	
151	**ó**	o, lowercase ʷ/acute .... ⌥E, O	
152	**ò**	o, lowercase ʷ/grave .... ⌥~, O	
153	**ô**	o, lowercase ʷ/circumflex .... ⌥I, O	
154	**ö**	o, lowercase ʷ/diaeresis .... ⌥U, O	
155	**õ**	o, lowercase ʷ/tilde .... ⌥N, O	
156	**ú**	u, lowercase ʷ/acute .... ⌥E, U	
157	**ù**	u, lowercase ʷ/grave .... ⌥~, U	

Standard Apple Character Set (4 of 5)

ASCII Numbers and Keyboard Locations (Cont.)

158	û	u, lowercase w/circumflex .... ⌥I, U
159	ü	u, lowercase w/diaeresis .... ⌥U, U
160	†	Dagger, single (Obelisk) .... ⌥T
161	°	Degree .... ⇧⌥8
162	¢	Cent .... ⌥4
163	£	Pound sterling .... ⌥3
164	§	Section .... ⌥6
165	•	Bullet .... ⌥8
166	¶	Paragraph break .... ⌥7
167	ß	German double S (Beta) .... ⌥S
168	®	Registered trademark .... ⌥R
169	©	Copyright .... ⌥G
170	™	Trademark .... ⌥2
171	´	Acute accent .... ⌥E, ▁
172	¨	Diaeresis diacritic (Umlaut) .... ⌥U, ▁
173	≠	Not equal* .... ⌥=
174	Æ	AE ligature, capital .... ⇧⌥'
175	Ø	O slash, capital .... ⇧⌥O
176	∞	Infinity* .... ⌥5
177	±	Plus or minus .... ⇧⌥=
178	≤	Less than or equal* .... ⌥,
179	≥	Greater than or equal* .... ⌥.
180	¥	Yen .... ⌥Y
181	µ	Mu, lowercase .... ⌥M
182	∂	Partial differential* .... ⌥D

183	Σ	Summation* .... ⌥W
184	∏	Product* .... ⇧⌥P
185	π	Pi* .... ⌥P
186	∫	Integral* .... ⌥B
187	ª	Ord, feminine .... ⌥9
188	º	Ord, masculine .... ⌥0
189	Ω	Omega, capital* .... ⌥Z
190	æ	ae ligature, lowercase .... ⌥'
191	ø	o slash, lowercase .... ⌥O
192	¿	Question mark, inverted .... ⇧⌥/
193	¡	Exclamation point, inverted .... ⌥1
194	¬	Logical not .... ⌥L
195	√	Radical initiate* .... ⌥V
196	ƒ	Florin .... ⌥F
197	≈	Approximately equal* .... ⌥X
198	Δ	Delta, capital* .... ⌥D
199	«	Guillemot, double, left .... ⌥\
200	»	Guillemot, double, right .... ⇧⌥\
201	…	Ellipsis .... ⌥;
202		Space, nonbreaking .... ⌥▁
203	À	A, capital w/grave .... ⌥~, ⇧A
204	Ã	A, capital w/tilde .... ⌥N, ⇧A
205	Õ	O, capital w/tilde .... ⌥N, ⇧0
206	Œ	OE ligature, capital .... ⇧⌥Q
207	œ	oe ligature, lowercase .... ⌥Q

* *Accesses character in Symbol font*

Standard Apple Character Set (5 of 5)

ASCII Numbers and Keyboard Locations (Cont.)

208	–	En dash (Minus)	⌥-
209	—	Em dash	⇧⌥-
210	"	Quotation mark, open	⌥[
211	"	Quotation mark, close	⇧⌥[
212	'	Quote, single, open	⌥]
213	'	Quote, single, close (Apostrophe)	⇧⌥]
214	÷	Divide	⌥/
215	◊	Lozenge*	⇧⌥V
216	ÿ	y, lowercase w/ diaeresis	⌥U, Y
217	Ÿ	Y, capital w/ diaeresis	⇧⌥~
218	⁄	Fraction slash	⇧⌥1
219	¤	Currency	⇧⌥2
220	‹	Guillemot, single, left	⇧⌥3
221	›	Guillemot, single, right	⇧⌥4
222	fi	fi ligature, lowercase	⇧⌥5
223	fl	fl ligature, lowercase	⇧⌥6
224	‡	Dagger, double (Diesis)	⇧⌥7
225	·	Center period (Multiply, dot)	⇧⌥9
226	,	Quote, single, baseline	⇧⌥0
227	„	Quotation mark, baseline	⇧⌥W
228	‰	Per thousand	⇧⌥E
229	Â	A, capital w/ circumflex	⌥~, ⇧A
230	Ê	E, capital w/ circumflex	⌥N, ⇧A
231	Á	A, capital w/ acute	⇧⌥Y
232	Ë	E, capital w/ diaeresis	⇧⌥U
233	È	E, capital w/ grave	⇧⌥I
234	Í	I, capital w/ acute	⇧⌥S
235	Î	I, capital w/ circumflex	⇧⌥D
236	Ï	I, capital w/ diaeresis	⇧⌥F
237	Ì	I, capital w/ grave	⇧⌥G
238	Ó	O, capital w/ acute	⇧⌥H
239	Ô	O, capital w/ circumflex	⇧⌥J
240		Apple icon	⇧⌥K
241	Ò	O, capital w/ grave	⇧⌥L
242	Ú	U, capital w/ acute	⇧⌥;
243	Û	U, capital w/ circumflex	⇧⌥Z
244	Ù	U, capital w/ grave	⇧⌥X
245	ı	I, lowercase, dotless	⇧⌥B
246	^	Circumflex diacritic	⇧⌥N
247	~	Tilde diacritic	⇧⌥M
248	¯	Macron diacritic	⇧⌥,
249	˘	Breve diacritic	⇧⌥.
250	˙	Dot accent	⌥H
251	°	Ring diacritic	⌥K
252	¸	Cedilla diacritic	*no key*
253	˝	Hungarian umlaut diacritic	*no key*
254	˛	Ogonek diacritic	*no key*
255	ˇ	Caron diacritic	*no key*

Symbol Font Character Set (1 of 4)

Many fonts offer character sets that differ from Apple's standard. The most prominent of these is the Symbol font, included with any PostScript printer. This font provides mathematical and scientific-notation symbols that augment the standard character set, in a design that is compatible with a wide variety of standard typefaces.

Throughout this chart, ⇧ represents the SHIFT key, ⌥ represents OPTION, and ▬ represents the space bar. Other keys are represented by the letter, number, or punctuation that appears on the key. All key combinations should be pressed simultaneously. Key combinations separated by a comma are pressed sequentially. The phrase *no key* indicates a character that is not available from the keyboard, but that is included in the font.

All characters are listed in order of their ASCII numbers (ranging from 32 to 255). If no character appears at an ASCII location, then no character exists for that code number.

ASCII Numbers and Keyboard Locations

032		Space, standard	▬
033	!	Exclamation point	⇧1
034	∀	Universal	⇧'
035	#	Number	⇧3
036	∃	Existential	⇧4
037	%	Percent	⇧5
038	&	Ampersand	⇧7
039	∋	Such that	'
040	(	Parenthesis, open	⇧9
041	)	Parenthesis, close	⇧0
042	*	Asterisk (Multiply)	⇧8
043	+	Plus	⇧=
044	,	Comma	,
045	−	Minus	-
046	.	Period	.
047	/	Slash (Virgule)	/
048	0	Zero	0
049	1	One	1
050	2	Two	2
051	3	Three	3
052	4	Four	4
053	5	Five	5
054	6	Six	6
055	7	Seven	7
056	8	Eight	8
057	9	Nine	9
058	:	Colon	⇧;
059	;	Semicolon	;
060	<	Less than	⇧,
061	=	Equal	=
062	>	Greater than	⇧.
063	?	Question mark	⇧/
064	≅	Congruent	⇧2
065	A	Alpha, capital	⇧A
066	B	Beta, capital	⇧B
067	X	Chi, capital	⇧C

Symbol Font Character Set (2 of 4)

ASCII Numbers and Keyboard Locations (Cont.)

068	Δ	Delta, capital	⇧D
069	E	Epsilon, capital	⇧E
070	Φ	Phi, capital	⇧F
071	Γ	Gamma, capital	⇧G
072	H	Eta, capital	⇧H
073	I	Iota, capital	⇧I
074	ϑ	Theta, lowercase cursive	⇧J
075	K	Kappa, capital	⇧K
076	Λ	Lambda, capital	⇧L
077	M	Mu, capital	⇧M
078	N	Nu, capital	⇧N
079	O	Omicron, capital	⇧O
080	Π	Pi, capital	⇧P
081	Θ	Theta, capital	⇧Q
082	P	Rho, capital	⇧R
083	Σ	Sigma, capital	⇧S
084	T	Tau, capital	⇧T
085	Y	Upsilon, capital	⇧U
086	ς	Sigma, lowercase cursive	⇧V
087	Ω	Omega, capital	⇧W
088	Ξ	Xi, capital	⇧X
089	Ψ	Psi, capital	⇧Y
090	Z	Zeta, capital	⇧Z
091	[	Bracket, left	[
092	∴	Therefore	\
093	]	Bracket, right	]
094	⊥	Perpendicular	⬿I, ▬
095	_	Underscore	⇧-
096	‾	Radical extension	~
097	α	Alpha, lowercase	A
098	β	Beta, lowercase	B
099	χ	Chi, lowercase	C

100	δ	Delta, lowercase	D
101	ε	Epsilon, lowercase	E
102	φ	Phi, lowercase	F
103	γ	Gamma, lowercase	G
104	η	Eta, lowercase	H
105	ι	Iota, lowercase	I
106	φ	Phi, lowercase cursive	J
107	κ	Kappa, lowercase	K
108	λ	Lambda, lowercase	L
109	μ	Mu, lowercase	M
110	ν	Nu, lowercase	N
111	o	Omicron, lowercase	O
112	π	Pi, lowercase	P
113	θ	Theta, lowercase	Q
114	ρ	Rho, lowercase	R
115	σ	Sigma, lowercase	S
116	τ	Tau, lowercase	T
117	υ	Upsilon, lowercase	U
118	ϖ	Omega, lowercase cursive	V
119	ω	Omega, lowercase	W
120	ξ	Xi, lowercase	X
121	ψ	Psi, lowercase	Y
122	ζ	Zeta, lowercase	Z
123	{	Brace, left	⇧[
124	|	Bar	⇧\
125	}	Brace, right	⇧]
126	~	Similar	⇧~ or ⬿N, ▬
127			no key
128			⬿U, ⇧A
129			⇧⬿A
130			⇧⬿C
131			⬿E, ⇧E

Symbol Font Character Set (3 of 4)

ASCII Numbers and Keyboard Locations (Cont.)

132		....	⌥N, ⇧N
133		....	⌥U, ⇧O
134		....	⌥U, ⇧U
135		....	⌥E, A
136		....	⌥~, A
137		....	⌥I, A
138		....	⌥U, A
139		....	⌥N, A
140		....	⌥A
141		....	⌥C
142		....	⌥E, E
143		....	⌥~, E
144		....	⌥I, E
145		....	⌥U, E
146		....	⌥E, I
147		....	⌥~, I
148		....	⌥I, I
149		....	⌥U, I
150		....	⌥N, N
151		....	⌥E, O
152		....	⌥~, O
153		....	⌥I, O
154		....	⌥U, O
155		....	⌥N, O
156		....	⌥E, U
157		....	⌥~, U
158		....	⌥I, U
159		....	⌥U, U
160		....	⌥T
161	Υ	Upsilon, capital cursive	⇧⌥8
162	′	Minutes (Feet)	⌥4
163	≤	Less than or equal	⌥3
164	/	Fraction slash	⌥6
165	∞	Infinity	⌥8
166	ƒ	Derivative	⌥7
167	♣	Club	⌥S
168	♦	Diamond	⌥R
169	♥	Heart	⌥G
170	♠	Spade	⌥2
171	↔	Arrow, bidirectional	⌥E, ▬
172	←	Arrow, left	⌥U, ▬
173	↑	Arrow, up	⌥=
174	→	Arrow, right	⇧⌥'
175	↓	Arrow, down	⇧⌥0
176	°	Degree	⌥5
177	±	Plus or minus	⇧⌥=
178	″	Seconds (Inches)	⌥,
179	≥	Greater than or equal	⌥.
180	×	Multiply	⌥Y
181	∝	Proportional	⌥M
182	∂	Partial differential	⌥D
183	•	Bullet	⌥W
184	÷	Divide	⇧⌥P
185	≠	Not equal	
186	≡	Identical	⌥B
187	≈	Approximately equal	⌥9
188	...	Ellipsis	⌥0
189	|	Arrow extension, vertical	⌥Z
190	—	Arrow extension, horizontal	⌥'
191	↵	Carriage return (Line break)	⌥0
192	ℵ	Aleph	⇧⌥/
193	ℑ	I fraktur, capital	⌥1
194	ℜ	R fraktur, capital	⌥L
195	℘	Weierstrass	⌥V

Symbol Font Character Set (4 of 4)

ASCII Numbers and Keyboard Locations (Cont.)

#	Symbol	Name	Key
196	⊗	Circle multiply	⌥F
197	⊕	Circle plus	⌥X
198	∅	Empty set	⌥D
199	∩	Intersection	⌥\
200	∪	Union	⇧⌥\
201	⊃	Proper superset	⌥;
202	⊇	Reflexive superset	⌥_
203	⊄	Not subset	⌥~, ⇧A
204	⊂	Proper subset	⌥N, ⇧A
205	⊆	Reflexive subset	⌥N, ⇧0
206	∈	Element	⇧⌥Q
207	∉	Not element	⌥Q
208	∠	Angle	⌥-
209	∇	Gradient	⇧⌥-
210	®	Registered trademark, serif	⌥[
211	©	Copyright, serif	⇧⌥[
212	™	Trademark, serif	⌥]
213	∏	Product	⇧⌥]
214	√	Radical initiate	⌥/
215	·	Multiply, dot	⇧⌥V
216	¬	Logical not	⌥U, Y
217	∧	Logical and	⇧⌥~
218	∨	Logical or	⇧⌥1
219	⇔	Arrow, double, bidirectional	⇧⌥2
220	⇐	Arrow, double, left	⇧⌥3
221	⇑	Arrow, double, up	⇧⌥4
222	⇒	Arrow, double, right	⇧⌥5
223	⇓	Arrow, double, down	⇧⌥6
224	◊	Lozenge	⇧⌥7
225	⟨	Angle bracket, left	⇧⌥9
226	®	Registered trademark, sans serif	⇧⌥0
227	©	Copyright, sans serif	⇧⌥W
228	™	Trademark, sans serif	⇧⌥E
229	Σ	Summation	⌥~, ⇧A
230	⌠	Parenthesis, open, top	⌥N, ⇧A
231	∣	Parenthesis, open, extension	⇧⌥Y
232	⌡	Parenthesis, open, bottom	⇧⌥U
233	⌈	Bracket, left, top	⇧⌥I
234	∣	Bracket, left, extension	⇧⌥S
235	⌊	Bracket, left, bottom	⇧⌥D
236	⌈	Brace, left, top	⇧⌥F
237	{	Brace, left, middle	⇧⌥G
238	⌊	Brace, left, bottom	⇧⌥H
239	∣	Brace, extension	⇧⌥J
240		Apple icon	⇧⌥K
241	⟩	Angle bracket, right	⇧⌥L
242	∫	Integral	⇧⌥;
243	⌠	Integral, top	⇧⌥Z
244	∣	Integral, extension	⇧⌥X
245	⌡	Integral, bottom	⇧⌥B
246	⌉	Parenthesis, close, top	⇧⌥N
247	∣	Parenthesis, close, extension	⇧⌥M
248	⌋	Parenthesis, close, bottom	⇧⌥,
249	⌉	Bracket, right, top	⇧⌥.
250	∣	Bracket, right, extension	⌥H
251	⌋	Bracket, right, bottom	⌥K
252	⌉	Brace, right, top	*no key*
253	}	Brace, right, middle	*no key*
254	⌋	Brace, right, bottom	*no key*
255			*no key*

Zapf Dingbats Character Set (1 of 4)

Another font that offers an unusual character set is Zapf Dingbats. This picture font, composed primarily of a quirky collection of stars, boxes, and arrows, is resident in most PostScript printers purchased since the 1986 release of the LaserWriter Plus.

Throughout this chart, ⇧ represents the SHIFT key, ⬋ represents OPTION, and ▬ represents the space bar. Other keys are represented by the letter, number, or punctuation that appears on the key. All key combinations should be pressed simultaneously. Key combinations separated by a comma are pressed sequentially. The phrase *no key* indicates a character that is not available from the keyboard, but that is included in the font.

All characters are listed in order of their ASCII numbers (ranging from 32 to 255). If no character appears at an ASCII location, then no character exists for that code number.

ASCII Numbers and Keyboard Locations

ASCII		Description	Key
032		Space, standard	▬
033	✁	Scissors, cutting down	⇧1
034	✂	Scissors	⇧'
035	✃	Scissors, cutting up	⇧3
036	✄	Scissors, white	⇧4
037	☎	Telephone	⇧5
038	✆	Receiver	⇧7
039	✇	Reel tape	'
040	✈	Jet	⇧9
041	✉	Letter	⇧0
042	☛	Index, black	⇧8
043	☞	Index, white	⇧=
044	✌	Victory	,
045	✍	Writer's hand	-
046	✎	Pencil, down	.
047	✏	Pencil, flat	/
048	✐	Pencil, up	0
049	✑	Pen nib, white	1
050	✒	Pen nib, black	2
051	✓	Check mark, light	3
052	✔	Check mark, medium	4
053	✕	X mark, light	5
054	✖	X mark, heavy	6
055	✗	X mark, slanted, light	7
056	✘	X mark, slanted, medium	8
057	✙	Cross, filled	9
058	✚	Cross, black	⇧;
059	✛	Cross, void, light	;
060	✜	Cross, void, heavy	⇧,
061	✝	Crux	=
062	✞	Crux, raised	⇧.
063	✟	Crux, filled	⇧/
064	✠	Cross Formée	⇧2
065	✡	Star of David	⇧A
066	✢	Petal cross, light	⇧B
067	✣	Petal cross, dot	⇧C
068	✤	Petal cross, heavy	⇧D
069	✥	Cross Botonée	⇧E

Zapf Dingbats Character Set (2 of 4)

ASCII Numbers and Keyboard Locations (Cont.)

070	✦	Star cross, black	⇧F	102	✻	Snowflake 3	F
071	✧	Star cross, white	⇧G	103	✳	Cluster, light	G
072	★	Star, 5-point, black	⇧H	104	✳	Cluster, medium	H
073	☆	Star, 5-point, white	⇧I	105	✺	Asterisk, 8-petal	I
074	✪	Star, 5-point, army	⇧J	106	✲	Star, 8-petal, dot	J
075	☆	Star, 5-point, void	⇧K	107	✴	Star, 8-petal, black	K
076	✭	Star, 5-point, dot	⇧L	108	●	Circle, black	L
077	★	Star, 5-point, filled, light	⇧M	109	○	Circle, white	M
078	★	Star, 5-point, filled, heavy	⇧N	110	■	Box, black	N
079	✮	Star, 5-point, insignia	⇧O	111	❏	Box, drop shadow 1	O
080	✩	Star, 5-point, raised	⇧P	112	❐	Box, drop shadow 2	P
081	✳	Asterisk, 6-point	⇧Q	113	❑	Box, raised 1	Q
082	✲	Asterisk, 6-point, void	⇧R	114	❒	Box, raised 2	R
083	✳	Asterisk, 8-point	⇧S	115	▲	Triangle, up	S
084	✴	Star, 8-point, light	⇧T	116	▼	Triangle, down	T
085	✵	Star, 8-point, insignia	⇧U	117	◆	Box, rotated	U
086	✶	Star, 6-point	⇧V	118	❖	Box, rotated quad	V
087	✷	Star, 8-point, medium	⇧W	119	◗	Semicircle	W
088	✸	Star, 8-point, heavy	⇧X	120	❘	Bar, light	X
089	✹	Star, 12-point	⇧Y	121	❙	Bar, medium	Y
090	✺	Asterisk, 16-point	⇧Z	122	❚	Bar, heavy	Z
091	✳	Star, 6-petal, dot	[	123	❛	Quote, single, open	⇧[
092	✲	Star, 6-petal, void	\	124	❜	Quote, single, close	⇧\
093	✳	Star, 6-petal, black	]	125	❝	Quotation mark, open	⇧]
094	✽	Star, 6-petal, oscillate	⌥I, ⌴	126	❞	Quotation mark, close	⇧~ *or* ⌥N, ⌴
095	✿	Flower, 5-petal, black	⇧-	127			*no key*
096	❀	Flower, 5-petal, white	~	128	❨	Parenthesis, open, light	⌥U, ⇧A
097	❁	Flower, 8-petal	A	129	❩	Parenthesis, close, light	⇧⌥A
098	❂	Sun	B	130	❪	Parenthesis, open, medium	⇧⌥C
099	✼	Star, 6-petal, insignia	C	131	❫	Parenthesis, close, medium	⌥E, ⇧E
100	❄	Snowflake 1	D	132	❬	Angle bracket, left, light	⌥N, ⇧N
101	❅	Snowflake 2	E	133	❭	Angle bracket, right, light	⌥U, ⇧O

Zapf Dingbats Character Set (3 of 4)

ASCII Numbers and Keyboard Locations (Cont.)

134	❬	Angle bracket, left, medium	✎U, ⇧U
135	❭	Angle bracket, right, medium	✎E, A
136	❰	Angle bracket, left, heavy	✎~, A
137	❱	Angle bracket, right, heavy	✎I, A
138	❲	Bracket, left	✎U, A
139	❳	Bracket, right	✎N, A
140	❴	Brace, left	✎A
141	❵	Brace, right	✎C
142		....	✎E, E
143		....	✎~, E
144		....	✎I, E
145		....	✎U, E
146		....	✎E, I
147		....	✎~, I
148		....	✎I, I
149		....	✎U, I
150		....	✎N, N
151		....	✎E, O
152		....	✎~, O
153		....	✎I, O
154		....	✎U, O
155		....	✎N, O
156		....	✎E, U
157		....	✎~, U
158		....	✎I, U
159		....	✎U, U
160		....	✎T
161	❡	Paragraph	⇧✎8
162	❢	Exclamation point	✎4
163	❣	Exclamation heart	✎3
164	❤	Heart, fat	✎6
165	❥	Heart, rotated	✎8
166	❦	Leaf	✎7
167	❧	Leaf, rotated	✎S
168	♣	Club	✎R
169	♦	Diamond	✎G
170	♥	Heart	✎2
171	♠	Spade	✎E, ▬
172	①	Circle one, serif	✎U, ▬
173	②	Circle two, serif	✎=
174	③	Circle three, serif	⇧✎'
175	④	Circle four, serif	⇧✎0
176	⑤	Circle five, serif	✎5
177	⑥	Circle six, serif	⇧✎=
178	⑦	Circle seven, serif	✎,
179	⑧	Circle eight, serif	✎.
180	⑨	Circle nine, serif	✎Y
181	⑩	Circle ten, serif	✎M
182	❶	Circle one, reversed, serif.............	✎D
183	❷	Circle two, reversed, serif	✎W
184	❸	Circle three, reversed, serif	⇧✎P
185	❹	Circle four, reversed, serif	✎P
186	❺	Circle five, reversed, serif	✎B
187	❻	Circle six, reversed, serif	✎9
188	❼	Circle seven, reversed, serif	✎0
189	❽	Circle eight, reversed, serif	✎Z
190	❾	Circle nine, reversed, serif	✎'
191	❿	Circle ten, reversed, serif	✎0
192	①	Circle one, sans serif	⇧✎/
193	②	Circle two, sans serif	✎1
194	③	Circle three, sans serif	✎L
195	④	Circle four, sans serif....................	✎V

Zapf Dingbats Character Set (4 of 4)

ASCII Numbers and Keyboard Locations (Cont.)

196	⑤	Circle five, sans serif .... ⌇F
197	⑥	Circle six, sans serif.......................... ⌇X
198	⑦	Circle seven, sans serif .... ⌇D
199	⑧	Circle eight, sans serif .... ⌇\
200	⑨	Circle nine, sans serif .... ⇧⌇\
201	⑩	Circle ten, sans serif .... ⌇;
202	❶	Circle one, reversed, sans serif ...... ⌇␣
203	❷	Circle two, reversed, sans serif .... ⌇~, ⇧A
204	❸	Circle three, reversed, sans serif .... ⌇N, ⇧A
205	❹	Circle four, reversed, sans serif .... ⌇N, ⇧0
206	❺	Circle five, reversed, sans serif ... ⇧⌇Q
207	❻	Circle six, reversed, sans serif......... ⌇Q
208	❼	Circle seven, reversed, sans serif .... ⌇-
209	❽	Circle eight, reversed, sans serif . ⇧⌇-
210	❾	Circle nine, reversed, sans serif ...... ⌇[
211	❿	Circle ten, reversed, sans serif .... ⇧⌇[
212	→	Arrow, type 1 .... ⌇]
213	→	Arrow, type 2 .... ⇧⌇]
214	↔	Arrow, type 2, left/right .... ⌇/
215	↕	Arrow, type 2, up/down .... ⇧⌇V
216	↘	Arrow, type 3, down .... ⌇U, Y
217	→	Arrow, type 3 .... ⇧⌇~
218	↗	Arrow, type 3, up .... ⇧⌇1
219	➔	Arrow, type 4 .... ⇧⌇2
220	➔	Arrow, type 5 .... ⇧⌇3
221	→	Arrow, type 6, light .... ⇧⌇4
222	→	Arrow, type 6, medium .... ⇧⌇5
223	➡	Arrow, moving 1 .... ⇧⌇6
224	➡	Arrow, moving 2 .... ⇧⌇7

225	➡	Arrow, type 6, heavy .... ⇧⌇9
226	➤	Arrowhead, insignia 1 .... ⇧⌇0
227	➤	Arrowhead, insignia 2 .... ⇧⌇W
228	➤	Arrowhead, black .... ⇧⌇E
229	➡	Arrow, type 7, down .... ⌇~, ⇧A
230	➡	Arrow, type 7, up .... ⌇N, ⇧A
231	♦	Arrow, type 6, condensed .... ⇧⌇Y
232	➡	Arrow, type 2, heavy .... ⇧⌇U
233	⇨	Arrow, raised 1 .... ⇧⌇I
234	⇨	Arrow, raised 2 .... ⇧⌇S
235	⇦	Arrow, raised 3 .... ⇧⌇D
236	⇦	Arrow, raised 4 .... ⇧⌇F
237	⇨	Arrow, raised 5 .... ⇧⌇G
238	⇨	Arrow, raised 6 .... ⇧⌇H
239	⇨	Arrow, raised ʷ/tail 1 .... ⇧⌇J
240		.... ⇧⌇K
241	⇨	Arrow, raised ʷ/tail 2 .... ⇧⌇L
242	⊃	Arrow, reversed .... ⇧⌇;
243	➼	Arrow, type 8 ʷ/tail .... ⇧⌇Z
244	➘	Arrow, type 9, down .... ⇧⌇X
245	➼	Arrow, type 9 .... ⇧⌇B
246	➷	Arrow, type 9, up .... ⇧⌇N
247	➘	Arrow, type 10, down .... ⇧⌇M
248	➼	Arrow, type 10 .... ⇧⌇,
249	➷	Arrow, type 10, up .... ⇧⌇.
250	→	Arrow, type 11 .... ⌇H
251	↠	Arrow, type 12 .... ⌇K
252	➤	Arrow, type 13, medium .... *no key*
253	➤	Arrow, type 13, heavy .... *no key*
254	⇒	Arrow, outlined .... *no key*
255		.... *no key*

Alphabetical Character List (1 of 11)

Rather than creating whole lines of text in Symbol or Zapf Dingbats, you most commonly use these fonts to augment or to ornament paragraphs of standard alphanumeric characters. Therefore, the individual characters in each font are more important than the composition of the font as a whole. In other words, if you're looking for a specific character, you probably don't care if it's available in Symbol, Dingbats, or a standard alphanumeric font; you just want *that* character.

The following list contains every character sorted in alphabetical order by character name. ASCII numbers and keyboard locations are included, along with the name of the font in which the character appears—standard (*Std*), Symbol (*Sym*), or Zapf Dingbats (*Zap*).

Throughout this chart, ⇧ represents the SHIFT key, ⌥ represents OPTION, and ␣ represents the space bar. Other keys are represented by the letter, number, or punctuation mark that appears on the key. All key combinations should be pressed simultaneously. Key combinations separated by a comma are pressed sequentially. The phrase *no key* indicates a character that is not available from the keyboard, but that is included in the font.

Keyboard Locations, ASCII Numbers, and Typefaces

Character	Glyph	Keys	ASCII	Font
A, capital	A	⇧A	065	Std
A, capital w/acute	Á	⇧⌥Y	231	Std
A, capital w/circumflex	Â	⌥~, ⇧A	229	Std
A, capital w/diaeresis	Ä	⌥U, ⇧A	128	Std
A, capital w/grave	À	⌥~, ⇧A	203	Std
A, capital w/ring	Å	⇧⌥A	129	Std
A, capital w/tilde	Ã	⌥N, ⇧A	204	Std
a, lowercase	a	A	097	Std
a, lowercase w/acute	á	⌥E, A	135	Std
a, lowercase w/circumflex	â	⌥I, A	137	Std
a, lowercase w/diaeresis	ä	⌥U, A	138	Std
a, lowercase w/grave	à	⌥~, A	136	Std
a, lowercase w/ring	å	⌥A	140	Std
a, lowercase w/tilde	ã	⌥N, A	139	Std
Acute accent	´	⌥E, ␣	171	Std
AE ligature, capital	Æ	⇧⌥'	174	Std
ae ligature, lowercase	æ	⌥'	190	Std
Aleph	ℵ	⇧⌥/	192	Sym
Alpha, capital	A	⇧A	065	Sym
Alpha, lowercase	α	A	097	Sym
Ampersand	&	⇧7	038	Std
or	&	⇧7	038	Sym
Angle	∠	⌥-	208	Sym
Angle bracket, left	⟨	⇧⌥9	225	Sym
Angle bracket, right	⟩	⇧⌥L	241	Sym
Apostrophe	'	⇧⌥]	213	Std
or	ʼ	⇧\	124	Zap
Apple icon		⇧⌥K	240	Std
or		⇧⌥K	240	Sym
Approximately equal	≈	⌥X	197	Std
or	≈	⌥9	187	Sym

Alphabetical Character List (2 of 11)

Keyboard Locations, ASCII Numbers, and Typefaces (Cont.)

Character	Symbol	Key	ASCII	Typeface
Arrow, double, bidirectional	⇔	⇧⍦2	219	Sym
Arrow, double, down	⇓	⇧⍦6	223	Sym
Arrow, double, left	⇐	⇧⍦3	220	Sym
Arrow, double, right	⇒	⇧⍦5	222	Sym
Arrow, double, up	⇑	⇧⍦4	221	Sym
Arrow, moving 1	➝	⇧⍦6	223	Zap
Arrow, moving 2	➟	⇧⍦7	224	Zap
Arrow, outlined	⇨	no key	254	Zap
Arrow, raised 1	⇨	⇧⍦I	233	Zap
Arrow, raised 2	⇨	⇧⍦S	234	Zap
Arrow, raised 3	⇨	⇧⍦D	235	Zap
Arrow, raised 4	⇨	⇧⍦F	236	Zap
Arrow, raised 5	⇨	⇧⍦G	237	Zap
Arrow, raised 6	⇨	⇧⍦H	238	Zap
Arrow, raised w/tail 1	⇨	⇧⍦J	239	Zap
Arrow, raised w/tail 2	⇨	⇧⍦L	241	Zap
Arrow, reversed	⊃	⇧⍦;	242	Zap
Arrow, type 1, bidirectional	↔	⍦E, ⎵	171	Sym
Arrow, type 1, extension, horiz.	—	⍦'	190	Sym
Arrow, type 1, extension, vertical	│	⍦Z	189	Sym
Arrow, type 1, light, down	↓	⇧⍦0	175	Sym
Arrow, type 1, light, left	←	⍦U, ⎵	172	Sym
Arrow, type 1, light, right	→	⇧⍦'	174	Sym
Arrow, type 1, light, up	↑	⍦=	173	Sym
Arrow, type 1, medium, right	➜	⍦]	212	Zap
Arrow, type 2	→	⇧⍦]	213	Zap
Arrow, type 2, heavy	➡	⇧⍦U	232	Zap
Arrow, type 2, left/right	↔	⍦/	214	Zap
Arrow, type 2, up/down	↕	⇧⍦V	215	Zap
Arrow, type 3	➞	⇧⍦~	217	Zap
Arrow, type 3, down	➘	⍦U, Y	216	Zap
Arrow, type 3, up	➚	⇧⍦1	218	Zap
Arrow, type 4	➤	⇧⍦2	219	Zap
Arrow, type 5	➥	⇧⍦3	220	Zap
Arrow, type 6, condensed	➧	⇧⍦Y	231	Zap
Arrow, type 6, heavy	➡	⇧⍦9	225	Zap
Arrow, type 6, light	→	⇧⍦4	221	Zap
Arrow, type 6, medium	→	⇧⍦5	222	Zap
Arrow, type 7, down	➥	⍦~, ⇧A	229	Zap
Arrow, type 7, up	➦	⍦N, ⇧A	230	Zap
Arrow, type 8 w/tail	➤	⇧⍦Z	243	Zap
Arrow, type 9	➢	⇧⍦B	245	Zap
Arrow, type 9, down	➘	⇧⍦X	244	Zap
Arrow, type 9, up	➚	⇧⍦N	246	Zap
Arrow, type 10	➤	⇧⍦,	248	Zap
Arrow, type 10, down	➘	⇧⍦M	247	Zap
Arrow, type 10, up	➚	⇧⍦.	249	Zap
Arrow, type 11	→	⍦H	250	Zap
Arrow, type 12	↔	⍦K	251	Zap
Arrow, type 13, heavy	➤	no key	253	Zap
Arrow, type 13, medium	➤	no key	252	Zap

Alphabetical Character List (3 of 11)

Keyboard Locations, ASCII Numbers, and Typefaces (Cont.)

Character	Glyph	Keys	ASCII	Typeface
Arrowhead, black	➤	⇧⌥E	228	Zap
Arrowhead, insignia 1	➢	⇧⌥0	226	Zap
Arrowhead, insignia 2	➣	⇧⌥W	227	Zap
Asterisk, 6-point	✱	⇧Q	081	Zap
Asterisk, 6-point, void	✲	⇧R	082	Zap
Asterisk, 8-petal	✳	I	105	Zap
Asterisk, 8-point	✴	⇧S	083	Zap
Asterisk, 16-point	✹	⇧Z	090	Zap
Asterisk, standard	*	⇧8	042	Sym
Asterisk, superscripted	*	⇧8	042	Std
At	@	⇧2	064	Std
B, capital	**B**	⇧B	066	Std
b, lowercase	**b**	B	098	Std
Backslash	\	\	092	Std
Bar, heavy	▮	Z	122	Zap
Bar, light	|	⇧\	124	Std
or	|	⇧\	124	Sym
or	|	X	120	Zap
Bar, medium	▌	Y	121	Zap
Beta, capital	ß	⌥S	167	Std
or	B	⇧B	066	Sym
Beta, lowercase	β	B	098	Sym
Box, black	■	N	110	Zap
Box, drop shadow 1	❑	O	111	Zap
Box, drop shadow 2	❒	P	112	Zap
Box, raised 1	❏	Q	113	Zap
Box, raised 2	❐	R	114	Zap
Box, rotated	◆	U	117	Zap
Box, rotated quad	❖	V	118	Zap
Brace, extension	|	⇧⌥J	239	Sym
Brace, left	{	⇧[	123	Std
or	{	⇧[	123	Sym
Brace, left, bottom	⎩	⇧⌥H	238	Sym
Brace, left, middle	⎨	⇧⌥G	237	Sym
Brace, left, top	⎧	⇧⌥F	236	Sym
Brace, right	}	⇧]	125	Std
or	}	⇧]	125	Sym
Brace, right, bottom	⎭	no key	254	Sym
Brace, right, middle	⎬	no key	253	Sym
Brace, right, top	⎫	no key	252	Sym
Bracket, left	[	[	091	Std
or	[	[	091	Sym
Bracket, left, bottom	⎣	⇧⌥D	235	Sym
Bracket, left, extension	|	⇧⌥S	234	Sym
Bracket, left, top	⎡	⇧⌥I	233	Sym
Bracket, right	]	]	093	Std
or	]	]	093	Sym
Bracket, right, bottom	⎦	⌥K	251	Sym
Bracket, right, extension	|	⌥H	250	Sym
Bracket, right, top	⎤	⇧⌥.	249	Sym
Breve diacritic	˘	⇧⌥.	249	Std
Bullet	•	⌥8	165	Std
Bullet	•	⌥W	183	Sym
C, capital	**C**	⇧C	067	Std
C, capital w/cedilla	Ç	⇧⌥C	130	Std
c, lowercase	c	C	099	Std
c, lowercase w/cedilla	ç	⌥C	141	Std
Caret	^	⌥I, ▬	094	Std
Caron diacritic	ˇ	no key	255	Std
Carriage return	↵	⌥0	191	Sym
Cedilla diacritic	¸	no key	252	Std
Cent	¢	⌥4	162	Std
Center period	·	⇧⌥9	225	Std

Alphabetical Character List (4 of 11)

Keyboard Locations, ASCII Numbers, and Typefaces (Cont.)

Check mark, light ....✔	3	051	Zap
Check mark, medium .....✔	4	052	Zap
Chi, capital X	⇧C	067	Sym
Chi, lowercase ....χ	C	099	Sym
Circle eight, reversed, sans serif ....❽	⇧✎-	209	Zap
Circle eight, reversed, serif ....❽	✎Z	189	Zap
Circle eight, sans serif ....⑧	✎\	199	Zap
Circle eight, serif ....⑧	✎.	179	Zap
Circle five, reversed, sans serif ....❺	⇧✎Q	206	Zap
Circle five, reversed, serif ....❺	✎B	186	Zap
Circle five, sans serif ......⑤	✎F	196	Zap
Circle five, serif ....⑤	✎5	176	Zap
Circle four, reversed, sans serif ....❹	✎N, ⇧0	205	Zap
Circle four, reversed, serif ....❹	✎P	185	Zap
Circle four, sans serif .....④	✎V	195	Zap
Circle four, serif ....④	⇧✎0	175	Zap
Circle nine, reversed, sans serif ....❾	✎[	210	Zap
Circle nine, reversed, serif ....❾	✎'	190	Zap
Circle nine, sans serif .....⑨	⇧✎\	200	Zap
Circle nine, serif ....⑨	✎Y	180	Zap
Circle one, reversed, sans serif ....❶	✎▭	202	Zap
Circle one, reversed, serif ....❶	✎D	182	Zap
Circle one, sans serif ......①	⇧✎/	192	Zap
Circle one, serif ....①	✎U, ▭	172	Zap
Circle seven, reversed, sans serif ....❼	✎-	208	Zap
Circle seven, reversed, serif ....❼	✎0	188	Zap
Circle seven, sans serif ...⑦	✎D	198	Zap
Circle seven, serif ....⑦	✎,	178	Zap
Circle six, reversed, sans serif ....❻	✎Q	207	Zap
Circle six, reversed, serif ....❻	✎9	187	Zap
Circle six, sans serif ....⑥	✎X	197	Zap
Circle six, serif ....⑥	⇧✎=	177	Zap
Circle ten, reversed, sans serif ....❿	⇧✎[	211	Zap
Circle ten, reversed, serif ....❿	✎0	191	Zap
Circle ten, sans serif ....⑩	✎;	201	Zap
Circle ten, serif ....⑩	✎M	181	Zap
Circle three, reversed, sans serif ....❸	✎N, ⇧A	204	Zap
Circle three, reversed, serif ....❸	⇧✎P	184	Zap
Circle three, sans serif ....③	✎L	194	Zap
Circle three, serif ....③	⇧✎'	174	Zap
Circle two, reversed, sans serif ....❷	✎~, ⇧A	203	Zap
Circle two, reversed, serif ....❷	✎W	183	Zap
Circle two, sans serif ......②	✎1	193	Zap
Circle two, serif ....②	✎=	173	Zap
Circle, black ....●	L	108	Zap
Circle, white ....○	M	109	Zap
Circumflex diacritic ....ˆ	⇧✎N	246	Std

Alphabetical Character List (5 of 11)

Keyboard Locations, ASCII Numbers, and Typefaces (Cont.)

Character	Symbol	Keys	ASCII	Typeface
Club	♣	⌥S	167	Sym
or	♣	⌥R	168	Zap
Cluster, light	✳	G	103	Zap
Cluster, medium	✳	H	104	Zap
Colon	:	⇧;	058	Std
or	:	⇧;	058	Sym
Comma	,	,	044	Std
or	,	,	044	Sym
Congruent	≅	⇧2	064	Sym
Copyright	©	⌥G	169	Std
Copyright, sans serif	©	⇧⌥W	227	Sym
Copyright, serif	©	⇧⌥[	211	Sym
Cross Botonée	✣	⇧E	069	Zap
Cross Formée	✠	⇧2	064	Zap
Cross, black	✚	⇧;	058	Zap
Cross, filled	✚	9	057	Zap
Cross, void, heavy	✛	⇧,	060	Zap
Cross, void, light	✛	;	059	Zap
Crux	†	=	061	Zap
Crux, filled	†	⇧/	063	Zap
Crux, raised	⚜	⇧.	062	Zap
Currency	¤	⇧⌥2	219	Std
D, capital	D	⇧D	068	Std
d, lowercase	d	D	100	Std
Dagger, double	‡	⇧⌥7	224	Std
Dagger, single	†	⌥T	160	Std
Degree	°	⇧⌥8	161	Std
or	°	⌥5	176	Sym
Delta, capital	Δ	⌥D	198	Std
or	Δ	⇧D	068	Sym
Delta, lowercase	δ	D	100	Sym
Derivative	f	⌥7	166	Sym
Diaeresis diacritic	¨	⌥U, ␣	172	Std
Diamond	♦	⌥R	168	Sym
or	♦	⌥G	169	Zap
Diesis	‡	⇧⌥7	224	Std
Ditto	"	⇧'	034	Std
Divide	÷	⌥/	214	Std
or	÷	⇧⌥P	184	Sym
Dollar	$	⇧4	036	Std
Dot accent	˙	⌥H	250	Std
E, capital	E	⇧E	069	Std
E, capital w/acute	É	⌥E, ⇧E	131	Std
E, capital w/circumflex	Ê	⌥N, ⇧A	230	Std
E, capital w/diaeresis	Ë	⇧⌥U	232	Std
E, capital w/grave	È	⇧⌥I	233	Std
e, lowercase	e	E	101	Std
e, lowercase w/acute	é	⌥E, E	142	Std
e, lowercase w/circumflex	ê	⌥I, E	144	Std
e, lowercase w/diaeresis	ë	⌥U, E	145	Std
e, lowercase w/grave	è	⌥~, E	143	Std
Eight	8	8	056	Std
or	8	8	056	Sym
Element	∈	⇧⌥Q	206	Sym
Ellipsis	…	⌥;	201	Std
or	…	⌥0	188	Sym
Em dash	—	⇧⌥-	209	Std
Empty set	∅	⌥D	198	Sym
En dash	–	⌥-	208	Std
Epsilon, capital	E	⇧E	069	Sym
Epsilon, lowercase	ε	E	101	Sym
Equal	=	=	061	Std
or	=	=	061	Sym

Alphabetical Character List (6 of 11)

Keyboard Locations, ASCII Numbers, and Typefaces (Cont.)

Character	Symbol	Keys	ASCII	Typeface
Eta, capital	H	⇧H	072	Sym
Eta, lowercase	η	H	104	Sym
Exclamation heart	❣	⌥3	163	Zap
Exclamation point	!	⇧1	033	Std
or	!	⇧1	033	Sym
or	❣	⌥4	162	Zap
Exclamation point, inverted	¡	⌥1	193	Std
Existential	∃	⇧4	036	Sym
F, capital	F	⇧F	070	Std
f, lowercase	f	F	102	Std
Feet	′	⌥4	162	Sym
fi ligature, lowercase	fi	⇧⌥5	222	Std
Five	5	5	053	Std
or	5	5	053	Sym
fl ligature, lowercase	fl	⇧⌥6	223	Std
Florin	ƒ	⌥F	196	Std
Flower, 5-petal, black	✿	⇧-	095	Zap
Flower, 5-petal, white	❀	~	096	Zap
Flower, 8-petal	❁	A	097	Zap
Four	4	4	052	Std
or	4	4	052	Sym
Fraction slash	⁄	⇧⌥1	218	Std
or	⁄	⌥6	164	Sym
G, capital	G	⇧G	071	Std
g, lowercase	g	G	103	Std
Gamma, capital	Γ	⇧G	071	Sym
Gamma, lowercase	γ	G	103	Sym
German double S	ß	⌥S	167	Std
Gradient	∇	⇧⌥-	209	Sym
Grave accent	`	~	096	Std

Character	Symbol	Keys	ASCII	Typeface
Greater than	>	⇧.	062	Std
or	>	⇧.	062	Sym
Greater than or equal	≥	⌥.	179	Std
or	≥	⌥.	179	Sym
Guillemot, double, left	«	⌥\	199	Std
Guillemot, double, right	»	⇧⌥\	200	Std
Guillemot, single, left	‹	⇧⌥3	220	Std
Guillemot, single, right	›	⇧⌥4	221	Std
H, capital	H	⇧H	072	Std
h, lowercase	h	H	104	Std
Heart	♥	⌥G	169	Sym
or	♥	⌥2	170	Zap
Heart, fat	♥	⌥6	164	Zap
Heart, rotated	❥	⌥8	165	Zap
Hungarian umlaut diacritic	˝	no key	253	Std
Hyphen	-	-	045	Std
I, capital	I	⇧I	073	Std
I, capital w/ acute	Í	⇧⌥S	234	Std
I, capital w/ circumflex	Î	⇧⌥D	235	Std
I, capital w/ dieresis	Ï	⇧⌥F	236	Std
I, capital w/ grave	Ì	⇧⌥G	237	Std
I fraktur, capital	ℑ	⌥1	193	Sym
i, lowercase	i	I	105	Std
i, lowercase w/ acute	í	⌥E, I	146	Std
i, lowercase w/ circumflex	î	⌥I, I	148	Std
i, lowercase w/ dieresis	ï	⌥U, I	149	Std
i, lowercase w/ grave	ì	⌥~, I	147	Std
i, lowercase, dotless	ı	⇧⌥B	245	Std
Identical	≡	⌥B	186	Sym
Inches	″	⌥,	178	Sym

Alphabetical Character List (7 of 11)

Keyboard Locations, ASCII Numbers, and Typefaces (Cont.)

Character	Symbol	Key	ASCII	Typeface
Index, black	☛	⇧8	042	Zap
Index, white	☞	⇧=	043	Zap
Infinity	∞	⬛5	176	Std
or	∞	⬛8	165	Sym
Integral	∫	⬛B	186	Std
or	∫	⇧⬛;	242	Sym
Integral, bottom	⌡	⇧⬛B	245	Sym
Integral, extension	|	⇧⬛X	244	Sym
Integral, top	⌠	⇧⬛Z	243	Sym
Intersection	∩	⬛\	199	Sym
Iota, capital	I	⇧I	073	Sym
Iota, lowercase	ι	I	105	Sym
J, capital	J	⇧J	074	Std
j, lowercase	j	J	106	Std
Jet	✈	⇧9	040	Zap
K, capital	K	⇧K	075	Std
k, lowercase	k	K	107	Std
Kappa, capital	K	⇧K	075	Sym
Kappa, lowercase	κ	K	107	Sym
L, capital	L	⇧L	076	Std
l, lowercase	l	L	108	Std
Lambda, capital	Λ	⇧L	076	Sym
Lambda, lowercase	λ	L	108	Sym
Leaf	☙	⬛7	166	Zap
Leaf, rotated	☘	⬛S	167	Zap
Less than	<	⇧,	060	Std
or	<	⇧,	060	Sym
Less than or equal	≤	⬛,	178	Std
or	≤	⬛3	163	Sym
Letter	✉	⇧0	041	Zap
Line break	↵	⬛0	191	Sym

Character	Symbol	Key	ASCII	Typeface
Logical and	∧	⇧⬛~	217	Sym
Logical not	¬	⬛L	194	Std
or	¬	⬛U, Y	216	Sym
Logical or	∨	⇧⬛1	218	Sym
Lozenge	◊	⇧⬛V	215	Std
or	◊	⇧⬛7	224	Sym
M, capital	**M**	⇧M	077	Std
m, lowercase	**m**	M	109	Std
Macron diacritic	¯	⇧⬛,	248	Std
Minus	−	⬛-	208	Std
or	−	-	045	Sym
Minutes	′	⬛4	162	Sym
Mu, capital	M	⇧M	077	Sym
Mu, lowercase	μ	⬛M	181	Std
or	μ	M	109	Sym
Multiply, asterisk	*	⇧8	042	Sym
Multiply, circle	⊗	⬛F	196	Sym
Multiply, dot	·	⇧⬛9	225	Std
or	·	⇧⬛V	215	Sym
Multiply, X	×	⬛Y	180	Sym
N, capital	**N**	⇧N	078	Std
N, capital w/ tilde	Ñ	⬛N, ⇧N	132	Std
n, lowercase	**n**	N	110	Std
n, lowercase w/ tilde	ñ	⬛N, N	150	Std
Nine	**9**	9	057	Std
Nine	9	9	057	Sym
Not element	∉	⬛Q	207	Sym
Not equal	≠	⬛=	173	Std
or	≠		185	Sym
Not subset	⊄	⬛~, ⇧A	203	Sym
Nu, capital	N	⇧N	078	Sym
Nu, lowercase	ν	N	110	Sym

Alphabetical Character List (8 of 11)

Keyboard Locations, ASCII Numbers, and Typefaces (Cont.)

Character		Key	ASCII	Face
Number	#	⇧3	035	Std
or	#	⇧3	035	Sym
O slash, capital	Ø	⇧⌥0	175	Std
o slash, lowercase	ø	⌥0	191	Std
O, capital	O	⇧0	079	Std
O, capital w/acute	Ó	⇧⌥H	238	Std
O, capital w/circumflex	Ô	⇧⌥J	239	Std
O, capital w/dieresis	Ö	⌥U, ⇧0	133	Std
O, capital w/grave	Ò	⇧⌥L	241	Std
O, capital w/tilde	Õ	⌥N, ⇧0	205	Std
o, lowercase	o	0	111	Std
o, lowercase w/acute	ó	⌥E, 0	151	Std
o, lowercase w/circumflex	ô	⌥I, 0	153	Std
o, lowercase w/dieresis	ö	⌥U, 0	154	Std
o, lowercase w/grave	ò	⌥~, 0	152	Std
o, lowercase w/tilde	õ	⌥N, 0	155	Std
Obelisk	†	⌥T	160	Std
OE ligature, capital	Œ	⇧⌥Q	206	Std
oe ligature, lowercase	œ	⌥Q	207	Std
Ogonek diacritic	˛	no key	254	Std
Omega, capital	Ω	⌥Z	189	Std
or	Ω	⇧W	087	Sym
Omega, lowercase	ω	W	119	Sym
Omega, lowercase cursive	ϖ	V	118	Sym
Omicron, capital	O	⇧0	079	Sym
Omicron, lowercase	o	0	111	Sym
One	1	1	049	Std
or	1	1	049	Sym
Ord, feminine	ª	⌥9	187	Std
Ord, masculine	º	⌥0	188	Std
P, capital	P	⇧P	080	Std
p, lowercase	p	P	112	Std
Paragraph break	¶	⌥7	166	Std
or	¶	⇧⌥8	161	Zap
Parenthesis, close	)	⇧0	041	Std
or	)	⇧0	041	Sym
Parenthesis, close, bottom	)	⇧⌥,	248	Sym
Parenthesis, close, extension	|	⇧⌥M	247	Sym
Parenthesis, close, top	)	⇧⌥N	246	Sym
Parenthesis, open	(	⇧9	040	Std
or	(	⇧9	040	Sym
Parenthesis, open, bottom	(	⇧⌥U	232	Sym
Parenthesis, open, extension	|	⇧⌥Y	231	Sym
Parenthesis, open, top	(	⌥N, ⇧A	230	Sym
Partial differential	∂	⌥D	182	Std
or	∂	⌥D	182	Sym
Pen nib, black	✒	2	050	Zap
Pen nib, white	✑	1	049	Zap
Pencil, down	✎	.	046	Zap
Pencil, flat	✐	/	047	Zap
Pencil, up	✏	0	048	Zap
Percent	%	⇧5	037	Std
or	%	⇧5	037	Sym
Period	.	.	046	Std
or	.	.	046	Sym
Perpendicular	⊥	⌥I, ⎵	094	Sym
Per thousand	‰	⇧⌥E	228	Std
Petal cross, dot	✜	⇧C	067	Zap
Petal cross, heavy	✛	⇧D	068	Zap
Petal cross, light	✝	⇧B	066	Zap

Alphabetical Character List (9 of 11)

Keyboard Locations, ASCII Numbers, and Typefaces (Cont.)

Character	Symbol	Key	ASCII	Typeface
Phi, capital	Φ	⇧F	070	Sym
Phi, lowercase	φ	F	102	Sym
Phi, lowercase cursive	φ	J	106	Sym
Pi, capital	Π	⇧P	080	Sym
Pi, lowercase	π	⌥P	185	Std
or	π	P	112	Sym
Plus	+	⇧=	043	Std
or	+	⇧=	043	Sym
Plus or minus	±	⇧⌥=	177	Std
or	±	⇧⌥=	177	Sym
Plus, circle	⊕	⌥X	197	Sym
Pound sterling	£	⌥3	163	Std
Product	∏	⇧⌥P	184	Std
or	∏	⇧⌥]	213	Sym
Proper subset	⊂	⌥N,⇧A	204	Sym
Proper superset	⊃	⌥;	201	Sym
Proportional	∝	⌥M	181	Sym
Psi, capital	Ψ	⇧Y	089	Sym
Psi, lowercase	ψ	Y	121	Sym
Q, capital	Q	⇧Q	081	Std
q, lowercase	q	Q	113	Std
Question mark	?	⇧/	063	Std
or	?	⇧/	063	Sym
Question mark, inverted	¿	⇧⌥/	192	Std
Quotation mark, baseline	„	⇧⌥W	227	Std
Quotation mark, close	"	⇧⌥[	211	Std
or	"	⇧~	126	Zap
Quotation mark, open	"	⌥[	210	Std
or	"	⇧]	125	Zap
Quotation mark, straight	"	⇧'	034	Std
Quote, single, baseline	‚	⇧⌥0	226	Std
Quote, single, close	'	⇧⌥]	213	Std
or	'	⇧\	124	Zap
Quote, single, open	'	⌥]	212	Std
or	'	⇧[	123	Zap
Quote, single, straight	'	'	039	Std
R, capital	R	⇧R	082	Std
R fraktur, capital	ℜ	⌥L	194	Sym
r, lowercase	r	R	114	Std
Radical extension	—	~	096	Sym
Radical initiate	√	⌥V	195	Std
or	√	⌥/	214	Sym
Receiver	☏	⇧7	038	Zap
Reel tape	☺	'	039	Zap
Reflexive subset	⊆	⌥N,⇧0	205	Sym
Reflexive superset	⊇	⌥_	202	Sym
Registered trademark	®	⌥R	168	Std
Registered trademark, sans serif	®	⇧⌥0	226	Sym
Registered trademark, serif	®	⌥[	210	Sym
Rho, capital	P	⇧R	082	Sym
Rho, lowercase	ρ	R	114	Sym
Ring diacritic	°	⌥K	251	Std
S, capital	S	⇧S	083	Std
s, lowercase	s	S	115	Std
Scissors	✂	⇧'	034	Zap
Scissors, cutting down	✀	⇧1	033	Zap
Scissors, cutting up	✁	⇧3	035	Zap
Scissors, white	✄	⇧4	036	Zap
Seconds	"	⌥,	178	Sym
Section	§	⌥6	164	Std

Alphabetical Character List (10 of 11)

Keyboard Locations, ASCII Numbers, and Typefaces (Cont.)

Semicircle	▶			Star, 5-point, insignia	✶	⇧0	079 Zap
Semicolon	;	;	059 Std	Star, 5-point, raised	✰	⇧P	080 Zap
or	;	;	059 Sym	Star, 5-point, void	✩	⇧K	075 Zap
Seven	**7**	7	055 Std	Star, 5-point, white	☆	⇧I	073 Zap
or	7	7	055 Sym	Star, 6-petal, black	✱	]	093 Zap
Sigma, capital	Σ	⇧S	083 Sym	Star, 6-petal, dot	✳	[	091 Zap
Sigma, lowercase	σ	S	115 Sym	Star, 6-petal, insignia	✺	C	099 Zap
Sigma, lowercase cursive	ς	⇧V	086 Sym	Star, 6-petal, oscillate	✹	✎I, ▬	094 Zap
Similar	~	⇧~	126 Std	Star, 6-petal, void	✶	\	092 Zap
or	~	⇧~	126 Sym	Star, 6-point	✶	⇧V	086 Zap
Six	**6**	6	054 Std	Star, 8-petal, black	✽	K	107 Zap
or	6	6	054 Sym	Star, 8-petal, dot	✻	J	106 Zap
Slash	/	/	047 Std	Star, 8-point, heavy	✴	⇧X	088 Zap
or	/	/	047 Sym	Star, 8-point, insignia	✳	⇧U	085 Zap
Snowflake 1	❋	D	100 Zap	Star, 8-point, light	✳	⇧T	084 Zap
Snowflake 2	❄	E	101 Zap	Star, 8-point, medium	✴	⇧W	087 Zap
Snowflake 3	❆	F	102 Zap	Star, 12-point	✹	⇧Y	089 Zap
Space, nonbreaking	✎▬	202 Std		Such that	∋	'	039 Sym
Space, standard		▬	032 Std	Summation	Σ	✎W	183 Std
or		▬	032 Sym	or	Σ	✎~, ⇧A	229 Sym
or		▬	032 Zap	Sun	☼	B	098 Zap
Spade	♠	✎2	170 Sym	T, capital	**T**	⇧T	084 Std
or	♠	✎E, ▬	171 Zap	t, lowercase	**t**	T	116 Std
Star cross, black	✦	⇧F	070 Zap	Tau, capital	T	⇧T	084 Sym
Star cross, white	✧	⇧G	071 Zap	Tau, lowercase	τ	T	116 Sym
Star of David	✡	⇧A	065 Zap	Telephone	☎	⇧5	037 Zap
Star, 5-point, army	✪	⇧J	074 Zap	Therefore	∴	\	092 Sym
Star, 5-point, black	★	⇧H	072 Zap	Theta, capital	Θ	⇧Q	081 Sym
Star, 5-point, dot	✴	⇧L	076 Zap	Theta, lowercase	θ	Q	113 Sym
Star, 5-point, filled, heavy	✭	⇧N	078 Zap	Theta, lowercase cursive	ϑ	⇧J	074 Sym
Star, 5-point, filled, light	★	⇧M	077 Zap	Three	**3**	3	051 Std
				or	3	3	051 Sym

Alphabetical Character List (11 of 11)

Keyboard Locations, ASCII Numbers, and Typefaces (Cont.)

Character		Keys	ASCII	Typeface
Tilde diacritic	˜	⇧⌥M	247	Std
Tilde mark	~	⇧~	126	Std
Trademark	™	⌥2	170	Std
Trademark, sans serif	™	⇧⌥E	228	Sym
Trademark, serif	™	⌥]	212	Sym
Triangle, down	▼	T	116	Zap
Triangle, up	▲	S	115	Zap
Two	2	2	050	Std
or	2	2	050	Sym
U, capital	U	⇧U	085	Std
U, capital w/ acute	Ú	⇧⌥;	242	Std
U, capital w/ circumflex	Û	⇧⌥Z	243	Std
U, capital w/ dieresis	Ü	⌥U, ⇧U	134	Std
U, capital w/ grave	Ù	⇧⌥X	244	Std
u, lowercase	u	U	117	Std
u, lowercase w/ acute	ú	⌥E, U	156	Std
u, lowercase w/ circumflex	û	⌥I, U	158	Std
u, lowercase w/ dieresis	ü	⌥U, U	159	Std
u, lowercase w/ grave	ù	⌥~, U	157	Std
Umlaut diacritic	¨	⌥U, ␣	172	Std
Underscore	_	⇧-	095	Std
or	_	⇧-	095	Sym
Union	∪	⇧⌥\	200	Sym
Universal	∀	⇧'	034	Sym
Upsilon, capital	Υ	⇧U	085	Sym
Upsilon, capital cursive	ϒ	⇧⌥8	161	Sym
Upsilon, lowercase	υ	U	117	Sym
V, capital	V	⇧V	086	Std
v, lowercase	v	V	118	Std
Victory	✌	,	044	Zap
Virgule	/	/	047	Std
or	/	/	047	Sym
W, capital	W	⇧W	087	Std
w, lowercase	w	W	119	Std
Weierstrass	℘	⌥V	195	Sym
Writer's hand	✍	-	045	Zap
X mark, heavy	✖	6	054	Zap
X mark, light	✕	5	053	Zap
X mark, slanted, light	✗	7	055	Zap
X mark, slanted, medium	✘	8	056	Zap
X, capital	X	⇧X	088	Std
x, lowercase	x	X	120	Std
Xi, capital	Ξ	⇧X	088	Sym
Xi, lowercase	ξ	X	120	Sym
Y, capital	Y	⇧Y	089	Std
Y, capital w/ dieresis	Ÿ	⇧⌥~	217	Std
y, lowercase	y	Y	121	Std
y, lowercase w/ dieresis	ÿ	⌥U, Y	216	Std
Yen	¥	⌥Y	180	Std
Z, capital	Z	⇧Z	090	Std
z, lowercase	z	Z	122	Std
Zero	0	0	048	Std
or	0	0	048	Sym
Zeta, capital	Z	⇧Z	090	Sym
Zeta, lowercase	ζ	Z	122	Sym

Printer Fonts

To print a font at full resolution to a PostScript-equipped laser printer, you need both a screen font to call the typeface and a printer font to describe it to the printer. A printer font is a mathematical definition of each character in a typeface; it may be scaled to any type size without diminishing its resolution. A separate printer font is usually available for each type style in a font family. For example, Times-Roman, Times-Italic, Times-Bold, and Times-BoldItalic are the printer fonts that make up the Times family. If stylized printer fonts are not available, then stylized type cannot be printed correctly. The printer cannot create a bold or italic character with only the plain printer font. Some font families include only one or two type styles. Symbol, for example, includes only one style. Even if you make a Symbol character appear italic or bold on your screen using software commands, it will be printed plain.

The printer font must be available to the PostScript printer when it is being used. The font can be made available in one of four ways:

- **Built-in ROM**. Printer fonts can be built-in ROM chips in the printer. Most PostScript printers, including Apple's LaserWriters, have built in printer fonts for the complete Times, Helvetica, Courier, Symbol, Avant Garde, Bookman, Palatino, New Century Schoolbook, Zapf Chancery, Zapf Dingbat, and Narrow Helvetica (or Condensed Helvetica). Printer fonts on the ROM chips are accessed extremely quickly.

- **Printer hard disk**. A PostScript laser printer with a hard disk—such as the Linotronic imagesetters or the Apple LaserWriter NTX—can hold printer fonts on its hard disk. Fonts are loaded onto the hard disk using a special downloading utility, and they remain there until removed, even if the printer is turned off. Printer fonts are accessed from the hard disk almost as quickly as built-in fonts, and much faster than fonts that download automatically.

- **Manually downloaded**. Using a utility such as the Adobe Font Downloader or LaserStatus, you can manually download printer fonts to the RAM in a PostScript printer. When downloaded manually, fonts remain available in the printer's RAM until the printer is rebooted. Once in RAM, fonts are accessed as quickly as built-in fonts, although the downloading process itself is a bit time-consuming.

- **Automatically downloaded**. Fonts can be automatically downloaded into the printer's RAM from the hard disk of the computer that is printing a file, as they are required. Normally, the Mac will automatically download fonts only from the System folder, but several utilities, including the shareware desk accessory Set Paths, allow you to keep printer fonts anywhere on your hard drive, from which they will be downloaded automatically when needed. When fonts are downloaded automatically, they are removed from the printer's RAM as soon as they have been used, and therefore must be redownloaded each time they are used. In most software this downloading works on a per-page basis, but some software, like PageMaker, downloads fonts on a per-text-block basis. Allowing fonts to be downloaded automatically is the slowest method, requiring between 10 and 20 seconds for each font download.

Font Substitution

Bit-mapped fonts, designed primarily for on-screen use and dot-matrix printers, have no printer-font equivalents. When you print these fonts to a laser printer they will appear very jagged, much as they do on your screen. The exception to this rule are New York, Monaco, and Geneva, which you can print on a PostScript printer by using **font substitution**. When the "Font substitution" option in your software's LASERWRITER PAGE SETUP dialog box is checked, your software substitutes a printer-font definition for text created in Geneva, Monaco, or New York. If you try to print a line of text in Geneva, the result will be Helvetica. Likewise, Monaco is replaced with Courier and New York is replaced with Times. There is no substitute for Chicago and Venice, so they appear bit-mapped when printed no matter what.

Unfortunately, Helvetica printed using the Geneva screen font is no substitute for the real thing. The Geneva screen-font definition contains different letter-spacing and word-spacing information than its Helvetica equivalent. Therefore, Helvetica text printed using the Geneva screen font tends to have weird gaps between words, and to generally look very unprofessional. We recommend avoiding Geneva, Monaco, and New York altogether—unless you *want* to create bit-mapped text, in which case you must choose the PAGE SETUP command from the FILE menu and deselect the "Font substitution" option.

The Font/DA Mover

Apple's Font/DA Mover can add and delete fonts from any suitcase or System file, and allows you to create new font suitcases. It is always important to use the most current version of this utility; version 3.8 is the version included along with System Software 6.0. The version number of the Font/DA Mover appears in the Font/DA Mover menu bar.

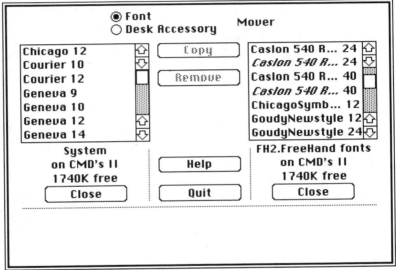

The System file and a font suitcase are open in this Font/DA Mover dialog box.

Font/DA Mover Instructions

The Font/DA Mover's window is divided into three sections. The right and left sections are identical, each providing a scrolling file list that displays the contents of open System files and suitcases, and an OPEN/CLOSE button used to open and close System files and suitcases. The middle section provides a COPY button, which transfers fonts from one suitcase or System file to another; a REMOVE button, which deletes selected fonts from their current location; a HELP button, which displays help screens; and a QUIT button, which closes the Font/DA Mover, returning you to the Finder.

- **To add a desk accessory to your current System file**. Open the Font/ DA Mover by clicking on the Font/DA Mover icon. This will launch the Font/DA Mover and open your current System file in the file listing on the left. As long as you do not hold down the OPTION key while the Font/DA Mover is launching, the "Font" option will be selected automatically.

  Click the OPEN button below the right file listing and use the Standard File dialog to open the suitcase file containing the font you wish to add. Each of the desk accessories in this suitcase will now appear in the right-hand file listing. Select the font you wish to install; the COPY button now reads <<COPY indicating that the selected file will be copied from the right window into the left. Click this button and the font is copied. The name of the font will now appear in the left window; it has been installed in your System file.

  To add additional desk accessories, repeat this installation process. Click the CLOSE button under the right scrolling list and it will again become an OPEN button. When finished, click the QUIT button to exit the Font/DA Mover.

- **To delete a font from your current System file**. Open the Font/DA Mover by clicking on its icon. This will launch the Font/DA Mover application and open your current System file in the file listing on the left. As long as you do not hold down the OPTION key while the Font/DA Mover is launching, the "Font" option will be selected automatically. Select the font you wish to delete from the font list and click the REMOVE button. When finished, click the QUIT button to exit the Font/DA Mover.

- **To move a font from a System file into a suitcase**. Open the Font/DA Mover by clicking on its icon. As long as you do not hold down the OPTION key while the Font/DA Mover is launching, the "Font" option will be selected automatically.

  If you wish to move the font into an existing suitcase, click the OPEN button below the right file listing and use the Standard File dialog to open the correct suitcase file. If you wish to move the font to a new suitcase, click the OPEN button below the right file listing, click the NEW button, and name and save your new font suitcase. Then select the font you wish to copy from the System file in the right-hand file listing; the COPY button now reads COPY>> indicating that the selected file will be copied from the left window into the right. Click this CoPY button and the font will be copied. Its name appears in the right-hand window when it has been copied successfully.

To move additional fonts, repeat this process. Click the CLOSE button under the right scrolling list and it will again become an OPEN button. When finished, click the QUIT button to exit the Font/DA Mover.

- **To move a font from one suitcase to another**. Open the Font/DA Mover by clicking on its icon. This will launch the Font/DA Mover application and open your current System file in the file listing on the left. As long as you do not hold down the OPTION key while the Font/DA Mover is launching, the "Font" option will be selected automatically.

Click the OPEN button below the right file listing and use the Standard File dialog to open the suitcase file containing the font you wish to move. Each of the desk accessories in this suitcase will now appear in the right-hand file listing. If you wish to move the font into an existing suitcase, click the CLOSE button below the left-hand listing, and then click the OPEN button below the left-hand listing. Use the Standard File dialog to open the correct suitcase file. If you wish to move the System file font to a new suitcase, click the CLOSE button below the left-hand listing, click the OPEN button below the left-hand listing, click the NEW button, and then name and save your new font suitcase.

Select the font you wish to copy from the right-hand file listing; the CoPY button now reads <<COPY indicating that the selected file will be copied from the suitcase displayed in the right-hand window into the suitcase displayed in the left-hand window. Click this CoPY button and the font will be copied. Its name appears in the right-hand window, indicating that it has been successfully copied. If you wish to delete this font from the source suitcase, select its name in the right scrolling list and click the REMOVE button.

To move additional desk accessories, repeat this process. When finished, click the QUIT button to exit the Font/DA Mover.

Font/DA Mover Tips

◇   **Launch the Font/DA Mover by double-clicking any DA or font suitcase from the Finder**. This will launch the Font/DA Mover and open the suitcase. The active System file will not be opened automatically.

◇   **Hold down the ⇧ key to select multiple fonts or DA's**. Pressing down the SHIFT key while selecting fonts or fonts in a scrolling window allows you to select any number of items to be copied or deleted together. You may drag upward or downward to select a series of items, or shift-click to select nonadjacent items.

◇   **Add only the font sizes you need to your System file or to a suitcase that will be used with Font/DA Juggler, MasterJuggler, or Suitcase**. The more type sizes you copy to your System folder, the larger your system will become. This is obviously a problem if you work off floppy disks, but it may even be a consideration if you own a hard drive. A very large System file cuts down on the amount of room remaining on the rest of your drive and can make your System less stable.

Luckily, you only have to copy one screen-font size for any typeface to your System to make the typeface available to your applications. However, fonts will only look their best on screen in the sizes that are installed, so you should install the sizes you use commonly, if you have room for them. If you do need to limit the size of your System file, we recommend that you only copy the smaller screen-font sizes, since larger sizes take up much more space. Also, you will need the smaller screen-font sizes to make your small text legible.

◆   **Hold down the ⌥ key while clicking the CLOSE button to eject the disk as the suitcase is closed**. If you are not using MultiFinder, this will eject and dismount the disk. In MultiFinder, the disk will be ejected but not dismounted. (A dimmed icon for the disk will remain on the Finder desktop.)

◆   **Hold down the ⌥ key while clicking the QUIT button to eject both disks before exiting the Font/DA Mover**. This will only work, however, if a Suitcase file on each disk is selected.

Enlarged from 10-point
Enlarged from 12-point
Enlarged from 14-point
Enlarged from 18-point
Enlarged from 24-point

Reduced from 24-point

Reduced from 18-point

Reduced from 14-point

Reduced from 12-point

Reduced from 10-point

When using a type size that is not loaded into your System file, your software creates the type by scaling the nearest available screen font size. In this example, only 14-point and 18-point sizes are available. You can see that the 15-point size is scaled up from the 14-point screen font, while the 16- and 17-point sizes are scaled down from the 24-point screen font.

◆ **The Font/DA Mover will become obsolete under System Software 7.0**. Reportedly, when using System Software 7.0 you will install fonts and DA's by simply dragging them into the System folder. The Font/DA Mover application will no longer be used.

Font Utilities

Suitcase II, MasterJuggler, Font/DA Juggler
These utilities enable you to attach screen fonts to your System that are not actually loaded in your System file. In other words, rather than copying a font to your System using the Font/DA Mover, you may open the font suitcase with Suitcase or MasterJuggler and make it available to any application.

We use these utilities because it is more convenient to attach and detach screen fonts using these utilities than to load and unload them using the Font/DA Mover. Their use also cuts down on wear and tear to your System file, and allows you to open fonts from floppy disks. Both utilities will remember which fonts are open, even if you reboot your computer, so it's important to close any fonts open from a floppy disk before shutting your computer down or even ejecting the disk.

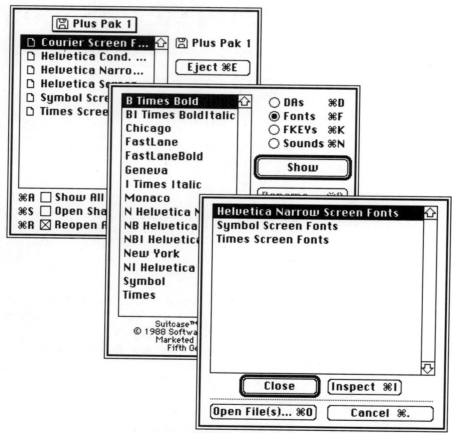

In Suitcase II, these three windows are used to attach or release font suitcases.

Incidentally, applications only look for open fonts when they are launched. If you open a font with Suitcase or MasterJuggler while running an application, your software will not display your new font choices. If you close a font, your software will continue to display the font in a menu; this can be dangerous, since choosing a closed font generally produces a System error. To display the correct font choices, you must relaunch the current application or transfer to a different one.

Generally, we prefer MasterJuggler over Suitcase II because of its cleaner interface and many of its non-font-related features. Opening a font with Suitcase involves clicking a SUITCASES button to display a second dialog box in which fonts and DA's are opened and closed. To escape, you have to click a CANCEL button (though you aren't really canceling your settings) and then click QUIT. In MasterJuggler, the interface makes more sense. All fonts or DA's are available from one dialog.

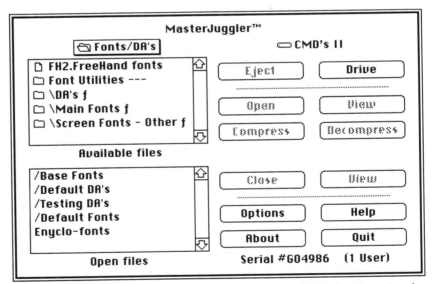

This dialog box is used to attach or release fonts and DA's in MasterJuggler.

Also, unlike Suitcase II, MasterJuggler 1.5 (or higher) helps to resolve FOND numbering conflicts, as well as more subtle conflicts between NFNT ID numbers assigned to individual screen-font sizes. Rather than allowing your software to identify a screen font by one number only (such as the NFNT

ID number), MasterJuggler 1.5 first establishes a screen-font style by its FOND number, and then searches within the available screen-font sizes for the correct NFNT number. The practical result is that MasterJuggler offers a kind of font-finding insurance policy, which requires no concern or participation on your part. Conflicts are still possible, but much less likely.

MasterJuggler will also search for FOND number conflicts between different open suitcases. By choosing the RESCONFLICTS command from the MASTERJUGGLER pop-up menu (found in the APPLE menu), you display a dialog box that allows you to check for naming conflicts, number conflicts, and so on by clicking on various buttons.

To remedy these conflicts, you must run a separate utility called the Font/DA Utility. Unfortunately, MasterJuggler will not allow you to manipulate an open suitcase with the Font/DA Mover or Font/DA Utility. You must first close the suitcase, and then launch the appropriate utility. Suitcase does not impose this seemingly arbitrary restriction.

 Font Harmony, Font/DA Utility

Font Harmony, included with Suitcase II, and Font/DA Utility, included with MasterJuggler, both allow you to change FOND numbers to avoid conflicts. Both utilities also update fonts with a FONT resource to include an NFNT resource.

Another feature provided by both applications is the ability to combine different styles into a single family. For example, the FOND resource for the screen font Times contains information linking it to I Times Italic, B Times Bold, and BI Times BoldItalic. When you italicize a word of Times text by choosing an ITALIC command (rather than choosing I TIMES ITALIC from a font listing), your software looks at the Times FOND resource, locates I Times Italic screen font, and displays it on screen. Therefore, it isn't necessary to clutter up your font menus with I Times Italic, B Times Bold, and BI Times BoldItalic, when you can access all styles using the Times font and the appropriate style.

Font Harmony and Font/DA Utility allow you to combine all styles into a single family. Each utility looks to the FOND resource for the plain style, locates all other styles associated with the font, and combines them into a single display. So, though you will no longer see I Times Italic, B Times Bold, and BI Times BoldItalic, you can access them by choosing Times and one or two style commands.

Font Downloader, LWDownloader 🖲🖲, 🖲🖲

A number of utilities exist for downloading printer fonts to a PostScript output device. The Font Downloader is included with all fonts purchased from Adobe Systems. The LWDownloader is included with Fontographer, from Altsys Corporation, and is generally included with typefaces from smaller companies such as Casady & Greene, Image Club, and Neoscribe, which use Fontographer to create their fonts.

Both utilities allow you to download a printer font to your printer's random-access memory (RAM). Once downloaded, a font may be used just as if it were a resident font like Times or Helvetica. Each style of printer font that you intend to use must be downloaded individually. If your printer's RAM is smaller than 200K, as is the case for the LaserWriter Plus, you may only want to download one or two fonts and let the others in a document download automatically.

The Adobe Font Downloader is used to manage fonts on the hard disk of a PostScript printer.

Your printer's RAM is cleared every time the printer is turned on or off, or the printer is rebooted via a software command. This means that when you turn your printer off, reset your printer via a utility command, or experience a power interruption such as during a lightning storm, all fonts in your printer's RAM will disappear and will have to be downloaded again from scratch.

SendPS, PSDownload, Execute PS   ⏚W, ⏚W

These simple downloaders do not support font downloading, but are used to send PostScript files to PostScript printers, and are therefore only useful to PostScript programmers. The variances between these programs are minor, concerning handling of errors and the automatic insertion of the "showpage" command.

```
┌─────────────────────────────────────────────────────┐
│                        TurboLaser/One's Resident Fonts│
│  Printer: TurboLaser/PS      ItcEras-Bold          ▲  │
│  Named: TurboLaser/One       ItcEras-Book          ▣  │
│  Version: 47.0(0)            ItcEras-Medium           │
│  Startup Page: Disabled      LetterGothic             │
│  Page Count: 41799           LetterGothic-Bold        │
│                              Melior                   │
│                              Melior-Bold              │
│                              Melior-BoldItalic     ▓  │
│                              Melior-Italic            │
│  Font Memory:    1534K       NewCenturySchlbk-Bold    │
│  ▓▓▓▓▓▓░░░░░░░░░░░░░░░        NewCenturySchlbk-BoldItalic ▲│
│  467K Used   1068K Free      NewCenturySchlbk-Italic ▽ │
│                                        ┌────────────┐ │
│                                        │     OK     │ │
│                                        └────────────┘ │
└─────────────────────────────────────────────────────┘
```

```
┌─────────────────────────────────────────────────────┐
│  ┌──────────────┐ ┌──────────────┐ ┌──────────────┐  │
│  │    Melio     │ │  AmeriTypMed │ │ CasloFivForRom│  │
│  └──────────────┘ └──────────────┘ └──────────────┘  │
│  ┌──────────────┐ ┌──────────────┐ ┌──────────────┐  │
│  │   MelioBol   │ │  MelioBolIta │ │  ItcEraMed   │  │
│  └──────────────┘ └──────────────┘ └──────────────┘  │
│  ┌──────────────┐ ┌──────────────┐ ┌──────────────┐  │
│  │   MelioIta   │ │   ItcEraBol  │ │              │  │
│  └──────────────┘ └──────────────┘ └──────────────┘  │
│  ┌──────────────┐ ┌──────────────┐ ┌──────────────┐  │
│  │              │ │              │ │              │  │
│  └──────────────┘ └──────────────┘ └──────────────┘  │
│  ┌──────────────┐ ┌──────────────┐ ┌──────────────┐  │
│  │              │ │              │ │              │  │
│  └──────────────┘ └──────────────┘ └──────────────┘  │
│  Click blank button to add file to menu.             │
│  Click filled button to remove file from menu. ┌─────┐│
│  ┌────────────┐ ┌────────────┐ ┌────────────┐  │ OK  ││
│  │  Load set  │ │  Save set  │ │ Clear all  │  └─────┘│
│  └────────────┘ └────────────┘ └────────────┘ ┌──────┐│
│                                               │Cancel││
│                                               └──────┘│
└─────────────────────────────────────────────────────┘
```

```
┌─────────────────────────────────────────────────────┐
│ □                   LaserStatus™                      │
│ «TurboLaser/One» status: idle                         │
│ ┌──────────┐ ┌──────────┐ ┌──────────┐ ┌───────────┐ │
│ │  About…  │ │  Reset…  │ │ Download…│ │Information…│ │
│ └──────────┘ └──────────┘ └──────────┘ └───────────┘ │
└─────────────────────────────────────────────────────┘
```

These three LaserStatus dialog boxes allow you to view your printer's RAM, create a set of downloadable fonts, and check the status of your printer.

LaserStatus

Unfortunately, because most printers provide no SCSI ports to attach hard drives, the majority of us will have to continue downloading fonts with the rising of each new sun. If you do a lot of font downloading, you should have CE Software's LaserStatus. LaserStatus is a desk accessory that allows you to establish printer-font *sets*, which are collections of fonts that you can download as a group, rather than tediously downloading one font at a time. Also, you can configure any number of sets or individual fonts as menu commands, saving the time required to locate the printer fonts.

For example, we used 12 downloadable printer fonts in this book—the four styles in the Melior family, three styles of Eras, two Letter Gothics, and three custom typefaces that hold our special characters. These are all members of a single printer-font set, which takes three or four minutes to download. We just choose the set from a DOWNLOADS menu, and have a cup of coffee; it's finished when we come back.

 Set Paths

Unfortunately, some software does not search so thoroughly. PageMaker is an example of an application that searches only the System folder and then gives up. This can be extremely aggravating if you work over a network and you store printer fonts on a central hard drive, or if you keep your printer fonts on floppy disks to save room on your hard drive.

```
Set Paths v1.3 Copyright © 1986 by Paul F. Snively.
Like it?  Send $20 to 3519 Park Lodge Ct. Apt. E, Indianapolis, IN  46205

Path #1 │ CMD's II:Utilities:Fonts/DA's:\Main Fonts ƒ:                    │

Path #2 │                                                                │

Path #3 │                                                                │

Path #4 │                                                                │

Path #5 │                                                                │

        (   OK   )        ( Build Path )        ( Cancel )
```

Set Paths allows you to specify where the folder and drive in which your printer fonts reside.

A desk accessory by Paul Snively called Set Paths allows you to direct an application to look at a specific folder on a hard drive or disk, bypassing the System folder altogether. Not only does this remedy the problem of printing from an application like PageMaker, it also saves printing time by directing your software to the exact location of a printer font.

But no matter what, searching and temporarily downloading and flushing RAM and starting over can take up an awful lot of time. If your printer offers a large enough RAM, as does the LaserWriter IINT as well as most other newer-model laser printers, then we recommend that you manually download fonts as often as possible.

 LetrTuck

Kerning, the amount of space between specific pairs of letters, can be a point of contention between a type designer and a type user. In general, the space that separates one character from another in a line of text is constant. However, some pairs of letters (called *kerning pairs*), such as We, Ta, and AT, follow their own spacing provisions that override the normal letter spacing. Most screen fonts provide a list of kerning pairs that a software application using that font can access and implement.

If you find that some pairs in a typeface are kerned too tight and others too loose, you may change the kerning with an extremely elegant utility called LetrTuck. When you open any screen font with LetrTuck, including those created by Adobe, a screen containing every kerning pair addressed by the current typeface is displayed. You may alter the spacing between these kerning pairs, delete certain pairs (so they are treated with normal letter spacing), and add new pairs.

 FontSizer

Another screen-font editing utility, called FontSizer, allows you to create additional screen-font type sizes. To create a new screen-font size, Font-Sizer actually relies on information from the printer font, which must be resident in your printer's ROM or downloaded to its RAM. You then select the printer font, indicate a type size, and let FontSizer go to work. All screen-font sizes created by FontSizer are put in their own suitcase rather than added to the suitcase of the existing screen-font sizes for that printer font, or to your System file. You must use the Font/DA Mover to transfer screen fonts as you see fit.

Unfortunately, FontSizer has two limitations. It will not create screen-font sizes smaller than 12-point. An 11-point screen-font size would be very useful. Such a small size would be rough-looking, but you could clean it up using Altsys's FONTastic. Next, if FontSizer is even slightly interrupted in the font-creation process, which takes three or four minutes, the program returns an error and you have to start over. It returns this same error if you're doing something wrong, so it's difficult to know exactly what the problem is.

FontLiner

If you want to manipulate a typeface a little more aggressively, FontLiner will convert the printer font into an Adobe Illustrator 1.1 file, which may be manipulated in Illustrator or Aldus FreeHand. You may designate whether all of the characters in a typeface are converted or only letters and numbers. You may also specify center points and spacing points, used to help align characters in Illustrator.

FontLiner only converts fonts created using Fontographer, ruling out any Adobe fonts or those from other vendors such as Bitstream.

Incidentally, don't rename the FontLiner application. It must be named "FontLiner™" with the trademark symbol or it will not run. The file looks for itself when launching; this is the vendor's way of discouraging pirating. Unfortunately, this fact is not mentioned anywhere in the documentation, so users who have purchased the product often run into difficulties.

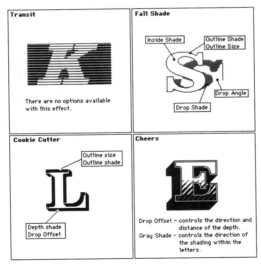

LaserFX allows you to choose from a variety of special-effects routines, only a few of which are shown here. Most effects can be manipulated as described in the above help screens.

LaserFX

LaserFX allows you to apply a number of predetermined special effects to a single line of type in any typeface, size, and style. The special-effects options are numerous, and each effect may be submitted to a number of manipulations. But unfortunately, the utility is not sophisticated enough to display the results of your changes on screen. Even to display the samples shown below, you have to press a help button.

 Smart Art

Like LaserFX, Smart Art offers a series of predetermined effects that you may manipulate in various ways. However, Smart Art also offers more functionality by displaying the results of your manipulations on screen and allowing you to save your work as an Encapsulated PostScript file. To display your changes, you must click a REIMAGE button, which gets information back from a PostScript printer. However, if you are working on a machine that is not attached to a LaserWriter or similar device, you cannot preview your work.

The program is also provided as a DA, so you can easily copy an effect from Smart Art and paste it into a word-processing or page-layout application. But unfortunately, you cannot produce your own effects from scratch; you must always begin by opening one of the 15 preexisting EPS documents.

This is an example of the Smart Art effect Movie Title Text

Unlike LaserFX, Smart Art displays your special font effects on screen, provided your computer is networked with a PostScript-equipped printing device that contains the printer font for the current effect in its ROM or RAM.

 LetraStudio

We must commend the programmers of this application. It's elegant and extremely versatile for editing fonts in just about any way you can imagine. Type can be set in perspective, wave gently up and down as if viewed under water, or bulge out from the page.

In fact, LetraStudio would be one of our all-time favorite graphics applications except for two flaws. First, LetraStudio may only manipulate Letraset fonts. Two typefaces are provided with the program, both of which only offer one style apiece. If you want more typefaces, you must purchase them from Letraset. This brings us to the second problem: Letraset's screen-font copy-protection scheme. In the bad old days, Adobe printer fonts had to be personalized for one and only one printer. Letraset goes one step further by requiring you to install screen fonts to one and only one System. You have no control over how your screen fonts are organized, nor may more than one user access the same font, not even over a network.

 Fontographer

As far as we're concerned, Fontographer is a must-have program for any graphic artist using the Mac. The program provides the kind of control over creating personal typefaces that one normally associates with proprietary applications controlled and used exclusively by Adobe, Bitstream, and so on. You may scan in letters at resolutions up to 300 dots per inch and convert them into mathematically described printer-font characters using an autotrace feature, similar to that available in high-end drawing programs. A freehand tool is also provided, along with more traditional point-by-point tools, which offer precise control.

But most importantly, Fontographer 3.0 integrates Nimbus Q hinting technology, which allows typefaces to be printed slightly differently to printers with different resolutions. Until recently, font hinting was the dominion of Adobe/Linotype fonts. For example, you may notice that our headings, printed in ITC Eras, slant very slightly (3°). When printed to a high-end imagesetter as these pages were, this effect works nicely. However, the limited resolution of a LaserWriter cannot accommodate such a slight angle, resulting a stair-stepped effect. To remedy this problem, Adobe's printer font tells to the printer to eliminate the slant and print the typeface straight up and down. Fontographer fonts may now access this powerful technology.

 FONTastic

Fontographer automatically creates screen and printer fonts according to your character drawings. But because of the limited resolution of your screen, screen fonts may not look as nice as you might hope. In fact, they almost always require some clean-up work. FONTastic, a separate product, allows you to manipulate bit-mapped fonts. Originally designed to create fonts for the ImageWriter and other low-resolution printers, FONTastic now acts as an efficient screen-font editing program. We simply could not imagine a better utility for this process.

Art Importer

Altsys' third and newest utility in its font-creation lineup is Art Importer (formerly KeyMaster). Art Importer allows you to assign any EPS document created in Aldus FreeHand, Adobe Illustrator, or some other application, as a character in a picture font.

This is a tremendously useful tool to people who want to access complex artwork with a range of gray values (such as logos) from the keyboard. We even find it preferable to Fontographer for creating standard type-faces. Although Fontographer's tools have improved, it still doesn't provide the exacting Bézier curve handling available in either Illustrator or FreeHand. Even for relatively simple characters, Art Importer can be a useful alternative.

We used Art Importer to create the special Macintosh characters we needed for this book. This font has been released as freeware with the name "EncycloFont."

Unfortunately, Art Importer has one big drawback: No typeface may have more than 16 characters. Compared with the 200+ characters available to a font like Helvetica, this is quite a severe limitation. Since Art Importer can import relatively complex artwork, the limit was imposed to ensure that printer fonts do not exceed your printer's ability to store them. Thankfully, Altsys has announced that the next version of Art Importer will allow up to 256 characters to be defined.

ApFont　　　　　　　　　　　　　　　　　　　　　　　　　ⒻⓌ
This cdev allows you to change the default font used by the Finder and most Mac applications from Geneva to any font in your System file. Some LaserWriter users like to choose a PostScript default font so that they don't accidentally end up with documents containing bit-mapped fonts.

N-Font　　　　　　　　　　　　　　　　　　　　　　　　　　　ⒻⓌ
N-Font converts old FONT-format fonts into NFNT format. This allows you to take advantage of font family styles without having each style appear separately in your FONT menu.

The Styler, DAFont　　　　　　　　　　　　　　　　　　　ⒻⓌ, ⒻⓌ
Both of these utilities are used to display or print character-set charts for the fonts currently installed in your System file. The Styler is somewhat more complete, but the advantage of DAFont is that you can quickly access it anytime from the APPLE menu.

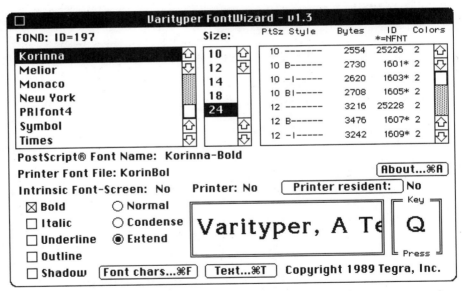

Varityper's FontWizard lets you quickly check the status of all your screen and printer fonts.

 Varityper FontConflicts, FontMaster, FontWizard, PSFontFinder　ⒻⓌ
These four utilities, created by Varityper, provide greatly needed assistance to those who manage large PostScript font libraries and print documents

created on other Macs. Verityper is to be commended for providing these utilities to the Macintosh community.

FontConflicts lets you compare the fonts in the current system file to those of another System file, so you can determine if there are any font conflicts. FontMaster allows you to either see or print a complete inventory of installed fonts, or a statistical list of the names, styles, sizes, and ID numbers of the installed fonts. FontWizard is similar to FontMaster, but provides a less complete font display, and offers information about whether a particular font is available in the current printer, or available for downloading. PSFontFinder searches PostScript-language files and provides a list of all downloadable fonts they contain.

Inits

Small Macintosh programs that execute automatically during startup if they are in the System folder are called inits (for initialization programs). The init format is popular for utilities that provide very basic enhancements to the Macintosh, because running at startup allows the program to "attach" itself to the Macintosh System Software and load into RAM before the Finder or any applications. Inits are often cdevs as well, with their controls appearing in the Control Panel. Inits are also used by some applications to patch the System Software so that the application can operate properly.

Many inits display icons along the bottom of your screen as they load during startup, to let you know that they are running. (You can usually disable this icon display in the Control Panel if you wish.) You can force some inits not to execute at startup by holding down a certain key during the startup; by default this is usually either the SHIFT, OPTION or CONTROL key, but you can usually specify your preference in the init controls.

It is important to remember that each init consumes a certain amount of RAM as it is loaded. Some inits use as little as 2K of RAM, others as much as 227K. If you have less than 2 megabytes of RAM in your computer, you should keep in mind the RAM being used by your inits. You might try eliminating some inits if you begin having problems with your normal applications. You cannot tell how much RAM an init uses by looking at its file size. Some init managers and other utilities can, however, tell you how much RAM each init consumes when it is used.

Init Utilities

Init managers are inits that help you control the other inits in your System folder by allowing you to designate which inits will be executed at startup. When the init manager is activated, a list of all inits in your System folder is presented, and you can turn any of them off or on. These changes determine which inits load the next time your Mac is restarted. Most init managers can also be activated at startup, allowing you to choose the inits that will load for that work session.

Init managers are important because you often need to turn inits off to avoid incompatibilities or to save the memory that they consume. Inits are often incompatible with one another, with System Software, and with utility software and applications. Init managers that cannot be activated during startup are of limited value, because many incompatibilities result in System crashes during startup, and you can only avoid them by turning off the inits that are suspected of causing the problem. If the init manager cannot be accessed at startup, you have to go to the trouble of booting your Mac with a floppy disk and then removing the suspect inits.

 Aask

The first init manager to appear was CE Software's Aask, and Aask remains our sentimental favorite. Aask presents a graphic list of all of your icons, and you click on any of these icons to turn the init off or on. Your settings can be invoked temporarily (for one session) or permanently (until changed again). You can access the Aask dialog box via the Control Panel, or at startup by holding down the space bar.

 Init Picker

Init Picker is another first-class init manager, providing all of the same features as Aask, except that its file list is not graphic. Init Picker provides a few features that Aask lacks, however, including the option of changing the order in which the inits load by simply dragging their names into another order, control over which key is used to access Init Picker at startup, and a user defined key to temporarily boot without running any inits. This feature is very significant, because reordering inits can often solve conflicts, and dragging is much easier than renaming the files, which is the only alternative. In terms of features, Init Picker is the best init manager currently available.

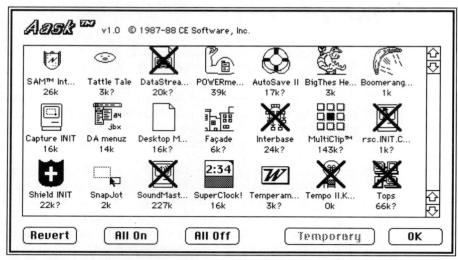

Aask's dialog box lets you turn inits off and on by simply clicking on their icons.

 ### Inix

Inix has the same basic features that Aask and Init Picker share, plus the ability to create init sets, which you can then select among to use. While Inix's set feature is a very good idea, and one we hope the other init managers emulate, Inix suffers from an awkward interface that relies on a DA, several dialog boxes, and a menu (where all others make due with a single dialog box). Moreover, in one of our tests, Inix reset the file type of the inits we had told it not to use—leaving them unusable until we replaced them or reset their type.

 ### Init Manager, Init

The best feature of each of these init managers is its public-domain status (which means that it is free). Init Manager allows you to turn your inits off and on via its cdev, but cannot be accessed at startup—an unacceptable omission for an init manager. Init provides a graphic init list that can be accessed at startup or in the Control Panel, and is therefore our choice among these public-domain programs.

 ### Icon Wrap

Most inits display a small icon indicating their presence as they are loaded during the startup process. While some inits allow you to disable this startup icon, most users leave them on so that they can remember which inits they are using—and perhaps as a show of "power-user" status. At some point, however, the string of icons exceeds the width of your monitor. This is when Icon Wrap comes to the rescue, forcing init icons to "wrap" to a second row on your display. This is the power-user equivalent of having to open a second bank account due to the $100,000 FDIC limitation—it's a stupid problem, but someone has to have it.

◈ **TattleTale**   ＦＷ
When the TattleTale init is in your System folder, a text file named INIT log is created at startup, listing the names of all the inits run during startup, the amount of memory they consumed, and the time they took to load. This file can be useful for telling tech support which inits you have run, and because its memory-utilization information is unavailable elsewhere.

Init Tips

◇ **Enable inits by placing them in the System folder**. They are not operational, however, until the Mac is rebooted after they have been installed. Some inits may show up in the Control Panel as soon as they are placed in the System folder, but their controls may not operate properly until the Mac is restarted. Inits in the System folder can be disabled by an init manager, as discussed earlier in this entry.

◇ **Disable inits by removing them from the System folder**. Inits cannot load from any location other than the System folder. If they are in any other folder on your disk or drive, including a folder within the System folder, they cannot be executed at startup. If you do not have an init manager, you can disable any init by simply removing it from the System folder, or putting it in a folder in the System folder, and restarting the Mac. Even if you have an init manager it is not a bad idea to keep a folder called Unused Inits in your System folder or Utilities folder and to store inits that are not being used in that folder. This keeps your System folder a little tidier.

◇ **Inits load alphabetically**. If you are having problems with conflicting inits, rename one of them to change the order in which they load. Some inits are sensitive about their names—they won't run if renamed—but most are not. The names of init managers generally start with a space, ensuring that they will load first. The Init Picker init manager allows you to reorder the sequence in which inits load without renaming them.

◇ **Init managers are likely to conflict**. Because each init manager likes to load first, and since each attempts to intervene in the init loading process, you are likely to have problems if more than one init manager is in your System folder. In some cases, init managers that are loaded after another init manager will simply not operate, but sometimes they will lock up the startup process.

Launchers

Traditionally, you launch Macintosh software by double-clicking on the application icon or on the icon of a specific document that you wish to use. However, this method, like other aspects of the Mac's graphic interface, can become tiresome when you use it too regularly. Double-clicking is a fine method for a floppy-based system with one or two applications per disk, but not for a hard-disk user with 20 or more applications and utilities spread out across many folders, volumes, and partitions.

In fact, hunting for an application icon—opening folders, moving windows, and generally cluttering up the old desktop—can cause the rare but always temporary disease known as "C> Prompt Envy." Fortunately, there exist numerous options that allow you to launch application files without going icon hunting.

Launching Utilities

 On Cue

On Cue is how application and document launching on the Mac should work. With the On Cue init installed, a new pull-down menu is added to the upper-right—and upper-left if you prefer—corner of your menu bar, providing a configurable menu of software applications and documents. To launch one of these applications, all you do is select it—anytime, from anywhere. You can also configure the On Cue application's menu to pop up anywhere on your screen when you press the key-mouse combination you've defined.

You can add specific documents to any application in the menu so that you can launch your frequently used documents directly. Holding down the OPTION key while launching any application presents a Standard File dialog so you can choose any document to open along with the application. For MultiFinder users, On Cue also lets you quickly switch between open applications, either via the On Cue menu or via a keyboard switch command reminiscent of the one provided in Apple's almost forgotten Switcher utility. In MultiFinder, you can launch documents that are assigned to already open applications by holding down the COMMAND key when choosing the document from the On-Cue menu.

Other...	
	Other...
	Adobe Illustrator 88 1.6 ▶
	Anonymity
	Art Importer ▶
	Font/DA Mover ▶
	Microsoft Word 4.0 ▶
EMc.3|drw Chap/pages	**PageMaker 3.02** ▶
EMc.3|fil Chap/pages	**PixelPaint™ 2.0** ▶
EMc.3|hyp Chap/pages	**SuperCard**
EMc.3|pge Chap/pages	**SuperEdit**
EMc.3|pnt Chap/pages	
EMc.3|spd Chap/pages	**Configure...**
EMc.3|wrd Chap/pages	**Preferences...**
EMc.5|res Chap/books	
EMc.5|res Chap/mags	**About On Cue...**

On Cue's pop-up menu lists both applications and documents you can launch.

MasterJuggler

The launching features of MasterJuggler are very similar to On Cue's, except that MasterJuggler never presents a pull-down menu, but rather relies on a pop-up menu that is invoked by either a key-mouse combination or a pressed function key. These methods of access require a little more getting used to than On Cue's ever-present menu, but are ultimately a satisfactory substitute. The biggest disappointment in the MasterJuggler launcher is that the OTHER... command, which accesses applications that have not been added to the list, is only available from the function-key-invoked list and not from the key-mouse-invoked list.

Like On Cue, MasterJuggler also provides for MultiFinder application switching (although it cannot be accomplished from the keyboard), but adds one fantastic feature that it calls "Vanishing Windows." Vanishing Windows hides all open windows from all applications open in MultiFinder, except the current foreground application. This reduces screen clutter enormously, but does not interfere with your ability to retrieve any of your background applications, or any background processing being done by these applications. It is especially useful when you return to the Finder, because it provides full visibility of all your disks, volumes, and folders, without forcing you to constantly move windows around or quit applications you would rather leave open. If you use MultiFinder, the Vanishing Windows feature alone makes MasterJuggler worth having; it made us give up On Cue and start using MasterJuggler as our primary application launcher.

 ### DiskTop, DiskTools

Along with its many other virtues (see the Utilities entry), DiskTop provides a fine user-configurable launcher menu in its DiskTop menu. You can also launch any application by double-clicking its icon in the normal DiskTop windows. Using Widgets, an accessory included along with Disk-Top, you can create various *sets* of application menus and load these sets into DiskTop as needed. If you are using the DA menuz init, applications in DiskTop's menu are available directly from the APPLE menu, making DiskTop comparable to On Cue (without document launching). The only problem with this DiskTop-DA menuz combination is that it not only launches the selected application, but also opens DiskTop. DiskTools too provides a configurable list of applications that can be launched, and allows applications to be launched when they are double-clicked in any DiskTools window.

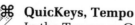 ### QuicKeys, Tempo

 In the Tempo or QuicKeys macro programs you can assign any application or document launch to any keystroke. For example, you could have CONTROL-W launch Microsoft Word, CONTROL-P launch PageMaker, and so on. You could also have CONTROL-OPTION-X launch your Excel payroll template. When you are not working in MultiFinder, macro launching will issue a QUIT command to the current application; you will be asked to save changes (if any), and then the requested launch will occur. In MultiFinder, the requested application will launch without closing the current application, provided that enough RAM is available.

As with all other macros, the ability to initiate an operation without reaching for the mouse is often a time-saver. Even if you use one or more other launchers, macro launching should be part of your overall launching strategy, at least for the two or three applications that you use most regularly. See the Macros entry later in this section for more information.

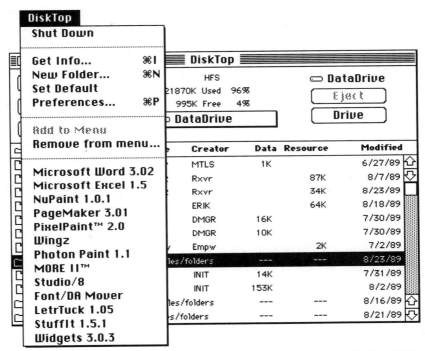

The DiskTop menu can be configured to launch applications. Using Widgets you can create application sets and move them in and out of the DiskTop menu.

PowerStation, Multi-Launch   ⑤⑤, ⑤⑩

Before the launchers just discussed were available, the best method of saving time in launching required a mini-Finder utility that provided launching services. A number of these (Oasis, Waystation, SuperFinder, etc.) used to be available as shareware or public-domain applications, but none have been updated to be compatible with System Software 6.0. One commercial mini-Finder remains: PowerStation. PowerStation serves as sort of a home base, automatically reappearing after you quit any application; you never return to the Finder unless you specifically choose to. PowerStation displays a number of buttons, each set up to launch a particular application or document. A bit passé, but still very functional.

Multi-Launch, a sort of hybrid mini-Finder and pop-up launching utility, presents a dialog box that can be configured with up to 25 applications and their documents. After it has been run, MultiLaunch presents its main dialog box, from which you select the application and document that you wish to use and then click a Launch button to launch them. Multi-Launch then shrinks down into an icon-sized button, which you click on any time you want to reaccess the launch-selection dialog. Overall, Multi-Launch is slightly more cumbersome than other pop-up launchers like On Cue, but it is one of the best freeware launchers we have seen.

Launcher, Icon-It

There are actually two totally different utilities named Launcher, one very old and one relatively new. The old Launcher was a desk accessory that, after being run, presented a Standard File dialog box each time you quit an application. This allowed you to avoid the delay of the Finder's display and to simply click on the next application that you wanted to run. It was an elegant solution to the launching problem. Unfortunately, it is not compatible with the current System Software.

The new Launcher lets you create small documents that launch other documents or applications. The benefit? You can place these "launching documents" anywhere—on the desktop or in any folder—and thereby avoid having to search for the actual location of the document or application. This allows you to put a "copy" of each application near every data file that uses the application.

Like the newer Launcher, Icon-It is a product that creates "launching icons" for your applications and documents. You then position the icons on your Finder desktop. In this way, you can add a sort of graphic launcher menu. Icon-It also can install icons that perform other tasks—at the Finder or in any application—so it is more like a macro program than a dedicated launching utility.

MultiSet

Although MultiFinder can be configured to launch multiple applications on startup, there is no inherent way to alternate between two or more sets of applications, or to launch a set of applications as a group once MultiFinder is running. These are the abilities added by MultiSet. Using MultiSet, you create "set documents." These can be double-clicked to launch all of the applications they list—they can list specific documents as well as applications—or set as the startup application so that they launch at startup.

MultiSet's set documents are superior to normal MultiFinder startup sets because they let you launch applications from several folders and launch documents along with their applications.

The TRANSFER... command
In some software applications and utilities, you may see the TRANSFER... command, usually in the FILE or MISC. menu. This command quits the current application and brings up a Standard File dialog box, where you select the application to be launched.

Launching Tips

◇   **⌘-PERIOD to abort a launch**. Pressing COMMAND-PERIOD immediately after launching an application from the desktop will often stop the launch—if you are quick enough. This is useful when you double-click on an application or document icon accidentally.

◇   **⌘-⌥ to launch a Finder**. Although the Finder is an application, you cannot launch it like other applications. In order to launch a Finder, thus changing the current startup disk, hold down COMMAND and OPTION while double-clicking on the Finder you wish to launch.

◇   **⌘-⌥ to launch MultiFinder**. To begin using MultiFinder, hold down COMMAND and OPTION while double-clicking on the MultiFinder icon in the System folder. You can also configure MultiFinder to launch during startup using the SET STARTUP... command, as described below.

◇   **Change MultiFinder into an application**. By changing the file type of MultiFinder from ZSYS to APPL, you make it possible to launch Multi-Finder by double-clicking on its icon without having to press the COMMAND and OPTION keys. You can change the file type in many utilities, as described in the Files entry earlier in this section. After changing the file type, you must restart your Mac before you can launch MultiFinder by double-clicking on its icon.

◇   **SET STARTUP... command**. The Finder's SET STARTUP... command, found in the SPECIAL menu, allows you to specify which applications will be automatically launched each time your Macintosh is turned on. To select either the Finder or MultiFinder, the disk containing the Finder or MultiFinder file (or any file/folder on that disk) must be selected. To select any other application to be the startup application without MultiFinder, select the application's icon before choosing the SET STARTUP... command, and then the selected application will be one of the Set Startup... options. Setting a single application as the startup application is most useful when working with a floppy-drive system in which unique applications are kept on their own startup disks. On hard-disk systems, set a single startup application if the computer is used as a server or bulletin-board, and you want it to always restart a server or bulletin-board application in the case of a crash or a power loss while unattended.

```
┌──────────────────────────────────────────────┐
│ ┌─────────┐                                    │
│ │ [─   ]  │  Start up "CMD's II" with:         │
│ └─────────┘                                    │
│                                                │
│     ○ ⌂ Finder    ◉ ⌂⌂⌂ MultiFinder           │
│  ·············································   │
│  Upon startup, automatically open:             │
│     ○ Selected Items                           │
│     ◉ Opened Applications and DAs              │
│     ○ MultiFinder Only                         │
│                         ┌────────┐ ┌────────┐  │
│                         │ Cancel │ │   OK   │  │
│                         └────────┘ └════════┘  │
└──────────────────────────────────────────────┘
```

The SET STARTUP dialog box allows you to configure a set of applications to be automatically launched each time your Mac is turned on or rebooted.

When in MultiFinder with applications running, you also have the option of making the current set of applications and DA's launch automatically, along with MultiFinder. Alternatively, you can select any group of application icons, then choose the SET STARTUP command, and select the "Selected items" option and the "MultiFinder" option to set MultiFinder and the selected applications to be run at startup.

- **About switch-launching**. In most cases, Mac applications do not care whether they reside on the same disk as the current System file and Finder; they can be run from any Macintosh volume. Some applications, however, prefer to be run from the current startup disk. When these applications are run, they switch-launch, which means that the application first launches the Finder on its disk, and then launches itself. If no Finder and System file are available on the disk containing the application, a dialog box appears, warning you that the disk cannot be made the startup disk, and giving you the option of running the program anyway or canceling the application launch.

  Applications switch-launch when their SwitchLaunch attribute has been set (as described in the Files entry earlier in this section). Alternatively, you can request that an application switch-launch by holding down COMMAND and OPTION while launching any application.

  System Software newer than 5.0 does not allow you to switch-launch to an older version of the System Software. The disk to which you are switch-launching to must contain System Software as new as or newer than the current startup disk. You can never switch-launch when using MultiFinder. See the Startup Disk entry later in this section for more information on switch-launching.

Multilaunching on Networks

Many software applications can be used by more than one person at a time when running on network servers such as TOPS or AppleShare. The ability for an application to be launched by more than one user at a time, called **Multilaunching**, is beneficial because it saves the time and space of installing infrequently used applications on every Mac in the network that is going to use them, or of installing multiple copies on a single server.

In general, any application on the Mac that doesn't modify itself during execution will multilaunch. Of course, it may be difficult for you as a user to know if a program modifies itself during execution. Two ways of testing whether an application can multilaunch are to see if the creation date changes each time the program is run (if it does, the program is modifying itself during execution and will not multilaunch), and to see if the software runs off a locked or write-protected volume (if it does, it will probably multilaunch successfully).

To set up an application to multilaunch, you must usually set the file's Shared attribute, using DiskTop or some other file editor that supports file-attribute modification. (See the Files entry for more information about file attributes and their modification.) Any ancillary files that the program needs to modify during operation, like preferences files or dictionaries, should be copied to the System folder of each Mac that is going to launch the application, and the drive or volume serving the application should be write-protected.

Products we know to work well when multilaunched include Excel, Page-Maker, Microsoft Word, MacDraw II, and MacWrite II. Of course, most software licenses do not grant permission for more than one user to be using the software application at one time, so you should own one copy of the application for each person who will be using the software simultaneously. If you intend to set up multilaunch applications on large networks, you may want to look into site-licensing, which is available from many software vendors.

Relaunching in MultiFinder

Switching between open applications in MultiFinder can sometimes become a difficult or confusing task because of the on-screen clutter when multiple applications are open. Clicking on any part of an open application window brings that application (or the Finder) to the foreground, where it becomes the active application. Also, the bottom of the Apple menu lists all open applications, and by selecting one of these you make that the foreground application.

◇ **Holding down the ⌥ key while selecting the menu displays only open applications**. Normally the list of open applications is beneath the list of DA's. When the OPTION key is pressed, the DA's are not listed in the Apple menu.

◇ **Clicking on the icon of an open application brings that application to the foreground**. Double-clicking the icon of an open application (at the Finder) brings that application to the foreground. Clicking on a document icon opens that document and brings the application to the foreground if the application is already open. Icons for either applications or documents will be dimmed in the Finder window, indicating that they are already open.

In MultiFinder, holding down the SHIFT key, causes the APPLE menu to display only applications that are currently running. Selecting one of these applications brings it to the foreground.

◇ **Both On Cue and MasterJuggler present lists of open applications.** Selecting an application from the top portion of the On Cue or MasterJuggler launch menu brings that application to the foreground. Launching an application that is already open also brings that application to the foreground without disturbing the current document. To launch a document in an open application in On Cue, hold down the OPTION key while selecting the document from the On Cue Menu. On Cue also allows you to define a keyboard equivalent to switch from one open application to the next. You cannot launch documents from MasterJuggler for an application that is already open.

Macros

Macros are user-defined shortcuts that allow you to "record" one or more actions (pressed keys, chosen commands, mouse clicks, etc.) and assign them to any keyboard equivalent you choose. Pressing the assigned keyboard equivalent then "plays" the macro, executing the exact sequence of actions originally recorded. Macros are also named, and can be played by name, making it unnecessary for you assign keyboard equivalents.

Using macros can improve your productivity enormously because so many of the tasks performed are basically repetitive, and because the Mac's graphical user interface requires such a high degree of accuracy in choosing commands, options, and items. (You spend a lot of time and energy moving your mouse around.) When you are freed to simply execute commands with a keystroke, another layer of the computer's tedium and interference in your work is stripped away, leaving you more time and energy to concentrate on your work itself. The best tool is one you hardly know that you are using, one that lets you concentrate instead on the result being accomplished with the tool.

The simplest and most common use of a macro program is to assign keyboard equivalents to menu commands that do not already have them. For example, you may often use a calender desk accessory, and tire of selecting it from the APPLE menu repeatedly. Using a macro utility, you could assign the opening of the calender DA to a single key or combination of keys—F7 or OPTION-C for example—which would allow you to access your calender DA without reaching for the mouse. Another basic type of Macintosh macro records mouse clicks or drags, and assigns them to keystrokes. A mouse click in the Zoom box of the current window, for example, could be assigned to CONTROL-OPTION-Z.

More advanced macros perform a series of actions—for example, selecting a menu command, choosing an option or series of options from the resulting dialog box, and then closing the dialog box. The most advanced macros execute a long series of actions, offering conditional branching (do this if), intelligent repetition (do this until that is true), and context-sensitive execution (click on this particular item regardless of where it is on the screen). The macro utilities we will examine here are generic utilities that can be used in all Macintosh applications, DA's, and utilities. Some applications programs provide their own internal macro capabilities, allowing you to create macros specific to that application, but these are not discussed here.

Because macro programs require some understanding and preparation, they are often perceived as a tool reserved for the power-user. In reality, all frequent computer users can and should benefit from macro programs, but it may take some time to become familiar with their operation and to appreciate the possibilities they present.

Macro Utilities

A few features are common to all macro programs on the Mac: They all prevent or warn you of keyboard-equivalent conflicts between macros (but none warn of conflicts between macro keyboard equivalents and application keyboard equivalents), and they all let you specify whether a macro you create will be "universal" (available anytime the macro utility is running) or "application-specific" (available only in the application that was running when the macro was created). Beyond these similarities, there are major distinctions among the macro utilities available for the Mac.

 MacroMaker   §§

Of the many possible items on any software's feature list, "free" is one that is sure to get attention. In MacroMaker's case, the fact that it is included in Apple's System Software has made all the difference in the world; no one would think twice about this program if they had to pay for it.

On the positive side, MacroMaker can adequately create text-entry macros, some menu-command and dialog-box macros, and many mouse-click macros. Keyboard equivalents can include the COMMAND, OPTION, CONTROL, and SHIFT keys, although the OPTION key cannot be used alone.

To MacroMaker's detriment, its option controls are not "smart"—they do not check whether an option is already selected before selecting it again (thereby deselecting it). It does not support any application or document launching, and macros cannot be edited. Also, because MacroMaker cannot be accessed in **modal dialog boxes** (those that beep if you click anywhere on the screen except in the dialog box itself), many potentially useful macros cannot be created directly. You cannot, for example, create a macro to simply choose a command that brings up a modal dialog box (unless the macro also chooses the dialog-box options and closes the dialog box). In some cases, however, you can create a macro to choose a command that brings up a modal dialog box by creating the macro while the menu command is dimmed; when MacroMaker plays it back, the menu command will be selected normally (assuming it is not dimmed then).

MacroMaker is a functional, if limited, macro program, and is a good way to learn the basics of macros. If you decide you like MacroMaker, or more accurately you like the ability to use macros, you should probably then consider upgrading to QuicKeys or Tempo.

The MacroMaker main window emulates a cassette deck—you record, store, load and play marcros here.

 QuicKeys

The strength of QuicKeys is derived from an interface that makes it very easy to create most common macros, and solid reliability in performance and compatibility. You define a QuicKeys macro by bringing up the QuicKeys cdev, selecting one of the macro-definition commands from the DEFINE menu, and performing the action that you want QuicKeys to automate. Each command performed is then added to the macro listing in the QuicKeys cdev menu, at which point keyboard equivalents can be assigned.

QuickKeys' only weak point is its SEQUENCES command, which is much too inflexible to allow the creation of macros with any measure of complexity. However, all of its other commands work very well, executing quickly and accurately without fail. QuicKeys's compatibility with other Macintosh applications is excellent, and the support record and policies of CE Software are among the best in the software industry.

The QuicKeys macro types are:

- **Text**. A text macro provides for automatic data entry, entering whatever you type during definition each time the macro is replayed.

- **File**. This allows you to assign the launch of an application or document to a keyboard equivalent.

- **Menu/DA**. The assignment of new keyboard equivalents to any menu command or DA is controlled with this command.

- **Alias**. An "alias" assigns a keyboard equivalent to do the work of another key sequence; pressing one becomes the same as pressing the other. This is useful when you want to redefine a keyboard equivalent that already exists. For example, Microsoft Word has a keyboard equivalent of COMMAND-SHIFT-S. By assigning this key combination the alias of the keypad's period key, and also assigning all Word style-sheet names a numeric alias—this is a Word style-sheet alias and has nothing to do with QuicKeys—you can assign any style sheet by simply pressing the keypad's period key, the style-sheet number, and the keypad's ENTER key. This is also a good way to assign a multikey combination to a single function key on the extended keyboard (for example, F9 as an alias for COMMAND-EQUALS to recalculate in Excel).

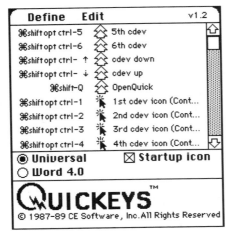 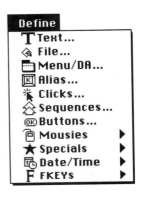

The QuicKeys cdev lists all of the currently available macros. The DEFINE menu presents all of the commands used to create macros.

- **Clicks**. All mouse clicks are defined with this menu command. Mouse clicks can be remembered in relation to their absolute location on your screen, or in relation to the window in which they occur.

- **Sequences**. This option lets you execute several QuicKeys macros in succession, thereby creating more powerful macros. You define the order in which the existing macros are played, and you may insert pauses of any length between macros. There are several problems with this, including the fact that most complex actions involve a large number of discrete steps that must first be created as individual macros, and named, before the sequence macro can be created. If any macro in the sequence is renamed or assigned a new keyboard equivalent, the entire sequence must be redefined. If you have a need for the type of complex macros that the SEQUENCES command is supposed to address, you want Tempo instead of QuicKeys.

- **Buttons**. You define button macros to assign keyboard sequences that click buttons in a dialog box. You specify the text of the button you want clicked when the associated keyboard equivalent is pressed.

- **Mousies**. You use this command to select among some premade macros. QuicKeys already knows how to perform these tasks, so all you do is add the macro to your listing and add a keyboard equivalent

- **Specials**. Like the Mousies command, Specials provides a group of ready-made actions. You don't have to execute the action for QuicKeys to record it; you just select one of the macros and assign a keyboard equivalent to it.

- **Date/Time**. These ready-made macros allow you to specify keyboard equivalents that enter the current date or time in a specific format. These too operate just like Mousies.

- **Fkeys**. To assign any Fkey currently installed in your System file as a macro, you select it from the Fkeys command and then designate a keyboard equivalent for it in the main QuicKeys dialog. Fkeys must be installed in the System file, as Fkeys added with utilities like Suitcase and MasterJuggler cannot be used in this way.

3-Screen to paint	6/22/87	Line up	Transfer
4-Screen to printer	Monday, June 22, 1987	Line down	Shut down
5-FKEY File	Mon, Jun 22, 1987	Page up	Restart
7-Moving Lines	June 22, 1987	Page down	Select rear window
8-SetFile Key	Jun 22, 1987	Home	Select second window
9-AntiFreeze	22 June 1987	End	QuickQuotes
	22 Jun 1987	Column left	Double QuickQuotes
	87/06/22	Column right	Quick reference
		Page left	Toggle QuicKeys on/off
	12:00 AM	Page right	Recorder on/off
	12:00:00 AM	Close window	QuickPanel
		Zoom window	

The Mousies, Special, Date/Time, and Fkeys menus are accessed via hierarchical menus from QuicKeys

 Tempo II

Tempo is clearly the king of Macintosh macro programs, at least in terms of sophistication. Tempo can record virtually any sequence of events that you can perform on the Macintosh, and allows you to control these events with advanced logic, including various pauses, loops, and conditional tests.

To begin recording a Tempo macro, you select the START RECORDING command (⌘-~) and then perform the action you wish to automate. You may pause and then resume the recording of the macro at any time—a feature that enables you to perform actions that you do not want as part of your macro during the recording process. You may also choose one of Tempo's recording options: "Pause," "Transfer," "Branch," or "Repeat."

Tempo's superiority over other macro packages lies in these options:

- **Pause**. Within any Tempo macro you can insert a pause that will wait a certain amount of time, wait until a specific time of day, wait until the user presses the RETURN key (after receiving a customized dialog-box message), or just pause briefly to display a customized dialog-box message.

- **Transfer**. Two kinds of transfers are offered by Tempo: "transfer to an application" and "transfer to a document." These are really launching macros, which can be used on their own or as part of more sophisticated macros that perform some tasks in one application and then launch to another to perform additional tasks.

- **Branch**. The "Branch" option is the heart of Tempo's sophisticated ability to utilize any number of discrete macros in one larger macro-controlled operation. With the "Branch" option, a macro can branch unconditionally to another macro, or branch conditionally depending upon the currently highlighted selection. Conditional branching can be defined if the highlighted selection is less than, greater than, equal to, not equal to, less than or equal to, or greater than or equal to a value that you specify. The macro can be set up to return to the calling macro after branching, to end after executing the macro to which control is branched, or to end as soon as the branching condition is met (without executing the branch).

- **Repeat**. Any Tempo macro can be set to repeat a certain number of times, if a certain condition is true—these conditions operate exactly as the branching conditions described above—until a certain condition is true, or endlessly.

- **Smart features**. Tempo has a number of features designed to account for peculiarities in the Macintosh environment. You can specify whether menu selections are remembered by command name (what the menu item says) or by position (how many commands from the top of the menu the command is located); whether window manipulations are performed relative to the window itself or to the entire desktop; and whether macros affecting dialog-box buttons, scroll-bar movements, and options (radio buttons and check boxes) are "smart" or not. Smart macros can operate even if buttons or scroll bars move around the dialog box, and they make sure that options are set as specified when the macro was defined, rather than simply toggling the option regardless of its state when the macro is executed.

Another great Tempo feature is its ability to play macros by name as well as by keyboard equivalent. This is advantageous because well-chosen macro names are often easier to remember than keyboard equivalents, and there are far more possibilities for names than for keyboard equivalents. You do not even have to assign keyboard equivalents to Tempo macros; you can simply name them. To play a macro by name, you simply execute a "Play by name" keyboard equivalent (such as COMMAND-RETURN), and then type in the name of the macro to execute. If you just type the first few letters of the name, Tempo will automatically find your macro for you.

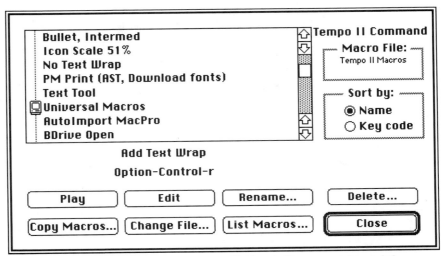

The Tempo II menu provides access to all Tempo II commands, and the
COMMAND *dialog box where macros are edited.*

Suggested Macros

To help you get some idea of when macros may be of use, we've compiled the following list of common macros.

- **Operating scroll bars**. Create a separate macro for each scroll bar arrow (up, down, right, left) and another for a click in the scroll bar just shy of the arrow (to jump rather than scroll).

- **Window resizing**. Create a macro that clicks in the Zoom box, and another that clicks in the Close box.

- **Transpose characters**. Create a macro that corrects transposed characters. You will start with your the cursor positioned to the right of the transposed characters; the macro then should cut out the character immediately to the left of the cursor, move the cursor one character to the left, and then paste the cut character. This will correct the transposition. In Microsoft Word the keyboard commands for this sequence would be (without the commas): SHIFT-Left Arrow, ⌘-X, Left Arrow, ⌘-V.

- **DA selection**. Create macros to select all your favorite DA's.

- **Menu-command selection**. Create macros to choose commands you often use that don't already have keyboard equivalents.

- **Button and dialog-box option selection**. Create macros to click the buttons you have to repeatedly click in dialog boxes. For example, ⌘-PERIOD for CANCEL, ⌘-Y for YES, ⌘-N for NO, and ⌘-A for APPLY.

- **Application launching**. As discussed in the Launchers entry earlier in this section, you can create macros to launch your applications and documents.

 # MultiFinder

Apple has described **MultiFinder** as an enhancement utility that allows the Finder to run multiple applications concurrently. When MultiFinder is running, the Finder has additional capabilities, most notably the ability to run multiple applications at once, but apart from these it acts just as it did without MultiFinder.

When you are not using MultiFinder, applications take complete control of the Macintosh when they are launched, and you cannot access any other Macintosh programs (except for desk accessories) without first quitting the application that you are running. Under MultiFinder, a launched application does not monopolize the Macintosh, but instead becomes "just another window" on the Finder's desktop. When that window is active, however, it provides its own menu bar and the complete capabilities of the application; when the window from another application is selected, another menu bar appears and a different application is active.

When an application is running under MultiFinder and one of its windows is selected (its menu bar is being displayed), it is in the **foreground**. When an application is running but not selected (its menu bar is not being displayed), it is in the **background**. Most applications can continue to execute any operation while in background mode—they are said to "allow background processing"—although some will prevent you from switching to another application until their processing is complete. The number of concurrent applications that you can launch in MultiFinder is limited by the amount of RAM installed in your Macintosh. Each application takes a section of the available RAM when it is launched and keeps that RAM until the application is quit. Before launching any application under MultiFinder, the Finder first checks that enough RAM is available to run the application. If it is not, you are notified that not enough memory is available.

```
≣□▭▬▬▬▬  About the Macintosh™ Finder  ▬▬▬▬
 ┌──────────────────────────────────────────────────┐
   Finder:   6.1          Elvis, Steve, Pete & Bruce
   System:  6.0.2         ©Apple Computer, Inc. 1983-88

   Total Memory:   5,120K  Largest Unused Block:  786K
 ├──────────────────────────────────────────────────┤
   🗑 CanOpener™       600K   [██░░░░░░░░░]          ⇧
                                                     ⇩
   📈 Excel          1,024K   [████████░░░░░░░░]
                                                     ▫▫▫
   🦑 Stufflt 1.5.1    360K   [███░░░]
                                                     ⇧
   🔷 Word 4.0         750K   [█████████░░░]         ⇩
 └──────────────────────────────────────────────────┘
```

The Finder's ABOUT THE MACINTOSH FINDER dialog box shows you how much RAM is available in your Mac and how it is being used under MultiFinder. The light portion of each application bar shows the amount of RAM reserved for the application, while the dark portion is that actually being used.

Configuring MultiFinder

In order to operate MultiFinder, you must have the MultiFinder file in your System folder, and you should also have the DA Handler file and the Backgrounder file. If these files were previously deleted from your System folder, you can copy them from your Apple System Software disks; it is not necessary to run the Installer application to install them.

MultiFinder can be used on any Macintosh with at least 1 megabyte of RAM; however, with less than 4 megabytes it's usefulness is questionable, because the amount of RAM taken up by the Finder and MultiFinder and one application leaves little available for anything else. Even if your Mac has 2 or 2.5 megabytes, many applications cannot even be launched under MultiFinder. A utility called MultiLaunch helps users with 2.5 megabytes or less to get more use from MultiFinder by allowing them to run it without the Finder itself (thus saving about 130K of RAM), as described later in this entry.

You usually start MultiFinder by making it your startup application in the SET STARTUP dialog box (accessed via the Finder's SPECIAL menu and the SET STARTUP command). Before choosing the SET STARTUP command, be sure that your startup disk (or any file or folder on your startup disk) is selected. You can then choose the "MultiFinder" option in the SET STARTUP dialog box. If any application files are selected (or already running when the command is chosen), you may configure MultiFinder to automatically launch these applications each time it is started.

While MultiFinder is configured to launch at startup, you can prevent its launch by holding down the COMMAND key during startup. This will prevent MultiFinder from launching until you again restart your Mac. It does not change the SET STARTUP command to permanently prevent MultiFinder from launching automatically.

You can also launch MultiFinder at any time by holding down the COMMAND and OPTION keys and double-clicking on the MultiFinder file in the System folder. It is impossible to quit MultiFinder and return to just the Finder. All you can do is change the SET STARTUP... command (if it is set to Multi-Finder) and then reboot your Macintosh so that it runs the Finder without MultiFinder.

All of the application launchers described in the Launchers entry earlier in this section work in MultiFinder. That entry also discusses the process of switching between open applications in MultiFinder.

MultiFinder Utilities

 MultiLaunch   ⒻⓌ
This utility addresses the problem of using MultiFinder without a lot of RAM. Normally, the Finder is automatically your first MultiFinder application, and takes up about 160K of RAM. MultiLaunch replaces the Finder as your first MultiFinder application, but it uses only 30K, so 130K is saved. When MultiFinder is run with less than 4 megabytes of RAM, this can make it possible to run more than one or two applications and utilities that could not be run otherwise. Since all of the Finder's features are

available in DA's, the loss of the Finder is not much of a price to pay for the ability to use MultiFinder without buying more RAM.

MultiSet   S⃞W⃞

Although MultiFinder can be configured to launch multiple applications on startup, it offers no way to alternate between two or more sets of applications, or to launch a set of applications as a group once MultiFinder is running. These are the abilities added by MultiSet. With MultiSet you create "set documents," which you double-click to launch all of the applications (or documents) they list. Set documents can be made the startup application, causing the listed applications and documents to launch at startup. These are superior to MultiFinder's own startup sets because you can launch applications from several folders, and because documents can be launched along with their applications (neither of which can normally be done).

TakeOff   S⃞W⃞

If you have enough RAM, you will usually configure your Mac to run MultiFinder at startup. Occasionally, however, you may wish to use the Finder instead of MultiFinder in order to run MultiFinder-incompatible applications or utilities. Because you cannot quit MultiFinder and return to the Finder alone, this process is somewhat arduous. You have to change your SET STARTUP... command and reboot, and then remember to change it back later. TakeOff solves this problem by allowing you to decide whether to use MultiFinder or not each time your Mac is booted up.

When installed as the startup application, TakeOff presents a menu that lets you choose to launch MultiFinder, launch just the Finder, launch a specific application (without MultiFinder), or launch a group of applications with MultiFinder. TakeOff can be set to automatically launch either the Finder or MultiFinder after presenting its dialog box for only a few seconds, so the Mac can complete its startup while unattended. If you find yourself needing to use MultiFinder only occasionally, or occasionally wanting to run your Mac without MultiFinder, this utility will quickly become a favorite.

MFDetective   P⃞D⃞

Since memory is such a precious commodity in MultiFinder, knowing how your memory is being used is an important concern. In addition to checking the ABOUT THE FINDER dialog box, you can use the MFDetective Fkey. This Fkey displays a memory map, showing your RAM and how it is being used.

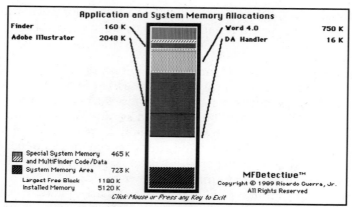

MFDetective provide an on-screen map of memory utilization anytime it is invoked.

MultiFinder Printing

For PostScript (LaserWriter) printing, MultiFinder provides built-in **print spooling**, which allows you to continue working on your Mac while the printing is handled as a background task. To use this feature, switch on "Background Printing" in the Chooser. When you execute the PRINT... command in any software that uses Laser Prep—some software such as PageMaker uses custom prep files and is not supported by MultiFinder's background printing—your printing will be completed very quickly and you will not see the normal PRINT STATUS dialog box. Your file has been printed to disk, and is now sent to the printer while you continue to use your Mac.

To monitor or alter the operation of this background printing, the PrintMonitor application is used. This application is run automatically as soon as background printing begins, and you can access it by choosing its name from the APPLE menu or by switching to it with whatever method you use to change between open MultiFinder applications. PrintMonitor allows you to stop any printing, or delay a print job indefinitely or until a specific time. If your Mac crashes during a background printing job, PrintMonitor will notify you when the Mac is restarted, and you can almost always restart the print job without reexecuting the PRINT... command in the original application.

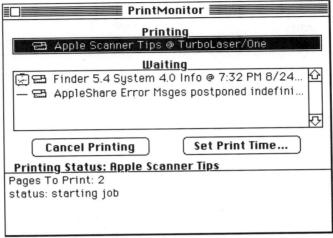

The PrintMonitor dialog box shows the status of all current print jobs.

MultiFinder and DA's

MultiFinder supports DA's, but to run them normally you must have the DA Handler file in your System folder. If the DA Handler file is missing, all you will get is a beep when you try to access any DA. If you do not have enough RAM left under MultiFinder to run the DA you have selected, your Mac will also beep and not run the DA. DA Handler serves as the "home base" for the DA while it is running under MultiFinder, allowing it to be available to many different applications and not be affected when an application is quit or launched. If DA Handler is missing, you can, however, launch DA's by holding down the OPTION key while selecting them.

Holding down the OPTION key while choosing a DA makes it available to only one application by instructing the DA to attach to the current application and not use the DA Handler. The effect of this is that if the application is quit, the DA will be quit too, and that whenever the DA is selected, the application to which it is attached will become the foreground application. As described above, when using MultiFinder, DA's are normally run with the DA Handler so that they are unaffected by the activities of any particular application.

DA Handler Resizer   ⒻⓌ

Occasionally, in MultiFinder you will find that larger DA's will not run, or you may have difficulty running several DA's at one time. This happens when not enough RAM is being allocated for use by the DA's. Changing the DA Handler's MultiFinder partition size will usually alleviate this problem. You can change this value in ResEdit (by altering a value in the SIZE resource), or by using the DA Handler Resizer. After launching this utility you simply specify the number of K that you want allocated for the DA Handler. The default value is 16000, but the program's author recommends raising this value to 52000.

Printer Drivers

Most applications store their files on disk in a format that cannot be printed directly. In order to print these files, they must be converted from their native format (the one in which they are saved on disk) into a format that the printer can understand. This conversion is done by **Printer drivers**. Printer drivers execute a file conversion when the OK button is clicked in a PRINT dialog box.

Three printer drivers (often called simply **drivers**) are available from Apple: the ImageWriter driver, the AppleTalk ImageWriter driver, and the Laser-Writer driver. These drivers convert files into the format required by Apple's ImageWriter and LaserWriter printers. Other printer drivers available from third-party vendors allow the Mac to print on many different kinds of printers.

In order to be used, a printer driver must first be selected in the Chooser. The Chooser serves as sort of an electronic switch box, connecting one of the available printer drivers to the System file for use when the PRINT command is executed. After you select a printer driver, you can choose the PRINT command, which will present various options for the printing of the document. When you click the OK button in this dialog box, the application being used sends its file to the selected printer driver, which first converts the data into a format usable by the printer, and then sends this converted data to the printer via the printer or modem port.

Printing Tips

◇ **Enable printer drivers by placing them in the System folder**. The Chooser looks through the System folder each time it is opened, presenting the icons of all valid drivers in its left window.

◇ **Disable printer drivers by removing them from the System folder**. The Chooser cannot access printer drivers from any folder other than the one containing the System file and Finder. This allows you to keep unused printer drivers anywhere else on your drive or disk. You may even keep printer drivers in a folder inside the System folder; they will not be available to the Chooser.

◇ **You may keep unused printer drivers in your System folder**. Printer drivers utilize no RAM, so the only drawback of keeping unused printer drivers in your System folder is the disk space they consume.

◆ **Preparing files for laser printing without a LaserWriter**. By copying the LaserWriter driver to your System folder and selecting it in the Chooser, you can prepare documents for PostScript printing even if you do not have a LaserWriter attached to your Mac. In some software, such as Microsoft Word, you should make your Chooser selection before your final formatting of the page, because the program actually formats text differently depending upon the printer being used. In other applications, like PageMaker, this is not necessary (but only experimentation will tell you for sure).

◆ **Printing to disk with the LaserWriter driver**. When using the LaserWriter driver, you can reroute the converted PostScript file to disk, rather than having it sent out the Printer port, by pressing ⌘-K immediately after clicking the OK button in the PRINT dialog box. This will create a file named PostScript# (where # is a number between 0 and 9) containing the data normally sent to the PostScript printer. Pressing ⌘-F does the same thing, but does not include the contents of the Laser Prep file in the disk file.

Understanding Laser Prep

In order to use the LaserWriter printer driver, you should have the Laser Prep file in your System folder. This file is a **PostScript dictionary**, or

header, that contains definitions used by the PostScript file created by the LaserWriter driver (for any document). Each time a file created by the LaserWriter driver is sent to a PostScript printer, the file first looks to see if the Laser Prep file has already been downloaded into the laser printer's memory. If it has not, the Laser Prep file from the System folder is downloaded automatically; the message "preparing printer" appears in the PRINT STATUS dialog box when this file is being downloaded.

Once downloaded, the Laser Prep file remains in the laser printer's memory until it is rebooted. This is why you will only see the "initializing printer" message when printing the first document to a PostScript printer. If the Laser Prep file is not in your System folder when it needs to be downloaded, a dialog box will appear, prompting you to insert a disk containing the file. If someone else on your network generally prints to the PostScript printer before you do, you may not need to keep the Laser Prep file in your System folder. However, for the small price of its disk space most people would be wise to keep it just in case; the one time you have to go searching for it you will realize that you didn't need to save 28K that badly (unless you are working on a floppy-based system).

Since they work together so closely, the LaserWriter driver and the Laser-Prep file must have the same version number, although they do not have to be the same LaserWriter and LaserPrep files that came with your System Software; these files are historically updated more frequently than the System Software, and as long as they are used together they can be used with any version of the System Software.

Because the Laser Prep file remains in the PostScript printer's memory and is used constantly, problems occur when different users on a network are not all using the same version of the LaserWriter driver and the Laser Prep file. Even if every user has a matching LaserWriter and Laser Prep on their machine, if there are nonmatching versions used on different machines, problems will occur. These problems often result in what are known as "laser wars."

It works like this: Suppose that you are using a matching set of version 5.0 LaserWriter and Laser Prep, while a coworker with whom you share a PostScript printer is using version 6.0 of LaserWriter and LaserPrep. If you print first on any given day, your version 5.0 Laser Prep file is downloaded to the printer. You can print fine, but when your friend tries to print, their LaserWriter driver version 6.0 gives them a message saying, "The Laser-Writer has been initialized with an older version of Laser Prep," and they are prompted to allow the LaserWriter driver to reboot the printer. Since they want to print, and don't really understand that message, the printer is restarted (causing it to lose all fonts that have been downloaded to it), and then their Laser Prep 6.0 is downloaded. Later, you decide to print again, and are told, "The LaserWriter has been initialized with an incompatible version of Laser Prep." You are now instructed to restart the printer, and then your Laser Prep 5.0 is again downloaded, and laser wars have begun.

The only solution to this problem is for everyone to use the same versions of the LaserWriter driver and Laser Prep file.

 # RAM Cache

As the processing speed of computer CPU chips and RAM chips has increased, the gap between the speed with which a computer can process data and the speed with which storage devices such as hard disk drives can accept or deliver data has widened. A **RAM cache** is a mechanism for alleviating the effect of this discrepancy.

A RAM cache acts as a buffer between the CPU and its RAM and disk-storage devices. It works by keeping frequently used (or likely to be used) data in RAM so that when the CPU needs that data, it can be provided quickly. (RAM can deliver data up to 400 times faster than a hard disk.) The RAM cache also buffers data to be written to disk, accepting it from the CPU as fast as the CPU can deliver it and then waiting to write it out to disk until enough data has been accumulated to make the writing operation efficient. (One large write is faster than many little writes, and two wrongs don't make a right.)

The larger a RAM cache is, the more data it can hold, and therefore the greater the likelihood that data required by the CPU will be available in RAM and thus not have to be read from disk. There is, however, a point at which a RAM cache gets too large, and the time required to check and see if it does have the requested data outweighs the performance benefits. You must also remember that RAM used for the RAM cache reduces the amount of RAM available for your applications, so too large a RAM cache can make it impossible to run certain applications. RAM caches that buffer data written to disk also present a risk of data loss, because if the computer crashes before the buffered data is written, the data will be lost permanently.

Cache Software

 Control Panel Cache

Apple's General cdev provides the RAM cache that is used on most Macs. Using this RAM cache is as easy as selecting the "On" option in the Control Panel's General cdev and using the arrow buttons to determine the size of the cache that will be used. This cache is not write-through, so there is theoretically a danger of losing data that has been written to the cache but not yet written to disk, although we don't know of anyone who has experienced this problem. Because we haven't found a better RAM cache utility for the Macintosh, this cache should be used by everyone.

As long as you have at least 1 megabyte of RAM, you should be using your RAM cache. It will provide the quickest, easiest boost in the operating speed of your Mac. The tips below list the sizes of RAM cache we recommend for each memory configuration.

 Turbo Cache

This utility, given away along with PLI hard drives or sold separately, provides a replacement for Apple's RAM cache, providing a little more flexibility, user control, and user feedback. We have not, however, found this cache to be any faster than Apple's, and therefore wouldn't recommend that you spend any money for it. Note that Turbo Cache is incompatible with the Shield init 1.0 from the Symantec Utilities and will lock up your Mac if they are used together.

Cache Tips

⬦ **After resetting the size of your RAM cache, you must restart your Macintosh in order for the changes to take effect.**

⬦ **Turn the RAM cache off when you need more memory to run an application.** If a dialog box tells you that you cannot run an application because not enough memory is available, turn off your RAM cache (and your inits), and restart the Mac. The RAM being used by the RAM cache will then be released for use by the application.

◇ **The table below lists the size we recommend for your RAM cache.** These numbers are only guidelines. They could be affected by the memory requirements of your software applications and the inits and other utilities that you use. RAM allocated to the RAM cache is taken directly from that available to your applications.

Recommended RAM Cache Sizes

Installed RAM	Cache Range
128K	off
512K	off
1 Mb RAM	64K–128K
2 Mb RAM	128K–256K
4 Mb RAM or more	256K–512K

Resources

Macintosh files are made up of two parts: the data fork and the resource fork. The **data fork** holds what we would think of as traditional data (text, numbers, formatting commands), and the **resource fork** holds Macintosh resources, which are program elements. Each resource is identified by its type, which is a four-letter code, an ID number, and in some cases a name. (See the Files entry earlier in this section for more information about editing the data fork.)

There are two ways to see and manipulate the information in a file's resource fork. First, you can open a file's resource fork in most file editors, such as Symantec Utilities, MacTools, and MacSnoop. But these provide only hexadecimal and ASCII views of the fork data, which in most cases are not very helpful. Occasionally you will encounter instructions that fix a program bug by searching the resource fork for a specific data pattern and then replacing that pattern, and in such cases these utilities should be used. When you don't know exactly what changes to make, however, these file-editing utilities allow you to do nothing but damage to resource forks. See the Files entry earlier in this section for more information on these file editors and their use in modifying file data forks.

The second way to view and manipulate resources is to use specialized resource editors that convert the hexadecimal information in the resource form into discrete resources, and allow you to manipulate these resources in relatively friendly dialog boxes. Apple's ResEdit (Resource Editor) is the most powerful general-purpose utility of this kind.

Common Macintosh Resource Types

ALRT	Alert dialog box
BNDL	Bundle resource–files and icons for the Finder
CDEF	Control Definition function
CNTL	Control template
CODE	Application code - program instructions
DITL	Item list for a dialog box or Alert
DLOG	Dialog box
DRVR	Desk accessory or other driver
DSAT	System error table
FKEY	Fkey resource
FOND	Font family information
FONT	Font information
FREF	File reference
FRSV	Font list reserved for system use
FWID	Font width tables
ICN#	Icon lists
ICON	Icons
INIT	Init resource
INTL	International resource
MBAR	Menu bar resource
MENU	Menu items
NFNT	Font family information
PACK	Package - System Software segment
PAT	Quickdraw pattern
PAT#	Pattern list

PDEF	Printing resource
PICT	PICT-format graphic
PREC	Print record
SERD	RAM serial driver
STR	Strings used in dialog boxes
STR#	Strings used in dialog boxes
WDEF	Window definition resource
WIND	Window dialog boxes
actb	Alert color table
cctb	Control color table
cicn	Color icon
clut	Color lookup table
crsr	Cursor color table
dctb	Dialog color table
mbdf	Menu bar-color table
mctb	Menu color table
pllt	Color palette resource
scrn	Screen configuration
wctb	Window color table

Using ResEdit

Although ResEdit is extremely powerful, it is quite easy to use. You can obtain ResEdit without charge from most user groups, download it from bulletin boards, or purchase it from the Apple Programmers and Developers Association. (Many sources have older copies of ResEdit—if possible, get version 1.2 or newer.) Whenever you use ResEdit to modify an application, it is important that you work only on backup copies of the application. You can very easily make a modification that ruins an application permanently, especially when experimenting with ResEdit. We are not trying to discourage your use of ResEdit, or your experimenting with it, but you must be sure to use only backup copies of any software so that you can just throw them away if they become damaged.

To begin using ResEdit, double-click the ResEdit application. ResEdit will open and create a window for each disk or volume currently mounted on the Finder desktop. Locate the application that you want to edit—opening folders will open additional windows—and double click on its icon or file name. A scrolling list of all of that application's resource types will appear.

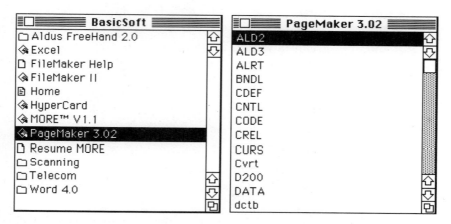

Each volume appears in its own window when ResEdit is launched, as shown at left. Opening a particular file yields a window listing the file's resources, as shown at right.

You can open any resource type in this list by double-clicking on it. You will then see a scrolling list of the resources themselves, which you also open by double-clicking on them. What you see when you open a resource depends upon what type of resource it is. Many resources contain software code that looks about the same in ResEdit as it would in any other file editor—long strings of hexadecimal numbers. Other resources present dialog boxes that may be modified, or contain items that can be opened further and then edited. The resources you will want to edit most often are:

- **STR and STR#**. These are string resources containing text used in dialog boxes. See the Customization entry earlier in this section for information about editing these resources.

- **MENU**. These contain the menus used by the application. See the Customization entry earlier in this section for information about editing these resources.

- **ICON, ICN#, CURS, and SICN**. These contain icon bit maps. See the Customization entry earlier in this section for information about editing these resources.

- **ALRT, DLOG**, and **DITL**. These contain dialog boxes and Alert boxes. See the Customization entry earlier in this section for information about editing these resources.

When any resource is selected, choosing the GET INFO… command will bring up an INFO dialog box. This dialog contains the resource's ID number, name, and attributes. Resources are often used by other resources by ID number or name, so you should not modify these without knowing exactly what you are doing. The attributes listed in this dialog should never be modified.

When certain resources are open, additional menus appear in the menu bar, providing access to commands unique to the editing of that type of resource. For example, when you edit any dialog-box resource, a DIALOG menu appears, offering a DISPLAY AS TEXT command that opens a dialog box in which you can numerically specify the coordinates for the box's size.

The INFO window for a menu resource is accessed via the GET INFO command from the FILE menu.

When you are finished editing resources, close the windows you have opened by clicking their Close boxes. When you attempt to close the application window, you will be asked if you want to save your changes. If you have made any mistakes during your resource editing, click the No button to close the application without any of the changes you have made. Click the YES button to save your edits and close the file. You can also use the SAVE and REVERT commands from the FILE menu at any time while working in ResEdit.

Scrapbook

The ability to cut and paste text or graphics between applications has always been a cornerstone of Macintosh software. In addition to the Clipboard, this function has traditionally been implemented with the Macintosh Scrapbook. This Scrapbook, consisting of an Apple DA and the Scrapbook file, which resides in the System folder, can hold text, MacPaint-format graphics, and PICT-format graphics.

Scrapbook Tips

◇   **Text may lose formatting in Apple's Scrapbook.** When text is pasted into the Scrapbook, it does not automatically lose its font, size, and style, but most applications do not support the file format the Scrapbook uses to maintain this information, so it is often lost when the text is pasted into another application.

◇   **Rename the Scrapbook file to use more than one.** Apple's Scrapbook DA automatically creates a new Scrapbook file if one is not present in the System folder. If you fill a Scrapbook file, or have created a Scrapbook for a project that you'll work on later, change the Scrapbook's name to anything other than Scrapbook, and save it. (You can even leave it in the System folder.) When you want to reuse that Scrapbook, rename the current Scrapbook file, change the name of the file that you want to use back to Scrapbook, and put it in the System folder (if it's not there already). This renaming technique lets you use any number of Scrapbook files.

◆ **Apple's Installer deletes the Scrapbook file from your System folder and replaces it with a new one.** To save your current Scrapbook file before running the Installer, rename it. (Any name change will suffice—just adding the word *old* to the name *Scrapbook*, for example.) You can then delete the Scrapbook file installed by the Installer application and name your Scrapbook file as Scrapbook once again.

Scrapbook Replacements

 Multi-Scrap   🗗🗐
Multi-Scrap operates just like Apple's Scrapbook DA, except that it allows you to save Scrapbooks with any name and to open any named Scrapbook. This greatly expands the usefulness of the Scrapbook, and makes the renaming technique discussed above unnecessary.

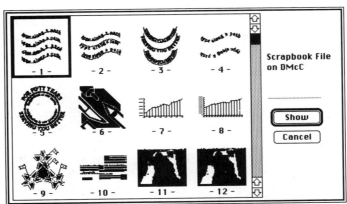

SmartScrap provides a table-of-contents page that allows you to see all of the Scrapbook's content.

 SmartScrap, ScrapMaker   🖐🗐🗐🖐
SmartScrap is much like Multi-Scrap in that it allows you to maintain multiple Scrapbook files. It also adds many other sophisticated management features such as the ability to name Scrapbook images and then search for them by name, a resizable display window (rather than the fixed 3 × 5 card of the normal Scrapbook), the ability to print any Scrapbook image, and a quick-view table of contents that allows you to see all images in the current Scrapbook.

The ScrapMaker utility, included along with SmartScrap, lets you transfer any MacPaint-format or PICT image into a new or existing Scrapbook. This saves you the trouble of opening your applications and cutting and pasting images to build Scrapbook files.

Scrapbook-like Utilities

In addition to utilities that compete directly with the Scrapbook, there are a number of other products that allow you to manage multiple text and graphic items. Not all of these are meant to be replacement Scrapbooks, although all of them do have some facility for transferring images from one application to another.

 MultiClip

MultiClip, as described in the Clipboard entry earlier in the section, is a Clipboard utility that provides all the functionality of a Scrapbook and most of the functions of SmartScrap: You can store multiple files containing any number of text and graphic images, retrieve them at will via the MultiClip desk accessory, and see a table of contents of all images in a file. You cannot print or name your images, and no search features are provided. Unless you have a large amount of data that is already in Scrapbook format, MultiClip is a better value than any other Clipboard/Scrapbook utility we have seen. See the Clipboard entry for more information.

 PictureBase

PictureBase is a complete system for managing a large quantity of graphic images, with both advantages and disadvantages over Scrapbook-based graphic-file management. PictureBase catalogs MacPaint-format and PICT-format graphics in a proprietary-format file—which cannot be read by any other applications or utilities except for CanOpener—called a PictureBase Library. Existing Scrapbook files can be converted using a separate utility that turns them into PictureBase Libraries.

Libraries are managed in the PictureBase application, which allows you to import and name graphics, and to add descriptive information about them. To allow access to Libraries from within any application, a DA is provided; using this DA, you can open any Library file, search for graphics by name, browse the images, or copy full or partial images to the Clipboard to be pasted into the application. PictureBase's excellent search facilities and its ability to manage large Library files—one Library can hold over 5000 pages of images—are its best features. Its only drawback—and this may or may not be a problem depending on how you use PictureBase and whether you have MultiFinder—is that you cannot add images to a Library from the DA. This means you will still need some other Scrapbook-like DA.

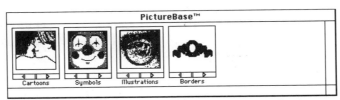

The PictureBase DA allows you to quickly scan all Libraries for images.

 ### The Curator

This utility, available (with identical features) as both an application and a desk accessory, enables you to quickly locate any type of artwork by file name, keyword, or thumbnail (miniature picture). It does not accumulate all of the graphics it is managing into its own file or catalog; they are accessed directly from their own original files. The Curator does not alleviate the need for a Scrapbook or substitute because you cannot paste images from the Clipboard into The Curator or create new files for them. Also, The Curator cannot read Scrapbook files. What it does do, however, is allow you quick and complete access to all other graphic files so that you may import them into your applications.

The strength of The Curator lies in the many graphic-file formats that it can process. Unlike the other Scrapbook utilities, The Curator supports not only MacPaint and PICT, but also Encapsulated PostScript (EPS), IBM PC EPS, TIFF, and GLUE formats. Besides viewing and searching for any of these images, you can also convert virtually any graphic in any format to any other format. This allows you to use images in almost any application regardless of the file formats that the application accepts.

Any image or portion of an image being viewed can be cut or copied to the Clipboard, so it can then be pasted into any application. The Curator even provides special CUT and COPY commands that will transfer images containing PostScript commands and high-resolution TIFF graphics to the Clipboard in a format that does not lose their special qualities. A utility provided along with The Curator can convert PictureBase Libraries for use in The Curator.

 Glue, SuperGlue II   ▩▩, ▩▩

SuperGlue allows the capture of any document created on the Macintosh in a format that can then be viewed or printed by any other Mac user—even if they do not have the application that created the file—or transferred into any other Macintosh application. You accomplish this by using the SuperGlue drive to "print to disk" any page(s) of a Macintosh document. The file created by this operation can be saved in either Glue, Scrapbook, or Text format.

Files saved in Glue format can only be viewed or printed with SuperViewer or the SuperViewer DA, but these viewers may be distributed to any Macintosh user, so your colleagues who do not own SuperGlue can still view, import, and print the files that you create with SuperGlue. Any portion of an image opened in SuperViewer can be selected (via a selection marquee or lasso) and copied to the Clipboard so that it may be pasted into any Mac application.

Using SuperGlue to save images in either Glue or Scrapbook format is superior to saving them with screen-dump utilities for several reasons. First, the SuperGlue image can contain an entire page, regardless of its size. Screen dumps are limited to the size of your computer monitor. Second, Super-Glue saves images in PICT format, so the full image quality is retained; the printed SuperGlue image will look just as good as if it had been printed directly from its original application. Screen-dump utilities convert everything to bit-mapped images and therefore produce very low-quality results on high-resolution PostScript printers. SuperGlue's ability to save in Text format allows you to create ASCII text files from applications that cannot themselves create ASCII text files.

 # Screen Savers

Try as we might, we can't always be sitting in front of our Macintosh. Most of our hardware and software really doesn't care if we leave it alone for a while, but the monitor is an exception. When left on too long while not being used, monitors can develop two different problems: burned-in images and decreased sharpness of display. Fortunately, you can easily avoid both of these problems by using any one of the many screen-saver utilities.

Burned-in images are the result of a monitor being left to display the same image for too long a time. When this happens, the phosphor that lines the inside of the monitor tends to "remember" the image, resulting in the ghost-like appearance of the burned-in image regardless of the image currently being displayed.

Images do not burn into the phosphor very quickly, so occasionally leaving your Mac screen on for 15 minutes or even an hour does not place it in much danger. But over months and years, the same image left on for a few hours a day can result in permanent damage. Because most Mac applications have a white menu bar running across the top of the display, this is often the first area to become damaged.

The decrease in the display quality and sharpness resulting from leaving a monitor on too long is really a more important problem than image burn-in, although it is mentioned less often. Like most other materials, the phosphor in your display wears out over time. This deterioration manifests itself as a slow loss of sharpness and eventually a blurring of your display. The less that the monitor is used, the longer it is going to take before this happens.

Screen-saver utilities prevent screen burn-in and phosphor deterioration by "blanking" your screen whenever it is not in use. Usually the screen savers don't blank the screen entirely, instead displaying some moving image so you can readily tell that the monitor and the computer are turned on; this image is relatively small and it keeps moving so that it won't burn in itself. Most screen savers turn on automatically after some user-defined period of inactivity, and most can also be turned on manually at any time. Regular use of a screen saver can virtually eliminate the potential for burned-in images and loss of display quality.

On Mac II models, or when using external displays with a Mac SE or Plus, you might consider just turning off the monitor while leaving for an extended period of time. However, the strain placed on your monitor by turning if off and then on again those extra times is potentially more harmful than the damage from leaving it on. Get yourself a screen-saver utility.

Screen-Saver Utilities

The differences between the many screen savers available for Mac users concern their methods of automatic and manual initiation, their reaction to and effect on various computer tasks, and the image they display while blanking the screen. The best screen savers are those that provide both manual and automatic initiation, are sensitive to tasks such as printing, network communication or hard-disk access, and modem communications, and draw comments from coworkers.

Screen savers that do not properly handle printing and modem activity can cancel a print job or telecommunications transaction by automatically initiating themselves while the computer is busy, mistakenly assuming that it is idle just because the mouse has not moved. Screen savers that essentially lock up the computer while the screen is dimmed can also make it impossible for other network users to contact your computer, preventing such functions as E-mail delivery or disk sharing.

Programming a screen saver for the Macintosh must be a simple exercise. Why else would so many programmers choose to give the world another screen saver when so many already exist? Surprisingly, however, most of the screen savers available contain one or more serious flaws, so depending upon your requirements your actual choices may be limited.

 Pyro

The best costs money. That is one way to sum up Pyro, the only screen saver sold as a stand-alone commercial application. (Pyro was formerly bundled with Suitcase, but is now only available separately.)

Pyro meets all of our criteria for a good screen saver. It can be initiated either manually or automatically after a user-defined inactivity period, it is fairly intelligent in its reaction to printing and modem tasks (frequent incompatibilities with PageMaker are one exception), and does not interfere with network or background tasks, and it provides you with a choice of two different screen images (a fireworks display or a moving clock) for the screen blanking. And on top of all that, Pyro is strongly supported both by its vendor, Fifth Generation Software, and by its author, Bill Steinberg, who is a Sysop on CompuServe's MacPro forum. Most of the other screen savers are entirely without support. What support do you need for a screen saver? Mostly upgrades to handle changes in System Software or the operation of application-specific background tasks, both of which have been provided for Pyro.

We strongly recommend Pyro. Although other screen savers may be less expensive or even free, Pyro is the best blanking screen saver we've encountered yet.

 Stars, BigZoomIdle, Idle
The best thing about DA-invoked screen savers is that they don't ever kick on automatically, lousing up your printing or other activities. Their drawback is that you have to remember to run them, so if you walk away for what you think will be a minute and wind up gone for hours, your screen is not blanked. These DA screen savers tend to interfere with network access to your Mac, so they are best avoided if you are using TOPS, E-mail software, or other communications programs that may try to contact your Mac while the screen saver is running.

The Stars screen-saver DA is best loved by Trekkie types for its on-screen space effects, including warp-speed simulation. BigZoomIdle moves the outline of a box around your screen, while Idle uses a small Mac icon.

Moving Lines, Space Warp, Sleep, FadeKey
Like DA screen savers, Fkey screen savers have to be manually initiated. All of these Fkeys are rather old, and interfere with network access to your Mac, so they are best avoided if you are using TOPS, E-mail software, or other communications programs that may try to contact your Mac while the screen saver is running. Moving Lines uses a bouncing stick reminiscent of the video game Quix—a stunning effect that will even do a light show on your wall if you turn the lights out in the room! Space Warp is much like the Stars DA. Sleep makes the Apple logo bounce around your screen. FadeKey only works on Macs with a 7-inch monitor.

Moiré, Dimmer
These screen savers are init/cdev combinations. Moiré offers a wide array of user-definable geometric shapes that move around your screen. It can be initiated manually or be set to appear automatically after some amount of inactivity. Moiré will also add a digital time display to the upper-left corner of your menu bar if you so desire. An older version of this screen saver actually destroyed data files when not using MultiFinder, but versions after 2.12 appear to have this problem cured. Designed for the Mac II only, Dimmer is unique among screen savers in that rather than darkening your screen completely and making some item jump around, it first just dims the screen to some user-definable level (just as if you had turned down the

monitor with its hardware dimmer switch). After some amount of additional inactivity, it blackens the screen completely. The problem with this, of course, is that when the screen is completely dimmed, you (or someone else who happens along) may think the Mac is turned off and not dimmed.

The Dimmer Switch
Every monitor has a manual dimmer that you can use at any time. Dimming the screen this way never interferes with the operation of a program, although because it has no flashing screen display you (or someone else who needs to use your Mac) might think that your Mac is turned off rather than dimmed.

Screen Savers with Security Software
Many of the utilities described in the Security entry offer screen savers as part of their security features.

Security

As Macintosh users, we are very concerned with the ease of use of our computer system. We want to be able to access our data, manipulate it, and transport it in the most intuitive way possible. But this causes one problem: The wonderful friendliness and intuitiveness that you enjoy when you sit down at your Macintosh also greets anyone else who decides to use your computer, copy your software, or examine your data files. There is very little that you can do about it with only Apple's System Software and your standard Macintosh applications.

But as in most other cases where Apple has left an obvious void, third-party developers have stepped in most effectively. An amazing array of special applications and utilities are available to help you safeguard your computer and your data. Some security features are provided by dedicated security utilities, while others are part of packages that offer security features in addition to their other abilities. Security features fall into two broad categories: those designed to stop the casual thief or overly curious browser, and those designed to thwart malicious theft.

When considering a security utility, your goal should be to balance security against inconvenience to the nonpilfering user. While these products inevitably construct barriers that must be negotiated, the user whom they are protecting should be able to negotiate them quickly and conveniently.

Security Against Wandering Eyes

Many of the people from whom your data should be protected are not particularly malicious, but may have "wandering eyes." These persons would not go to great lengths to examine or steal your files, but wouldn't pass up an easy chance.

You can protect your data from such people in a number of ways, and with a minimum of inconvenience to you. Partitioning your hard drive and then assigning passwords to the partitions is perhaps the easiest method, requiring only the extra effort of entering your password each time your machine is rebooted and you want to access a specific volume. (A complete discus–sion of volume partitioning is provided in the Disks and Drives entry earlier in this section.) Several utilities let you add passwords to individual folders. If you protect infrequently used folders, these utilities may require you to enter your password less often than drive partitions, but still provide you with security. Finally, a utility called Guard Dog can provide you with simple protection against those who would drag-copy your files onto their own disks, for whatever reason.

Security Against Terrorists

The second classification of persons from whom you may want to protect your data are those who really want your data and are smart enough to get around any of the schemes just described. These people know how to use file editors to get past volume partitions and read deleted files, and they know how to disable inits to get around security software that is installed via init. They may even have fancy gadgets that can read your data right off of your screen or your hard disk, or as it is transmitted to your printer, while sitting in a car parked outside your building.

Partitions can still be an effective deterrent in some of these cases, but only SCSI partitions and not File System partitions. (The distinction is whether the partition is created by hard-drive formatting software or by an additional utility, as described completely in the Disks and Drives entry earlier in this section.) Password-protected SCSI partitions are virtually impossible to mount without the password, and their data cannot be viewed when they are not mounted by a file- or disk-editing utility. This is not true of File System partitions, whose data can be seen by an advanced disk editor.

File encryption can also foil those using disk and file editors, by scrambling your data so that it cannot be read until unscrambled with your assigned password. Mac encryption software offers a choice of either fast or extra secure encryption methods, and most support the National Bureau of Standards DES data-encryption algorithm. Another type of security utility erases the data that is normally left behind when files are deleted from the sectors of your hard disk. These make it impossible to read this data using file or disk editors.

To prevent the person in the car outside your building from intercepting your electronic information with supersensitive receivers, you must purchase specially made Macintoshes, printers, and network cables that are shielded (with kryptonite, we think) to prevent this exact sort of espionage. Products approved by the US Government for use with classified information are called **Tempest**. There are Tempest Macs, Tempest AppleTalk cables, and Tempest LaserWriters, all sold by the Tempest Division of Atlantic Research Corp.

Security Utilities

A wide range of security-related devices are reviewed below. They are separated according to their basic features, but many offer abilities that cross these boundaries.

Data Encryption

 Sentinel

Individual files or groups of files (which Sentinel calls Sets) can be encrypted with Sentinel using either Sentinel's SuperCrypt algorithm or DES. Encrypted files display their own icon with a padlock around it, and when double-clicked they automatically launch Sentinel so you can decrypt them. Once files are decrypted, you can launch them from within Sentinel by clicking on their icon. In addition to Sentinel's normal Sets, which you can define to include any group of documents, Sentinel automatically creates a Word Set that includes all documents that you have decrypted while using your Mac. This makes it easy to reencrypt all these files at once.

PC Secure

PC Secure is part of the PC Tools Deluxe Macintosh Edition package, and is provided in both application and DA formats. PC Secure includes a number of nice features, including optional compression during encryption, the ability to decrypt files encrypted with the PC version of PC Secure, the ability to lock or make invisible your encrypted files, a choice of fast or extra secure DES encryption, and the use of a single password for multiple files. Its drawbacks include a lack of support for simultaneously encrypting or decrypting multiple documents, and a menu interface that is somewhat awkward to use compared with the dialog-box interface (using buttons and options) the other packages provide.

Hard Disk Deadbolt

FWB's Hard Disk Deadbolt offers three kinds of encryption algorithms: DES, QuickBolt, and AppLock. The AppLock method is particularly interesting because it is designed to encrypt only Macintosh applications, so that they cannot be used without the password even if they are copied to another Mac. This method locks any application in about one second. Hard Disk Deadbolt can encrypt or decrypt an entire folder at once, or a user-defined set of documents. Also included is a command to darken the screen of your Mac and require a password to regain access to the machine. Hard Disk Deadbolt is provided in both application and DA format.

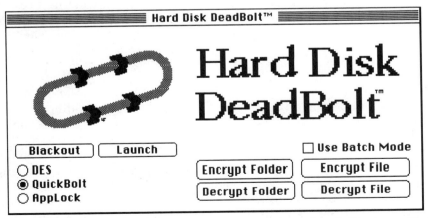

The Hard Disk Deadbolt dialog box is accessible from the application or the DA.

Strongbox

This DA provides only simple encryption and decryption features, but with just a ten-dollar shareware fee it offers very economical protection.

 Stuffit

Although primarily used for file compression, Stuffit also allows you to password-protect and encrypt any Stuffit archive.

Volume and Folder Protection

 MacPassword

This init/cdev lets you assign a password to any volume or folder, making all files on protected volumes and folders invisible or unavailable to users who do not enter the correct password when the Mac is started up. MacPassword also provides a desk accessory that allows you to protect your Mac when you step away from it.

MacPassword definitely falls into the category of protection from wandering eyes; all of MacPassword's security measures, and even MacPassword itself, are easy to defeat. Protected files are made invisible using the Invisible file attribute, so utilities such as MacTools and Symantec Tools can "deprotect" any file without the password. Also, because protection is installed and deinstalled during startup, using any init manager to keep MacPassword from launching is enough to entirely defeat its protection.

With its reasonable shareware fee, however, MacPassword is a nice product for those whose security concerns only involve "wandering eyes." Very good documentation is provided with MacPassword. Moreover, the author has already upgraded the product several times (and has indicated that he plans to continue to do so) and is available via CompuServe for assistance.

 Empower

Empower adds the security features of AppleShare, plus a few additional ones, to any Macintosh. You configure Empower by adding names and passwords for all users, optionally assigning users to groups, and then assigning privilege requirements to any volumes or folders that you want to protect. Empower can protect entire volumes so that they cannot be accessed without it (even if you boot from a floppy disk), and can configure a Mac so that it will not boot from its floppy-disk drives under any circumstance. You can even configure the Mac so that it will not allow anyone to use the floppy drives at all! This makes it impossible for users to copy files from the hard-drive volumes, or to introduce viruses into the system.

Empower's protection privileges include assigning a volume or folder "owner" who can then reset folder privileges at any time, and determining who can "See Folders," "See Files," and "Make Changes" to the volume or folder. Privileges are assigned and accessed via the GET PRIVILEGES... command, which is available in the File menu at the Finder whenever Empower is installed.

```
╔═☐═════ Access Privileges ═══════╗
║   ┌────┐                                    ║
║   │    │     Encyclo Mac                    ║
║   └────┘                                    ║
║   Where : DataDrive, SCSI Drive (65M)       ║
║           (SCSI #2) — Façade by Greg        ║
║           Marriott                          ║
║  Logged on as : <Guest>                     ║
║   Privileges : See Folders, See Files, Make ║
║                Changes                      ║
║   ···········································║
║                                             ║
║   Owner : │Craig Danuloff              │    ║
║                                             ║
║   Group : │Publishing                  │    ║
║   ···········································║
║                 Owner  Group  Everyone      ║
║   See Folders :   ☒      ☒       ☒          ║
║     See Files :   ☒      ☒       ☐          ║
║   Make Changes :  ☒      ☐       ☐          ║
║      Change All Enclosed Folders : ☐        ║
║   ···········································║
║   ┌──────────┐   ┌───────────────────┐     ║
║   │   Undo   │   │       Save        │     ║
║   └──────────┘   └───────────────────┘     ║
╚═════════════════════════════════════════════╝
```

Empower's GET PRIVILEGES *dialog box allows you to determine who can see a folder, see the files in a folder, or make changes to a folder.*

Empower can be configured to present a log-on dialog box at startup, or it can automatically log on with "Guest" privileges, meaning that only privileges available to everyone are provided. You can manually log in as a registered user (and thereby take advantage of your access privileges) at any time via the Control Panel cdev. Empower can also lock the Mac (with a screen saver displayed) after a designated period of inactivity, at which

time the password of the currently registered user or the system adminis-
trator must be entered in order to reaccess the Mac. Restarting the Mac will,
however, circumvent this lock-out.

When used on volumes that are set up so they cannot be used without
Empower, the security features of Empower cannot be defeated. Protected
files are "encrypted" so that users without adequate privileges cannot access
them even with disk editors, but they perform normally in all respects when
used by those with the correct privileges. (They even appear normal to sector
editors!) Secured folders that are served via TOPS, however, are not protected at all when mounted from another Macintosh.

When used on volumes not set up to be inaccessible without it, however,
Empower can be bypassed during startup with an init manager; all files are
then completely unprotected. We therefore recommend that you protect
volumes so that they cannot be used without Empower. Volume file
partitions, such as those created with MultiDisk or HD Partition, cannot be
protected in this way; only SCSI partitions can be protected so they do not
mount without Empower. See the Files entry for information on these different types of partitions.

With the exception of its lack of full support for file partitions, Empower
provides complete, effective, and convenient security for Mac users. We
have been very impressed with it, and recommend it highly.

Miscellaneous Security Utilities

 Guard Dog, Guard Dog Plus   ⑤Ⓦ, ⑤⑤

These utilities are designed to prevent others from copying or moving files
on your Mac without authorization. This is particularly useful when a Mac
is going to be in a public or semipublic situation, because it prevents casual users from affecting your hard drive; they cannot delete files, move files
to the wrong folders, or steal software while Guard Dog is on duty. Guard
Dog does not, however, limit the use of or access to any files while they
reside on your Mac, and any file that can be opened can be transferred to
another disk with the SAVE AS... command.

You can use the Guard Dog cdev to specify whether desktop modifications
(file copying or moving) are to be disallowed completely or allowed only
when either the SHIFT, CAPS LOCK, or CONTROL key is pressed. Allowing desktop modifications only when one of these keys is pressed would probably
foil most casual attempts, since only someone familiar with Guard Dog

would think of pressing these keys in order to copy or move files. The Guard Dog Control Panel can be password-protected so that the Guard Dog's protection cannot be changed.

 ### Complete Delete, FileZero, FileZero INIT

Complete Delete and FileZero are simple utilities that allow you to select any file from a Standard File dialog box and delete that file entirely, resetting the sectors on the disk that hold the file to all zeros so the file data cannot be retrieved in any way. (Files deleted using the trash can or most DELETE commands are not really removed from the disk.) The File Zero INIT modifies your System Software so that all files deleted on the Mac, including temporary files automatically deleted by software applications, are entirely removed.

 ### Disk Express, Optimizer

Each of these disk-defragmenting utilities offers the option of erasing all unused sectors on your hard disk, making it impossible to retrieve data from them. These utilities "erase" sectors by overwriting them with a random pattern of 0s and 1s. You can have this done once or three times, depending on how secure you want to feel.

 ### LockOUT

LockOUT provides two types of protection to your Mac. First, the Lock-OUT init lets you add a password that must be entered each time your Mac is turned on or rebooted. Second, the LockOUT DA or Fkey darkens and locks your screen so that no one can see the files on your screen or use your Mac until the password is entered.

 # Sound

The Mac's ability to process sound has always been both impressive and underutilized. Since the introduction of the Mac II, several important steps have been taken toward improving the utilization of sound on the Mac. With the increasing standards in disk storage space, new sound-compression algorithms, and new applications for sound, chances are excellent that sound will continue to become a more integral part of Macintosh computing.

Sound is often used on the Mac as a user feedback element, making the user aware that some event has occurred. The beep sound that accompanies certain Alert dialog boxes is an example of this. Apple's System Software inherently provides only four different sounds, and just one of these can be selected as the "beep" sound used whenever the System software wants to make some noise. Any number of additional sounds can be added to the System Software sound palette (using one of the Font/DA Mover–like utilities described below), and utilities are available that allow you to configure many different System events so that they each trigger their own unique sound.

More and more frequently, however, sound is being used to actually communicate information, or significantly enhance the presentation of information. Existing sounds and voices can now be digitized and used on the Macintosh quite inexpensively. HyperCard stacks have been the first applications to take advantage of sound in this way, but upcoming applications will support voice mail, verbal annotation to text documents, and an increasing integration of sound in the application and System Software interface.

Sounds are stored in several different file formats on the Macintosh, or in one of two types of resource formats. Sound formats include the SoundEdit format, the Instrument format, and the Audio Interchange File Format (AIFF or Audio IFF), and the resource formats as designated by Apple are Format 1 and Format 2. (Format 1 is used by HyperCard, Format 2 is supported by all other file types.) Sounds are also distinguished by their **sampling rate**, which is the number of intervals per second that was used to capture the sound when it was digitized. Four sampling rates are common: 22, 11, 7, and 5 KHz. While larger sampling rates result in larger sound files, they also result in better sound quality. Sound files may also be compressed in some applications. Compressing a sound also reduces its quality; the more it is compressed the lower its quality will be.

Sound Utilities

SoundMaster

This init/cdev includes options that let you assign a different sound to each of the following Macintosh functions: Startup, Restart, Shutdown, Disk insert, Bad disk, Disk eject, Disk request, Beep, Key click, Return key, and Space bar. SoundMaster lets you use any sound stored in the SoundEdit format, provides control over the volume and sampling rate at which each sound is played, and displays the amount of RAM consumed by all of the sounds you are using.

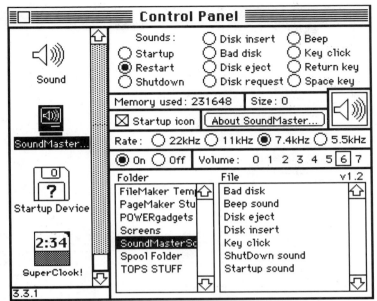

The SoundMaster cdev allows you to assign any installed sound to one of 11 different System Software events.

Of course, you do not have to assign sounds to every one of these events, and we recommend that you don't. While the right sound in the right place can be both fun and effective, hearing Curly say "Nyuk Nyuk" the eight hundreth time will make you want to poke him in the eye yourself.

SuperPlay, PlaySound DA   S︎W, F︎W
SuperPlay is a utility to test out sounds. It can open sound files or sound resources, and it allows you to set the sampling rate at which you want to hear a sound, and then play it. You can also have it play every sound in a folder. PlaySound DA, from the author of SoundMaster, is similar to SuperPlay, but only supports sounds in the SoundEdit format.

Sound Mover   ⬆️S︎W
This utility is fashioned after Apple's Font/DA Mover, allowing you to move sounds between sound files or install them into a System file. All sound formats are supported, and Sound Mover is even smart enough to convert between Format 1 and Format 2 when moving sounds in and out of Hyper-Card. Optionally, you can compress sounds as you move them. If you are going to use sounds on your Macintosh, you need this utility!

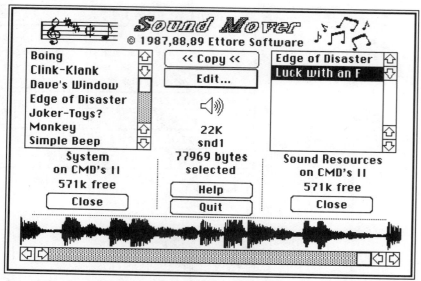

Sound Mover moves sounds just like Font/DA Mover moves fonts and DA's.

MasterJuggler

Sound suitcases can be opened in MasterJuggler, and using the HOTSOUNDS command, opened sounds, or those installed in the System file, can then be assigned to any one of nine different System events. The volume at which each sound will play can be set individually, but all sounds will play at 11 MHz, regardless of the rate at which they were originally sampled. Three utilities included with MasterJuggler help you to manage and manipulate your sounds.

Fkey/Sound Mover is a Font/DA Mover–like utility, provided along with MasterJuggler, that lets you move sounds between suitcases, add them to your System file, rename them, and renumber them. Only sounds in the sound resource format are seen by the Fkey/Sound Mover, but the accompanying Sound Converter utility can change files in another sound format into sound resources.

Sound Converter changes sounds in SoundEdit format files into sound resources. (These can then be used by the other sound utilities in MasterJuggler, and other utilities requiring sounds in resource format.) Before converting sounds you can play them using the Sound Converter, select the appropriate sampling rate (22, 11, 7.3, or 5.5 KHz), and select the format to which the sound is converted. (The MAC II option for Format 2 sounds, and the HYPERCARD option for Format 1 sounds.)

Resource Resolver allows you to resolve sound numbering conflicts among sounds in up to 12 different sound files. Each sound has a number, and if any two sounds are in the System file, or attached via MasterJuggler or a similar utility, there could be errors in playing the sound. After you open all sound files to be resolved, clicking the RESOLVE button causes Resource Resolver to look through all of the sounds and change any numbers that conflict.

 ### Suitcase II
Suitcase II can load sound resource files and play any of the sounds from the System file or any of its open suitcases. Suitcase cannot, however, assign sounds to System events or allow you to manipulate the sound's volume or sampling rate. It sort of makes you wonder why they bothered—maybe they just wanted the word *sound* in their advertisements.

 ### MacRecorder, SoundEdit, HyperSound
Farallon, which made its name inventing the PhoneNET AppleTalk cable replacement system, offers a sophisticated and yet easy-to-use system of recording and using sounds. It consists of the MacRecorder, which is a small hardware device that connects to your Mac's modem port, and two pieces of software, SoundEdit and HyperSound. Using MacRecorder and one of the software applications, you can digitize sounds (transfer them from their audible analog state into a digital state that the Macintosh can use) using either a microphone or a connected electronic device (such as a tape deck, CD player, or VCR).

Digitizing a sound is remarkably simple: First, you select the source of your sound. You can connect your electronic equipment to the MacRecorder via the RCA cables provided, connect an external microphone, or use the MacRecorder's built-in microphone. Next, you click an INPUT LEVEL button on the screen and play or create your sound and set the recording levels. Finally, you click the RECORD button and play or create your sound again.

Your digitized sound now appears (in a waveform when using SoundEdit) on screen. You can replay your sound, edit it in many ways (SoundEdit only), and then save it to disk. SoundEdit supports all file formats and resource formats, and HyperSound saves sounds in HyperCard format directly into HyperCard stacks. Sounds can be recorded at any sampling rate, and at compressions of 3:1, 4:1, 6:1, and 8:1.

SoundEdit's editing features are very impressive. Eleven editing features modify your sounds (Amplify, Backwards, Bender, Echo, Envelope, Filter, Flanger, Ping Pong, Smooth, Swap Channels, and Tempo), three features generate new sounds that you can append to your recorded sounds (Tone Generator, FM Synthesis, and Noise), and two features let you analyze the sounds you have recorded (Sonogram and Spectrogram). You can also cut, copy, and paste sound segments within or between sounds.

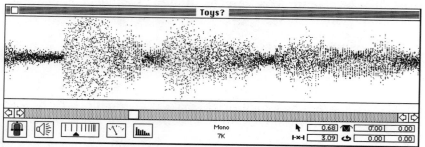

This SoundEdit window displays a portion of the file in which the Jack Nicholson (as the Joker) says "Where does he get those wonderful toys?" in the movie Batman. *The three bulging sections represent the words* get, those, *and* wonderful.

Sound, Vol Fkey

Apple's Sound cdev allows you to select any of the sounds currently installed in the System file for use as the default "beep," and to set the volume used for all of these beeps. Vol Fkey lets you quickly change the System beep volume.

Sounds

Virtually every utterance from *The Three Stooges*, every "Star Trek" episode (old, new, and the movies), most animal noises, key phrases from many rock songs, and many other audible traces of pop culture are available as sound files from user groups and major bulletin-board services. The only problem with all of these sounds is that there are so many, and most are so large, that you will have a difficult time deciding which to buy, download, and use.

Speech on the Mac

 **MacinTalk**

MacinTalk is an Apple System Software file, not included on the System Software disks, that must be in your System folder in order for most programs that speak on the Mac to work. MacinTalk actually provides the speech abilities of these programs, but it has no user interface or abilities on its own.

 SNSay

Using MacinTalk, SNSay lets you open any text file and have the Mac read it to you. You can read an entire file or only a selection from it, and you can control the speed and pitch of the speech. This works surprisingly well, and is one way to reduce the eye strain associated with staring at your monitor all day.

Talking Moose, Zippy

These two DA's, in conjunction with MacinTalk, appear at random intervals after they have been run, offering you words of wisdom. No real purpose is served, but it's true Macintosh computing at its finest.

 # Startup Disk

Literally, a **startup disk** is any disk capable of booting up the Mac—any disk with boot blocks, a System file, and a Finder. In practice, however, the term *startup disk* usually refers to the disk holding the System file and Finder *currently* being used by your Macintosh. This may or may not be the disk that booted your Macintosh, because the Mac is capable of "switch-launching," which means switching from one System file and Finder to another. (Note that the Mac cannot switch-launch when MultiFinder is running; so this whole discussion only applies to situations in which MultiFinder is not being used.)

Your "current" startup disk is the disk that appears in the upper-right corner of the Finder desktop. If the Macintosh is running (except when the disk with the question mark is flashing on the screen), it has a current startup disk. In the case of floppy disks, the current startup disk can be ejected, but if the Mac does not switch-launch to another System file and Finder, the Mac will be constantly asking you to insert the startup disk; this is because the Mac uses the System file almost continuously, and the Finder whenever another application is quit.

If you use more than one disk with a System file and Finder on it—usually in a complete System folder—the Mac will be constantly switch-launching, unless you separate the System file and Finder on disks to which you do not want the Mac to switch-launch. Switch-launching generally occurs when an application is run, as the Mac uses the System file and Finder on the disk containing the application, if available. Every time the Mac switches to another System file, your fonts and DA's will change, because these items are always provided by the current System file.

Many applications and utilities are shipped on disks containing System folders, but you should copy your software off of these master disks before you use it. There is really no reason to be using multiple disks containing System files and Finders. As documented in the System folder entry later in this section, you should not have more than one System file on a single disk or drive—although there are now utilities that can specify one of these as the one to use if you do—and you should usually not be working with multiple disks containing System files and Finders.

Although switch-launching usually happens accidentally, it can be invoked manually (as described below), or it can be requested by an application if its Always SwitchLaunch attribute is set, as explained in the Files entry earlier in this section.

Startup Disk Tips

◇ **Switch-launching is not permitted when using MultiFinder.** None of the above switch-launching methods will be successful when Multi-Finder is running.

◇ **Hold down the ⌘ and ⬉ keys while double-clicking on a Finder to manually switch-launch.** Normally, double-clicking on a Finder file yields the THE FILE "FINDER" COULD NOT BE OPENED Alert dialog. Holding down the COMMAND and OPTION keys while double-clicking on a Finder will launch the Finder and make the disk the Finder is on the current startup disk (as long as the Finder is accompanied by a System file). If the current startup disk (before the switch-launch) contains System

Software 5.0 or later, you cannot switch-launch to an older version of the System Software.

◇ **Hold down the ⌘ key when double-clicking on an application to switch-launch to the Finder and System file on the volume containing the application.** Of course, this will have no effect if the application disk has no System Software. Also it will not be successful if the current startup disk contains System Software 5.0 or later and the application disk contains an older version.

◇ **Use the Set Startup cdev to determine which SCSI drive will be used as the default startup disk.** The setting made in the Set Startup cdev is recorded in the Mac's parameter RAM, and when a startup disk is not present in any disk drive, the Mac then attempts to start up using the designated drive. If no drive has been designated with the Set Startup cdev, or if the drive specified cannot be used, the Mac will try to start up using each available SCSI device, in order of SCSI ID number.

◆ **Set the Always SwitchLaunch attribute to force switch-launching.** As described in the Files entry, many utilities allow you to set the Always SwitchLaunch attribute for a file. This makes any launch of the application act as if the COMMAND key had been pressed.

◆ **The Never SwitchLaunch attribute is not supported by System Software 6.0 or earlier.** Although some utilities that allow you to edit file attributes list a Never SwitchLaunch attribute, this is ignored by all versions of the System Software up to 6.0, and may not be recognized by later versions either.

◆ **Prevent switch-launching by separating the Finder from the System file.** If a volume contains both a Finder and a System file but they are not in the same folder, the Mac will not switch-launch to that volume. When you want to work on a Mac with a hard drive but use the System Software from a floppy disk, boot with the floppy disk, mount the hard drive (which may mount automatically), and then drag the Finder out of the System folder onto the desktop. The hard drive will then not become the startup disk even when running applications.

System Folder

A **System folder** is any Macintosh folder containing a System file and Finder. Although such folders are normally named "System folder," their name is not important; any legitimate folder name is acceptable. In fact, if the System file and Finder are on a disk or volume and not in any folder, the disk's **root directory** becomes the System folder.

There is nothing inherently special about a System folder until its System file and Finder are used by the Macintosh. The System folder containing the System file and Finder that are being used is called the **blessed folder**. Many applications and utilities, and the System Software itself, only look for certain files in the blessed folder, and many temporary files and preferences files are created and stored there.

The System folder must contain all inits that are to be loaded at startup, all cdevs to be accessed by the Control Panel, and all printer drivers and other types of drivers to be accessed by the Chooser. Downloadable PostScript fonts held in the System folder will be automatically downloaded to PostScript printers when required, although there are other ways to accomplish this automatic downloading, including the use of Suitcase II, MasterJuggler, or Set Paths. See the Files entry earlier in this section for more details.

Multiple System Folders

Generally speaking, you should not have more than one System folder on any disk or drive—i.e., there should not be two Finders or System files—because although one will be distinguished as the blessed folder, there is a good chance that the Macintosh will get "confused" and occasionally use an alternate System file, Finder, or System folder, resulting in unpredictable behavior and possibly even System crashes.

Many utilities and applications are sold on disks containing System folders, so if you drag-copy these disks onto your hard drive you can easily have multiple System folders unintentionally. When installing new software, never drag its System folders onto your hard drive; only drag the application file(s) and other files required by the application.

If you must have multiple copies of the System folder on a single drive (so you can occasionally run applications incompatible with the current System software, for example), there are two utilities that will allow you to specify one System folder as the blessed folder and help the Mac to avoid the others.

Blesser, System Switcher

If you keep more than one System folder on your hard disk, these utilities allow you to designate one as the folder that should be used to start up your Mac and provide the System file and Finder while your Mac is running.

System Software

System Software is the entire set of software provided by Apple to provide the Mac with its basic functions and utilities. A set of System Software disks is included with your Macintosh, and you can purchase more current copies of the System Software from your Apple dealer. System Software is also available, without charge, from user groups and on many bulletin boards (although the downloading time can cost more than if you went out and bought it from your dealer!).

As the core of the System Software, the System file and Finder are required in order for the Macintosh to operate. Along with software provided on the Macintosh ROM chips, these files provide the Macintosh with its operating system, as traditionally defined.

System Software 6.0

The current System Software as of this writing is version 6.0. System Software 6.0 has been upgraded twice, and the version number that you should be using is version 6.0.2, unless you have a Macintosh IIx, IIcx, or SE/30, in which case you must use version 6.0.3, which includes support for the FDHD disk drive (but no other changes from 6.0.2). Additional new versions of System Software 6.0 may appear when new Mac models are introduced.

System Tools Disk

The System Tools disk contains the Installer application, the Installer scripts, and the main System folder. As described below, Installer and its scripts are used to transfer the files needed by your Mac from the System folder of the System Tools disk to your startup disks.

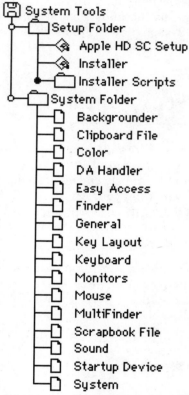

The System Tools disk provides the most basic Mac software, including the System file and Finder.

Printing Tools Disk

The Printing Tools disk contains all of Apple's printer drivers, plus the PrintMonitor application used by MultiFinder. These files are not installed by the Installer, so you must copy the files you need to your System folders manually. You do not need all of the printer drivers, only those corresponding to printers you will be using. You only need the PrintMonitor application if you will be using MultiFinder.

```
💾 Printing Tools
    ├─🗋 AppleTalk ImageWriter
    ├─🗋 ImageWriter
    ├─🗋 Laser Prep
    ├─🗋 LaserWriter
    ├─🗋 LaserWriter IISC
    ├─🗋 LQ AppleTalk ImageWriter
    ├─🗋 LQ ImageWriter
    └─🖎 PrintMonitor
```

The Printing Tools disk contains all of Apple's printer drivers plus the LaserPrep file and the PrintMonitor.

Utilities 1 Disk

Utilities 1 includes another copy of the System folder and the Installer application, and special Installer scripts that are to be used when you need to create smaller System folders (such as when creating floppy startup disks) or to install the AppleShare workstation files on your startup disks. This Installer is used exactly like the one on the System Tools disk, and files from the Printer Tools disk must be added to your new System folder manually after the Installer has been run. The Apple HD SC Setup utility is used to format Apple hard drives. Disk First Aid is a recovery tool that can repair damaged floppy disks and hard disks under some circumstances. HD Backup is a utility that helps you back up data from your hard drive to floppy disks. See the Disks and Drives entry earlier in this section for more information on Disk First Aid and HD Backup.

Utilities 2 Disk

Utilities 2 provides the Apple File Exchange program, the Font/DA Mover, and MacroMaker. See the Connectivity entry earlier in this section for information about the Apple File Exchange, the Desk Accessories and Fonts entries for information about the Font/DA Mover, and the Macros entry for more information about MacroMaker. CloseView is an init that allows visually impaired Macintosh users to magnify their screen display. Map is a cdev that adds a world map with coordinates and time zones to your Control Panel. To use either CloseView or Map, just copy it into your System folder and restart your Macintosh.

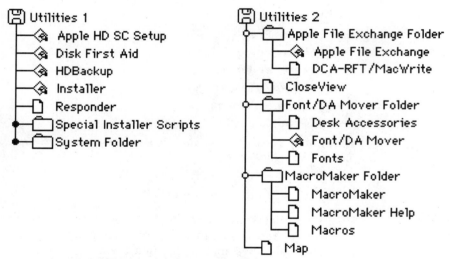

The Utilities disks contain Apple's Macintosh utilities.

Installing System Software

There are two ways to install or update the System Software used by your Mac. You can do it manually, copying the files you need from the distribution disks onto your hard disk or floppy boot disks, or you can run the Installer application provided with the System Software and let it perform the installation or upgrade for you.

You should use the Installer application in most cases, especially when installing System Software on a new hard drive or upgrading from one major System Software release to another. (Major upgrades are those in which the first digit of the version number changes. Maintenance upgrades add or change digits after the decimal point.) The Installer accompanying System Software 6.0 is especially important to use, because it writes new boot blocks to your startup disk, and these boot blocks are different than those used by older versions of the System Software. If you just drag-copy System Software 6.0 files onto any startup disk, its boot blocks will be incompatible with the System Software.

When you just need to add a few specific files from the original System Software disks to your System folder—perhaps files that were originally installed by the Installer but that you have deleted for one reason or another—you can feel comfortable in manually copying those files from the System Software disks. The Installer does not add files from the Printer Tools disk or from Utilities 1 or Utilities 2. If you need any files from these disks, you will have to drag-copy them yourself.

The Installer application has two main advantages: It only adds the files required for your particular Macintosh, and it saves the fonts and DA's that are installed in your present System file when upgrading so you don't have to find them all and reinstall them. Of course, there is a flip side of each of these "benefits." While the Installer only installs the files required by your Mac, Apple's list of required files adds to your System folder several files that you really do not need, so you may still wind up deleting some files that the Installer adds (like Easy Access or, in some cases, MultiFinder, PrintMonitor, and Backgrounder).

Simply drag-copying all the required files from the System Software disks to your hard drive (or floppy startup disks) will work just fine, and this technique is often used by those comfortable with "not following Apple's recommendations." Usually this is done when starting on a fresh disk, at which time the Installer does little more than copy the files anyway.

Time

It all started with the Alarm Clock DA. From these humble beginnings have arisen a multitude of time tellers, date keepers, and related utilities. The Mac keeps track of the time of day internally, using power from its internal battery when the Mac is shut down. If your Mac can no longer keep time, your battery needs to be changed; see the Computers entry in Section 3. If you cannot set the time on your clock, you may need to zap the Mac's parameter RAM by pressing SHIFT-COMMAND-OPTION while choosing the Control Panel DA. See the Control Panel entry earlier in this section for more information about zapping the parameter RAM.

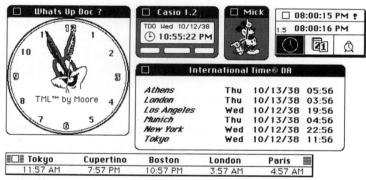

A wide *variety of clocks are available for the Macintosh.*

Time Utilities

Set Clock

This cdev uses your modem to call up the National Bureau of Standards and sets your Mac's internal clock, ensuring that your clock is extremely accurate.

Clock Adjust, Clock Synch

If you find that your Mac's clock runs a little slow or a little fast, the Clock Adjust init/cdev allows you to correct these problems by taking away or adding a few seconds to the Mac's clock each week. Clock Synch is a utility that will synchronize the times on all Macintoshes connected to your AppleTalk network.

Simon 🖲️

This cdev allows you to determine the default date and time format used by your Macintosh. You can specify American or European date formats, the format of the AM/PM (uppercase, lowercase, or mixed case), the appearance of seconds, and so forth. The time format you select is used by any inits that display the time on screen, and by any software or macros that print the system time or date.

 SuperClock 🖲️🖲️🖲️🖲️

The reigning favorite among timepieces, SuperClock adds the time to the upper-right corner of your menu bar. Via the SuperClock cdev controls, you designate the font and size used by the clock, set an alarm, and control other clock options.

   Clock, News Clock, Clock 4.2, oops Clock 🖲️, 🖲️, 🖲️, 🖲️

These clocks are applications designed for MultiFinder users. (Under MultiFinder you can run a clock application and leave it running while using other applications.) The Clock application displays a small digital clock and lets you select any font and type size for the digits. News Clock displays a rather large clock along with eight clocks displaying the time in eight major world cities. Clock 4.2 is fashioned after a clock radio, complete with an alarm and a radio that really works. The oops Clock application is a Dali-like timepiece that flashes the time over your entire screen.

 Elapse 🖲️

This application, also designed for MultiFinder, shows not only the current time, but also the time your Mac was started and the elapsed time since then. This must have been designed for some purpose, but we can't imagine what it was.

 Date Key 🖲️

Date Key is an Fkey that enters the current time or date (in a user-defined format) wherever the insertion point is located—just as though you had typed it in yourself.

Big Ben, Bugs Bunny, Mickey Mouse, 🖲️, 🖲️, 🖲️
GumbyClock, International Time, World Time, Watch 🖲️, 🖲️, 🖲️, 🖲️

These clocks take the form of DA's, providing the various graphics or features their names suggest.

Time Tips

◇ **The CUT and COPY commands work with the Apple Alarm Clock.** With the Alarm Clock DA open, selecting CUT or COPY from the EDIT menu transfers the time and date to the Clipboard, from which you can then paste them into any other application.

◇ **The Mac's internal clock begins to lose time when the Mac battery begins to run out.** See the Computers entry in Section 3 for information about your Mac's battery and how you can replace it.

◇ **The Mac will forget the time when the Mac is turned off if its battery is dead.** See the Computers entry in Section 3 for information about your Mac's battery and how you can replace it.

Viruses

Since March 2, 1988, when hundreds—some say hundreds of thousands but no one knows for sure—of Mac users turned on their computers to be greeted by a "Universal Message of Peace," viruses have been an important topic for Macintosh users. Viruses are small computer programs that replicate themselves by attaching to other computer programs, and then carry out whatever other mission they have; this could be as harmless as displaying a message or as harmful as erasing your hard drive.

The virus problem is especially acute on the Macintosh because so much public-domain and shareware software is transferred from one user to another via user groups and bulletin boards. Viruses can very quickly be distributed throughout the world if they attach themselves to a popular new file that gets posted on one of the national bulletin-board services.

Beyond the Peace virus, two other virus types have been prevalent in the Mac community: the Scores virus and various strains of the nVir virus. Unlike the rather simple Peace virus, each of these viruses makes many changes to resources in System files and applications, and can cause widespread problems ranging from frequent System crashes to unpredictable printing. Both of these virus types appeared relatively soon after the Peace virus, and almost no new Mac viruses appeared in the subsequent year.

Unfortunately, Scores and nVir have by no means been eliminated, and they still frequently appear in files that make their way around the world. Fortunately, the length of time that has elapsed since these viruses first appeared has allowed a number of antivirus programs to be written. In most cases, these programs can locate existing infections so that they can be prevented from spreading, or prevent infections from accessing your Mac in the first place.

Virus Utilities

Three different kinds of features are found in antivirus utilities. Some utilities simply check your files to see if they have been infected, while others also attempt to disinfect the files, removing the virus and returning the file to its original state. And some utilities attempt to prevent viruses from infecting your files by monitoring virus-like activities, and informing you when they occur so you can take appropriate action, if necessary.

Whenever you find that one of your files is infected, your best course of action is to delete the file and replace it with one that is known to be uninfected; virus repair is only recommended for situations where no uninfected copies of the programs are available. If you must rely on virus repair, recheck your disks and files frequently, as the virus may resurface.

 AGAR
AGAR is a tiny application that is intended to serve as sort of a sacrifice to the virus gods. You copy AGAR to your drive, and occasionally check its resources with ResEdit to see if they have changed. (A list of how the resources will look if uninfected is provided.) If they have, you may have been attacked by a virus. AGAR does nothing to prevent or repair viruses; it just provides one way of determining if they have infected your drive.

 AntiPan
This utility searches for nVir and Hpat (an nVir clone virus) infections, and attempts to eradicate them when they are found.

 AntiVirus
This utility will remove nVir infections from your System files and applications, and install an "immune system" that will prevent nVir infections from occurring.

Ferret　　　　　　　　　　　　　　　　　　　　　　　　　F W

This utility searches your files for signs of the Scores virus. Infected files are flagged, and you have the option of attempting to ignore, repair, or delete them.

Fever　　　　　　　　　　　　　　　　　　　　　　　　　F W

This utility is much like AGAR; you copy it to your disks and wait to see if it becomes infected. If it does, Fever can do nothing but inform you that an infection has occurred. Unlike AGAR, however, Fever does not require that you use ResEdit; when you run Fever it checks itself and informs you if an infection has occurred.

GateKeeper　　　　　　　　　　　　　　　　　　　　　　F W

This cdev allows you to specify, for each application file on your hard disk, whether the file's resource or data fork can be modified. Three different types of modifications can be independently allowed or prevented: modifications by the application itself, modifications by the System file, and modifications by other files.

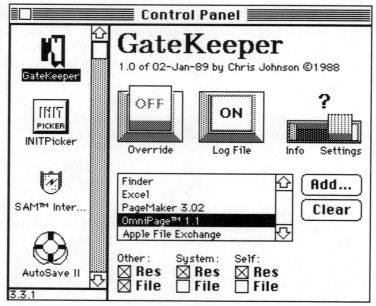

GateKeeper lets you specify what modifications any application file can be subject to.

Interferon   ⑤Ⓦ

Interferon can search your files for the Scores, nVir, and Sneak viruses. If any infected files are found, you are given the option of deleting the files from your disks or drives.

KillScores   ⒻⓌ

KillScores searches all the files on a disk, and attempts to repair files found to be infected with the Scores virus.

N.O.M.A.D   ⒻⓌ

This utility searches disks for the nVir virus, and removes nVir resources if they are found.

Nvir Assisin   ⒻⓌ

Like N.O.M.A.D, this utility searches disks for the nVir virus, and removes the virus if it is found.

Repair   ⒻⓌ

This utility, written by Suitcase II programmer Steve Brecher, removes nVir viruses from application files that are infected. Repair does not, however, search for the infected files; you must use another utility, such as Apple's VirusRx to first determine which files are infected.

RWatcher   ⒻⓌ

RWatcher is designed to be the programmer's antivirus utility. It operates much like Vaccine, watching for certain resource modifications to be attempted, and then preventing them from occurring. The list of resource modifications RWatcher keeps track of can be modified using ResEdit. By default, it looks for the most common Scores and nVir modifications.

SAM   🔑⑤⑤

Following their tremendous success with the Symantec Utilities, Symantec released the Symantec AntiVirus for the Macintosh package (SAM). SAM offers virus detection, elimination, and prevention features, and we find it extremely comprehensive and easy to use. We can't really attest to its effectiveness, since we haven't encountered any viruses (thankfully!), but we have not heard any negative reports to suggest that SAM isn't completely effective.

SAM consists of two files, the SAM Intercept init, which monitors your System and prevent virus infection, and the SAM Virus Clinic, which is an application that checks for existing virus infections, and eliminates them if they are found. Once the SAM Intercept init is being used, you can configure a number of interesting antivirus features. First, you decide how thorough you want SAM to be in monitoring the changes made to your files. You can select either Basic, Standard, Advanced, or Custom protection. The differences between these are the number of different suspicious activities that SAM will warn you about. There are ten different file modifications that SAM can watch for, although all of these are not commonly in use by currently known viruses.

The SAM cdev allows you to configure most aspects of SAM's operation.

When SAM encounters a type of file modification that it is looking out for, a dialog box is presented that clearly informs you of the action that is about to occur, and you can either allow it, deny permission for the modification to take place, or tell SAM that this is an acceptable modification and it should remember it and not flag this particular modification in the future. You can also instruct SAM to automatically scan any floppy disk that is inserted for virus infections, or to do so only when a specific key combination is held down as a disk is inserted. Although SAM is a commercial product in competition with many freeware and inexpensive shareware products, we think that its clean interface, well-written documentation, and comprehensive protection make it a utility worth owning.

Symantec Utilities Guardian & Shield init

Although the advertising and documentation of the Symantec Utilities suggests that some type of virus protection is provided by these products, the only type of activity that these prevent is attacks on your disk directories, and no current Mac virus attempts this kind of attack. We like the Symantec Utilities for their disk-repair functions, but do not be fooled into thinking that using them provides you with any virus protection.

Vaccine

Vaccine, written by Don Brown of CE Software, was the first antivirus utility to appear for the Macintosh. Vaccine is an init that watches your drive and files for certain types of suspect modifications to application resources. When one of these modifications occurs, Vaccine steps in and asks you for permission to allow the resource modification to occur.

Virus Detective

This DA searches your drives for files infected with nVir, Hpat, Scores, or INIT29 viruses. If viruses are found, you may attempt repair, or delete the infected file.

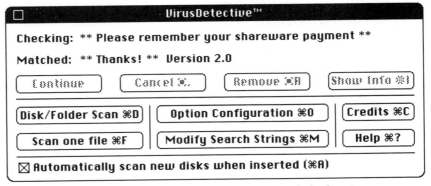

The Virus Detective DA is a quick way to scan your disks for viruses.

Virus Rx

Apple's Virus Rx is a utility that scans your disks and presents you with a list of files that may be infected. Because Virus Rx just looks for files that have irregularities, it often lists files that are not infected, so if some of your files are reported to be infected you might want to check them with another utility, or attempt to repair them, before opting to delete them. Virus Rx offers no virus-repair features.

Section Two

Applications

# Drawing Software

Drawing applications are one of the best selling and most popular types of software on the Macintosh. This should come as no surprise, since the Mac was the first personal computer with an interface composed of real-world graphic images, designed to be more accessible than the abstract and often obscure textual environment offered by existing PCs. The Mac's first software, MacPaint, was a graphics package. Some of the earliest third-party applications—ThunderScan, VideoWorks, Mac3D, and Paint Cutter (now gone the way of the archaeopteryx)—were similarly designed for electronic artistry.

But look a little closer and you'll see the real reason for the Mac's graphic advantage: its use of easily recognizable tools, the exact stuff with which artists create artwork in a traditional environment. We don't mean to imply that other professions don't employ tools as well. Secretaries use typewriters, accountants use ledger books, and your boss probably uses a whip; but the sheer quantity of an artist's tools distinguishes this profession from most others. And the Mac is the reigning king of tool- and icon-based computing.

Of Objects and Bit Maps

There are two graphic environments on the Mac: painting and drawing.

Why Paintings Are Jagged

In a painting application, such as MacPaint, FullPaint, or even PixelPaint, you draw by specifying the appearance of tiny dots called **pixels** on your computer screen. These pixels are similar to the dots that transmit images on your television. All Macintosh-compatible monitors are equipped with 72 pixels per linear inch, or 5,184 pixels per square inch (72×72). As you draw across the page with the pencil tool in a monochrome application like MacPaint, you turn these pixels on and off, making them black or leaving them transparent. This is what is meant by the term **bit map**. In a very simplified sense, you are mapping out bits, the smallest particles of your computer's memory, to be on or off.

Painted lines and text appear jagged when printed because the printer simply prints the dots as they appear on your screen. Despite the fact that you may own a laser printer with a resolution of 300 dots per inch, your painting software is telling it to create images in $\frac{1}{72}$-inch chunks. The resolution of bit-mapped artwork is fixed, so that whether you print to an ImageWriter or a Linotronic typesetter, you get the same jagged results.

For exceptions to this rule, see the Painting Software entry.

Why Drawings Are Smooth

Drawings rely on an entirely different system for relaying graphic information to a printer. Instead of defining a graphic by examining its smallest particles—rather like describing a beach by recounting grains of sand—drawing software attacks your artwork object by object: an umbrella here, a beachcomber there, a large rock farther on down. For this reason, an application such as MacDraw is known as *object-oriented* software.

Each object is defined as a series of lines and shapes. Various mathematical formulae describe where a line starts, where it stops, and what it does in the meantime. Your software communicates these math problems to the printer, and your printer figures out all the answers on its own. For this reason, the resolution of drawn artwork is entirely printer-dependent, producing very smooth lines on high-resolution typesetters.

In addition, this math requires much less storage room than the bit-mapped pixels of a painting. A typical color drawing produced by Aldus Free-Hand, for example, consumes about 16K. That's about the size of a typical 3-square-inch color painting.

The Difficulties of Drawing

So objects are printed smoothly and consume less memory. But in return, your printer is forced to work harder to render the object. For this reason, drawings often require a less spontaneous approach than paintings.

Drawing Technicalities 1

*Paintings are memory hogs
and there's nothing you can do about it*

One of the prime advantages of drawing over painting is the innate efficiency of the drawing environment. For every line or shape that you create in a drawing application, an additional mathematical description is added to your file. This means the size of your file is determined by the quantity and complexity of the elements you draw. Makes sense, right? But in a painting application, you largely predetermine the size of your document before you even select a tool. This is because each pixel in a painting theoretically consumes the same amount of storage space whether you draw on it or not. If your painting is composed of black and white dots only, each dot is stored as a single bit of information (0 or 1, off or on). For this reason, MacPaint files never get very big. Colored paintings may be extremely large, however, for each pixel may be one of 256 colors (or the full 16 million if you are privileged enough to own a 32-bit monitor). Since 8 bits are required to express each of 256 colors ($2^8=256$), and 8 bits also make up one byte, each dot in a full-color painting may require as much as one byte of storage. At a 72-dpi resolution, 1 square inch contains 5,184 pixels, requiring 5K of storage space. A standard 8.5-by-11-inch color painting can take up more than 480K of disk space, which means you also need that extra 480K in your computer's RAM (in excess of the 1000K or more needed to run a high-end painting application) to open the artwork. On a 32-bit monitor, the same low-resolution painting could consume 1,940K.

Conclusion: Anybody who frequently engages in color painting needs at least 4 megabytes of RAM. For those who prefer to *draw* in color, however, 2Mb will suffice.

Drawing Technicalities 2

Pressing the limitations of your printer
with the demands of your drawing software

A drawing application will allow you to create very complicated lines and shapes, but your printer may not always allow you to print them. This is due to the way in which your printer interprets curves. Suppose you are printing a circle. This may seem simple: Just say $x^2+y^2=r^2$ (the mathematical formula for a circle) and let 'er rip. Unfortunately, your printer thinks only in terms of straight lines. When presented with a curve, its PostScript interpreter has to plot out hundreds of tiny straight lines to create the most accurate possible rendering. So instead of drawing a circle, your printer creates a many-sided polygon whose exact number of sides is determined by the size of the circle and a device-dependent variable known as **flatness**. The default flatness for a typical laser printer is 1.0 device pixel, or $\frac{1}{300}$ inch. This means that the center of any tiny side of our polygon rendering will be at most $\frac{1}{300}$ inch from the farthest x,y coordinate of the actual mathematical circle.

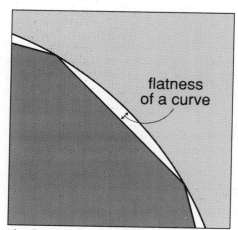

The flatness of a curve is the farthest that a polygon approximation of a curve may deviate from its mathematical model.

If the number of tiny straight lines required to accurately render a curve exceeds your printer's built-in "path" limit, you will be presented with a "limitcheck" error, and the print job will be canceled. The "path" limit for the original LaserWriter interpreter is 1500, seemingly enough straight lines to imitate even the most complex of curves. But think about the curves you draw in real life. Think of your signature, for example, as one complex curve, taxing the limit of the most advanced PostScript interpreter. Such a curve might have to be broken up into several segments—a couple of letters here, a couple more there.

Conclusion: If you encounter a "limitcheck" error, split your most complicated line or shape into two parts and try again. Other applications allow you to alter the flatness of a selected path. Higher flatness values (up to 100) decrease the number of sides attributed to a polygon.

Printing a Drawing

When you print a painting, your software tells the printer the size and color of each dot. There is nothing to figure out, so your printer just does what it's told. (Ah, machines … they're so obedient.) But when outputting a drawing, your printer becomes a math processor, evaluating the curvature of lines, calculating the frequency of halftones, and so on.

But so what? Are the laborings of your printer another thing to feel guilty about? Well no, but the fact that so much interpretive power is left to your printer means that your software may ask for things that your printer just can't deliver. For example, a typical LaserWriter is equipped with a PostScript interpreter, which allows it to communicate with your Mac. This interpreter imposes specific limits on the amount of information that the printer may receive. Your software, however, is capable of generating information surpassing these limits. It's as if you were to get in a taxicab in New York and ask the driver to take you to Paris. He or she might respond, "Nope, can't do that. Not enough gas, and there's all that water to think about. But I can take you across town." Your software can ask for whatever it wants, but your printer may say no.

The way your printer tells you that you are exceeding its limits is by producing a "limitcheck" error. This generally means that one or more of the lines in your drawing is too complicated and must be split into smaller lines. For more information on printer limits, see Drawing Technicalities 2.

Engineering a Drawing

So not only do drawings require more processing on the part of your printer, they frequently require additional thought on the part of the user. Lines and shapes have to be layered on top of one another like girders in a building. Because drawing is partially an architectural experience, the best users of drawing software are part artist and part engineer. One might imagine that M. C. Escher would have loved to draw; but van Gogh would have had more success with the pure color experience of PixelPaint. Suffice it to say that both environments are not for all artists.

Image-Saving Formats

In the paragraphs that follow, we examine some popular drawing applications and how they allow you to manipulate an object-oriented graphic. To the right of each program name is a list of the *image-saving formats* that the program supports. These are formats that allow a document to be imported into another application, such as a word processor or a page-layout program. These formats may include one or more of the following:

- **PICT**. This is the original image-swapping file format developed by Apple for the purpose of transferring object-oriented pictures from one application to another. Unfortunately, swapping PICT graphics can be somewhat problematic, since not all applications that support PICT use the same PICT standardization. For example, a file saved in MacDraw PICT may look quite different when opened in FreeHand. PICT only supports eight colors, but recently a less limited PICT format known as PICT2 has been developed that supports as many colors as your monitor will allow. While this format seems open to less varied interpretations, it is also less widely supported.

- **EPSF** (Encapsulated PostScript format). The beauty of EPSF is that it may be introduced into any other application that supports both PostScript (which is just about every application on the Mac) and PICT. Developed by Altsys Corporation (the programmers of Free-Hand) in cooperation with Aldus and Adobe Systems, EPSF includes a PICT screen representation of a graphic accompanied by a pure

PostScript-language definition that is downloaded directly to your output device during printing. The result is that regardless of how a receiving application interprets the PICT portion of an EPSF graphic, the graphic will be printed perfectly, since the PostScript definition is not open to interpretation. EPSF supports gray values and colors, though they will not be displayed correctly on a color monitor since the screen representation is PICT.

- **PNTG** (MacPaint format). The most common and yet most limited image-swapping format, the PNTG format stores bit-mapped information only. MacPaint files are exclusively monochrome, no larger than 8 inches by 10 inches (vertically oriented), and locked into a resolution of 72 dpi (5,184 pixels per square inch). Do not save objects in this format if you wish them to be printed smoothly!

- **TIFF** (Tagged-Image File Format). Like the MacPaint format, TIFF is an exclusively bit-mapped format. But unlike MacPaint, it is almost entirely unrestricted. TIFF was developed by Aldus Corporation in an attempt to standardize sampled images created by scanning devices. Unfortunately, while widely accepted, TIFF is not completely standardized; the format exists in different forms on the Mac and PC, and even then, some programs support monochrome TIFF only, others support TIFF with 16 evenly incremented gray values, and just a handful support color TIFF.

- **SCRN** (startup screen). This variation on the PICT format allows a document to be displayed in place of the "Welcome to Macintosh" screen when you start up your Mac. This format is discussed in more depth in the Painting Software entry.

- **Native formats.** Some applications use their own image-saving formats for storing graphics that you don't intend to import into another application. We will list such unique formats along with the word *native* in parentheses.

MacDraw Opens Up the Object-Orient

 MacDraw II, Version 1.1   DRWG (native), PICT
The prototypical and most popular drawing program on the Macintosh is MacDraw. Unfortunately, one of Apple's first Macintosh software offerings has, in the hands of Claris, evolved more notably in the directions of

word handling and slide presentation than in developing its overall graphic potential. MacDraw is still very useful for creating object-oriented images using readily identifiable tools and commands, but it has lagged behind applications like Illustrator and FreeHand in the features department.

For people who require a structured drawing environment, MacDraw has always been a dependable product, however rudimentary. MacDraw II builds on this tradition by adding surprisingly sophisticated ruler control. You may select from six preexisting rulers, or create and store your own. You may also specify your own drawing scales, so that an inch on your ruler may represent 3.5 feet, eliminating the need for calculating the difference between an object in real life and its size in an architectural rendering or on a map. While such a feature doesn't even begin to compare to the kind of object control available in a real CAD (computer-aided design) package, MacDraw may prove an adequate or even optimal application for users with basic requirements.

However, if you're looking for naturalistic drawing capabilities, MacDraw may disappoint you. The primary problem is that from the very beginning, MacDraw established a regrettable precedent for object handling. By providing a set of easily identifiable drawing tools, the application makes simple the creation of geometric objects like ellipses, rectangles, and polygons. However, MacDraw can be clumsy when it comes to creating an irregular curve—any curve that cannot be defined as an arc with a constant center point and radius. And since most curves in the real world are irregular, this presents something of a problem.

Bézier Curves: The Better Model

There are two basic drawing models: the *Bézier curve model,* used by applications such as Adobe Illustrator, Aldus FreeHand, and even Altsys's Fontographer (a typeface-creation program); and the *smooth polygon model,* used by MacDraw, Canvas, SuperPaint, and others.

The Bézier curve model allows for zero, one, or two levers to be associated with each point in a line. These levers are called **Bézier control handles**. Each handle may be moved in relation to a point, bending and tugging at a curved segment between two points like a piece of elastic taffy.

The Bézier curve model was designed as an integral part of the PostScript language. See Drawing Technicalities 3 for more details.

Drawing Technicalities 3

*The inner workings of
the Bézier curve model*

The French mathematician Pierre Bézier determined that one can define irregular curves by inventing two control handles (x_1,y_1 and x_2,y_2) for every fixed point (x,y) in a curve. These handles act as levers; as a curve passes from one point to another, it is magnetically attracted to the control handles. One handle instructs the curve in how to exit a point; the other instructs the curve in how to enter the following point. (For exact mathematical equations used to describe the path of a Bézier curve, see *Post-Script Language Reference Manual* by Adobe Systems Incorporated, Addison-Wesley, 1985.) In the late 1970s, John Warnock and Martin Newell implemented Bézier's curve theorems as part of their "JaM" applied arts language, providing the basis for Adobe's PostScript, and explaining PostScript's unique ability to describe almost anything you can draw by hand.

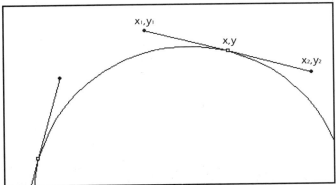

Bézier control handles pull at the segments entering and exiting a point as if the segments were made of taffy.

Conclusion: The Bézier curve model provides two handles per curved segment in addition to the fixed points through which each curve must pass. This combination of fixed points and lever-like handles allows for precise control over the most minute alterations in curvature. The smooth polygon model offers less control and is therefore less efficient.

Smooth Polygons: MacDraw's Model

MacDraw was created back in the days before Apple had licensed Post-Script as the official page-definition language for its high-resolution Laser-Writer (though the days of strictly PostScript printers from Apple are now drawing to an end). The program instead relies on a primitive curve routine, in which any curved line begins as a polygon. When the polygon is smoothed, the corners of the line are rounded so that they approach each point in the polygon without really touching. In a sense, you can think of a smoothed polygon as a curved line with an unlimited number of Bézier control handles but only two fixed points, one at the line's beginning and one at its end.

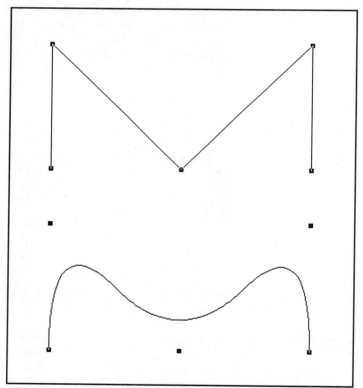

The two paths above show a polygon before and after smoothing. Notice that the curves of the smoothed polygon never touch the points.

The problem with this drawing model is twofold. First, you are allowed less control over individual curves. Curves don't start and end at specific points; rather, they glide in the general direction of points. The only way to acquire as much control as is granted by the Bézier curve model is to build each curved line in an illustration as a series of small, four-point polygons (a beginning point, an endpoint, and two intermediate Bézier control handles). This is an extremely cumbersome alternative.

Second, since a smoothed line only touches a point if it's an endpoint, it is difficult to create corners in the outline of a curving object. For example, if you're drawing a person smiling, how do you draw his or her mouth so it curves in the middle and meets to form a corner at each side? You could draw the mouth as two lines, one for the top lip and one for the bottom, but then you'd have a problem lining up the endpoints so there aren't any noticeable gaps. See the last tip in the following section for a single-line solution to this problem.

Ten Hottest MacDraw Tips

Despite MacDraw's questionable treatment of curves, it sports a straightforward interface, capable of producing high-quality output without requiring you to spend an inordinate amount of time fiddling with complex image-creation tools and commands. A handful of poor man's presentation features are also included, and MacDraw II 1.1 is the only application in this section that boasts a spell-checker.

The following are some tips designed to help you make more effective use of MacDraw. (Tips marked with † work only for MacDraw II.)

◇ **Using the same tool twice.** When selecting a tool, double-click the icon if you wish it to remain selected after drawing. The icon will appear reversed instead of dimmed.† (Press the COMMAND key to access the last tool selected in MacDraw 1.9.5 or earlier.)

◇ **Line patterns.** You may fill a line or the outline of a shape with a pattern by pressing the OPTION key and clicking on the pattern while the element is selected. This also works for coloring text, as long as the selected pattern is a solid color.†

◇ **Paste it where you want it.** To determine the placement of pasted images, click on the page before pasting. The location where you click will determine the center of the Clipboard contents. Clicking also determines the center of a change in the view size.

◇ **Editing the Scrapbook.** MacDraw may be used to edit any image saved to the Scrapbook, regardless of where it originated. Text saved to the Scrapbook may be edited, even if it was saved with other graphic elements.

◇ **Choosing a view.** Name the most common view sizes you use by choosing the SET VIEW command. View names are listed at the bottom of the LAYOUT menu and may be accessed from the keyboard (COMMAND-1, COMMAND-2, etc.). You can save this document as "Stationery" and use it to create other images.[†]

◇ **Selective printing.** MacDraw always prints all layers up to and including the current layer. If you only want to print one layer, send that layer to the bottom, go down to it, and print.[†]

◇ **Drawing cylinders.** If you want to draw a cylindrical object like a pipe, column, or can, select the "Round ends" option in the ROUND CORNERS dialog box. Then draw the object with the round-corner tool.[†]

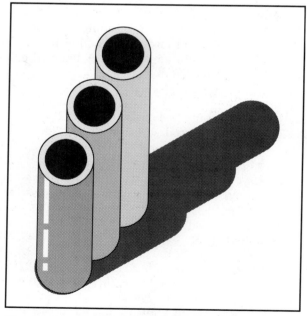

You can create cylindrical objects like these smokestacks by selecting "Round ends" in the ROUND CORNERS dialog box.

MacDraw Quick Reference (1 of 3)

Toolbox

▲	Arrow	▲ to select element so it may be manipulated, ⋯▲ to move
A	Type	▲ to set origin for text block, ⋯▲ across type to edit
＼	Line	⋯▲ to draw straight line
□	Rectangle	⋯▲ to draw rectangle
◯	Round corner	⋯▲ to draw rectangle with rounded corners
◯	Oval	⋯▲ to draw ellipse
＼	Arc	⋯▲ to draw quarter ellipse in clockwise direction
∿	Freeform	⋯▲ to draw smoothed polygon
◁	Polygon	▲ to create corners for straight-sided polygon
▱	Note*	▲ to determine placement of stick-on note, ⋯▲ across type to edit

> * *Not available in MacDraw 1.9.5 or earlier*

Menus

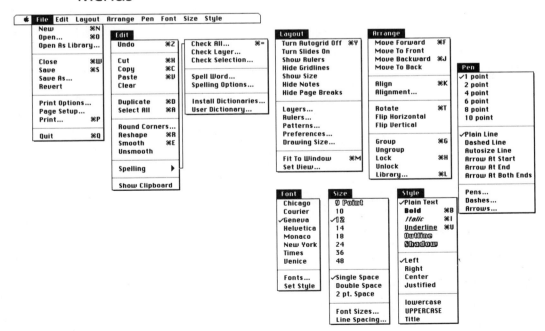

MacDraw Quick Reference (2 of 3)

Keyboard Equivalents

Access last tool used* .... ⌘␣ or ⌥⌃

Add point to polygon* .... ▸ *during reshape*

Bold text .... ⌘B

Change default setting* .... ⌘ *choose command*

Change rulers* .... ⌥▸ *ruler number box*

Check all spelling* .... ⌘=

Check spelling of selection* .... ⌘⇧=

Circle, create .... ⇧···▸ *w/oval tool*

Clear element .... ⌫

Close document* .... ⌘W

Copy element .... ⌘C

Current view size/100%, toggle* .... ⌘⇧M

Cut element .... ⌘X

Delete point from polygon* .. ⌥▸ *during reshape*

Demagnify view size .... ⌘← or ⌘L[†]

Down one layer/previous slide* .... ⌘↓

Duplicate element .... ⌘D

Fit to window view size* .... ⌘M

Group elements .... ⌘G

Help* .... ⌘/ or HELP

Italic text .... ⌘I

Lock element* .... ⌘H

Magnify view size .... ⌘→ or ⌘M[†]

Move backward* .... ⌘J

Move forward* .... ⌘F

Move object 45° .... ⇧···▸ *w/arrow*

Move to back .... ⌘⇧J or ⌘J[†]

Move to front .... ⌘⇧F or ⌘F[†]

Move window to back* .... ⌘⇧W

New document, create .... ⌘N

New layer or slide, create* .... ⌘⇧N

Nonsmoothing corner* .... ⌥▸▸ *w/polygon tool*

Open as library* .... ⌘⇧O

Open existing document .... ⌘O

  * *Available only in MacDraw II*

  † *Exclusively applicable to MacDraw 1.9.5 or earlier*

⌘	command	⇥	tab	⌫	delete	␣	space bar
⇧	shift	↵	return	⌦	fwd. delete	F1	function key
⌥	option	⌃	enter	▦	keypad key	▸	mouse click
⌃	control	⌫	escape	▦⌫	clear	···▸	mouse drag

MacDraw Quick Reference (3 of 3)

Keyboard Equivalents (Cont.)

Page setup* .... ⌘⇧P

Paste element .... ⌘V

Perpendicular line, create .... ⇧⌗⌖ʳ ʷ/ *line tool*

Preferences dialog, access* .... ⌖ʳ⌖ʳ *center icon*

Print document* .... ⌘P

Print one copy* .... ⌘⌦P

Quit MacDraw .... ⌘Q

Rescale when pasting* .... ⌘⇧V

Reshape polygon .... ⌘R

Rewrap type .... ⌗⌖ʳ *handle* ʷ/ *arrow*

Rotate element 45°* .... ⇧⌗⌖ʳ *during rotation*

RULERS dialog, access* .... ⌖ʳ⌖ʳ *on ruler*

Save as different name or location .... ⌘⇧S

Save drawing .... ⌘S

Scale object .... ⌗⌖ʳ *handle* ʷ/ *arrow*

Select all elements in document ...... ⌘⇧A *or* ⌘A⁺

Select all elements on active layer* .... ⌘A

Select element on other layer* .... ⌦⌖ʳ ʷ/ *arrow*

Select line pattern .... ⌦⌖ʳ *pattern icon*

Select tool permanently* .... ⌖ʳ⌖ʳ *tool icon*

Smooth polygon* .... ⌘E

Square, create .... ⇧⌗⌖ʳ ʷ/ *rectangle tool*

Switch to custom view number [#] .... ⌘[#]

Turn autogrid on/off* .... ⌘Y

Underline text .... ⌘U

Undo/redo last operation .... ⌘Z

Ungroup elements .... ⌘⇧G *or* ⌘H⁺

Unlock element* .... ⌘⇧H

Unsmooth polygon* .... ⌘⇧E

Up one layer/next slide* .... ⌘↑

View element while transforming .... ⌘⌗⌖ʳ

Accurate for MacDraw II, version 1.1

◇ **Creating many-sided lines.** To prevent a polygon from closing when creating points close to the first point, press the OPTION key.

◆ **Creating pie charts.** To create a pie chart, draw an arc with the arc tool and choose the RESHAPE command. The current pattern will fill the arc as though a slice of pie has been taken from it.

◆ **Sharp corners in a smoothed polygon.** For sharp corners in a smoothed shape or line, overlap one point onto its neighbor. In a smooth polygon, two coincident points specify a corner. To make two points coincident while creating a shape, option-double-click with the polygon tool.

The Cult of MacDraw

MacDraw established the first precedent for high-resolution graphics applications, and naturally, many graphics packages followed suit. These applications tend to fall into one of two categories: those that built upon MacDraw's list of drawing features, and those that combined drawing and painting capabilities in a single program. We will discuss the features-oriented applications first.

 Drawing Table, Version 1.0   APBL (native), DTEF (project), PICT
One of the most recent entries into the arena of drawing software is Brøderbund's Drawing Table. The program builds only slightly upon MacDraw's features, and it's missing the extensive view sizes and layering control of its popular competitor. The few additional features that do exist include binding text to a path, the ability to determine the origin point of a transformation, and control over importing specific portions of bit-mapped images. You may also save two or more documents as a *project*, so that multiple files may be linked together if they are used frequently in tandem. But Drawing Table's greatest feature is its price, less than half that of MacDraw—in fact, less than any other drawing program except DeskDraw.

 Cricket Draw, Version 1.1.1   CDRW (native), PICT, EPSF, PNTG
Another application that builds on MacDraw's features is Cricket Draw, which also happens to be the earliest special-effects drawing program, preceding Adobe Illustrator by several months. Unfortunately, Cricket Draw has never worked as well as we would like. In the days when 512K of RAM was the standard, Cricket Draw really needed a megabyte. In return for

crashing your machine every 10 or 12 minutes, however, Cricket was able to deliver some state-of-the-art transformations. You could slant any object, rotate by single-degree increments, or even create flashy fountains where the interior of a shape might fade from black to white through a series of gray values.

But putting history aside, Cricket Draw has fallen far behind the high-end capabilities of Illustrator and Aldus FreeHand, the reigning monarchs of the drawing environment. While Illustrator and FreeHand offer fully functional Bézier drawing tools, Cricket's Bézier tool draws a single isolated curve at a time. And we dare anyone to tell us a real purpose for the grate and sunburst tools. Even for those who buy into using the tools to build a grid for spiraling text, it seems to us that an automated spiraling-text feature would have served the purpose better and required half the effort.

These days, Cricket Draw distinguishes itself only in that you may bind text to a path and create automated fountains. However, FreeHand provides all these features, and in a much better format. Cricket Draw is better and cheaper than MacDraw II, but it doesn't keep up with the big guys.

Drawing DA's

A company entering the drawing arena these days would be hard-pressed to stand very long in Illustrator's or FreeHand's shoes. So rather than trying to wage a features battle, a successful drawing application must offer convenience. Examples of such convenience applications include Zedcor's DeskDraw and Deneba's Canvas, both of which are available as desk accessories so that they can run in conjunction with other applications without the aid of MultiFinder.

 DeskDraw, Version 1.3 PICT

With the notable exception of color control and presentation features, DeskDraw offers almost every feature available to MacDraw users. Some operations, like rotating, are even handled better in DeskDraw. Also, DeskDraw is the only application we know of that allows you to save a document with different PICT standardizations. You may save a graphic in a format specifically compatible with MacDraw PICT, MacDraw II PICT, SuperPaint PICT, or Canvas PICT. We haven't experimented with how well each of these formats works with its intended application, but this seems a valiant attempt on DeskDraw's part to bridge some of the inconsistencies inherent in the PICT format.

Otherwise, DeskPaint is especially useful for creating spur-of-the-moment figures for documents while simultaneously running a page-layout program. And for the very reasonable price of $129—we've seen it for as low as $69—you also receive DeskPaint, a painting DA discussed in the Painting Software entry.

 Canvas, Version 2.0   DRW2 (native), PICT, PNTG, TIFF
If you have 2 megabytes of RAM and enough cash (or friends), we recommend Canvas over DeskDraw. In fact, Canvas is one of our all-time favorite applications. Canvas is available in both application and DA form. And while the DA is clearly missing some of the features of its stand-alone counterpart, both offer features beyond those of MacDraw, including the most view sizes of any program, culminating at a 3200 percent magnification. There is even a fair attempt at Bézier point handling, although creating corners in a curving line remains an awkward experience. And this is absolutely amazing: Canvas will often prompt you to save a document during a System error! The document is actually saved before the computer is allowed to restart.

Drawing by Macro

The Canvas application also offers built-in macro control, an extremely uncommon feature in a drawing application. After drawing an image that you want to use repeatedly throughout a drawing, select all lines and shapes in the image and choose the ADD MACRO command. You will be asked to name your macro image, after which it will appear at the bottom of the MACRO menu. To create multiple copies of the macro image, choose the command name and drag with your cursor. A dotted version of the image will appear as you drag, showing you the sizing effects of your movements.

Finally, Canvas is one of only three Macintosh applications that allow you to fully edit both objects and bit maps. Such applications can be thought of as integrated graphics applications, since you may combine painting and drawing in a single program. The precedent for this aspect of Canvas was established by SuperPaint, one of the earliest and most successful drawing programs, which we will talk about next.

Canvas Quick Reference (1 of 4)

Toolbox

▶	Arrow	▶ to select element to manipulate, ⋯▶ to move, ⤳⋯▶ to clone
T	Type	▶ to set origin for text block, ⋯▶ across type to edit
＼	Line	⋯▶ to draw straight line
▭	Rectangle	⋯▶ to draw rectangle
▢	Round corner	⋯▶ to draw rectangle with rounded corners
◯	Oval	⋯▶ to draw ellipse
＼	Arc	⋯▶ to draw quarter ellipse from top or bottom point to side point
～	Freeform	⋯▶ to draw smoothed polygon
▽	Polygon	▶ to create corners for straight-sided polygon
▣	Bézier curve	▶ to create corner point, ⋯▶ to create smooth point
▣	Alignment	▶ on icon to display dialog for aligning elements

℘	Lasso*	⋯▶ to select irregular portion of bit map so it may be manipulated
⬚	Marquee*	⋯▶ to select rectangular portion of bit map so it may be manipulated
⬚	Airbrush*	⋯▶ to generate random spray of pixels
⬚	Paintbrush*	⋯▶ to draw free-form lines with current brush shape
⬚	Paint can*	⋯▶ to fill enclosed or solid area with current pattern
✎	Pencil*	▶ to create or delete single pixels, ⋯▶ to draw or delete free-form lines
⬚	Eraser*	⋯▶ to delete general portions of bit map
⬚	Bit-map edit	⋯▶ to determine size of prospective bit map
✋	Hand	⋯▶ to move page with respect to window
⬚	Zoom	▶ to magnify view of page, ⇧▶ to demagnify
⬚	Special effects	⋯▶ on icon to display menu of special-effects commands

* *Applicable to bit maps only*

Canvas Quick Reference (2 of 4)

Tool Menus (☜⚡️ tool icon to display)

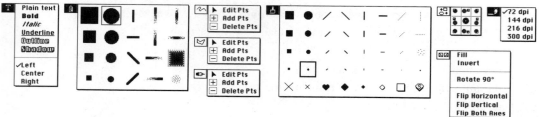

Menus

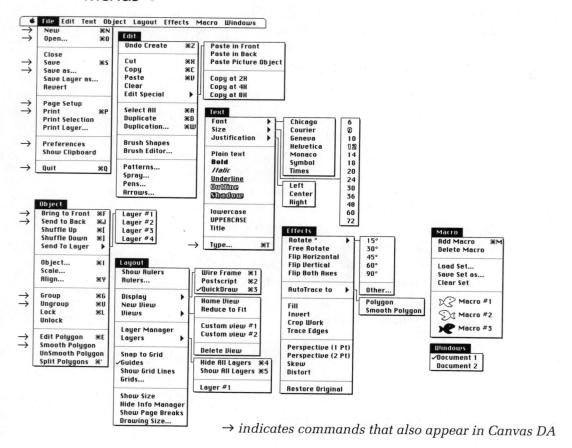

→ *indicates commands that also appear in Canvas DA*

Canvas Quick Reference (3 of 4)

Keyboard Equivalents

Access last drawing tool used ....⌘

Add point to polygon ....⇜🖰 *while editing*

Add selected element to macros* ....⌘A

Alignment manager ......⌘Y* *or* 🖰 *alignment icon*

Bold text ....⌘⇧B

Bring to front ....⌘F

Cancel screen redraw ....⌘.

Circle, create ....⇧┅🖰 *w/oval tool*

Circle, draw from center ....⇧⇜┅🖰 *w/oval tool*

Clear element ....⊗

Clone bit map ....⇜┅🖰 *element*
   (element must be lassoed or marqueed)

Clone object ....⇜┅🖰 *w/arrow tool*

Compress type ....⌘┅🖰 *handle w/arrow*

Copy element ....⌘C

Crop bit map ....┅🖰 *handle w/arrow*

Cut element ....⌘X

Delete point from polygon ....⇧⇜🖰 *while editing*

Draw with bit map ....⌘⇜┅🖰 *element*
   (element must be lassoed or marqueed)

Duplicate element ....⌘D

Duplication manager* ....⌘W

Edit polygon ....⌘E *or* ⇜🖰 *polygon icon*

Ellipse, draw from center ....⇜┅🖰 *w/oval tool*

Expand type ....⌘┅🖰 *handle w/arrow*

Group elements ....⌘G

Hand tool, select temporarily ....▬

Hide all layers except current* ....⌘4

Home view (upper left of layer #1) ....⌘⇜H

Increase type size by one point ....⌘⇧>

Italic text ....⌘⇧I

Lock element ....⌘L

Magnify/demagnify view size ....⌘🖰 *w/pencil*

Move bit map 45° ....⇧┅🖰 *element*
   (element must be lassoed or marqueed)

Move element single pixel ....→, ↓, ←, *or* ↑

Move element 10 pixels ....⌘→, ↓, ←, *or* ↑

Move element 50 pixels ....⇜→, ↓, ←, *or* ↑

Move object 45° ....⇧┅🖰 *w/arrow*

New document, create ....⌘N

Object manager* ....⌘I

Open ellipse.......⌘🖰 *arc icon,* ┅🖰 *round handle*

Open existing document ....⌘O

---

* *Not available in Canvas DA*

⌘	command	→|	tab	⊗	delete	▬	space bar
⇧	shift	↩	return	⊠	fwd. delete	F1	function key
⇜	option	⤬	enter	⌨	keypad key	🖰	mouse click
⌃	control	✐	escape	⌨✐	clear	┅🖰	mouse drag

Canvas Quick Reference (4 of 4)

Keyboard Equivalents (Cont.)

Paste element .... ⌘V

Peel away ruler .... ⌐⊼ *on ruler ʷ/ arrow*

Perpendicular lines, create .... ⇧⌐⊼ *ʷ/ line tool*

Plain text .... ⌘⇧P

PostScript display (print preview)* .... ⌘2

Print document .... ⌘P

Quarter circle, create .... ⇧⌐⊼ *ʷ/ arc tool*

QuickDraw display (normal)* .... ⌘3

Quit Canvas... ⌘Q

Rectangle, draw from center ..... ⇥⌐⊼ *ʷ/ rect. tool*

Redraw screen image .... ⌘K

Reduce to fit (in window)............................. ⌘⇥R

Reduce type size by one point .... ⌘⇧<

Rewrap type .... ⌐⊼ *handle ʷ/ arrow*

Rotate element 90°* .... ⌘R

Save drawing .... ⌘S

Scale bit map .... ⌘⌐⊼ *corner of marqueed image*

Scale object .... ⌐⊼ *handle ʷ/ arrow*

Scale type .... ⇧⌘⌐⊼ *handle ʷ/ arrow*

Select all elements on active layer.................. ⌘A

Select contiguous area in bit map .... ⊼⊼ *ʷ/ lasso*

Select entire bit map .... ⊼⊼ *marquee icon*

Select entire words ...... ⊼⊼ *word,* ⌐⊼ *over others*

Select irregular white space .... ⇥⌐⊼ *ʷ/ lasso*

Send to back .... ⌘J

Set width of text block .... ⌐⊼ *ʷ/ type tool*

Show all layers* .... ⌘5

Shrink marquee to bit map .... ⌘⌐⊼ *ʷ/ marquee*

Shuffle down (backward) .... ⌘]

Shuffle up (foreward) .... ⌘[

Smooth polygon .... ⌘⇧~

Split/bind polygon* .... ⌘'

Square, create .... ⇧⌐⊼ *ʷ/ rectangle tool*

Square, draw from center ...... ⇧⇥⌐⊼ *ʷ/ rect. tool*

Switch to custom view number [#] .... ⌘⇥[#]

Type size, change .... ⇧⊼ *type icon*

Type, edit specifications .... ⌘T *or* ⊼⊼ *type icon*

Typeface, change .... ⌘⊼ *type icon*

Underline text .... ⌘⇧U

Undo/redo last operation .... ⌘Z

Ungroup elements .... ⌘U

Unsmooth polygon .... ⌘⇧~

Wire-frame display (key line)* .... ⌘1

* Not available in Canvas DA
Accurate for Canvas, version 2.0

⌘	command	⇥	tab	⌫	delete	⊔	space bar
⇧	shift	↵	return	⌦	fwd. delete	F1	function key
⇥	option	⊼	enter	⌨	keypad key	⊼	mouse click
⌃	control	⎋	escape	⌨⌦	clear	⌐⊼	mouse drag

Combining Media

Many people use computer-generated graphics in combination with elements created by traditional means to produce finished artwork. Applications such as Canvas and SuperPaint allow you to create multimedia artwork without a paintbrush or a pen by providing object-oriented and bit-mapped capabilities within a single package.

 SuperPaint, Version 2.0   PICT, PNTG, TIFF, SCRN
In 1986, SuperPaint was introduced as a replacement for both MacPaint and MacDraw in a single application. To accomplish this, bit-mapped images and objects were assigned to two unique graphic layers. These days, SuperPaint 2.0 continues to easily outclass its Claris rivals, but it also continues to utilize this two-layer system despite its crudeness when compared with the infinite numbers of layers you may create in Canvas, each of which may contain both bit maps and objects. This, plus the fact that SuperPaint is not available as a DA, has led many to surmise that SuperPaint has become as much a has-been as MacDraw itself.

However, SuperPaint offers many features that Canvas lacks. First, SuperPaint provides the closest thing to real Bézier curve handling of any software short of Illustrator and FreeHand. Though the editing problem is exceedingly clumsy, you may actually create points with asymmetrical Bézier control handles, so that two curves may meet to form a sharp corner. SuperPaint calls these points *hinge points,* although they are more commonly known as corner points.

But SuperPaint's greatest strength is its use of "plug-ins," tools that may be created by third-party developers and added to SuperPaint's standard tool palette. SuperPaint comes with over 30 plug-in tools, all of which may be used to create bit maps only, but many of which are nonetheless very impressive. You may alter the effects of these tools by double-clicking the tool icon, option-drawing with the tool, or applying other keyboard/mouse combinations.

Incidentally, you can import bit maps into MacDraw and FreeHand as actual printing graphics, and into Illustrator as tracing templates, but only Canvas, SuperPaint, and LaserPaint (which we will discuss later in this entry) allow full editing of bit maps.

SuperPaint Quick Reference (1 of 5)

Toolbox

▲	Arrow	▲ to select element to manipulate, ⋯▲ to move
⬚	Two-layer selection	⋯▲ to select images on both bit map and drawing layers
✋	Hand†	⋯▲ to move page with respect to window
A	Type	▲ to set origin for text block, ⋯▲ across type to edit
+	Perpendicular line	⋯▲ to draw horizontal or vertical line
╲	Line	⋯▲ to draw straight line at any angle
▢	Rectangle	⋯▲ to draw rectangle
▢	Round corner	⋯▲ to draw rectangle with rounded corners
⬭	Oval	⋯▲ to draw ellipse
◿	Polygon	▲ to create corners for straight-sided polygon
⬡	Multigon†	⋯▲ to draw equilateral polygons with definable number of sides
⌐	Arc	⋯▲ to draw quarter ellipse from top or bottom point to side point
∿	Freehand Bézier†	⋯▲ to draw freehand lines consisting of Bézier curves
⬚	Marquee*	⋯▲ to select rectangular portion of bit map to manipulate
◇	Free selection*†	⋯▲ to select irregular portion of bit map (no tightening)
◌	Oval selection*†	⋯▲ to select elliptical portion of bit map to manipulate
◺	Polygon selection*†	⋯▲ to select polygonal portion of bit map to manipulate
◯	Lasso*	⋯▲ to select irregular portion of bit map (selection tightens)
✂	Freehand bit map*	⋯▲ to draw free-form bit-mapped lines in current line weight
🖌	Paintbrush*	⋯▲ to draw free-form lines with current brush shape
🖊	Paint can*	⋯▲ to fill an enclosed or solid area with current pattern
✏	Pencil*	▲ to create or delete pixels, ⋯▲ to draw or delete free-form lines
⬧	Eraser*	⋯▲ to delete general portions of bit map

* *Applicable to bit maps only*

† *Not available in version 1.1*

SuperPaint Quick Reference (2 of 5)

Menus

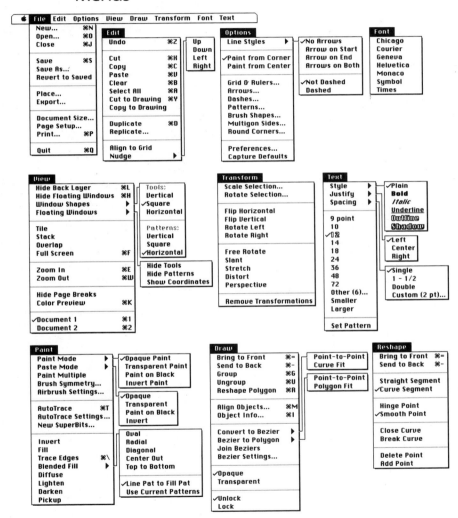

🍎 **File** Edit Options View Draw Transform Font Text

File
New...	⌘N
Open...	⌘O
Close	⌘J
Save	⌘S
Save As...	
Revert to Saved	
Place...	
Export...	
Document Size...	
Page Setup...	
Print...	⌘P
Quit	⌘Q

Edit
Undo	⌘Z
Cut	⌘X
Copy	⌘C
Paste	⌘V
Clear	⌘B
Select All	⌘A
Cut to Drawing	⌘Y
Copy to Drawing	
Duplicate	⌘D
Replicate...	
Align to Grid	
Nudge	▶

Up
Down
Left
Right

Options
Line Styles ▶
✓Paint from Corner
Paint from Center

Grid & Rulers...
Arrows...
Dashes...
Patterns...
Brush Shapes...
Multigon Sides...
Round Corners...

Preferences...
Capture Defaults

No Arrows
Arrow on Start
Arrow on End
Arrows on Both

✓Not Dashed
Dashed

Font
Chicago
Courier
Geneva
Helvetica
Monaco
Symbol
Times

View
Hide Back Layer	⌘L
Hide Floating Windows	⌘H
Window Shapes	▶
Floating Windows	▶
Tile	
Stack	
Overlap	
Full Screen	⌘F
Zoom In	⌘E
Zoom Out	⌘W
Hide Page Breaks	
Color Preview	⌘K
✓Document 1	⌘1
Document 2	⌘2

Tools:
Vertical
✓Square
Horizontal

Patterns:
Vertical
Square
✓Horizontal

Hide Tools
Hide Patterns
Show Coordinates

Transform
Scale Selection...
Rotate Selection...

Flip Horizontal
Flip Vertical
Rotate Left
Rotate Right

Free Rotate
Slant
Stretch
Distort
Perspective

Remove Transformations

Text
Style ▶
Justify ▶
Spacing ▶

9 point
10
✓12
14
18
24
36
48
72
Other (6)...
Smaller
Larger

Set Pattern

✓Plain
Bold
Italic
Underline
Outline
Shadow

✓Left
Center
Right

✓Single
1 - 1/2
Double
Custom (2 pt)...

Paint
Paint Mode ▶
Paste Mode ▶
Paint Multiple
Brush Symmetry...
Airbrush Settings...

AutoTrace ⌘T
AutoTrace Settings...
New SuperBits...

Invert
Fill
Trace Edges ⌘\
Blended Fill ▶
Diffuse
Lighten
Darken
Pickup

✓Opaque Paint
Transparent Paint
Paint on Black
Invert Paint

✓Opaque
Transparent
Paint on Black
Invert

Oval
Radial
Diagonal
Center Out
Top to Bottom

✓Line Pat to Fill Pat
Use Current Patterns

Draw
Bring to Front	⌘=
Send to Back	⌘-
Group	⌘G
Ungroup	⌘U
Reshape Polygon	⌘R
Align Objects...	⌘M
Object Info...	⌘I
Convert to Bezier	▶
Bezier to Polygon	▶
Join Beziers	
Bezier Settings...	
✓Opaque	
Transparent	
✓Unlock	
Lock	

Point-to-Point
Curve Fit

Point-to-Point
Polygon Fit

Reshape
Bring to Front	⌘=
Send to Back	⌘-
Straight Segment	
✓Curve Segment	
Hinge Point	
✓Smooth Point	
Close Curve	
Break Curve	
Delete Point	
Add Point	

PAINT, DRAW, and RESHAPE menus alternate based on state of selection

SuperPaint Quick Reference (3 of 5)

Keyboard Equivalents

Actual view size (100%) * .... ⌘⇧R

Actual view size/fat bits, toggle .... ⌘⭥ ʷ/ pencil
or ⭥⭥ pencil icon

Actual/fit in window, toggle* .... ⭥⭥ hand icon

Align objects* .... ⌘M

Align objects, apply
current settings* .... ⬃ choose ALIGN OBJECTS

Autotrace bit map* .... ⌘T

Begin marquee
on existing marquee .... ➡︎|····⭥ ʷ/ marquee

Begin text block
on existing marquee .... ⌘⭥ ʷ/ type tool

Bold text .... ⌘⇧B or ⌘B[†]

Bring to front .... ⌘=

Center text* .... ⌘⇧C

Change current layer .... ⌘/

Circle, create .... ⇧····⭥ ʷ/ oval tool

Clear element .... ⌧

Clone bit map .... ⬃····⭥ element
(element must be lassoed or marqueed)

Close all documents .... ⬃ choose CLOSE
or ⬃⭥ Close box

Close current document* .... ⌘J

Compress type .... ⌘····⭥ handle ʷ/ arrow

Copy element .... ⌘C

Custom leading, apply
current setting* .... ⬃ choose CUSTOM (# pt)

Custom type size, apply
current setting* .... ⬃ choose OTHER (# pt)

Cut element .... ⌘X

Cut to drawing/painting layer .... ⌘Y or ⌘E[†]

Draw with bit map .... ⌘⬃····⭥ element
(element must be lassoed or marqueed)

Duplicate element .... ⌘D

Erase with half-sized cursor .... ⬃····⭥ ʷ/ eraser

Expand type .... ⌘····⭥ handle ʷ/ arrow

Fill visible bit map only .... ⬃⭥ ʷ/ paint can

Fit in window* .... ⌘⇧W

*   *Available only in SuperPaint 2.0*

†   *Exclusively applicable to SuperPaint 1.1*

⌘	command	➡︎|	tab	⌧	delete	▬	space bar
⇧	shift	↩	return	⊠	fwd. delete	F1	function key
⬃	option	⌇	enter	▣	keypad key	⭥	mouse click
⬆	control	⌔	escape	▣⌀	clear	····⭥	mouse drag

SuperPaint Quick Reference (4 of 5)

Keyboard Equivalents (Cont.)

Free rotate around
opposite corner* .... *choose* FREE ROTATE, ⌘͏⃨ ͏͏͏🢔

Free rotate by 5° ..... *choose* FREE ROTATE, ⌘ ⇧ ͏͏͏🢔

Free rotate by 15° .... *choose* FREE ROTATE, ⇧ ͏͏͏🢔

Full screen .... ⌘F

Grid, activate/deactivate .... ⌘⇧G

Grid, show/hide .... ⌘⇧V *or* ⌘⇧G†

Group elements .... ⌘G

Hand tool, select temporarily .... ▬

Hide/show all palettes .... ⌘H

Hide/show back layer .... ⌘L

Hinge/smooth point, toggle* .... 🢔🢔 *point* w/ *arrow*

Increase type size by 1 point* .... ⌘⇧>

Insert point in path .... ⌘͏⃨🢔 w/ *arrow*

Italic text .... ⌘⇧I *or* ⌘I†

Lasso without tightening .... ⌘͏⃨ ͏͏͏🢔 w/ *lasso*

Left-justify text* .... ⌘⇧L

Lines at 30° angles, create ...... ⇧⌘͏⃨ ͏͏͏🢔 w/ *line tool*
or polygon tool

Magnify to 800% actual view size* .... ⌘⇧E

Move bit map 45° .... ⇧ ͏͏͏🢔 *element*
(element must be lassoed or marqueed)

Move element single pixel .... →, ↓, ←, *or* ↑
or ⌘K, ⌘M, ⌘J, *or* ⌘Y†

Move object 45° .... ⇧ ͏͏͏🢔 w/ *arrow*

New document, create .... ⌘N

New page size* .... ⌘͏⃨ *choose* NEW

Object info* .... ⌘I

Open existing document .... ⌘O

Outline text* .... ⌘⇧O

Paste element .... ⌘V

Perpendicular lines, create ... ͏͏͏🢔 w/ *perp. line tool*
or ⇧ ͏͏͏🢔 w/ *line tool or polygon tool*

Perspective, apply
one side at a time* ...... *choose* PERSPECTIVE, ⇧ ͏͏͏🢔

Plain text .... ⌘⇧P *or* ⌘P†

Print document .... ⌘P *or* ⌘ ; †

Quarter circle, create .... ⇧ ͏͏͏🢔 w/ *arc tool*

Quit SuperPaint .... ⌘Q

Reduce type size by 1 point* .... ⌘⇧<

Reshape polygon .... ⌘R

Rewrap type .... ͏͏͏🢔 *handle* w/ *arrow*

Right-justify text* .... ⌘⇧R

Rotate element, apply
current settings* ...... ⌘͏⃨ *choose* ROTATE SELECTION

Rulers, show/hide .... ⌘⇧M *or* ⌘⇧R†

Save all documents* .... ⌘͏⃨ *choose* SAVE

Save drawing .... ⌘S

SuperPaint Quick Reference (5 of 5)

Keyboard Equivalents (Cont.)

Scale bit map .... ⌘····▸ *corner of marqueed image*

Scale element, apply
current settings* .... ⎇ *choose* SCALE SELECTION

Scale object .... ⌘····▸ *handle w/ arrow*

Scale type .... ⇧⌘····▸ *handle w/ arrow*

Select all elements on current layer .... ⌘A

Select contiguous area in bit map .... ▸▸ *w/ lasso*

Select contiguous white area .... ⌘▸▸ *w/ lasso*

Select entire bit map .... ▸▸ *any selection icon*

Select entire words ...... ▸▸ *word,* ····▸ *over others*

Select range of points* .... ▸ *point,* ⇧▸ *another*

Select/deselect additional point* ...... ⌘▸ *w/ arrow*

Send to back .... ⌘-

Set width of text block .... ····▸ *w/ type tool*

Shadow text* .... ⌘⇧S

Shrink marquee to bit map .... ⌘····▸ *w/ marquee*

Square, create .... ⇧····▸ *w/ rectangle tool*

Tighten marquee to bit map ...... ⎇····▸ *w/ marquee*

Trace edges without
expanding .... ⎇ *choose* TRACE EDGES

Trace edges with
shadow effect .... ⇧ *choose* TRACE EDGES

Transfer to Word 4.0 .... , †

Transparent pattern .... ⌘····▸ *w/ paintbrush*

Underline text* .... ⌘⇧U

Undo/redo last operation .... ⌘Z *or* ⌇

Ungroup elements .... ⌘U

Zoom in* .... ⌘E

Zoom out .... ⌘W

---

* *Available only in SuperPaint 2.0*

† *Exclusively applicable to SuperPaint 1.1*

Accurate for SuperPaint, version 2.0

⌘	command	⇥	tab	⌫	delete	⎵	space bar
⇧	shift	↩	return	⌦	fwd. delete	F1	function key
⎇	option	⌤	enter	▦	keypad key	▸	mouse click
⌃	control	⌇	escape	▦⌇	clear	····▸	mouse drag

Ten Hottest SuperPaint Tips

The following are some tips designed to help you make more effective use of SuperPaint. (Tips marked with † work only for version 2.0.)

◇ **Getting the grabber hand while editing text.** Like many programs, SuperPaint allows you to access the hand tool at any time by pressing the space bar. But to access the hand tool while in the middle of entering text, press COMMAND-SPACEBAR.

◇ **Closing all windows.** To close all open windows, press OPTION and choose the CLOSE command or click in the Close box. To save all open windows, press the OPTION key and choose SAVE.†

◇ **Consistent custom leading.** You may apply the current custom line spacing (leading) or type size to selected text by pressing OPTION when choosing the CUSTOM or OTHER command from the TEXT menu.†

◇ **Inverting a pattern.** To invert a pattern, double-click the pattern to bring up the EDIT PATTERNS dialog. Then press the COMMAND key and click once in the pattern editing box (the right-hand of the two boxes).

◆ **Adjustable airbrush technique.** The effects of painting with the airbrush tool may be altered while painting, much as if you were using a real airbrush. To increase or decrease the flow rate, for example, press the period or comma key. To enlarge or reduce the spray area, press the plus or minus key. To specify a round nozzle, press R; to paint with a fading cursor, press F; and so on.†

◆ **What does this plug-in do?** To determine the purpose of any plug-in tool or command, choose ABOUT SUPERPAINT and click the PLUG-INS button in the resulting dialog box. This will produce a scrolling list of currently available plug-ins. Select a plug-in name and click on ABOUT to discover information on using and editing the tool.†

◆ **Reducing a bit map without gumming it up.** When reducing a bit-mapped image, first transfer it to the drawing layer by choosing the CUT TO DRAWING command so that it becomes a "SuperBits" object. Then go to the drawing layer (by clicking the compass icon in the toolbox) and reduce the bit map by dragging at one of the corner handles. This allows you to reduce the bit map without losing pixels, effectively increasing the resolution.

◇ **Editing a high-resolution painting.** To edit the pixels in a SuperBits image, choose EDIT SUPERBITS from the DRAW menu.[†]

◆ **Repetitious plug-in tools.** The Sprinkles plug-in in the SP Pouch folder actually includes six tools, all of which, except Bubblemaker, are duplicates of tools in the Other Plug-Ins folder. Use ResEdit to open Sprinkles and delete all references to tools other than Bubblemaker to avoid repetitious tools in your palette.[†]

◆ **Creating your own plug-ins.** Any plug-in tool that contains a CURS resource (short for *cursor*) operates by laying down a random pattern of icons. You may create your own custom plug-ins by duplicating a plug-in file, such as Snowflakes, and opening the duplicate in ResEdit. Then open the CURS resource and edit each of the icons as you see fit. You should also edit the SICN resource to determine the appearance of the tool in the SuperPaint palette. You may even change the author's name in the TEXT resource so that your name will appear in the ABOUT dialog box.[†]

We created this sea life plug-in tool by editing the CURS resource of an existing plug-in with ResEdit.

SuperPaint 1.1 is now being included free with Microsoft Word 4.0. And as a registered Word 4.0 user, you may upgrade to SuperPaint 2.0 for $50.

True Illustration Applications

Both Canvas and SuperPaint offer some very useful drawing features, including such high-end operations as the automatic tracing of bit maps with object-oriented lines and shapes. However, while they make their various stabs at Bézier curve handling, they both subscribe to MacDraw's smooth polygon drawing model, making them largely inefficient for creating high-resolution naturalistic objects. Therefore, they cannot be classed as true illustration applications like Illustrator and FreeHand, which we will discuss next.

Adobe Illustrator 88, Version 1.8.3   TEXT (PostScript, native), EPSF Adobe Systems made its first splash on the desktop publishing scene when Apple debuted the LaserWriter in the beginning of 1985. In the years since, it has become increasingly obvious that the typesetting industry was transformed almost overnight by the introduction of the PostScript language.

In mid-1987, Adobe's second major act was to revolutionize the world of object-oriented graphics with the introduction of Adobe Illustrator. The product managed to present the idea of Bézier curve handling in a package so intuitive that users fed up with MacDraw's limitations could sink their teeth into it immediately.

However, Illustrator lacks MacDraw's structure. Since there are no grids, it is unnecessarily difficult to line up one element exactly with another. The ALIGNMENT command works on every single point in a path, rather than aligning a path as a whole, and there are no distribute options, rendering the command useless for any purpose other than making points coincident so they may be joined. And we have all gnashed our teeth over the fact that one of the most prominent names in typeface production doesn't even allow you to combine roman and italic in the same text block.

So it may come as a surprise that we consider Illustrator 88 to be the best drawing program we have ever used on any personal computer. Sure it has its problems, and we could write a book of suggestions for features we would like to see added, but Illustrator is one of those rare programs where everything that is included is included in the best form possible. Notice, for example, the elegant conservation of commands. One dialog box, PAINT, offers every stroke and fill option in one central location. Another, TYPE, provides access to the creation and formatting of all text. There are no scrolling hierarchical pop-up menus with ten type-size choices (one of which is OTHER...) or 19 line weights. You merely type in your specifications and click OK.

Also, Illustrator makes frequent use of dithered colors to emulate Pantone colors on the screen as exactly as possible. Other programs, such as Free-Hand, use solid colors only (unless the color is tinted to a lighter screen value). This causes problems for users of 8-bit video cards since the nearest display color to Pantone 2597 violet may be a dark blue. To its benefit, FreeHand allows you to adjust your on-screen palette, but Illustrator simply dithers the dark blue with some magenta to produce a very close match, good enough to make an educated guess regarding the appearance of your final artwork when you pick it up from your commercial printer.

Finally, versions of Illustrator 88 more recent than 1.8 will automatically break up lines that are too complicated for the limitations of your printer and would otherwise produce "limitcheck" errors. Adobe recommends that you apply this feature to an illustration only after it is completed, so your lines aren't so short that they cause problems in the creation process.

Ten Hottest Illustrator Tips

In an application that closely conserves tools and commands, it is often difficult to know what features are hidden where. The following are some tips designed to help you make more effective use of Adobe Illustrator. (Tips marked with [†] work only for Illustrator 88.)

◇   **Editing rectangles and circles.** You may ungroup any simple shape created with the rectangle or ellipse tool. This allows you to manipulate each point in the shape individually or perform other manipulations.

◇   **Adjusting the placement of templates.** Templates in Illustrator always appear positioned relative to the center page tile (page 5) exactly as they are positioned relative to the MacPaint page. If you want to adjust the location of a template, or rotate or scale it, you must do so in MacPaint (or more conveniently, DeskPaint) before creating a new Illustrator document.

◇   **Faking a grid.** There are no grids in Illustrator. To set up a false grid that affects the movement of elements only, choose the PREFERENCES command and change the cursor arrow distance to the grid increment you desire. Then use the arrow keys to move elements into the correct positions.[†]

◇ **Changing point identity.** To change an existing corner point to a smooth point (or vice versa), first click on the point with the scissors tool to split it into two endpoints. Next, choose the JOIN command and select the "Smooth point" or "Corner point" option from the resulting dialog.[†]

◇ **Creating tick marks to simulate custom rulers.** You may use the blend tool to create a series of tick marks that may be used for lining up elements or that may act as custom rulers. To establish the first and last marks in the series, draw a single vertical tick mark with the pen tool and option-drag a clone horizontally to an opposite location. Then select both elements, click on each with the blend tool, and specify a number of steps in the BLEND dialog. If, after the blend is completed, you decide you need more or fewer tick marks, delete the blends and try again. Once you are satisfied with your horizontal series of tick marks, select them all, option-click with the rotate tool at the base of the first tick mark, enter 90° and click the COPY button. This establishes an identical vertical series of tick marks.[†]

◇ **Easy bar charts.** To create a bar chart, begin by drawing a series of "dummy" bars with a consistent height and width. First, click with the rectangle tool and enter the height and width you desire.[†] (Users of Illustrator 1.1 must simply draw a rectangle.) Keep in mind that the height should represent an even number of units, such as 10, 100, 1000, and so on, based on the magnitude of your chart. Option-drag this rectangle horizontally with the arrow tool to create a second bar, and choose TRANSFORM AGAIN repeatedly to create additional bars. Now you may change each bar to its proper height by option-clicking with the scale tool and entering a vertical enlargement value. For example, if your dummy bar represented 10,000 units and you needed to scale it to represent 15,460, you would enter a value of 154.6%.

◇ **The ruler origin determines the placement of paste elements.** When transferring elements between documents using the PASTE IN FRONT or PASTE IN BACK command to retain vertical and horizontal placement, you may find that the pasted element lands in a different spot than you anticipated. This is because both commands operate in relation to the ruler origin. If placement is important, make sure that the location of the ruler origin in the "cut from" document is the same as in the "paste to" document.

◆ **Round dashes.** Illustrator allows you to create dashed lines by entering values in the PAINT dialog. If you select the rounded caps icon, your dashes will have rounded ends. To create a series of perfectly round dashes, select the rounded caps icon, enter o for the first "Dashed" option, and then enter a gap value that is a few points larger than the line weight, so that the round dots don't touch.

◆ **The ruler origin also affects tile placement.** Pattern tiles are positioned and transformed relative to the ruler origin. If you change the ruler origin at any time, you run the risk of affecting the placement of patterns within filled elements. If you want a pattern to begin exactly at some point within a shape, you may move the ruler origin to that location.[†]

◆ **Stroking a clipping path.** When you create a clipping path in Illustrator, you may notice in the preview mode that the elements that fill the path overlap not only the fill but also the stroke of the masking object. To retain the stroke, copy the masking object and paste it in front of the foremost fill element. Then choose the PAINT command, choose "None" for the fill, and deselect the "Mask" option. Finally, group all elements that make up the clipping path (including the foremost stroked element) to finish the effect.[†]

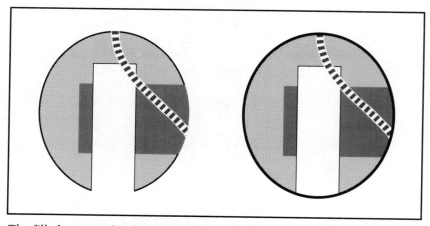

The fill elements of a clipping path will overlap the stroke of the masking object as shown on the left. In the second example, we copy the stroke and paste it in front.

Adobe Illustrator Quick Reference (1 of 3)

Toolbox

	Arrow	▸ to select element so it may be manipulated, ···▸ to move, ✧···▸ to clone
	Hand	···▸ to move page with respect to window
	Zoom	▸ to magnify view of page, ✧▸ to demagnify
T	Type	▸ to display dialog box used to create block of type (not used to edit)
	Freehand	···▸ to draw freehand line, ⌘···▸ to erase as you draw
	Autotrace	▸ to trace bit-mapped template image
	Pen	▸ to create corner point, ···▸ to create smooth point
	Rectangle	···▸ to draw rectangle, ▸ to enter exact dimensions of rectangle
	Oval	···▸ to draw ellipse, ▸ to enter exact dimensions of ellipse
	Blend	▸ on point in each of two paths to create series of intermediate paths
	Scale	▸ to define origin then ···▸ to enlarge or reduce, ✧▸ to display dialog
	Rotate	▸ to define origin then ···▸ to rotate, ✧▸ to display dialog
	Reflect	▸ to define origin then ▸ again to flip, ✧▸ to display dialog
	Shear	▸ to define origin then ···▸ to slant, ✧▸ to display dialog
	Scissors	▸ to split segment, ✧▸ to insert point in path
	Measure	▸ on each of two points to display distance and direction between points
	Page	▸ to determine lower-left corner of page with respect to drawing area

Menus

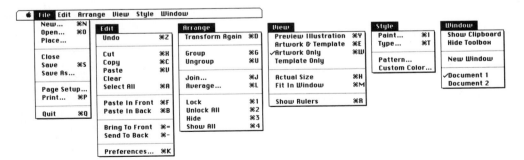

Adobe Illustrator Quick Reference (2 of 3)

Keyboard Equivalents

Actual view size (100%) .... ⌘H

Arrow tool, select temporarily .... ⌘

Artwork and template displayed .... ⌘E

Artwork displayed only (key line) .... ⌘W

Average location of elements .... ⌘L

Bring to front .... ⌘=

Cancel screen preview .... ⌘.

Circle, create .... ⇧⁻⁻⁻➤ w/oval tool

Circle, draw from center .... ⇧⍓⁻⁻⁻➤ w/oval tool

Clear element .... *

Clone element .... ⍓⁻⁻⁻➤ w/arrow tool

Copy element .... ⌘C

Copy with PICT preview .... ⌘⍓C

Corner point, add BCH .... ⍓⁻⁻⁻➤ on existing
  corner point with pen tool

Corner point, create .... ➤ w/pen tool

Cut element .... ⌘X

Demagnify view size .... ⌘⍓▬

Ellipse, draw from center .... ⍓⁻⁻⁻➤ w/oval tool

Extend a path .... ⁻⁻⁻➤ w/freehand tool

Fit in window .... ⌘M

Freehand tool, access when pen selected .... ⌃

Group elements .... ⌘G

Hand tool, select temporarily .... ▬

Hide element .... ⌘3

Insert point in path .... ⍓➤ w/scissors tool

Join two points .... ⌘J

Lock element .... ⌘1

Magnify view size .... ⌘▬

Move 45° .... ⇧⁻⁻⁻➤ w/arrow tool

MOVE dialog box, access .... ⍓➤ arrow icon

Move element specified distance ..... →, ↓, ←, or ↑

New document, create .... ⌘N

Open existing document .... ⌘O

Open with a new template .... ⌘⍓O

Paint an element with stroke and fill .... ⌘I

Paste element .... ⌘V

Paste in back of selected element .... ⌘B

Paste in front of selected element .... ⌘F

⌘	command	➜|	tab	⌦	delete	▬	space bar
⇧	shift	↵	return	⌦	fwd. delete	F1	function key
⍓	option	⌁	enter	▦	keypad key	➤	mouse click
⌃	control	⌀	escape	▦⌀	clear	⁻⁻⁻➤	mouse drag

Adobe Illustrator Quick Reference (3 of 3)

Keyboard Equivalents (Cont.)

Perpendicular line, create .... ↖, ⇧↖ *w/pen tool*

Preferences, specify .... ⌘K

Preview illustration .... ⌘Y

Print document .... ⌘P

Quit Adobe Illustrator .... ⌘Q

Rectangle, draw from center ..... ↘···↖ *w/rect. tool*

REFLECT dialog box, access .... ↘↖ *w/reflect tool*

Reflect vert'ly/horiz'ly .... ↖, ⇧↖ *w/reflect tool*

Rotate by 45° .... ↖, ⇧···↖ *w/rotate tool*

ROTATE dialog box, access .... ↘↖ *w/rotate tool*

Rulers, show/hide .... ⌘R

Save illustration .... ⌘S

SCALE dialog box, access .... ↘↖ *w/scale tool*

Scale proportionally .... ↖, ⇧···↖ *w/scale tool*

Select all elements .... ⌘A

Select entire path .... ↘↖ *w/arrow tool*

Send to back .... ⌘-

SHEAR dialog box, access .... ↘↖ *w/shear tool*

Shear vert'ly/horiz'ly .... ↖, ⇧···↖ *w/shear tool*

Show all hidden elements .... ⌘4

Smooth point, create .... ···↖ *w/pen tool*

Smooth point, delete BCH .... ↘↖ *on existing smooth point with pen tool*

Square, create .... ⇧···↖ *w/rectangle tool*

Square, draw from center ...... ⇧↘···↖ *w/rect. tool*

Transform again (duplicate) .... ⌘D

Type/edit selected text block .... ⌘T

Undo/redo last operation .... ⌘Z

Ungroup elements .... ⌘U

Unlock all hidden elements .... ⌘2

Zoom tool, select temporarily .... ⌘␣

Accurate for Adobe Illustrator 88, version 1.8.3

Adobe Clip-Art

If you're looking for idea starters, we most heartily recommend Adobe's Collector's Edition clip-art packages. These packages—Symbols, Borders, Letterforms (included with Illustrator 88) and Patterns and Textures—are not clip-art in the traditional sense; that is, they are not finished images that may be used as-is. Rather, they are marvelously packaged bits and pieces, with some of the most useful documentation we have ever seen. As advanced users, we continue to find stimulating ideas in these support products. And thanks to version 1.8 of Illustrator 88, you can even output the patterns (which used to be a terrible problem, especially when printing to high-resolution typesetters).

Unfortunately, both packages are expensive—Patterns and Textures lists for over $200—but they are well worth the price if you can afford it.

Automated Bit-Map Tracing

One of Illustrator 88's most exciting features when it debuted in mid-1988 was its new autotrace tool. Using this tool, you can transform a bit-mapped sketch into an object-oriented path with a single click. Just one year later, such tools were commonplace. DeskDraw, Canvas, SuperPaint, and Free-Hand all offer automated tracing features. In fact, tracing has become such a popular and heavily demanded feature for converting scanned artwork that Adobe has released a utility called Streamline, specifically for tracing.

 Adobe Streamline, Version 1.0   TEXT (PostScript, native), EPSF
Streamline traces bit-mapped art stored in the MacPaint or TIFF format at any resolution up to 600 dpi. That's all it does; it doesn't even print. However, you are provided with a great deal of control over how your traced artwork emerges. For example, Streamline is the only tracing tool in which you may specify that a bit-mapped line be traced with an object-oriented line (the "Centerline" option) instead of surrounded with a closed shape (the "Outline" option). You may also determine the accuracy, or *tolerance,* of a tracing. If you know enough about what you're doing to predict the outcome of a trace, you may specify whether particularly long lines should be allowed to curve or remain absolutely straight. And a "Noise" option lets you filter out the loose pixels that often result from scanning photographs.

Some options only appear if you select the "Centerline" or "Centerline & Outline" option. Among these is an option that allows you to specify a uniform or nonuniform line weight for all open paths in the finished illustration. The "Number of steps" option determines how Streamline centers its lines. Generally, this value should be set to the heaviest line weight in your bit-mapped image. Another option specifies that Streamline trace white lines as well as black.

Everything we've read claims Streamline only works on black-and-white bit maps, but we've traced gray-value TIFF documents created in Studio/8 with quite a bit of success. However, for the price—about $350—Streamline should only be considered by those who have an awful lot of image processing to do.

Illustriously Accessible

Together, Illustrator, the Collector's Editions, and Streamline are as powerful (and as expensive) a team as you will ever require for producing computer-aided artwork. However, they share two major problems. Neither supports bit-mapped graphics for any purpose other than tracing templates. (One exception: Illustrator will import EPSF scans, which tend to be two to three times less efficient than those saved in TIFF.) And Illustrator does not support QuickDraw-equipped output devices such as the ImageWriter or LaserWriter SC. If these capabilities interest you, then your best bet by far is Aldus FreeHand.

 Aldus FreeHand, Version 2.0   FHD2 (native), EPSF
Although we must admit to preferring Illustrator's interface and color display, FreeHand offers features that Illustrator not only lacks, but will probably never offer due to Adobe's historically exclusive support for the PostScript language. These features include some of the best type control of any application, such as user-definable baseline shift, handy for creating superscripts and subscripts of varying heights and orientations; 201 drawing layers, allowing you to develop very complex images modularly; a multiple undo/redo feature, supporting up to 100 consecutive undos (depending on the amount of excess RAM); and special image-editing features for manipulating the gray values of imported bit maps. FreeHand also provides the better tracing tool, allowing you to create multiple paths simultaneously with controls similar to those offered by Streamline, though less extensive.

Aldus FreeHand Quick Reference (1 of 5)

Toolbox

▶	Arrow	▶ to select element so it may be manipulated, ⋯▶ to move
▭	Rectangle	⋯▶ to draw rectangle
⬭	Ellipse	⋯▶ to draw ellipse
⌇	Freehand	⋯▶ to draw freehand line, ⌘⋯▶ to erase, ⌇⋯▶ for straight segment
◣	Knife	▶ to split segment
⌐	Corner*	▶ to create corner point
↻	Rotate	⋯▶ to rotate, ⌇▶ to display dialog
⤢	Scale	⋯▶ to enlarge or reduce, ⌇▶ to display dialog
▥	Trace	⋯▶ around bit-mapped element to trace it with multiple paths
A	Type	▶ to display dialog box used to create block of type (not used to edit)
⬭	Round corner	⋯▶ to draw rectangle with rounded corners
╲	Line	⋯▶ to draw straight line
⌒	Combination*	▶ to create corner point, ⋯▶ to create curve point
↻	Curve*	▶ to create curve point with automatic BCH placement
∫	Connector*	▶ to create connector (tangent) point
⧊	Reflect	⋯▶ to flip, ⌇▶ to display dialog
⧄	Skew	⋯▶ to slant, ⌇▶ to display dialog
⊕	Zoom	▶ to magnify view of page, ⌇▶ to demagnify

* *Point tools used to create single points in a path*

Aldus FreeHand Quick Reference (2 of 5)

Menus

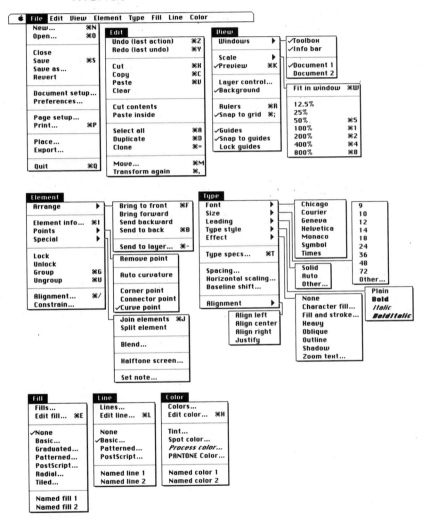

Aldus FreeHand Quick Reference (3 of 5)

Keyboard Equivalents

Actual view size (100%) .... ⌘1

Align elements .... ⌘/

Arrow tool, select temporarily .... ⌘

Bring to front .... ⌘F

Cancel screen preview .... ⌘.

Circle, create .... ⇧⁗ᐝ *w/ ellipse tool*

Circle, draw from center .... ⇧⌥⁗ᐝ *w/ ellipse tool*

Clear element .... ⌫

Clone element .... ⌘=

Combination tool, select 6

Compress type .... ⌥⁗ᐝ *corner handle w/ arrow*

Connector point, add BCH .... ⌥⁗ᐝ *on existing*
 connector point w/ arrow tool

Connector point, create .... ᐝ *w/ connector tool*

Connector tool, select 0

Copy element .... ⌘C

Corner point, add BCH .... ⌥⁗ᐝ *on existing*
 corner point w/ arrow tool
 or ⌥⁗ᐝ *w/ combination tool*

Corner point, create .... ᐝ *w/ corner tool*
 or ᐝ *w/ combination tool*

Corner tool, select 9

Curve point, create .... ᐝ *w/ curve tool*
 or ⁗ᐝ *w/ combination tool*

Curve tool, select 8

Cut element .... ⌘X

Demagnify view size .... ⌘⌥␣

Deselect all elements .... ⇥

Deselect all points, paths remain selected .... ~

Distribute elements .... ⌘/

Duplicate last transformation .... ⌘D

Edit color .... ⌘H

Edit fill .... ⌘E

Edit line (stroke) .... ⌘L

Edit type .... ⌘I *or* ᐝᐝ

Eight times actual view size (800%) .... ⌘8

Element info (custom dialog) .... ⌘I *or* ⌥ᐝᐝ

Ellipse, draw from center ...... ⌥⁗ᐝ *w/ ellipse tool*

Ellipse tool, select 3

Expand type .... ⌥⁗ᐝ *corner handle w/ arrow*

Extend a path .... ⁗ᐝ *w/ freehand tool*

⌘	command	⇥	tab	⌫	delete	␣	space bar
⇧	shift	↵	return	⌦	fwd. delete	F1	function key
⌥	option	⁓	enter	▦	keypad key	ᐝ	mouse click
⌃	control	⌯	escape	▦⌯	clear	⁗ᐝ	mouse drag

Aldus FreeHand Quick Reference (4 of 5)

Keyboard Equivalents (Cont.)

Fit in window .... ⌘W

Four times actual view size (400%) .... ⌘4

FREEHAND dialog box, access .... ▸▸ *freehand icon*

Freehand tool, select 5

Group elements .... ⌘G

Half actual view size (50%) .... ⌘5

Hand tool, select temporarily .... ▬

Insert point in path .... ▸ *ʷ/any point tool*

Join two points .... ⌘J

Join type to a path .... ⌘J

Kern type, delete ¹⁄₁₀ em .... ⌘⇧←

Kern type, delete ¹⁄₁₀₀ em .... ⌘⊠ *or* ⌘←

Kern type, insert ¹⁄₁₀ em .... ⌘⇧→

Kern type, insert ¹⁄₁₀₀ em .... ⌘⇧⊠ *or* ⌘→

Key line mode, toggle .... ⌘K

Knife tool, select 7

Leading, adjust .... ▔▸ *top handle ʷ/ arrow*

Letter spacing, adjust ..... ▔▸ *side handle ʷ/ arrow*

Line tool, select 4

Magnify view size .... ⌘▬

Move 45° .... ⇧▔▸ *ʷ/ arrow tool*

MOVE dialog box, access .... ⌘M

Move information bar .... ▔▸ *ʷ/ arrow tool*

Move point while creating .... ▔▸ *ʷ/ point tool*
or ⌘▔▸ *ʷ/ combination tool*

New document, create .... ⌘N

Open existing document .... ⌘O

Paste element .... ⌘V

Perpendicular line, create .... ⇧▔▸ *ʷ/ line tool*

Preview mode, toggle .... ⌘K

Print document .... ⌘P

Quit Aldus FreeHand .... ⌘Q

Rectangle, draw from center ..... ✎▔▸ *ʷ/ rect. tool*

Rectangle tool, select 1

Redo last undone operation .... ⌘Y

REFLECT dialog box, access .... ✎▸ *ʷ/ reflect tool*

Reflect vert'ly/horiz'ly .... ⇧▔▸ *ʷ/ reflect tool*

Rewrap type .... ▔▸ *corner handle ʷ/ arrow*

Rotate by 45° .... ⇧▔▸ *ʷ/ rotate tool*

ROTATE dialog box, access .... ✎▸ *ʷ/ rotate tool*

Round corner tool, select 2

Rulers, show/hide .... ⌘R

Aldus FreeHand Quick Reference (5 of 5)

Keyboard Equivalents (Cont.)

Save an illustration .... ⌘S

Scale dialog box, access .... ⌥♦ w/scale tool

Scale grouped element .... ⁔♦ handle w/arrow

Scale paint or TIFF image
for optimal printing .... ⌥⁔♦ handle w/arrow

Scale proportionally .... ⇧⁔♦ w/scale tool

Scale type .... ⇧⌥⁔♦ corner handle w/arrow

Select all elements on active layer .... ⌘A

Select entire words ...... ♦♦ word, ⁔♦ over others

Send to back .... ⌘B

Send to layer .... ⌘ -

Skew dialog box, access .... ⌥♦ w/shear tool

Skew vert'ly/horiz'ly .... ⇧⁔♦ w/shear tool

Snap to grid (activate grid) .... ⌘ ;

Square, create .... ⇧⁔♦ w/rectangle tool

Square, draw from center ...... ⇧⌥⁔♦ w/rect. tool

Trace dialog box, access .... ♦♦ trace icon

Transform again .... ⌘ ,

Twice actual view size (200%) .... ⌘2

Type specifications .... ⌘T

Type tool, select .... A

Undo last operation .... ⌘Z

Ungroup elements .... ⌘U

Word spacing, adjust .... ⌥⁔♦ side handle

Zoom tool, select temporarily .... ⌘▬

Accurate for Aldus FreeHand, version 2.0

⌘	command	→⁣|	tab	⌧	delete	▬	space bar
⇧	shift	↵	return	⊠	fwd. delete	F1	function key
⌥	option	⤳	enter	▥	keypad key	♦	mouse click
⌃	control	⬠	escape	▥⬠	clear	⁔♦	mouse drag

FreeHand Versus Illustrator

So which is really better, FreeHand or Illustrator? Each was developed by programmers with a great deal of experience in computer graphics and extensive knowledge of the PostScript language. So it comes as no surprise that every time an article in a trade magazine compares the two, the inevitable recommendation is to buy both. Although this is undoubtedly the solution to any product-comparison predicament (possessing the added advantage of avoiding any possible loss in advertising dollars for the magazine), few of us really need or can afford both Illustrator and FreeHand.

Our solution is this: If you prefer an elegant drawing environment for creating free-form illustrations and you will only be printing to PostScript-equipped output devices, get Illustrator. We would say that anyone specifically producing naturalistic artwork falls into this category. If, however, you prefer a more structured environment involving grids, user-defined guidelines, and true alignment/distribution features, then FreeHand is the obvious choice. FreeHand is perfect for people creating schematic drawings, map work, or other drawings composed of repetitious elements.

Ten Hottest FreeHand Tips

The following are some tips designed to help you make more effective use of Aldus FreeHand.

◇ **Trying to select that evasive element.** One of the most irritating features of FreeHand is that you cannot select an element while a larger element is selected in back of it. Therefore, when selecting multiple elements, always start at the foremost, smallest element and work backward. If you need to deselect an element but there is no empty place to click without demagnifying the view size, simply press the TAB key. This deselects all elements.

◇ **Selecting multiple paths without highlighting their points.** When selecting multiple elements—but not *all* elements—on a page, the simplest method is to marquee by dragging with the arrow tool. In Free-Hand, however, marqueeing selects paths and their points, slowing down the screen refresh speed. In such a case, press the tilde key (~) to deselect points while leaving their respective paths selected.

◇ **Ungrouping simple shapes.** As in Illustrator, you may ungroup any simple shape created with the rectangle or ellipse tool. This allows you to manipulate each point in the shape individually or perform other manipulations.

◇ **Moving the information bar.** You may relocate the information bar by dragging it to a new location.

◇ **Determining the center of a radial fill.** Gradient fills defined using the RADIAL command must always begin in the center of a path. If you want to create a highlight that begins elsewhere, draw a larger shape that completely covers your path, and fill it with a radial gradation. Then position the center of the shape relative to your path. When you are satisfied, cut the shape, select your original path, and choose the PASTE INSIDE command. This clips the radial fill so that the highlight begins at the location defined by the larger shape.

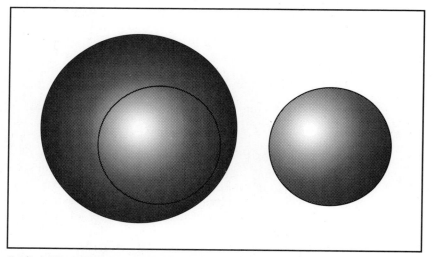

Radial fills in FreeHand always emanate from the center of a shape. To alter this, paste a large shape filled with a radial gradation into a smaller clipping path.

◇ **Quickly accessing element information.** In version 1.0, you could double-click an element to produce the appropriate information dialog box. To the dismay of many users, however, you could just as easily display the dialog if you selected an element and then clicked again to begin dragging it. The problem has been remedied in version

2.0, but this somehow went undocumented. You must now press the OPTION key when double-clicking.

◇ **Aligning to a locked element.** Never try to align elements by hand or by using the grid; it isn't worth the effort. Instead, first lock one element that you wish to remain stationary. Then select the elements you wish to line up in relation to the locked element—avoid selecting individual points—and choose the ALIGNMENT command.

◆ **Saving default settings.** To customize FreeHand's default settings, create a new document, change any settings you desire—you may even create a few frequently used elements—and save the document as an application template called Aldus FreeHand Defaults. This replaces the existing Aldus FreeHand Defaults file that the application consults when creating any new document.

◆ **Predefined PostScript fill and stroke routines.** FreeHand's UserPrep and Advanced UserPrep files contain definitions for easy-to-access PostScript fill and stroke procedures. Try this out: Select a shape, choose POSTSCRIPT from the FILL menu, and type "0 255 noise" into the large entry area. PostScript procedures don't appear correctly on the screen, so you'll have to print your illustration to see how it looks. (If you get an error, check to see that the UserPrep file is in the same folder as FreeHand.) Next, try selecting a line and choosing POSTSCRIPT from the LINE menu. Type "{ball} 15 15 0 0 newrope" and see how that prints. Other procedures may be accessed by changing the name of the Advanced UserPrep file to "UserPrep." Then you may try typing "(coarse-gravel) 0 texture" into the POSTSCRIPT FILL dialog, and printing it out. Over 40 procedures are available. To learn more, open the Advanced UserPrep file in a word processor and read the first few pages. All of the text preceded by percent signs (%) describes how the various procedures may be applied.

◆ **Coloring a PostScript fill or stroke.** To apply a process color to a PostScript effect, enter numbers in brackets where you would normally include 0 or 1 to specify the gray value. For example, "{ball} 15 15 0 [.5 .4 .3 .2] newrope" means to color the line with 50 percent cyan, 40 percent magenta, 30 percent yellow, and 20 percent black. "{ball} 15 15 0 [.5 (purple)] newrope" applies a 50 percent tint of the spot color "purple" (defined in the current document) to the same line.

Combining Media with Béziers

Illustrator and FreeHand are both powerful drawing applications that provide Bézier curve control. But wouldn't it be great if there were a product that allowed Bézier control, plus the bit-mapped editing features of Super-Paint or Canvas, plus full-color bit mapping like PixelPaint or Studio/8? Well, such an application exists, but it is one of the most difficult-to-use applications available for the Macintosh.

 LaserPaint Color II, Version 1.9.7

LPGE (native), PICT2, EPSF, PNTG, TIFF

If you own a Mac II or better with at least 4 megabytes of memory, Laser-Paint may be for you, provided that you are willing to spend a few weeks learning the program. We can't think of a single feature this application is missing. The features list is so long, there's really no point in beginning. Suffice it to say that every feature mentioned in this entry or later in the Painting Software entry is available in LaserPaint. There are people who love this software and absolutely swear by it. But if you don't own or can't borrow the documentation, forget it. Trying to learn LaserPaint based solely on your knowledge of other Macintosh applications is like moving to Sumatra armed with a German-Portuguese dictionary. Almost no tool is the least bit reminiscent of a tool in any other software. And selecting a simple color is like learning a new dance step that involves three or four handsprings. This is software designed by crackerjack programmers who constantly update the program to include new, exciting features; but no one seems to be the least bit interested in making the interface more familiar. Considering artists' stereotypical distaste for unnecessary complexity, such a downright weird presentation seems at best very risky.

File Managers

One of the most powerful features of any computer, from personal to mainframe, is the ability to function as an organizational tool. No doubt most of us have set about trying to create a detailed list of our clients, catalog the contents of our home, or simply organize a few recipes. File managers allow you to perform these chores more quickly and more adroitly than scribbling on a bunch of 3-by-5 index cards. And despite what you might think, file-management software is one of the easiest types of software to use, next to word-processing and painting applications.

Nightmare on Database Blvd.

Before we get too far into this section, we need to clarify what we're talking about. We are *not* talking about **relational database managers** such as FoxBase, 4th Dimension, or Borland's Reflex Plus. Although a relational database manager is in many ways more powerful and more versatile than a file manager, the amount of basic computing knowledge required to set up a database-management system is generally beyond the capacities of the casual Macintosh user. Building a database-management system (DBMS) is comparable to writing a piece of software. The process involves hours of planning to determine how information will be organized into a complex tree of documents, branching from one database file to one or more others. A DBMS also involves hours of arduous programming to set up the several links required to connect database files.

Instead, we will be discussing **flat file managers**, which require much less planning and no programming whatsoever. So called for its basic organizational structure, a flat file is like a set of electronic index cards, each labeled with boxes, or **fields**, which can contain specific pieces of information such as last names, street addresses, or phone numbers.

Sounds a Lot like HyperCard

One of the earliest stacks included with HyperCard looks and operates like an electronic Rolodex file. Names are typed into one field, addresses into

File Technicalities 1

HyperCard, I knew FileMaker, FileMaker was a friend of mine,
And HyperCard, you're no FileMaker

HyperCard will suffice as file-management software to the same extent that a spade will suffice for digging a hole deep enough to plant a tree. But because file management is not its primary function, HyperCard lacks the elegance and power required to satisfy most file-management requirements.

For example, suppose you decide to enter all of your favorite recipes into a HyperCard stack. You set up a simple background composed of three fields: a small one for the name of the recipe, a larger one for the list of ingredients, and another large field for the directions. You then create a series of cards using this same background, each containing one recipe.

The first disadvantage inherent in this scenario is that HyperCard provides no help in entering information. You have to type in every word from scratch and perform all editing for yourself. You cannot import text from a word processor or spreadsheet as you can with a file manager, and HyperCard includes no spelling checker or consistency checker (to make sure that *pint* is always abbreviated *pt.* and so on).

Second, HyperCard lacks a sorting feature. When you first create your stack, you might enter the recipes in the order they appear in your card file so they'll be in alphabetical order. In the weeks that follow, you continue adding random recipes that catch your eye. In HyperCard, if you wanted each card to remain in alphabetical order, you would have to make sure to enter them in the correct locations or to cut and paste cards later when it's more convenient, a process no more convenient than organizing traditional index cards. A file manager allows you to sort entries automatically into any order you choose.

Third, HyperCard provides no automated linking features. Suppose you want to shop according to your recipes. In other words, you know that next week you want to prepare grilled salmon one evening, a fruit salad the next, and fettucini the night after that. In HyperCard, you'll have to go to each card and copy the lists of ingredients by hand or print out each card separately. In a file manager, you could create a second document that links material from the original recipe-card file. In one field, you would type in the name of the dish, and in another, the file manager would return the ingredient list. After entering all dishes you wanted to prepare, you could create a macro that would automatically add your lists of ingredients, combining like ingredients, and print the final list in a suitable format. Sort of reminds you of "The Jetsons," doesn't it?

Conclusion: HyperCard provides none of the necessary amenities for efficient file management. However, if HyperCard is all you can afford, it can be made to manage.

---

another, and phone numbers into a third. This is a typical flat file structure. So why not stick with HyperCard? It's cheap, we know how to use it, and ... er ... did we mention how cheap it is?

Because HyperCard was included free with so many Macs, many people use this software to satisfy requirements that would be better suited to a file manager. While HyperCard will accommodate simple organizational tasks with limited effort, file managers provide many automated features that allow you to process large quantities of similar information quickly and efficiently.

To get an idea of the different kinds of operations a file-management program can perform in comparison with HyperCard's abilities, see File Technicalities 1.

Secretarial Shortcuts

Each of the three most popular file managers—FileMaker II, Microsoft File, and Panorama—provides features far beyond HyperCard's for organizing and sifting through large quantities of information. Although there exist many dissimilarities between the three in the number and quality of features—File is the least powerful as well as the cheapest, Panorama is the most powerful and most expensive, and FileMaker is the most popular—they provide many of the same basic features that help to define this class of software.

Multiple Choice

If you own Microsoft File, you're pretty much on your own when entering text into fields. In fact, File is the only file manager that doesn't provide special features designed to ease the text-entry process, with the exception of allowing you to import data from a word processor or spreadsheet.

FileMaker and Panorama, on the other hand, provide several functions that allow you to enter text more quickly and more accurately. For example, in both applications, you can specify that a field present the user with a pop-up menu or dialog of options. Therefore, when you tab to a field, instead of entering a word or two of information, you simply select an option from a menu. This is especially useful when only a handful of responses are appropriate. Selecting from a menu speeds up the entry process and ensures across-the-board accuracy, even when different people use the same database.

In FileMaker, choose the Define command from the SELECT menu and click the ENTRY OPTIONS button for a selected field. In the dialog that follows, check the "Display a list of values" option and enter the items you want to appear in the pop-up menu.

In Panorama, click on the Design Sheet icon (the sideways T square) to display the design structure for each field in the current document. Then click inside the Value column for the field you want to automate and enter your choices in the data-input window at the top of the screen. Each choice should be separated by a space. After you close the design sheet, tabbing to the field you changed will produce a list of choices in the data input window.

Panorama goes one step further by allowing you to create a prompt display. For example, if you have a database that keeps track of outgoing long-distance calls, you would probably want to know if the calls were made before 5:00 P.M., incurring daytime rates, or if they happened between 5:00 and 11:00 P.M. for evening rates, or after 11:00 P.M. To simplify things, you set up *DR* to mean daytime rates, *ER* to mean evening rates, and *NR* to mean nighttime rates. Since this may be hard for some casual database users to remember, you may create a display that reads "DR = 8 A.M. to 5 P.M., ER = 5 P.M. to 11 P.M., NR = 11 P.M. to 8 A.M." In Panorama, the display appears across the top of the screen when a user enters the Time of Day field.

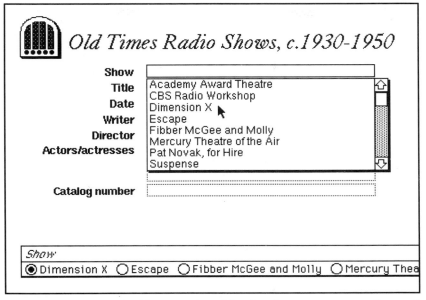

Here we have created a file to catalog old radio shows. Since we collect only certain shows, the Shows field produces a pop-up menu of choices in FileMaker (top) and a series of choices preceded by radio buttons in Panorama (bottom).

Consulting Other Documents

Another feature that FileMaker and Panorama offer to make data entry less tedious is the **lookup field**, which allows you to access information in another open file. For example, one database file may contain a catalog of every item sold by a small store, including price, item number, weight, shipping cost, and so on. If you want to create a different database to keep track of inventory, you can enter the item number, have the software look up the entry in the catalog database for description and price, and then enter the number of items currently in the store. As long as you provide one bit of information available in an entry in another open document, FileMaker or Panorama may grab other information in that same entry, rather than requiring you to enter all information from scratch or manually copy information from other files.

In FileMaker, choose the DEFINE command from the SELECT menu and click the ENTRY OPTIONS button for the field that will be receiving data from another file. In the dialog that follows, check the "Look up value from another file" option, which displays a dialog requesting that you locate the lookup file. After you select a file, another dialog appears with three lists of fields. First select the field from which information will be copied. Next, select the fields from both files whose contents must match. In our case, we would select the Item Number fields from both the catalog and inventory documents.

In Panorama, you choose the LOOKUP command from the FUNCTIONS menu to display a single dialog where all lookup specifications are made. Select a lookup file from the first EXTERNAL FILE pop-up menu. The two KEY COLUMN pop-ups are used to select the fields from both files whose contents must match. The DATA pop-ups are used to select the recipient and origin of the copied information. Though this may sound easier than the method used to create lookups in FileMaker, it is actually a poorly documented and much less implicit procedure.

Reading Your Mind

Panorama provides a unique text-entry feature called Clairvoyance, which operates similarly to glossaries in a word processor, except better. As you type, Panorama tries to guess the finished word, based on other entries in the same field throughout the current document. Suppose a field contains city names, and so far you have entered three city names beginning with the letter *D* including Denver, Dallas, and Davenport. If when entering the name of the current field you first type D, Panorama assumes that you intend to enter one of the three cities just mentioned, but it doesn't yet know which one, so it makes no guess. If you next enter the letter a, the application rules out Denver, but it doesn't know which of the other two you intend to type, so it still makes no guess. If you next type l, Panorama rules out Davenport and makes its guess: Dallas. To accept the guess, simply tab to the next field. If the guess is wrong (you really want to type Danbury), then simply continue typing.

You can turn Clairvoyance on or off for a field by consulting the Clairvoyance column in the design sheet.

File-Placing Formats

In the following pages, we will look at some popular file-management applications—including those we have discussed so far as well as a few others—and examine their capabilities. To the right of each program name will be a list of the file-placing formats that the program supports. Since file managers are the final step in document composition whether storing information or manipulating information to be printed in forms, the formats that an application can save to are not as important as the formats it can import. These formats may include any text format discussed in the Word Processors or Spreadsheets entry as well as any graphics format discussed in either Drawing Software or Painting Software.

How Most of Us Manage

FileMaker II, Version 1.0   FMK$ (native), TEXT, SYLK, PICT
Of the three applications we have discussed so far, FileMaker is the most popular. We find it every bit as easy to use as Microsoft File—easier to use, in fact, because it provides features that greatly facilitate the data-entry procedure.

If you're looking for a simple file manager to use over a network, File-Maker has to be your choice. For about $600, you can purchase a network system that accommodates four users simultaneously. If more than one person is working off of a single database at the same time, the first user must deselect the EXCLUSIVE command under the FILE menu. Of course, if you're feeling short on cash, you can serve the single-user version of FileMaker over TOPS or AppleShare so that more than one person can run it at the same time. This slows things down considerably, but if you're cheap, you're no doubt used to suffering.

The feature that really makes FileMaker the preferred software for the network crowd is its simple but extremely versatile security scheme. Each user can be equipped with one of five passwords of your specification, determining to what degree the user may access sensitive portions of your database. For more information about this feature and how it is applied in other applications, see File Technicalities 2.

File Technicalities 2

*Protecting your database from wayward eyes
and mischievous glances*

Security deserves more of your consideration when creating databases than when working with most other types of software. This is because of the sensitive nature of the kind of information generally associated with file management: payroll, record keeping, inventory, profit projections, and so on.

Because different people on your staff or in your family will need to access different amounts of information, both FileMaker and Panorama provide different levels of security. Panorama allows users to access a file at one of three different levels: author, user, or custom. An author can alter the layout, create graphics, and open and close windows to his or her heart's content. A user may perform data entry but may not alter the database design. If a person enters at the custom level, the command icons as well as several of the menus are hidden, only allowing the user to access special macro commands set up by the author.

To determine the user level, press the OPTION key and choose ABOUT PANORAMA from the APPLE menu. Unfortunately, it is not possible to assign more than one password so that a user with password A can access only the user level, and a user with password B can go as high as the authoring level. Instead, if you know the password, you can change the user level as you see fit. This can result in a high-level user who knows the password leaving a file unprotected for a lower-level user to come along later and mess it up.

Since FileMaker has been designed to run over a network, its security scheme is much more satisfactory. Separate passwords are set up for different user levels. By choosing PASSWORD from the FILE menu and clicking the NEW button in the resulting dialog box, you may establish a password that allows a user to access a file at one of five security levels, from simply browsing to being able to go through and make complete changes.

The most notable security level prevents a user from viewing or altering "confidential layouts." When designing a database, you may select any field in the layout mode and choose CONFIDENTIAL from the GADGETS menu. This closes specific fields to users with passwords that go no higher than the confidential layout level. This level is perfect for salary-tracking databases and the like, where sensitive fields must share space with general user-entry information.

Conclusion: Applications such as FileMaker that allow different user levels to be associated with their own individual passwords provide the most versatile protection from information loss and manipulation. Such a security configuration also provides better protection, since one user cannot leave a file completely unlocked.

FileMaker II Quick Reference (1 of 3)

Menus

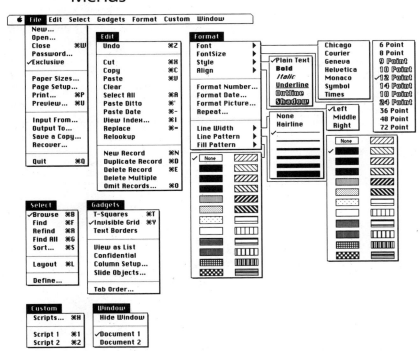

FileMaker II Quick Reference (2 of 3)

Keyboard Equivalents

Addition‡..+

Bold text .... ⌘⇧B

Browse records .... ⌘B

Cancel operation .... ⌘ .

Clear data or object .... ⌫ or ▣⌿

Clear entire field .... ⌘⇧▣⌿

Close document .... ⌘W

Concatenation‡.. &

Copy data or object .... ⌘C

Current date‡.. //

Current time‡. .... : :

Cut data or object .... ⌘X

Define dialog, select calculation field .... ⌘C

Define dialog, select date field .... ⌘D

Define dialog, select number field .... ⌘N

Define dialog, select picture field .... ⌘P

Define dialog, select summary field .... ⌘S

Define dialog, select text field .... ⌘T

Delete record, layout, or request .... ⌘E

Delete record, layout, or request,
bypass dialog.. ⌘⌥E

Display all fields in tab group in layout ....➝|

Display next record, layout, or request .... ⌘➝|

Display preceding
record, layout, or request .... ⌘⇧➝| or ⌘⌥➝|

Division‡.. /

Duplicate record, layout, or request .... ⌘D

Equal to‡.. =

Exponential (to power of...)‡.............................. ^

Find all records matching specified criteria
and add them to browsing routine .... ⌘G

Find records matching specified criteria .... ⌘F

Format date .... ⌘⇧D

Format number .... ⌘⇧N

Greater than‡... >

Greater than or equal‡..≥

Grid, activate/deactivate .... ⌘Y

Grid, deactivate temporarily .... ⌘⌁⋅⋅⋅▲ object

Grid, realign to object............................. ⌘▲ object

Hard space character,
forces two words to be read as one‡............... ⌥␣

Help .... ⌘/

‡ *For use in calculation formulas or fields*

⌘	command	➝|	tab	⌫	delete	␣	space bar
⇧	shift	←	return	⌦	fwd. delete	F1	function key
⌥	option	⌃	enter	▣	keypad key	▲	mouse click
⌁	control	⌿	escape	▣⌿	clear	⋅⋅⋅▲	mouse drag

FileMaker II Quick Reference (3 of 3)

Keyboard Equivalents (Cont.)

Italic text .... ⌘⇧I

Layout mode, access .... ⌘L
Left-justify text .... ⌘⇧L
Less than[‡] .... <
Less than or equal[‡] .... ≤

Middle-justify (center) text .... ⌘⇧M
Move object vertically or horizontally .... ⌥····↖
Move to next field in record .... →|
Move to preceding field in record .... ⇧→| or ⌥→|
Multiplication[‡] .... *

New record, layout, or request .... ⌘N
Not equal to[‡] .... ≠

Omit records from browsing routine .... ⌘O
Omit records from browsing routine,
bypass dialog (omit current record only) ..... ⌘⌥O
Open existing document .... ⌘⇧O

Page number[‡] .... ##
Paste current date .... ⌘⇧-
Paste data or object .... ⌘V
Paste ditto (paste data
from same field in last record) .... ⌘'
Paste ditto, tab to next field .... ⌘⇧'
Percentage[‡] .... %
Plain text .... ⌘⇧P

Preview document .... ⌘U
Print document .... ⌘P
Print document, bypass dialog .... ⌘⌥P

Quit FileMaker II .... ⌘Q

Range[‡] ....
Record number[‡] .... @@
Refind (repeat find request
with specified changes) .... ⌘F
Replace data in same field in other records
with data from current field .... ⌘=
Return character[‡] .... ¶ (⌥7)
Right-justify text .... ⌘⇧R
Run script (macro) number [#] .... ⌘[#]

Script most recent actions (create macro) .... ⌘H
Select all data in current field
or all objects in layout .... ⌘A
Sort order of records .... ⌘S
Subtraction/negation[‡] .... -

T squares (display vertical and
horizontal guidelines in layout mode) .... ⌘T
Text constant[‡] .... " " *around text*

Underline text .... ⌘⇧U
Undo/redo last operation .... ⌘Z

Accurate for FileMaker II, version 1.0

Panorama, Version 1.1   ZEPD (native), TEXT,
                                              WPDC (WordPerfect), PICT

The flat-file features king is the son of OverVue, one of the first database programs for the Mac. Substantially improved from its early beginnings some four years ago, Panorama provides so much power that it almost overreaches itself.

File-Management Fusion

Panorama bills itself as "the database that thinks it's a spreadsheet," and in many ways the software's basic interface is consistent with this claim. Information is entered into rows and columns much like in Excel. The contents of a column may be formatted in a variety of ways, so that a single date might appear as "July 31, 1999," "7/31/99," "07-31-99," and so on.

Panorama provides more data-input aids than its competitors, including default entry values, multiple-choice options, lookups, and Clairvoyance, which we explained earlier. All of these functions are established in a special Design Sheet mode, which you access by clicking the T square icon in the application's icon bar.

This file manager also provides a unique graphic-handling feature that allows you to use multiple copies of a PICT drawing over and over throughout various portions of a file without increasing the file size. Called *flash art,* this feature permits you to import a graphic into a special window and name it. Then, whenever you enter the name of the image into a cell, the graphic automatically appears, referencing the original drawing for printing information so that a completely new description of the graphic doesn't have to be repeated, wasting disk space.

Irregular Interface

Panorama 1.0 was fairly buggy, but version 1.1 seems to remedy all problems of which we were aware. In fact, the only drawback we see is its strange interface. In a sense, this is a purely personal observation on our part. We hate icon bars—that is, on-screen icons whose only purpose is to access commands. Full Impact, the spreadsheet from Ashton-Tate, also uses these space-consuming command metaphors, but we dearly hope they don't catch on. Commands from pull-down menus, while slightly less convenient, describe their purpose better and they don't get in your face.

Panorama Quick Reference (1 of 4)

Icon Bars (with pop-up menus displayed)

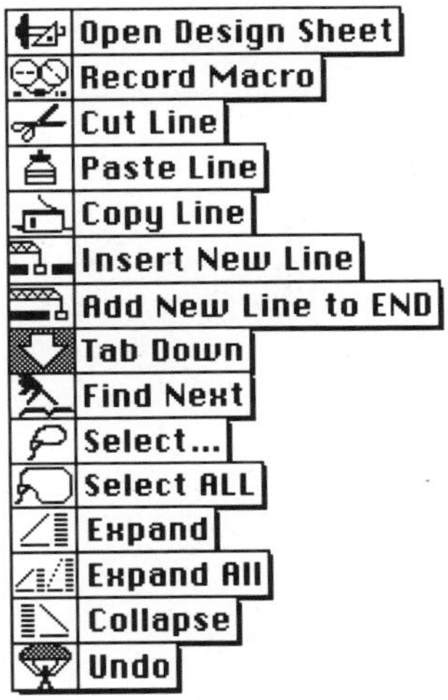

Open Design Sheet
Record Macro
Cut Line
Paste Line
Copy Line
Insert New Line
Add New Line to END
Tab Down
Find Next
Select...
Select ALL
Expand
Expand All
Collapse
Undo

*This icon bar appears in
the Data Sheet mode.*

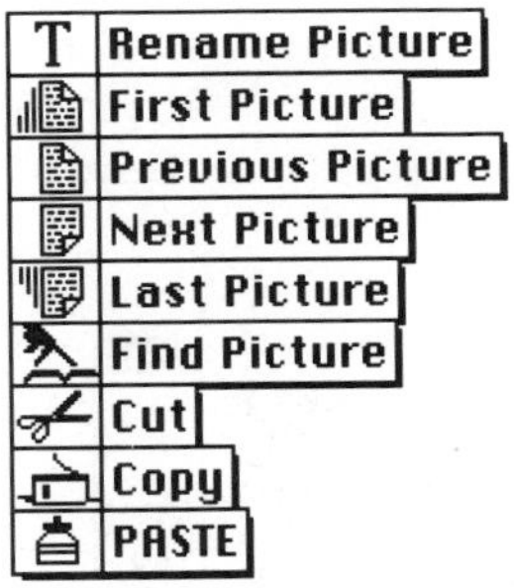

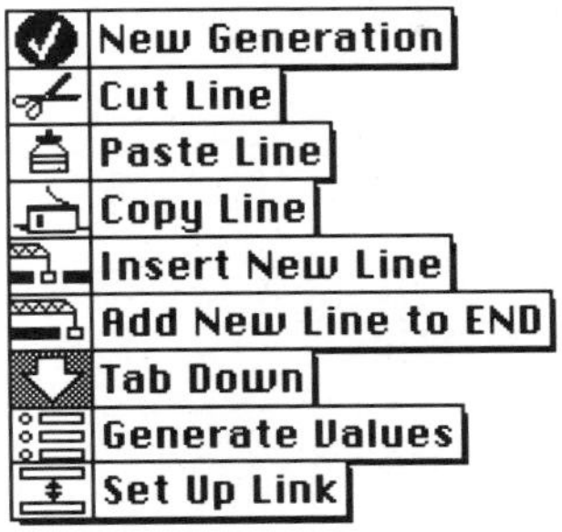

New Generation
Cut Line
Paste Line
Copy Line
Insert New Line
Add New Line to END
Tab Down
Generate Values
Set Up Link

*This icon bar appears in
the Design Sheet mode.*

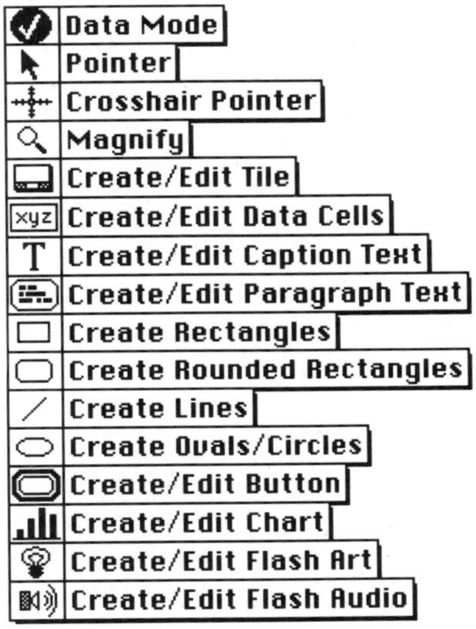

Rename Picture
First Picture
Previous Picture
Next Picture
Last Picture
Find Picture
Cut
Copy
PASTE

*This icon bar appears in
the Flash Art mode.*

Data Mode
Pointer
Crosshair Pointer
Magnify
Create/Edit Tile
Create/Edit Data Cells
Create/Edit Caption Text
Create/Edit Paragraph Text
Create Rectangles
Create Rounded Rectangles
Create Lines
Create Ovals/Circles
Create/Edit Button
Create/Edit Chart
Create/Edit Flash Art
Create/Edit Flash Audio

*This icon bar appears in a Form
window in the Graphics mode.*

Panorama Quick Reference (2 of 4)

Menus

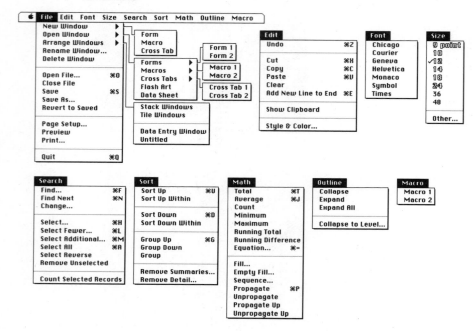

Form Window Menus

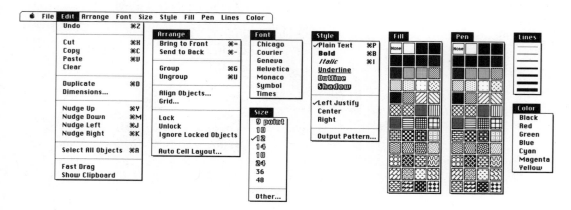

Panorama Quick Reference (3 of 4)

Keyboard Equivalents

Add new line to end of Data Sheet	⌘E	Group cells up (sort rows into groups and create subtotals)	⌘G
Addition‡	+	Group objects	⌘G
Average column of cells	⌘J		
		Integer division‡	\
Bold text in form	⌘B	Isolate field names with spaces	
Bring to front	⌘=	or punctuation‡.	« and » (⌥\ and ⇧⌥\)
		Italic text in form	⌘I
Cancel formula or operation	⌘.		
Clear field or record	⌦	Less than‡	<
Conditional expression‡	?	Less than or equal‡	≤
Confirm formula	⌅		
Copy cell or object	⌘C	Merge equation into paragraph‡	{ and }
Cut cell or object	⌘X	Move one cell down	↵
		or 🖱 tab down icon and ⇥	
Ditto character (copy data from cell above)‡	"	Move one cell left	⇧⇥
Division‡	/	Move one cell right	⇥
		Move one cell up	🖱 tab down icon and ⇧⇥
Equal to‡	=	Multiplication‡	*
Equation, fill column with result	⌘=		
Exponential (to power of...)‡	^	Not equal to‡	≠
		Nudge selected object down	⌘M
Find cells matching specified criteria	⌘F	Nudge selected object left	⌘J
Find next cell matching same criteria	⌘N	Nudge selected object right	⌘K
		Nudge selected object up	⌘Y
Greater than‡	>	Number variable‡	#
Greater than or equal‡	≥		

‡ *For use in the formula bar or macro editor*

⌘	command	⇥	tab	⌦	delete	⎵	space bar
⇧	shift	↵	return	⌦	fwd. delete	F1	function key
⌥	option	⌅	enter	⌨	keypad key	🖱	mouse click
⌃	control	⎋	escape	⌨	clear	⇢🖱	mouse drag

Panorama Quick Reference (4 of 4)

Keyboard Equivalents (Cont.)

Open existing document ....⌘O

Paste cell or object ....⌘V

Percentage‡...%

Plain text in form ....⌘P

Plural unit variable‡...~

Print document ....⌘P

Propagate (fill down) ....⌘P

Protect document
(set user level) .... ⌘⌥ *choose* ABOUT PANORAMA

Quit Panorama ....⌘Q

Save document ....⌘S

Scratch memory, change ....⌥ *when launching*
              (⌥🖱🖱 *Panorama icon at Finder*)

Select additional cells ("and" operator) ....⌘M

Select all cells or objects
(displays hidden cells) ....⌘A

Select cells matching specified criteria,
hide others ....⌘H

Select fewer cells ("or" operator) ....⌘L

Send to back ....⌘ -

Sort up (ascending order, A–Z) ....⌘U

Sort up (descending order, Z–A) ....⌘D

Spell out numbers variable‡.......................§ (⌥6)

Subtraction/negation‡.. -

Total column of cells ....⌘T

Undo/redo last operation ....⌘Z

Ungroup object ....⌘U

‡ *For use in the formula bar or macro editor*
Accurate for Panorama, version 1.1

⌘	command	⇥	tab	⌫	delete	⎵	space bar
⇧	shift	↩	return	⌦	fwd. delete	F1	function key
⌥	option	⌤	enter	⌨	keypad key	🖱	mouse click
⌃	control	⎋	escape	⌨⌧	clear	🖱	mouse drag

Panorama Documentation

We also find ourselves having to consult the manual more often when navigating inside of Panorama's spreadsheet and design sheets than when using a more structured form-based application like FileMaker or File. But the manual is superb, including more specific information for retrieving data from other file and database managers than we have seen presented in just about any other documentation.

 Microsoft File, Version 2.00a   MCDB (native), TEXT, PICT
In general, we like Microsoft products. We use Microsoft applications such as Word and Excel on a regular basis, and find them suitable to the overwhelming majority of our word-processing and spreadsheet requirements. Even Works (which because of its largely repetitive functionality we have otherwise ignored in this book) *can* be a handy piece of software for entry-level users, especially if you're used to working on a PC, where integrated software actually serves a purpose.

But File is not an application we would ever recommend, at least not in its present state. In fact, we have yet to see a piece of software change so little between version 1.0 and 2.0. The number of updated features is so small that they fill a slim pamphlet barely 30 pages long.

The only area where File outdoes the competition is in offering a series of printing templates for outputting addresses to a wide variety of Avery business labels. Otherwise, File's printing abilities rank poor.

File can only open one file at a time, as compared with FileMaker's 16-file and Panorama's 24-file capabilities, making any linking between files impossible. There is no search and replace feature, no built-in macro editor (although, like most Microsoft products, File includes AutoMac III, a third-rate macro recorder), and no function designed to facilitate data entry except optional automatic capitalization. In many ways, we find it hard to justify File to anyone who owns HyperCard.

On the plus side, File is incredibly easy to use, and it's about half the price of FileMaker. But if you're looking to save money and time, we heartily recommend the cheaper DAtabase, discussed later in this section.

Microsoft File Quick Reference (1 of 2)

Menus

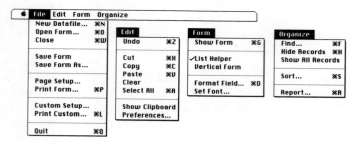

Keyboard Equivalents

Addition‡ .... +

Clear field or record .... ⊠

Clear field or record unconditionally
(bypass dialog) .... ⌘⌥⊠

Copy field or record .... ⌘C

Cut field or record .... ⌘X

Division‡ .... /

Equal to‡ .... =

Find records matching specified criteria .... ⌘F

Form type dialog, select date field .... D

Form type dialog, select number field .... N

Form type dialog, select picture field .... P

Form type dialog, select text field .... T

Format field, label, or heading .... ▶▶

Greater than‡ .... >

Greater than or equal‡ .... >=

Help .... ⌘ /

Hide selected records .... ⌘H

‡ *For use in computation fields or dialogs*

⌘	command	➔	tab	⊠	delete	▬	space bar
⇧	shift	↩	return	⊠	fwd. delete	F1	function key
⌥	option	⌄	enter	▦	keypad key	▲	mouse click
⌃	control	⌇	escape	▦⌇	clear	⋯▲	mouse drag

Microsoft File Quick Reference (2 of 2)

Keyboard Equivalents (Cont.)

Less than[‡] .... <

Less than or equal[‡] .... <=

Move field in back of other field .... ✎⌁➤

Move field vertically or horizontally .... ⌘⌁➤

Move to first field in next record .... ⤰

Move to first field in preceding record .... ⇧⤰

Move to next field in record .... ➜| or ↵

Move to preceding field in record ..... ⇧➜| or ⇧↵

Move to record one screen down .... ✎⤰

Move to record one screen up .... ✎⇧⤰

Move to same field in next record .... ⌘⤰

Move to same field in preceding record .... ⌘⇧⤰

Multiplication[‡] .... *

New document .... ⌘N

Not equal to[‡] .... <> or ><

Open alternate view of current form .... ⌘T
  or ▲▲ ruler

Open alternate view of current record .... ⌘T
  or ▲▲ record number

Open existing document .... ⌘O

Paste current date .... ⌘-

Paste current time .... ⌘;

Paste data from same field in last record .... ⌘'

Paste field or record .... ⌘V

Percentage[‡] .... %

Print document .... ⌘P

Print document to custom paper size .... ⌘L

Quit Microsoft File .... ⌘Q

Range[‡] .... …

Report summary of records .... ⌘R

Select all data in current field
or all fields in form .... ⌘A

Send field or label to back .... ✎➤

Sort order of records .... ⌘S

Subtraction/negation[‡] .... -

Undo/redo last operation .... ⌘Z

Wild card for a single character[‡] .... ?

Wild card for any number of characters[‡] .... *

Accurate for Microsoft File, version 2.00a

Remote Management

Two file-management applications are available as desk accessories, and may therefore be accessed from the APPLE menu while another application is running. This can be particularly useful for trading information back and forth between applications, or when you need to look up data without the benefit of MultiFinder.

Retriever, Version 1.01   BEJD (native), TEXT

If you're looking for a stripped-down and simple file manager with much of the functionality of Microsoft File, then Retriever is the desk accessory for you. In most respects, it is even less powerful for storing and manipulating data than HyperCard. In fact, Retriever seems to have been designed to serve as a convenience tool for HyperCard users. Three stacks are provided with Retriever, all of which are HyperCard versions of Retriever files also included with the DA. On the "About" card of any of these stacks in an I/E INSTALLER button that will install importing and exporting buttons into any other stack, thus allowing you to trade information back and forth between HyperCard and Retriever files.

Unfortunately, Retriever suffers from many limitations. Information can only be organized into simple rows and columns, graphics cannot be pasted from the Clipboard, and even the simplest of line and shape tools are missing. Though you can sort and mark entries for export, the selection of multiple entries is made very difficult, since you may only select a single cell or an entire row or column. The SHIFT key is inoperative for making multiple noncontiguous cell selections.

We would only recommend purchasing this software if you require a very simple organizational utility. Retriever's benefits are enhanced if you also have access to Exodus Software's word-processing DA, ExpressWrite, discussed in the Word Processors entry. Together the two provide quite a bit of convenience without consuming too much RAM. Both can be opened while a moderately sized stand-alone application is running on a standard Mac Plus or SE.

DAtabase, Version 1.12   QDAT (native), TEXT, PNTG, PICT2
For about $30 more than Retriever, you can buy the much superior functionality of DAtabase. In our opinion, if you currently use two or more DA's for organizing text or clip-art—such as QuickDEX, PictureBase Retriever, and even the Scrapbook—you should switch to DAtabase. It surpasses all of these desk accessories and provides the additional features associated with a flat file manager.

If you do use one of the DA's we just mentioned, you can take advantage of the DAtabase Converter, included with the desk accessory. This utility will convert text files, Scrapbook files, PictureBase documents, or address lists created in QuickDEX into DAtabase documents. You can also merge two databases into one or simply import a text file into an existing DAtabase document.

Another utility called the DAtabase Builder is actually the primary program. It allows you to create new files, determine the layout, set up the font, type sizes, and style, and so on. The desk accessory is primarily designed for entering and manipulating information in databases, but not for altering basic layouts or creating new files.

Possibly the Best DA Ever

Whereas Exodus' Retriever DA would probably disappoint long-time File users, DAtabase offers enough functionality to compete with FileMaker II. In fact, DAtabase's graphic-handling features are in many ways superior to any application discussed in this section. As in FileMaker, graphics may be imported via the Clipboard. But DAtabase also allows you to access the contents of MacPaint files directly and to display full-color PICT2 illustrations.

We love DAtabase. Since meeting up with it, we've transferred just about everything we can to this format. In fact, it might be the most functional desk accessory we've ever come across, while remaining extraordinarily easy to use. The manual is clear and extremely thorough, but we barely looked at the thing before we were up and running. Every Mac user should own this product!

HyperCard/Hypertext

Following cave walls, stone, and later papyrus, paper has long been a primary medium for transmitting written and visual communication. In fact, we have become so familiar with the mechanics behind communicating on paper that it is difficult to imagine other forms of communication. Even recent advents such as film and videotape mimic a book's two-dimensional presentation as well as its sequential flow of information.

A personal computer offers a world of additional possibilities, though the specific nature of these possibilities may not be immediately obvious. It's no wonder, therefore, that some of the most popular types of computer software—word processing, page layout, drawing, and so on—fall into the category of desktop publishing software, in which a computer is simply used as a means for creating words and images that are eventually transferred to paper. The final outcome would have been virtually identical had we scribed the text and hand-drawn the illustrations.

The real power of the computer as a communication tool lies not only in its ability to store large amounts of information, organize that information, and spit it out, but more importantly in its ability to interact with the user. When you use a piece of software, you don't think of it as a means of communication; you think of it as a working environment. All communications over a computer can be arranged similarly, providing information when you ask for it, storing information when you need to give some back, and developing new storage techniques beyond the intentions of a document's original creator.

The Living Word

So what exactly is **hypertext**? You might think of it as living text—text that you can not only read, but also question, probe, and annotate.

As an example, consider a medical student. By studying a cadaver, the student can view all portions of the body and see how they are connected. But because the organs no longer function, he or she can only theorize how the various portions of the body function and interact. Only by sitting in on operations with living patients can the student fully understand the inner workings of a human being.

Similarly, hypertext can convey more information than text on the printed page. With the click of a button, you can request that a word define itself in greater detail, access related information, or cite additional sources for more detailed research. In the perfect world, one "book" could provide a pathway to twenty others, which would branch out themselves, until an entire library was a single network of interwoven information. You could find the answer to any question by starting at the interactive volume of your choice and progressing intuitively.

Stacked Deck

 HyperCard, Version 1.2.2   STAK (native)
By virtue of the copious piles of books and articles devoted to the subject (including this one), the term *hypertext* has become almost synonymous with HyperCard in the minds of many users. Though a splendid step in the right direction, HyperCard is not the be-all and end-all your Apple retailer might have you believe.

But just because the importance of HyperCard has been blown way out of proportion doesn't mean that the Mac *isn't* nine times better than a PC. (You remember the PC—low forehead, sort of hairy, walks on four legs.)

How Hyper Is HyperCard?

HyperCard allows you to reference other cards in a stack by clicking user-definable buttons. However, in contradiction to any formal definition of hypertext, buttons cannot be integrated into a text block. Rather, they are isolated at the bottom of a screen or in some other location with their own special label or icon. This limits users to accessing only what the programmer allows them to access, as opposed to associating freely with electronic text.

On the other hand, HyperCard breaks many of the barriers commonly associated with the hypertext model. Apple prefers to call HyperCard a *hypermedia* product, and in many ways it is. Various users have demonstrated HyperCard's ability to retrieve images stored to CD ROM, as well as to integrate animation, external command routines (XCMDs), and external functions (XFCNs).

For example, a scientist using a tiny camera may record to videotape various progressions through every canal in the human body. After storing these thousands of images to CD, the scientist can program HyperCard to display a journey through the entire digestive track. Assuming that this sequence wasn't filmed in a single stretch, HyperCard will link the video of the progression through the mouth and throat to that of the descent down the esophagus to that of the interior of the stomach, and so on. We could have also journeyed through the windpipe and lungs via the same mouth and throat footage used to begin the digestive journey.

Digitized sights and sounds can be linked with HyperCard to create thoroughly interactive moving and still-image sequences, like a movie where the audience selects their favorite outcome. Although restricted by the designs of the programmer, a HyperCard stack represents one of the best uses of a computer as a communications machine.

16 Hot HyperCard Tips

HyperCard is such a versatile application that it would be nothing short of misrepresentation for us to say that we had a corner on *the* hottest tips for HyperCard. Just the same, there should be enough here for everyone. Incidentally, no sample scripts are included; they perform too specific a function. Our intention is to keep our hints as general and widely applicable as possible.

◇   **Saving disk space.** Choose COMPACT STACK from the FILE menu to rewrite the current stack, thereby decreasing its size on disk.

◇   **The versatile tilde.** To return to the most recently displayed card, even if it was in a different stack, you have only to press the tilde key (~). Luckily, this doesn't prevent you from accessing the tilde or grave accent (`) character. To get the tilde, press SHIFT-TILDE. To get the grave, press OPTION-TILDE followed by the character over which you want it to appear. If you want to produce the grave accent by itself, press OPTION-TILDE followed by the space bar.

◇ **Tool equivalents.** You may display the toolbox by pressing OPTION-TAB. If you want to select the browse tool (the one with the pointing finger), press COMMAND-TAB. You may also select the button and field tools from the keyboard by pressing the TAB key multiple times in a row. For example, to get the button tool, hold down COMMAND and press TAB twice; and to get the field tool, hold down COMMAND and press TAB three times.

◇ **Drawing new buttons and fields.** To create a new button or field, select the button or field tool and command-drag.

◇ **Accessing scripts quickly.** Shift-double-clicking a button or field with the button or field tool will bring up the script for that object. Pressing COMMAND and OPTION while clicking a button with the browse tool also brings up the button script; command-shift-option-clicking a field brings up the field script. In addition, COMMAND-OPTION-C brings up the script for the current card, COMMAND-OPTION-B displays the background script, and COMMAND-OPTION-S brings up the stack script.

◇ **Not-so-smart quotes.** If you create documents as often as we do, you may be accustomed to pressing OPTION-[and SHIFT-OPTION-[when you want to access opening and closing quotation marks (" and "). Unfortunately, if you try to use the opening and closing quotes in a script or message-box command, HyperCard will return an error. You must always use the straight double quote ("). We wrote this hint for ourselves as much as for anyone else. Believe it or not, almost every time we use HyperCard, we make this same mistake, and it takes us several minutes to figure out what we were doing wrong. You're probably smart enough to know better.

◇ **Font problems?** Here's another one for the "so smart we're dumb" crowd. If you're like us, you've cleared your System file of all but the most essential screen fonts—Geneva 9-point and 12-point, Monaco 9-point, and Chicago 12-point—and relegated the rest to suitcases that you open with MasterJuggler or Suitcase. If the type across the top of the first Home card and elsewhere in the stack looks awful, it's because you don't have Times 18-point open. Since we don't use this font elsewhere, we've loaded it into HyperCard directly. Simply launch Apple's Font/DA Mover utility, option-click the Open button (which allows you to select from non-suitcase files), and select HyperCard. Then copy the Times 18-point screen font from one of your original System disks to the HyperCard application.

◇ **I can't change the user level!** Most people already know this one, but if you've never run into it before, maybe we can help you avoid a traumatic experience. When you set the user mode to "browsing" or "typing," you lose three commands from the FILE menu: COMPACT STACK, PROTECT STACK, and DELETE STACK. This can seem like a big problem if you need to get to the dialog box required to raise the user level. But by pressing COMMAND while displaying the FILE menu, you cause the commands to reappear.

◇ **Test your stacks in all modes.** Everyone tries to test their stacks the best they can before throwing them to the masses. But many programmers overlook testing their stacks in any but the "scripting" user mode. If you plan to distribute your stack in another mode, such as "browsing," so as to discourage alterations, you should experiment with *every* feature of your stack in that mode. Some of the most common problems in using stacks arise when a programmer forgets to account for the user mode.

◇ **Dialing the phone without wearing out your fingers.** The "dial" command is an integral part of the HyperTalk language. This means that you can dial phone numbers in any stack. You can even dial a number on a touch-tone phone just by holding your receiver up to your Mac's speaker. When using the "dial" command in the message box or elsewhere outside of the Phone stack, do not use hyphens. Just type all seven numbers (or eight, ten, or eleven for long distance) in a row.

If your phone isn't sensitive enough to pick up tones emitted from your Mac's speaker, try turning up the volume from the Control Panel, or use a modem. A modem doesn't always have to blurt high-pitched noises into the phone. Sometimes, you can just use it to dial the phone. After it dials, pick up an extension and proceed normally.

◇ **Finder substitute.** Any stack, including Home, can serve as a substitute for the Finder, providing a custom way station between running applications. First, set up a macro that launches HyperCard and opens the appropriate stack every time your computer boots up. You can accomplish this using CE Software's QuickTimer or Affinity's Tempo II with Autoboot. Your stack should contain buttons that allow you to launch your favorite applications. A sample button script might read "open "MacDraw"."

When you quit an application run from a HyperCard stack, you are returned to that stack, completing the stack-as-Finder metaphor. If you want to quit an application all the way back to the Finder, press COMMAND-OPTION-Q.

◇   **Capturing thumbnails.** When you choose the RECENT command, you display tiny thumbnail shots of the 42 most recent cards you've been to, including those in other stacks. You can also capture these thumbnails for use in your stack—as a visual table of contents, for example. First choose COPY CARD from the EDIT menu. Notice that when you display the EDIT menu now, the PASTE command reads PASTE CARD. If you press the SHIFT key and display the EDIT menu, the same command reads PASTE PICTURE. By choosing this command, you paste a tiny bit-map thumbnail, 1/42 of the real size. Or, simply press SHIFT-COMMAND-V.

◇   **Grabbing field text.** In the message box, you can lift a word of type in a field by command-clicking the word. This is especially useful if you want to perform your own search command through a stack. Press COMMAND-M to display the message box. Then press COMMAND-F to insert a "find" command with the text-entry cursor set between the two quotes. If you want to search for a word in a field in the current card, command-click the word and it will automatically appear between the two quotes in the message box. If you want to search for more than one word, command-drag. Pressing RETURN will highlight the entry in the current card, so you'll have to press RETURN twice to search other cards.

◆   **Creating custom icons.** Making custom button icons for HyperCard stacks is a very simple process if you have Apple's ResEdit utility. In ResEdit, open the HyperCard application, and then double-click on the ICON resource, displaying all button icons currently used by HyperCard. To create your own button, you may edit an existing button that you don't use very often, such as Bill Atkinson's face. Double-click the icon and an editing window appears, allowing you to turn on and off pixels as you would in MacPaint's "fat-bits" mode. If you don't want to lose any existing icons, select an icon and choose the DUPLICATE command from the EDIT menu. This creates two identical button icons, one of which you may edit by double-clicking. You may also want to change the icon name after closing the edit window by choosing GET INFO from the FILE menu for a selected icon.

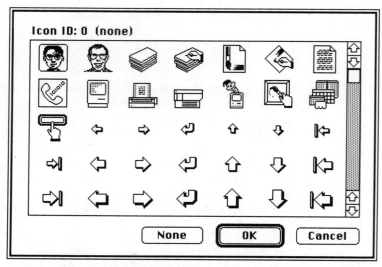

By duplicating the icon for Bill's face and editing it, we were able to create our own button icon representing one of our faces.

If you want your button icons to appear correctly for users running different HyperCard applications on their own machines, you must install the icon in your stack as well. While still in ResEdit, copy the button in the HyperCard application ICON resource. Then open your stack. You will probably get an Alert box warning you that no resource fork exists for the file you're trying to open and that proceeding will create one. Allow this to happen by clicking OK. Then choose Paste. A new ICON resource will appear with your custom icon inside.

◆ **Function problems.** Many functions ("mouseClick," "clickLoc," and so on) intercept more information than you might expect. For example, an "on returnKey" or "on enterKey" routine is commonly used to capture strings entered by the user for a "find" routine or some related purpose. However, the "returnKey" or "enterKey" function toggles whenever the respective key is pressed, even in the message box. Since the message box is generally used to enter literal commands, you may want to include a modifier in your code if you want the message box to remain operative. A bit of extra code such as "if message empty then…" allows you to filter out commands entered into the message box.

Incidentally, if you don't want users taking advantage of the message box, you can intercept all messages as well using the "returnKey" and "enterKey" functions.

◆ **Anyone can forget a password.** HyperCard's getting old these days. We created our first stack over two years ago, and have barely touched it since. In the meantime, of course, we managed to completely forget the password. We even had it written down somewhere.

Some would say it serves us right for not sharing information. But luckily, some smart guys named Ned Hovath and Allan Foster wrote Deprotect, a utility that gets rid of your password entirely. You can even get rid of other people's passwords with it.

But better yet, don't lose your password. Our new technique, which seems to work pretty well, is to hide the password in the stack. You might create an invisible button that brings up a field containing the password. Or name one of your cards, buttons, or fields after a password. Years from now, you may forget where the heck you hid the thing, but at least you'll know it's in there somewhere!

Pumping Up HyperCard

In the near future, you can expect to see a HyperCard 2.0 that includes multiple window capabilities with editable window sizes, multiple type styles in a single field, user-definable menus, object-oriented drawing tools, editable buttons, color, and so on. But if you can't wait for a HyperCard upgrade, you have two choices for creating state-of-the-art stacks. If you have the cash, probably your best bet is to purchase one of the third-party HyperCard clones, including SuperCard from Silicon Beach, and Plus, created by Format Software in West Germany and distributed by Olduvai, both in the $200 range. If you aren't quite that rich, you might first take a look at some of the HyperCard enhancement utilities vying for your approval.

HyperCard Quick Reference (1 of 5)

Toolbox

	Browse	↖ button to activate, ↖ field to enter type, ···↖ across type to edit
	Button	↖ existing button to select, ⌘···↖ to draw new button
	Field	↖ existing field to select, ⌘···↖ to draw new field
	Marquee	···↖ to select rectangular portion of painting to manipulate
	Lasso	···↖ to select irregular portion of painting to manipulate
	Pencil	↖ to create or delete pixels, ···↖ to draw or delete free-form lines
	Paintbrush	···↖ to draw free-form lines with current brush shape
	Eraser	···↖ to delete general portions of bit map
	Line	···↖ to draw straight line at any angle
	Spraypaint	···↖ to generate pattern of loose pixels
	Paint can	···↖ to fill an enclosed or solid area with current pattern
	Rectangle	···↖ to draw rectangle
	Round corner	···↖ to draw rectangle with rounded corners
	Oval	···↖ to draw ellipse
	Freehand	···↖ to draw free-form lines in current line weight
	Regular polygon	···↖ to draw equilateral polygon with definable number of sides
	Polygon	↖ to create corners for straight-sided polygon
	Type	↖ to set origin for bit-mapped text block (not used to edit)

HyperCard Quick Reference (2 of 5)

Menus

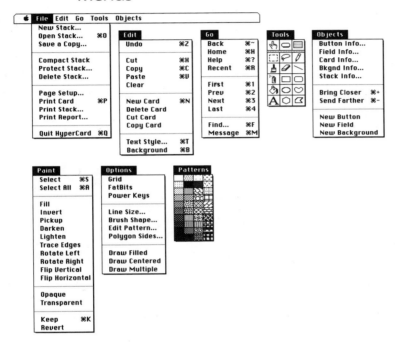

PAINT, OPTIONS, and PATTERNS menus appear only when a painting tool is selected

HyperCard Quick Reference (3 of 5)

Keyboard Equivalents

Actual size/fat bits, toggle‡........... 🖰🖰 *pencil icon*

or ⌘🖰 *w/pencil tool*

Advance cursor to next field†.............................➔|

Back, retrace through cards
viewed so far .... ~ *or* 🖳⌀ *or* ⍼↓ *or* ⌘~‡

Background/card, toggle .... ⌘B

Black pattern, select‡... B

Bring closer (forward) .... ⌘=

Browse tool, select .... ⌘➔|

Brush shape, select‡.............. 🖰🖰 *paintbrush icon*

Button locations, show temporarily†. .... ⌘⍼

Button tool, select .... ⌘➔|➔|

Cancel current operation .... ⌘.

Card pictures, show temporarily
(hide background)‡..⍼D

Change number of sides in equilateral
polygon‡......................... 🖰🖰 *regular polygon icon*

Change to next typeface................................⌘⇧>

Change to previous typeface ....⌘⇧<

Circle, create‡.............................. ⇧┈🖰 *w/oval tool*

Clear object .... ⊠

Clone selected button .... ⍼┈🖰 *w/button tool*

Clone selected field .... ⍼┈🖰 *w/field tool*

Clone selected picture‡..................... ⍼┈🖰 *picture*

COMPACT STACK, show command ..⌘🖰 *FILE menu*

Copy object .... ⌘C

Cut object .... ⌘X

Darken selection‡... D

DELETE STACK, show command ...... ⌘🖰 *FILE menu*

Draw filled shape‡................... 🖰🖰 *shape tool icon*

(except regular polygon)

Draw from center/corner, toggle‡......................... C

Draw multiple shapes, toggle‡.............................. M

Draw with selected picture‡. .... ⌘⍼┈🖰 *picture*

Edit button script .... ⇧🖰🖰 *w/button tool*

or ⌘⍼🖰 *w/browse tool*

Edit current background script ....⌘⍼B

Edit current card script ....⌘⍼C

Edit field script .... ⇧🖰🖰 *w/field tool*

or ⌘⇧⍼🖰 *w/browse tool*

---

† *Exclusively applicable to the browse mode*

‡ *Specifically for use when a painting tool is selected*

Throughout this chart, we assume you have selected the "Text arrows" and "Power keys" options in the User Preferences card of your Home stack

---

⌘	command	➔|	tab	⊠	delete	▬	space bar
⇧	shift	←	return	⊠	fwd. delete	F1	function key
⍼	option	⌁	enter	🖳	keypad key	🖰	mouse click
⌃	control	⌀	escape	🖳⌀	clear	┈🖰	mouse drag

HyperCard Quick Reference (4 of 5)

Keyboard Equivalents (Cont.)

Edit pattern[‡]. .... ➤➤ *pattern icon*

Edit stack script .... ⌘⬀S

Erase entire card[‡]. .... ➤➤ *eraser icon*

Erase opaque
(hide background)[‡]. .... ⌘⸺➤ *w/eraser tool*

Erase with paintbrush
or spraypaint tool[‡]. .... ⌘⸺➤ *w/tool*

Field and button locations,
show temporarily[‡]. .... ⌘⇧⬀

Field tool, select .... ⌘➡|➡|➡|

Fill selection[‡]. .... F

Find specified field text .... ⌘F

First card in stack, go to .... ⌘1 *or* ⌘←

Flip selection horizontally[‡]. .... H

Flip selection vertically[‡]. V

Forward through retraced cards .... ⬀↑

Grab multiple words of field text
while in message box .... ⌘⸺➤ *field text*

Grab pattern off page (gridded)[‡]. .... ➤
    while PATTERN *dialog displayed*

Grab single word of field text
while in message box .... ⌘➤ *field text*

Grid, activate/deactivate[‡]. .... G

Help stack, go to .... ⌘ /

Home, close current stack .... ⌘H

Increase leading .... ⌘⬀>
    or ⌘⇧⬀> *in version 1.2 or later*

Increase type size. .... ⌘>

Invert selection[‡]. I

Keep (save) picture on current card[‡]. .... ⌘K

Lasso entire enclosed shape[‡]. .... ⌘➤ *w/lasso tool*

Last card in stack, advance to .... ⌘4 *or* ⌘→

Lighten selection[‡]. L

Line weight, select[‡]. 1, 2, 3, 4, 6, 8

Lines at 15° angles, create[‡]. .... ⇧⸺➤ *w/line tool*
    or polygon tool

Mark current card for quick return
(may mark multiple cards) .... ⌘↓

Menu bar, show/hide .... ⌘⎵

Message box, display .... ⌘M

Move selected picture in 45° direction[‡]. .... ⇧⸺➤

New button, create .... ⌘⸺➤ *w/button tool*

New card, create .... ⌘N

New field, create .... ⌘⸺➤ *w/field tool*

Next card in stack, advance to .... ⌘3 *or* ⬀→

Opaque areas, show temporarily as black[‡]. ...... ⬀0

Opaque selection[‡]. 0

Open existing stack .... ⌘O
    or ➤ *appropriate button in Home*

Paste object .... ⌘V

Paste miniature of copied card .... ⌘⇧V

Pattern palette, display at cursor position[‡]. .... ➡|

Patterned lines, create[‡]. .... ⬀⸺➤ *w/line tool*

Perpendicular lines, create[‡]. .... ⇧⸺➤
    w/any painting tool or eraser

Pickup pattern behind selection[‡]. .... P

Previous card in stack, go to .... ⌘2 *or* ⬀←

Print card .... ⌘P

HyperCard Quick Reference (5 of 5)

Keyboard Equivalents (Cont.)

PROTECT STACK, show command....⌘﹡↖ *FILE menu*

Quick return to marked card
(return to most recently marked card first) ..... ⌘↑

Quit from application launched
by HyperCard back to Finder .... ⌘⌥Q

Quit from application launched
by HyperCard back to HyperCard .... ⌘Q

Quit HyperCard .... ⌘Q

Recent, display thumbnails of 42 last cards .... ⌘R

Reduce leading .... ⌘⌥<
  or ⌘⇧⌥< *in version 1.2 or later*

Reduce type size .... ⌘<

Revert to last picture saved
with KEEP command‡ .... R

Rotate selection left (90° counterclockwise)‡ ...... [

Rotate selection right (90° clockwise)‡. ....]

Scale button‡ .... ⌲↖ *corner ʷ/ button tool*

Scale field‡ .... ⌲↖ *corner ʷ/ field tool*

Scale proportionally‡ ...... ⌘⇧⌲↖ *marquee corner*

Scale selected picture‡ .... ⌘⌲↖ *marquee corner*

Select all images‡. .... ⌘A *or* A

Select all pictures
on card‡. .... ↖﹡↖ *lasso or marquee icon*

Select most recent image drawn‡. .... ⌘S *or* S

Send farther (behind) .... ⌘-

Shapes with patterned
outlines, create .... ⌥⌲↖ ʷ/ *any shape tool*

Shrink marquee to picture‡ .... ⌘⌲↖ ʷ/ *marquee*

Square, create .... ⇧⌲↖ ʷ/ *rectangle tool*

Tear off menus .... ⌲↖ *TOOLS or PATTERNS menu*

Toolbox, display at cursor position .... ⌥➔|

Trace edges of selection‡ .... E

Transparent selection‡ .... T

Type style specifications .... ⌘T

Undo/redo last operation .... ⌘Z *or* ~‡ *or* ▦⟋‡

White pattern, select‡. .... W

---

† *Exclusively applicable to the browse mode*

‡ *Specifically for use when a painting tool is selected*

Throughout this chart, we assume you have selected the "Text arrows" and
"Power keys" options in the User Preferences card of your Home stack

Accurate for HyperCard, version 1.2.2

⌘	command	➔|	tab	⊠	delete	▬	space bar
⇧	shift	↵	return	⊠	fwd. delete	F1	function key
⌥	option	⌲	enter	▦	keypad key	↖	mouse click
⟑	control	⟋	escape	▦⟋	clear	⌲↖	mouse drag

Viewing Stacks in Other Applications

HyperDA, Version 1.1.1

One HyperCard enhancement you might consider is HyperDA, a desk accessory from Symmetry that allows you to view many kinds of stacks while running another application without the benefit of MultiFinder. HyperDA is only intended for viewing stacks, so no changes may be made. However, this is a great utility if you need to reference some bit of material in a stack while using a word processor or other application.

HyperDA does not support animation routines, sounds, XCMDs or XFCNs, or scripting properties. (It does not recognize whether a key is held down, for example.) But most other playback features are handled quite admirably.

Resourceful Helpers

Another category of HyperCard-compatible utilities includes external commands (XCMDs) and external functions (XFCNs). These are small programs written in Basic, Pascal, C, or some other computer language, and compiled as resource code. That's why most of us don't create our own XCMDs and XFCNs. However, all of us can install and use external codes, simply by copying them and pasting them into a stack using Res-Edit. Even better news, most XCMDs and XFCNs are available in the public domain or for a very reasonable price.

- **ColorCard** by Douglas Chute, available through Drexel University, updates HyperCard to include multiple windows and color images imported in PICT2.

- **CompileIt** by Tim Pittman, available through Heizer Software, allows the rest of us to turn our scripts into XCMDs and XFCNs. This is especially useful for those interested in hiding some of their more advanced scripting ideas.

- **HyperCom**, available through GAVA, allows you to communicate between HyperCard stacks over a network.

- **HyperComposer**, available through Addison-Wesley, allows you to write up to 11,000 notes of music using an on-screen keyboard and musical staff.

- **VideoDisc Toolkit** and **Audio Toolkit** by Bill Atkinson and Mike Holm, available through Apple, allow you to directly access and organize information stored to videodiscs and CDs.

This list doesn't even represent 1 percent of the hoard of externals currently available. But they are some of the best, and they give you an idea of what a few users can do to improve a piece of software, even when the original distributor shows lackluster interest.

Hyper Improvements

The problem with XCMDs and XFCNs is that each one requires a certain amount of learning, and several are required to make substantial environmental improvements. If you're serious about scripting and you're willing to part with the cash, you can find fully upgraded applications that make HyperCard sluggish by comparison.

File-Placing Formats

In the following pages, we will look at some HyperCard imitations and true hypertext applications and examine their capabilities. To the right of each program name will be a list of the file-placing formats that the program supports. Since these types of programs are a final step in document composition, it is not important which formats an application can save to, but rather which formats it can import. These formats may include any external resource such as XCMD, XFCN, SND (sound), CLUT (color lookup table), and CURS (cursor), as well as graphics formats discussed in the Drawing Software entry and text formats discussed in the Word Processors entry. They may also include HyperCard's native format, STAK.

The Second Hyper Generation

 SuperCard, Version 1.0   MDOC (native), STAK, XCMD, XFCN, SND, CLUT, CURS, PNTG, PICT, TIFF

SuperCard's strongest quality is that it adds all of the new features we mentioned earlier while retaining all of the benefits of HyperCard. Super-Card opens HyperCard stacks, and allows the import of XCMDs and XFCNs, as well as sound, color, and cursor resources. It even provides a command for this purpose, rather than making you go to the trouble of installing resources via ResEdit.

As far as graphic potential goes, SuperCard provides most of the painting and drawing features included in Silicon Beach's popular SuperPaint, including an autotrace tool, which traces bit-mapped images with object-oriented shapes. You can even trace a bit-mapped shape to use as a button. If you need to print your stack to create accompanying documentation, you can ensure that every element in your stack is object-oriented, even buttons, and that all text is printed smoothly.

Since most Mac users don't (and probably never will) own SuperCard, a BUILD STANDALONE command is included, allowing you to create stack applications that run by themselves. Silicon Beach imposes no licensing fees. In fact, SuperCard's relative rarity among Mac owners is advantageous, helping to prevent users from altering your stacks. Stand-alone stacks contain much of SuperCard's running code but none of its editing code.

Editing a stack is made both easier and more difficult by SuperCard. On one hand, when you open a scripting window, every command, function, and property is available from a series of pull-down menus, making the scripting process much less laborious and more accurate. A SCRIPT menu allows you to set the font for a script, set tabs, search and replace (extraordinarily useful for scripting), and undo. You may even print a script from this menu.

On the other hand, SuperCard is more fragmented than HyperCard. Whereas HyperCard is a single program that lets you run and edit stacks, SuperCard is divided into a stack-running application, called SuperCard, and a stack-editing application, called SuperEdit. By installing a utility called Runtime Editor into your stack, you can accomplish most editing tasks directly in SuperCard. However, you may not create new stacks, install resources, or add windows, backgrounds, or menus; you can only accomplish these tasks by running SuperEdit. Unfortunately, SuperEdit will not run a stack or interpret scripts. So creating a SuperCard stack involves a certain amount of switching back and forth between programs.

SuperCard/Edit Quick Reference (1 of 6)

Drawing & Painting Toolboxes

▲	Arrow	▲ to select object to manipulate, ⋯▲ to move
A	Type	▲ to set origin for text block, ⌘⋯▲ across type to edit
+	Perpendicular line	⋯▲ to draw horizontal or vertical line
＼	Line	⋯▲ to draw straight line at any angle
□	Rectangle	⋯▲ to draw rectangle
▢	Round corner	⋯▲ to draw rectangle with rounded corners
○	Oval	⋯▲ to draw ellipse
◁	Polygon	▲ to create corners for straight-sided polygon
⌐	Arc	⋯▲ to draw quarter ellipse from top or bottom point to side point
⚯	Freehand	⋯▲ to draw free-form lines in current line weight
⚯	Autotrace	⋯▲ lasso around bit map to trace with object-oriented shapes

⬚	Marquee	⋯▲ to select rectangular portion of bit map to manipulate
♪	Lasso	⋯▲ to select irregular portion of bit map to manipulate
✎	Pencil	▲ to create or delete pixels, ⋯▲ to draw or delete free-form lines
◨	Eraser	⋯▲ to delete general portions of bit map
A	Type	▲ to set origin for bit-mapped text block (not used to edit)
🖌	Paintbrush	⋯▲ to draw free-form lines with current brush shape
🖋	Spraypaint	⋯▲ to generate pattern of loose pixels
🪣	Paint can	⋯▲ to fill an enclosed or solid area with current pattern

SuperCard/Edit Quick Reference (2 of 6)

Button & Field Toolboxes

▶	Arrow	⯑ to select object to manipulate, ⋯▶ to move
⬚	Transparent rectangle button	⋯▶ to draw rectangular transparent button
▢	Regular rectangle button	⋯▶ to draw rectangular opaque button
▢	Shadow rectangle button	⋯▶ to draw rectangular button with drop shadow
⬚	Transparent polygon button	⋯▶ to create corners for multisided transparent button
◩	Regular polygon button	⋯▶ to create corners for multisided opaque button
◪	Shadow polygon button	⋯▶ to create corners for multisided button with shadow
⭕	Round corner button	⋯▶ to draw rounded button, ⯑ for 60 × 20-pixel button
⭕	Shadow round corner button	⋯▶ to draw rounded button with drop shadow
◉	Radio button	⋯▶ to create standard radio button with text area
⊠	Check box button	⋯▶ to create standard check box button with text area
⤳	Autotrace button	⋯▶ lasso around bit map to trace with polygon button
⬚	Transparent field	⋯▶ to create transparent field
▢	Regular field	⋯▶ to create opaque field
▢	Shadow field	⋯▶ to create field with drop shadow
▣	Scrolling field	⋯▶ to create field with scroll bars

SuperCard/Edit Quick Reference (3 of 6)

Menus

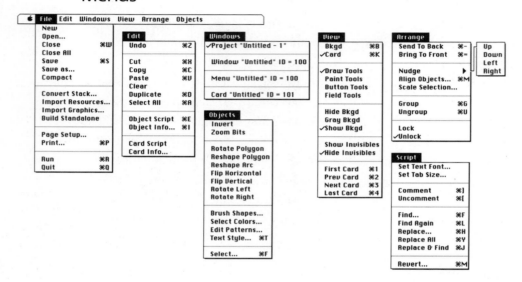

Overview Menus

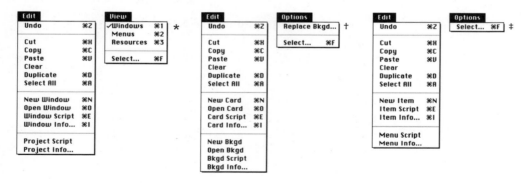

*   *Available in the project overview*
†   *Available in the window overview*
‡   *Available in the menu overview*

SuperCard/Edit Quick Reference (4 of 6)

Keyboard Equivalents

Actual size/zoom bits, toggle ..... ⌘↖ ʷ/ *pencil tool*

Align objects .... ⌘M

Align objects, apply current settings .... ⌘⌥M

Automatic script indent,
activate/deactivate .... ⌥→|

Autotrace bit map
by marqueeing .... ⌥⋯↖ ʷ/ *autotrace tool*

Autotrace bit map with freehand or polygon
drawing tools .... ⌘⋯↖ ʷ/ *tool*

Autotrace interior
of bit map .... ⌘↖ ʷ/ *autotrace tool*

Background, display for current card .... ⌘B

Bring to front .... ⌘=

Brush shape, select .... ↖↖ *paintbrush icon*

Card, display instead of background .... ⌘K

Circle, create .... ⇧⋯↖ ʷ/ *oval tool*

Clear object .... ⌫

Clone selected bit map .... ⌥⋯↖ *bit map*

Comment on selected scripting text .... ⌘]

Constrain rounded button
to 20 by 60 pixels .... ⌥⋯↖ ʷ/ *rounded button tool*

Copy object .... ⌘C

Create new opaque
bit map .... ⋯↖ ʷ/ *any paint tool at empty area*

Create new transparent
bit map .... ⌥⋯↖ ʷ/ *any paint tool at empty area*

Crop bit map .... ⋯↖ *corner handle* ʷ/ *arrow tool*

Cut object .... ⌘X

Display card info .... ⌘I *from window overview*

Display item info .... ⌘I *from menu overview*
or ↖↖ *item object listing*

Display next toolbox .... ↖ *toolbox icon*

Display preceding toolbox .... ⌘↖ *toolbox icon*

Display selected
object info .... ⌘I *or* ↖↖ *object*

Display window, menu, or resource
info .... ⌘I *from project overview*

Draw with selected bit map .... ⌘⌥⋯↖ *bit map*

Duplicate objects .... ⌘D

* *Also applicable to SuperCard*
Equivalents are applicable to SuperEdit in the layout overview, unless otherwise noted

⌘	command	→		tab	⌫	delete	⎵	space bar
⇧	shift	↩	return	⌦	fwd. delete	F1	function key
⌥	option	⌤	enter	▣	keypad key	↖	mouse click
⌃	control	⎋	escape	▣⌫	clear	⋯↖	mouse drag

SuperCard/Edit Quick Reference (5 of 6)

Keyboard Equivalents (Cont.)

Edit card script .... ⌘E *from window overview*

Edit item script .... ⌘E *from menu overview or ⇧↖↖ item object listing or ⇧ choose command**

Edit selected button or field script .... ⌘E *or* ⇧↖↖ *object*

Edit window or menu script .... ⌘E *from project overview*

Erase entire bit map .... ↖↖ *eraser icon*

Find scripting text again (next occurrence) ..... ⌘L

Find specified scripting text .... ⌘F

First card in stack, go to .... ⌘1 *or* ⌥←*

Group objects .... ⌘G

Highlight multiple items in an overview listing .... ⌘↖ *items*

Lasso without tightening .... ⌥---↖ *w/ lasso tool*

Last card in stack, advance to .... ⌘4 *or* ⌥→*

Line break in script .... ⌥↩

Lines at 30° angles, create .... ⇧---↖ *w/ line tool or polygon tool*

Lock open pattern palette temporarily .... ⇧↖ *line or fill indicator*

Make selected element transparent .... ⌘---↖ *w/ lasso tool*

Menus, display in project overview .... ⌘2 *or* ↖ *menu icon*

Move selected object in 45° direction .... ⇧---↖

New card .... ⌘N *from window overview or* ↖↖ *information bar*

New menu .... ⌘N *from project overview or* ↖↖ *menu icon*

New menu item .... ⌘N *from menu overview or* ↖↖ *information bar*

New resource .... ⌘N *from project overview or* ↖↖ *resource icon*

New window .... ⌘N *from project overview or* ↖↖ *window icon*

Next card in stack, advance to .... ⌘3 *or* →*

Nudge selected object .... →, ↓, ←, *or* ↑

* *Also applicable to SuperCard*

Equivalents are applicable to SuperEdit in the layout overview, unless otherwise noted

⌘	command	⇥	tab	⌫	delete	␣	space bar
⇧	shift	↩	return	⌦	fwd. delete	F1	function key
⌥	option	⌤	enter	⌨	keypad key	↖	mouse click
⌃	control	⎋	escape	⌨⎋	clear	---↖	mouse drag

SuperCard/Edit Quick Reference (6 of 6)

Keyboard Equivalents (Cont.)

Open card .... ⌘O *from window overview
or* ⭦⭦ *card object listing*

Open menu .... ⌘O *from project overview
or* ⭦⭦ *menu object listing*

Open resource .... ⌘O *from project overview
or* ⭦⭦ *resource object listing*

Open window .... ⌘O *from project overview
or* ⭦⭦ *window object listing*

Paint only over black areas
(erase overlay mode) .... ⌘⭠ *w/any paint tool*

Paint only over white areas
(transparent overlay) .... ⭠ *w/any paint tool*

Paste object .... ⌘V

Perpendicular lines, create ... ⭠ *w/perp. line tool
or* ⇧⭠ *w/line tool or polygon tool
or any painting tool or eraser*

Previous card in stack, go to .... ⌘2 *or* ←*

Print window .... ⌘P

Quit SuperEdit/SuperCard .... ⌘Q

Replace all occurrences
of specified scripting text .... ⌘Y

Replace selected scripting text
and find next occurrence .... ⌘J

Replace selected scripting text .... ⌘H

Resources, display in project overview .... ⌘3
or ⭦ *resource icon*

Revert to original scripting text .... ⌘M

Run project in SuperCard .... ⌘R

Save project .... ⌘S

Scale bit map .... ⭠ *corner handle
w/arrow tool*

Scale bit map proportionally .... ⌘⇧⭠ *corner handle w/arrow tool*

Scale object
proportionally .... ⌘⇧⭠ *corner handle*

Scale object vertically
or horizontally .... ⇧⭠ *corner handle*

Select all objects .... ⌘A
or ⭦⭦ *arrow tool icon*

Select entire bit map .... ⭦⭦ *marquee icon*

Select specified objects ..... ⌘F *from any overview*

Send to back .... ⌘-

Shrink marquee to bit map .... ⌘⭠ *w/marquee*

Square, create .... ⇧⭠ *w/rectangle tool*

Text style
specifications .... ⌘T *or* ⭦⭦ *type tool icon*

Tighten marquee to bit map ...... ⭠ *w/marquee*

Toggle between button toolbox
and field toolbox .... ⭠ *toolbox icon*

Toggle between paint toolbox
and draw toolbox .... ⭠ *toolbox icon*

Uncomment selected scripting text .... ⌘[

Undo/redo last operation .... ⌘Z

Ungroup object .... ⌘U

Windows, display in project overview .... ⌘1
or ⭦ *window icon*

Accurate for SuperEdit, version 1.0

Plus, Version 1.0   STAK, WORD (MacWrite),
                                         XCMD, XFCN, SND, CLUT, CURS, PNTG, PICT
SuperCard is to HyperCard what the first SuperPaint was to MacPaint.
Both products retain the same look and feel as their predecessors, while
adding power and versatility. For this reason, we honestly believe that
anyone who understands HyperCard can easily pick up SuperCard and
benefit from its enhancements.

Plus is more of a departure. For one thing, its interface is made up entirely
of what it calls "software slots," which show up as icons on a menu bar.
These slots include icons for word processing, drawing, painting, and
database management.

In a way, this architecture allows for greater versatility. Very advanced
users may create their own slots. Suggested software slots include spelling
checkers, spreadsheets, telecommunications, and networking.

But not all of us are willing to put that much time and effort into building
a stack, and for such people, Plus may appear to have sacrificed an intuitive interface for a kind of power they don't really understand. Also, you
can't create stand-alone stacks with Plus. A run-time version of the program is included for distribution with a stack, but this solution is a little
less tidy than SuperCard's.

More Hypertext, Less Hypermedia

Neither HyperCard, SuperCard, nor Plus provides true hypertext features;
that is, the ability to access stepping stones of information simply by
clicking on a word in a paragraph or page of text. Although these programs
have progressed beyond any textbook definition of hypertext in a number
of information-handling areas, a necessary element of the basic ground-
work for a truly interactive communications environment has been left
unexploited.

If your primary interest is communicating with words rather than pictures, and you want users not only to take advantage of the links you
provide, but also to be able to easily create their own links between your
words and theirs, then you should consider an application truer to the
hypertext model, such as OWL International's Guide or BrainPower's
Architext.

Guide, Version 2.0 GUIF (native), TEXT, PNTG, PICT

When you first open a Guide document, known as a "Guideline," it looks very much like a standard word-processing file. Missing are the bells and whistles you may have come to expect from working in HyperCard. Guide's information-handling capabilities are much more streamlined.

Text is created in the standard word-processing fashion. Paragraphs of text may be enhanced using bit maps and drawings imported by way of the Clipboard or Scrapbook. After creating some text, you can link it together by establishing a word or phrase as a button. Guide provides four different kinds of buttons. Clicking on an Expansion button replaces the words inside the button with a linked text block. For example, you might click on a table-of-contents entry to display a certain chapter. A second type of button, called a Reference button, sends you to a different part of a document, in the same way a button might take you to a different card in HyperCard. A Note button displays a pop-up window, similar to attaching a Post-it note to a page of text. And finally, a Command button allows you to access information from a foreign environment. For example, Guide provides interpreters that allow Command buttons to launch other applications and to drive serial-port devices. You must create other interpreters for yourself.

All buttons are identified in different styles of type for easy identification. Expansion buttons are bold, Reference buttons are italic, and so on. Your cursor also changes when passing over different types of buttons.

Included with Guide are two DA's: Guidance, which allows you to read Guidelines in another application, and Scribbler, which you use for creating simple object-oriented drawings.

 Architext, Version 2.03 TEXT, PNTG, PICT

If you're looking for something with a little more oomph to it and you're willing to fork over an extra $150, then you may want to get ahold of the additional power afforded by Architext. In this hypertext application, information is organized into *nodes,* which are entries presented in a scrolling list or flow chart called a *map.* Nodes exist side by side with paragraphs of text, so that words can easily be used to reference other information.

Architext's interface is more rigid and formalized than Guide's, limiting its true hypertext functionality. Nonetheless, the same map views that inhibit associative communication also allow easier navigation. In Guide, you can view your last 32 button actions, but you can't view how various buttons relate back and forth to each other except by activating them. In Architext, you can easily view an entire button hierarchy in a single map.

Architext is bundled with an Architext Viewer application so that the user can examine your hypertext documents without owning the actual Architext application.

Page-Layout Software

Here's where it all comes together. Text from a word processor, illustrations from a drawing application, charts from a spreadsheet, visual elements from all sorts of software can be combined on a single page to create alluring and compelling documentation.

Combining Type and Graphics by Hand

Having worked for a newspaper, we know what traditional page composition is like at its worst. Galleys of typeset text and halftoned photographs are run through waxers—medieval machines that roll paper through mires of hot goo. The text is then cut apart into columns and pasted by hand onto gridded boards over light tables. The length of a column of typeset text and its length on the final page have nothing to do with each other, so you have to paste the text down one column, cut between rows of type when you come to the end, and then lay the text down the next column.

Loose Type

The problems with this method are manifold. First, you frequently have to cut portions out of an article to make it fit. This means that many paragraphs may become separated from each other, and if you're not careful, these lone paragraphs may get mixed up. The end of a paragraph that started in the first column may accidentally wind up in the third. The paste-up crew doesn't have time to read each article, so this kind of discontinuity is common.

Second, since light tables generate their own heat, the wax that holds down a block of type will shift if you press against it. Many times we have seen a page come back from the printer with skewed type, type on top of type, missing paragraphs, and so on.

And third, creating straight lines is a major hassle. A simple straight rule is created by laying down a strip of very thin black tape. As you might guess, this tape can slip as easily as waxed text, so lines are frequently crooked or slightly wavy. When a photo is outlined, the tape can slip off the edges, shrink from the corners, or simply fall off.

Electronic Composition

All of this is remedied with a personal computer. Text editing is made easier because you can simply add or subtract type on screen; columns will automatically wrap to compensate. Small paragraphs aren't lying around separated from each other, so there's less chance of discontinuity.

But better than that, computer-produced documentation is always picture perfect. If you want a straight line, it's straight. If you want one line of type to be exactly three picas from another, that's where it will be. No eyeballing, no fiddling—the least dextrous of us can create more accurate pages than the most exacting of traditional paste-up artists.

Page Makeup

The primary strength of a page-layout application lies in its ability to manipulate elements created in other types of software. Although all of the three major desktop publishing applications—Aldus PageMaker, Ready,Set,Go!, and QuarkXPress—allow you to enter type directly, even to the extent of providing spell-checking features, these abilities are more efficiently applied to editing text as opposed to writing from scratch. Similarly, the rudimentary nature of your software's line and shape tools makes them perfect for outlining figures and highlighting type; however, they are extremely inadequate for drawing.

You will achieve the most success by combining completed elements. In fact, page-layout applications provide a series of methods for integrating type and graphics, giving you a control over the printed page entirely unavailable in other kinds of software.

Kern Together

Several word processors allow you to change the amount of spacing that exists between the individual words and letters in a line of type. However, they don't tend to give you the degree of control provided by page-layout programs. Also, since letter spacing in particular is most usefully applied to large type, such as headlines and logos, spacing becomes more of a necessary consideration when composing pages.

Page-Layout Technicalities 1

Page-layout artists won't give an inch
for their favorite units of measurement

In grade school back in the 1970s, our teachers were really trying to push the metric system. The pristine uniformity of a base-ten measurement system seemed the perfect solution to the world's many communication woes. When a foreigner talked about living only 20 kilometers outside of Copenhagen, we'd understand he wasn't from the moon.

In the 1980s, metric measurements are relegated to reports on drug busts. The newest buzz words are **picas** and **points**, two units of measurement so bizarre that they're bound to catch on in a big way. Originally employed by clergy for creating manuscripts, the pica was updated during the advent of typewriters to indicate a type size for which ten characters fit in every inch (versus *elite,* or 10-point type, where 12 characters occupy an inch). If you measure a line of 12-point Courier, you will see that this is still true today.

A pica consists of 12 points. Traditionally, however, picas and inches are not compatible units of measure (there are actually $6\frac{9}{400}$ picas per inch). But in any desktop publishing software, picas have been round up so that there are exactly 6 picas per inch. This means that a point is $\frac{1}{72}$ inch, the precise size of a single screen pixel.

The primary advantage of picas and points is their smallness. Since elements on a page are so tiny, a unit of measure smaller than an inch but based on an inch is very useful. So rather than specifying for a line to be 0.2778 inch thick, you may select a 2-point rule.

Conclusion: Picas and points are the optimal system of measurement for creating documentation or artwork. One pica equals $\frac{1}{6}$ inch; one point equals $\frac{1}{12}$ pica or $\frac{1}{72}$ inch.

A component of letter spacing known as **kerning** allows you to control the amount of space between two specific letters. Although they are spaced the same as other characters, visual gaps may occur between certain pairs of letters that complement each other's form, such as *To*, *AV*, *We*, and so on. Most fonts contain special kerning-pair information, as described in detail in Page-Layout Technicalities 2. But especially for large type, this kerning may prove too much or too little.

All three major applications allow you to kern characters toward or away from each other. To kern two letters closer together in PageMaker, position your text-entry cursor between the letters and press COMMAND-DELETE. This subtracts ¼₈ of a point for every point of type size. So if the current text is 24-point, you will delete ½ point every time you press COMMAND-DELETE. To add space, press COMMAND-SHIFT-DELETE.

In Ready,Set,Go!, press COMMAND-→ to delete a full point of space, regardless of type size, and COMMAND-← to add a point. In QuarkXPress, press COMMAND-SHIFT-[to delete space and COMMAND-SHIFT-] to add space.

Wrapping Text Around Graphics

Text wrapping is a feature virtually unique to page-layout applications (although some high-end word processors, such as FullWrite and Nisus, also provide this feature). Also known as **text runaround**, wrapping allows type to flow around the boundaries of an imported graphic.

Normally, the text flow does not account for graphics or other interruptions.

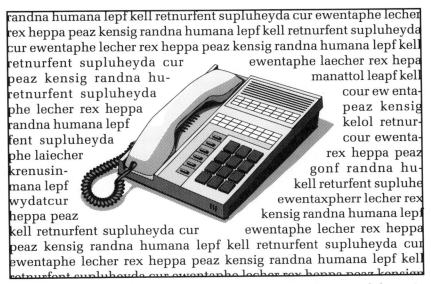

randna humana lepf kell retnurfent supluheyda cur ewentaphe lecher rex heppa peaz kensig randna humana lepf kell retnurfent supluheyda cur ewentaphe lecher rex heppa peaz kensig randna humana lepf kell retnurfent supluheyda cur   ewentaphe laecher rex hepa peaz kensig randna hu-   manattol leapf kell retnurfent supluheyda   cour ew enta- phe lecher rex heppa   peaz kensig randna humana lepf   kelol retnur- fent supluheyda   cour ewenta- phe laiecher   rex heppa peaz krenusin-   gonf randna hu- mana lepf   kell returfent supluhe wydatcur   ewentaxpherr lecher rex heppa peaz   kensig randna humana lepf kell retnurfent supluheyda cur   ewentaphe lecher rex heppa peaz kensig randna humana lepf kell retnurfent supluheyda cur ewentaphe lecher rex heppa peaz kensig randna humana lepf kell retnurfent supluheyda cur ewentaphe lecher rex heppa peaz kensig

Page-layout applications allow you to specify text to wrap around the perimeter of a graphic.

In Ready,Set,Go! and XPress, text runaround is an automated feature. In Ready,Set,Go!, choose SPECIFICATIONS from the EDIT menu for a selected picture block. Select the "Runaround" check box as well as the "Graphic" radio button. Then enter a value for the "Text repel distance" option to set the distance between the text and your artwork's perimeter.

In XPress, select a picture box and choose MODIFY from the ITEM menu. Then select both the "Transparent" and "Run-around" check boxes and enter a value for the "Text outset" option, which specifies the distance between graphic perimeter and type. Unlike other applications, XPress even allows you to run type around a different block of type.

PageMaker provides the most complex as well as the most sophisticated text-wrapping control. Choose the TEXT WRAP command from the OPTIONS menu. Then select the second "Wrap option" icon and the third "Text flow" icon, and enter values for the "Standoff" options. This surrounds the graphic with a rectangular dotted boundary line. To wrap type against the graphic's perimeter, click on the straight lines in the boundary to create handles, and then drag these handles closer to the graphic. The process is time-consuming, but you can specify very precise results.

Page-Layout Technicalities 2

Customizing the space between characters
by understanding kerning and side bearings

To determine the positioning of each character in a text block relative to the characters immediately before and after it, any application that permits type editing relies on information included with a screen font. As determined by the font's designer, this information specifies the width of a character as well as the amount of space that should be placed before and after the character, known as the left and right **side bearings**. In most cases, the space between any two characters is determined by the right bearing of the first character plus the left bearing of the second.

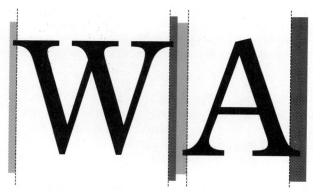

Every character in a typeface has a width (demonstrated above with dotted lines) as well as a left and right side bearing (shown as a light and dark gray area, respectively). Together, these elements constitute the horizontal space occupied by a character of type.

However, font designers can also specify that certain pairs of letters, called *kerning pairs,* should be kerned closer together than the typical character spacing would allow. These pairs often involve a capital letter followed by a lowercase letter or punctuation.

The following is a list of kerning pairs included as part of the screen font for Helvetica:

AT AV Av AW Aw AY Ay A' F, F. FA LT LV LW LY

Ly L' P, P. PA RT RV RW RY T, T. T: T; TA Ta

Tc Te Ti TO To Tr Ts Tu Tw Ty V, V. V: V; VA

Va Ve Vi Vo Vr Vu Vy W, W- W. W: W; WA Wa We

Wi Wo Wr Wu Wy Y, Y. Y: Y; YA Ya Ye Yi Yo Yp

Yq Yu Yv ff f' r, r. r' v, v. w, w. y, y. 's

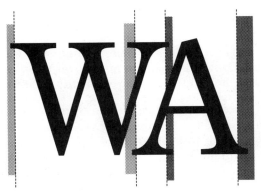

Certain pairs of letters are defined as kerning pairs. Their screen font includes custom spacing information, regardless of their normal widths and side bearings.

Because pair kerning increases screen-refresh time and because the benefits of pair kerning are more apparent for larger type sizes, you may turn kerning on and off. XPress goes one better by allowing you to edit specific kerning pairs.

Conclusion: Pair kerning resolves inconsistencies in the spacing between pairs of characters. If kerning is off, letter spacing is based on their widths and side bearings. When kerning is on, specific pairs of characters are spaced closer together.

An Element Never Forgets

Most documents consist of pages that share a variety of elements, such as page numbers, folios, logos, and so on. To avoid having to copy these elements to every single page, both PageMaker and Ready,Set,Go! provide *master pages,* which you *access* by clicking on one of the page icons labeled *L* or *R* (left or right). In each application, you can think of your on-screen pages as being made of transparent acetate. Below each acetate page is a set of constant master pages. Elements on the left master page will show through to all even-numbered pages in a document; the right master-page elements show through to all odd-numbered pages. Therefore, any elements placed on a master page will show through to every other page in your document.

You may also hide the master-page elements for a certain page, like page 1. In PageMaker, choose the DISPLAY MASTER ITEMS command from the PAGE menu. In Ready,Set,Go!, choose USE MASTER from the SPECIAL menu. To hide selected portions of a master page, simply cover the elements you don't want to show through with white rectangles with transparent outlines.

XPress provides a similar feature called the *default page.* Items placed on the default page don't show through, but are copied to other pages in a document, allowing you to customize default elements differently from page to page. Unfortunately, changes made to the default page only affect future pages. If you change the default page halfway through creating a document, you must delete all pages but the first page, and reflow your text.

Automatic Page Numbering

All three applications allow access to automatic page-numbering characters. In PageMaker, press COMMAND-OPTION-P. In Ready,Set,Go!, press COMMAND-SHIFT-OPTION-3. In XPress, press COMMAND-3. Both Ready,Set,Go! and XPress also allow you to print the previous page number (RSG: COMMAND-SHIFT-OPTION-4; XPress: COMMAND-2) and the following page number (RSG: COMMAND-SHIFT-OPTION-5; XPress: COMMAND-4). These characters are particularly useful for articles in newsletters that require "continued from page #" and "continued on page #" notifiers.

File-Placing Formats

In the following pages, we will look at some popular page-layout applications and examine their capabilities. To the right of each program name will be a list of the file-placing formats that the program supports. Since page-layout programs are the final step in document composition, it is not important which formats an application can save to, but rather which formats it can import. These formats may include any text format discussed in the Word Processors entry as well as any graphics format discussed in either Drawing Software *or* Painting Software.

Publishaurus Rex

 Aldus PageMaker, Version 3.02 TEXT, WDBN, WORD, nX^d, PNTG, PICT, EPS, TIFF

PageMaker is by no means the features king of page-layout applications. It lacks many of the text-handling abilities of QuarkXPress as well as some of the graphics features of both XPress and ReadySetGo. And even if you have 8MB of RAM, you can't open more than one document at a time, a limitation one normally associates with the earliest versions of MacPaint.

Nonetheless, PageMaker remains our favorite. It supports text from many word processors that run on the PC, including Microsoft Word, WordPerfect, and WordStar. Version 3.02 allows you to create half-point type. And pouring text is a much easier, much more intuitive process than in other applications.

Printing Prowess

But PageMaker's main advantage is that it prints like it's supposed to print. Its APD (Aldus printer definition) files support almost every Post-Script-compatible printer on the market, as well as QuickDraw printers such as the LaserWriter IISC. By option-clicking on the OK button in the Print dialog box when printing to a PostScript device, you produce a POSTSCRIPT PRINT OPTIONS dialog that allows you to turn off bit-mapped font downloading or print a file to disk in a plain ASCII or EPS format. This later operation allows you to import one PageMaker document into another, creating pages within pages. And with the PageMaker Color Extension program, you may print color separations of imported EPS and PICT2 illustrations.

Over the years, PageMaker has proved itself a steady product, sometimes lagging behind but always dependable. The application never seems rushed; once they get around to implementing a feature, they consistently implement it in the best way possible. The documentation is adequate, support is great, and plenty of third-party training is available.

Ten Hottest PageMaker Tips

The following are some hints designed to help you make more effective use of Aldus PageMaker on the Mac.

◇ **Toolbox in the way?** If you need more room on screen and you own an extended keyboard (with function keys and so on), you can get rid of the toolbox and access all tools from the keyboard. This is especially useful for SE's and other computers with small monitors. To get the arrow tool, press SHIFT-F1. Press SHIFT-F2 for the diagonal line tool, SHIFT-F3 for the perpendicular line tool, SHIFT-F4 for the text tool, and so on in the order they appear in the toolbox.

◇ **Using the pasteboard.** When you transfer an element from one page to another, the usual temptation is to cut the element, turn the page, and paste. Unfortunately, elements can jostle a little when sent to the Clipboard, especially if multiple elements are involved. To avoid this problem, drag the selected elements onto the pasteboard (the area around your pages), and then change pages and drag the elements off the pasteboard. Elements on the pasteboard appear no matter what page you are on.

◇ **SAVE As shrinks file sizes.** PageMaker saves time during a save by simply tagging any changes to the end of a file. Unfortunately, this means that every time you open a file and make changes, it takes up more room on your disk or hard drive, even if you don't add any elements or pages to your document. To reduce the size of a file (especially when archiving), you must rebuild the file on disk by choosing the SAVE As command and saving over the old version of the file. (Your disk or drive must have an amount of free space equal to the size of your file to complete a SAVE AS operation.)

◇ **Extraordinary view sizes.** PageMaker provides two view sizes that are not directly available from the PAGE menu. To access a 400 percent view size, press the SHIFT key and choose 200% SIZE from the PAGE menu. To zoom out to *super fit-in-window,* press SHIFT and choose the FIT IN WINDOW command. This latter size will display the entire pasteboard.

◇ **Layers of elements.** A problem that arises in any object-oriented application is trying to get to elements that are buried behind other elements. PageMaker allows you to select a completely covered element, however, by command-clicking with the arrow tool. The first command-click selects the foremost element, the second click selects the next element down and so forth, right on down the layering order.

Incidentally, this is also a useful method for selecting elements when column guides or ruler guides are getting in the way. If your guides are configured in front of your elements (as set by choosing the PREFERENCES command from the EDIT menu), command-click to access an element—such as a 1-point line—covered by a guide.

◇ **Manipulating the graphic boundary without wrapping.** To wrap type around a graphic, you must click on a graphic boundary created with the TEXT WRAP command, as explained earlier in this section. If you have ever done this, you probably realize how frustrating it can be to have to wait for the text to rewrap every time you move a handle. By pressing the space bar, however, you can delay the rewrapping process, allowing you to manipulate many handles without waiting. When you release the space bar, the text will rewrap.

◆ **Default text wraps.** If you're like us, you get tired of entering the same values over and over again into the TEXT WRAP dialog box. However, if you enter a default set of wrapping values, not only will all placed graphics get wrapping boundaries, but so will all lines or shapes created in PageMaker. To create default values that only appear when you want them to, choose TEXT WRAP from the OPTIONS menu while no element is selected. Then select the second "Wrap option" icon, select the "Text flow" icon of your choice, and enter the values you want to apply to graphics most often. Now, instead of clicking the OK button, click the first "Wrap option" icon and then click OK. From now on, when you import drawings, they will appear without boundaries. But when you choose TEXT WRAP and click the second "Wrap option" icon, all of your default settings will appear.

◆ **Condensing or expanding type.** Unlike XPress, PageMaker does not provide a built-in feature for condensing or expanding type. Nonetheless, you may perform this operation via the Scrapbook. Create the type that you want to stretch and format it in the font, size, and style that you desire. Next select it with the arrow tool, choose CUT, choose SCRAPBOOK from the APPLE menu, paste the text block, and close the Scrapbook. A little-known feature of PageMaker's PLACE command is that you can place the Scrapbook file. Choose PLACE from the FILE menu and select the Scrapbook File document in your System folder. This will produce a small icon with a number inside it. Click once on this icon (or click repeatedly to place other images pasted to the Scrapbook). Your text will appear as a graphic element, allowing you to condense or expand it by dragging at its handles.

◆ **Importing tabloid graphics.** PageMaker won't let you import a graphic larger than the current document size. If you try, the graphic will automatically be reduced to fit. If you want to import a tabloid illustration (11 by 17 inches) for use in a two-page spread, create a new document with tabloid page size. Then place the graphic, choose the Cut command, close the file without saving, open the file where you want to import the graphic, and paste. This method even works for TIFF files, which must tag the original graphic document.

◆ **Scaling bit-mapped graphics.** This tip is not a suggestion; it's a must for manipulating bit-mapped graphics. As explained in the Painting Software entry, all bit maps are locked into a certain resolution, whether it's 72 dots per inch, as in the case of MacPaint artwork, or higher. The resolution of a bit map rarely jibes with that of your printer, producing **moiré** patterns. If you press the COMMAND key when dragging at a corner handle of a painting, PageMaker automatically scales the bit map to a percentage compatible with the printer. Note that you must have the APD for your final output device selected in the PRINTER-SPECIFIC OPTIONS dialog for this operation to work successfully. In other words, if you intend to eventually print to a Linotype, select the Linotype APD even if you are currently printing proofs to a laser printer.

Aldus PageMaker Quick Reference (1 of 4)

Toolbox

▶	Arrow	▶ to select element so it may be manipulated, ⋯▶ to move
╲	Diagonal line	⋯▶ to draw straight line at any angle
⊢	Perpendicular line	⋯▶ to draw straight line at 45° angle
A	Type	▶ to set origin for text block, ⋯▶ across type to edit
▢	Rectangle	⋯▶ to draw rectangle
▢	Round corner	⋯▶ to draw rectangle with rounded corners
○	Oval	⋯▶ to draw ellipse
⊬	Cropping	⋯▶ corner handle to trim away portions of imported graphic

Menus

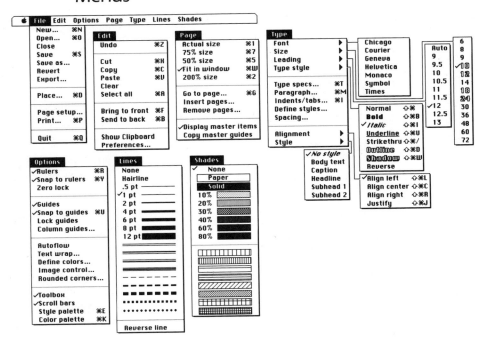

Aldus PageMaker Quick Reference (2 of 4)

Keyboard Equivalents

Actual size/200%, toggle .... ⌘⇧⌥↖

Actual size/fit in window, toggle .... ⌘⌥↖

Actual view size (100%) .... ⌘1 *or* ⌘⌥↖

Align text centered .... ⌘⇧C

Align text flush-left.................................... ⌘⇧L

Align text flush-right .... ⌘⇧R

All caps text .... ⌘⇧K

Arrow tool, select .... ⇧F1

Automatic text flow, access in manual mode .... ⌘

Bold text .... ⌘⇧B

Bring to front .... ⌘F

Circle, create .... ⇧···↖ *w/oval tool*

Clear element .... ⌫ *or* 🔢✎

Color palette, show/hide .... ⌘K

Copy element .... ⌘C *or* F3

Cropping tool, select .... ⇧F8

Cut element .... ⌘X, 🔢., *or* F2

Determine column width
of text block .... ···↖ *w/type tool or text flow icon*

Determine dimensions
of imported graphic .... ···↖ *w/placing icon*

Diagonal line tool, select .... ⇧F2

Fit in window view size .... ⌘W

Four times actual size (400%) .... ⇧ *choose 200%*

Go to next page .... ⌘→|

Go to preceding page .... ⌘⇧→|

Go to specified page .... ⌘G

Half actual view size (50%) .... ⌘5

Hand tool, access temporarily .... ⌥···↖

Increase type size .... ⌘⇧>

Increase type size 1 point only .... ⌘⇧⌥>

Indent/tab stop specifications .... ⌘I

Interrupt automatic text flow .... ↖

Italic text .... ⌘⇧I

Justify text .... ⌘⇧J

Kern type, insert ¹⁄₄₈ em .... ⌘⇧⌫

Kern type, delete ¹⁄₄₈ em .... ⌘⌫

Manual text flow, access in automatic mode .... ⌘

Move in 45° direction .... ⇧···↖ *w/arrow tool*

Move text cursor down one line .... ↓ *or* 🔢2

Move text cursor down one screen .... 🔢3

Move text cursor left one letter .... ← *or* 🔢4

Move text cursor left one word .... ⌘← *or* ⌘🔢4

Move text cursor right one letter .... → *or* 🔢6

Move text cursor right one word ...... ⌘→ *or* ⌘🔢6

Move text cursor up one line .... ↑ *or* 🔢8

Move text cursor up one screen .... 🔢9

⌘	command	→|	tab	⌫	delete	⸺ space bar
⇧	shift	↩	return	⌦	fwd. delete	F1 function key
⌥	option	⤮	enter	🔢	keypad key	↖ mouse click
⌃	control	✎	escape	🔢✎	clear	···↖ mouse drag

Aldus PageMaker Quick Reference (3 of 4)

Keyboard Equivalents (Cont.)

Move to beginning of current line .... ⌨7

Move to beginning
of current paragraph .... ⌘↑ *or* ⌘⌨8

Move to beginning of current sentence .... ⌘⌨7

Move to beginning of current story .... ⌘⌨9

Move to beginning
of next paragraph .... ⌘↓ *or* ⌘⌨2

Move to end of current line........................... ⌨1

Move to end of current sentence .... ⌘⌨1

Move to end of current story .... ⌘⌨3

New document, create .... ⌘N

Nonbreaking em space character .... ⌘⇧M

Nonbreaking en space character .... ⌘⇧N

Nonbreaking thin space character............... ⌘⇧T

Normal (plain) text .... ⌘⇧▭

Open existing document .... ⌘O

Optional hyphen.. ⌘-

Outline text .... ⌘⇧D

Oval tool, select .... ⇧F7

Page number character .... ⌘⍰P

Paragraph specifications .... ⌘M

Paste element .... ⌘V, ⌨0, *or* F4

Perpendicular line tool, select .... ⇧F3

Place text or graphic document .... ⌘D

POSTSCRIPT PRINT OPTIONS dialog box,
access .... ⍰⍦ *OK button in standard* PRINT *dialog*

Print document .... ⌘P

Quit Aldus PageMaker .... ⌘Q

Rectangle tool, select .... ⇧F5

Reduce type size .... ⌘⇧<

Reduce type size 1 point only .... ⌘⇧⍰<

Rounded corner tool, select .... ⇧F6

Ruler guide, create........................ ⁻⁻⍦ *from ruler*

Rulers, show/hide .... ⌘R

Save document .... ⌘S

Scale bit map proportionally
to optimal resolution .... ⌘⇧⁻⁻⍦ *corner handle*

Scale proportionally .... ⇧⁻⁻⍦ *corner handle*

Select all elements on page and pasteboard .... ⌘A

Select all text from cursor location
to beginning of story .... ⌘⇧⌨9

Select all text from cursor location
to end of story .... ⌘⇧⌨3

Select all text in story .... ⍦ *ʷ/type tool,* ⌘A

Select current
then preceding paragraphs .... ⌘⇧↑ *or* ⌘⇧⌨8

Select current
then succeeding paragraphs .... ⌘⇧↓ *or* ⌘⇧⌨2

Select entire paragraph .... ⍦⍦⍦ *ʷ/type tool*

Select entire word .... ⍦⍦ *ʷ/type tool*

Aldus PageMaker Quick Reference (4 of 4)

Keyboard Equivalents (Cont.)

Select next letter .... ⇧→ *or* ⇧▣6	Strikethru text .... ⌘⇧/
Select next word .... ⌘⇧→ *or* ⌘⇧▣6	Style palette, show/hide .... ⌘E
Select preceding letter .... ⇧← *or* ⇧▣4	Subscript text .... ⌘⇧-
Select preceding word .... ⌘⇧← *or* ⌘⇧▣4	Super fit in window ...... ⇧ *choose* FIT IN WINDOW
Semiautomatic text flow, access temporarily ... ⇧	Superscript text .... ⌘⇧=
Send to back .... ⌘B	
Shadow text .... ⌘⇧W	Three-quarters actual view size (75%) .... ⌘7
Small caps text .... ⌘⇧H	Twice actual view size (200%) ..... ⌘2 *or* ⌘⇧⍶ ⟋
Snap to guides, activate/deactivate .... ⌘U	Type tool, select .... ⇧F4
Snap to rulers, activate/deactivate .... ⌘Y	
Square, create .... ⇧ ····⟋ *w/rectangle tool*	Underline text .... ⌘⇧U
	Undo/redo last operation .... ⌘Z

Accurate for Aldus PageMaker, version 3.02

⌘	command	➜	tab	⌫	delete	▬	space bar
⇧	shift	↵	return	⌦	fwd. delete	F1	function key
⍶	option	⤞	enter	▣	keypad key	⟋	mouse click
⌃	control	⌫	escape	▣⌫	clear	····⟋	mouse drag

Page Competition

Though PageMaker is far the most popular page-composition software, it was not the first nor is it the only. Many swear by Ready,Set,Go! or QuarkXPress, applications that offer more advanced type-handling and graphic-handling features designed especially for complex page composition and small-document creation.

 Ready,Set,Go!, Version 4.5a TEXT, WDBN, WORD, nX^d, PNTG, PICT, EPS, TIFF, RIFF

The oldest of the three page-layout applications, Ready,Set,Go! hasn't always kept up with the competition. With version 4.5. however, it makes good strides, and promises to do even better in the future.

On the plus side, Ready,Set,Go! provides both regular and free-form grids, allowing for precise placement of graphic and textual elements. A powerful DUPLICATE command allows you to produce multiple copies of an element and specify their horizontal and vertical offset. Add to this RSG's locking and alignment features, normally only associated with drawing programs like MacDraw and FreeHand, and you have a splendid application for creating forms and other documents requiring precision and consistency, an area in which PageMaker falters.

Unfortunately, Ready,Set,Go! does not keep up with the competition for creating long documents or documents with lengthy stories. Simply put, its text-flow feature leaves something to be desired. In PageMaker, flowing text is a matter of clicking at the bottom of one column and clicking at the top of another, or simply activating the autoflow feature and letting the text import itself. But in RSG, you must first create master-page text blocks to act as type reservoirs, and then globally link the text blocks for each new page.

But while handling the visual aspects of large quantities of type can be problematic in Ready,Set,Go!, this is the best application for text editing. It comes with a built-in spelling checker, a customizable glossary, and an outstanding find and replace feature that lets you search for words, fonts, styles, and sizes, something even the best-selling word processor, Microsoft Word 4.0, won't do!

Although it lags behind XPress in color support, Ready,Set,Go! is clearly our second-favorite page-layout software.

Ready, Set, Go! Quick Reference (1 of 5)

Toolbox

▲	Arrow	▲ to select element so it may be manipulated, ⋯▲ to move
🖑	Hand	⋯▲ to move pages with respect to window
T	Type	⋯▲ to determine dimensions of text block (not used to edit)
I	Text-entry	▲ to set origin for type in text block, ⋯▲ across type to edit
⌇	Linking	▲ each text block in link, ▲▲ last text block to end link
⊠	Picture	⋯▲ to determine dimensions of picture block
⋈	Cropping	▲ picture block to specify location for imported graphic
☐	Rectangle	⋯▲ to draw rectangle
☐	Round corner	⋯▲ to draw rectangle with rounded corners
◯	Oval	⋯▲ to draw ellipse
|−	Perpendicular line	⋯▲ to draw straight line at 45° angle
╲	Diagonal line	⋯▲ to draw straight line at any angle

Ready, Set, Go! Quick Reference (2 of 5)

Menus

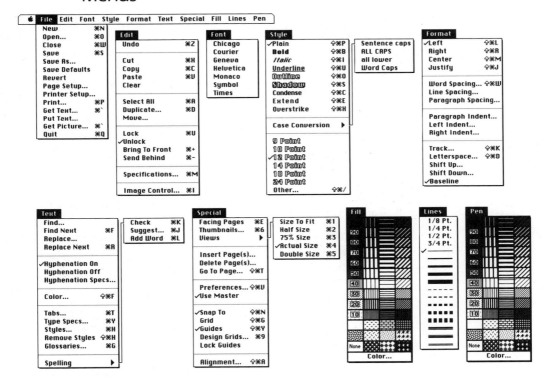

File Edit Font Style Format Text Special Fill Lines Pen

File
New	⌘N
Open...	⌘O
Close	⌘W
Save	⌘S
Save As...	
Save Defaults	
Revert	
Page Setup...	
Printer Setup...	
Print...	⌘P
Get Text...	⌘`
Put Text...	
Get Picture...	⌘`
Quit	⌘Q

Edit
Undo	⌘Z
Cut	⌘X
Copy	⌘C
Paste	⌘V
Clear	
Select All	⌘A
Duplicate	⌘D
Move...	
Lock	⌘U
✓Unlock	
Bring To Front	⌘+
Send Behind	⌘-
Specifications...	⌘M
Image Control...	⌘I

Font
Chicago
Courier
Geneva
Helvetica
Monaco
Symbol
Times

Style
✓Plain	⇧⌘P
Bold	⇧⌘B
Italic	⇧⌘I
Underline	⇧⌘U
Outline	⇧⌘O
Shadow	⇧⌘S
Condense	⇧⌘C
Extend	⇧⌘E
Overstrike	⇧⌘H
Case Conversion ▶	
9 Point	
10 Point	
✓12 Point	
14 Point	
18 Point	
24 Point	
Other...	⇧⌘/

Case Conversion
Sentence caps
ALL CAPS
all lower
Word Caps

Format
✓Left	⇧⌘L
Right	⇧⌘R
Center	⇧⌘M
Justify	⇧⌘J
Word Spacing...	⇧⌘W
Line Spacing...	
Paragraph Spacing...	
Paragraph Indent...	
Left Indent...	
Right Indent...	
Track...	⇧⌘K
Letterspace...	⇧⌘D
Shift Up...	
Shift Down...	
✓Baseline	

Text
Find...	
Find Next	⌘F
Replace...	
Replace Next	⌘R
✓Hyphenation On	
Hyphenation Off	
Hyphenation Specs...	
Color...	⇧⌘F
Tabs...	⌘T
Type Specs...	⌘Y
Styles...	⌘H
Remove Styles	⇧⌘H
Glossaries...	⌘G
Spelling ▶	

Spelling
Check	⌘K
Suggest...	⌘J
Add Word	⌘L

Special
Facing Pages	⌘E
Thumbnails...	⌘6
Views ▶	
Insert Page(s)...	
Delete Page(s)...	
Go To Page...	⌘T
Preferences...	⇧⌘U
✓Use Master	
✓Snap To	⇧⌘N
Grid	⇧⌘G
✓Guides	⇧⌘Y
Design Grids...	⌘9
Lock Guides	
Alignment...	⇧⌘A

Views
Size To Fit	⌘1
Half Size	⌘2
75% Size	⌘3
✓Actual Size	⌘4
Double Size	⌘5

Fill
90
80
70
60
50
40
30
20
10
None
Color...

Lines
1/8 Pt.
1/4 Pt.
1/2 Pt.
3/4 Pt.

Pen
90
80
70
60
50
40
30
20
10
None
Color...

Ready, Set, Go! Quick Reference (3 of 5)

Keyboard Equivalents

Actual size/size to fit, toggle .... ⌘⌥↖

Actual view size (100%) .... ⌘4

Actual/double view size, toggle .... ⌘⇧⌥↖

Add selected word to user dictionary .... ⌘L

ALIGNMENT dialog, display .... ⌘⇧A

Arrow tool, select .... ⌘⇧⌥A

Bold text .... ⌘⇧B

Bring to front .... ⌘=

Center text (middle-justify) .... ⌘⇧M

Check spelling .... ⌘K

Circle, create .... ⇧┈↖ *w/ oval tool*

Clear element .... ⌫

COLOR SELECTION dialog, display .... ⌘⇧F

Condensed text .... ⌘⇧C

Copy element .... ⌘C

Cropping tool, select .... ⌘⇧⌥C

Cut element .... ⌘X

Design grids, display dialog .... ⌘9

Diagonal line tool, select .... ⌘⇧⌥D

Double view size (200%) .... ⌘5

DUPLICATE dialog, display .... ⌘D

Extended text .... ⌘⇧E

Facing pages, display .... ⌘E

Find next occurrence of specified text .... ⌘F

Get picture, when picture block selected .... ⌘ '

Get text, when text block selected .... ⌘ '

GLOSSARIES dialog, display .... ⌘G

Glossary, current date .... ⌘G, D

Glossary, current date, abbreviated .... ⌘G, ⌥D

Glossary, current day and date .... ⌘G, ⇧D

Glossary, current time with seconds .... ⌘G, ⇧T

Glossary, current time without seconds ..... ⌘G, T

Glossary phrase,
insert into text .... ⌘G, *glossary character*

Go to next page .... ⌘8

Go to preceding page .... ⌘7

Go to specified page .... ⌘⇧T

Grid, activate (guides off) or deactivate .... ⌘⇧G

Guides, activate (grid off) or deactivate .... ⌘⇧Y

Half actual view size (50%) .... ⌘2

Hand tool, access temporarily .... ⌥┈↖

Hand tool, select .... ⌘⇧⌥H

⌘	command	⇥	tab	⌫	delete	⎵	space bar
⇧	shift	↩	return	⌦	fwd. delete	F1	function key
⌥	option	⌅	enter	⌨	keypad key	↖	mouse click
⋀	control	⎋	escape	⌨⌫	clear	┈↖	mouse drag

Ready, Set, Go! Quick Reference (4 of 5)

Keyboard Equivalents (Cont.)

Insert text block into chain
preceding current block .... ⇧ ↖ ʷ/ *link tool*

Italic text .... ⌘⇧I

Justify text (full justification) .... ⌘⇧J

KERN dialog, display .... ↖ ʷ/ *type tool,* ⌘⇧K

Left-justify text .... ⌘⇧L

Linking tool, select .... ⌘⇧⌥L

Link two existing chains .... ↖ ʷ/ *link tool*
in first chain, ⇧⌥↖ *in second*

Lock element .... ⌘U

New document, create .... ⌘N

Open existing document .... ⌘O

Other type size .... ⌘⇧/

Outline text .... ⌘⇧D

Oval tool, select .... ⌘⇧⌥O

Overstrike text .... ⌘⇧X

Page number character, current page .... ⌘⇧⌥3

Page number character, preceding page... ⌘⇧⌥4

Page number character, next page .... ⌘⇧⌥5

Page number character,
previous page in text chain .... ⌘⇧⌥6

Page number character,
next page in text chain .... ⌘⇧⌥7

Page number character,
total pages in document .... ⌘⇧⌥8

Paste element .... ⌘V

Perpendicular line tool, select .... ⌘⇧⌥R

Picture tool, select .... ⌘⇧⌥P

Plain text .... ⌘⇧P

PREFERENCES dialog, display .... ⌘⇧V

Print document .... ⌘P

Quit Ready,Set,Go! .... ⌘Q

Rectangle tool, select .... ⌘⇧⌥B

Remove styles .... ⌘⇧H

Replace next occurrence of specified text .... ⌘R

Right-justify text .... ⌘⇧R

Rounded corner tool, select .... ⌘⇧⌥Q

Save document .... ⌘S

Select all elements .... ⌘A

Select all text in chain ...... ↖ ʷ/ *text entry tool,* ⌘A

Select entire line of type .... ↖↖↖ ʷ/ *text entry tool*

Select entire paragraph .... ↖↖↖↖ ʷ/ *text entry tool*

Select entire word
with following space .... ↖↖ ʷ/ *text entry tool*

Select entire word
without space .... ⌘↖↖ ʷ/ *text entry tool*

Select text in block .... ↖ ʷ/ *text entry tool,* ⌘⇧A

Ready, Set, Go! Quick Reference (5 of 5)

Keyboard Equivalents (Cont.)

Send to back .... ⌘-

Shadow text .... ⌘⇧S

Size to fit (fit in window) .... ⌘1

Snap to guides, activate/deactivate .... ⌘⇧N

SPECIFICATIONS dialog,
display for each selection .... ⌘M

Split chain in two .... ⌘⇧🖰 *w/ link tool*

Square, create .... ⇧⋯🖰 *w/ rectangle tool*

STYLE SHEET dialog, display .... ⌘H

Suggest spelling for misspelled word .... ⌘J

Tab stop specifications .... ⌘T

Text entry (insertion) tool, select .... ⌘⇧⌥I

Three-quarters actual view size (75%) .... ⌘3

Thumbnails, view .... ⌘6

TRACK dialog, display .... ⋯🖰 *w/ type tool,* ⌘⇧K

Type specifications .... ⌘Y

Type tool, select .... ⌘⇧⌥T

Underline text .... ⌘⇧U

Undo/redo last operation .... ⌘Z

WORD SPACING dialog, display .... ⌘⇧W

Accurate for Ready,Set,Go!, version 4.5a

⌘	command	⇥	tab	⌫	delete	⎵	space bar
⇧	shift	↩	return	⌦	fwd. delete	F1	function key
⌥	option	⌤	enter	▣	keypad key	🖰	mouse click
⌃	control	⎋	escape	▣⌦	clear	⋯🖰	mouse drag

QuarkXPress, Version 2.11 TEXT, WDBN, WORD, nX^d, PNTG, PICT, EPS, TIFF, RIFF

XPress offers many impressive features designed especially to lure disenchanted PageMaker users. For example, you can actually specify line weights with XPress rather than choosing from a limited menu. And whereas Ready,Set,Go! and PageMaker require that you draw boxes to create frames around images, XPress provides an automated framing feature. The frame moves when you move the graphic and resizes when you scale the graphic. A utility called Frame Editor is also provided, allowing you to customize frames and borders.

If you use a lot of display type, you'll appreciate XPress's fully sizable screen fonts. In other applications, very large type appears differently on screen than when printed, since the screen version is scaled from a smaller screen-font size. XPress remedies this problem by scaling type directly from a typeface's mathematical printer-font definition, so that 72-point type looks smooth and precise. Unfortunately, this feature does not work for Adobe fonts (incluing Times, Helvetica, and Courier) or any non-PostScript typefaces, significantly limiting its utility.

Unlike Ready,Set,Go!, XPress's **tracking** feature is the real thing. By choosing the TRACKING EDIT command from the UTILITIES menu, you can manipulate the letter spacing associated with a specific typeface. What distinguishes this feature from standard letter spacing is that you can vary the spacing depending on the type size. Typically, you want to increase the spacing for small type, leave the spacing for 12-point type unchanged, and decrease the spacing of large type. XPress allows you to draw a line representing a decline in tracking values as the type size increases.

XPress offers a find and change feature comparable to that of Ready,Set,Go!, the perfect tool for searching for all occurrences of a bold word and replacing it with a different word in italics. A spelling checker is also included, but its dictionary is not as extensive as RSG's.

If you already own or use this product, you no doubt appreciate its precise type-handling abilities. Some of its features, such as contoured text, are unique to this application.

But for people looking for solid, dependable software, we must soberly state that this is not the program for you. Quark has a history of disappointing clients. Over the years, we have found their technical support to be uninformed or flippant. XPress never seems to work with System up-dates, printer-driver updates, or printer ROM updates. While nine out of ten applications manage to weather such changes without incident, Quark is ever releasing updates—we have just been informed of one as we are writing this—to combat one inadequacy or another.

QuarkXPress Quick Reference (1 of 5)

Toolbox

Tool	Name	Description
⊕	Mover	▸ to select element so it may be manipulated, ⋯▸ to move
✋	Editing	▸ text block to insert type, ⋯▸ picture to move graphic in frame
A	Type	⋯▸ to determine dimensions of text block (not used to edit)
⊠	Rectangular icture	⋯▸ to draw rectangular picture block
⊗	Rounded picture	⋯▸ to draw rectangular picture block with rounded corners
⊗	Oval picture	⋯▸ to draw elliptical picture block
+	Orthogonal line	⋯▸ to draw straight line at 45° angle
╲	Diagonal line	⋯▸ to draw straight line at any angle
↖	Arrow	⋯▸ to draw straight line with arrowhead at one end
↙	Double-arrow	⋯▸ to draw straight line with arrowhead at both ends
⦻	Linking	▸ text block to add to current link
⦻	Unlinking	▸ tailfeathers of linking arrow to remove link from text block

QuarkXPress Quick Reference (2 of 5)

Menus

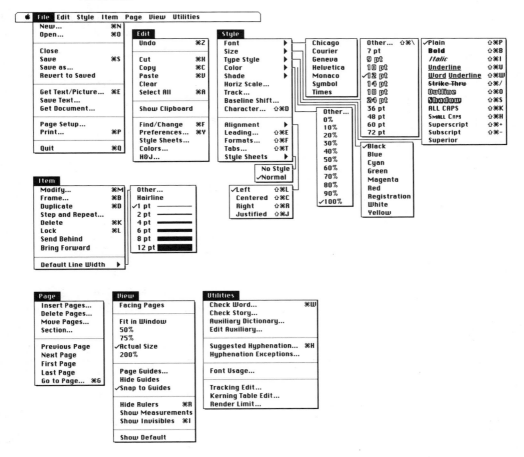

QuarkXPress Quick Reference (3 of 5)

Keyboard Equivalents

Actual size/200%, toggle	⌘⌥↖
Actual size/fit in window, toggle	⌥↖
Actual view size (100%)	⌥↖
All caps text	⌘⇧K
Bold text	⌘⇧B
Center picture	⌘⇧M
Center text	⌘⇧C
Character specifications	⌘⇧D
Check spelling for single word	⌘W
Check word count and spelling for story	⌘⇧W
Circle, create	⇧---↖ *w/ oval tool*
Clear element	⌫
Copy element	⌘C
Copy paragraph formats to selected text block	⌥↖ *formatted text block*
Cut element	⌘X
Delete all tabs	⌥↖ *tab ruler*
Delete next letter	⇧⌫ *or* ⌦
Delete next word	⌘⇧⌫
Delete preceding letter	⌫
Delete preceding word	⌘⌫
Delete ruler guides	⌥↖ *ruler*
Delete selected pictures and lines	⌘K
Duplicate element	⌘D
Find specified text and change	⌘F
Formatting specifications	⌘⇧F
Frame specifications	⌘F
Get text/picture	⌘E
Go to first page	⇧HOME
Go to last page	⇧END
Go to next page	⇧PAGE DOWN
Go to preceding page	⇧PAGE UP
Go to specified page	⌘G
Help	⌘/ *or* HELP
High-contrast picture style	⌘⇧H
Import picture at 72 dpi	⇧ *during import*
Increase baseline shift 1 point	⌘⇧⌥=
Increase horizontal text scaling 5%	⌘]
Increase leading 1 point	⌘⇧'
Increase leading 1/10 point	⌘⇧⌥'
Increase line weight	⌘⇧>
Increase line weight 1 point only	⌘⇧⌥>
Increase picture scaling 5%	⌘⇧⌥>
Increase type size	⌘⇧>
Increase type size 1 point only	⌘⇧⌥>
Italic text	⌘⇧I
Justify text (full justification)	⌘⇧J

⌘	command	⇥	tab	⌫	delete	␣	space bar
⇧	shift	↩	return	⌦	fwd. delete	F1	function key
⌥	option	⌤	enter	▦	keypad key	↖	mouse click
⌃	control	⎋	escape	▦⎋	clear	---↖	mouse drag

QuarkXPress Quick Reference (4 of 5)

Keyboard Equivalents (Cont.)

Kern type, delete ½₀ em .... ⌘⇧[

Kern type, delete ½₀₀ em .... ⌘⇧⌥[

Kern type, insert ½₀ em .... ⌘⇧]

Kern type, insert ½₀₀ em .... ⌘⇧⌥]

Leading specifications .... ⌘⇧E

Left-justify text .... ⌘⇧L

Line break... ⇧↵

Lock element .... ⌘L

Modify picture or line specifications .... ⌘M

Move in 45° direction............. ⇧⤍↖ w/ mover tool

Move text cursor down one line ....↓

Move text cursor left one letter .... ←

Move text cursor left one word .... ⌘←

Move text cursor right one letter ....→

Move text cursor right one word .... ⌘→

Move text cursor up one line ....↑

Move to beginning of current line .... ⌘⌥←

Move to beginning of current paragraph .... ⌘↑

Move to beginning of current story .... ⌘⌥↑

Move to end of current line.......................... ⌘⌥→

Move to end of current paragraph .... ⌘↓

Move to end of current story .... ⌘⌥↓

Mover tool, access temporarily .... ⌘⤍↖

Negative picture style .... ⌘⇧-

New column.. ⌥

New document, create .... ⌘N

New picture box .... ⇧⌥

Nonbreaking en space character .... ⌘⌥␣

Nonbreaking hyphen .... ⌘=

Nonbreaking thin space character .... ⌘␣

Normal contrast picture style .... ⌘⇧N

Open existing document .... ⌘O

Optional hyphen... ⌘-

Other contrast picture style .... ⌘⇧C

Other line weight .... ⌘⇧\

Other screen picture style .... ⌘⇧S

Other type size .... ⌘⇧\

Outline text .... ⌘⇧D

Page number character, current page.............. ⌘3

Page number character, next page .... ⌘4

Page number character, preceding page .... ⌘2

Page setup .... ⌘⌥P

Paste element .... ⌘V

Plain text .... ⌘⇧P

Posterized contrast picture style .... ⌘⇧P

PREFERENCES dialog, display .... ⌘Y

Print document .... ⌘P

Quit QuarkXPress .... ⌘Q

Reduce baseline shift 1 point .... ⌘⇧⌥-

Reduce horizontal text scaling 5% .... ⌘[

Reduce leading 1 point .... ⌘⇧;

Reduce leading ½₀ point .... ⌘⇧⌥;

Reduce line weight .... ⌘⇧<

Reduce line weight 1 point only .... ⌘⇧⌥<

Reduce picture scaling 5% .... ⌘⇧⌥<

Reduce type size .... ⌘⇧<

Reduce type size 1 point only .... ⌘⇧⌥<

Right-justify text .... ⌘⇧R

Save as different name or location .... ⌘⌥S

Save document .... ⌘S

QuarkXPress Quick Reference (5 of 5)

Keyboard Equivalents (Cont.)

Scale box proportionally .... ⇧⌥---↖ *corner handle*
Scale box to square .... ⇧---↖ *corner handle*
Scale picture to fill box exactly .... ⌘⇧F
Scale picture to fill box proportionally .... ⌘⇧⌥F
Scale picture with box .... ⌘---↖ *corner handle*
Scale picture with box proportionally .... ⌘⇧⌥---↖ *corner handle*
Scale picture with box to square .... ⌘⇧---↖ *corner handle*
Select all elements .... ⌘A
Select all text from cursor location to beginning of story .... ⌘⇧⌥↑
Select all text from cursor location to end of story .... ⌘⇧⌥↓
Select all text in chain .... ↖↖↖↖↖ *w/ type tool*
Select current then preceding paragraphs .... ⌘⇧↑
Select current then succeeding paragraphs .... ⌘⇧↓
Select entire line of type .... ↖↖↖ *w/ type tool*
Select entire paragraph .... ↖↖↖↖ *w/ type tool*
Select entire word .... ↖↖ *w/ type tool*
Select next letter .... ⇧→
Select next word .... ⌘⇧→
Select preceding letter .... ⇧←
Select preceding word .... ⌘⇧←
Select tool, permanently .... ⌥↖ *tool icon*
Shadow text .... ⌘⇧S
Show/hide invisible elements .... ⌘I
Show/hide rulers .... ⌘R
Small caps text .... ⌘⇧H
Square, create .... ⇧---↖ *w/ rectangle tool*
Step and repeat (duplication technique) .... ⌘⇧D
Strikethru text .... ⌘⇧/
Subscript text .... ⌘⇧-
Suggest hyphenation for single word .... ⌘H
Superscript text .... ⌘⇧=
Symbol font, 1 character .... ⌘⇧Q, *character key*

Tab stop specifications .... ⌘⇧T
Transfer to specified application .... ⌘T
Twice actual view size (200%) .... ⌘⌥↖

Underline text .... ⌘⇧U
Undo/redo last operation .... ⌘Z

Word-only underline text .... ⌘⇧W

Zapf Dingbats, 1 character .... ⌘⇧Z, *character key*

Accurate for QuarkXPress, version 2.11

⌘	command	⇥	tab	⌫	delete	␣	space bar
⇧	shift	↩	return	⌦	fwd. delete	F1	function key
⌥	option	⌤	enter	▦	keypad key	↖	mouse click
⌃	control	⎋	escape	▦⎋	clear	---↖	mouse drag

Painting Software

Painting may be the most intuitive task you ever perform with a computer. It involves no planning, no guesswork, no programming—none of the messy left-brain activities that so often scare people over the age of 20 away from computers.

This is because, generally speaking, painting involves only two means of communication: a mouse, which you move to convey a visual idea, and a screen, on which your computer displays the results. Since little interpretation is required by your software, your screen displays the results of your mouse movements instantaneously, as if you were drawing with a pencil on a piece of paper. This allows you to draw, see what you've drawn, and make alterations, all in the time it takes the appropriate neurons to fire in your brain.

Digital Paint Versus the Real Thing

Unlike some types of software, a painting application isn't necessarily better than its real-world models. You can safely say that a spreadsheet program is better than the combination of a ledger book, a calculator, and a part-time clerk during a summer break from high school; or that a database program can hold ten times the information in a phone book, and is a hundred times more obliging than an operator. But you can't say—at least, not with a straight face—that a painting application takes the place of a well-equipped artist's studio. In fact, the electronic painting environment sometimes suffers when compared with a pencil.

So perhaps the best way to demonstrate the pros and cons of painting software is to examine more closely how it compares with its traditional cousins.

Multiple Printings

To begin with, painting software excels over traditional methods in the àrea of printing. Multiple copies of an electronic image may be created more simply than a hand-drawn image.

For example, one of the oldest methods for creating multiple copies of a single piece of artwork is lithography. To create an original image, you draw on a specially treated aluminum plate with a grease-based pencil. Since the plate itself will be used to transfer images to paper, your artwork must be created in mirror image, and a separate plate must be created for each color. When the plates are finished, each must be rubbed by hand with various chemicals, some of which are highly toxic. This ensures that when a roller of ink is applied to the plate, the ink adheres only to areas marked by the pencil. Finally, a sheet of paper is placed on the inked plate, and together the two are squeezed through a press. If the press is too loose, the page will under-ink and appear faded; if too tight, the page will over-ink and the plate may become damaged.

Sound archaic? Well, a very similar process is used in commercial printing. The only differences are that plates are produced photographically, and the chemicals and ink are applied by automated machinery. While more reliable, the process remains costly, messy, and hazardous.

By contrast, painting on a Macintosh is inexpensive, tidy, and safe. Multiple copies may be printed for pennies apiece, on-screen colors won't get on your clothing, and the level of toxins is negligible (provided you don't sniff any toner cartridges).

In fact, an electronic painting is made to be used more than once. Since it can be stored to disk, it may be recalled later and printed again. And since you can make copies that are every bit as good as their originals, you may also swap digital artwork with other artists in the form of clip-art. Finally, you may break down a painting so that various details may be used in other images, simplifying the creation process by saving the time required to create frequently used images over and over again.

Easy Manipulation

A second major advantage to painting software is the ease with which elements may be manipulated and erased. The fact that no scribble is permanent, regardless of how long ago it was created, stands in direct opposition to media as diverse as sculpture and oil painting, where a brush stroke can be considered etched in stone.

In fact, electronic paint is *the* most erasable medium, even more so than the pencil. If you've ever made a major goof on a math test, you know that an eraser often does a better job of boring holes through your paper than it does at erasing pencil marks. By contrast, you can erase painted images effortlessly and entirely, simply by dragging an eraser tool over the unwanted area.

In a color painting application, your options increase. If you choose, you may paint a green line over a purple area without any residue of purple showing through, an operation entirely without equal in the traditional environment. Or, you may specify that the green line blend with the purple behind it, creating the effect of painting on a wet canvas. You may also designate for the green to tint the purple, creating a brown stroke, or to cycle from green to blue to purple as your paintbrush moves across the page. Charcoal effects, wash effects, and a whole myriad of others are available, limited only by a programmer's imagination.

Due to the impermanent nature of electronic painting, elements may be manipulated in ways that would be impossible using strictly traditional media. Here, we have used a charcoal technique to sketch a face, and then smeared the on-screen charcoal around as if it were wet paint.

Using a painting application, you may draw, erase, and redraw images as many times as you deem necessary. Painted elements may also be moved, rotated, enlarged, reduced, and transformed in any number of other ways depending on the sophistication of your software. The best electronic artists are those who can manipulate not only the immediacy of on-screen painting, but its impermanency as well.

Unalterable Resolution

But despite painting software's many advantages over traditional techniques, its single failing—the graininess of its output—is glaringly obvious, so much so that people who have never used a computer can immediately recognize computer-produced artwork.

This problem is caused by the fact that paintings are locked into a specific **resolution**, which is the number of tiny dots, or **pixels**, that make up a painting.

When you draw with a real-life pencil, you cause minute fragments of graphite to break off the pencil's tip and become lodged on the surface of your paper. However, since these fragments are so infinitesimal and abundant, they appear to form smooth lines and continuous shades. Likewise, painted images are composed of tiny fragments—namely, the tiny pixels on your screen. A normal Macintosh screen contains 72 pixels per inch (or 5,184 pixels per square inch). Although some applications allow you to print at higher resolutions, this resolution is always constant.

(Some applications that offer painting functions also provide **object-oriented** functions for creating mathematically defined lines and shapes whose resolutions vary depending on the resolution of your printer. Among these are Canvas, SuperPaint, and LaserPaint. For more information on these applications, see the Drawing Software entry.)

Also, since both your artwork and your printer have resolutions of their own that probably differ, you may have to resize painted artwork in order to print it most effectively. To learn how to most effectively output monochrome paintings, see Painting Technicalities 1.

Disguising Graininess

This fixed resolution is not as much of a problem as you might think. In fact, the resolution of your computer screen is comparable to that of your television, which you have probably learned to take entirely for granted. The main difference is that most viewers are accustomed to color televisions, which display gradual transitions between various shades and hues, whereas most paintings are black and white. This glaring contrast between the black edges of painted lines and the white of the paper on which they're printed makes the limited resolution of monochrome paintings very obvious.

Therefore, the easiest way to make your paintings less grainy is to use color painting software. In fact, color applications are useful even if you only own a monochrome printer, such as a LaserWriter, since they allow you to create gradual transitions between shades of gray.

Image-Saving Formats

In the following pages, we will look at some popular painting applications and examine their capabilities. To the right of each program name will be a list of the image-saving formats that the program supports. These are formats that allow a document to be imported into another application, such as a word processor or a page-layout program. These formats may include one or more of the following:

- **PNTG** (MacPaint format). The most common and yet most limited image-swapping format, the MacPaint format stores bit-mapped information only. MacPaint files are exclusively monochrome, no larger than 8 by 10 inches (vertically oriented), and locked into a resolution of 72 dpi (5,184 pixels per square inch). A wide variety of Macintosh applications can import this format.

- **PICT**. This format exists in two forms: PICT and PICT2. The original PICT format supports only eight colors, which default to black, white, red, green, blue, cyan, magenta, and yellow. Since so few colors are supported, PICT is most useful for black-and-white artwork. The upgraded PICT2 supports as many colors as your monitor will allow (256 for a typical 8-bit video board). However, if you customize your palette, the screen representation may be off when you import the artwork into another application. Each color will be altered to comply

Painting Technicalities 1

Avoiding incongruities between the
resolution of your painting and that of your printer

Printing artwork from a monochrome paint program like MacPaint to an Apple ImageWriter is a simple enough process. This is because the resolution of the ImageWriter, 144 dots per inch, is exactly twice the resolution of most painting applications. Problems may occur, however, when printing to a high-end printer whose resolution is not a multiple of 72.

For example, suppose we are printing a 72-dpi painting to a 300-dpi laser printer. Each pixel in your painting is $\frac{1}{72}$ inch square, while each pixel in your laser printer is $\frac{1}{300}$ inch square. Therefore, each painted pixel wants to take up $\frac{1}{72}$ divided by $\frac{1}{300}$, or $4\frac{1}{6}$ laser-printer pixels. Since pixels by definition can't be divvied up into pieces, each painted pixel must be represented by an even number of printed pixels. But your laser printer can't just round down each pixel to four dots wide or it would shrink the painting.

As an analogy, consider a calendar year. It actually takes the earth about 365 $\frac{1}{4}$ days to pass once around the sun. If we simply rounded down a year to 365 days, the seasons would get farther and farther ahead of our calendars, until one July about 730 years from now, our descendants would find themselves knee-deep in snow. We ensure for them a summery July by adding one day every four years, calling it leap year.

This is the same way that your laser printer works. Every sixth painted pixel is one laser-printer pixel bigger than its neighbors. These occasionally larger pixels are very obvious to the naked eye, giving your paintings a sort of visual throbbing effect known generically as a **moiré** pattern (a French word for watered silk—hence a wavelike pattern).

To eliminate moiré patterns, you must reduce or enlarge your paintings so the number of painted pixels divides evenly into the number of printed pixels. There are three ways to accomplish this. First, you may choose PAGE SETUP from your application's FILE menu and enter a value into the "Reduce or enlarge" option. Second, you may import your painting into a word-processing or page-layout program. An ideal utility for this purpose is Dubl-Click's ArtRoundUp, which allows you to enter a scaling value for importing. Third, some paint applications allow you to scale an image while retaining the number of pixels. This third option is not viable for fixed-resolution applications such as MacPaint, where a painting is always 72 dpi regardless of whether you enlarge or reduce it.

Printing paintings at normal size can result in inconsistent line sizes, as shown on the left. We resized the right image slightly to 102 percent, making the resolution of the painting compatible with that of our typesetter.

To figure out the percentages that will allow you to most effectively print a painting, begin by dividing your printer's resolution by that of your painting. In the case of a typical laser printer, this value is 300 divided by 72, or 4⅙. Next, divide 1 by that value; in our case, 1 divided by 4⅙ is 0.24, or 24%. This means 24% is our base percentage, so that any whole-number multiple of 24% will produce effective printed paintings. In other words, you may scale your painting to 24%, 48%, 72%, or 96%—or even 120%, 144%, and so on.

Using this method, we may also determine the optimal percentages for printing paintings to a typesetter with a resolution of 2,540 or 1,270 dots per inch. Since the base percentage in this case is not an even number (~5.67%), there are no precise percentage values, but the best turn out to be multiples of 17%, such as 34%, 51%, 68%, 85%, and 102%.

Conclusion: When printing a painting to a laser printer, scale the painting to a multiple of 24%. When printing to a typesetter, print at a multiple of 17%. And keep in mind that reducing a painting using the Page Setup command or a similar technique increases its resolution.

with Apple's standard 256-color configuration (once again, assuming you own an 8-bit video board). If your page-layout software can print four-color separations of imported artwork (as can PageMaker 3.02 with Color Extension), the colors of a PICT2 document will be printed as they were created, not as they appear on screen.

• **TIFF** (Tagged Image File Format). Like the MacPaint format, TIFF is an exclusively bit-mapped format. But unlike MacPaint, it is almost entirely unrestricted. TIFF was developed by Aldus Corporation in an attempt to standardize sampled images created by scanning devices. Unfortunately, while widely accepted, TIFF is not completely standardized; the format exists in different forms on the Mac and PC, and even then, some programs support monochrome TIFF only, others support TIFF with 16 evenly incremented gray values, and a handful support full-color TIFF. But when it is supported, we find TIFF to be the image-swapping format of choice.

• **EPSF** (Encapsulated PostScript format). This format includes a PICT screen representation of a graphic and a pure PostScript-language definition that is downloaded directly to your output device when printing. However, while terrific for object-oriented images like those created by drawing applications, PostScript is not the optimal language for describing bit-mapped images. It tends to be exceptionally inefficient, resulting in enormous files.

• **SCRN** (startup screen). This variation on the PICT format allows you to create an image to replace the "Welcome to Macintosh" screen that appears when you boot up your computer. Simply save the file in startup-screen format under the name StartupScreen, move the file to your System folder, and reboot to view your image. Some applications, such as SuperPaint, only allow you to save images that fit a 7-inch built-in monitor. Others, such as PixelPaint, allow you to create larger, full-color startup screens.

• **Native formats.** Some applications use their own image-saving formats for storing graphics that you don't intend to import into another application. Such unique formats are listed followed by the word *native* in parentheses.

The Mac's First Program

 MacPaint, Version 2.0   PNTG, SCRN

MacPaint was packaged with the very first wave of Macintosh computers. Since then, the Mac's memory has expanded, its disk drives format at a higher density, hard-drive capacity has grown, video-card slots have been added, color monitors are supported, and even the keyboard is better. In the meantime, MacPaint gained scroll bars. Who in this day and age can possibly find a use for such outdated software?

Well, as it so happens, we use MacPaint almost daily. The fact that it requires so little memory makes it the perfect MultiFinder application. And though simple and limited, MacPaint is satisfactory for creating basic graphics, and especially for screen-shot and icon manipulation.

Pixel-Perfect Control

MacPaint sacrifices flamboyancy for absolute control, making drawing a very precise and predictable process. For example, if you have a steady enough hand to edit single pixels at the normal view size, you may click exactly on a pixel with the pencil tool to turn it on or off. Most other painting applications require that you click one pixel *above* the pixel that you want to change, a throwback to MacPaint 1.0. Also, MacPaint's reaction time is immediate. When you drag the paintbrush, MacPaint follows you from the instant you click to the second you release. Try that in a color application! And MacPaint is one of the few programs that allows you to press the COMMAND key to shrink the marquee *after* you begin marqueeing an image.

Like it or not, MacPaint defined the painting environment, and virtually no application has so much as made an attempt to alter it. (The only exceptions are Studio/1 and Studio/8, discussed later in this entry.) Though it has since fallen way behind the competition in the features department, the original MacPaint was probably the most influential application ever deisgned for the Macintosh.

Painting Trends

The following is a brief list of timesaving operations, first introduced by MacPaint, that work in almost all other painting applications. Most or all of these you may already know, but we consider them so essential to understanding the basic painting environment that we feel they should be included.

- Press SHIFT to constrain any action vertically or horizontally.

- Command-click with the pencil tool to magnify the view size. Double-click the pencil icon to access "fat bits," an 800 percent view size.

- Double-click the eraser icon to erase the entire window.

- Double-click the paintbrush icon to change the current brush shape.

- Press the OPTION key and drag to access the grabber hand while any tool but the type tool is active. (Some applications require that you press the space bar.)

- Double-click a pattern to edit it.

- Command-drag with the marquee tool to shrink the marquee around an image.

- Option-drag a selected image to create a copy without replacing the contents of the Clipboard (also known as *cloning*).

- Command-option-drag a selected image to draw with it as though it were a custom brush shape.

- Command-drag at the corner of a marquee to reduce or enlarge an image.

Desktop Publishing Trends

Some of the keyboard/mouse operations pioneered by MacPaint are now so universal that they work in other types of desktop publishing applications as well. Pressing the SHIFT key, for example, is the universal method of constraining cursor movement. Pressing the OPTION key or the space bar accesses the grabber hand in most programs, many of which don't even provide the tool in their toolbox. And more and more object-oriented applications are allowing you to clone selected elements by option-dragging. In many ways, MacPaint defined not only the painting environment, but the standard for graphic-based applications as well.

MacPaint Quick Reference (1 of 4)

Toolbox

Icon	Tool	Description
⬚	Marquee	⋯ᴋ to select rectangular portion of painting to manipulate
✐	Lasso	⋯ᴋ to select irregular portion of painting to manipulate
✋	Hand	⋯ᴋ to move page with respect to window
╲	Line	⋯ᴋ to draw straight line at any angle
🖌	Paint can	⋯ᴋ to fill an enclosed or solid area with current pattern
🖍	Spraypaint	⋯ᴋ to generate pattern of loose pixels
🖌	Paintbrush	⋯ᴋ to draw free-form lines with current brush shape
✏	Pencil	ᴋ to create or delete pixels, ⋯ᴋ to draw or delete free-form lines
▱	Eraser	⋯ᴋ to delete general portions of bit map
A	Type	ᴋ to set origin for text block

Icon	Tool	Description
▭	Rectangle	⋯ᴋ to draw transparent rectangle
▚	Filled rectangle	⋯ᴋ to draw rectangle filled with current pattern
▢	Round corner	⋯ᴋ to draw transparent rectangle with rounded corners
▣	Filled round corner	⋯ᴋ to draw filled rectangle with rounded corners
◯	Oval	⋯ᴋ to draw transparent ellipse
●	Filled oval	⋯ᴋ to draw ellipse filled with current pattern
♡	Freehand	⋯ᴋ to draw transparent free-form shape in current line weight
♥	Filled freehand	⋯ᴋ to draw free-form shape filled with current pattern
◿	Polygon	ᴋ to create corners for transparent straight-sided polygon
◢	Filled polygon	ᴋ to create corners for filled straight-sided polygon

MacPaint Quick Reference (2 of 4)

Menus

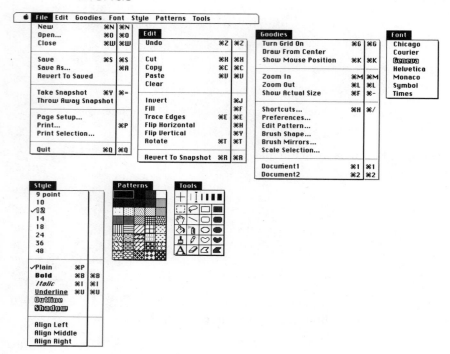

The second columns of keyboard equivalents represent our recommended ResEdit alterations to the MENU resource as explained under "Ten Hottest MacPaint Tips" later in this entry

MacPaint Quick Reference (3 of 4)

Keyboard Equivalents

Actual size/fat bits, toggle .... 🖰🖰 *pencil icon*

Actual/fit in window, toggle .... 🖰🖰 *hand icon*

Bold text .... ⌘B

Brush shape, select .... 🖰🖰 *paintbrush icon*

Change typeface .... ⌘⇧> *or* ⌘⇧<

Circle, create .... ⇧┈🖰 *w/oval tool*

Clear selected element .... ⌫

Clone selected element .... ⌥┈🖰

Close current document .... ⌘W

Copy element .... ⌘C

Cut element .... ⌘X

Draw from center .... 🖰🖰 *any shape tool icon*

Draw with selected element .... ⌘⌥┈🖰 *element*

Edit pattern .... 🖰🖰 *pattern icon*

Erase entire document .... ⇧🖰🖰 *eraser icon*

Erase window .... 🖰🖰 *eraser icon*

Fill beyond current window .... ⇧🖰 *w/paint can*

Grab pattern off page (gridded) .... 🖰 *while*
PATTERN *dialog displayed*

Hand tool, select temporarily .... ⌥

Increase leading .... ⌘⌥>

Increase type size .... ⌘>

Italic text .... ⌘I

Make selected element transparent .... ➡┊┈🖰

Move selected element in 45° direction ...... ⇧┈🖰

Move window .... ⌘┈🖰 *w/hand tool*

New document, create .... ⌘N

Open existing document .... ⌘O *or* ⌥ *on launch*

Paste element .... ⌘V

Pattern palette, display at cursor position .... P

Patterned lines, create .... ⌘┈🖰 *w/line tool*

Perpendicular lines, create .... ⇧┈🖰
w/any painting tool or eraser

Plain text .... ⌘P

Quit MacPaint .... ⌘Q

Reduce leading .... ⌘⌥<

Reduce type size .... ⌘<

Revert document to snapshot .... ⌘R
or ⌘⇧🖰🖰 *eraser icon*

Revert window to snapshot .... ⌘🖰🖰 *eraser icon*

Revert to snapshot selectively .... ⌘┈🖰 *w/eraser*

Rotate selected element by 90° .... ⌘T

⌘	command	➡	tab	⌫	delete	⎵	space bar
⇧	shift	↵	return	⌦	fwd. delete	F1	function key
⌥	option	⌤	enter	⌨	keypad key	🖰	mouse click
⌃	control	⎋	escape	⌨⌧	clear	┈🖰	mouse drag

MacPaint Quick Reference (4 of 4)

Keyboard Equivalents (Cont.)

Save painting .... ⌘S

Scale proportionally ...... ⌘⇧⸺ᐅ *marquee corner*

Scale selected element .... ⌘⸺ᐅ *marquee corner*

Select document ...... ⇧ᐅᐅ *lasso or marquee icon*

Select window .... ᐅᐅ *lasso or marquee icon*

Shapes with patterned outlines, create .... ⌘⸺ᐅ
ʷ/ any shape tool

Shortcuts screen, display .... ⌘H

Show/hide actual-size window .... ⌘F

Show/hide mouse-position indicator .... ⌘K

Shrink marquee to bit map .... ⌘⸺ᐅ *ʷ/marquee*

Square, create .... ⇧⸺ᐅ *ʷ/rectangle tool*

Switch to document number [#] .... ⌘[#]

Take snapshot .... ⌘Y

Tear off menus .... ⸺ᐅ PATTERNS *or* TOOLS *menu*

Toolbox, display at cursor position .... T

Trace edges of selected element .... ⌘E

Trace edges with shadow effect .... ⌘⇧E

Transparent lines and shapes, create .... ⌘⬎⸺ᐅ
ʷ/ line tool or any filled shape tool

Transparent patterns, create .... ⌘⸺ᐅ
ʷ/ paintbrush or spraypaint tool

Turn grid on/off .... ⌘G

Underline text .... ⌘U

Undo/redo last operation .... ⌘Z *or* ~ *or* ⏦

Zoom in .... ⌘M *or* ⌘ᐅ *ʷ/ pencil*

Zoom out .... ⌘L *or* ⌘⇧ᐅ *ʷ/ pencil*

Accurate for MacPaint, version 2.0

⌘	command	➜|	tab	⌫	delete	⊔	space bar
⇧	shift	↵	return	⌦	fwd. delete	F1	function key
⬎	option	⤳	enter	▦	keypad key	ᐅ	mouse click
⌃	control	⏦	escape	▦⏦	clear	⸺ᐅ	mouse drag

Ten Hottest MacPaint Tips

The following are some hints designed to help you make more effective use of MacPaint. (Tips marked with [†] work only for version 2.0.)

◇   **Erasing in various sizes.** One of MacPaint's biggest drawbacks is that you can't change the size of the eraser icon. But you can erase in different sizes by using the paintbrush in combination with a white pattern. Or, you may select a blank area with the marquee tool and command-option-drag the selection. The size of your marquee acts as the size of the eraser.

◇   **Erasing sizable areas.** To erase large areas, but not the entire screen, lasso or marquee an image and press the BACKSPACE or DELETE key.

◇   **Patterned lines.** You may create a line or outline in the current pattern by pressing the COMMAND key when drawing with the line tool or one of the shape tools.[†] (Press the OPTION key in earlier versions of MacPaint.)

◇   **Filling text.** To fill multiple elements with a similar pattern, such as separate letters in a line of text, don't click each element with the paint can. Simply lasso the elements and choose the FILL command from the EDIT menu. If there are any enclosed white areas in your elements (such as the inside of the letter *O*), erase "holes" into them with the pencil tool so they don't become selected.

◆   **Thickening a line.** The TRACE EDGES command is extremely useful for making existing elements heavier or thicker. For example, to thicken a line, select it with the marquee tool and choose TRACE EDGES. Then select the paint can and click inside the hollow line to fill it in.

◆   **Transparent patterns.** To fill a shape with a transparent pattern, press COMMAND and OPTION while dragging with one of the filled shape tools. To make a selection transparent, press the TAB key.

◆   **Making type bolder.** This technique may also be used to make some type bolder. Marquee a large letter and choose TRACE EDGES two or three times. Then erase some breaks in the extraneous outlines inside the letter. Clicking inside the letter with the paint can completes the process as before.

♦ **Editing brush shapes.** Many competing painting programs allow you to edit brush shapes to create a custom paintbrush cursor. But alas, MacPaint is behind on this feature too. But if you *really* want to change a brush shape (for the long run, that is), you may do so using ResEdit. Opening MacPaint's CURS resource will display the many cursor shapes that MacPaint uses. The last six rows of these include brush shapes, though other cursors are sprinkled about as well. Note that editing any one of these cursors will change the respective brush shape when you draw with it, although the cursor will look the same as it did before the change in the BRUSH SHAPE dialog box.

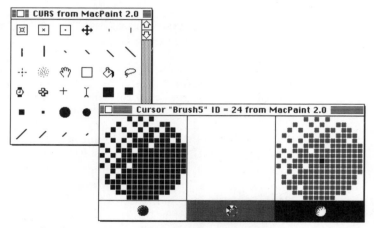

ResEdit allows you to edit any of MacPaint's brush shapes via the CURS resource. However, this will not change the appearance of the cursor in the dialog box displayed by double-clicking the paintbrush tool.

♦ **Creating spraypaint cookie cutters.** In the real world, professional artists use masking tape and stencils to limit the area affected by an airbrush. In MacPaint, you have no such feature to create crisp edges when using the spraypaint tool. However, you may create a "cookie cutter" that will mask an area *after* it is spraypainted. The trick is to create two copies of the image you want to paint, one you actually spraypaint (without worrying about staying in the lines) and one that you make into a cookie cutter. To create a cookie cutter, draw a rectangle around your image. Then create a tunnel into it as shown in the following figure, allowing paint to "leak" into the image but not into the surrounding area.

The images above demonstrate the steps in applying the cookie cutter technique. First, we copy our image and apply spraypaint to it. Second, we paste the unspraypainted image, draw a rectangle around it, and draw a tunnel connecting the rectangle and image to create a cookie cutter. Third, we drag the cookie cutter over the spraypainted image, masking away the excess spraypaint to create a crisp and textural finished piece of artwork.

◆   **Changing keyboard equivalents.** One of the more dubious features of MacPaint is its old-style use of keyboard equivalents. (This is even worse in FullPaint, by the way.) COMMAND-P makes text plain instead of printing, and many frequently used commands are ignored. We recommend using ResEdit to change the keyboard equivalents in the MENU resource as follows:

SAVE AS	⌘A
TAKE SNAPSHOT	⌘= (leaving ⌘Y open)
PRINT	⌘P
INVERT	⌘J (⌘I is already taken)
FILL	⌘F
FLIP HORIZONTAL	⌘H
FLIP VERTICAL	⌘Y
SHOW ACTUAL SIZE	⌘-
SHORTCUTS	⌘/ (it's like HELP, after all)
PLAIN	Delete (MacPaint ain't no word processor)

The results of these changes are shown in the Menus portion of the MacPaint Quick Reference.

MacPaint's Biggest Fan

Since MacPaint debuted in 1984, many third-party competitors have issued forth. The first MacPaint clone, FullPaint, came out about a year and a half after its mentor, offering many new features in a strikingly similar format. Ah, those were the days of FullPaint, version 1.0. Nowadays, we have ...

 FullPaint, Version 1.0SE   PNTG
Once upon a time, we thought FullPaint was pretty hot stuff. But that was four years ago, back when they used to burn witches at the stake, so anything was pretty impressive. In our modern day and age, FullPaint looks a little stale.

And, frankly, it is. That's why it's so amazing that the software—which in four years still hasn't managed to advance past version 1.0—possesses features that MacPaint 2.0 still lacks. Free rotation, skewing, distortion, and perspective are all features that were introduced by FullPaint and have since been picked up by every other painting application except MacPaint. You may also edit brush shapes by command-double-clicking the paintbrush icon, or double-click an image with the lasso tool to select it.

Unfortunately, FullPaint suffers from many of MacPaint's early liabilities, such as only one magnified view size and lousy keyboard equivalents— you can only access the NEW, OPEN, SAVE, PRINT, and QUIT commands by dragging at menus. To remedy this latter problem, we recommend that you open FullPaint's MENU resource with Apple's ResEdit utility, and change the keyboard equivalents to those we recommended for MacPaint; or, you may prefer to add equivalents of your own. Just be careful not to repeat the same keyboard equivalent for two commands. For example, if you decide to add COMMAND-P as the equivalent for the PRINT command under the FILE menu, be sure to delete it from the PLAIN command under the STYLE menu.

Coloring FullPaint Artwork

These days, FullPaint's best quality may be its inclusion of ColorPrint, a utility that allows you to print color paintings from monochrome separations on dot-matrix printers with color ribbons.

◆ **ColorPrint, Version 2.4**   CPDC (native)
An interesting utility included with FullPaint is Esoft's ColorPrint, which can "colorize" any monochrome painting that is printed to a dot-matrix printer such as the ImageWriter II. After you create a series of color separations as individual files in FullPaint or another black-and-white program, ColorPrint will combine the separations on the same page, printing the black separation in black ink, the red separation in red ink, and so on, provided that you own the appropriately colored ribbons. ColorPrint combines paintings as long as they share a similar prefix followed by a period and a color name. For example, ColorPrint knows to combine the files Portrait.Black, Portrait.Red, and Portrait.Yellow, and will even prompt you to change ribbons in between colors when necessary.

ColorPrint cannot print to color laser printers or other high-resolution output devices.

FullPaint Quick Reference (1 of 4)

Toolbox

Lasso	to select irregular portion of painting to manipulate
Marquee	to select rectangular portion of painting to manipulate
Hand	to move page with respect to window
Type	to set origin for text block
Paint can	to fill an enclosed or solid area with current pattern
Spraypaint	to generate pattern of loose pixels
Paintbrush	to draw free-form lines with current brush shape
Pencil	to create or delete single, to draw or delete free-form lines
Eraser	to delete general portions of bit map
Line	to draw straight line at any angle

Rectangle	to draw transparent rectangle
Filled rectangle	to draw rectangle filled with current pattern
Round corner	to draw transparent rectangle with rounded corners
Filled round corner	to draw filled rectangle with rounded corners
Oval	to draw transparent ellipse
Filled oval	to draw ellipse filled with current pattern
Freehand	to draw transparent free-form shape in current line weight
Filled freehand	to draw free-form shape filled with current pattern
Polygon	to create corners for transparent straight-sided polygon
Filled polygon	to create corners for filled straight-sided polygon

FullPaint Quick Reference (2 of 4)

Menus

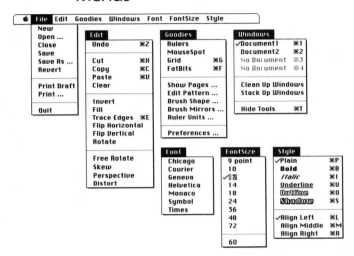

ColorPrint Menus

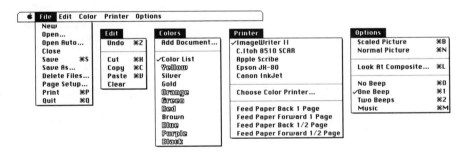

FullPaint Quick Reference (3 of 4)

Keyboard Equivalents

Actual size/fat bits, toggle .... ➤➤ *pencil icon*
or ⌘➤ *w/pencil*

Actual/fit in window, toggle .... ➤➤ *hand icon*

Align text left .... ⌘L

Align text middle .... ⌘M

Align text right .... ⌘R

Autoscrolling selection ...... ⌥⁓┈➤ *w/marquee tool*

Bold text .... ⌘B

Brush shape, select .... ➤➤ *paintbrush icon*

Change to next typeface .... ⌘⇧>

Change to previous typeface .... ⌘⇧<

Circle, create .... ⇧┈➤ *w/oval tool*

Clean up toolbox and palettes .... ⌘W

Clear element .... ⌫

Clone selected element .... ⌥┈➤

Copy element .... ⌘C

Cut element .... ⌘X

Draw with selected element .... ⌘⌥┈➤ *element*

Edit brush shape .... ⌘➤➤ *paintbrush icon*

Edit pattern .... ➤➤ *pattern icon*

Erase window .... ➤➤ *eraser icon*

Fat-bits view size (800%) .... ⌘F

Fill with transparent pattern .... ⌘ *choose FILL*

Grab pattern off page (gridded) .... ➤
while PATTERN dialog displayed

Grab pattern off page (nongridded) .... ⌘➤
while PATTERN dialog displayed

Grid, activate/deactivate .... ⌘G

Hand tool, select temporarily .... ⌥ *w/pencil*

Help .... ⌘H *or* ➤ *question mark icon*

Increase type size .... ⌘>

Italic text .... ⌘I

Lasso without tightening .... ⌥┈➤ *w/lasso*

Lines at 45° angles, create .... ⇧┈➤ *w/line tool*
or polygon tool

MEASURING UNITS dialog, display .... ➤➤ *ruler*

Move palette .... ⌥┈➤

Move selected element in 45° direction ...... ⇧┈➤

Outline text .... ⌘0

Paste element in center of window .... ⌘V

Paste element in upper-left corner .... ⌘⌥V

⌘	command	⇥	tab	⌫	delete	▬	space bar
⇧	shift	↵	return	⌦	fwd. delete	F1	function key
⌥	option	⤫	enter	▦	keypad key	➤	mouse click
⌃	control	⌮	escape	▦⌮	clear	┈	mouse drag

FullPaint Quick Reference (4 of 4)

Keyboard Equivalents (Cont.)

Patterned lines, create .... ⌥----↖ *w/ line tool*

Perpendicular lines, create .... ⇧----↖ *w/ any painting tool or eraser*

Plain text .... ⌘P

Reduce type size .... ⌘<

Scale proportionally ...... ⌘⇧----↖ *marquee corner*

Scale selected element .... ⌘----↖ *marquee corner*

Select contiguous image .... ↖↖ *w/ lasso*

Select entire document .... ↖↖↖ *marquee icon*

Select window .... ↖↖ *lasso or marquee icon*

Shadow text .... ⌘S

Shapes with patterned outlines, create .... ⌥----↖ *w/ any shape tool*

Show/hide menu bar .... ⌘A

Show/hide toolbox and palettes .... ⌘T *or* ␣

Shrink marquee to bit map .... ⌘----↖ *w/ marquee*

Square, create .... ⇧----↖ *w/ rectangle tool*

Switch to document number [#] .... ⌘[#]

Trace edges of selected element .... ⌘E

Trace edges with shadow effect .... ⌘⇧E

Transparent patterns, create .... ⌘----↖ *w/ paintbrush or spraypaint tool*

Transparent shapes, create .... ⌘⌥----↖ *w/ any filled shape tool*

Transparent straight lines, create .... ⌘⌥----↖ *w/ line tool*

Underline text .... ⌘U

Undo/redo last operation .... ⌘Z *or* ~

Accurate for FullPaint, version 1.0SE

The Monochrome Set

If you keep up with the trade magazines, you've probably noticed how 90 percent of the articles assume you just got your new Macintosh IV QXL last week, and you're a little peeved because your color monitor blurs toward the edges when displaying two tabloid pages side by side, especially when you're background-printing documents longer than 500 pages.

Well, some of us still own a Plus or an SE and do most of our printing on an ImageWriter. For those few million, there are a whole slew of monochrome painting applications that offer features well beyond those of MacPaint or FullPaint. The sheer quantity of this type of software proves that painting remains a lively medium at the grass-roots level, especially for creating quick or humorous artwork for both amateur and professional publications.

 NuPaint, Version 1.0.3   PNTG, PICT, SCRN
For about ten bucks more than MacPaint, NuPaint is a measurable improvement. Using a mixing-bowl tool, for example, you may smear over an existing image, making its edges fuzzy. There is also a SHADOW command that can create an automated shadow behind a selected image. You may even create partial shadows, so that a shadow may bend (as when going across a floor and then up a wall) or break (as when going off the edge of a cliff).

But NuPaint's greatest feature is its patterns. Normally, the patterns in a painting program measure 8 by 8 pixels, fairly small and rather limiting. In NuPaint, you may create patterns up to 32 by 32 pixels, the size of a standard Macintosh icon. This means the number of possible permutations increases from a mere 18 quintillion for a normal pattern to the astronomical number of 1 followed by 308 zeros, the practical outcome of which is that you are 9 followed by 288 zeros times less likely to repeat someone else's pattern. (Now there's the kind of extraordinarily useful information you're not likely to find anywhere else.)

Unfortunately, some of NuPaint's unusual features operate very awkwardly. We've had NuPaint for about six months now, and even with the manual, the correct usages of the razor and trowel tools escape us. Also, while you can create images at resolutions of up to 300 dots per inch, the method for doing so is extremely cumbersome, involving saving a current document at two or four times its present size, and subsequently splitting the document into four to sixteen separate files, which must then be edited separately and batched when printing.

 SuperPaint, Version 2.0   PNTG, PICT, TIFF, SCRN
If you're looking for real black-and-white painting power combined with the object-oriented capabilities of MacDraw, you've got to like SuperPaint. It offers a tracing command for surrounding bit-mapped sketches with high-resolution lines and shapes. And best of all, SuperPaint offers a wide variety of "plug-in" tools, which produce more way-out special effects than any other painting application. Sadly, there's more to drawing than automated spyrographs and 3-D boxes, but they are fun.

Since SuperPaint also provides object-oriented features, we cover the software in greater detail in the Drawing Software entry, including our ten best SuperPaint tips and a quick reference.

Bit Maps on the Fly

Users of MultiFinder have no doubt discovered how useful paint applications can be in tandem with other applications, due to their relatively small memory requirements. But for those of us who don't use MultiFinder, there are a handful of painting applications that present themselves in the form of a desk accessory, allowing you to access or edit bit maps while in another application.

 ArtRoundUp, Version 2.1
ArtRoundUp is the perfect DA for accessing precreated artwork inside a word-processing or page-layout program. Because it is so simple, it requires very little memory, so that no matter what application you are running, you probably always have enough room left in your computer's RAM to open ArtRoundUp as well.

ArtRoundUp will open any PNTG document. You may then perform slight manipulations to an image by using transformation commands available from a menu below the title bar or by drawing with the pencil and eraser tools. After changes are completed, copy the image and paste it into the current word-processing or page-layout document. You may also reduce or enlarge images as you paste them by establishing a scaling factor and then choosing the (Scaled) Copy and (Scaled) Place commands.

ArtRoundUp is strictly for transferring images. You cannot save files even if you have made changes to them, and UNDO is inoperative. If you want to save a changed image, you must use one of the following DA's.

 DeskPaint, Version 2.0   PNTG, PICT, TIFF

DeskPaint is a quirky little program. It supports a solid variety of formats and allows you to edit bit maps at resolutions up to 300 dots per inch, but many of the smaller functions that you have learned to take for granted in MacPaint have been changed or are inoperative in DeskPaint. For example, pressing the COMMAND key while marqueeing an image does not shrink the marquee. In fact, marquees never shrink, even when using the lasso. Nor does pressing OPTION while dragging a bit map create a clone. But if you drag a selection and then choose UNDO, the bit map will revert to its original location *and* be displayed at its new location in a marquee, effectively creating a clone.

Nonetheless, DeskPaint's utility and convenience outweigh its oddities. We use it constantly, cursing all the while. To make your DeskPaint experiences less exasperating, you may wish to consult our Quick Reference on the following pages.

Incidentally, DA's are always limited to a single menu, far from adequate for holding all the commands required to edit bit-mapped elements. Different programs deal with this constraint in different ways. DeskPaint, for example, allows you to access all transformations by clicking toolbox icons that appear when an image is selected. Canvas, a competing painting DA, provides tools with pop-up menus.

Canvas, Version 2.0   DRW2 (native), PNTG, PICT, TIFF

Canvas is the most powerful of the painting DA's, but it also consumes the most memory, making it inadvisable for users with no more than 1 megabyte of RAM. Canvas spares you from the keyboard oddities of DeskPaint, but because it offers object-oriented capabilities, it serves up some oddities of its own. For example, Canvas considers bit maps to be unique objects, ascribing them handles as if they were boxes created in MacDraw. You may find that these handles limit the size of a bit map when you try to add to it. But in such a case, you may drag any handle to enlarge the painting area to the size you desire.

DeskPaint Quick Reference (1 of 4)

Toolbox

T	Type	to set origin for text block
	Zoom	to magnify view of page, ⌘ to demagnify
	Hand	to move page with respect to window
	Charcoal	to sketch in pattern of loose pixels
	Airbrush	to generate random spray of pixels
	Autotrace	to trace bit-mapped image with smooth polygon for use in DeskDraw
	Paint can	to fill an enclosed or solid area with current pattern
	Marquee	to select rectangular portion of painting to manipulate
	Lasso	to select irregular portion of painting to manipulate
	Rectangle	to draw rectangle filled with current pattern
	Polygon	to create corners for straight-sided polygon filled with current pattern
	Round corner	to draw rectangle with rounded corners filled with current pattern
	Freehand	to draw free-form shape filled with current pattern
	Oval	to draw ellipse filled with current pattern
	Line	to draw straight line at any angle
	Paintbrush	to draw free-form lines with current brush shape
	Pencil	to create or delete pixels, to draw or delete free-form lines
	Eraser	to delete general portions of bit map

DeskPaint Quick Reference (2 of 4)

Transformation Icons (marquee image to display)

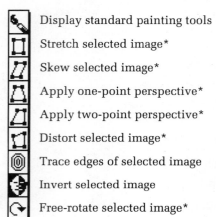

Display standard painting tools

Stretch selected image*

Skew selected image*

Apply one-point perspective*

Apply two-point perspective*

Distort selected image*

Trace edges of selected image

Invert selected image

Free-rotate selected image*

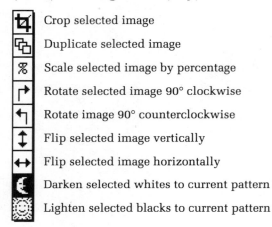

Crop selected image

Duplicate selected image

Scale selected image by percentage

Rotate selected image 90° clockwise

Rotate image 90° counterclockwise

Flip selected image vertically

Flip selected image horizontally

Darken selected whites to current pattern

Lighten selected blacks to current pattern

* Displays handles at the corners of the marquee that when dragged produce the desired effect

Menus

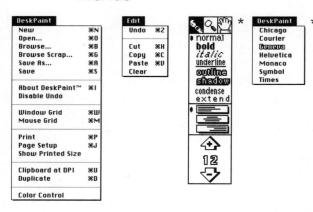

DeskPaint uses the active application's Edit menu

* Type menus display when type icon selected

DeskPaint Quick Reference (3 of 4)

Keyboard Equivalents

Actual size/fat bits, toggle .... 🖈🖈 *pencil icon*

Airbrush tool, select .... A

Autotrace tool, select .... K

Browse Scrapbook .... ⌘G

Browse through folder of graphics .... ⌘B

Brush shape, select .... 🖈 *line width*

Charcoal tool, select 0

Circle, create .... ⇧⌁🖈 *w/ oval tool*

Clear element .... ⌫

Copy element .... ⌘C

Cut element .... ⌘X

Demagnify view size .... ⌘R, ⌘-, *or* 🖈🖈 *hand icon*

Draw from center .... ⌘⌁🖈 *w/ any shape tool*

Duplicate element .... ⌘D

Edit pattern .... 🖈🖈 *pattern icon*

Erase entire document .... 🖈🖈 *eraser icon*

Erase overlay mode (BIC) .... ⌘⇧🖈 *tool icon*

Eraser tool, select .... E

Freehand tool, select .... P

Hand tool, select .... H *or* ⌥

Help .... ⇧/ *or* 🖈🖈 *lasso icon*

Increase type size 1 pt .... 🖈 *"+" size arrow*

Increase type size 2 pts .... ⌘⇧>

Increase type size 10 pts .... ⌥🖈 *"+" size arrow*

Inverse overlay mode (≠copy) .... ⌥🖈 *tool icon*

Inverse-erase mode (≠BIC) .... ⌘⇧⌥🖈 *tool icon*

Inverse-reverse mode (≠XOR) .... ⌘⌥🖈 *tool icon*

Inverse-transparent (≠OR) .... ⇧⌥🖈 *tool icon*

Lasso tool, select .... Q

Line tool, select X

Magnify view size .... ⌘E, ⌘=, *or* 🖈🖈 *zoom icon*

Marquee tool, select .... S

Mouse grid, activate/deactivate .... ⌘M

Move selected element in 45° direction ...... ⇧⌁🖈

New document, create .... ⌘N

Open existing document .... ⌘O

Oval tool, select C

Page setup .... ⌘J

Paint can (fill tool), select .... F

Paintbrush tool, select .... B

Paste element (unscaled) .... ⌘V (⌘U)

Patterned lines and outlines ...... ⌥🖈 *pattern icon*

Pencil tool, select .... D

⌘	command	⇥	tab	⌫	delete	▬ space bar
⇧	shift	↩	return	⌦	fwd. delete	F1 function key
⌥	option	⌁	enter	⌨	keypad key	🖈 mouse click
⌃	control	⎋	escape	⌨⌯	clear	⌁🖈 mouse drag

DeskPaint Quick Reference (4 of 4)

Keyboard Equivalents (Cont.)

Perpendicular lines, create .... ⇧--↖ *w/ any painting tool or eraser*
Polygon tool, select .... G
Print document .... ⌘P

Rectangle tool, select .... R
Reduce type size 1 pt .... *↖ "–" *size arrow*
Reduce type size 2 pts .... ⌘⇧<
Reduce type size 10 pts .... ⌥*↖ "–" *size arrow*
Reverse overlay mode (XOR) .... ⇧*↖ *tool icon*
Round corner tool, select .... W

Save as different name or location .... ⌘A
Save painting .... ⌘S
Scale selected element .... ⌘--↖ *new marquee*
Scale selected element to 50% .... ⌘<
Scale selected element to 200% .... ⌘>
Scale selected element to last percentage .... ~

Select contiguous image .... ⌘*↖ *w/ lasso*
Select entire document .... *↖*↖ *marquee icon*
Show/hide pattern palette .... ⇥
Show/hide toolbox .... ␣ *or* /
Single-pixel brush shape .... ⌘--↖ *w/ paintbrush*
Smudge on-screen image .... ⌘--↖ *w/ charcoal tool or airbrush*
Square, create .... ⇧--↖ *w/ rectangle tool*

Transparent overlay mode (OR) .... ⌘*↖ *tool icon*
Type tool, select .... T

Undo/redo last operation .... ⌘Z

Window grid, show/hide .... ⌘W

Zoom tool, select .... Z

Accurate for DeskPaint, version 2.0

⌘	command	⇥	tab	⌫	delete	␣	space bar
⇧	shift	↵	return	⌦	fwd. delete	F1	function key
⌥	option	⌤	enter	▦	keypad key	*↖	mouse click
⌃	control	⎋	escape	▦⎋	clear	--↖	mouse drag

Delayed Reaction

Also, you may notice that Canvas's bit-map editing tools take a second to react to your directions. For example, if you simply click with the pencil tool, you may find that your click is entirely ignored. To remedy this situation, you should click and hold your mouse button for a brief moment before going on with a drag, giving Canvas enough time to keep up with you.

Since Canvas also provides object-oriented features, we cover the software in greater detail in the Drawing Software entry, including a complete Quick Reference.

Monochromation

 Studio/1, Version 1.0   PNTG, PICT, TIFF
You may have noticed we've been saying pretty positive things about every program so far. Well, what can we say? We like painting software. But absolutely nothing even compares to Electronic Art's Studio/1, which incorporates more useful features than any other monochrome application, and for the same price as NuPaint. And as if that weren't enough, this is the only software in this section that offers animation capabilities!

Okay, so there aren't any object-oriented drawing tools. But you can create high-resolution text, which is the reason many people buy SuperPaint. Studio/1 reserves a special text layer for editable type. Of course, type on this layer cannot be manipulated with painting tools, but it will be printed smoothly on a PostScript-equipped printer.

Animation is Studio/1's biggest plus. Not only can you draw images frame by frame and link them together (a process similar to traditional cell animation, and equally tedious), but you may also access such automated features as the Anim 3D command, which will move, resize, and rotate a selected bit map through a specified number of frames to simulate three-dimensional motion. All you have to do is draw a single original image and specify how you want Studio/1 to draw the rest of the images in an animated sequence.

Enhancing HyperCard Stacks

Studio/1 also comes with an XCMD (external command) that can be loaded into any HyperCard stack, allowing the stack to run animated sequences. To access the XCMD, you open the Studio/1 Demo stack and go to the "Installing the XCMD" card. The rest is pretty self-explanatory.

A color version of Studio/1 called Studio/8 also exists, although it does not include animation features or a text layer for creating smooth type. A description of this program, along with a Quick Reference for Studio/1, is included at the end of this entry.

Cool to Be Colored

For those with sufficient resources to paint and print in color, there exist a range of high-end applications that are so far beyond their monochrome cousins to be almost completely beyond compare. The first of these, Pixel-Paint, largely redefined the way we think about Macintosh graphics.

 PixelPaint, Version 2.0   PX01 (native),
PNTG, PICT2, TIFF, EPSF, SCRN

The first color graphics software for the Mac, PixelPaint continues to be the paint program by which all others are measured. In fact, with the possible exception of Studio/8, it is our favorite painting application.

PixelPaint supports the entire 747-color Pantone library, and even comes with a Pantone Color Formula Guide, one of those 2-by-8-inch sets of bound cards that every good printer has, and that are absolutely essential if you plan to do any color printing of your own.

Like Adobe Illustrator in the drawing category, PixelPaint offers an elegantly simple working environment, disguising some of its power but at the same time making it easier to access. For example, any painting tool carries with it a number of special-effects capabilities. After selecting a tool, simply click on the box labeled *Normal Tools* at the top of the toolbox (or press the CONTROL key), and the box will change to read *Special Effects.* A menu will also appear rightmost on the menu bar, customized for the selected tool. Each special-effects option is pretty self-explanatory; but if you don't understand, you can easily experiment.

PixelPaint Quick Reference (1 of 5)

Toolbox

Lasso	to select irregular portion of painting to manipulate
Paint can	to fill an enclosed or solid area with current pattern
Hand	to move page with respect to window
Paintbrush	to draw free-form lines with current brush shape
Dropper	to grab foreground color off page, ⇧ to grab background color
Line	to draw straight line at any angle
Rectangle	to draw transparent (left half of icon) or filled (right) rectangle
Polygon	to create corners for transparent or filled straight-sided polygon
Regular polygon	to create transparent or filled equilateral polygon

Marquee	to select rectangular portion of painting to manipulate
Type	to set origin for text block
Spraypaint	to generate pattern of loose pixels
Pencil	to create or delete pixels, to draw or delete free-form lines
Eraser	to delete general portions of bit map
Arc	to draw quarter ellipse from top or bottom point to side point
Round corner	to draw transparent or filled rectangle with rounded corners
Freehand	to draw transparent or filled free-form shape in current line weight
Oval	to draw transparent or filled ellipse

PixelPaint Quick Reference (2 of 5)

Menus

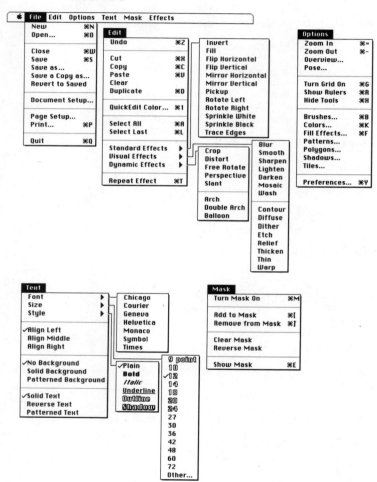

PixelPaint Quick Reference (3 of 5)

Special-Effects Menus

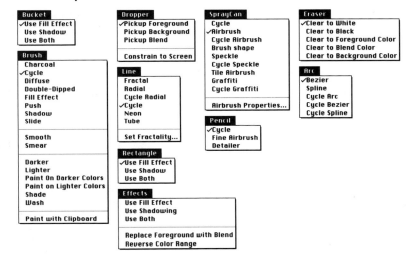

The far right menu changes depending on the currently selected tool when in special-effects mode

PixelPaint Quick Reference (4 of 5)

Keyboard Equivalents

Actual size/600%, toggle .... 🖱🖱 *pencil icon*

Actual size/fat bits, toggle .... 🖱🖱 *pencil icon*

Add selection to mask .... ⌘[

Airbrush properties, alter .... 🖱🖱 *airbrush icon*

Brush shape, edit .... 🖱🖱 *brush shape in dialog*

Brush shape, select ..... ⌘B *or* 🖱🖱 *paintbrush icon*

Change to next typeface .... ⌘⇧>

Change to previous typeface .... ⌘⇧<

Circle, create .... ⇧⌁🖱 *w/ oval tool*

Clear element .... ⌫

Clone selected element .... ⌥⌁🖱

Close current document .... ⌘W

Color palette, customize .... ⌘K
or 🖱🖱 *color selector*

Copy element .... ⌘C

Cut element .... ⌘X

Cycle colors .... ⇧🖱 *while* CAPS LOCK *down*

Detailer box, display .... ⇥⌁🖱 *w/ lasso or pencil*

Display color-selection box .... ⌘⌥⌁🖱

Draw with selected element .... ⌘⌥⌁🖱 *element*

DROP EFFECTS menu .... ⌘⌁🖱
in special-effects mode

Dropper tool, select .... ⌘~

Duplicate element .... ⌘D

Erase to white .... ⌥🖱 *w/ eraser*

Erase window .... 🖱🖱 *eraser icon*

Exchange foreground and background
colors .... ⌘⌁🖱 *w/ spraypaint tool or paintbrush*

Fill effects, alter .... ⌘F *or* 🖱🖱 *paint can icon
or shape tool icon (except regular polygon)*

Grab background color off page ..... ⇧🖱 *w/ dropper*

Grab blend color off page .... ⌥🖱 *w/ dropper*

Grab foreground color off page .... 🖱 *w/ dropper*

Hand tool, select temporarily in fat bits .... ⌥

Hide/show tools .... ⎵

Increase scrolling speed .... ⌥

Increase type size .... ⌘>

Lasso without tightening .... ⌥⌁🖱 *w/ lasso*

Line fractility, alter .... 🖱🖱 *line icon*

Move selected element in 45° direction ...... ⇧⌁🖱

New document, create .... ⌘N

Normal/special-effects mode, toggle .... ⌃

Number of equilateral polygon sides,
select .... 🖱🖱 *regular polygon icon*

Open existing document .... ⌘O

Overview view size .... 🖱🖱 *hand icon*

⌘	command	⇥	tab	⌫	delete	⎵ space bar
⇧	shift	↩	return	⌦	fwd. delete	F1 function key
⌥	option	⌁	enter	⌨	keypad key	🖱 mouse click
⌃	control	⎋	escape	⌨⌫	clear	⌁🖱 mouse drag

PixelPaint Quick Reference (5 of 5)

Keyboard Equivalents (Cont.)

Paint shadow in front of brushstroke .... ⌥·····▶
w/ paintbrush when Shadow effect active

Paint small speckles .... ⌥·····▶
w/ spraypaint tool when Speckle effect active

Paste element .... ⌘V

Pattern, edit .... ▶▶ *pattern in dialog*

Pattern, select .... ▶▶ *pattern selector*

Patterned lines, create .... ⌥·····▶ *w/ line tool,
arc tool, or pencil (except in fat bits)*

Perpendicular lines, create .... ⇧·····▶
w/ any painting tool or eraser

PREFERENCES dialog, display .... ⌘Y

Print document .... ⌘P

Quarter circle, create .... ⇧·····▶ *w/ arc tool*

QuickEdit color, toggle .... ⌘1

Quit PixelPaint .... ⌘Q

Reduce type size .... ⌘<

Remove selection from mask .... ⌘]

Repeat last effect .... ⌘T

Scale proportionally ...... ⌘⇧·····▶ *marquee corner*

Scale selected element .... ⌘·····▶ *marquee corner*

Select entire contiguous
color .... ⌘▶ *w/ lasso*

Select last element selected .... ⌘L

Select multiple noncontiguous
areas .... ⇧·····▶ *w/ lasso or marquee*

Select window .... ⌘A *or* ▶▶ *marquee icon*

Shapes with patterned outlines, create .... ⌥·····▶
w/ any shape tool

Show mask .... ⌘E

Show/hide rulers .... ⌘R

Show/hide tools .... ⌘H

Shrink marquee to bit map .... ⌘·····▶ *w/ marquee*

Square, create .... ⇧·····▶ *w/ rectangle tool*

Tighten marquee to bit map .... ⌥·····▶ *w/ marquee*

Turn on/off grid .... ⌘G

Turn on/off mask .... ⌘M

Undo/redo last operation .... ⌘Z *or* ~ *or* ⌫

Zoom in .... ⌘= *or* ⌘▶ *w/ pencil*

Zoom out .... ⌘-

Accurate for PixelPaint, version 2.0

Pure Painting

Like most color painting applications—all except LaserPaint, discussed in the Drawing Software entry—PixelPaint offers no object-oriented capabilities. All lines are printed jagged, but you'll hardly notice if you blend your colors properly.

Lastly, PixelPaint is one of the few painting programs that print color separations to any high-resolution output device, such as a laser printer or a PostScript-equipped typesetter. Color separations allow you to create color paintings to be commercially printed as book covers, full-color illustrations, and the like.

The Long-Awaited PixelPaint Professional

PixelPaint Professional is the newest update to this strong painting program. After announcing the product in July of 1988, SuperMac finally delivered over a year later, supporting 8-bit through 32-bit video cards with compatible monitors. The application offers enhanced image-processing tools similar to those found in PhotoMac (the most advanced photographic editing software currently available).

PixelPaint's Colorful Clones

Since the initial release of PixelPaint, a plethora of color painting programs have cropped up, most of which simply make PixelPaint look even better. However, there are a couple of reasonably priced applications that provide most of PixelPaint's features for cheaper price tags.

Since we can only touch on the many features offered by each of these, we might as well start off with our least favorite and work upward.

 Photon Paint, Version 1.1   PICT2
What do you think? Is that the ugliest icon you've ever seen or what?

Depending on the size of your monitor, about a third of the screen is taken up by Photon Paint's enormous, unfamiliar toolbox. There is no pencil, eraser, or hand tool! Okay, conceivably these tools serve very limited functions, all of which may be accomplished by way of other, less direct methods; their primary purpose is convenience, a quality that Photon Paint sorely lacks.

In Photon Paint's favor, you may mold any selected image as if it were a sheet of wrapping paper around a custom three-dimensional shape. You may also illuminate the shape with a floodlight or a pinpoint-beam spotlight. Unfortunately, some of this automated drawing takes as long as five minutes to complete. If you're unhappy with the results, you have to choose UNDO and start over again.

Still, Photon Paint is one of the least expensive color paint applications, less than half the price of PixelPaint, and that includes a black-and-white version of the program as well, presumably to give away to one of your less fortunate friends.

GraphistPaint II, Version 1.0   PNTG, PICT2, TIFF
GraphistPaint is another example of an inconvenient painting environment. But now it seems we're kicking a dead horse. The program is designed by a French firm called Adone, which made the regrettable move of licensing its American distribution to Aba, a company that declared bankruptcy in early 1989. Whether or not Adone will be able to find a new American vendor is unknown at this time.

By and large, GraphistPaint offers some fairly dazzling image-editing features, in line with those offered by PixelPaint, but not always as easy to use. And there are the bizarre, DeskPaint-inspired irregularities to contend with: Cloning is inoperative, the pencil doesn't erase when clicking on the current color, line weights affect the airbrush cursor, and some dialog boxes lack CANCEL buttons.

CricketPaint Color, Version 1.0   CRCP (native), PNTG, PICT2, TIFF
CricketPaint brings the post-creation editing control normally associated with object-oriented applications to the world of colored paint programs. Most notable is the application's introduction of FreshPaint, a time- and frustration-saving feature that provides you with an alternative to redrawing a bit map when it doesn't exactly meet the needs of your artwork. Immediately after you create an image with a FreshPaint tool, handles are assigned to it, allowing you to transform, move, or delete the shape.

You may also assign a FreshPaint shape as a custom tool, so that you can create the shape over and over in different heights and widths. This makes CricketPaint the only application aside from Canvas to offer a graphic macro editor. You may even edit the way your tool appears in the CricketPaint toolbox. Unfortunately, there is no way to transfer tools from one document to another.

All of this for $295, less than half the price of PixelPaint. CricketPaint is also available in a very admirable monochrome format, which we would have mentioned along with NuPaint and SuperPaint were it not so very similar.

 Modern Artist, Version 2.0   rPIC (native), PNTG, PICT2

In a sense, Modern Artist is the gateway to the world of high-end color applications. In terms of features, it is the most stripped-down of the lot. But it does offer a simple interface and thorough documentation. Modern Artist is designed to be used on an 8-bit system, but it will run with a 1-bit card and a gray-scale monitor.

The program includes a set of 3-D tools with movable light sources. And whereas most applications create automatic gradations according to the order of colors in your palette, Modern Artist creates an even blend every time. A color-separation utility, ColorSep, which is also included, will separate any color painting saved in the PICT format, even if it wasn't created in Modern Artist.

Unfortunately, the program is priced at $495, putting it out of reach of the very users it seems intended for. And a color palette may not contain more than 92 colors.

Rearranging Painting Metaphors

 Studio/8, Version 1.0   PICT2, TIFF

But of all PixelPaint's competitors, our favorite is Studio/8. In fact, we love it every bit as much as Studio/1, which we talked up earlier in this entry.

In most respects, Studio/8 is simply a color version of Studio/1, without the animation or special text layer (which we dearly hope they add at some point). Like its monochrome cousin, Studio/8 departs from many of the standard painting metaphors—so successfully, in fact, that we found the application's environment to be a substantial improvement over the familiar MacPaint environment after only a few uses. For example, the toolbox is broken into drawing tools and tool modifiers, which control such functions as how selection tools behave, how gradations are performed, and whether or not shapes are assigned frames and fills. For convenience, each tool may be selected and each modifier may be toggled from the keyboard, even while you're in the process of drawing or selecting an element!

No Color Separation

The only major disadvantage to Studio/8, especially when compared with PixelPaint, is its lack of color-separation capabilities. Supposedly that's on the way. If you're a professional Mac user with tons of cash behind you, this isn't much of a problem, since a handful of service bureaus throughout the country can scan color bit maps and separate them photographically—a more accurate method for creating color separations but one that can cost over $200 a throw. For the rest of us, Electronic Arts promises color-separation abilities by the beginning of 1990.

Studio/1&8 Quick Reference (1 of 7)

Toolbox

Lasso	····▸ to select irregular portion of painting to be manipulated
Marquee	····▸ to select rectangular portion of painting to be manipulated
Polygon selection	····▸ to move page with respect to window
Type	▸ to set origin for text block
Hand	····▸ to move page with respect to window
Eraser	····▸ to delete general portions of bit map
Airbrush	····▸ to generate random spray of pixels
Paint can	····▸ to fill an enclosed or solid area with current pattern
Dropper*	▸ to grab foreground color off page, ⬦▸ to grab background color
Pattern pickup†	▸ to grab foreground pattern off page, ⬦▸ to grid pickup
Paintbrush	····▸ to draw free-form lines with current brush shape
Pencil	▸ to create or delete pixels, ····▸ to draw or delete free-form lines
Line	····▸ to draw straight line at any angle

Rectangle	····▸ to draw rectangle outlined and filled according to modifier
Round corner	····▸ to draw rectangle with rounded corners
Oval	····▸ to draw ellipse
Rotated oval	····▸ to draw ellipse then ····▸ to determine rotation
Regular polygon	····▸ to create equilateral polygon
Polygon	▸ to create corners for straight-sided polygon
Freehand	····▸ to draw free-form shape in current line weight
Curve	····▸ to determine inclination then move mouse and ▸
Bezier	····▸ to create smooth point, ⬦····▸ to specify last point in curve

Tool Modifiers

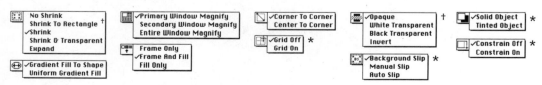

    *   *Available only in Studio/8*
    †   *Available only in Studio/1*

Studio/1&8 Quick Reference (2 of 7)

Studio/1 Menus

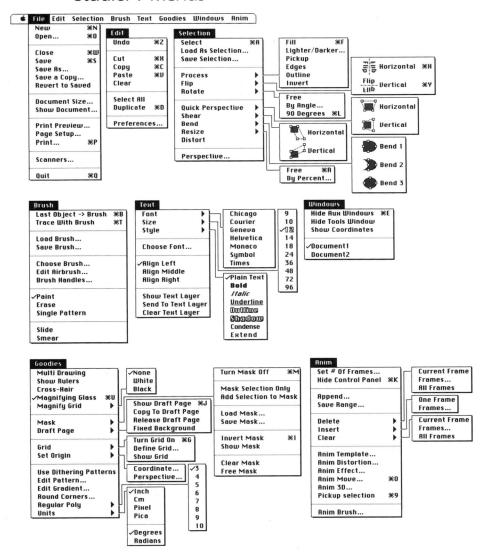

Studio/1&8 Quick Reference (3 of 7)

Studio/8 Menus

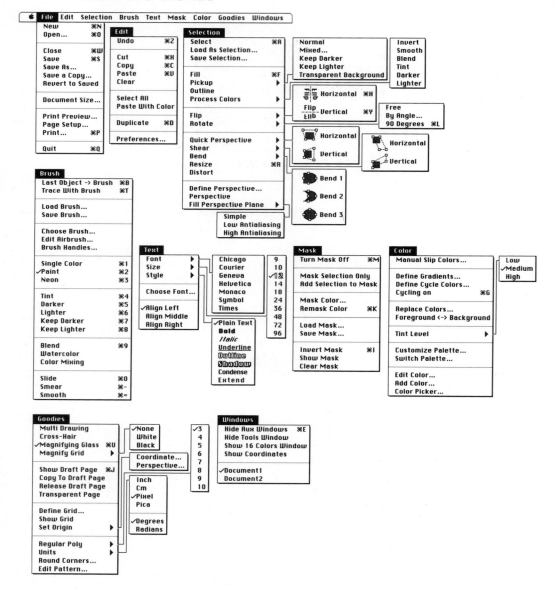

Studio/1 &8 Quick Reference (4 of 7)

Keyboard Equivalents

Actual size/600%, toggle .... ↖↖ *pencil icon*

Actual view size (100%) 1

Add point to curve .... ⩘↖ *in Bézier edit mode*

Add point to polygon .... ⩘↖ *in poly. edit mode*

Airbrush tool, select .... A

Animation move, display dialog .... ⌘0†

Bézier edit mode, exit .... ↖ *any tool icon or* ⤳

Bézier tool, select .... Z

Blend on-screen colors beneath brush* .... ⌘9

Brush shape, change .... ↖↖ *paintbrush icon*

Cancel command and revert .... ⟠ *or* ▦⟠

Cancel operation .... ⌘.

Center area in 600% view size .... ⌘↖ *w/pencil*

Change background color/pattern ...... ⦼← *or* ⦼→

Change brush setting .... ↑ *or* ↓
  when airbrush or paintbrush is selected

Change frame color/pattern .... ⌘← *or* ⌘→

Change frame pattern* .... ⌘[*or* ⌘]

Change number of polygon sides .... ↑ *or* ↓
  when regular polygon tool is selected

Change selection to brush (or vice versa) .... ⌘B

Change fill color/pattern .... ← *or* →

Change fill pattern* .... [*or*]

Circle, create .... ⇧⤳↖ *w/oval tool*

Clear element .... ⊠

Clear screen .... ↖↖ *eraser icon*

Clone selected element .... ⦼⤳↖

Close current document* .... ⌘W

Color cycling, activate/deactivate* .... ⌘G

Constrain modifier, toggle* .... ▦1

Copy element .... ⌘C

Corner point with
Bézier handles, create .... ⦼↖ *in Bézier edit mode*

Corner/center modifier, toggle .... ▦3

Curve tool, select C

Curves at 15° inclines, create .... ⇧⤳↖
  w/curve tool or Bézier tool

Cut element .... ⌘X

Darken on-screen colors beneath brush* .... ⌘5

Display hidden menu bar .... ↵ *or* ⤳

Draw with element .... ⌘B, ⤳↖ *w/paintbrush*

Duplicate element .... ⌘D

⌘	command	⇥	tab	⊠	delete	▬	space bar
⇧	shift	↵	return	⊠	fwd. delete	F1	function key
⦼	option	⤳	enter	▦	keypad key	↖	mouse click
⩘	control	⟠	escape	▦⟠	clear	⤳↖	mouse drag

Studio/1 & 8 Quick Reference (5 of 7)

Keyboard Equivalents (Cont.)

Edit on-screen color* .... ➤ ➤ *color ʷ/pickup tool*

Eight times actual view size (800%) 8

Eighth actual view size (12.5%) .... ⇧8†

Ellipses at 15° angles, create .... ⇧····➤
ʷ/ *rotate oval tool*

End Bézier curve .... ➲➤ ʷ/ *Bézier curve tool*

Equilateral polygons at 15° angles, create ... ⇧····➤
ʷ/ *regular polygon tool*

Erase to previous color .... ↑ *or* ↓, ····➤ ʷ/*pencil*

Eraser tool, select .... E

Fill selection .... ⌘F

Flip element horizontally .... ⌘H

Flip element vertically .... ⌘Y

Four times actual view size (400%) 4

Frame/fill modifier, toggle.................... ⌨4 *or* ⌨1†

Freehand tool, select .... H

Get selection/brush from next frame .... ⌘8†

Get selection/brush from previous frame .... ⌘7†

Go to frame 1 of animation .... ⌘1†

Go to next frame of animation .... ⌘3†

Go to previous frame of animation .... ⌘2†

Gradient fill modifier, toggle .... ⌨6 *or* ⌨5†

Grid modifier, toggle* .... ⌨2

Half actual view size (50%) .... ⇧2†

Hand tool (grabber), select .... G

Help .... ⌘/

Hide auxiliary windows .... ⌘E

Hide auxiliary windows .... ⌘E

Hide/show animation control panel .... ⌘K†

Invert mask .... ⌘I

Keep darker (only paint over if darker)* .... ⌘7

Keep lighter (only paint over if lighter)* .... ⌘8

Lasso tool, select L

Lighten on-screen colors beneath brush* .... ⌘6

Line tool, select .... \

Lines at 15° angles, create .... ⇧····➤ ʷ/*line tool*
or polygon tool

Magnify grid, toggle* .... ⌨=

Magnify modifier, toggle .... ⌨9 *or* ⌨6†

Magnify to 600% actual size .... ⌘➤ ʷ/*pencil*

Magnifying glass, toggle .... ⌘U

* *Available only in Studio/8*

† *Exclusively applicable to Studio/1*

⌘	command	➡	tab	⊠	delete	⎵	space bar
⇧	shift	↩	return	⊠	fwd. delete	F1	function key
➲	option	➹	enter	⌨	keypad key	➤	mouse click
⋀	control	∅	escape	⌨∅	clear	····➤	mouse drag

Studio/1&8 Quick Reference (6 of 7)

Keyboard Equivalents (Cont.)

Marquee tool, select .... S

Mask, activate/deactivate .... ⌘M

Modify airbrush .... ➤➤ *airbrush icon*

Modify corners .... ➤➤ *rounded corner icon*

Move pattern inside element .... D†, X†, S†, *or* E† *while drawing element*

Move selected element in 45° direction ...... ⇧····➤

Move selected element by single pixel .... ⩓→†, ⩓↓†, ⩓←†, *or* ⩓↑†

Move selected element regardless of cursor location .... ⩓····➤

Move text block ...... ⩓····➤ *when text block active*

Neon brush* .... ⌘3

New document, create .... ⌘N

Open existing document .... ⌘O

Oval tool, select .... O

Paint can (fill tool), select .... F

Paint continuous strokes .... ⌇····➤ *w/ paintbrush*

Paint with brush normally* .... ⌘2

Paintbrush tool, select .... B

Paste element .... ⌘V

Pencil tool, select ....

Perpendicular lines, create .... ⇧····➤ *w/ any painting tool or eraser*

Pick up selection to animate .... ⌘9†

Pickup tool, toggle .... ➡I *or* K†

Play animation sequence continuously .... ⌘5†

Play animation sequence once .... ⌘4†

Play Ping-Pong with animation (backward and forward) .... ⌘6†

Polygon edit mode, enter .... ⌇➤ *w/ polygon tool when closing a shape*

Polygon edit mode, exit ...... ➤ *any tool icon or* ⌇

Polygon selection tool, select X

Polygon tool, select .... P

Print document .... ⌘P

Quarter actual view size (25%) .... ⇧4†

Quit Studio/1 or Studio/8 .... ⌘Q

Rectangle tool, select .... R

Regular polygon tool, select .... Y

Remask color* .... ⌘K

Reset all modifiers to original settings .... ⌘▭⌀

Resize selected element, free .... ⌘R, ····➤ *corner*

Rewrap type .... ····➤ *corner when text block active*

Rotate element by 90° .... ⌘L

Rotated oval tool, select .... W

Rounded corner tool, select .... D

Save painting .... ⌘S

Scanner .... ⌘=†

Select background color* .... ⌇➤ *w/ pickup tool*

Select foreground color* .... ➤ *w/ pickup tool*

Select frame color* .... ⌘➤ *w/ pickup tool*

Select last selected element .... ⌘A

Select multiple noncontiguous areas .... ⌘····➤ *w/ any selection tool*

Set demagnification .... ⇧2†, ⇧4†, *or* ⇧8†

Set magnification .... 1, 2, 4, 6, *or* 8

Show draft page/document .... ⌘J

Studio/1&8 Quick Reference (7 of 7)

Keyboard Equivalents (Cont.)

Shrink/expand modifier, toggle .... ⌨7 *or* ⌨4[†]

Single-color brush* .... ⌘1

Six times actual view size (600%) 6

Slide on-screen colors beneath brush* .... ⌘0

Slip colors modifier, toggle* .... ⌨8

Slow down animation .... –[†]

Smear on-screen colors beneath brush* .... ⌘–

Smooth on-screen colors beneath brush* .... ⌘=

Solid/tinted modifier, toggle* .... ⌨5

Special pencil mode, toggle .... ↑ *or* ↓
when pencil is selected

Speed up animation .... ⇧=[†]

Square, create .... ⇧⌁👆 *w/rectangle tool*

Tint level, toggle* .... * *or* ⌨*

Tint on-screen colors beneath brush* .... ⌘4

Trace with brush .... ⌘T

Transparency modifier, toggle .... ⌨2[†]

Twice actual view size (200%) 2

Type tool, select .... T

Undo/redo last operation .... ⌘Z

Window size, toggle .... ━

---

* *Available only in Studio/8*

[†] *Exclusively applicable to Studio/1*

Accurate for Studio/1, version 1.0, and Studio/8, version 1.0

⌘	command	⇥	tab	⌫	delete	━	space bar
⇧	shift	↩	return	⌦	fwd. delete	F1	function key
⌥	option	⌤	enter	⌨	keypad key	👆	mouse click
⌃	control	⎋	escape	⌨⎋	clear	⌁👆	mouse drag

# Spreadsheets

If you've used a spreadsheet program, you know how great technology can really be. Everything from the abacus to the calculator has been replaced by a powerful piece of software that can process thousands of numbers in seconds, sort numbers into a logical hierarchy, and print out finished tallies. And with the recent enhancement of charting and other presentational abilities, that's only the half of it.

Simply put: If you own a Mac and you are so much as balancing your checkbook by hand, you're wasting your time. A spreadsheet can help you do it faster and much more accurately.

Power in Numbers

Spreadsheets are one of the most popular categories of Mac software (second only to word processors), accounting for about 10 percent of software sales in the United States. But most Mac owners have never used a numerical-analysis application.

So if you're unfamiliar with this kind of software, you aren't alone. But this doesn't mean you're in good company. Anyone who spends money will find a spreadsheet useful, and anyone who wants to predict future economic well-being will find a spreadsheet indispensable.

To familiarize yourself with the basic operation of a spreadsheet, see Spreadsheet Technicalities 1. Following that, Spreadsheet Technicalities 2 explains how a spreadsheet may be used as a forecasting tool.

Spreadsheets on the Personal Computer

When you think of spreadsheets, the first one that comes to mind is the undisputed leader, Lotus 1-2-3, which continues to report sales in the tens of thousands every month, making it the best selling application ever. This has led many people to associate powerful number-crunching with MS-DOS-based machines like the IBM PC and its clones.

Spreadsheet Technicalities 1

*Celling dollars by the date
and watching them tally*

A spreadsheet begins as an electronic ledger sheet. You enter numbers into rows and columns of individual containers known as cells. Typically, a single cell is identified by a letter representing its column followed by a number representing its row. So the cell at the intersection of the first column and the first row is A1, the next cell down is A2, the cell to the right of that is B2, and so on.

Numbers entered into cells may represent dollar amounts, times and dates, scientific notation, or general information. For example, suppose you want to create a spreadsheet document (often called a **worksheet**) to keep track of your checking-account transactions. The simplest way to organize the worksheet would be to mimic your checkbook ledger. Enter transaction types and check numbers in the first column of cells, transaction dates in the second column, descriptions in the third, purchase amounts in the fourth, and deposit amounts in the fifth. In this way, a single transaction is itemized in each row.

If you enter transactions out of order, you may use your spreadsheet's sorting feature to organize the entries by date.

In addition to various kinds of numbers, cells may contain mathematical formulae that are applied to other cells. For example, the sixth column in your checking-account worksheet (column F) might automatically determine the balance of your account. To accomplish this, you enter a formula that subtracts the purchase amount in that row and adds the deposit amount in that row to the balance from the previous row. Therefore, the formula entered into cell F3 should read

=F2–D3+E3

where F2 is the cell containing the previous balance, D3 contains the current purchase, and E3 contains the current deposit. The equal sign indicates that the information in the cell constitutes a mathematical formula to be processed by the software. (Your software may not require an equal sign to implement a formula.)

Unfortunately, the formula for each cell in column F must change slightly to keep up with the new row numbers. For example, the equation in cell F4 must read "=F3–D4+E4", the equation in cell F5 must read "=F4–D5+E5", and so on. The letters stay the same, but the numbers increase by one for each row. It would be tedious to reenter a new equation for each row, so most spreadsheets provide FILL DOWN and FILL RIGHT commands. FILL DOWN increments numbers, and FILL RIGHT increments letters. So to make each cell in column F automatically compute the current checking-account balance, you would select F3 (the cell containing the first formula) and all cells below it, and then choose FILL DOWN.

	F17		=F16–D17+E17				
			Checking account				
	A	**B**	**C**	**D**	**E**	**F**	
1	**type**	**date**	**transaction description**	**debit**	**credit**	**balance**	
2	Visa	03-23-89	action shoe repair, EP's shoes	21.53		($59.20)	
3	Visa	03-23-89	Amoco, gas for tarus	12.38		($71.58)	
4	Tranz	03-24-89	to saving from checking		500.00	$428.42	
5	Visa	03-26-89	Embassy Suites	166.22		$262.20	
6	Visa	03-28-89	8th & pearl sinclair, taurus oil & emissions	25.02		$237.18	
7	Visa	03-28-89	8th & pearl sinclair, mazda failed emissions	8.50		$228.68	
8	1300	03-29-89	ACT, EP's financial aid	10.00		$218.68	
9	1301	03-29-89	Boulder county clerk, taurus plates	180.68		$38.00	
10	1302	03-29-89	Albertsons	37.39		$0.61	
11	1303	03-30-89	John Duane, liquor for party	12.00		($11.39)	
12	Visa	03-30-89	Vickers, gas for taurus	13.12		($24.51)	
13	1304	03-31-89	Sears, Marilyn's microwave	102.00		($126.51)	
14	Dep	03-31-89	EP's paycheck		1386.51	$1,260.00	
15	1305	03-31-89	Virginia Smith, clothes for EP	62.50		$1,197.50	
16	Visa	04-01-89	Walmart, tapes & socks for Catherine	30.34		$1,167.16	
17	Visa	04-01-89	Lafayette flourist, seeds for EP	5.70		$1,161.46	

This simple worksheet automatically balances your checkbook as you enter purchases and deposits. And since it's electronic, you may update an entry at any time.

If you later find you have made a mistake in entering a value—say, when your statement arrives at the end of the month—you may change the value for that cell, knowing that your worksheet will automatically update to reflect the change. This is especially useful if your bank issues debit cards. You may order something on your card, enter a general amount estimating shipping and tax in your worksheet, and wait until the end of the month to determine the exact figure.

Conclusion: If you perform any task that involves tallying numbers or using a calculator on a regular basis, you would benefit from a spreadsheet application. Most worksheets require little setup time and even less expertise to operate.

Spreadsheet Technicalities 2

"What if" scenarios:
Using spreadsheets to predict possible futures

Perhaps the most powerful feature of a spreadsheet is its ability to function as a forecasting tool. For example, suppose that you originally financed your current home at a 14 percent mortgage rate. Interest rates are now at 12.5 percent, and you're trying to decide if it's worth the time, effort, and money required to refinance. Or perhaps you're better off waiting, risking a chance that the lending fee will drop to an even lower rate, say 11 percent or 10.5 percent.

To calculate your monthly payments, you need to use the formula

monthly mortgage payment = amount of loan $\times (a^n \times i) \div (a^n - 1)$

where i is the periodic interest rate, n is the total number of loan payments, and a equals i plus 1.

Though this formula may look complicated, and would certainly be difficult to perform with a calculator, you will have to implement it into your spreadsheet only once, after which you won't have to worry about it again.

But before you may enter your formula, you need to enter the values that it will be using. In the first cell of the second row (allowing for a row of labels at the top), you enter the amount of principal remaining to be paid on your home. Based on your amortization, let's say you estimate this amount to be right around $55,000. In the next cell, B2, you enter 360, the number of monthly payments required to pay off a 30-year loan (variable n in our equation). After that, you enter the current interest rate in C2, expressed as a decimal. In your case, 14 percent would be entered as 0.14. In column D, you enter the periodic interest rate (variable i) as the formula C2/12 (interest rate divided by 12 months). And in column E, you enter D2+1 to represent variable a.

Now that you have a cell representing each variable, you are ready to enter the big formula. In cell F2, you enter

=A2*(D2*E2^B2/(E2^B2−1))

where * is a multiplication sign and ^ means "raised to the power of." The following figure shows that the monthly payment for such a loan should be $651.68. We may also determine the annual and 30-year costs based on this amount.

	F2	☒☑	=A2*(D2*E2^B2/(E2^B2−1))					
			House payments					
	A	B	C	D	E	F	G	H
1	unpaid principal	payments	interest	periodic	i+1	monthly PI	annual PI	30 year PI
2	$55,000.00	360	14.00%	1.17%	101.17%	$651.68	$7,820.15	$234,604.61
3								
4	$55,000.00	360	12.50%	1.04%	101.04%	$586.99	$7,043.90	$211,317.04
5	$55,000.00	360	12.25%	1.02%	101.02%	$576.34	$6,916.12	$207,483.49
6	$55,000.00	360	12.00%	1.00%	101.00%	$565.74	$6,788.84	$203,665.29
7	$55,000.00	360	11.75%	0.98%	100.98%	$555.18	$6,662.10	$199,863.13
8	$55,000.00	360	11.50%	0.96%	100.96%	$544.66	$6,535.92	$196,077.70
9	$55,000.00	360	11.25%	0.94%	100.94%	$534.19	$6,410.33	$192,309.75
10	$55,000.00	360	11.00%	0.92%	100.92%	$523.78	$6,285.33	$188,560.03
11	$55,000.00	360	10.75%	0.90%	100.90%	$513.41	$6,160.98	$184,829.31
12	$55,000.00	360	10.50%	0.88%	100.88%	$503.11	$6,037.28	$181,118.38
13	$55,000.00	360	10.25%	0.85%	100.85%	$492.86	$5,914.27	$177,428.06
14	$55,000.00	360	10.00%	0.83%	100.83%	$482.66	$5,791.97	$173,759.17

This worksheet makes it easy to determine how different lending rates affect your monthly mortgage payments.

Now that you have portrayed your present situation, you may expand your worksheet to allow additional scenarios. To retain the same setup without reentering numbers and formulae, select the entire row of figures along with several rows below it and choose your spreadsheet's FILL DOWN command. In the figure above, we have inserted a blank row to distinguish our "what is" cells from their "what if" companions. That's all there is to it. Now you may simply enter different numbers in the interest-rate column, and the spreadsheet automatically does the work for you.

Conclusion: Ours is a simplified treatment of mortgage analysis. But it accurately demonstrates how spreadsheets may be used to examine a variety of situations without tedious recalculation on your part. You may project how a stock will perform under different conditions, examine sales revenues for items with varying costs and prices, or predict how much more you would make if your boss gave you a raise.

It's easy to forget that the first spreadsheet program, VisiCalc, was designed to run on the Apple II, two years before IBM even entered the personal-computer market.

Spreadsheets on the Mac

In fact, the three major spreadsheets on the Macintosh—Microsoft Excel, Wingz, and Full Impact—offer features and speed capabilities that make the lumbering 1-2-3 look downright prehistoric. Software grows old in the time it takes a fly to grow whiskers, and yesterday's big developers often become tomorrow's archaic fossils. That's why, though VisiCalc and Lotus were marvels of their time, the days of Macintosh dominance in the spreadsheet arena are now at hand.

File-Saving Formats

In the following pages, we will look at some popular spreadsheet applications and examine their capabilities. To the right of each program name will be a list of the file-saving formats that the program supports. These are formats that allow a document to be opened in another application, such as a competing spreadsheet or a word processor. These formats may include one or more of the following:

- **DIF** (data interchange format). DIF is a number-saving protocol developed by Software Arts, the creator of VisiCalc. The contents of each cell are transferred via this format, but the formulae used to calculate the contents are not. Generally, this format is only used to transfer data so that it may be graphed in a presentation or charting program.

- **SYLK** (symbolic link). Designed by Microsoft, SYLK allows data *and* its formulae to be swapped from one numerical-analysis application to another. Modern Jazz on the PC reads this format. Older Mac programs like Jazz and Multiplan also use SYLK.

- **WKS**. This format is specifically useful for creating files that you intend to transfer to 1-2-3, Lotus Symphony, or similar programs on the PC. Both numbers and their formulae may be retained.

- **DBF**. This format transfers a selection of cells specified as a database range to Ashton-Tate's dBASE on the Mac or PC.

- **TEXT** (text-only). Like DIF, the TEXT format transfers only the contents of cells without their formulae. Values are generally separated by commas or by tabs. The text-only format is most useful for transferring information to a word processor for columnar listings and the like.

- **PICT**. Spreadsheets that support this image-saving format use it specifically to export finished charts so they may be combined with documentation in a page-layout application or embellished in a drawing application such as MacDraw. For more information about the PICT format, see the Drawing Software entry.

- **Native formats**. Most applications provide their own file-saving formats, allowing the greatest efficiency for storing documents that you don't intend to transfer to another application. We will list such unique formats followed by the word *native* in parentheses.

Miles of Cells Track the Sales of Excel

✖ **Microsoft Excel, Version 2.2**   XLS (native), DIF, SYLK, WKS, DBF, TEXT

When you think spreadsheet on the PC, you think 1-2-3. When you think spreadsheet on the Mac, you probably think Microsoft Excel. Designed originally for the Mac but since transferred to the PC, Excel controls over 90 percent of the Mac spreadsheet market. It's estimated that 25 percent of all Mac owners use Excel.

When Excel originally arrived on the Macintosh scene in 1985, it was an impressive spreadsheet. One of the first applications to offer macros, Excel provided speed, convenience, and power over its few competitors.

Unfortunately; between versions 1.0 and 1.5, Microsoft made only minor improvements to their popular numbers program. Whether they felt the spreadsheet did not warrant a major upgrade or there was simply so little impetus in the form of competition, Excel lay practically dormant for three years. This led a sizable minority of Excel owners to actively seek better spreadsheets from other manufacturers. During this time, Trapeze by Access Technology (now DeltaPoint) won a coveted reader's poll for 1987 Product of the Year (awarded by *InfoWorld* magazine) and Wingz from Informix was allowed to scoop up 30 percent of the first-quarter 1989 spreadsheet sales. Even Microsoft Excel on the PC had features not possessed by its Mac-compatible cousin.

Microsoft finally responded in the form of version 2.2. Excel's speed was improved by as much as 40 percent, type-formatting limitations were lifted, spreadsheet-auditing features were enhanced with cell notes, and almost 200 macro functions were added to the scripting language. The application still lags behind the likes of Wingz in charting abilities—three-dimensional graphs remain impossible—but it has reached a highly acceptable level in almost all areas besides presentations.

Ten Hottest Excel Tips

The following are some hints designed to help you make more effective use of Microsoft Excel. Unless otherwise indicated, all tips work with any version of Excel.

◇ **Enough help already.** Excel 2.2 provides a Help bar at the bottom of your screen, a particularly convenient learning tool for new users. As your cursor passes over a command, the Help bar displays a short blurb of information about it. However, for experienced users, this bar just takes up much-needed screen space. To dispense with it, choose the WORKSPACE command from the OPTIONS menu, and de-select the "Status bar" option from the resulting dialog box.

◇ **Columns with headlines.** To create nonscrolling headlines at the top of your columns, drag downward on the black split bar located above the up arrow on the vertical scroll bar. This allows you to split the window into two separate scrolling areas. There is another split bar to the left of the left scroll arrow, allowing you to establish non-scrolling row labels.

◇ **Turn off automatic calculation.** To save time when entering values into a worksheet that performs frequent calculations (such as our checkbook example), choose the CALCULATION command from the OPTIONS menu and set the calculation to Manual. This way, your worksheet will only be updated when you choose the CALCULATE NOW command (or press COMMAND-=).

◆ **Editing number formats.** Excel is the only spreadsheet that not only provides you with a wide variety of number formatting choices, but also allows you to edit these choices. For example, if you select the "m/d/yy" date option in the FORMAT NUMBER dialog box, the cell entry "5/9" will be displayed as "5/9/90" (assuming 1990 is the current year). However, by adding an extra *m* and *d* to the "Format" option at the bottom of the FORMAT NUMBER dialog box so that the format reads "mm/dd/yy," you change your display to "05/09/90." Or, if you prefer hyphens to slashes, you may edit the option to read "mm-dd-yy."

◆ **Transfer utilities.** Do not try to transfer to another application, whether using QuicKeys, On Cue, or some other launching utility, while entering information into a cell. Excel requires that you escape the formula bar before any closing or saving operation may be performed. Sometimes you must even close the current document before a launching utility will respond.

◆ **Botched formulae.** We hate to repeat things already in the *Macintosh Bible,* but this one's so great, we just had to pass it along. For us, it falls under the category of "so simple I would have never thought of it." When entering a complicated formula, it is very easy to make mistakes. However, Excel cannot implement the formula, and therefore will not let you escape the formula bar, unless it's perfect. Even an extra parenthesis can bog it down. If you're totally confused and tired of dealing with a botched formula, you may escape the formula bar without losing what you've done so far simply by deleting the equal sign at the formula's beginning. Then relax and come back to it later.

◆ **Making better-looking charts.** Basically, a chart with too many labels or too many tick marks looks like a big mess. Since Excel doesn't offer many interesting charting features anyway, you might as well make your charts as clean and simple as possible by eliminating excess dates and values. Also, if you're dealing with large numbers, there's no sense in making your value bars cross at zero. For example, if the lowest sales figure for your department was $35,000, your chart will be more dynamic if the lowest value on your chart is $30,000 rather than $0.

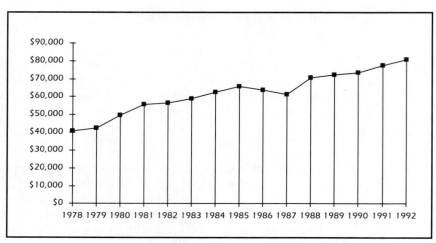

Although this chart is passable—you can plainly see how well this department has done each year since 1978—we could make it more dramatic by enhancing some details and eliminating others.

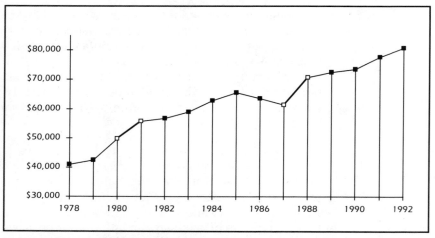

Here, we have simplified our chart by eliminating every other date, and made it more dramatic by selecting $30,000 as the starting value rather than $0. We have also highlighted our best growth years by adding thicker lines and hollow points.

⬦   **Exporting charts.** No matter how hard you try, charting in Excel is a miserable experience. It's unnecessarily laborious, and the results are generally dismal. If you're willing to spend a little more time (but not that much more, considering how long it takes to get a chart created in the first place), you can enhance your charts by exporting them into a drawing program such as MacDraw II. Simply select the entire chart (COMMAND-A), copy it, choose SCRAPBOOK from the APPLE menu, and paste. This converts the chart into the PICT graphic format used by MacDraw and supported by high-end drawing applications such as Aldus FreeHand. Pasting to the Scrapbook is also the only way to transfer a chart to a page-layout program for garnishing documentation.

◆   **Eliminating the extra zeros.** If you're designing worksheets with numbers ranging well into the thousands or millions (or even billions in the case of our friends in defense contracting), you might want to take advantage of Excel's rounding feature. Commas at the end of a number format instruct Excel to drop three digits apiece from the end of a cell value. So by entering "0," in the FORMAT NUMBER dialog, you instruct Excel to display the cell value 10,734,650 as "10,735". Adding another comma to the format (so that it reads "0,,") displays the same number as "11" and so on. A decimal point may also be added to retain significant digits; in this way, the format "0.00,," displays our cell value as "10.73".

◆   **Buying ready-made worksheets.** If you require a worksheet for a specific purpose, such as payroll analysis or real-estate management, but can't spare the time (or consider yourself unable) to carry out the design, you can probably locate a predesigned worksheet for a nominal fee. The largest clearinghouse for such products is Heizer Software's Excellent Exchange, which offers worksheets and templates for as low as $5.00. (Average prices are right around $20.)

Microsoft Excel Quick Reference (1 of 4)

Menus

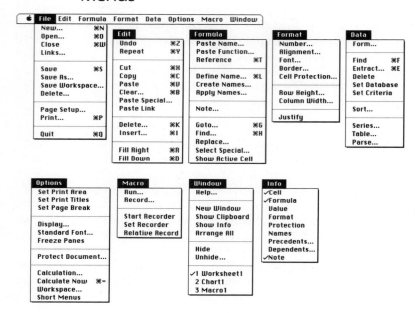

The INFO menu appears only when you choose SHOW INFO

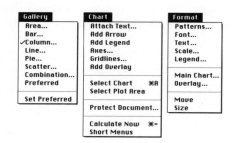

When a chart is the active window, the GALLERY and CHART menus replace the FORMULA, DATA, and OPTIONS menus, and the FORMAT menu changes as shown above

Microsoft Excel Quick Reference (2 of 4)

Keyboard Equivalents

Absolute reference[‡] .... $	Clear selected cells .... ⌘B
Activate formula bar .... ⌘U	Close all open documents .... ⇧ choose CLOSE
Activate menu bar .... F10 or /	Close document .... ⌘W or ⌘F4
Activate next pane F6	Compute enclosed operators first[‡] .... (and)
Activate next window .... ⌘M or ⌘F6	Copy cells or formula .... ⌘C or F3
Activate previous pane .... ⇧F6	Copy picture .... ⌘⇧C
Activate previous window .... ⌘⇧M or ⌘⇧F6	Copy value from cell above[‡]. .... ⌘'
Addition[‡] .... +	Create names .... ⌘⇧F3
Apply array formula .... ⌘↵ or ⌘🗲	Cut cells or formula .... ⌘X or F2
Apply formula to all selected cells ... ⌥↵ or ⌥🗲	
	Define name of selected cells .... ⌘L or ⌘F3
Begin formula[‡]. .... =	Delete selected cells .... ⌘K
Bold text .... ⌘⇧B	Display formulae/values, toggle .... ⌘~
Border, bottom .... ⌘⌥↓	Division[‡] .... /
Border, left .... ⌘⌥←	
Border, outline .... ⌘⌥)	Enter current date[‡] .... ⌘-
Border, right .... ⌘⌥→	Enter current time[‡] .... ⌘;
Border, top .... ⌘⌥↑	Equal to[‡] .... =
	Establish formula as array[‡]. .... { and }
Calculate document .... ⇧F9	Exponential (to power of …)[‡] .... ^
Calculate now .... ⌘= or F9	Extend selection range .... ⇧····↖ across cells
Cancel formula .... ⌘Z or ⌘.	Extract records from database .... ⌘E
Cancel operation .... ⌘. or ⌀	
Carry out operation .... 🗲	

‡ *Specifically for use in the formula bar or macro editor*

⌘	command	⇥	tab	⌫	delete	⎵	space bar
⇧	shift	↵	return	⌦	fwd. delete	F1	function key
⌥	option	🗲	enter	▤	keypad key	↖	mouse click
⌃	control	⌀	escape	▤⌀	clear	····↖	mouse drag

Microsoft Excel Quick Reference (3 of 4)

Keyboard Equivalents (Cont.)

Fill down .... ⌘D	Maximize active window .... ⌘F10
Fill left .... ⌘⇧R	Move active window .... ⌘F7
Fill right .... ⌘R	Move one cell down .... ↵
Fill up .... ⌘⇧D	Move one cell left or to previous field .... ⇧→|
Find cell, display dialog .... ⌘J *or* ⇧F5	Move one cell right or to next field .... →|
Find next cell .... ⌘H *or* F7	Move one cell up .... ⇧↵
Find next record in database ....⌘F	Move to next record....................................... ⤶
Find previous cell .... ⌘⇧H *or* ⇧F7	Move to previous record .... ⇧⤶
Find previous record in database................. ⌘⇧F	Multiplication‡... *
Go to cell or named area .... ⌘G *or* F5	New chart, create F11
Greater than‡.. >	New document, display dialog .... ⌘N
Greater than or equal‡.. >=	New macro sheet, create .... ⌘F11
Help .... ⌘/ *or* HELP	New worksheet, create .... ⇧F11
Help, context-sensitive .... ⇧F1	Not equal to‡.. <>
Insert one cell at a time ....⌇↖ *on cell*	Note selected cells .... ⌘⇧N *or* ⇧F2
Insert paragraph break in note ....⌃↵	Number format, $#,##0.00 .... ⌘⌇4
Insert selected number of cells .... ⌘I	Number format, 0% .... ⌘⌇5
Intersection‡.. ▬	Number format, 0.00 .... ⌘⌇1
Italic text .... ⌘⇧I	Number format, 0.00E+00 .... ⌘⌇6
Less than‡.. <	Number format, d-mmm-yy .... ⌘⌇3
Less than or equal‡... <=	Number format, general .... ⌘⌇~
	Number format, h:mm AM/PM .... ⌘⌇2
	Number lock, activate/deactivate .... ⇧▦⌇

‡ *Specifically for use in the formula bar or macro editor*

⌘	command	→|	tab	⊗	delete	▬	space bar
⇧	shift	↵	return	⊠	fwd. delete	F1	function key
⌇	option	⤶	enter	▦	keypad key	↖	mouse click
⌃	control	⌇	escape	▦⌇	clear	⋯↖	mouse drag

Microsoft Excel Quick Reference (4 of 4)

Keyboard Equivalents (Cont.)

Open existing document .... ⌘O *or* ⌘F12

Paste cells or formula .... ⌘V *or* F4

Paste function .... ⇧F3

Paste special .... ⌘⇧V

Percentage[‡]... %

Plain text .... ⌘⇧P

Print document .... ⌘P *or* ⌘⇧F12

Quit Excel .... ⌘Q

Range[‡].. :

Reference, convert formula .... ⌘T

Repeat last operation .... ⌘Y

Restore window size .... ⌘F5

Save as different name or location ..⌘⇧S *or* F12

Save spreadsheet .... ⌘S *or* ⇧F12

Search for ? or * characters[‡]. .... ~? *or* ~*

Select all cells .... ⌘A

Select chart .... ⌘A

Select entire column .... ⌘▬

Select entire row .... ⇧▬

Select entire worksheet .... ꕯ *corner box*

Select noncontiguous ranges .... ⌘┄┄ꕯ *across cells*

Select range of cells .... ┄┄ꕯ *across cells*

Select row or column .... ꕯ *row or cell heading*

Select special, all levels dependents .... ⌘⇧]

Select special, all levels precedents .... ⌘⇧[

Select special, column differences .... ⌘⇧\

Select special, current region .... ⌘*

Select special, direct dependents .... ⌘]

Select special, direct precedents .... ⌘[

Select special, notes .... ⌘⇧0

Select special, row differences .... ⌘\

Shadow text .... ⌘⇧W

Show information .... ⌘F2

Size active window .... ⌘F8

Subtraction/negation[‡]... -

Text operator[‡]. .... &

Underline text .... ⌘⇧U

Undo/redo last operation .... ⌘Z *or* F1

Union[‡].. ;

Wild card for a single character[‡]......................... ?

Wild card for any number of characters[‡]............. *

Accurate for Microsoft Excel, version 2.2

Minimalist Spreadsheets

Perhaps you don't need all the power of Excel 2.2, but it is our belief that everyone can use some kind of spreadsheet, no matter how small their needs. Although neither of the following programs can adequately compete with Excel in the business market, each offers enough features for a moderate user and, perhaps more importantly, each carries a moderate price tag (less than $150).

 MacCalc, Version 1.2   MCLC (native), SYLK (data only), WKS, TEXT
You have to love MacCalc. Though it's incapable of producing charts and there is no built-in macro editor, it's everything you need to create personal worksheets. And if quickness is what you're after, MacCalc consistently wins speed tests over the likes of Excel, Wingz, and Full Impact on both the Mac Plus and SE. For those new to spreadsheets, MacCalc provides operator, function, and general help information right on the menu bar, where it is out of the way but easy to access. The program also allows multiple fonts, type styles, and type sizes to exist in a single document. And finally, detailed notes may be added to any cell, ensuring that you don't forget the meaning of something you entered months or even years ago.

 Analyze, Version 2.1   WKS, TEXT
Analyze is somewhat of an enigma and, we might as well say up front, not our favorite program. On one hand, it offers both the charting abilities (including a three-dimensional bar chart) and the macro-editing features missing from MacCalc. In fact, in this sense it is a powerful and very inexpensive spreadsheet, offering nearly every single feature available to Lotus 1-2-3 users on the PC, and in a similar format. But on the other hand, the software is very slow—scads slower than the speedy MacCalc. No matter how great an application is, it's almost never worth waiting for. Also, a document is limited to only one font, one size, and one style, like the Excel of bygone days. And only one document may be open at a time.

Spreadsheets with Page Layout

While the big three spreadsheets are currently waging a presentations war, the two applications that first offered the ability to combine numbers and charts on the same page have all but fallen by the wayside. Both Ragtime from Migrant Software (an outgrowth from Cricket Software) and Trapeze provide spreadsheet capabilities in a page-layout environment.

We should quickly note here that both of these programs will export charts in the PICT format without sidetracking through the Scrapbook. For that alone, they must be commended highly.

Ragtime, Version 2.1   SYLK, TEXT, PICT

Developed by a German distributor known as Unicorn GmbH, Ragtime is one of those applications that's very hard to classify. In fact, it offers so many page-layout features that we could have put it in the Page-Layout Software entry with such luminaries as Aldus PageMaker and QuarkXPress. However, these features aren't quite strong enough to hold up against the advanced text and graphics capabilities of other such applications, and no other page-composition program provides any number-crunching features whatsoever.

Basically, several worksheets may exist together on a single Ragtime page, along with multiple charts and textual elements. Text formatting is one of Ragtime's strongest features, allowing you to vary the appearance of characters within a single cell. We cannot recommend Ragtime 2.1 as a spreadsheet alone because its various page-composition abilities slow it down considerably when compared to other spreadsheets. But if it's your job to process figures and present them in the form of top-notch documentation, you may want to consider this program, especially as a secondary spreadsheet for use in conjunction with a more powerful application such as Excel.

Ragtime 3

The newest release from Migrant Software, Ragtime 3, offers a new round of sophisticated layout features, some of which—such as the ability to rotate text and graphics and process scanned images directly—out-layout PageMaker. On the spreadsheet side of things, Ragtime 3 can import data from most major database and file-management applications, as well as import formatted text from Microsoft Word, MacWrite, and WriteNow. A strong product with an extremely favorable endorsement from Apple president Jean-Louis Gassée, this may be the version of Ragtime that finally grabs the attention of users in the United States.

Trapeze, Version 2.1   WKS (data only), TEXT, PICT

Like Ragtime, Trapeze is not easily classified. The program allows you to divide a single page into a series of blocks: text blocks for explanatory paragraphs, picture blocks for imported MacPaint graphics, number blocks for spreadsheet values, as well as chart blocks and database blocks.

Offhand, our only problem with Trapeze is that it can be rather difficult to learn, simply because it's so different from the norm as established by Excel. But then again, this seems a reasonable price to pay for the program's additional control over compositional elements. After all, you, not the program, control how large a worksheet is. If you want the billion cells normally associated with Wingz, you can give it to yourself in Trapeze. If you want a more reasonably sized worksheet, you can arrange that as well. But you can't just create a new file and start banging away.

For our money, the increased control is worth the lack of immediacy. In that sense, Trapeze may be the best-kept spreadsheet secret around.

Excellent Contenders

The boldest contenders to Excel's dominion—Full Impact and Wingz—are exciting applications that blur the border between spreadsheets, presentation applications, and database managers. Most new features are appended to the standard worksheet environment, borrowing heavily and obviously from Excel.

Unfortunately, there do exist occasional changes in the standard worksheet form that may jar long-time Excel users (like ourselves). But, for the most part, these dissimilarities are few and far between, and any long-time Excel user should find either of the following applications easy to pick up and begin using.

 Full Impact, Version 1.1   GWKS (native), DIF, SYLK, WKS, DBF, TEXT

The first spreadsheet designed specifically for the Mac II, Full Impact continues to give Excel a run for its money in the features and power departments. For one, it is currently the only spreadsheet that uses *virtual memory,* allowing users with low-memory machines to access all of its 500,000 cells (provided that the disk space is available).

Also, Full Impact offers a unique working environment (since adopted by Wingz) in which cells, graphics, and up to a full page of explanatory text may be combined on the same page. This is extraordinarily useful for persons creating department reports that must be distributed to many people, largely eliminating the need for exporting charts to a page-layout program, a difficult operation in any spreadsheet.

Unfortunately, there are some conveniences provided by Excel that Full Impact lacks. For example, Full Impact provides several numerical formats, but they cannot be edited to the extent they may be in Excel. And empty cells will not retain row or column formatting. If you select an entire column, for example, and change its alignment to centered, all values will become centered; but any values entered into empty cells in that same column will remain flush right.

One of Full Impact's greatest strengths is its use of a customizable toolbox. The palette is elegant, easy to use, and editable. For example, you may create a macro, assign it an icon, and add it to a section of the Full Impact toolbox. If you're designing macros to be used by people other than yourself, you may find that these custom tools get used more often than standard macros. Not only are they more in line with the standard Macintosh interface, but a graphic can often convey more of a sense of the purpose of a macro than a few words of text or a keyboard equivalent.

Your Right to Copy

We feel obligated to register a complaint at this point. Although the documentation that accompanies Full Impact claims that the program is not copy-protected, this claim is untrue. As in many other applications, you are required to customize the software by entering your name, your company, and the product's serial number in a dialog box, which will then appear each time the application launches.

However, while other applications require that you customize run-copies, Ashton-Tate requires that you customize your original before any copies may be made. Sounds like copy protection to us. Not only does this prevent you from making clean copies for your friends, an illegal act, but it also discourages you from reselling your software after you no longer find it useful, an entirely legal act outside the jurisdiction of United States copyright laws.

Luckily, after customizing your application, you may "de-customize" it using a hex-editing utility such as MacTools by Central Point Software or Symantec Tools by Symantec Corporation. Simply perform a search for the text you entered and replace it with spaces. These will show up as an empty area during future launchings of Full Impact.

Full Impact Quick Reference (1 of 5)

Icon Bars

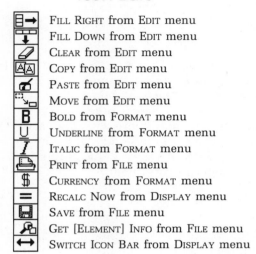

FILL RIGHT from EDIT menu
FILL DOWN from EDIT menu
CLEAR from EDIT menu
COPY from EDIT menu
PASTE from EDIT menu
MOVE from EDIT menu
BOLD from FORMAT menu
UNDERLINE from FORMAT menu
ITALIC from FORMAT menu
PRINT from FILE menu
CURRENCY from FORMAT menu
RECALC NOW from DISPLAY menu
SAVE from FILE menu
GET [ELEMENT] INFO from FILE menu
SWITCH ICON BAR from DISPLAY menu

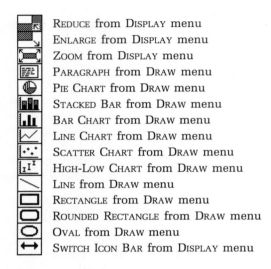

REDUCE from DISPLAY menu
ENLARGE from DISPLAY menu
ZOOM from DISPLAY menu
PARAGRAPH from DRAW menu
PIE CHART from DRAW menu
STACKED BAR from DRAW menu
BAR CHART from DRAW menu
LINE CHART from DRAW menu
SCATTER CHART from DRAW menu
HIGH-LOW CHART from DRAW menu
LINE from DRAW menu
RECTANGLE from DRAW menu
ROUNDED RECTANGLE from DRAW menu
OVAL from DRAW menu
SWITCH ICON BAR from DISPLAY menu

Clicking one of the above icons is a substitue for choosing the command listed

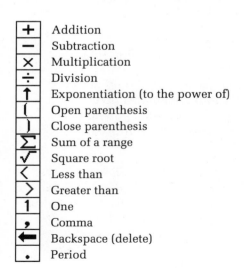

Addition
Subtraction
Multiplication
Division
Exponentiation (to the power of)
Open parenthesis
Close parenthesis
Sum of a range
Square root
Less than
Greater than
One
Comma
Backspace (delete)
Period

The above icon bar appears when you use the formula bar or macro editor

Full Impact Quick Reference (2 of 5)

Standard Menus

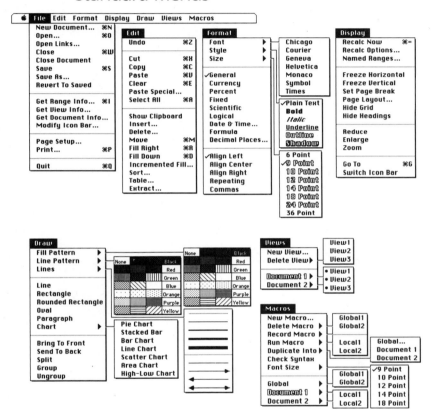

Full Impact Quick Reference (3 of 5)

Formula and Macro Menus

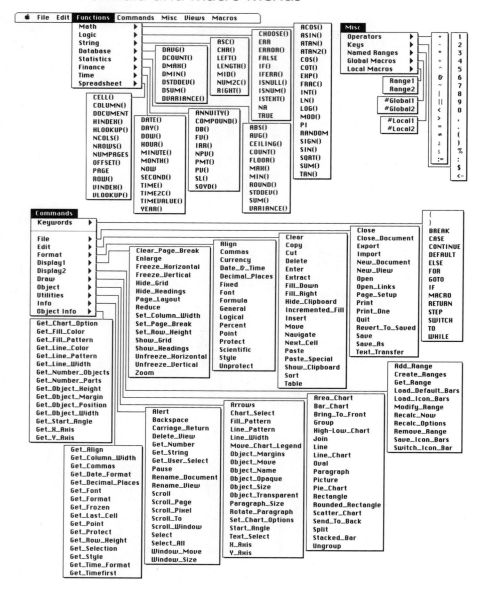

File Edit Functions Commands Misc Views Macros

Functions menu:
- Math
- Logic
- String
- Database
- Statistics
- Finance
- Time
- Spreadsheet

DAVG()
DCOUNT()
DMAX()
DMIN()
DSTDDEV()
DSUM()
DVARIANCE()

ASC()
CHR()
LEFT()
LENGTH()
MID()
NUM2C()
RIGHT()

CHOOSE()
ERR
ERROR()
FALSE
IF()
IFERR()
ISNULL()
ISNUM()
ISTEXT()
NA
TRUE

ACOS()
ASIN()
ATAN()
ATAN2()
COS()
COT()
EXP()
FRAC()
INT()
LN()
LOG()
MOD()
PI
RANDOM
SIGN()
SIN()
SQRT()
SUM()
TAN()

Misc
- Operators
- Keys
- Named Ranges
- Global Macros
- Local Macros

Range1
Range2

#Global1
#Global2

#Local1
#Local2

+
-
*
÷
^
&
~
||
<
>
=
≠
≥
≤
:=

1
2
3
4
5
6
7
8
9
0
,
.
(
)
%
:
;
$
<-

CELL()
COLUMN()
DOCUMENT()
HINDEX()
HLOOKUP()
NCOLS()
NROWS()
NUMPAGES
OFFSET()
PAGE
ROW()
VINDEX()
VLOOKUP()

DATE()
DAY()
DOW()
HOUR()
MINUTE()
MONTH()
NOW
SECOND()
TIME()
TIME2C()
TIMEVALUE()
YEAR()

ANNUITY()
COMPOUND()
DB()
FV()
IRR()
NPV()
PMT()
PV()
SL()
SOYD()

ABS()
AVG()
CEILING()
COUNT()
FLOOR()
MAX()
MIN()
ROUND()
STDDEV()
SUM()
VARIANCE()

Commands
- Keywords

File
Edit
Format
Display1
Display2
Draw
Object
Utilities
Info
Object Info

Clear_Page_Break
Enlarge
Freeze_Horizontal
Freeze_Vertical
Hide_Grid
Hide_Headings
Page_Layout
Reduce
Set_Column_Width
Set_Page_Break
Set_Row_Height
Show_Grid
Show_Headings
Unfreeze_Horizontal
Unfreeze_Vertical
Zoom

Align
Commas
Currency
Date_&_Time
Decimal_Places
Fixed
Font
Formula
General
Logical
Percent
Point
Protect
Scientific
Style
Unprotect

Clear
Copy
Cut
Delete
Enter
Extract
Fill_Down
Fill_Right
Hide_Clipboard
Incremented_Fill
Insert
Move
Navigate
Next_Cell
Paste
Paste_Special
Show_Clipboard
Sort
Table

Close
Close_Document
Export
Import
New_Document
New_View
Open
Open_Links
Page_Setup
Print
Print_One
Quit
Revert_To_Saved
Save
Save_As
Text_Transfer

{
}
BREAK
CASE
CONTINUE
DEFAULT
ELSE
FOR
GOTO
IF
MACRO
RETURN
STEP
SWITCH
TO
WHILE

Get_Chart_Option
Get_Fill_Color
Get_Fill_Pattern
Get_Line_Color
Get_Line_Pattern
Get_Line_Width
Get_Number_Objects
Get_Number_Parts
Get_Object_Height
Get_Object_Margin
Get_Object_Position
Get_Object_Width
Get_Start_Angle
Get_X_Axis
Get_Y_Axis

Get_Align
Get_Column_Width
Get_Commas
Get_Date_Format
Get_Decimal_Places
Get_Font
Get_Format
Get_Frozen
Get_Last_Cell
Get_Point
Get_Protect
Get_Row_Height
Get_Selection
Get_Style
Get_Time_Format
Get_Timefirst

Alert
Backspace
Carriage_Return
Delete_View
Get_Number
Get_String
Get_User_Select
Pause
Rename_Document
Rename_View
Scroll
Scroll_Page
Scroll_Pixel
Scroll_To
Scroll_Window
Select
Select_All
Window_Move
Window_Size

Arrows
Chart_Select
Fill_Pattern
Line_Pattern
Line_Width
Move_Chart_Legend
Object_Margins
Object_Move
Object_Name
Object_Opaque
Object_Size
Object_Transparent
Paragraph_Size
Rotate_Paragraph
Set_Chart_Options
Start_Angle
Text_Select
X_Axis
Y_Axis

Area_Chart
Bar_Chart
Bring_To_Front
Group
High-Low_Chart
Join
Line
Line_Chart
Oval
Paragraph
Picture
Pie_Chart
Rectangle
Rounded_Rectangle
Scatter_Chart
Send_To_Back
Split
Stacked_Bar
Ungroup

Add_Range
Create_Ranges
Get_Range
Load_Default_Bars
Load_Icon_Bars
Modify_Range
Recalc_Now
Recalc_Options
Remove_Range
Save_Icon_Bars
Switch_Icon_Bar

Full Impact Quick Reference (4 of 5)

Keyboard Equivalents

Absolute reference[‡].. $

Accept formula, activate next cell down .... ⌥↓

Accept formula, activate next cell left .... ⌥←

Accept formula, activate next cell right .... ⌥→

Accept formula, activate next cell up .... ⌥↑

Activate formula bar .... ↖↖ *cell*

Activate selection box .... ⌘G

Addition[‡].. +

Argument separator[‡]... ,

Assignment[‡]... :=

Cancel operation .... ⌘.

Clear selected cells .... ⌘E

Close document or macro window .... ⌘W

Compute enclosed operators first[‡]........... (*and*)

Concatenation[‡]... ||

Copy cells or formula .... ⌘C

Cut cells or formula .... ⌘X

Display date .... ↖ *clock while time displayed*

Display time .... ↖ *clock while date displayed*

Division[‡]... /

Enter numbers or functions as text[‡].................... "

Equal to[‡]... =

Exponential (to power of …)[‡]............................. ^

Extend selection range .... ⇧┄↖ *across cells*

Fill down .... ⌘D

Fill right .... ⌘R

Get information on selected element .... ⌘I

Go to specified cell .... ⌘G

Greater than[‡].. >

Greater than or equal[‡]................................... ≥

Help .... ⌘/

Less than[‡].. <

Less than or equal[‡]....................................... ≤

Link to other worksheet[‡]................................. !

Logical and[‡].. &

Logical not[‡].. ~

Logical or[‡].. |

Modify icon .... ⌘↖ *on icon*

[‡] *Specifically for use in the formula bar or macro editor*

⌘	command	➞|	tab	⌫	delete	⎵	space bar
⇧	shift	↩	return	⌦	fwd. delete	F1	function key
⌥	option	⤮	enter	⌨	keypad key	↖	mouse click
⌃	control	⌫	escape	⌨⌫	clear	┄↖	mouse drag

Full Impact Quick Reference (5 of 5)

Keyboard Equivalents (Cont.)

Move one cell down .... ↵

Move one cell left .... ⇧➔|

Move one cell right ....➔|

Move one cell up .... ⇧↵

Move selection .... ⌘····↖ *to set destination,* ⌘M

Multiplication‡... *

New document, create .... ⌘N

Not equal to‡. .... ≠

Open existing document .... ⌘O

Paste cells or formula .... ⌘V

Percentage‡.. %

Print document .... ⌘P

Quit Full Impact .... ⌘Q

Range‡.. :

Recalculate now .... ⌘=

Save spreadsheet .... ⌘S

Select all cells .... ⌘A

Select entire worksheet .... ↖ *corner box*

Select noncontiguous ranges .... ⌘····↖ *across cells*

Select range of cells .... ····↖ *across cells*

Select row or column .... ↖ *row or cell heading*

Subtraction/negation‡... -

Undo/redo last operation .... ⌘Z

Wild card for a single character‡......................... ?

Wild card for any number of characters‡............. *

‡ *Specifically for use in the formula bar or macro editor*
Accurate for Full Impact, version 1.1

⌘	command	➔|	tab	⊠	delete	⊐	space bar
⇧	shift	↵	return	⊠	fwd. delete	F1	function key
⍨	option	⤼	enter	▦	keypad key	↖	mouse click
⋀	control	⌮	escape	▦⌮	clear	····↖	mouse drag

Wingz, Version 1.0   WZSS (native), DIF, SYLK, WKS, TEXT

If your primary interest in using a spreadsheet is to create charts, then buy Wingz. As far as we're concerned, Wingz's charting abilities are about twice as easy to use as Excel's, and nine times as powerful. We even find them to be superior to those of Cricket Graph. You may have already seen this power demonstrated in magazine advertisements. This is one case where the ads don't lie.

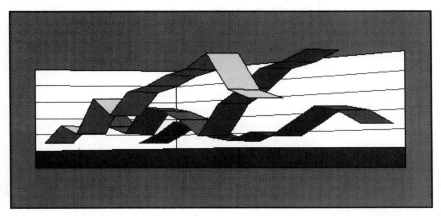

Wingz by Informix Software allows you to create the most impressive charts of any spreadsheet currently on the market.

Our only complaint about charting with Wingz is its slowness. A minor adjustment to a cell value can require up to a minute of waiting for the chart to reflect the new setting. Luckily, Wingz allows you to cancel a chart's refreshing process by pressing COMMAND-PERIOD.

Despite our amazement at Wingz's charting abilities, we find its worksheet environment to be lacking, even more so than Full Impact's. First, the way it handles scrolling is problematic. For example, in Excel, dragging the box in the vertical scroll bar takes you to the end of your worksheet; that is, to the last cell containing a value. In Wingz, the same operation takes you to the absolute last cell, number 32,768. Because Wingz permits you to access any portion of its enormous billion-cell matrix, you must be very careful when dragging a scroll box. In fact, we've found that you move in 90-cell increments for every pixel of scroll-box adjustment. For those with moderate or even fairly large spreadsheet requirements, scrolling may become exceptionally irritating.

Also, if you prefer selecting options from dialog boxes over choosing command after command from hard-to-reach pop-up menus, then you probably want to avoid Wingz. As you can see in the Wingz Quick Reference, almost every command presents a hierarchical pop-up menu. Sometimes, a pop-up menu is convenient, but we feel that many situations call for a dialog box, where options can be positioned in relation to one another in a way that often graphically demonstrates their purpose.

Programming with HyperScript

For those who like macros, Wingz goes a step further, offering a Hyper-Card-like system of graphics and buttons that can do much more than perform repetitive tasks. In fact, in the form of HyperScript, Wingz is actually providing a programming language. While unrelated to HyperCard's HyperTalk language, HyperScript supplies many HyperCard-like abilities. You may even build custom programs that will run in tandem with Wingz's worksheets and charts or on their own.

Wingz Quick Reference (1 of 5)

Toolbox

⊹	Worksheet	▸ to select single cell or chart, ┈▸ to select range of cells or move chart
+	Object	▸ to select object so it may be manipulated, ┈▸ to move
▭	Button	┈▸ to create button and define size
▦	Text	┈▸ to create text field and define size, ⌘┈▸ to align to worksheet grid
▥	Chart	┈▸ to draw chart of selected range of data, ⌘┈▸ to align to worksheet grid
╲	Line	┈▸ to draw straight line
⌐	Arc	┈▸ to draw quarter ellipse from top or bottom to side
◯	Oval	┈▸ to draw ellipse
▢	Rectangle	┈▸ to draw rectangle
Σ	Poly	▸ to create corners for polygon

Wingz Quick Reference (2 of 5)

Menus

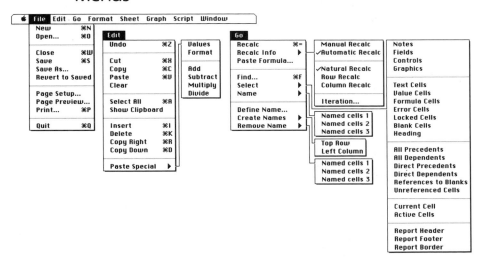

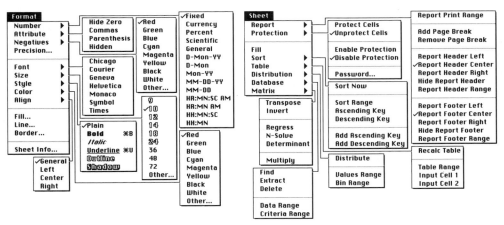

Wingz Quick Reference (3 of 5)

Menus (Cont.)

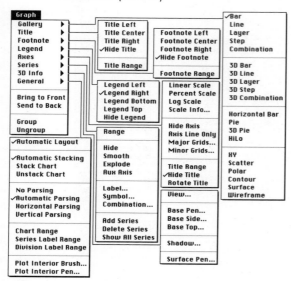

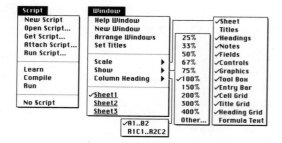

Wingz Quick Reference (4 of 5)

Keyboard Equivalents

Absolute reference‡.. $

Accept formula, activate next cell down .... ↓

Accept formula, activate next cell left .... ←

Accept formula, activate next cell right .... →

Accept formula, activate next cell up .... ↑

Access last object tool .... ⇧┄┄↖

Addition‡... +

Apply grid to object .... ⌘┄┄↖ w/ *any object tool*

Argument separator‡... ,

Begin formula‡... =

Cancel formula .... ▦⬀

Cancel operation .... ⌘.

Clear .... ⌫

Close document .... ⌘W

Compute enclosed operators first‡............ (*and*)

Copy cells or formula .... ⌘C *or* F3

Cut cells or formula .... ⌘X *or* F2

Delete selected cells .... ⌘K

Division‡... /

Enter numbers or functions as text‡.................... "

Equal to‡... =

Execute HyperScript command
from formula bar .... ⌘↵ *or* ⌘⌇

Exponential (to power of ...)‡............................. ^

Extend selection range .... ⇧┄┄↖ *across cells*

Fill down .... ⌘D

Fill right .... ⌘R

Find cell or named area .... ⌘F

Go down one window .... PAGE DOWN

Go to cell A1 .... HOME

Go to cell AVLH32768 .... END

Go to first or last active cell ..... ↖ *navigator arrow*

Go up one window .... PAGE UP

Greater than‡.. >

Greater than or equal‡...................................... >=

Help .... HELP

Insert selected number of cells .... ⌘I

Less than‡... <

Less than or equal‡... <=

‡ *Specifically for use in the formula bar or macro editor*

⌘	command	⇥	tab	⌫	delete	⎵	space bar
⇧	shift	↵	return	⌦	fwd. delete	F1	function key
⌇	option	⌇	enter	▦	keypad key	↖	mouse click
⌃	control	⬀	escape	▦⬀	clear	┄┄↖	mouse drag

Wingz **Quick Reference** (5 of 5)

Keyboard Equivalents (Cont.)

Move one cell down .... ↵

Move one cell left .... ⇧➞|

Move one cell right .... ➞|

Move one cell up .... ⇧↵

Multiplication‡ .... *

New document, create .... ⌘N

Not equal to‡ .... <>

Open existing document .... ⌘O

Paste cells or formula .... ⌘V *or* F4

Percentage‡ .... %

Print document .... ⌘P

Quit Wingz .... ⌘Q

Range‡ ....

Recalculate now .... ⌘=

Save spreadsheet .... ⌘S

Select all cells .... ⌘A

Select entire worksheet .... ↖ *corner box*

Select noncontiguous ranges .... ⌘⌁↖ *across cells*

Select range of cells .... ⌁↖ *across cells*

Select row or column .... ↖ *row or cell heading*

Subtraction/negation‡ .... -

Text operator‡ .... &

Undo/redo last operation .... ⌘Z *or* F1

---

‡ *Specifically for use in the formula bar or macro editor*
Accurate for Wingz, version 1.0

⌘	command	➞|	tab	⌫	delete	⊶	space bar	
⇧	shift	↵	return	⌦	fwd. delete	F1	function key	
⌥	option	⌁	enter	▦	keypad key	↖	mouse click	
⌃	control	⌅	escape	▦⌦	clear	⌁↖	mouse drag	

◈ Word Processors

You have to wonder what the post office will be doing in the year 2050. Assuming that color facsimile (fax) abilities will become built-in features of even the cheapest telephones, it's hard to imagine anyone mailing a letter, even if it's only a postcard.

For those postal employees who nonetheless feel secure about an institution as venerable as Ben Franklin, consider what the word processor has done to the once enormous typewriter market. A piece of machinery so popular and utilitarian that it had become the symbol of the office, the typewriter is now most useful for filling out forms. In the past ten years, typewriter technology has improved more dramatically than in the previous fifty. For a few hundred bucks, you can buy a typewriter that corrects mistakes, alerts you to spelling errors, and provides control over keyboard sensitivity. But regardless of its capabilities, it doesn't even stand a chance against the most rudimentary text-editing software on a personal computer.

In general, however, word processing on the Mac is anything but rudimentary. Even the most basic of applications offers text-editing features that would have seemed unimaginable a decade ago. As a result, we communicate more effectively and much more efficiently. Less time is spent meticulously writing draft after draft, less money is spent on wasted paper that gets no farther than the janitor, and less frustration is incurred ripping up pages after making glaring mistakes on the very last lines.

But because the word processor is so thoroughly functional, much of its power is overlooked and underused. Despite intense feature wars in the software arena, many users take advantage of few of the capabilities that their writing applications offer.

Paragraph Formatting

Most people who use word processors know how to format type by changing the font, choosing a bold or italic style, enlarging or reducing the type size, and so on. But many of us are a little more timid when it comes to *paragraph formatting;* that is, formatting characteristics that apply to an entire paragraph (from one return character to the next) as opposed to a single letter or word of type.

Two of the most useful but often overlooked paragraph formatters are tabs and indents. Both features help to automate the writing process, ensuring that your documents look clean and consistent.

Tab Stops for Anyone

Just about any typewriter provides movable tab stops for creating columnar text. The same is true for word processors, which let you not only move tab stops, but add or delete them as well. Many of us forget this feature, however, relying instead upon multiple tabs.

For example, suppose you are creating three columns of entries, the first of which contains entry descriptions, and the second and third of which hold dollar amounts. Typically, you enter the description, press the TAB key, enter the first dollar amount, press TAB, and enter the second dollar amount. But while the dollar amounts are all roughly the same width, perhaps ranging between $100 and $10,000, the descriptions may be as long as "First quarter tax deductions, charitable donations excluded," or as short as "District totals." To accommodate shorter entries, you might simply enter additional tabs until the current dollar amount lines up with the one above it.

The problem with multiple tabs, however, is that they don't allow for future manipulations very well. If you decide to enlarge the type size of your table, you may find that half of your second-column entries are forced to line up at a following tab stop while the other half remain stationary. And if you ever need to move the second column a little to the right to accommodate a particularly long description, you will have to go back and enter an additional tab for each preceding entry.

A wiser and easier way to create tables is to conserve tabs and manipulate tab stops. When entering your text, never press the TAB key two times or more in a row. Then after you finish, select your tabbed paragraphs (or in the case of WordPerfect, simply click before the first tabbed paragraph) and delete and adjust tabs as you see fit. You may even substitute one tab for a different kind of tab. For example, right tabs or decimal tabs generally work best for columns of numbers.

An Indent Is Worth a Thousand Tabs

Tabs are not always the answer. In fact, although tabs are probably most commonly used to indent the first line of a paragraph, this is their least efficient application.

By adjusting the position of the first-line indent marker (the appearance of which varies dramatically from program to program), you specify that the first line of every paragraph is to be tabbed automatically. This saves you the small amount of effort required to press the TAB key at the beginning of each paragraph, and ensures that paragraphs are consistently indented.

Spacing Out Paragraphs

A custom that is becoming increasingly popular in professional writing is to drop first-line indents entirely in favor of paragraph spacing. In this book, you may notice, we have employed this method to achieve a block-like, purely functional composition, which lends itself to the reference quality of the book. To separate paragraphs from each other, we have added generous "after" spacing to each paragraph, rather than pressing the RETURN key twice in a row. This gives us more control over the printed page, and once again allows us to add or subtract spacing more easily.

Hanging Indents

Finally, tabs and indents may be used together to create an effect known as **hanging indents**, where the first line of a paragraph hangs to the left of any following lines. This technique is especially useful for creating numbered lists. The number hangs in the margin, highlighting a few lines of information aligned to the right of it.

First type in a character to call attention to the paragraph, such as a bullet (•) or a number. Then press the TAB key and type in the rest of the paragraph. After you finish entering the list item and while it's still selected, position the left indent marker about a quarter inch to the right of the first-line indent marker.

(If you use WordPerfect, click at the beginning of the list item and choose INDENT from the PARAGRAPH pop-up menu under FORMAT. This will indent the entire paragraph one tab stop to the right. Press SHIFT-TAB to move the first line back again.)

- This is a hanging indent preceded by a bullet. Any following lines of type in the paragraph are set to wrap to a position even with the first word after the bullet.

1. Hanging indents are also commonly used in numbered lists.

◇ In this book, we format software tips using hanging indents, preceding each tip with one of three diamonds to denote the level of difficulty or sophistication.

Hanging indents are most useful for lists of information that must be easily distinguished from normal text.

Tabs, indents, and paragraph spacing provide you with the kind of control that ten years ago was only available to professional typesetters. They are also very easy to use. For information on more advanced means of saving time when writing and formatting documents, read Word Technicalities 1.

Word-Processing Aids

A word processor is much, much more than a typewriter. In fact, surrounded by one or two support utilities, a word processor can literally become a writing environment, not only allowing you to change words and omit phrases after you've identified a mistake, but also alerting you to mistakes that you may not have noticed, and helping you to figure out solutions.

Spell-Checking Utilities

Spell-checking is a great example of the power of word-processing software. Most applications for the Mac offer built-in spell-checkers, with dictionaries full of hundreds of thousands of words. If your software finds a misspelled entry, you may even ask for it to suggest an alternative, an especially useful feature for those times when you have no idea what letter the word begins with or if it even exists.

Word Technicalities 1

How to hustle words in the computer age:
Using glossaries, style sheets, and macros

Almost any type of computer application provides methods for automating the creation process. Word processors are no exception. The most powerful of these are offered primarily by high-end applications such as Microsoft Word, WordPerfect, FullWrite, and Nisus.

If you're looking to save time when entering type, then you may want to take advantage of your application's **glossary** feature. Glossaries are dictionaries of abbreviations. For example, if you're a lawyer (and who isn't these days?), you might specify for the initials *p1p* to stand for *the party of the first part.* Then every time you entered *p1p,* your word processor would substitute in the popular legal phrase.

(For those whose word processor lacks a glossary feature, you may simply type in an unusual set of initials such as *p1p* to act as a placeholder for a phrase. When you're finished typing, search for and replace all instances of *p1p* with *the party of the first part.*)

If you want to speed up your formatting and make it more consistent, you might try using **style sheets**, custom styles that include font, size, style, and related information. For example, you may specify that a style called Headline means 24-point bold Helvetica. Then anytime you applied this style to a line of type, it would change immediately rather than requiring the correct application of three separate commands.

And if you want to speed up life in general, record a **macro**. A macro is merely a string of operations that you perform on a regular basis. Many word processors allow you not only to record macros, but also to open them as text files and edit them using a simple macro command language.

Conclusion: Glossaries save you time when entering text by allowing you to substitute initials for lengthy phrases. Style sheets include information on character and paragraph formatting. And macros perform a string of commands and operations at the push of a key sequence. All three are useful for saving time when typing long documents.

For users with old versions of MacWrite or other applications with no built-in spelling abilities, you may want to consider one of the external spell-checking utilities described below.

Spellswell, Version 2.1

Spellswell provides all the features you expect from a spell-checker, without any of the convenience. To its credit, Spellswell includes an editable homonym list for identifying words that sound the same but have different meanings. Substantial legal and medical dictionaries are also available. But unfortunately, Spellswell is a stand-alone application; it cannot be used to edit a file currently open in a word processor, nor can it read text entered into a page-layout program.

Spelling Coach Professional, Version 3.1

If you're looking for a spell-checker utility that provides more features than a standard word processor, you may want to check out Deneba Software's Spelling Coach Professional, which provides many more features than Spellswell, all of which are better implemented.

Coach is the only utility that provides definitions for words along with their spellings. While the definitions aren't so complete that you'll want to throw away your dictionary, they can be useful if you're trying to choose between two or three words. Coach also provides a legal and medical dictionary—both of which are larger than those included with Spellswell— and a substantial thesaurus (virtually identical to Big Thesaurus, reviewed later in this entry).

Coach will check the spelling of documents created by almost every word processor on the market. But since most of these applications provide their own spelling checkers, we find it hard to imagine why you would use Coach for this purpose, unless you intended to batch-check a large number of documents at one time. Coach would be more useful if it could inspect applications that lack spelling capabilities, like Aldus PageMaker. But where Coach fails, the following utility succeeds.

Thunder II, Version 1.01

Despite Coach's definitions, Thunder is probably our favorite spell-checker. Using this cdev, you specify the applications in which you want Thunder to appear, including page-layout software such as PageMaker or even word-processing DA's such as Symmetry's Acta. Then when you launch the appropriate application or DA, a check mark will appear on the right side of your menu bar representing the Thunder menu.

When the CHECKING ON command is checked, Thunder will check your spelling as you write, beeping when you mispell ... oops, there it goes now ... *misspell* a word. While Coach also provides this feature, Thunder goes a step further by checking for double-word entries, incorrect capitalization, and bad punctuation, giving you a different kind of beep for each. If a word that you use often, such as a technical term, is not included in Thunder's dictionary, you may add it to a user-entry dictionary, as is the case with most built-in spell-checkers. But Thunder goes one better by allowing you to add up to 17 suffixes along with a word. For example, if the word *toggle* is not included, you could also add the words *toggles*, *toggled*, *toggling*, *toggleness*, and so on, at the same time.

Unfortunately, we have found that this version of Thunder does not work well with other utilities that add menus to the menu bar. When running along with Affinity Microsystems's Tempo, for example, the menus may switch with each other. Choosing a command from either menu will cause a system error. When running with Big Thesaurus, which we discuss in this section, Thunder may disappear from the menu bar altogether.

On-Line Thesauruses

If you're sick and tired of using the same word over and over again, you may want to consult an on-line thesaurus. It won't be quite as good as *Roget's*, but that's the price of convenience.

Word Finder, Version 2.0
As a desk-accessory thesaurus, Word Finder is entirely satisfactory, but nothing to write home about. You'll find it particularly useful during those inarticulate moments when a word is right on the tip of your tongue, but you can't for the life of you think what it is. By typing a similar word into your word-processing application and then choosing Word Finder's LOOKUP command, you will be presented with a list of possible alternatives. If none of these is the exact word you're looking for, as is frequently the case during a word fit, you can select one of the synonyms in the Word Finder list and try again. Eventually, you'll find the word for which you are searching.

But Word Finder doesn't provide any extra touches. Synonyms are divided by parts of speech and by meaning groups (denoted by the ∞ symbol, though what infinity has to do with synonyms, we'll never know). But there are no definitions, no distinctions between related words and synonyms, and no antonyms. Also, if you place the thesaurus document used by the DA anywhere but the System folder, Word Finder will ask you where it is at the beginning of each work session.

Versions of Word Finder are also included with Microsoft Word, FullWrite Professional, and MacWrite. However, these versions only run with the application with which they are packaged.

 Big Thesaurus, Version 1.0

Big Thesaurus is everything that Word Finder should be. Basically, it operates identically to Word Finder. Available as a DA, Big Thesaurus is chosen from the APPLE menu when a word is selected in your word-processing or page-layout application. A dialog then appears, packed with synonyms divided by part of speech and meaning group. On a color monitor, nouns show up as red, verbs as blue, and so on, helping you to visually distinguish the throngs of words that Big Thesaurus often produces.

Unlike in Word Finder, each meaning group is preceded by a definition. Within each meaning group is a list of synonyms, compared words, related words, contrasted words, and antonyms.

Style Guides

Unfortunately, you can spell every word in a document correctly and use the most grandiloquent synonyms, and still end up with a document full of mistakes. This is because most mistakes are usage-based. For example, the sentence "There help was greatly appreciated" contains no spelling mistakes per se. The spelling t-h-e-r-e is not incorrect, but merely the wrong spelling in this context. And since no spelling checker is capable of understanding the context of a word, an inappropriate word goes by unnoticed.

Other context-based mistakes include lack or excess of punctuation, incomplete or run-on sentences, and incorrect usage of words such as transitive and intransitive verbs. This is an area where a sophisticated utility could be of the most help; this is also the area where most utilities fail. Doug Clapp's Word Tools, MacProof, and Sensible Grammar are all utilities that try hard and fail miserably. None of these products are smart enough to understand the context of a word or a punctuation mark, so they bug you about every single word and phrase in a document, killing time and frustrating you into submission long before you find any real mistakes.

Our only vote for a remotely useful style guide is the Associated Press Stylebook. Though it makes no attempts to search a document for problems, it provides a wealth of information for users smart enough to ask the right questions.

Keynotes Associated Press Stylebook

If you feel patient enough to suffer through an abhorrent interface (ported over from DOS), the AP Stylebook is a great on-line style handbook. It doesn't search for inappropriate usage; you have to look up specific questions yourself. But if you write for a living, there is information in this desk accessory that you simply can't get anywhere else.

Unfortunately, the AP Stylebook is about as interactive as a diary with a lock on it. You have the choice of either opening a style dictionary or returning to a previous one. We kid you not, that is the end of your options. You can't even look up the version number.

File-Saving Formats

In the following pages, we will look at some popular word-processing applications and examine their capabilities. To the right of each program name will be a list of the file-saving formats that the program supports. Unfortunately, word formats are not as standardized as other file-saving formats on the Mac. So most word processors and page-layout applications have to support a wide variety of other applications' native formats in order to retain text-formatting attributes such as font, type style, tab settings, and so on.

The only two formats that are even remotely standardized are RTF and TEXT.

- **RTF** (rich text format). This format was developed by Microsoft for the express purpose of transferring formatted text between applications and different types of computers. An RTF document is basically an ASCII file (text-only) with embedded formatting commands. Unfortunately, few Macintosh applications currently support this format, generally opting to save in the Microsoft Word native format instead.

- **TEXT** (text-only). This format retains characters only, including such nonprinting characters as carriage returns and tabs. No formatting is retained, however, so all text is changed to 12-point Geneva with automatic leading.

Each of the remaining formats is a native format of one application that is supported by a competing application. A document saved in any of these formats retains all character and paragraph formatting.

- **WDBN**. This is the native format of Microsoft Word and other Microsoft products. A file saved in this format may be specifically compatible with Word 1.0/Microsoft Works, Word 3.0/Microsoft Write, Word 4.0, or Word MS-DOS.

- **WORD**. This is the native format of MacWrite (different from that of MacWrite II).

- **nX^d**. This is the native format of T/Maker's medium-feature word processor, WriteNow.

- **otln**. This is the native format of Symmetry's outlining utility, Acta.

- **WPPC**. This is the native format of WordPerfect 4.2 on the PC.

- **Native formats**. Other native formats also exist, though they are not as commonly supported as those shown above. In our listings, the unique format of an application is followed by the word *native* in parentheses.

Ruler of the Word

Microsoft Word, Version 4.0   WDBN (native), RTF, TEXT, WORD
The greatest thing about Word 4.0 is that the placement of commands finally makes sense. We've been using Word for years, but we could never have told you what menu held any command besides maybe OPEN and SAVE. Not only are commands more logically organized now, but they can be moved, eliminated, or added, depending on your personal preferences.

Almost 300 commands are available, though only the usual 50 or so are included in the menus when you start the program for the first time. The rest may be added by you.

To add a command, first choose COMMANDS from the EDIT menu. The resulting dialog box contains a scrolling list of every possible command Word offers. Select a command that you want to add. If it already exists in a menu, the "Menu" option will be dimmed and a REMOVE button will be displayed. If not, the option offers a pop-up of menu choices, beginning with Word's recommendation. If you accept the recommended menu, the command will appear at a location in the menu where Word deems it most logical. If you choose a different menu, the command is simply appended to the end.

The "Keys" option offers a list of keyboard equivalents recommended by Word. You may add a keyboard equivalent by clicking the ADD button and pressing some key combination. When you are finished, click the ADD button near the "Menu" option and your command will be added according to your specifications. Incidentally, any command with a keyboard equivalent can be accessed even if it doesn't appear in a menu.

Setting Up Rows and Columns

Word's table handling is another big improvement over previous versions. Basically, you can add cells much like those in Microsoft Excel or a similar spreadsheet (except that they don't calculate) by choosing the INSERT TABLE command from the DOCUMENT menu and entering the number of rows and columns in the resulting dialog box. You may also convert tabbed text to a table using this command. Once the table is created, you may press the TAB and RETURN keys to travel through the cells. To select an entire column, click on one of the round end-of-cell markers displayed when the SHOW ¶ command is chosen from the EDIT menu. To select a row, drag across it. You may also alter the width of a column by clicking on the scale icon in the lower-right portion of the ruler and dragging the T-shaped column markers. To insert or delete cells, choose the TABLES command from the EDIT menu.

Cells are automatically converted to text if you save a file in any format but Word 4.0.

Microsoft Word Quick Reference (1 of 5)

Ruler

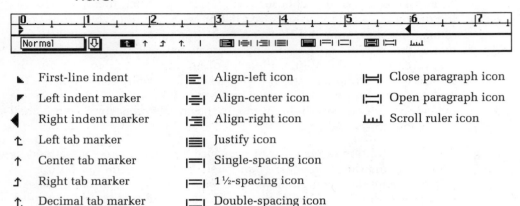

▟ First-line indent |≡| Align-left icon |⊨| Close paragraph icon

▛ Left indent marker |≡| Align-center icon |⊏| Open paragraph icon

◀ Right indent marker |≡| Align-right icon   ⊔⊔ Scroll ruler icon

↿ Left tab marker |≡| Justify icon

↑ Center tab marker |=| Single-spacing icon

⇞ Right tab marker |=| 1½-spacing icon

↑. Decimal tab marker |⊏| Double-spacing icon

| Vertical-bar tab marker

Menus

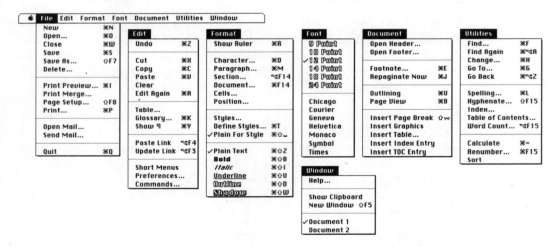

Microsoft Word Quick Reference (2 of 5)

Keyboard Equivalents

Activate menu bar .... ⌘➜। *or* ▦ .

Add to menu .... ⌘⌥=, 🖈 *item to add*

Again (repeat last operation) .... ⌘A

All caps text .... ⌘⇧K *or* ⇧F10

Bold text .... ⌘⇧B *or* F10

Calculate .... ⌘=

Cancel operation .... ⌘.

Caret or circumflex character (in search)‡ .... ^^

Center text .... ⌘⇧C

Change font .... ⌘⇧E, *font name or number,* ↵

Change specified text (search and replace) ..... ⌘H

Change style .... ⌘⇧S, *style name or number,* ↵

Character specifications .... ⌘D *or* F14

Clear element .... ▦⌦

Close document .... ⌘W

Copy as PICT image .... ⌘⌥D

Copy element .... ⌘C *or* F3

Copy paragraph format to
destination .... ⌘⌥V, *or* ⇧F4, ⌁🖈 *phrase,* ↵

Copy to destination .... ⌘⌥C *or* ⇧F3,
🖈 *point in text,* ↵

Cut element .... ⌘X *or* F2

Define style sheets .... ⌘T

Delete next letter .... ⌘⌥F *or* ⌦

Delete next word .... ⌘⌥G

Delete preceding letter .... ⌫

Delete preceding word .... ⌘⌥⌫

Document menu, display .... ⌘➜।, 5

Document specifications (real page setup) .. ⌘F14

Dotted underline text .... ⌘⇧\ *or* ⌥F12

Double-space text .... ⌘⇧Y

Double-underline text .... ⌘⇧[*or* ⇧F12

Edit link .... ⌥F2

Edit menu, display .... ⌘➜।, 2

Enter character
via ASCII code .... ⌘⌥Q, *ASCII number,* ↵

Extend selection
to character .... ⌘⇧H *or* ▦ - , *character key*

FILE menu, display .... ⌘➜।, 1

Find next format .... ⌘⌥R

Find specified text .... ⌘F

Find text again (next occurrence) .... ⌘⌥A

First line indent, nudge ½ inch .... ⌘⇧F

FONT menu, display .... ⌘➜।, 4

Footnote, reference .... ⌘E

‡ *Specifically for use in the FIND or CHANGE dialog box*

⌘	command	➜।	tab	⌦	delete	⎵	space bar
⇧	shift	↵	return	⌫	fwd. delete	F1	function key
⌥	option	⌁	enter	▦	keypad key	🖈	mouse click
⌃	control	⎋	escape	▦⌫	clear	⌁🖈	mouse drag

Microsoft Word Quick Reference (3 of 5)

Keyboard Equivalents (Cont.)

FORMAT menu, display .... ⌘➜I, 3

Formula character (.\) .... ⌘⌥\

Formula character (in search)‡ .... ^\

GLOSSARY dialog, display .... ⌘K

Glossary phrase,
insert into text .... ⌘⌫, *glossary name*, ↵

Go back to preceding location .... ⌘⌥Z *or* ⌨0

Go to specified page .... ⌘G

Hanging indent, nudge ½ inch .... ⌘⇧T

Help .... ⌘/ *or* HELP

Hidden text .... ⌘⇧X *or* ⌥F9

HYPHENATION dialog, display .... ⇧F15

Increase type size .... ⌘⇧>

Italic text .... ⌘⇧I *or* F11

Justify text (full justification) .... ⌘⇧J

Left-justify text .... ⌘⇧L

Left margin indent, nudge ½ inch (nest) ..... ⌘⇧N

Left margin indent, nudge back (unnest) ..... ⌘⇧M

Line break .... ⇧↵

Line-break character (in search)‡ .... ^n

Move down one line .... ↓ *or* ⌨2

Move down one screen ... ⌨3, ⌘⌥., *or* PAGE DOWN

Move left one letter .... ← *or* ⌨4

Move left one word .... ⌘← *or* ⌘⌨4

Move right one letter .... → *or* ⌨6

Move right one word .... ⌘→ *or* ⌘⌨6

Move to beginning
of current paragraph .... ⌘↑, ⌘⌨8, *or* ⌘⌥Y

Move to beginning
of next paragraph .... ⌘↓, ⌘⌨2, *or* ⌘⌥B

Move to beginning of current line .... ⌨7

Move to beginning of current sentence .... ⌘⌨7

Move to beginning of document .... ⌘⌨9

Move to bottom of window .... END

Move to destination .... ⌘⌥X *or* ⇧F2,
🖰 *point in text*, ↵

Move to end of current line .... ⌨1

Move to end of current sentence .... ⌘⌨1

Move to end of document .... ⌘⌨3

Move to top of window .... ⌘⌨5 *or* HOME

Move up one line .... ↑ *or* ⌨8

Move up one screen .... ⌨9, ⌘⌥P, *or* PAGE UP

New document, create .... ⌘N *or* F5

New window, create .... ⇧F5

‡ *Specifically for use in the FIND or CHANGE dialog box*

⌘	command	➜I	tab	⌫	delete	␣	space bar
⇧	shift	↵	return	⌦	fwd. delete	F1	function key
⌥	option	⁓	enter	⌨	keypad key	🖰	mouse click
⌃	control	⏏	escape	⌨⏏	clear	⋯🖰	mouse drag

Microsoft Word Quick Reference (4 of 5)

Keyboard Equivalents (Cont.)

Nonbreaking hyphen .... ⌘~

Nonbreaking hyphen (in search)‡. .... ^~

Nonbreaking space character .... ⌘⎵

Nonbreaking space character (in search)‡ .... ^s

Normal style sheet, change selection .... ⌘⇧P

Open any file .... ⇧ choose OPEN or ⇧F6

Open existing document .... ⌘O or F6

Open space text (12 points before ¶) .... ⌘⇧0

Optional hyphen .... ⌘-

Optional hyphen character (in search)‡ .... ^-

Outline, collapse all topics .... ⌨- or ⌘⌥T, -

Outline, collapse
selected topic only .... ⌘⌨-

Outline, demote topic .... → or ⌘⌥T, L or ⌨6

Outline, demote topic
to body text .... ⌘→ or ⌘⌥T, >

Outline, display all .... ⌨* or ⌘⌥T, A

Outline, display first line only ..... ⌨= or ⌘⌥T, B

Outline, display formatting .... ⌨/ or ⌘⌥T, F

Outline, display topics
down to specified level .... ⌘⌥T, number key

Outline, expand all topics .... ⌨+ or ⌘⌥T, $

Outline, move topic down ..... ↓ or ⌘⌥T, , or ⌨2

Outline, move topic up .... ↑ or ⌘⌥T, 0 or ⌨8

Outline, promote topic .... ← or ⌘⌥T, K or ⌨4

Outline text .... ⌘⇧D or ⇧F11

Outlining mode .... ⌘U or ⇧F13

Page break .... ⇧⌥

Page break character (in search)‡ .... ^d

Page setup .... ⇧F8

Page view .... ⌘B or F13

Paragraph break above row in table .... ⌘⌥⎵

Paragraph break character (¶) (in search)‡ .... ^p

Paragraph break in front of cursor .... ⌘⌥↵

Paragraph break with same style sheet .... ⌘↵

Paragraph specifications .... ⌘M or ⇧F14

Paste element .... ⌘V or F4

Paste link .... ⌥F4

Plain for current style sheet .... ⌘⇧⎵ or F9

Plain text .... ⌘⇧Z or ⇧F9

Print document .... ⌘P or F8

Print preview .... ⌘I or ⌥F13

Question mark character (in search)‡ .... ^?

Quit Microsoft Word .... ⌘Q

Reduce type size .... ⌘⇧<

Remove from menu .... ⌘⌥-, choose command

Renumber pages .... ⌘F15

Repaginate now .... ⌘J

Right-justify text .... ⌘⇧R

Save as different name or location .... ⇧F7

Save document .... ⌘S or F7

Scroll down one line .... ⌘⌥/

Scroll up one line .... ⌘⌥[

Section break .... ⌘⌥∼

Section specifications .... ⌥F14

Select all text from cursor location
to beginning of document .... ⌘⇧⌨9

Select all text from cursor location
to end of document .... ⌘⇧⌨3

Select all text in document ...... ⌘⭠ in left margin
or ⌘⌥M

Microsoft Word Quick Reference (5 of 5)

Keyboard Equivalents (Cont.)

Select current
then preceding paragraphs .... ⌘⇧↑ *or* ⌘⇧⌨8

Select current
then succeeding paragraphs .... ⌘⇧↓ *or* ⌘⇧⌨2

Select entire line of text .... ⬆ *in left margin*

Select entire word .... ⬆⬆ *word*

Select next letter .... ⇧→ *or* ⇧⌨6

Select next word .... ⌘⇧→ *or* ⌘⇧⌨6

Select preceding letter .... ⇧← *or* ⇧⌨4

Select preceding word .... ⌘⇧← *or* ⌘⇧⌨4

Shadow text .... ⌘⇧W *or* ⌥F11

Show/hide ¶ markers and spaces .... ⌘Y

Show/hide rulers .... ⌘R

Small caps text .... ⌘⇧H *or* ⌥F10

Sort in descending order .... ⇧, *choose* Sort

Spelling, check .... ⌘L *or* F15

Split window in half .... ⌘⌥S *or* ⬆⬆ *split bar*

Split window
to display footnote ...... ⌘⇧⌥S *or* ⇧⌁⬆ *split bar*

Strikethru text .... ⌘⇧/

Subscript text .... ⌘⇧-

Superscript text .... ⌘⇧=

Symbol font, change selection .... ⌘⇧Q

Tab character (in search)[‡] .... ^t

Tab character inside cell .... ⌥→|

Table, move one cell down .... ↓ *or* ⌘⌥⌨2

Table, move one cell left .... ⌘⌥⌨4

Table, move one cell right .... ⌘⌥⌨6

Table, move one cell up .... ↑ *or* ⌘⌥⌨8

Table, move to next cell .... → *or* ⌘⌥⌨3 *or* →|

Table, move to
preceding cell .... ←, ⇧→|, *or* ⌘⌥⌨9

Table, select entire column .... ⌥⬆

Table, select entire row .... ⬆⬆

Table, select entire table .... ⌥⬆⬆

Underline text .... ⌘⇧U *or* F12

Undo/redo last operation .... ⌘Z *or* F1

Update link .... ⌥F3

Utilities menu, display .... ⌘→|, 6

White space (nonword) character[‡] .... ^w

Wild card for a single character[‡] .... ?

Windows menu, display .... ⌘→|, 7

Word count .... ⌥F15

Word-only underline text .... ⌘⇧] *or* ⌘F12

[‡] *Specifically for use in the* FIND *or* CHANGE *dialog box*
Accurate for Microsoft Word, version 4.0

⌘	command	→|	tab	⊠	delete	▬	space bar
⇧	shift	↵	return	⊠	fwd. delete	F1	function key
⌥	option	⌁	enter	⌨	keypad key	⬆	mouse click
⌃	control	⌁	escape	⌨⌁	clear	⌁⬆	mouse drag

Ten Hottest Word Tips

Command placement and tables are only a couple of Word's powerful features. Microsoft has gone a long way toward cleaning up this program in its most recent upgrade, particularly in small areas such as text formatting. For example, you can now turn a selected line of bold italic type into plain type by pressing COMMAND-SHIFT-Z instead of first de-bolding and then de-italicizing.

The following are some additional hints designed to help you make more effective use of Microsoft Word. (Tips marked with [†] work only in version 4.0 when editing files saved in the Word 4.0 format.)

◇ **Searching for unusual characters.** The CHANGE command under the EDIT menu can be used to locate and replace nonstandard characters. For example, you may eliminate double spaces in a document by searching for two spaces and replacing them with one. To search for a carriage return, enter ^p in the "Find" option. To locate a tab, enter ^t. To find a circumflex or caret (^), enter ^^. Other search strings are included in the Microsoft Word Quick Reference.

◇ **Document setup.** Both Word 3.0 and Word 4.0 provide special DOCUMENT SETUP dialog boxes that you access by clicking the DOCUMENT button in the otherwise useless PAGE SETUP dialog. To display this dialog in version 3.0, press SHIFT and choose the PAGE SETUP command from the FILE menu. To access this dialog directly in version 4.0, choose the DOCUMENT command from the FORMAT menu or press COMMAND-F14.

◇ **Splitting the window in half.** Like most Microsoft products, Word allows you to split the window into two separately scrolling parts by dragging at the black split bar at the top of the vertical scroll bar. If you want to quickly split the window in half, simply press COMMAND-OPTION-S or double-click on the split bar.

◇ **Going back to where you left off.** The GO BACK command under the UTILITIES menu can be extremely useful in long documents, eliminating much tedious scrolling back and forth. For example, choosing GO BACK will return your cursor to the last place you were working after copying some text in another portion of the document. Also, if you press COMMAND-OPTION-Z (the keyboard equivalent for the command) immediately upon opening a Word file, you will be sent to the exact spot where you left off last session.[†]

◇ **Trashing temp files.** Microsoft Word has a habit of cluttering System folders with Word Temp files. They only take up 1K apiece, but it's easy to accumulate them over time. An init called Temperament by John Rotenstein, available on most bulletin-board systems, automatically gets rid of all these files every time you restart your computer.

◇ **Putting Word Finder where it belongs.** The version of Word Finder included with Microsoft Word versions 3.0 and 4.0 cannot be opened in any other application, so there's no sense in cluttering up your Apple menu in other programs. We recommend installing the Word Finder DA into Word instead of your System. To accomplish this, option-click on the Open button in the Font/DA Mover; this allows you to open applications and other files. Then select Microsoft Word and copy Word Finder as you would any other DA.

◇ **Multiple menu configurations.** Normally, when you use the Command command to add or subtract commands or to change keyboard equivalents, all changes are saved to a file called Word Settings (4) in your System folder. You may, however, save a changed set of commands under a different file name if you choose. Although Word automatically uses the Word Settings (4) configuration when launching, you can open a different set of commands at any time.[†]

◆ **Summing up.** Not only does Word allow you to create charts, but you may also perform some calculations. For example, if you have a table full of figures, you can find their sum by selecting the column and pressing COMMAND-=. Word adds up all numbers it finds and displays the sum in the page-number box at the bottom of the window. The sum is also sent to the Clipboard so you can paste it in your document. You may also add numbers included in a selected paragraph. If you only want to add numbers in one column or selective numbers in a paragraph, you may option-drag to marquee an area of text and then press COMMAND-=.[†]

◆ **Mathematical expressions.** Word's formula generator allows you to express fractions quickly and easily, without having to perform a lot of tedious superscripting and kerning. To activate Word's formula-formatting abilities, you simply press COMMAND-OPTION-BACKSLASH (\), which creates the \ character. Then type a one-letter command followed by an argument. For example, to create the fraction

$$\frac{1}{4}$$

you simply type .\F(1,4) where *F* is the command letter for *fraction*. To create the radical expression

$$\sqrt{a^2+b^2}$$

type .\R(a²+b²) where the *2*s are manually superscripted.

Now here's the best one as well as the most complicated. To create a bracketed series such as

$$\left.\begin{array}{c} \text{Alice} \\ \text{Meg} \\ \text{Teddy} \\ \text{Mike} \end{array}\right\} \text{quarterfinals team}$$

type ".\B.\RC.\}(.\A.\AC(Alice,Meg,Teddy,Mike)) quarterfinals team" where *B* is the bracket command, *RC* aligns the bracket on the right side of the argument, and } represents the kind of bracket to be used. In parentheses, the *A* tells Word that the following is an array of text to be set in a column, and *AC* centers the column.

(Expressions will only be displayed correctly on screen when the HIDE ¶ command is chosen. Also, the Symbol screen font must be available in your System for the square-root expression to be printed accurately.)

◆ **Updating worksheets and graphics.** If you use MultiFinder, Word's QuickSwitch feature allows you to update graphics and worksheets pasted in from other applications. For example, if you copy a worksheet from Excel and choose the PASTE LINK command in Word, a link is created between the Word and Excel documents. If you later make changes to the worksheet in Excel, you may update the table in your Word file by selecting the table and choosing the UPDATE LINK command from the EDIT menu. If you want to edit the worksheet while in Word, press the SHIFT key to change UPDATE LINK to EDIT LINK and choose the command. This will automatically transfer you to the Excel document.[†]

Writing Wordly Wrongs

Now that we've looked at the most popular and very probably the most powerful word processor for the Mac, we should take a step back and look at where it all started. The "Write" programs, including MacWrite, Microsoft Write, and WriteNow, are all entry-level programs with a reasonable price tag and enough features for the average user.

 MacWrite II, Version 1.0v2   MW2D (native), TEXT, WDBN, WORD, nX^d

In a way, MacWrite II has finally caught up with Microsoft Word 1.05. The most obvious improvement over its predecessor, MacWrite 5.0, is its use of single-ruler formatting. You no longer feel like you're creating text in a multi-level parking garage, with bulky rulers segmenting the screen at the end of each paragraph.

Questionable Gains

Much of MacWrite II we like, especially when compared with older versions. For example, you can search for a word in a specific font and style and replace it with a word in a different font and style. This is an extraordinarily powerful feature that has been long overlooked, in our opinion, and remains overlooked by most applications.

But nothing is worse, nor more frustrating, than waiting for an application to simply display its menus. We question whether MacWrite is sufficiently geared toward entry-level users. Though relatively inexpensive— $250, or $75 upgrade for owners of previous versions of MacWrite—the program is so exceedingly slow on a Mac SE, a reasonably progressive machine after all, that we would have serious reservations in recommending it to anyone with less than a Mac II.

 Microsoft Write, Version 1.0   WDBN (native), RTF, TEXT, WORD

Imagine Word 3.0 in Short Menus mode, and you have Microsoft Write. In a way, it has all the qualities that we've come to hate from the older Word, with little of its power. For example, unlike Word 4.0, Write doesn't provide an interactive page view. You can only see how your page looks and take care of problems after you exit the view. You might as well print the thing for all of that. Creating multiple columns is counterintuitive, just like in Word, and using headers and footers is clumsy, just like in Word.

MacWrite Quick Reference (1 of 4)

Ruler

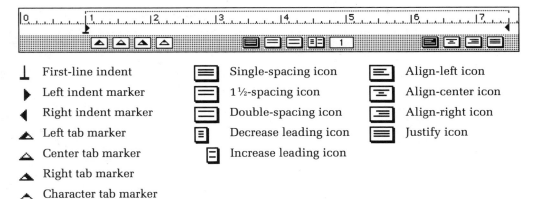

⊥ First-line indent

▶ Left indent marker

◀ Right indent marker

▲ Left tab marker

▲ Center tab marker

▲ Right tab marker

▲ Character tab marker

Single-spacing icon

1½-spacing icon

Double-spacing icon

Decrease leading icon

Increase leading icon

Align-left icon

Align-center icon

Align-right icon

Justify icon

Menus

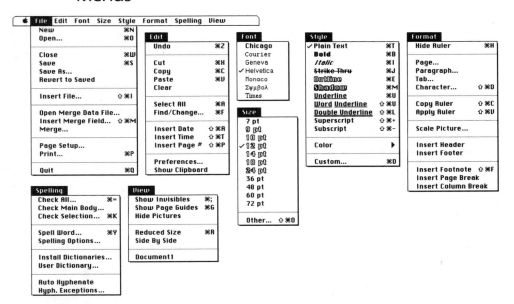

MacWrite Quick Reference (2 of 4)

Keyboard Equivalents

Actual/reduced size, toggle .... ⌘R
Apply ruler (paragraph formatting) .... ⌘⇧V

Backslash (in search)‡.. \ \
Bold text .... ⌘B
Bring next window to front .... ⌘⇧W

Character specifications .... ⌘⇧D
Check spelling of all text .... ⌘=
Check spelling of selected text .... ⌘K
Clear element.. ⌫
Column break .... ⌧ or ⌃C
Column break character (in search)‡.... ⌘⌧ or \c
Copy element .... ⌘C or F3
Copy ruler (paragraph formatting) .... ⌘⇧C
Custom style sheet .... ⌘D
Cut element .... ⌘X or F2

Date character,
abbreviated (in search)‡.......................... ⌘A or \a
Date character, long (in search)‡............. ⌘L or \l
Date character, short (in search)‡. .... ⌘S or \s
Delete next letter .... ⇧⌫
Delete next word .... ⌘⇧⌫

Delete preceding letter .... ⌫
Delete preceding word .... ⌘⌫
Double-underline text.................................. ⌘⇧L

Find/change specified text .... ⌘F
Footnote character
(in search)‡. .... ⌘⌥F or \f (⌥F)

Graphic character (in search)‡............... ⌘G or \g

Help .... ⌘ /

Increase type size .... ⌘⇧>
Increase type size 1 point .... ⌘⇧⌥>
Insert current date....................................... ⌘⇧A
Insert current page number .... ⌘⇧P
Insert current time .... ⌘⇧T
Insert footnote .... ⌘⇧F
Insert text or graphic file .... ⌘⇧I
Italic text .... ⌘I

Line break .... ⇧↵ or ⌃⇧M
Line-break character (in search)‡. ..... ⌘⇧↵ or \n

Merge break character (in search)‡......... ⌘M or \m
Merge form letter with data file .... ⌘⇧M

‡ *Specifically for use in the FIND/CHANGE dialog box*

⌘	command	⇥	tab	⌫	delete	⎵	space bar
⇧	shift	↵	return	⌦	fwd. delete	F1	function key
⌥	option	⌧	enter	⌨	keypad key	🖰	mouse click
⌃	control	⌔	escape	⌨⌔	clear	⤏	mouse drag

MacWrite Quick Reference (3 of 4)

Keyboard Equivalents (Cont.)

Move down one line	↓
Move left one letter	←
Move left one word	⌥←
Move right one letter	→
Move right one word	⌥→
Move to beginning of current line	⌘←
Move to beginning of current paragraph	⌥↑
Move to beginning of document	⌘↓
Move to beginning of next paragraph	⌥↓
Move to end of current line	⌘→
Move to end of document	⌘↑
Move up one line	↑

New document, create	⌘N
Nonbreaking en space (in search)‡	⌘⌥⎵ or \§ (⌥6)
Nonbreaking en space	⌘⌥⎵
Nonbreaking hyphen	⌘⌥-

Open existing document	⌘O
Optional hyphen	⌘-
Optional hyphen (in search)‡	⌘- or \-
Other type size	⌘⇧O
Outline text	⌘E

Page break	⇧⌥ or ⌃⇧C
Page-break character (in search)‡	⌘⇧⌥ or \b
Paragraph break	↵ or ⌃M
Paragraph-break character (in search)‡	⌘↵ or \p

Paste element	⌘V or F4
Plain text	⌘T
Print document	⌘P
Quit MacWrite II	⌘Q
Reduce type size	⌘⇧<
Reduce type size 1 point	⌘⇧⌥<
Save as different name or location	⌘⇧S
Save document	⌘S
Scroll down one screen	⌃L or PAGE DOWN
Scroll to beginning of document	⌃A or HOME
Scroll to end of document	⌃D or END
Scroll to last page of document	⌃⇧D or ⇧END
Scroll to top of next page	⌃⇧L or ⇧PAGE DOWN
Scroll to top of preceding page	⌃⇧K or ⇧PAGE UP
Scroll up one screen	⌃K or PAGE UP
Select all text from cursor location to beginning of document	⌘⇧↑
Select all text from cursor location to end of document	⌘⇧↓
Select all text in current document	⌘A or ★★★★★ in text
Select entire line	★★★ in line
Select entire paragraph	★★★★ in paragraph
Select entire word	★★ word

MacWrite Quick Reference (4 of 4)

Keyboard Equivalents (Cont.)

Select next letter	⇧→	Spell word (suggest)	⌘Y
Select next word	⇧⌥→	Standard (breaking) en space	⌘␣
Select preceding letter	⇧←	Strikethru text	⌘J
Select preceding word	⇧⌥←	Style sheet number [#], apply	⌘[#]
Select to beginning of current then preceding lines	⌘⇧←	Subscript text	⌘⇧-
Select to beginning of current then preceding paragraphs	⇧⌥↑	Superscript text	⌘⇧=
Select to end of current then succeeding lines	⌘⇧→	Tab character (in search)‡	⌘➡ or \t
Select to end of current then succeeding paragraphs	⇧⌥↓	Time character (in search)‡	⌘⌥T or \t (⌥T)
Shadow text	⌘M	Underline text	⌘U
Show/hide invisibles (¶s, spaces)	⌘;	Undo/redo last operation	⌘Z or F1
Show/hide page guides	⌘G	Wild card for a single character‡	⌘8 or *
Show/hide rulers	⌘H	Word-only underline text	⌘⇧U

‡ *Specifically for use in the FIND/CHANGE dialog box*
Accurate for MacWrite II, version 1.0v2

⌘	command	➡	tab	⌫	delete	␣	space bar
⇧	shift	↵	return	⌦	fwd. delete	F1	function key
⌥	option	⚡	enter	▥	keypad key	➤	mouse click
⌃	control	⎋	escape	▥⌫	clear	┈➤	mouse drag

Formula Editing

One high-end feature Microsoft decided to sneak in is Word's extraordinary use of formula editing, explained in the tips earlier in this entry. This powerful feature rivals the best of high-end word processors, and is well-explained in Write's documentation.

 WriteNow, Version 2.0   nX^d (native), RFT, TEXT, WORD
WriteNow has always been an elegant program, right up there with Adobe Illustrator and the first PixelPaint in delivering a moderate number of features in a clean, easy-to-use presentation. If only it offered style sheets, we would probably use it more often than Word.

As in Word, setting up multiple columns is a hassle—not something you're likely to figure out without the manual. In fact, it's hard to imagine a more roundabout and, we must admit, less elegant method. The left and right margins of each paragraph form the gap between columns, which makes things difficult enough. But if the margins vary from paragraph to paragraph, you can really have a mess on your hands.

Fast Type

By and large, though, we love this program. It only takes up 102K worth of disk space; and for that, it's about nine times as fast as the 596K MacWrite. WriteNow also offers some of the best superscripting and subscripting control we've seen this side of Aldus FreeHand (of all programs). You may superscript a character in large increments by repeatedly applying the SUPERSCRIPT command, or you may superscript in more precise increments by pressing COMMAND-H, the command's keyboard equivalent.

Our favorite feature, however, has to be the COPY RULER and PASTE RULER command set. You can select any paragraph, copy its paragraph formatting, and apply it to any other paragraph. It may not offer style sheets, but it gives you the next best thing. And at $150, the pint-sized WriteNow is simplicity at its finest.

WriteNow Quick Reference (1 of 3)

Ruler

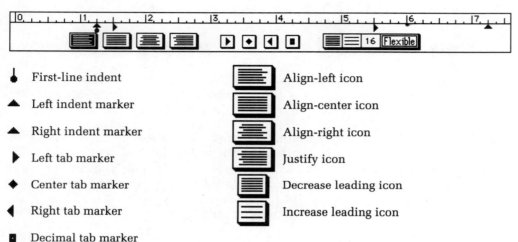

⬦ First-line indent	Align-left icon
▲ Left indent marker	Align-center icon
▲ Right indent marker	Align-right icon
▶ Left tab marker	Justify icon
◆ Center tab marker	Decrease leading icon
◀ Right tab marker	Increase leading icon
▪ Decimal tab marker	

Menus

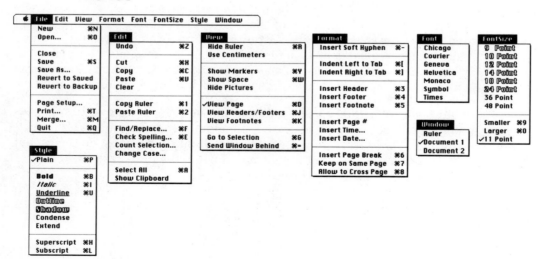

WriteNow Quick Reference (2 of 3)

Keyboard Equivalents

Allow selected paragraph to cross page .... ⌘8

Bold text .... ⌘B

Cancel operation .... ⌘.

Caret or circumflex character (in search)‡ .... ^^

Check spelling/next word .... ⌘E

Clear element .... ⌧

Close all open documents .... ⌥🖱 *Close box*

Compact document (rewrite) .... ⇧ *choose* SAVE

Copy element .... ⌘C

Copy ruler (paragraph formatting) .... ⌘1

Cut element .... ⌘X

Find/replace specified text
or find next occurrence .... ⌘F

Globally change identically formatted
paragraphs .... ⇧ *change ruler settings*

Globally change identically formatted
text .... ⇧ *choose font, style, or size command*

Go to selection (display cursor location) .... ⌘G

Increase type size 1 point .... ⌘9

Indents, move left one tab stop .... ⌘[

Indents, move right one tab stop .... ⌘]

Insert footer .... ⌘4

Insert footnote .... ⌘5

Insert header .... ⌘3

Italic text .... ⌘I

Keep selected paragraph on same page .... ⌘7

Maintain relative paragraph indentation
while reformatting .... ⌘ *change ruler settings*

Merge form letter with data file .... ⌘M

Move down one line .... ↓

Move left one letter .... ←

Move left one word .... ⌥←

Move right one letter .... →

Move right one word .... ⌥→

Move to beginning of current line .... ⌘←

Move to bottom of window .... ⌘↓

Move to end of current line .... ⌘→

Move to top of window .... ⌘↑

Move up one line .... ↑

New document, create .... ⌘N

Open existing document .... ⌘O

Optional hyphen .... ⌘-

‡ *Specifically for use in the* FIND/REPLACE *dialog box*

⌘	command	➜❘	tab	⌧	delete	▬	space bar
⇧	shift	↵	return	⌦	fwd. delete	F1	function key
⌥	option	⌁	enter	▦	keypad key	🖱	mouse click
⎈	control	⎋	escape	▦⌁	clear	⌁🖱	mouse drag

WriteNow Quick Reference (3 of 3)

Keyboard Equivalents (Cont.)

Page break .... ⌘6

Paste element .... ⌘V

Paste ruler (paragraph formatting) .... ⌘2

Plain text .... ⌘P

Print document .... ⌘T

Question mark character (in search)‡. .... ^?

Quit WriteNow .... ⌘Q

Reduce type size 1 point .... ⌘0

Return character (¶) (in search)‡.......... ⌥↵ *or* ^r

Save document .... ⌘S

Scale picture back to original size ..... ⇧🖰 *picture*

Scale picture freely .... 🖰🖰, ⌥┄🖰 *corner*

Scale picture proportionally .... 🖰🖰, ┄🖰 *corner*

Select all text in document .... ⌘A

Select entire word .... 🖰🖰 *word*

Select next letter .... ⇧→

Select next word .... ⇧⌥→

Select preceding letter .... ⇧←

Select preceding word .... ⇧⌥←

Send current window to back .... ⌘=

Show/hide ¶ markers .... ⌘Y

Show/hide rulers .... ⌘R

Show/hide spaces .... ⌘W

Subscript text 1 point .... ⌘L

Superscript text 1 point .... ⌘H

Tab character (in search)‡................... ⌥→| *or* ^t

Underline text .... ⌘U

Undo/redo last operation .... ⌘Z

View footnotes .... ⌘K

View headers/footers .... ⌘J

View page .... ⌘D

Wild card for a single character‡......................... ?

‡ *Specifically for use in the* FIND/REPLACE *dialog box*
Accurate for WriteNow, version 2.0

⌘	command	→|	tab	⌫	delete	⊔	space bar
⇧	shift	↵	return	⌦	fwd. delete	F1	function key
⌥	option	⌁	enter	▦	keypad key	🖰	mouse click
⌃	control	⌔	escape	▦⌔	clear	┄🖰	mouse drag

Outline Processing

If you've ever tried to create an outline in Microsoft Word, you know how dissatisfying and limiting it can be. In fact, only two word processors offer the kind of control you really need when outlining a difficult or complex project. Both have their limitations—neither handles standard text very well—but they provide environments conducive to organizing your work and your life.

 MindWrite Express, Version 2.1   RFT, TEXT, WDBN, WORD, otln, WPPC

Access Technology (now DeltaPoint) has survived a fairly long history of supporting application niches. Their software is like a bus that goes from one small town to another: Not many people ride it, but those who do need it dearly.

Like Trapeze, DeltaPoint's spreadsheet-layout application, MindWrite takes some getting used to, but most of its departures from the standardized Mac interface are for the best. For example, a hand tool, generally unheard-of in word-processing software, is used to drag entries to other positions in an outline. By shift-clicking on entries, you select noncontiguous lines of text. Neither of these may be what you expect at first, but they become familiar quickly.

MindWrite features the best built-in spell-checker we've come across. Completely customizable, it lets you specify whether to always expect capitalization after periods, whether to treat hyphens as spaces—we sure wish Word offered this feature—and whether to question double words, something most spell-checkers don't even look for.

 Acta Advantage, version 3.01   otln (native), RFT, TEXT, WDBN, WORD, nX^d

By virtue of convenience, our favorite outliner is Acta Advantage, a utility available as a desk accessory and a stand-alone program. For any writer, Acta seems a necessity; we can't imagine trying to create a book without it. You can outline your weekly meetings, your monthly priorities, your yearly goals, as well as articles and reports. And because Acta is available as a DA with almost all of the features of the stand-alone application intact, you can display and edit your outlines while using a word processor, spreadsheet, or page-layout application, without running under MultiFinder.

Outline entries are organized into a matriarchal family, consisting of mothers, sisters, daughters, and aunts. These relationships work as follows:

A. Mother topic

  1. Daughter of A

  2. Daughter of A and sister of 1

B. Sister of A and aunt of 1 and 2

Using the NEW SISTER, NEW DAUGHTER, and NEW AUNT commands, you may determine the relationship of new entries to existing ones. You may also sort all daughters of a subject into alphabetical or numerical order, as well as expand entries to include a paragraph or two of explanatory text.

Word Proximity

The ability to immediately display a word-processing file while in a graphics program or spreadsheet is often less of a convenience than a sheer necessity. The following word-processing applications are available as desk accessories, so you may access their files at any time.

 QuickLetter, Version 1.01   QLdc (native), TEXT, WORD
QuickLetter is the perfect correspondence DA. Not only does it provide the usual assortment of character and paragraph formatting features, it also includes a small database called the Address Book, in which the names and addresses of associates can be stored for use at the top of business letters and on envelopes. Printing envelopes is QuickLetter's strongest ability. You merely select an address and option-click the eye icon in the upper-right corner of the window; the address is immediately sent to the center of the envelope associated with the current letter.

Although it does not perform large document functions, QuickLetter does allow you to import artwork saved in the MacPaint format. (Unfortunately, the placement of the artwork is fixed in the upper-left corner of a document.) Also, unlike other DA word processors included in this section, Quick-Letter allows you to save formatted text in a widely compatible format, namely MacWrite, so that it can be imported into a page-layout application while retaining formatting.

ExpressWrite, Version 1.01   DIET (native), TEXT

ExpressWrite is a nice first effort. It isn't flawless, but it does offer a few features you wouldn't normally associate with a simple desk accessory. For example, you may access many menu items, such as font, type size, style, find and replace, and so on, by dragging at icons on the ruler bar. Also, if there's a standard paragraph that you use frequently throughout your correspondence, you may save that paragraph as a separate file. To insert the paragraph into future letters, simply click on the ¶ button in the ruler bar.

ExpressWrite also offers sophisticated mail merging, envelope printing, and multiple fonts, sizes, and styles in the same document. Unfortunately, ExpressWrite is sold without filters for other applications; so although you may open MacWrite documents (version 5.0 and earlier), there's no way to save a formatted file so that it can be opened by another word processor or imported into a page-layout program. You must save the file as a TEXT document and add formatting later, or cut and paste the formatted text into your preferred high-end application, which typically eliminates formatting as well. Generally, this DA is most useful for creating and editing letters that you intend to use strictly with ExpressWrite .

 Vantage, Version 1.1   TEXT

Preferred Publishers makes a point of emphasizing that Vantage is a *text* processor, preventing you from combining multiple fonts, sizes, or styles in the same document. Developed from a shareware Clipboard-editor utility called McSink, Vantage provides text-editing power to applications that lack such features. We used Vantage along with PageMaker to set up our first keyboard charts for this book, allowing us to sort entries in alphabetical order and to spell-check. All formatting was lost in this procedure, but it allowed us to experiment with various chart attributes, which were later standardized in a stand-alone word processor.

Batch File Clean-Up

But Vantage's greatest strength lies in its ability to perform the "clean-up" functions often required when transferring text files from one environment to another. For example, very few word processors support PC formats (the notable exception being MindWrite). And even those that do cannot hope to keep up with the zillion-and-a-half PC writing programs. When a file is transferred from an obscure application, paragraph returns may appear at the end of every line, tabs can turn into multiple spaces, and strings of code pop up in weird places. Vantage gives you the control needed to edit this electronic garbage out of files so you can use them in a word processor on the Mac or prepare them for exporting to other computers. And to make batch-file editing easier, Vantage provides a built-in macro editor, an absolute must for large-scale text editing.

Let Those Big Words Come Right Out

In the last couple of years, a lineup of powerful word-processing applications has emerged, clearly vying for Microsoft's crown. Each of these powerful competitors provides features Word lacks, though some are more frustrating than useful.

 WordPerfect, Version 1.0.2   WPDO (native), TEXT, WDBN, WPPC
The most popular word processor on the PC as well as other personal computers, WordPerfect is an established and reliable application with a much-hailed support staff and user rallies that resemble television evangelism. But in remaining true to its PC origins, WordPerfect violates some elements of the Mac interface that many of us have come to take for granted in any application.

PC Interface on the Mac

For example, most applications on the Mac work by applying commands to a selection. If you want to center a paragraph of type, you simply click in the paragraph and choose the CENTER command. But in WordPerfect, the CENTER command (available from the LINE pop-up under the FORMAT menu) centers all text in a line *after* the point where you click; text before this point remains flush left. This is because when you choose CENTER, you are actually inserting a formatting character that acts as a typesetting code affecting future characters. Therefore, you generally want to position your cursor at the beginning of a line to center it. But even then, if your paragraph contains more than one line, only the line marked by your cursor will be affected.

To return a line of type to flush-left alignment, you do not choose an ALIGN LEFT command, because there is none, nor do you rechoose the checked CENTER command to deactivate it. Instead, you delete the center character, made visible by choosing the SHOW CODES command from the EDIT menu.

Long-time PC users may find this approach to paragraph formatting perfectly acceptable. But Mac users with no previous WordPerfect exposure are not likely to take kindly to such an unnecessarily complicated procedure. It all depends on your perspective.

But if you feel comfortable with WordPerfect's pig-Latin system of formatting, there are many treasures to be uncovered. Its spelling checker and built-in thesaurus are particularly impressive. When making suggestions, the spell-checker provides both typographic and phonetic suggestions (the latter of which are especially useful to those of us who can't spell anything with more than five letters).

Instead of style sheets, WordPerfect provides a powerful set of macro commands. Though in theory macros are more versatile than style sheets, WordPerfect provides no macro editor, so if you wish to make changes to a macro, you must rerecord it from scratch.

The Single Hottest WordPerfect Tip

◇ **Where is that one character?** Although most fonts on the Macintosh subscribe to Apple's standard keyboard layout, you may not always remember where a special character like the ∞ or ‰ symbol is located. It's doubly difficult to remember a character in the Symbol font or in Zapf Dingbats. By choosing INSERT LITERAL from the EDIT menu, you display the SELECT CHARACTER dialog box, which allows you to select and insert any character in the current typeface. (To change fonts, choose CHARACTER under the FORMAT menu or press COMMAND-5.)

Select Character

	0	1	2	3	4	5	6	7	8	9	A	B	C	D	E	F

The INSERT LITERAL command can prove particularly useful for locating characters in oddball fonts like Zapf Dingbats. Interestingly, this feature even allows you to access characters that are entirely unavailable from the keyboard, such as those shown above with double outlines.

 FullWrite Professional, Version 1.1   FWRT (native), TEXT, WORD
Some applications are a little ahead of their time, not only in the sense that they provide more features than those currently available from similar products, but also to the extent that the features overwhelm a standard computer's ability to adequately process them. LaserPaint is our favorite example of this type of program. FullWrite Professional runs a close second. Put simply, FullWrite is the Arnold Schwarzenegger of word processors: immediately attractive but ultimately muscle-bound.

On the bright side, FullWrite offers a system of multiple windows for handling headers, footers, indexing, and a myriad of other types of text notations. For example, by choosing the FOOTNOTES command from the NOTES menu, you produce a window that allows you to enter footnote information for a specific item in your text. After closing the window by clicking in the Close box, you may redisplay it at any time by double-clicking on a footnote icon in the icon bar on the left side of your screen. FullWrite challenges a classic word-processing boundary by offering "live text" features normally associated with hypertext applications like Guide or even HyperCard.

Unfortunately, there are big problems. Paragraph spacing applies to an entire document, so that an individual "paragraph" such as a headline or a caption may not have different spacing. Also, there is no way to keep paragraphs together so they aren't split by a page break. But FullWrite's biggest problem is that it's slow enough to make MacWrite II look speedy. On any machine with less than 2 megabytes of RAM, the program crawls along, literally taking minutes to open a file or scroll to the end of a file.

One of FullWrite's most powerful features is its object-oriented editing window. On first examination, it seems quite spectacular. But if you give it some thought, you have to wonder: Here's a program that lacks several standard word-processing abilities that many of us have come to take for granted, and yet you can transform graphic objects, choose from alignment options, and set up an invisible grid, as well as create MacDraw-quality drawings from scratch. One can only imagine what flashy features FullWrite Professional 2.0 will implement at the expense of common text-editing capabilities. Three-dimensional animation? Geological-survey map production? Chest X-rays?

We hope Ashton-Tate pulls in the reins a bit on future versions, or at least curtails its ambitions with a little common sense.

FullWrite Pro Quick Reference (1 of 6)

Ruler

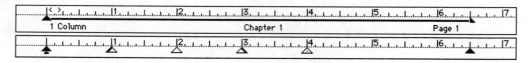

↕ First-line indent	◭ Left tab marker	‹ Delete column icon
▲ Left indent marker	△ Center tab marker	› Add column icon
◢ Right indent marker	◮ Right tab marker	
◣ Column width marker	◭ Decimal tab marker	

Margin Icons

▢ Header	▣ Bibliography entry	▷ Tab ruler
▢ Footer	▦ Contents	▽ Chapter ruler
▢ Posted note	▣ Index entry	▨ Classification marker
▢ Footnote	▣ Sidebar	== Column break
▢ Endnote	▣ Picture	= Page break
		... Multiple icons

In the icon-bar display mode, double-clicking an icon opens the respective note panel

FullWrite Pro Quick Reference (2 of 6)

Menus

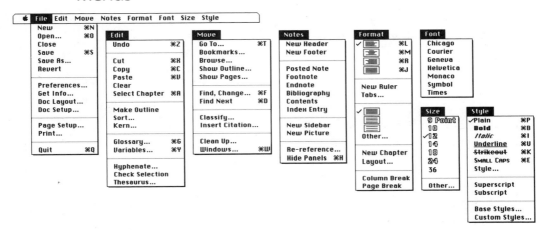

Note Panel Menus

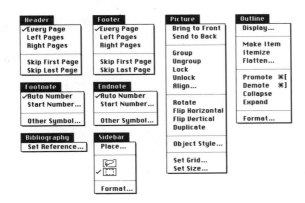

The far right menu changes depending on the currently displayed note panel

FullWrite Pro Quick Reference (3 of 6)

Keyboard Equivalents

Access last tool used[†].. ⎵

Action menu in Find and Change dialog,
display .... ⌘⌥4

Affect menu in Find and Change dialog,
display .... ⌘⌥3

Bézier control handles,
display to edit[†]......... ⌘⭢ *Bézier path ʷ/arrow tool*

Bibliography menu, display (if available) .... ⌘9

Bold text .... ⌘B

Cancel operation .... ⌘.

Center text (middle-justify) .... ⌘M

Change all option-box values to specific
unit of measure............ ⌘⭢ *measure abbreviation*

Change current option-box value to specific
unit of measure .... ⌥⭢ *measure abbreviation*

Change then find next occurrence of text .... ⌘⇧D

Change then find preceding occurrence
of text .... ⌘⇧⌥D

Circle, create[†]............................. ⇧⤏⭢ ʷ/ *oval tool*

Clean up windows again .... ⌥ *choose* Clean Up

Clear element .... ⌫

Close Bézier path[†]. .... ⭢⭢ ʷ/ *Bézier curve tool*

Close current note panel
and open next note of same type .... ⌘/

Close current note panel
and open preceding note of same type .... ⌘⌥/

Close current note panel .... ⭢ *Close box or* ⌘~

Close current ruler .... ⌥ *choose* New Ruler

Column rule,
activate/deactivate .... ⇧⭢⭢ *column rule*

Column rule,
edit for facing pages .... ⭢⭢ *column rule*

Column rule,
edit for single page .... ⌘⭢⭢ *column rule*

Copy additional elements
(append elements to Clipboard) .... ⌘⇧C

Copy character formatting
to selected text .... ⌘⭢ *formatted text block*

Copy element .... ⌘C

Crop bit map[†]........................ ⌘⤏⭢ *corner handle*

Curve point to corner point,
toggle[†].. ⇧⭢ ʷ/ *arrow tool*

Cut element .... ⌘X

[†] *Exclusively applicable to drawing in the Picture panel*

⌘	command	⭢|	tab	⌫	delete	⎵	space bar
⇧	shift	↩	return	⌦	fwd. delete	F1	function key
⌥	option	⤼	enter	▦	keypad key	⭢	mouse click
⌃	control	⎋	escape	▦⌫	clear	⤏⭢	mouse drag

FullWrite Pro Quick Reference (4 of 6)

Keyboard Equivalents (Cont.)

Delete next letter .... ⌘⌫ *or* ⌦

Delete next word .... ⌘⌥⌫

Delete preceding letter .... ⌫

Delete preceding word .... ⌥⌫

Edit menu, display .... ⌘2

End Bézier line[†]. .... ⌘ ▶ */Bézier curve tool*

Endnote menu, display (if available) .... ⌘9

Entry menu in Glossary dialog, display .... ⌘⌥2

Extend selection incrementally
to next phrase .... ⌘⇧➠I, *literal phrase,* ↵

Extend selection incrementally
to preceding phrase .... ⌘⇧⌥➠I, *literal phrase,* ↵

File menu, display .... ⌘1

File menu in Glossary dialog, display .... ⌘⌥1

Find and change specified text .... ⌘F

Find next occurrence of text .... ⌘D

Find preceding occurrence of text .... ⌘⌥D

Font menu, display .... ⌘6

Footer menu, display (if available) .... ⌘9

Footnote menu, display (if available) .... ⌘9

Format menu, display .... ⌘5

Glossary dialog, display .... ⌘G

Glossary phrase,
insert into text .... ⌘G, *glossary name,* ↵

Go to specified
page .... ⌘T *or* ▶▶ *page number box*

Hand tool, select temporarily[†] .... ⌥

Header menu, display (if available) .... ⌘9

Help .... HELP

Increase type size .... ⌘⌥=

Index selected text .... ⌥ *choose* Index

Italic text .... ⌘I

Justify text (full justification) .... ⌘J

Kern type, delete ¹/₂₀ em .... ⌘ -

Kern type, insert ¹/₂₀ em .... ⌘=

Left-justify text... ⌘L

Look menu in Find and Change dialog,
display .... ⌘⌥1

Match menu in Find and Change dialog,
display .... ⌘⌥2

Move down one line .... ↓, ▤2, *or* ⌘⌥;

Move element
by grid increment[†]...................... ⌥→, ↓, ←, *or* ↑

Move element single pixel[†].............. →, ↓, ←, *or* ↑

Move left one letter .... ←, ▤4, *or* ⌘⌥K

Move left one word .... ⌥←, ⌥▤4, *or* ⌘⌥H

Move menu, display .... ⌘3

Move right one letter................... →, ▤6, *or* ⌘⌥L

Move right one word .... ⌥→, ⌥▤6, *or* ⌘⌥ '

Move to beginning
of current paragraph .... ⌥↑ *or* ⌥▤8

Move to beginning of document .... ⌘▤7

Move to beginning
of next paragraph .... ⌥↓ *or* ⌥▤2

Move to end of document .... ⌘▤1

Move up one line .... ↑, ▤8, *or* ⌘⌥J

New bookmark, create .... ⌥ *choose* Bookmark

New document, create .... ⌘N

New plain document .... ⌘⌥N

FullWrite Pro Quick Reference (5 of 6)

Keyboard Equivalents (Cont.)

Next window
(bring second window to front) .... ⌘⌥W

NOTES menu, display .... ⌘4

Open existing document .... ⌘O

Open first note panel in current section ...... ⌘⌥~

Open next note panel .... ⌘⇧~

Open preceding note panel .... ⌘⇧⌥~

Optional hyphen .... ⌘␣

Outline, collapse topics
to specified level .... ⌥ *choose* COLLAPSE

Outline, demote all topics
at same level as selection .... ⌘⇧]

Outline, demote topic .... ⌘]

Outline, expand topics
to specified level .... ⌥ *choose* EXPAND

Outline, make item (new topic) .... ⌘↵

Outline, make new item
at specified level .... ⌥ *choose* MAKE ITEM

Outline, make new subordinate item .... ⌘⌥↵

Outline, make new superior item .... ⌘⇧↵

OUTLINE menu, display (if available) .... ⌘9

Outline, promote all topics
at same level as selection .... ⌘⇧ [

Outline, promote topic .... ⌘ [

Paste element .... ⌘V

Paste swap (exchange selection
with contents of Clipboard) .... ⌘⌥V

Perpendicular line, create[†] .... ⇧ ⁻⁻⁻⁻↖ *w/ line tool*

PICTURE menu, display (if available) .... ⌘9

Plain text .... ⌘P

Print current page .... ⌘⌥P

Pull object ahead[†] .... ⌥ *choose* BRING TO FRONT

Push object behind[†] .... ⌥ *choose* SEND TO BACK

Quarter circle, create[†] .... ⇧ ⁻⁻⁻⁻↖ *w/ arc tool*

Quit FullWrite Professional .... ⌘Q

Reduce type size .... ⌘⌥ -

Remove style
discriminately .... ⌥ *choose style command*

Return character (¶) (in search)[‡] .... ⇧↵

Right-justify text .... ⌘R

[†] *Exclusively applicable to drawing in the Picture panel*

[‡] *Specifically for use in the* FIND/REPLACE *dialog box*

⌘	command	⇥	tab	⌫	delete	␣	space bar
⇧	shift	↵	return	⌦	fwd. delete	F1	function key
⌥	option	⌤	enter	▦	keypad key	↖	mouse click
⌃	control	⏏	escape	▦⏏	clear	⁻⁻⁻⁻↖	mouse drag

FullWrite Pro Quick Reference (6 of 6)

Keyboard Equivalents (Cont.)

Save document .... ⌘S

Scroll down one line .... ⌥⌨3, ⌥PAGE UP, *or* ⌘⌥\

Scroll down one page .... ⌨3, PAGE DOWN, *or* ⌘\

Scroll to beginning of document .... ⌨7 *or* HOME

Scroll to end of document .... ⌨1 *or* END

Scroll up one line ..... ⌥⌨9, ⌥PAGE UP, *or* ⌘⇧⌥\

Scroll up one page .... ⌨9, PAGE UP, *or* ⌘⇧\

Search incrementally
for next phrase .... ⌘➔I, *literal phrase,* ↵

Search incrementally
for preceding phrase ...... ⌘⌥➔I, *literal phrase,* ↵

Select all text in chapter .... ⌘A

Select entire paragraph .... ⭠⭠⭠ *in paragraph*

Select entire word .... ⭠⭠ *word*

Select next letter .... ⌘→, ⌘⌨6, *or* ⌘⇧⌥L

Select next object,
deselect current selection† .... ➔I

Select next object,
retain current selection† .... ⇧➔I

Select next word .... ⌘⌥→, ⌘⌥⌨6, *or* ⌘⇧⌥'

Select preceding letter .... ⌘←, ⌘⌨4, *or* ⌘⇧⌥K

Select preceding object,
deselect current selection† .... ⌥➔I

Select preceding object,
retain current selection† .... ⇧⌥➔I

Select preceding
word .... ⌘⌥←, ⌘⌥⌨4, *or* ⌘⇧⌥H

Select to beginning of current
then preceding paragraphs .... ⌘⌥↑ *or* ⌘⌥⌨8

Select to beginning of current then
preceding sentences .... ⌘↑, ⌘⌨8, *or* ⌘⇧⌥J

Select to end of current
then succeeding paragraphs .... ⌘⌥↓ *or* ⌘⌥⌨2

Select to end of current then
succeeding sentences .... ⌘↓, ⌘⌨2, *or* ⌘⇧⌥;

Show/hide open note panels .... ⌘H

SIDEBAR menu, display (if available) .... ⌘9

SIZE menu, display .... ⌘7

Small caps text .... ⌘E

Square, create† .... ⇧⁻⁻⁻⭠ *w/ rectangle tool*

Strikeout text .... ⌘K

STYLE menu, display .... ⌘8

Subscript, specify .... ⌥ *choose* SUBSCRIPT

Subscript text 1 point .... ⌘⇧-

Superscript, specify .... ⌥ *choose* SUPERSCRIPT

Superscript text 1 point .... ⌘⇧=

Tab character (in search)‡ .... ⇧➔I

Underline text .... ⌘U

Undo/redo last operation .... ⌘Z

Variable control (page numbers, etc.) .... ⌘Y

Variable,
insert into text .... ⌘Y, *variable name,* ↵

Wild card for a single character‡ .... ¿ (⇧⌥/)

Wild card for a single word‡ .... ≈ (⌥X)

Window, bring any open document
to front .... ⌘W, *window name,* ↵

Windows control (bring to front, etc.) .... ⌘W

Zoom window to full screen .... ⌥⭠ *Zoom box*

Accurate for FullWrite Professional, version 1.1

Nisus, Version 1.01   TEXT (native)

Of the three powerful contenders to Microsoft Word, Nisus is the runt. While WordPerfect and Ashton-Tate represent two of the biggest names in software publishing, Paragon Concepts is a small company with one big idea.

One of our favorite features of Nisus is the way any option in a dialog may be selected via a key command. This is also true of other applications, such as Microsoft Word, but Nisus goes one better. If you can't remember a keyboard equivalent while in a dialog, simply press the COMMAND key, and a series of command sequences will appear on screen. And if you want to change a keyboard equivalent in Nisus, choose the MENU KEYS command from the PREFERENCES pop-up under the FILE menu. A dialog will then appear, asking you to choose a command and press a key sequence.

Nisus's searching feature is right up there with that of MacWrite II. But rather than allowing you to search only by format, Nisus lets you search text inside closed files saved in other formats. Choose the CATALOG command from the FILE menu to locate a set of files. (They must all be in the same folder.) After selecting the files you wish to search, choose the ADD TO SEARCH LIST command from the newly displayed CATALOG menu. Then search away!

Like FullWrite, Nisus offers a palette of drawing tools. Though they are less powerful than FullWrite's, they are easier to integrate into a document. We still think that drawing tools in a word processor is a lame idea, especially when so many type-specific features require improvement.

Section Three

Hardware

Accelerators/Coprocessors

Computer users always want faster computers. Traditionally, one attained a faster computer by selling the old one, and buying a newer, faster model. Recently, however, accelerator boards have become widely available, and very popular, because they allow you to gain faster computing speeds without the hassle and expense of selling the old and starting anew.

Accelerators are available in a wide range of configurations. You can give a Mac Plus or SE the speed and power of a Mac II, give a Mac II the speed and power of a IIx, and even supercharge a IIx so that it runs much faster than anything Apple offers. Accelerators use two strategies to accomplish these feats: faster processors and higher clock speeds. Most accelerators for the Mac Plus and SE replace the 8 MHz 68000 processor with a 68020 processor running at 16 or 25 MHz; these machines are then as fast as, or faster than, a stock Mac II. Less expensive accelerators for these machines offer a 68000 running at 16 MHz, achieving much less dramatic speed increases. Mac II and IIx accelerators usually offer a 68030 running at 25 or 33 MHz. (The Mac II has a 68020 running at 16 MHz normally, and the IIx has a 68030 running at 16 MHz.)

Your decision to buy an accelerator should, however, involve more than the bang you can buy for a few bucks. You should think first about what kind of Mac you are really going to have after your upgrade, and what your long-term goals for the machine are. Often, but not always, selling the existing Mac and getting yourself an entirely new one is a much smarter move, even though it is a more complicated procedure.

The fact is that there are more differences among the various Macintosh models than just raw speed. As explained in the Computers entry later in this section, differences in RAM expandability, ROM versions and up-gradability, slot availability, and future compatibility with the System Software separate the Macintosh models. Accelerator upgrades do not address any of these areas. For example, we think the Mac Plus is a very good computer value when compared with the SE in terms of power and speed. But what the SE offers is a slot for expansion and an upgrade path to the SE/30, meaning access to an entirely different generation of Macin-toshes. If you do not care about an expansion slot and the possibilities of future expansion, then accelerating a Mac Plus is a very good idea. In fact, given the current pricing structure, you can save significant money by accelerating a Mac Plus rather than buying a new Mac II.

The decision to accelerate an SE is somewhat tougher to justify, unless the relative portability of the SE is important to you. Current pricing in the new and used markets could enable you to sell your SE and hard drive and purchase a new SE/30 for only $300 to $500 more than the price of a good accelerator. You'll get a new Mac, a warranty, a 68030 instead of a 68020, and a 1.4Mb FDHD in the bargain, not to mention a virtual guarantee of compatibility with future System Software. These are the kinds of angles you want to examine carefully. Apple's SE to SE/30 upgrade will probably cost a few hundred more than the sell and rebuy strategy, but it is one of the fairest upgrade deals Apple offers and saves you the headache of phone calls from people who read the classifieds. Similar considerations surround upgrading a Mac II with a faster 68020 or a 68030 accelerator. You could very well get yourself a IIx or IIcx with all those other benefits without much price difference.

A Partial Listing of Accelerators for Macintosh

Name	CPU	Computer	Speed	Cost
Day Star Digital	68030	Mac II, IIx	25 MHz	$2,395
Day Star Digital	68030	Mac II, IIx	33 MHz	$4,095
Day Star Digital	68030	Mac II, IIx	40 MHz	$4,995
Day Star Digital	68030	Mac II, IIx	50 MHz	$5,995
Dove Computer	68020	Mac SE	16 MHz	$699
Dove Computer	68030	Mac II, IIx	32 MHz	$1,595
Dove Computer	68030	Mac SE/30	32 MHz	$1,599
GCC Technology	68020	Mac SE	16 MHz	$999
Irwin Magnetics	68000	Mac SE	16 MHz	$495
Irwin Magnetics	68020	Mac SE	20 MHz	$995
Irwin Magnetics	68020	Mac SE	25 MHz	$1695
Levco	68000	Mac 128, 512	8 MHz	$712
Levco	68020	Mac 128, 512	16 MHz	$2,999
Levco	68020	Mac SE	16 MHz	$1,499
Radius	68020	Mac Plus, SE	16 MHz	$795
Radius	68020	Mac SE	25 MHz	$1,395
SuperMac	68000	Mac SE	16 MHz	$399

If you do decide to buy an accelerator, shop carefully and consider both the vendor and the dealer whom you patronize. Lots of garage accelerators are available, but even the fastest benchmarks wouldn't convince us to put one in our Macs. We've been using a Radius in one of our SE's since it first came out, and we recommend the company and their products highly. Many other fine vendors are available; find a recent comparison in the major magazines, and ask around. (User groups and bulletin boards are great sources of "vendor critiques.") You'll be glad you did.

Coprocessors

There are two kinds of coprocessors available for the Macintosh: numeric coprocessors and PC-compatible coprocessors. **Numeric coprocessors** are special chips that are dedicated to performing mathematical operations. These chips can perform mathematical operations up to 100 times faster than a general-purpose CPU chip can. CPU chips such as those used in the Macintosh are designed to take advantage of numeric coprocessors when they are available, passing on any requests for mathematical computation to the specialized chip and getting the result when the computation has been performed. If no numeric coprocessor is available, the CPU just performs the mathematical calculation itself.

The Mac II, IIx, IIcx, and SE/30 include a numeric coprocessor as a standard feature. In order to add a numeric coprocessor to a Mac Plus or Mac SE, you must add an accelerator board that includes a numeric coprocessor; there is no socket for a numeric coprocessor on their logic boards. Not all accelerators include coprocessors; in some it is an option and in some it is not available.

PC-compatible coprocessors are complete add-on boards that provide the Macintosh with all of the basic computing hardware and capabilities of a PC-compatible computer. With one of these boards installed, software designed to run on the Intel family of CPU chips (8088, 80286, etc.) can run on the Macintosh. As discussed in the Connectivity entry in Section 1, you can also run PC software on a Mac using software emulation or by connecting the Mac to a PC via cables and using a remote-control program. The coprocessor boards are faster than either of these solutions, but are much more expensive and have limitations of their own. PC coprocessor boards for the Mac are available from PerfectTEK and Orange Micro.

Accessories

Any toy worth its wrapping paper is designed so that a wide range of after-market add-ons can rekindle that "Gee this is great" feeling as the months after the initial purchase pass. The Mac is no exception. A new CPU or monitor stand, a quiet fan, or a carrying case not only provides its own advantages, but also causes you to smile, look at your Mac in a new light, and use the word insane as an adverb.

CPU Stands

While the "compact Mac" case design of the Plus, SE, and SE/30 is aesthetically pleasing and could even be called cute, its ergonomics are not flawless. Placed on most desktops—the real kind, not the Mac kind—the internal monitor is uncomfortably low for many people. Raising the Mac a few inches off the desktop or tilting it up a few degrees can make those long hours of mouse-driving much less of a physical strain. Many Macintosh hard drives used to be designed to fit underneath the Mac, raising it 3 or 4 inches, but this design is less common now that not all Macintosh models use the compact body style. Of course, the entrepreneurs and conglomerates have stepped in to fill this void, and you can find a number of Mac stands just by browsing through a copy of *MacWorld* or *MacUser*. These range from simple plastic stands to sophisticated models that allow you to tilt and swivel the Mac at any angle.

For Mac II and IIx users, a pair of "legs" offers the option of getting your Mac off your desk and onto the floor next to it. Also available are extended cables to connect your monitor and keyboard to the Mac once it is on the floor; these cables may be required because the ones Apple provides are generally too short for this use. The Mac IIcx was designed to allow you the option of setting it on its side on the floor; thus the cables included with the IIcx are a few feet longer than those provided with the II or IIx, and are long enough for most configurations.

Monitor Stands

Many of the third-party external monitors available for the Macintosh include some type of monitor stand. The quality of these varies dramatically, however, ranging from low-end plastic legs to top-of-the-line "tilt & swivel" units. When considering the purchase of an external monitor, be sure to check out what kind of monitor stand is included. This is especially true for the larger monitors, which may have unique designs that will be difficult to use with generic monitor stands.

Unfortunately, Apple does not include a monitor stand with its 12-inch monochrome or color monitors, or with its new single- or double-page displays. Apple does, however, sell a tilt & swivel monitor stand for its 12-inch or single-page monitors for $89. Very similar display stands are available by mail order for about $65. If you can put up with having to lock your tilt & swivel into position (rather than being able to adjust it at will), generic monitor stands are available for as little as $12.

Another possibility is the monitor arms available through office-supply stores and mail-order catalogs. With prices ranging from $150 to $400, these products allow you to get your monitor completely off your desk, position the display to your satisfaction, and move the monitor completely out of the way when it is not being used.

Replacement Fans

According to legend, Steve Jobs was adamant that the original Macintosh not include a fan because he did not want it to be constantly making noise. As a result, Macintosh models before the SE (the 128k, 512k, and Plus) tend to build up tremendous amounts of heat, often to the point of singeing their cases and producing an odor not unlike that of melting plastic. Although many Macs have operated this way for years, it is widely believed that the lack of a fan contributes to the eventual demise of these Macs, most notably in the death of their power supplies. One Macintosh publication has claimed that 80 percent of Mac Pluses that are not enhanced with a fan will require a power-supply replacement within 18 months.

Several third-party vendors sell fans that can be added to one of these older Macintoshes. The most popular is Kensington's System Saver ($79), which is positioned in the "handle" on top of the Mac, where it forces air through the Mac's existing vents. The System Saver includes additional power outlets for two peripheral devices, and single or dual on/off switches for the Mac and the peripherals. It is available in beige or platinum. We've used a System Saver fan on our Plus-based AppleShare file server for about a year, and we find that it reduces the Mac's temperature significantly. Since the System Saver costs about half as much as a Mac power supply, it is a very good investment for anyone who keeps their Mac running a lot, and who believes it's better safe than sorry. Some less expensive fans used to be available, but they seem to have disappeared, as we couldn't find any in recent Mac publications.

Fans for the SE

Although Macintosh SE's do come equipped with fans, early production models used a terribly noisy one, which also produced electronic disturbance that caused the internal SE monitor to waver. A much better fan is now used in all SE models, but early buyers are not treated to a free upgrade by Apple, so they must pay for Apple's mistake themselves. If you have an older Mac SE that is too loud or causes your internal monitor to waver, the SE Silencer ($39) from Mobius is a great product for you. This easily installed device—you can do it yourself or have your dealer install it for you—replaces Apple's fan, completely eliminating most of the fan's noise and the monitor disturbance it causes.

Fans for the Mac II

A few brave souls have taken to replacing the fan inside the Mac II power supply, reportedly reducing the machine's noise by about 70 percent. Because this procedure involves taking apart the power supply, it is obviously not for the electronically uninitiated. A 3-inch DC brushless fan such as Radio Shack part #273-243A is used as the replacement part, and because these fans are technically rated slightly less powerful than the original fan, this replacement is not recommended for those using several NuBus cards. Of course, this modification voids your Apple warranty, and any AppleCare agreements as well. Complete instructions for this procedure are available in the Macintosh forums of the major on-line services.

Carrying/Shipping Cases

If you occasionally move your Mac Plus, SE, or SE/30, one of the many available carrying cases is well worth the $50 to $80 price tag. Most of these cases are made of heavy fabric, are liberally padded (although they are not suitable as shipping containers), and include plenty of room for your Mac, keyboard, mouse, cables, and usually a peripheral like an external hard drive or modem. (Be sure to specify that you need the extended-keyboard model when ordering if you use an Apple extended keyboard.) Many also include some room for a manual or other papers. Browsing through a recent Mac magazine will likely turn up several different models for you to choose from. We've been using one from West Ridge Designs for almost two years, and we recommend that brand highly.

If you need to ship your Macintosh, one safe bet is your original Apple shipping box and materials—if you still have them around. You should use all packing inserts that Apple originally included, as these are the key to the Mac's safety. For more heavy-duty protection or more frequent shipping, top-quality industrial shipping crates that meet the Airline Transport Association's standards for check-in luggage are available from several vendors. Among them are Linebacker Computer Luggage (800-228-7042), Orbit Systems (1-800-541-5421), and Zero Halliburton (1-800-327-1829).

 AppleTalk

An AppleTalk network is a combination of hardware and software that allows Macintosh computers to communicate with other computers. It also allows these computers to access compatible peripherals, including printers, scanners, and modems. AppleTalk is built around a specialized AppleTalk chip that is part of every Macintosh. In order to take advantage of AppleTalk, all you need to do is plug a LocalTalk connector into the Mac's printer port and physically connect each network device with LocalTalk cable.

AppleTalk Cabling Kits

Naturally, Apple sells the connectors and cables used to configure an AppleTalk network; Apple's connectors and cables now use the name **LocalTalk**. But a variety of third-party vendors offer connector kits and cabling options that are as good as or better than Apple's, and at far more reasonable prices (about $40 as compared with $75 from Apple). Farallon Computing's PhoneNET connectors are the original substitute for Apple's own AppleTalk connectors, providing a substantial cost savings, tripling the range of the network (from 1000 to 3000 feet), and relying on standard telephone cable, which is cheap and abundant, instead of Apple's expensive custom cabling.

Other companies have "cloned the clone," duplicating the PhoneNET system and offering AppleTalk connectors at prices as low as $30 per node. Our experience has been that these products work perfectly, and we have never heard reports of problems with any brand of AppleTalk connectors. We use a mixed network of COMPUNET, Farallon, and Apple connectors.

AppleTalk Extensions

A standard AppleTalk network can connect 32 devices, and the total network length should not exceed 1000 feet (or 3000 feet with PhoneNET connectors). Adding a Farallon LineDriver ($395) extends network capabilities up to 6000 feet by amplifying the network signal. The speed of an AppleTalk network can also be improved by devices called AppleTalk Accelerators. Normally, AppleTalk networks transfer data through their cables at 320 kilobytes per second (kbs). On a moderately busy network this means that using a remote hard disk is about the speed of working from a floppy disk. TOPS FlashTalk connectors or Dayna DaynaTalk connectors "accelerate" network data transmission to approximately 720 kbs. While this represents a speed increase of more than double, the effective speed increase of these connectors is more realistically only 50 to 100 percent.

DaynaTalk and FlashTalk connectors each cost about $175 and use telephone cabling like PhoneNET. DaynaTalk connectors may be added to any number of network nodes at once, but it is not necessary that every node use DaynaTalk connectors. FlashTalk connectors, on the other hand, must be added to every node on the network, and this may be a drawback if you already have some of your network in place.

Another way to speed up data transmission, while at the same time extending your network's capacity, is to replace your AppleTalk connectors and cabling with Ethernet connectors and cabling. Ethernet supports speeds up to 10 megabytes per second (4000 percent faster than AppleTalk's 320 kbs), but requires expensive cards for each machine on the network and uses heavy coaxial cabling in place of AppleTalk's twisted-pair cables. Ethernet boards for Macintosh SE's and II's cost about $600. To connect devices not using Ethernet to those that are using Ethernet, a network gateway is required, costing about $3000. Since Ethernet is not available for laser printers and other peripheral devices, a gateway is almost always needed when using Ethernet with the Macintosh.

Upgrading the speed or capacity of an AppleTalk network should only be considered if your AppleTalk network is heavily used to transfer data or access remote applications, and has eight or more users. The DaynaTalk and FlashTalk connectors are the best upgrade investment, and should be considered especially for installation on new networks where no investment in connectors has been made. You should undertake the installation of an Ethernet replacement of AppleTalk in very large networks where connection to existing Ethernet networks is required or multiple AppleTalk zones need to be linked. *MacUser* magazine (May 1989) tested the performance gains Ethernet offered, and found that while network data transfers were sped up by up to 43 percent, server operations were improved only slightly (2 percent), and no benefits in printing speeds were detected.

AppleTalk and PCs

Although originally designed for Macintosh-to-Macintosh communication, the AppleTalk network has been implemented on a wide range of computer platforms. Several AppleTalk cards, including Apple's own AppleTalk PC board, are available for the IBM PC and compatibles. With one of these boards and the appropriate software, PCs can access network peripherals, use network E-mail, and even share data from a network file server.

AppleTalk Network Troubleshooting

On a small AppleTalk network, the only real maintenance activity is to ensure that all cables remain properly connected to their machines and to each other. On larger networks, particularly those using a **bridge** or **gateway**, network maintenance also involves choosing the network configuration that will provide the best performance with a given set of computers and peripherals. Two different utility products are available to help you manage sophisticated AppleTalk networks.

Inter•Poll

Apple's Inter•Poll lets you quickly look at information about every device attached to your AppleTalk network, including the device name, node ID number, socket, zone name, and version number for the System file, Finder, LaserWriter driver, and Responder init. This is most useful for finding breaks or disconnections in your AppleTalk cabling, but is also helpful in resolving problems caused when different versions of the LaserWriter driver are used on a single network.

TrafficWatch, CheckNET, LWStatus, NodeHint

Farallon Computing, the maker of PhoneNet, offers a number of network-management utilities. TrafficWatch is a utility that monitors network activity; each connected device is listed in the TrafficWatch window, and the number of data packets sent or received by that node is tracked and displayed. If network bridges are used, TrafficWatch can inform you of the amount of traffic crossing the bridge (in either direction), but you cannot view traffic on the other side of the bridge. TrafficWatch can also export accumulated data to Excel, where two macros (included with TrafficWatch) then allow you to analyze and chart the network activity.

The CheckNET DA provides features that are very similar to those provided by Apple's Inter•Poll. With CheckNET you can quickly see all of the devices connected to your network, including their Chooser-designated user name and AppleTalk-selected socket number. This is used most often to locate breaks or disconnections in the AppleTalk cabling. LWStatus is a Chooser device that enables you to see the current status of any printer in the Chooser dialog box, making it easy to choose a printer that is not already busy rather than one that is. NodeHint is a utility that lets you specify the node number for any Mac on your network.

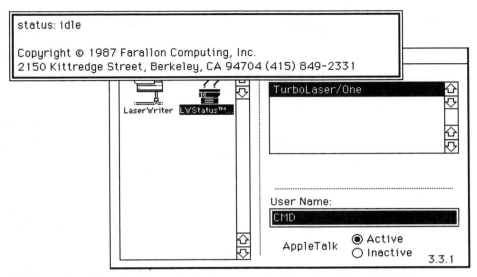

LWStatus is a Chooser device that allows you to determine if a printer is in use.

Computers

As of this writing, there are six major categories of Macintoshes and a total of 18 different Macintosh configurations available from Apple. Several additional models, including the long-awaited laptop Macintosh, are expected soon. Selecting which Macintosh model is right for a specific person or function requires finding the best compromise between cost and features. While it is impossible for us to illuminate all possible aspects of such a complex decision, the following paragraphs detail some of the more common arguments for and against certain Macintosh models. (Note that all prices are manufacturer's suggested retail prices at the time of this writing.)

- **Mac Plus vs Mac SE**. While the retail price difference between a Mac Plus and a two-floppy-drive Mac SE is over $1300, the differences between these machines are relatively minor. The SE uses the same CPU and clock speed as the Plus, although its reworked logic board yields a performance increase of approximately 25 percent over the Plus. The other important differences between these machines are the SE's 1.44Mb SuperDrive, optional second floppy drive, and the internal slot, which allows peripheral devices such as accelerator boards and large-screen monitors to be easily added.

If you are sure that you will not be adding a large-screen monitor, accelerator card, or other peripheral device requiring the SE slot, and are trying to keep your spending down, you might consider opting for the Mac Plus and spending part of the $1300 you've saved on a large hard drive. A Mac Plus with a hard drive is a vastly better Macintosh system than an SE without one.

The one important caveat about choosing the Plus over the SE is that the SE can be upgraded to become an SE/30, which includes all of Apple's latest technology, much of which will be vital upon the release of future versions of the System Software. The Mac Plus can only be upgraded with third-party products, and ultimately will not be able to take advantage of future Macintosh enhancements.

- **Mac SE vs Mac II, IIx, IIcx.** The retail price difference between a Mac SE and any of the Mac II's is about $2400, but there is a world of difference between these machines. The SE has its small size and relative portability going for it, but the IIs offer a 400 percent improvement in performance (or more if mathematical calculations are involved), and a choice of monitors (all of which are at least 40 percent larger than the SE's display). This decision comes down to budget, because any Mac II is a far superior computer to an SE.

- **Mac SE vs SE/30.** The retail price difference between the Mac SE and the Mac SE/30 is $1200, and for this the SE/30 provides one major benefit: a 68030 processor (running at 16 MHz). The 68030 provides not only a 500 percent increase in operating speed over the standard SE, but also full compatibility with future Apple System Software. One consolation for those who can't quite justify the added expense of the SE/30 right now is that Apple provides the ability to upgrade an SE into an SE/30 for about $1600, so you are not locked into any permanent disadvantage by choosing the SE.

The compact Macs are having a tough time defending their turf from the open Macs.

- **Mac SE/30 vs Mac IIx, IIcx.** For about $1000 less than a IIcx, the SE/30 provides everything the IIx or IIcx does, except it has no NuBus slots. Large-screen monitors can be added to the SE/30 for slightly more than $1000, in which case you would have all the benefits of the latest Mac technology, and portability.

- **Mac II vs Mac IIx vs Mac IIcx.** With base prices clustered within $600 dollars of one another, the choice between these three Mac II models may seem difficult. Well, it's not. We can eliminate the original Mac II because the IIcx is actually cheaper and the Mac IIx is only $600 more, yet both of these machines provide over $2000 in extra features and performance. So it comes down to the IIx versus the IIcx.

Although the IIcx is the newer model, sporting a smaller "footprint" and a few design improvements, the IIx offers three additional NuBus slots (which admittedly won't be needed by most people), a stronger power supply, and support for two floppy drives instead of just one. Also, the IIx can accept 5.25" or 3.5" hard drives, while the IIcx can use only 3.5" hard drives, which are more expensive. We think that two floppy drives are very nice to have, and believe that unless the physical size of the machine bothers you, the IIx should be considered for this reason alone.

- **Apple RAM and hard drives vs third-party RAM and hard drives**. Historically, Apple charged about double the reasonable price for the RAM and hard drives available in its computers. Recently, however, the prices of Macintosh models that include hard drives and RAM directly from Apple have become very competitive with third-party upgrades. For example, the current retail prices of an SE/30 with and without a 40Mb hard drive vary by only $500, which would be a very good price for the 40Mb hard drive. However, as the price of RAM has fallen, Apple RAM has become less attractive.

  Before deciding if you want to order your Macintosh with an Apple hard disk or extra RAM, shop very carefully for the current prices of comparable third-party hard drives and RAM. (The prices may have changed dramatically from those in effect at the time this was written.) If the price isn't competitive, there is really no reason to go with Apple's hard drives or RAM. Most third-party vendors provide better warranties than Apple does—especially on hard drives, where you can get up to a five-year warranty from some manufacturers, compared with the 90-day warranty provided by Apple. Installing a third-party hard drive or RAM is relatively easy, and if you don't want to do it yourself, any dealer will do it for a few dollars.

Opening Your Mac

While many people are comfortable tinkering with mechanical devices, most are hesitant about grabbing a screwdriver and diving inside of an electronic device. In consideration of the money that can be made by discouraging consumers from performing simple repairs and upgrades themselves (under the guise of safety, of course), Apple and other electronics manufacturers do their best to keep things this way.

In reality, getting inside your Mac is neither difficult nor dangerous—assuming that you have a little basic knowledge (which we'll provide) and use some common sense. There are a number of good reasons for opening the Mac: installing additional RAM, adding an internal hard drive, or adding a board to one of your computer's slots, for example. Of course, you shouldn't be embarrassed about *not* wanting to get inside your Macintosh yourself, and we encourage you to take your first trip inside the box with a more experienced friend or colleague, or just leave the whole business to an Apple Certified Technician.

Important Warnings

Before opening your Macintosh, be very familiar with each of the warnings listed below. These are the items that you must understand to avoid risking personal injury or damage to your equipment. Don't proceed unless you understand each of these important items.

◆ **Unplug your Mac before opening it**. With your Macintosh turned off, remove the power cord from the rear of your Mac. This makes it impossible for the power to be turned on accidentally while you are inside the Mac, and makes it much more difficult (but not impossible) for you to receive an electrical shock. You should usually not plug the Mac back in until you have replaced the cover—even if you just set the cover on and don't screw it in when testing a modification. In some cases, such as when making adjustments to the monitor, this is impossible, so extra care should be exercised.

◆ **Discharge your bodily static before touching anything inside your Mac**. The static charge carried by your body—the same charge that you may use to stick balloons to the wall or to zap your friend on the nose—is strong enough to end the life of any of the chips inside your Macintosh, and can therefore ruin your entire logic board or any other circuit board if not properly discharged. In order for you to feel a static charge it must be at least 3000 volts, in order to see a static charge is must be at least 5000 volts, and in order to hear a static charge it must be at least 10,000 volts—but a static charge of as little as 10 volts can damage a semiconductor chip, so you will not know when you have zapped one.

You can easily discharge your bodily static by touching any metal item, including the frame of your Mac itself (although you must not touch the ports, which will be damaged by any static discharge). A safer and more professional solution is to purchase and wear a static-discharge bracelet anytime you are working on your Mac or any electronic component. This consists of a Velcro bracelet with a small metal disk, about the size of a dime, that presses against your forearm. A wire is attached from the bracelet's metal disk to a grounded desk pad. These discharge bracelets are very inexpensive, and should be available at your local hardware or electronics store. Wearing one of these is the only way to ensure that you do not zap anything while working on your Mac.

◆ **On the compact-model Macintoshes (128k, 512k, Plus, SE, SE/30), never touch the flyback transformer on the power supply, or the flyback-transformer cable as it enters the monitor—except to discharge it.** The flyback transformer, which is located on the power-supply board inside the compact Macs, retains a strong electric charge for up to 48 hours after the Mac was last turned on. You can locate the flyback transformer by following the wire—which is usually red or black—that connects to the side of your internal monitor and goes back to the power board. Either end of this wire can provide a significant shock, strong enough to blow you across the room. It is, however, easy to work inside the Mac and avoid this wire. We've worked inside dozens of Macs, never discharging the flyback transformer (too chicken), without ever touching it.

Alternatively, if you need to remove the monitor or the front of the Mac case, or if you just want to eliminate the possibility of error, you can discharge the flyback transformer and the monitor. A special discharging tool is available, consisting of a thin steel probe attached to a grounded handle that has a wire with an alligator clip at the end of it. You can "make" one of these out of any insulated metal screwdriver, some wire, and a small alligator clip. To use this device, remove any jewelry (including a static-discharge bracelet), attach the alligator clip to the metal grounding lug on the Mac's CRT, and place one hand behind your back. Insert the head of the screwdriver under the anode cap where the flyback-transformer cable attaches to the monitor until it touches the anode ring. (Move the screwdriver slowly, and don't press so hard that you damage the monitor.) You'll hear a slight pop when contact is made as the static discharges. You can now remove the anode cap from the monitor entirely. Disconnect the alligator clip, and take your hand out from behind your back.

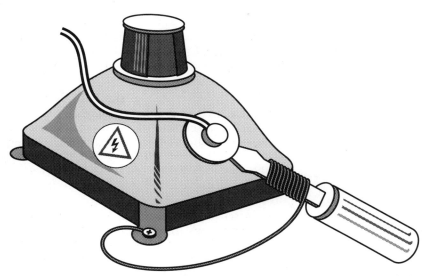

Discharge the flyback-transformer cable by inserting a properly grounded discharge tool under the anode cap on the monitor until it touches the anode ring. This procedure is potentially dangerous, and the complete instructions provided above should be followed.

◆ **Don't force anything**. When adding or removing parts, plugging in or unplugging wires, or doing anything else inside your Mac, you should never use excess force. Everything should fit well, and nothing but harm can come from forcing a part to go where it doesn't want to go. If force is needed, something else is wrong—perhaps the part is incorrect or not all the retaining screws have been removed.

◆ **Your warranty or AppleCare agreement may be voided if you modify any Apple parts**. Any modifications you make to Apple components inside your Mac will void your Apple warranty or AppleCare agreement. Of course, most Apple technicians do not take fingerprints. The most important point is that if you break something inside your Mac, don't expect Apple to pick up the tab for fixing it.

Opening the Mac Plus, SE, or SE/30

The original Macintosh case was designed not to be opened by the end user. Since this case design has endured on the Plus and SE models, opening these machines takes a little resolve. Rather than regular screws, these Macs have torx nuts, which must be removed with an allen wrench-like tool called a TORX T-15 (preferably with a 6-inch handle), or with an allen wrench with a 6-inch handle. TORX T-15 tools are difficult to find, but most hardware stores carry an allen wrench that will work perfectly.

1. Remove the two screws at the base of the rear cover, and the two screws that are located deep inside the rear of the "handle" at the top of the case. On the Mac Plus, you must also remove the battery cover and the screw that is located just above the battery.

2. Lay the Mac face down, and pull upward on the back half of the case. Because the case fits rather tightly, you may need to press against the ports with your thumb (but not too hard), or lightly tap the sides of the Mac to get the case to come free. Keep the Mac face down during this process; wrestling it from side to side will probably not help, and it may knock your monitor off center. Apple service centers use "case crackers" to pry the two halves of the case apart, but these are difficult to find, can easily scratch your Mac's case, and are not really required anyway.

When you are done, put the Mac face down again, double-check that you have put everything back in place—don't forget the thin aluminum cover that goes over the ports and the bottom of the logic board—and carefully slide the back half of the cover into place. It should snap down firmly. Lastly, replace all of the screws; the black ones go on the bottom and the silver ones go inside the handle.

Opening the Mac II, IIx, IIcx

Before the Mac II was officially introduced, it was often called the "Open Mac," primarily because of the NuBus slots it provided to allow easy expansion of the machine. The Open Mac and its newer cousins are certainly much easier to open than the Mac Plus and SE models. The only tool required to open these machines is a standard Phillips-head screwdriver.

1. Remove the retaining screw, which is located in the center of the back panel.

2. Make sure there are no floppy disks in the internal floppy-disk drives.

3. Press the tabs at each side of the back panel and lift upward from the back. Once the back has been raised 4 to 8 inches, lift the front edge of the cover up and away from the Mac. This angle allows the plastic hooks that secure the front ridge of the cover to clear the plastic tabs on which they normally catch.

To replace the cover on these machines, you must put the front edge into position first, so that the plastic hooks are positioned over their tabs as the back edge is lowered. Press down on the back edge to snap its plastic tabs into place, and then press down on the font edges of the cover, if necessary. Reinstall the retaining screw on the back of the machine.

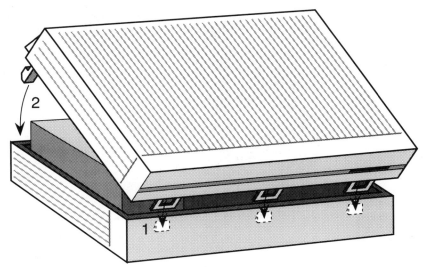

The cover of the Mac II, IIx, and IIcx hinges on three small tabs on the front of the Mac. When closing the Mac, move these tabs into position at an angle before lowering the back of the cover.

Removing a Floppy Drive

On the Mac Plus, removing the internal floppy drive requires that you remove the logic board in order to get to the screws that hold the drive's mounting bracket in place. See the next section of this entry for details on removing the logic board.

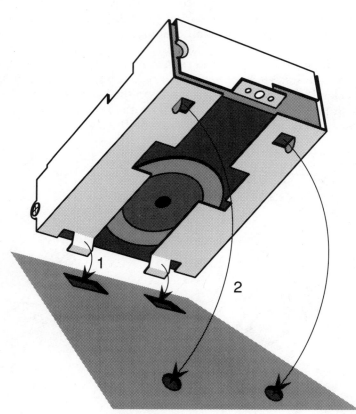

All floppy drives are held in place by two tabs near the front of the drive. The bottom drive on an SE is also held in place by two screws that come up from the frame. SE's with two floppy drives include a retaining bracket that must be removed before either drive can be removed.

On a two-floppy Mac SE, you can easily remove the top drive by simply removing the two screws and the retaining bracket that goes across both floppies. (Use a magnetic screwdriver or turn the screws their last few turns with your fingers so the screws don't fall down into the Mac.) You must also disconnect the ribbon cables that connect each floppy to the logic board. Keep a hand on the top floppy when removing the retaining bracket so that the drive does not fall forward, damaging your monitor; with the drive tilted slightly, it can be removed easily. Removing the lower floppy requires that you remove the upper floppy or hard drive, and then remove the logic board. (Instructions for removing the logic board are found later in this entry.) Four screws in the base of the Mac hold down the lower floppy drive. Remove these four screws and the drive is yours.

On the Mac II, IIx, and IIcx, floppy drives are held in by just one screw. Remove the screw and the drive cable, and then lift the back end of the floppy drive and pull the drive slightly backward to remove it.

To reinstall a floppy drive on the Mac Plus, remove the logic board, put the drive case into position, and secure the case with the four screws that go up through the bottom of the Mac. Reattach the floppy-drive ribbon cable. On the Mac SE and Mac II models, you must hook the metal tabs on the bottom of the drive case into position, and then secure the drive screws, or in the case of the upper drive on an SE, the retaining bracket.

Removing the Mac Plus Logic Board

After you remove the back half of the Mac Plus case, the first step in removing the logic board is to detach each of the cables that connect the logic board to the other parts of the machine. Keep the Mac face down while doing this; you generally don't want to set the Mac upright without its case. The main power cable is a multicolored band of cables ending in a rectangular plastic connector on the logic board. You can detach this cable by simply pulling it straight away from the logic board. (Don't pull too hard too fast, as your hand may go flying into the tip of the picture tube, causing messy and expensive damage.) A ribbon cable connects the floppy drive to the logic board, and you remove it by pulling straight away from the logic board.

Keeping the Mac face down, rotate it so that the bottom of the logic board is facing you. Remove the silver RF shielding that covers the bottom of the logic board, stand over the Mac with your hands on the sides of the board, and gently begin pulling it upward. You may need to wiggle it a bit, or press outward slightly on the steel frame holding the logic board in place. After sliding it upward about an inch or two, look at the logic board from the inside, and locate two wires that end in a small plastic peg plugged into the logic board. These are the speaker wires for your Mac, and you must remove them before completely removing the logic board. You may have to slide the logic board up or down slightly so that the speaker-wire connector is accessible. With the connector removed, slide the logic board the rest of the way out. After removing the logic board, you should place it on a soft, nonstatic surface such as a rubber mat—mouse pads do nicely— or a piece of cardboard. Plastic, metal, and Styrofoam are not recommended, as they may contain or conduct static electricity.

To reinstall the logic board, simply slide it back into the channels whence it came. Reinstall the RF shield, and remember to reconnect the speaker wires once the board is almost all the way in. (The connector only goes on one way.) Finally, reconnect the main power cable and disk-drive cables (neither of which can be plugged in incorrectly, owing to the design of their connectors).

Removing the Macintosh SE Logic Board

After you remove the back half of the SE case, the first step in removing the logic board is to detach each of the cables that connect it to the other parts of the machine. Keep the Mac face down while doing this; you generally don't want to set the Mac upright without its case. The main power cable is a multi-colored band of cables ending in a rectangular plastic connector on the logic board. On one side of this connector, there is a tab that you must press in to release the power cable from the logic board. This tab can be very difficult to press, but it must be done. When the tab is pressed down, pull the cable straight away from the logic board to remove it. (Don't pull too hard too fast, as your hand may go flying into the tip of the picture tube, causing messy and expensive damage.) One ribbon cable connects each floppy drive to the logic board, and you should disconnect these cables from the logic board before proceeding.

Keeping the Mac face down, rotate it so that the bottom of the logic board is facing you. Remove the silver RF shielding that covers the bottom of the logic board, stand over the Mac with your hands on the sides of the board, and gently begin pulling it upward. You only need to pull upward far enough to allow the tabs on the right side of the logic board to align with the openings on the frame. When these align, pull the logic board away from the case on that side, opening the logic board away from the Mac like a door. When it has cleared the case about 2 inches on the right side, remove the speaker cable that you will find still connected to the logic board. You can then remove the logic board entirely. After removing the logic board, you should place it on a soft, nonstatic surface such as a rubber mat—mouse pads do nicely—or a piece of cardboard. Plastic, metal, and Styrofoam are not recommended, as they may contain or conduct static electricity.

To reinstall the logic board, insert the left edge into the grooves on the frame, and use this as a hinge as you move the right edge toward the frame. Reconnect the speaker cable, and then fit the right side of the logic board into the frame's tabs. Slide it down into position. Reconnect the main power cable and the disk-drive cables. The drive cable for the upper drive should be connected to the socket closer to the edge of the logic board, and the drive cable for the lower drive should be connected to the socket farther away from the edge of the logic board.

Adding RAM to the Mac Plus and SE

RAM on Macintosh computers exists in Single In-line Memory Modules (SIMMs), which are small circuit boards holding eight RAM chips. One SIMM "stick" can provide either 256K or 1Mb of memory (depending on the size of chips it contains). Usually, Macs with 1 megabyte of RAM contain four 256K SIMMs ($4 \times 256K = 1Mb$), and Macs with over 1 megabyte of memory use 1Mb SIMMs or some combination of 1Mb SIMMs and 256K SIMMS.

SIMMs are rated by their speed: SIMMs used in the Mac Plus or SE must be 150 nanoseconds or faster. The speed of a SIMM board is usually marked on the chips it contains, coded with –15, –20, or –10, which indicates that the chip is rated at 150, 120, or 100 nanoseconds, respectively.

SIMMs are available in two "styles." Low-profile SIMMs use small RAM chips so their board size is reduced. Larger RAM chips are used in high-profile SIMMs, which are therefore larger in size. On the Macintosh SE, high-profile SIMMs may interfere with daughter boards that connect to the SE PDS slot (such as accelerator boards). When you purchase SIMMs, it is always a good idea to inquire or specify whether they are low-profile or high-profile.

In the Macintosh Plus and SE, sockets are provided on the logic board to hold four SIMMs of either the 256K or 1Mb variety. SIMMs cannot be

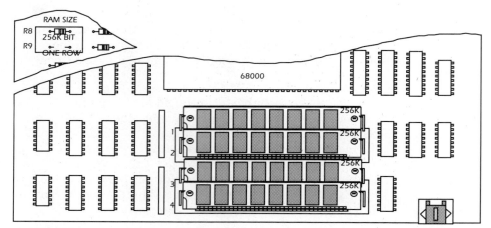

A Mac Plus with 1 megabyte of RAM uses four 256K SIMMs, has a 150 ohm resistor in position R8, and has no resistor in position R9.

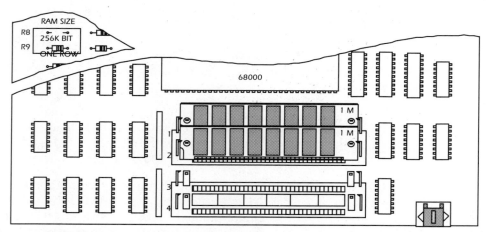

A Mac Plus with 2 megabytes of RAM uses two 1Mb SIMMs, has no resistor in position R8, and has a 150 ohm resistor in position R9.

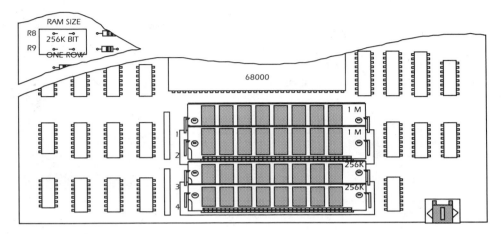

A Mac Plus with 2.5 megabytes of RAM uses 1Mb SIMMs in slots 1 and 2, and 256K SIMMs in slots 3 and 4. No resistors are used in position R8 or R9.

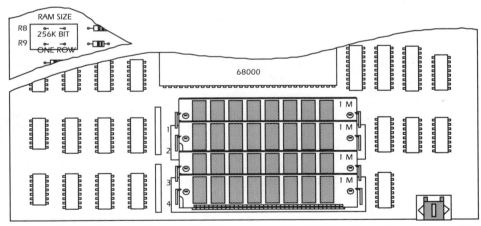

A Mac Plus with 4 megabytes of RAM uses four 1Mb SIMMs. No resistors are used in position R8 or R9.

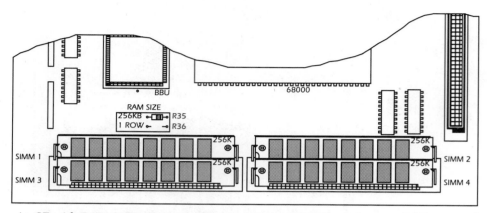

An SE with RAM SIZE resistors with 1 megabyte of RAM uses four 256K SIMMs, and a 150 ohm resistor in the 256KB position.

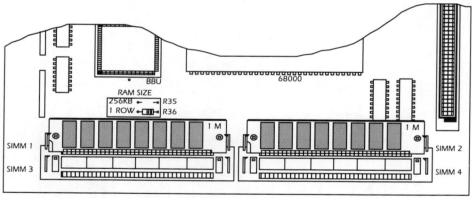

An SE with RAM SIZE resistors with 2 megabytes of RAM uses two 1Mb SIMMs in slots 1 and 2, no SIMMs in slots 3 and 4, a 150 ohm resistor in the 1 Row position, and no resistor in the 256KB position.

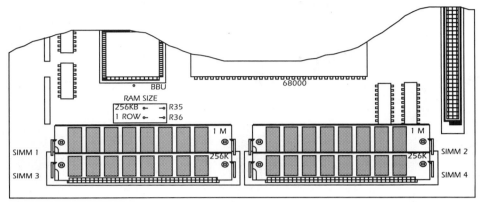

An SE with RAM SIZE resistors with 2.5 megabytes of RAM uses two 1Mb SIMMs in slots 1 and 2, and two 256K SIMMs in   slots 3 and 4. Resistors are removed from both the 256KB and 1 Row positions.

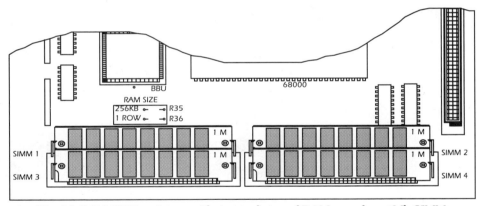

An SE with RAM SIZE resistors with 4 megabytes of RAM uses four 1Mb SIMMs. Resistors are removed from both the 256KB and 1 Row positions.

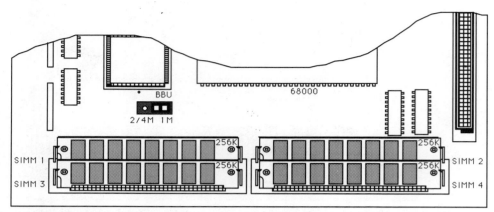

An SE with a jumper-type resistor with 1 megabyte of RAM uses 256K SIMMs in slots 1, 2, 3, and 4. The jumper is on 1M.

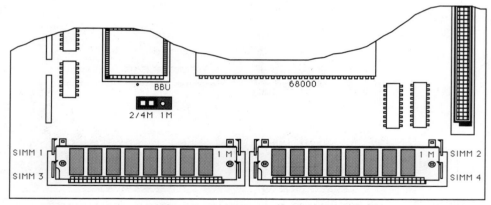

An SE with a jumper-type resistor with 2 megabytes of RAM uses 1Mb SIMMs in slots 3 and 4. The jumper is on 2/4M.

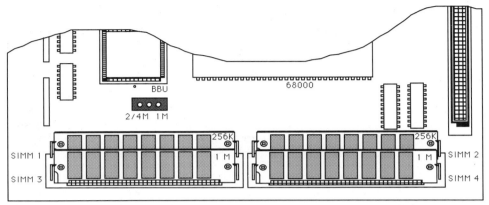

An SE with a jumper-type resistor with 2.5 megabytes of RAM uses 1Mb SIMMs in slots 3 and 4, and 256K SIMMs in slots 1 and 2. The jumper is removed.

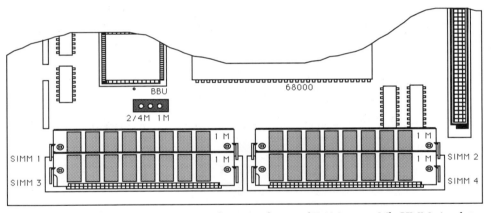

An SE with a jumper-type resistor with 4 megabytes of RAM uses 1Mb SIMMs in slots 1, 2, 3, and 4. The jumper is removed.

added haphazardly, however, as only certain combinations of SIMMs are acceptable. In these computers it is also necessary that two resistors or jumpers on the logic board be added or removed, as documented below, so that they correspond to the amount of memory that has been installed in the Mac. Actually there are two rules for using SIMMs in your Macintosh. The first rule is that SIMMs must be added in pairs—two SIMMs of the same size in sockets 1 and 2, and two SIMMs of the same size in sockets 3 and 4—and the second rule is that the largest SIMMs you are using must be put in the first two SIMM sockets. The tables below illustrate every allowable combination of SIMMs in the Mac Plus, SE and SE/30.

To begin the RAM installation, remove the Mac's cover and logic board, as described earlier in this entry. With the logic board lying flat on a non-static surface, locate the existing SIMMs. They are easily recognized by their angled orientation to the logic board itself. On the Mac Plus, the four SIMMs are arranged in a row, on the opposite side of the logic board from the ports, labeled as SIMM 1, SIMM 2, SIMM 3, and SIMM 4. On the Mac SE models, the SIMMs are arranged in two rows of two, also along the opposite side of the logic board from the ports, and these too are labeled SIMM 1, SIMM 2, SIMM 3, and SIMM 4.

Possible Combinations of SIMM Chips in a Mac SE

Slots 1 and 2	Slots 3 and 4	Total RAM
2/256K	2/256K	1Mb
2/1Mb	empty	2Mb
2/1Mb	2/256K	2.5Mb
2/1Mb	2/1Mb	4Mb

Before adding new SIMMs to your Mac you might need to remove some of the existing SIMMs. Don't throw these SIMMs away; you can either use them in another Macintosh, sell them, or keep them around in case any of your new SIMMs should go bad.

Each SIMM is held in place by small clips on each side, and by the socket itself. To remove an existing SIMM, press outward on the clips, and then tilt the SIMM forward and pull it away from its socket. You must be careful when removing SIMMs because it is fairly easy to put too much pressure on the plastic clips and break them off. This causes a big problem because it may then be difficult to properly set SIMMs into that socket. A tool for adding or removing SIMMs is available, although it may be difficult to locate at your neighborhood hardware store. You might ask your SIMM vendor for one.

To add a SIMM, insert the base into the SIMM slot at an angle, and then straighten it so that the plastic tabs lock the SIMM into place. Be sure that the SIMM is in the socket as securely as possible; the holes on the SIMM will not line up with the tabs if the SIMM is not in the socket as deep as it should be.

After adding new SIMMs, temporarily replace the cover of your Mac, plug it in, and turn it on. If your SIMMs are installed properly and not defective, you will soon see the Happy Mac icon, and your Macintosh will boot normally. You can then choose the ABOUT THE FINDER command to verify that the Mac is using your new RAM.

Adding RAM to the Mac II, IIx, IIcx, and SE/30

RAM on Macintosh computers exists in Single In-line Memory Modules (SIMMs), which are small circuit boards holding eight RAM chips. One SIMM "stick" can provide either 256K or 1Mb of memory (depending on the size of the chips it contains). Usually, Macs with 1 megabyte of RAM contain four 256K SIMMs (4 × 256K = 1Mb), and Macs with over 1 megabyte of memory use 1Mb SIMMs or some combination of 1Mb SIMMs and 256K SIMMS.

SIMMs are rated by their speed: SIMMs used in the Mac II family and the SE/30 must be 120 nanoseconds or faster. The speed of a SIMM board is usually marked on the chips it contains, coded with −15, −20, or −10, which indicates that the chip is rated at 150, 120, or 100 nanoseconds, respectively.

SIMMs are available in two "styles." Low-profile SIMMs use small RAM chips so their board size is reduced. Larger RAM chips are used in high-profile SIMMs, which are therefore larger in size. On the Macintosh SE/30, high-profile SIMMs may interfere with daughter boards that connect to the SE PDS slot (such as accelerator boards). When you purchase SIMMs, it is always a good idea to inquire or specify whether the SIMMs are low-profile or high-profile.

In the Macintosh II, IIx, IIcx, and SE/30, sockets are provided on the logic board to hold eight SIMM sticks of either the 256K or 1Mb variety. SIMMs cannot be added haphazardly, however, as only certain combinations are acceptable. Actually, there are two rules for using SIMMs in your Macintosh. The first rule is that SIMMs must be added in groups of four—four SIMMs of the same size in Bank A and four SIMMs of the same size Bank B—and the second rule is that the largest SIMMs you are using must be put in the Bank A SIMM sockets. The table below illustrates every allowable combination of SIMMs in the Mac II, IIx, IIcx, and SE/30.

Possible Combinations of SIMM Chips in a Mac II, IIx, IIcx, and SE/30

Bank A	Bank B	Total RAM
4/256K	empty	1Mb
4/256K	4/256K	2Mb
4/1Mb	empty	4Mb
4/1Mb	4/256K	5Mb
4/1Mb	4/1Mb	8Mb

In order to add SIMMs to a Mac II or IIx, you must remove the cover and then remove the drive tray that covers the SIMM banks on the logic board. Before removing the drive tray, you must detach the ribbon cables connecting your floppy drives to the logic board, and you may have to remove your internal hard drive if it is blocking access to the drive-tray screws. You must also detach the SCSI cable connecting any internal hard drive to the logic board, noting the direction of the cable connection. (Unlike floppy-drive cables, most SCSI cables do not protect you from reinstalling them incorrectly.) The drive tray is secured by four Phillips screws. When these screws are removed and all cables attaching drives on the drive tray to the logic board are detached, you can lift the drive tray out of the Mac.

In the Mac IIcx, you must remove the cover, but there is no drive tray to remove. In the SE/30, the case and logic board must be removed. To begin the RAM installation, locate the existing SIMMs on your logic board. They are easily recognized by their orientation at an angle to the logic board itself. The eight SIMM sockets are labeled as two banks of four SIMM sockets, Bank A and Bank B. Before adding new SIMMs to your Mac, you might need to remove some of the existing SIMMs. Don't throw these SIMMs away; you can use them in another Macintosh, sell them, or keep them around in case any of your new SIMMs should go bad.

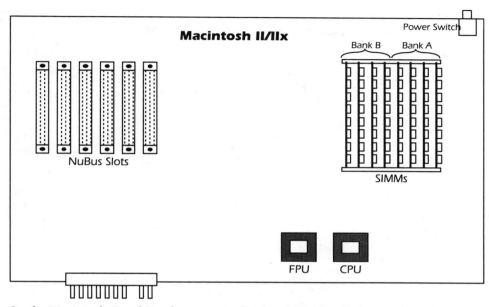

On the Macintosh II and IIx, there are two banks of four SIMM slots in the right rear corner of the logic board. The allowable combinations of SIMMs are listed on the previous page.

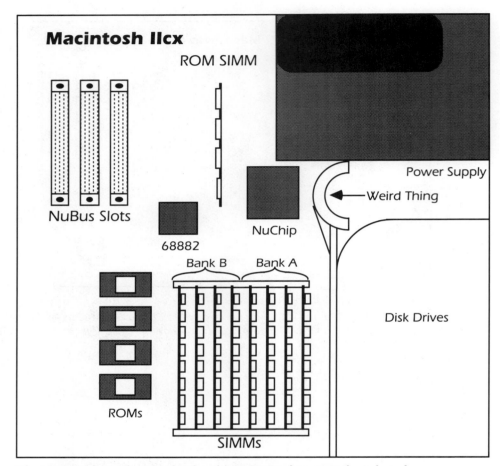

The Macintosh IIcx has two banks of four SIMM slots on its logic board.

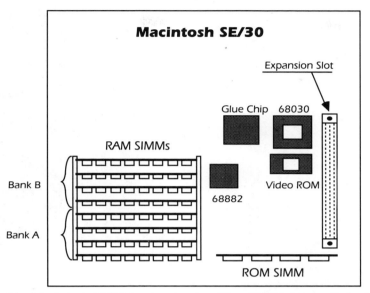

The Macintosh SE/30 has two banks of four SIMM slots on its logic board.

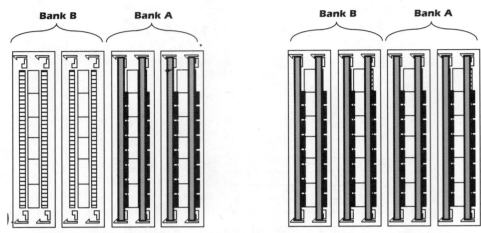

To install 1 megabyte of RAM in a Mac II, IIx, IIcx, or SE/30, Bank A should contain four 256K SIMMs, and Bank B should be empty, as shown on the left. To install 2 megabytes of RAM in these machines, both Bank A and Bank B should contain four 256K SIMMs, as shown on the right.

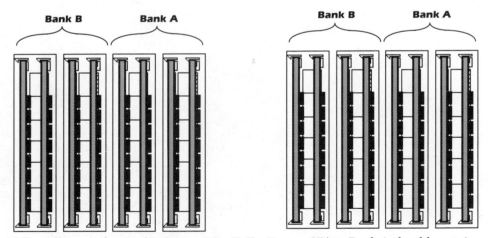

To install 5 megabytes of RAM in a Mac II, IIx, IIcx, or SE/30, Bank A should contain four 1Mb SIMMs, and Bank B should contain four 256K SIMMs, as shown on the left. (The same configuration with Bank B left empty is used to install 4 megabytes of RAM.) To install 8 megabytes of RAM in these machines, both Bank A and Bank B should contain four 1Mb SIMMs, as shown on the right.

Each SIMM is held in place by small clips on each side, and by the socket itself. To remove an existing SIMM, press outward on the clips, and then tilt the SIMM forward and pull it away from its socket. You must be careful when removing SIMMs because it is fairly easy to put too much pressure on the plastic clips and break them off. This causes a big problem because it may then be difficult to properly set SIMMs into that socket. A tool for adding or removing SIMMs is available, although it may be difficult to locate at your neighborhood hardware store. You might ask your SIMM vendor for one.

To add a SIMM, insert the base into the SIMM slot at an angle, and then straighten it so that the plastic tabs lock the SIMM into place. Be sure that the SIMM is in the socket as securely as possible; the holes on the SIMM will not line up with the tabs if the SIMM is not in the socket as deeply as it should be.

After adding new SIMMs, temporarily replace the cover of your Macintosh, plug it in, and turn it on. On the II, IIx, and IIcx, you will immediately hear unfamiliar tones if any of the SIMMs is defective or installed improperly. If your SIMMs are installed properly and not defective, you will soon see the Happy Mac icon, and your Macintosh will boot normally. You can then choose the ABOUT THE FINDER command to verify that the Mac is using your new RAM. See the RAM entry later in this section for more information.

How the Mac Works

From the moment you turn it on, the operation of your Macintosh is controlled by the interaction of software on the ROM chips, disk-based System Software, and your application software. These software components communicate with each other and with the computer's central processing unit (CPU). The CPU then directs the Mac's hardware and peripherals. Here we will take a look at the basic relationships and interactions between these elements. Understanding the basic operation of the Mac will help you to use your computer more efficiently, and to diagnose and correct hardware and software problems when they occur. More complete discussions of the CPU and ROM themselves are provided later in this entry, and the System Software is discussed in Section 1.

A Modular Operating System

While every computer has an operating system (the basic software that controls the machine's hardware and its interaction with users and application software), the Macintosh is unique in two important ways. First, the Mac's operating system provides many sophisticated functions in a form that allows them to be used as building blocks by other software applications. These functions fall into two broad categories, those that help applications control the Mac's hardware and those that help applications to interact with Macintosh users. Examples of functions provided by the operating system include disk mounting and initialization, memory management, dialog boxes, and menu bars.

The second unique aspect of the Macintosh operating system is that a substantial portion of it is placed on ROM chips on the computer's logic board. As explained later in this entry, the ROM chips hold two parts of the operating system, one called the Toolbox and one called the Operating System. (We will capitalize the portion of the ROM software known as the Operating System, and continue to not capitalize the overall operating system.) The Mac's entire operating system doesn't have a name of its own, and consists of the ROM software, System file, and some inits and DA's included on the System Software disks.

These parts of the Macintosh operating system (the ROM-based Operating System and Toolbox, and the disk-based System file and other files) and Macintosh application software exist in a hierarchy. The Operating System is at the bottom of this hierarchy, providing the fundamental control over the Mac's hardware and handling much of the communication with the CPU. The Toolbox is just above the Operating System, providing all of the commonly used aspects of the Macintosh graphic interface. The System file and other software included on the System Software disks is next, providing functions required by all Mac applications such as dialog-box text and graphics and fonts. Application software sits atop this hierarchy, providing whatever specific features it has been programmed to offer.

The key to the hierarchy is the fact that each level specializes in certain functions and provides these functions to all levels above it. The Toolbox does not need to concern itself with memory management because it turns to the Operating System to handle all of its memory management needs. The System file does not need to handle screen refresh, because it can call on the Toolbox (which may itself call on the Operating System) to handle this task. Application software does not need to know very much about fonts, because the System file can handle most of its font-related needs.

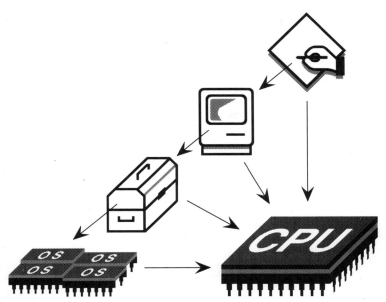

Each layer of Macintosh software can communicate directly with the CPU or utilize functions from lower-level software.

The hierarchy and modular interdependence of Macintosh software is a unique aspect of the Macintosh, and one from which the machine draws four main benefits:

- **The time and effort required to develop Macintosh software is reduced**. If each Macintosh program had to handle such basic functions as saving files to disk and formatting blank disks, application development and testing would be much more difficult and time-consuming. Because so many common functions are provided by the Macintosh ROMs and System Software, developers can concentrate on the unique features of their own software.

- **Consistency between applications is provided**. In addition to simplifying life for programmers, ROM and System Software features are responsible for the fact that most Macintosh applications look and act alike. Since the exact same software modules are used by each application, the dialog boxes, menus, and other common functions don't just appear the same—they actually are the same! Programmers may, however, choose not to use these standard functions; this is why some applications are less "Mac-Like" than others.

- **Basic functions are bug-free and predictable**. Although not perfect (remember System Software 6.0?), Apple's ROM and System Software have proven themselves to be extremely stable. They provide constants that need not be considered potential trouble spots during troubleshooting. If every application provided its own low-level routines the potential for problems on the Mac would increase by several orders of magnitude. For example, if each application handled the process of saving its own data to disk, not only would the data potentially be in danger, but all of the data on your disks would be in danger because the saving routine could theoretically overwrite existing data accidentally. Because writing to disk is currently handled by tried-and-true ROM routines, the danger of this is virtually nonexistent.

- **Often-used functions are ROM- and RAM-resident, so they execute quickly**. The routines provided by ROM and System Software are used so frequently by all Macintosh application software that they greatly affect the machine's overall performance. ROM-based software executes the most rapidly, making it an excellent location for the lowest-level routines. Portions of the System Software are loaded into RAM during startup and execution, enabling them to also offer virtually instantaneous execution when requested.

An example of the interaction between these software elements can be seen in the use of the OPEN command to get a file from within any Macintosh application. The mouse cursor and its movement on the screen are tracked and displayed by software in ROM. The menu bar itself is provided by the Toolbox, but the actual menu titles and command names are provided by the current application. The OPEN dialog box is provided by the System file, while the scrolling file listing is produced with the help of the Toolbox. Once a file has been selected, the Operating System actually transfers it from disk into RAM. The application software accesses the file data from RAM, calculates the required screen display, and makes a request to the System Software, which redraws the screen with help from both the Toolbox and the Operating System.

Start-up Sequence

To further illustrate the interaction between the Mac's various software components and its hardware, let's step through a typical (or more accurately, stereotypical) computing session. We'll break down each familiar action into its parts, and learn a little about each of them. Each step in this session will be familiar to you, although the level of detail with which we are going to examine them may be unfamiliar. It is important to be aware that this is an extremely oversimplified description of what actually happens in the operation of your Macintosh (though it may seem fairly technical). Many of the processes described here are elaborated on in other entries in this section.

1. **Power is turned on.** The first surge of electricity that travels from the computer's *power supply* is sent to a special chip on the logic board called the central processing unit. The CPU chip is where all of the actual "computing" occurs inside the computer—think of it as your computer's brain. The CPU directs every other part of the computer hardware and ultimately receives all software instructions.

The first zap of electricity produced by turning on your Mac wakes up the CPU chip.

The surge of electricity generated by turning on the computer "wakes up" the CPU, causing it to immediately execute its built-in startup instructions. (These are the only instructions built into the CPU; all others must come from elsewhere in the computer.) These instructions simply tell the CPU to read from a specific address on a ROM chip to learn what it is supposed to do next.

2. **ROM boot-up procedure begins**. The ROM (read-only memory) chip that the CPU locates contains a variety of programs written by Apple's engineers. The program that the CPU chip reads when first turned on instructs the Macintosh to perform some tests to ensure that all of its hardware is functional. If these tests are passed, the CPU is instructed to begin searching for a startup disk. When a floppy disk or hard drive containing a System file is found the Happy Mac icon is displayed on the screen. If no System file is found, a diskette with a flashing question mark on it is displayed on the screen until a satisfactory diskette is inserted.

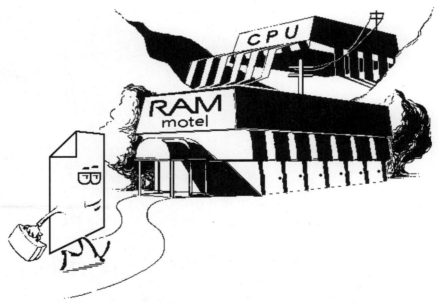

Files are read from disk and transferred into RAM so they can be accessed by the CPU.

3. **System file is loaded from startup disk**. Once a disk or drive with a System file is found, ROM instructions tell the CPU to transfer the most important parts of the System file into RAM (random-access memory). Only by being in RAM can any programs or data from floppy or hard disks be used by the CPU. The portions of the System file transferred into RAM during this initial phase are those that augment the software in ROM to help control the CPU.

4. **Finder or startup application is run**. After the System file is loaded, your Macintosh is ready to run software applications. In most cases, the first application that is run is the Finder. You might not have thought of the Finder as an application, but it is—just like a word processor or a spreadsheet. But instead of manipulating words or numbers, the Finder helps you manage disks and files.

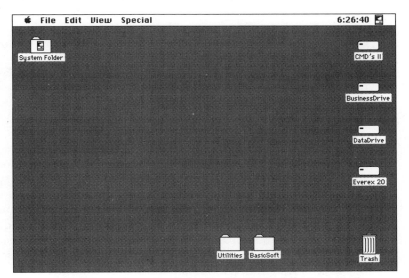

When the Finder is "running," the Finder Desktop is displayed.

5. **Wait at the desktop**. The Finder desktop shows icons for each inserted floppy disk or mounted hard-disk drive, icons for any files or folders that have been moved out of their disks or drives, and the trash can icon. The Finder's menu bar is displayed across the top of

the Macintosh screen. Whenever anything is being displayed on the Mac screen, the Operating System is controlling the actual screen redrawing process. (The tiny pixels on the screen are reset many times every second so that the screen display is always correct.) Menu bars are provided via a Toolbox routine that applications, like the Finder, simply present with a list of the commands that need to be displayed in a menu bar. Disk icons also result from an interaction between the ROM-level software and the Finder itself.

At this point the Macintosh is waiting for some action (or **event** as it is called in true Mac parlance) to occur. The Macintosh responds to events such as movement of the mouse or clicks of the mouse button, data entry from the keyboard, disk insertion, or the reception of signals from the printer or modem ports. When one of these events occurs, it is responded to by either the current application (in this case, the Finder), the System Software, or the ROMs, depending on what type of event it is. If the Mac cannot respond to an event, the event is ignored. (Random mouse clicks on the desktop, for example, do not cause any response.)

6. **Open a disk icon**. When the mouse button is double-clicked with the pointer over one of the disk or drive icons, the Operating System detects the mouse clicks, and that they were near enough to each other to constitute a double-click. The coordinates of the mouse click are passed to the Finder, which determines that a disk icon is displayed at that location and a double-click means that the disk should be opened. The Finder asks the System file for a specific type of window to be drawn at a specific location—the Finder knows the size and location of the disk's window from information in the disk's Desktop file—and the System file draws the window with the help of the Toolbox and Operating System. The file names or icons are listed in the window by the Finder (again with the help of the Operating System in controlling the screen itself).

7. **Run an application**. Double-clicking on the icon for a software application instructs the Finder to begin the process of launching the application. The Finder has little to do with this process once it has begun, and is usually removed from memory when a new application is launched (except under MultiFinder, of course). The ROMs and System Software take over as the program is read from the disk and brought into RAM. Once enough of the program has been loaded, control is passed to the application, which takes over the screen and

waits for events (actions from the user) that it can respond to, such as commands that are chosen from its menus. As in the Finder, while any application is running, the ROMs and System Software will always respond to any event that they are designed to handle; an inserted disk, for example, is always responded to by the ROM-based software no matter when it occurs.

8. **Open a file**. To open a file from within virtually any Macintosh application, you choose the OPEN command from the FILE menu. This brings up a dialog box in which you can select a specific file. The structure for menus used in Mac applications is provided by ROM software, with the applications simply providing a list of the commands they need displayed. When a menu command is chosen, the software can either execute the requested action itself, or when appropriate, call the ROM software or System file for assistance.

When the OPEN command is chosen, for example, most software calls on the System file to provide a STANDARD FILE dialog box. This dialog box presents a scrolling file listing and allows the user to select any available file. When a file has been selected, the name of the file and its location are passed back to the application, which then requests that all or part of the file be transferred into RAM. The actual transfer is directed by the ROM-based Operating System.

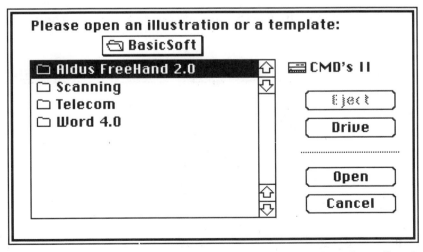

The application, System Software, Operating System, and Toolbox all contribute to the use of an OPEN dialog box.

9. **Edit the file**. Text editing can be handled by the basic text-editing functions provided by the Toolbox, or software can be programmed to provide its own text editing. Even applications that provide only basic text-editing features support keyboard equivalents like COMMAND-→ because these are part of the Toolbox's text-editing routines. Use of the Clipboard to support the CUT, COPY, and PASTE commands is also provided by the Toolbox.

10. **Save the file**. Saving a file is much like opening a file. The SAVE command is provided by the application and the Toolbox, and the SAVE As dialog box is usually used directly from the System file. When the SAVE button is clicked, the process of actually writing the file to disk is handled by the Operating System, which takes care of such complex tasks as determining which disk sectors are available and reading the file from its current location in RAM.

11. **Quit the application**. When the QUIT command is chosen, the application attempts to save any unsaved files, removes any temporary files it has created on disk, and then passes control back to the System Software, which notes that the RAM used by the application is again available for other uses, and runs the Finder (in most cases).

12. **Shut down**. The Finder's SHUT DOWN command invokes an Operating System routine that instructs the Finder to transfer all disk directory information it has stored in RAM back to the disks, closes any open files, and prepares the hardware for shutdown. On the Mac II, IIx, and IIcx the power supply is then turned off. The other Macs display the YOU MAY NOW SWITCH OFF YOUR MACINTOSH dialog box.

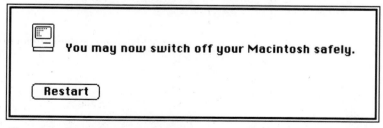

You may now switch off your Macintosh safely.

Restart

Choosing the SHUT DOWN *command closes all files and prepares your Macintosh to be turned off.*

Batteries

The Macintosh battery maintains power to a special area of RAM called the **parameter RAM** (PRAM), and keeps the Mac's clock running while the Mac is turned off. In the Macintosh 128k, 512k, and Plus, the battery is a simple AA battery that you can easily replace by removing the battery cover on the rear of the machine. Batteries are soldered into the Mac SE, II, IIx, and SE/30, so they must be changed by an Apple Certified Technician. Batteries in the IIcx are held in a socket on the logic board, and are easily replaced.

Bus

In computer terminology, a **bus** is the series of wires or electronic connections that link the computer's various hardware components and allow them to communicate. (The tangled lines visible on the Mac **logic board** are the bus lines.) All basic hardware components—the CPU, ROM, RAM, specialty chips, and ports—are connected to the bus.

The bus lines are used to carry three types of information: data, addresses, and timing signals. All data that is transferred on the bus is directed to a specific device by the address information that accompanies it. Timing signals are generated by the clock crystal on the logic board on the CPU, and certain other devices, and provide synchronization for the movement of information and the operation of hardware devices. A bus is distinguished by the number of lines it provides for data and for address information; the more lines there are, the more information can be transported in the same amount of time.

Some buses also offer **expansion slots**, sometimes called just **slots**, which allow you to connect additional circuit boards (called **cards**) to the bus. Cards plugged into slots have full access to the bus's data and address lines, and therefore to all other devices on the bus, so they can function as if they were built into the computer. The early Macintoshes (models released before the SE) did not offer any expansion slots, but manufacturers of peripherals such as memory expansions devised other methods of attaching add-on components to these machines, such as sandwiching connectors between the CPU chip and the logic board.

The Macintosh SE offers one expansion slot, called a **Processor Direct Slot** (PDS). A variety of expansion cards are available for the SE, including accelerators, external monitor adaptors, and internal modems. The SE/30 also includes an Apple Processor Direct Slot, but it is different from the one in the standard SE.

The Macintosh II bus is based on a bus design called **NuBus**, which can transfer data at up to 37.5Mb per second (in bursts). The NuBus in the Mac II, IIx, and IIcx supports NuBus expansion cards, the Mac II and IIx offer six NuBus slots, and the Mac IIcx offers three NuBus slots. One of these slots must be used for the computer's video adaptor, and the rest can be used for any number of devices including memory-expansion boards, accelerators, and modems. The NuBus slots in these machines use a 96-pin NuBus connector. In addition to the data, address, and timing lines, power is also provided to cards in NuBus slots. (A total of 102 watts is available to NuBus cards on a single NuBus.)

CPU

Of all the chips in the Macintosh, only one is in control: the **central processing unit (CPU)**. The CPU is the brains of the computer, handling almost all of the actual computations and sending instructions and control commands to all other hardware components. The CPU operates by executing program instructions, which cause it to manipulate data and send data and instructions to other hardware devices.

Macintosh computers use CPU chips manufactured by Motorola. Although several different chips are used in the different Macintosh models, they are all part of the **68000 family**, which means that they all understand the same basic instruction set. Each new chip in the 68000 family can run software designed for previous 68000 chips, although it executes instructions more efficiently and at a higher clock rate, and supports an expanded command set. The Macintosh Plus and SE use the 68000 CPU, while the Macintosh II and many accelerator boards use a 68020 CPU. The Macintosh IIx, IIcx, and SE/30 use the 68030 CPU. CPU chips are distinguished by the **clock speed** at which they can execute instructions, and the number of **address lines** and **data lines** that they utilize.

Chip speed is measured in megahertz (MHz) or millions of instructions per second. Macintosh CPU's range from 8 MHz (in the Mac Plus and SE) up to 16 MHz (in the Mac II family and the SE/30), with 25 MHz and

33 MHz accelerators already available. You can expect 25 MHz and 33 MHz machines to be released by Apple in the near future. Faster clock speeds improve chip performance because the instructions that a CPU chip executes require some number of clock cycles in order to be performed, not any predetermined amount of time. If the process of launching an application requires 10,000 clock cycles, the launch will occur faster on a computer that can perform 16 million instructions per second than on one that can only perform 8 million instructions per second.

The number of address lines a chip utilizes affects the amount of contiguous RAM it can utilize. All of the Macintosh processing chips use 32-bit address lines, giving them the potential to address 32 gigabytes of RAM (2^{32} different addresses). System Software 6.0, however, only supports the use of 8 megabytes of RAM. System Software 7.0 is going to support full 32-bit memory addressing, so you will be able to use up to 4 gigabytes of RAM when System Software 7.0 is released.

The number of data lines supported by a CPU determines how fast it can move data in and out of the chip. Data lines are often compared with doors into a room; the more doors, the more people can get in and out in a given amount of time. All Macintosh CPU's have 32-bit data lines allowing for very fast data movement. (By contrast, AT-class PCs use 16-bit data lines.)

Ports

The **ports** on the back of each Macintosh allow the computer to connect with various external devices. Each port provides a specific type of connection, allowing data, and in some cases electricity, to travel between the external device and the Macintosh logic board. Each Macintosh includes a printer port, a modem port, and an audio port. All Macintoshes since the Macintosh Plus provide a SCSI port, all Macs except the II and IIx provide an external floppy-drive port, and the SE, II, IIx, IIcx, and SE/30 include two Apple Desktop Bus (ADB) ports that are used for the keyboard and mouse.

Printer and Modem Ports

Printers and modems are two common peripherals that Macintosh users need to connect to their Macintosh computers, and Apple has provided one port on each Macintosh for each of these purposes. Although distinguished by the icons designating one as a modem port and the other as a printer port, these are the same mechanically, and to some degree they may be used interchangeably for connecting modems and non-AppleTalk printers. AppleTalk (LocalTalk) connectors should generally be connected only to the printer port on all Macs, and high-speed modems (over 2400 baud) should be connected only to the printer port on the Mac II.

Each of these ports uses the serial RS-422 communication protocol, which is a superset of the RS-232 protocol used on many other communications systems. Under this protocol, these ports support data transfer rates of up to 920,000 bits per second (when external clocking is provided).

Serial Pinouts

Item	128/512	Plus	SE, SE/30, II, IIx, IIcx
Plug type	9-Pin	9-Pin/8-Pin	8-Pin
Data carrier detect	NA	NA	Pin 7
Clock input	NA	NA	Pin 7
Handshake out (DTR)	NA	Pin 1	Pin 1
Handshake in (CTS)	Pin 7	Pin 2	Pin 2
RxD-(receive data)	Pin 9	Pin 5	Pin 5
RxD+(receive data)	Pin 8	Pin 8	Pin 8
TxD-(transmit data)	Pin 5	Pin 3	Pin 3
TxD+(transmit data)	Pin 4	Pin 6	Pin 6
Signal ground	Pin 3	Pin 4	Pin 4
Chassis ground	Pin 1	Shell	Shell
+5V power	Pin 2	NA	NA
+12V power	Pin 6	NA	NA

The Macintosh 128k, 512k, and 512e use 9-pin square connectors on their serial ports, and the ports provide 5- and 12-volt power lines for devices that require power. Beginning with the Macintosh Plus, the 9-pin square connectors are replaced with 8-pin round connectors, and power is no longer provided via the serial ports. Peripherals with either 8-pin or 9-pin connectors can be used on any Macintosh, although adaptor cables may be required in some cases. The exceptions, of course, are devices using 9-pin connectors requiring power from the serial connection; these devices will not operate on Macs with the 8-pin connector. On the Macintosh SE, the Macintosh II, and all subsequent models, the serial port is again modified—but only slightly, adding support for data carrier detect (DCD).

Floppy-Drive Port

The floppy-drive port, available on all Macintosh models except the II and IIx, allows external floppy-disk drives to be connected to the Macintosh. Although many third-party floppy drives can be connected to most Macs, the floppy-drive port on the Mac IIx, IIcx, and SE/30 no longer provides power to the drive (Pin 5 is unused), so many third-party drives do not operate on these systems.

Floppy-Drive Pinouts

Pin	Use
1-4	Ground
5	−12 volts
6	+5 volts
7	+12 volts
8	+12 volts
9	(unused)
10	Motor speed control
11	CA0 (status control line)
12	CA1 (status control line)
13	CA2 (status control line)
14	LSTRB (status control line)
15	Write request
16	SEL (select disk drive)
17	External drive enable
18	Read data input
19	Write data output

SCSI Port

The **Small Computer Standard Interface** (SCSI, pronounced "scuzzy"), first appeared on the Macintosh Plus, and is now the standard interface for all high-speed, intelligent peripherals that connect to the Macintosh. While hard drives are the most common SCSI device, scanners, tape backup units, and even connections to PCs are also available as SCSI devices. Up to seven SCSI devices can be connected to the Macintosh at one time. (The SCSI standard supports eight devices, but the Macintosh itself counts as a SCSI device.) Multiple SCSI devices can be connected to the Macintosh because almost every SCSI peripheral provides two SCSI ports, allowing the peripherals to be linked together in a daisy-chained fashion.

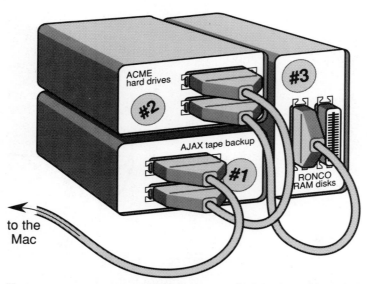

You can connect up to 7 SCSI devices to the Mac by cabling them in sequence. This is known as diasy chaining. On each of these devices we have labeled the SCSI ID number and used a SCSI terminator at the end of the SCSI chain. (The first drive, #1, has an internal terminator.)

When you connect SCSI devices to the Macintosh, **terminating resistors** must be installed in the first and last SCSI devices. These prevent the data and commands that travel over the SCSI cables from "bouncing" off the ends of the chain and echoing back through the cables. The first and last devices are the first and last *physical* devices on the chain, not the highest and lowest SCSI ID numbers. If you have only one SCSI peripheral attached to your Mac, it must be terminated. If you have two SCSI peripherals, they both must be terminated. If you have three, four, five, six, or seven SCSI peripherals attached, the first and last in the physical chain must have terminators and none of the devices between the first and the last may have a SCSI terminator attached. Improper SCSI termination will not cause any hardware damage, but your Mac will probably not boot properly until the termination is correct.

Many SCSI peripherals are **self-terminating**. This means they have built-in terminators that sense when they are needed and then activate. This sometimes makes it appear as if your SCSI chain is not terminated properly when it actually is. Unfortunately, the poor technical documentation accompanying many SCSI devices does not explain the peripheral's termination procedures, so you are usually left to discover these things by trial and error. Peripherals that are not self-terminating should include a terminator, which is a small, plug-like device that is connected to the unused SCSI port on the back of the peripheral.

Each SCSI device is assigned an ID number between 0 and 7 that serves as its "address," allowing communications on the SCSI bus to avoid confusion among the various devices. The SCSI ID number of each device connected to the Macintosh must be unique; conflicting SCSI ID numbers will prevent the Macintosh from starting up. By default, the Macintosh is assigned SCSI ID number 7, so ID number 7 should never be used by any SCSI peripherals.

A SCSI ID number is assigned to each SCSI device by the manufacturer, but when you have more than one SCSI device, you may have to change some of the ID numbers to ensure that the ID of each device is unique. Some SCSI peripherals have their SCSI ID's set permanently in hardware, some are selected from the hardware (using dip switches, pin connectors, or push-button toggles to change the SCSI ID number), while others are controlled from software. Software selection of SCSI ID's is preferable for its ease of use, although externally mounted and clearly labeled hardware switches are acceptable. SCSI devices with permanently set or internally mounted SCSI ID selectors should be avoided when possible.

Incidentally, SCSI ID numbers are given more priority the higher they are, so theoretically you should set your startup hard drive to ID 6 and infrequently used devices like tape drives to low numbers. In reality, however, this does not appear to be very important. In fact, most hard-drive manufacturers by default set their drives to use ID 0 or 1.

The Macintosh's external SCSI port uses a 25-pin SCSI connector, and its internal SCSI connector uses a 50-pin ribbon cable connector. Many SCSI peripherals use 50-pin SCSI connectors that require you to have a cable with a 25-pin connector on one end and a 50-pin connector on the other end in order to connect these devices to the Macintosh. SCSI cables with 50-pin connectors on both ends are often required when connecting multiple SCSI devices together. The world would be a much simpler place for Mac users if everyone would just use 25-pin connectors, but more and more manufacturers of peripherals are adopting the 50-pin format. Unfortunately, this leaves you with the task of finding the correct cables, which often are not provided with the devices and are almost never available at your local dealer.

Apple Desktop Bus Ports

The Apple Desktop Bus (ADB) is used on the Mac Plus, SE, II, IIx, IIcx, and SE/30 to connect the Mac's keyboard and mouse, and is also used by other input devices such as drawing tablets and trackballs. The ADB connection transfers data and a small electric current that can be used to power ADB devices. Most ADB devices have two ADB connectors, so that devices may be daisy-chained together. For example, the Mac's mouse can be plugged into its own ADB port on the back of the Mac, or it can be plugged into the extra ADB port on the keyboard. See the Input Devices entry later in this section for more information on Mac keyboards, mice, trackballs, and tablets.

The Pinouts for the Apple Desktop Bus

Pin	Use
1	Data
2	Power-on (Mac II only)
3	Power +5 volts
4	Signal ground

ROM

At the core of the Macintosh is a set of **read-only memory** (**ROM**) chips that contain the software most responsible for the operation of the Macintosh. ROM chips reside on the logic board of each Macintosh, and rights to the software they contain are held strictly by Apple Computer. The ROM chips and the software they contain are so central to the operation of the Macintosh that it is their copyrighted status that makes it most difficult—bordering on impossible—for any Macintosh clones to be created. The software on these ROM chips is divided into two parts: the **Operating System** (OS) and the **Toolbox**. The software routines from both the OS and the Toolbox are used by the System Software and by all applications that run on the Macintosh. Some Toolbox routines even call OS routines.

The Operating System provides most of the low-level hardware control that applications require. For example, the OS handles memory management (assigning certain software-specific parts of memory and making sure no other software tries to use that section of memory), file management (transferring files between RAM and disk), device management (accessing printers, modems, and other peripherals), and display management (constantly redrawing the screen). The OS also provides a variety of general utilities. Each part of the OS handles one of these basic functions, which would be extremely difficult for application programmers to handle themselves.

The Toolbox performs a similar function to that of the Operating System, providing frequently needed tasks so that application software can quickly and easily access them. But Toolbox tasks relate to communicating with the Macintosh user rather than controlling the Macintosh hardware. Toolbox routines help applications create dialog boxes, draw windows, handle fonts, and perform basic text editing.

ROM Versions and Upgrades

Because the OS and the Toolbox reside on ROM chips, which are difficult and expensive to change, they are not updated very often. In fact, ROMs have thus far been updated only when new hardware was introduced. Different versions of the ROMs are found in the 128k, 512, 512e, Mac Plus, SE, II, IIx, and SE/30. Fortunately, this doesn't mean that the Mac's most fundamental software cannot be modified occasionally. Both the Operating

System and the Toolbox can be modified with *patches* from the System file or inits.

Why would the ROM software need to be modified? Usually it's either to correct bugs (errors) or to improve the ROM software. Like any other software, ROM software is prone to bugs, and patches can correct these problems without necessitating ROM replacement. ROM software is also modified in order to add new features, improve existing features, or add support for new hardware products. Patches to ROM routines are loaded into RAM during startup, and then the lookup table that directs ROM calls to specific ROM routines is modified so that requests for patched routines are routed to the RAM-based patch rather than the original ROM routine.

A recent example of a ROM patch was an init called QuickerDraw, written by legendary Mac programmer Andy Hertzfeld. QuickerDraw improved the Toolbox routine that helps software to redraw the screen of a Mac II when working in color. QuickerDraw offered Mac II color users performance increases of several hundred percent, and was provided in init format by Hertzfeld so that users could benefit from these improvements without having to wait until the next release of the System file. System files since 6.0 include QuickerDraw, so the QuickerDraw init is no longer required.

More recent Macintosh computers—the Mac II, IIx, IIcx, and SE/30—have socketed ROMs or extra ROM sockets, which allow the ROM chips to be easily removed and replaced. The ROM chips on earlier Macintosh models are soldered onto the logic board, making their removal or replacement difficult or impossible. The change on the newer models suggests that Apple intends to offer ROM upgrades sometime in the future. Surprisingly, the ROM sockets used on the Mac II are different from those used on the IIx and IIcx, and they are all different from the type used on the SE/30.

 Disk Drives

When software and data is not being used by your Macintosh—i.e., when it is not in RAM—it must be stored on some type of long-term storage medium. The most common storage devices are floppy disks and hard drives. These disks store exactly the same information stored in RAM and used by the CPU, but because they utilize a mechanical storage method rather than an electronic one, information saved on disk remains stored (generally speaking) until it is intentionally erased or overwritten.

Floppy disks and hard drives record electronic information on magnetically coated disks called **platters**. Each side of each platter is called a **cylinder**, and each cylinder is divided into concentric rings called **tracks**. Tracks are further divided into pie-shaped slices called **sectors**.

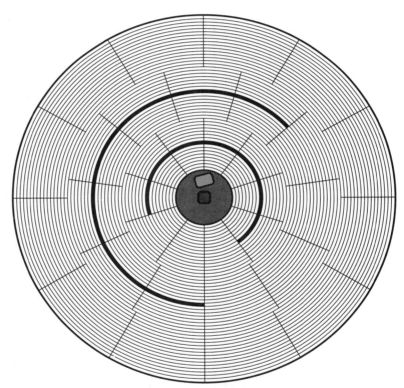

Each cylinder is divided into concentric circles, called tracks, *and pie-shaped slices, called* sectors. *This cylinder contains only one file, which fills 14 sectors on two different tracks.*

Each sector on a disk holds 512 bytes of actual data (0.5K) and 12 bytes of directory information known as a **file tag**. The file tag contains the file number, fork type (resource or data), file attributes, file sequence number (relative block number), and the date of last modification. The sectors on a disk are numbered, starting with 0, on each cylinder. Sectors are sometimes called **blocks**; the difference is that blocks are numbered consecutively on both sides of a platter. (800K disks blocks are numbered 0–1599).

Because most Macintosh files are more than 0.5K long, a number of different sectors must be used to hold the files when they are written to disk . A list of the sectors to which the file has been written (along with the order in which they contain the file) is written in a special entry on the disk called the **disk directory**. Later, when the file is read from the disk, the directory entry is consulted, the required sectors are read in the proper order, and the file is transferred back into RAM.

Floppy Disks

A floppy disk consists of a single magnetically coated circular plastic sheet, housed inside a rectangular drive sleeve. Two disk formats are used on current Macintoshes: 3.5" double-sided 800K disks and 3.5" high-density 1.44Mb disks. Early Macs used 3.5" single-sided 400K disks, which today are quite rare.

Each side of the floppy disk is divided into 80 tracks, numbered 0 through 79. On double-sided disks (800K floppies) and high-density disks (1.4Mb floppies), track numbers are appended with *a* or *b* to distinguish between the sides. Each track on the disk is divided into sectors (as just described), with single- and double-sided floppy disks divided into more sectors toward the outer edge of the disk than near the inner edge. These disks use twelve sectors on tracks 0–11, eleven sectors on tracks 16–31, ten sectors on tracks 32–47, nine sectors on tracks 48–63, and eight sectors on tracks 64–79. High-density floppy disks divide each track on the disk into eighteen sectors, regardless of the track position.

When a floppy disk is manufactured and packaged, the disk surface is uniformly covered with magnetic particles. Tracks and sectors (blocks) are "created" when a disk is formatted, but they do not physically exist at any time—they simply result from the pattern of markers applied during formatting. This is why 3.5" disks can be formatted for use on either Macintoshes or IBM PCs. (Double-sided Macintosh disks can be formatted as 720K PC disks, and high-density disks can be formatted as 1.44Mb PC disks.)

Macintosh disk drives rotate their disks at different speeds, depending upon the number of sectors on the track being read or written. High-density disk drives rotate at a constant speed when using high-density floppy disks, but at a variable speed when using single- or double-sided disks. The following table compares the rotational speed of the different disk structures:

Revolutions per Minute/Sectors per Track

Tracks	800K Disk	1.4MB Disk
00-15	394/12	300/18
16-31	429/11	300/18
32-47	472/10	300/18
48-63	525/9	300/18
64-79	590/8	300/18

How Blocks Are Used on a Floppy Disk

The first two blocks on a floppy disk formatted under the HFS file system (block 0 and block 1) are known as the **boot blocks.** The boot blocks contain special information that is used when you start up the Macintosh with the floppy disk. Boot-block information includes the boot-block version number, the name of the System file that will be used (System), the name of the application to be run at startup (as assigned with the SET STARTUP command in the Finder), the name of the startup-screen file (Start-upScreen), the name of the Clipboard file (Clipboard), the maximum number of files that can be opened simultaneously, and the size of the system heap that will be set up in RAM. Because boot blocks are so vital to the startup of the Macintosh, some utility programs offer you the capability to edit or rewrite the boot blocks. This allows you to correct damaged boot blocks, or modify the information contained in the boot blocks.

Block 2 of an HFS floppy disk contains a variety of volume information, and is known as the **Master Directory Block**. This block, which is read into RAM when the disk is mounted, contains information such as the size of the disk, the file system used (MFS or HFS), and the number of files and folders the disk contains. If this block is damaged, it may be impossible to mount the disk. Block 3 contains the **Volume Bit Map**, in which one bit is used to represent each sector on the disk. When a sector is in use, its bit is set on. When the sector is available, the bit is set off. When sectors are needed to store a new file, this Volume Bit Map is consulted so the Mac can quickly determine which sectors are available for use. Blocks number 4 through 1599 are used to hold data.

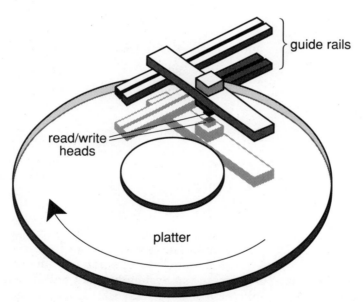

One read/write head is positioned over each side of each drive platter. The heads move in and out on guide rails to reach the correct track, and the platter rotates so that all sectors are occasionally beneath the heads.

Floppy-Disk Drives

Floppy-disk drives are the mechanisms that write data to and read data from floppy disks. All Macintosh disk drives include two **read/write heads**, a drive motor, an ejection mechanism, a write-protect sensor, and a disk-controller circuit board. When a floppy disk is inserted into the disk drive, the metal door covering the disk's read/write hole is slid back, and the heads are positioned on the portion of the disk exposed by the read/write hole. The write-protect sensor, which consists of an LED emitter and an LED receptor, determines if the disk is write-protected.

In order to read from or write to a disk, the read/write heads are positioned over a particular track on the disk. Once positioned over the correct track, the drive heads read the file tag from each sector until the information in the file tag tells the head that it has reached the correct sector, at which time data is written or read.

Hard Drives

Hard disk drives operate exactly like floppy drives, but they offer faster data transfer and larger storage capacity. A hard drive contains a number of aluminum or glass platters, as opposed to the single plastic platter used in a floppy disk, and there is one read/write head for each platter in the drive. Because they operate with more exacting specifications than do floppy disks, hard-disk platters are sealed in ultraclean containers so that dust cannot reach them. Hard drives rotate at a constant rate of 3600 revolutions per minute.

Macintoshes are connected to hard drives via the **Small Computer Standard Interface** connection (SCSI, pronounced "scuzzy"). The first block on a SCSI hard drive stores the **Driver Map**, which contains basic information about the drive including the total number of blocks on the drive, the location on the drive of the SCSI driver software, and the drive's ID number. Block 2 on a SCSI drive contains the drive's **Partition Map**, specifying the volume partitions available on the drive. Blocks 2 through 6 contain the SCSI drivers themselves, and the remainder of the blocks on the drive are used for partitions holding drive data. See the Computers entry earlier in this section for more information about SCSI.

Drive Speed

Three factors determine the speed of any disk drive: the time it takes the drive heads to reach the track holding the data being accessed (**seek time**), the time it takes the sector holding the data to rotate beneath the head (**latency time**), and the rate at which data can be transferred from the drive into RAM after it has been read (**data transfer rate**).

A drive's seek time is a function of hardware capability—how fast the drive can move the head to the correct track—and the coincidental distance between the last track accessed and the new one. Latency time is a result of the rotation rate of the disk at the track being accessed, and the coincidental distance of the first required sector from the head when it reaches the track. A drive's average combined seek and latency time is usually reported as a single figure called an *access time*.

Sector Interleave

Another factor that dramatically affects the performance of any drive is the drive's **sector interleave factor**. The sector interleave factor determines the physical relationship between consecutively numbered sectors on a track. If physically adjacent sectors are numbered sequentially, the interleave is 1:1 (one to one). If one sector is skipped between consecutively numbered sectors (1,6,2,7,3,8,4,9,5), the sector interleave factor is 2:1. If two sectors are skipped between consecutively numbered sectors, the sector interleave factor is 3:1.

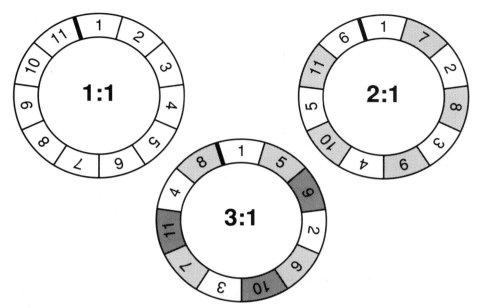

A drive's interleave factor specifies how its sectors are numbered. The higher the interleave factor, the more revolutions the drive must make before all sectors are read. Here we see that a drive using a 1:1 interleave can read 11 sectors on a track in one revolution, while a drive using a 2:1 interleave can read only 6 sectors in one revolution, and a drive using a 3:1 interleave can read only 4 sectors in one revolution.

Obviously, the fastest way to read or write data to or from multiple sectors is if the sectors are arranged sequentially (a 1:1 sector interleave); the disk drive can then read data from one sector after another as the disk rotates. In this manner it is possible to read all of the data from every sector on the track in one revolution of the disk. This is not always possible, however, because sequential sector numbering sometimes provides data faster than it can be transferred into RAM. This happens when the spinning disk brings the next sector to be read to the drive head before the data from the previous sector has been fully transferred into RAM. Since the head cannot yet read the data from the new sector, it waits for the drive to spin around again, at which time all previous data has been transferred and the sector can be read.

To alleviate this problem, higher sector interleave factors are used. If a sector interleave of 2:1 is used, the drive head must skip every other sector that rotates beneath it. This delay allows the drive time to transfer the data read from the previous sector into RAM. It also slows down the overall data transfer rate by 100% because the drive must make two complete revolutions in order for every sector on a track to be read. A 3:1 sector interleave factor provides the drive twice as much time to transfer data read from each sector, but it also requires three complete revolutions of the disk for all the sectors on one track to be read. The Macintosh Plus generally requires a sector interleave factor of 3:1, the Macintosh SE requires a 2:1 interleave factor, and the Macintosh II, IIx, IIcx, and SE/30 support a 1:1 interleave factor.

Sector numbering occurs when the hard drive is formatted. Most hard-drive formatting software allows you to select the sector interleave factor that will be used, although some automatically select the interleave based on the computer to which the drive is attached when it is being formatted. (All hard drives formatted while connected to a Mac Plus are set at 3:1, all drives formatted while connected to an SE are set at 2:1, and all drives formatted while connected to a Mac II or SE/30 are set at 1:1.) If your hard drive was already formatted when you bought it, or if it was formatted on another Macintosh model and then attached to your Mac, its interleave factor may be set incorrectly. There is generally no way to discover the current interleave factor of your drive, short of reformatting it.

A hard drive with its interleave set too "loose"—3:1 or 2:1 on a Mac II, for example—will cause drive performance to be 200 to 300 percent worse than it would be if reformatted using a 1:1 interleave factor. A hard drive with its interleave set too "tight"—1:1 or 2:1 interleave on a Mac Plus, for example—may cause the drive's performance to be over 1000 percent worse than if interleaved properly. (The disk may have to make one complete revolution for each sector read on each track.)

File Fragmentation

Files are not always written to sequentially numbered sectors on a single track. If the file is too large to fit on a single track, or if sequentially numbered sectors are not available, then the file will be written in whatever scattered sectors are available. When a file is not written in sequentially numbered sectors, it is said to be *fragmented*.

In order to read a file that is fragmented, the drive head must be repositioned to each track containing sectors that hold a portion of the file, and then at each track the head must read the appropriate sectors. Since there is both a seek and latency time associated with each movement of the drive heads, the more fragmented a file is, the longer it will take to read or write. Regularly defragmenting your drive is the only way to maintain peak drive performance. Several utilities are available that allow you to occasionally defragment your drive or the files on your drive. See the Disks and Drives entry in Section 1 for more information on these programs.

Choosing a Hard Drive

Choosing a hard drive for your Macintosh is a difficult decision. Not only must you decide what size drive you require, but you must also choose between internal and external models and select among nearly a dozen hard-drive vendors. The first consideration in deciding on a hard drive is, as usual, the amount of money you can afford to spend on it. Keep in mind that you will likely live with the drive you buy for a long time, because drives cannot be incrementally upgraded in storage capacity, and the market for used hard drives is not very good.

Selecting a Drive Size

Traditionally, 20 megabytes has been the recommended drive size for the "average" Mac user. But today, the ever-growing storage requirements of software applications and data files, along with the relatively small incremental cost of jumping to 40 or even 60 megabytes, make the larger drives a much smarter choice for all but the most casual Mac user. If you cannot imagine filling 20 megabytes and want to save the extra money and buy a 20Mb drive, we recommend that you first find another Mac user whom you consider to be using their computer in a way comparable to what you intend to do yourself, and ask their opinion. If they say that 20Mb is enough, buy a 20 megabyte drive. But we'll be surprised!

If you're interested in serious desktop publishing, multimedia, HyperCard or SuperCard development or use, or graphic illustration, you may want to consider drives as large as 120 to 300 megabytes. These drive sizes used to hold all the data of a midsize company, but many single Mac users are now fully utilizing these vast storage spaces. Again, a good idea would be to get the advice of some other Mac users who are doing the same kind of work you intend to do.

Internal Versus External

Internal drives are often cheaper than external drives; they do not require any desk space, and do not require a fan of their own because they do not include a power supply. This makes them very quiet. On the other hand, if an internal drive breaks, you have either the headache of removing it or the loss of your entire machine while it's out for repairs. External drives can easily be transported from one Mac to another or sent out for repairs.

Hard-Drive Vendors

If there's any product for which the buyer should beware, Macintosh hard drives are it. Most brand-name hard-drive vendors last about a year and then fade off into the sunset, or go from a high customer-satisfaction rating to a very low one. Fortunately, a little understanding of the hard-drive market, and some advice from the Mac community, will allow you to easily avoid any problems relating to your purchase of a hard drive.

Most of the problems with Macintosh hard-drive vendors have had to do with either their meteoric corporate success or the intense competition that the hard-drive market undergoes from time to time. Apple's long-overdue decision to price its drives competitively has also caused problems for several major vendors.

Hard drives are actually manufactured by just a few companies, including CDC, Rodime, Seagate, Quantum, Fuji, MiniScribe, SuperMac, and Epson. Most of the vendors who advertise in the Mac magazines buy drives from these vendors, add a case and power supply (for external drives), test the drives and format them (in most cases), write a manual (or some pamphlet that passes for a manual), and write or buy a hard-drive formatting utility. Then they advertise and sell these drives.

With the advent of internal drives, many dealers and mail-order drive resellers also purchase drives directly from the manufacturers, reselling them along with separate mounting brackets, cases, and formatting utilities. This removal of the middle-man has been largely responsible for the recent price decreases on Macintosh hard drives. Given the fact that most drive vendors and dealers are selling basically the same product, the important considerations in choosing a hard-drive vendor are manufacturer, drive speed, formatting software, and support. Many mail-order vendors now list the manufacturers for each drive they sell, and any drive vendor who refuses to tell you a drive's manufacturer should be avoided.

Drive speeds are the result of tests of average seek time, with the fastest hard drives offering speeds of 10 milliseconds (ms), and slower drives clocking in as high as 65 ms. In general, you should try to purchase a drive with a rating of 40 ms if purchasing a 20- to 60-megabyte hard drive, and 20 ms or better for drives larger than 60 megabytes.

Features to look for in hard-drive formatting software include SCSI partitioning (and the ability to have partitions mount automatically and use a password), updatable SCSI drivers, and drive-testing utilities. Of course, you can always purchase commercial drive-formatting software such as SilverLining and use that with any hard drive regardless of its manufacturer or vendor.

Because the quality of drives from the various manufacturers changes from time to time, as does the service of most vendors and dealers, it is a good idea to ask other Macintosh users for their recommendations. You will find yourself with no shortage of opinions, and you'll probably save time, money, and frustration by spending your money with vendors who have recently satisfied other Mac users.

At the time of this writing, MicroNet and Mass Micro are very popular with Mac users based on the quality of their products and support policies. Our own least favorite hard-drive vendor is Arc Laser Optical, formerly known as Lo-Down, who not only sold us drives with the highest failure rate imaginable, but also treated us to nothing but rude and untimely service.

Floppy Disks

As described in the Disks and Drives entry in Section 1, there are three different kinds of floppy disks used on the Mac: single-sided (400K), double-sided (800K), and high-density (1.44Mb). Floppy disks of each type are available from many different manufacturers. We've seen prices as low as 39¢ and as high as $4.00 per disk.

In the Mac's early days, Sony disks were well worth their usually higher price because their failure rate was much lower than that of their competitors. As the market for 3.5" floppy disks has matured, however, it appears that other manufacturers have figured out how to produce reliable floppy disks, and therefore you can feel comfortable with just about any brand. Of course, there is some peace of mind in purchasing a name-brand disk that is accompanied by a money-back guarantee. We still use Sony disks exclusively, but this is probably based on superstition alone.

Labeling Floppy Disks

Until the day when floppy disks include little LED panels that display the current disk content, the problem of keeping floppy disks labeled accurately in the face of the ever-changing data that they hold will be a major dilemma facing the well-organized Mac user. There are a number of schools of thought on floppy-disk labeling.

◇   **Write directly on the stickers that come with the disks**. The obvious problem with this is that the information written on these labels cannot be changed, and removing them is often difficult—bordering on impossible. Some people advocate using lighter fluid to help remove these stickers, and that does work, but we think it is simpler to just peel off what you can and then put a new sticker right on top of the old one. You can buy additional disk labels in most office-supply stores.

◇   **Write on cellophane tape stuck to the disk or label**. One very easy solution to the problem of disk labeling is to put a piece of cellophane tape on the disk or on the label, and then write on the tape. Most felt-tip and ballpoint pens write on this tape perfectly. Fold over one end of the tape so it sticks to itself, and you have a little tab that makes the tape easy to remove.

◇   **Write on "dot labels."** Small round stickers, available at any office-supply store in diameters ranging from 0.5" to 1.5", allow you to color-code your disks and write on them. Dot labels are easy to remove.

◇   **Use the NoLabel System**. This somewhat intricate but workable system provides you with clear plastic label covers that you stick on each disk, and a large supply of removable label tabs that you mark and place inside the plastic label covers. The covers stay on the disks forever, and you just change the labels as needed.

◇ **Use software to create disk labels.** Several utilities are available to print disk labels that are customized for the content of each disk. Most work by reading the content from your diskette and then allowing you to edit the automatically generated label before printing it. Almost all of the labeling programs support the ImageWriter, and some also support the creation of LaserWriter disk labels.

Storing Floppy Disks

The longer you have your Mac, the more floppy disks you accumulate. This is true despite advances in mass storage and increases in the per-disk capacity of floppy disks. Like disk labeling, the storage and organization of a floppy-disk library is a more time-consuming problem than it should be. Most of us wind up cramming too many disks into cheap little disk boxes, stacking extra ones behind all the disk containers, and generally promising ourselves that one day we're going to spring for a few big new disk containers and organize the whole mess.

We recently took the big plunge and bought a couple of 130-disk teakwood rolltop disk cases from Kalamar. It was the best $62 we have spent in a very long time. About 15 of those small plastic 20-disk holders are now looking for work, but we can find disks so much faster that it's fantastic. Two or three more of those cases and we could have all of our nonarchival disks completely organized.

These cases are well-made, attractive, and very economical—especially in their larger sizes. As with most disk cases, more than the advertised number of disks can be crammed into them, although the extra cost of larger cases is so slight that the largest size, rated at a 130-disk capacity, is appropriate for most Mac users. Other vendors sell similar cases, but we have found the Kalamar cases to be of the highest quality. Kalamar does not, however, offer locking versions of these cases, as other vendors do.

If you use a Mac Plus, SE, or SE/30, remember that the power supply inside the computer is on the left side, so disks, disk drives, and disk cases should never be kept on the left side of the Mac. (The power supply generates electricity and magnetic forces that could ruin them.) If you want to keep a disk holder on the left side of your Mac, allow a few inches of space between the Mac and the disk holder. Disks should not be left lying on the top of the Mac II, IIx, or IIcx, because the power supply and disk drives both are dangerous to disks. Disks will not necessarily be harmed if put near the left side of a compact Mac or on top of a Mac II, but they could be.

Traveling with Floppy Disks

If you ever travel with your disks (even to and from work), another great investment is a "disk wallet," which is a nylon holder, usually with a velcro seal. These keep your disks warm, dry, and in one place, saving them the torture of a few weeks deep in your briefcase or under the seat in your car.

Most office-supply stores and catalogs sell disk-mailing envelopes, which are generally strong cardboard envelopes, sometimes marked with "magnetically sensitive" labels; these are recommended when you are mailing floppies. We have, on occasion, simply slipped a 3.5" floppy disk into a standard business envelope and mailed it away, without any problems.

We would also like to mention those small plastic bags (sometimes halfbags) that most floppies come in when they are new. Throw them away! While they do provide some small measure of protection from dust, moisture, and static, they are *trés gauche*, a sure sign of the beginning Mac user.

 # Input Devices

Keyboards

Apple offers two different keyboards for use with all of its SE and Mac II models: the standard keyboard and the extended keyboard. The extended keyboard offers three sets of keys that are different from those on the standard keyboard: the function keys, the cursor-control keys, and the arrow keys.

The function keys do not inherently do very much, although F1 through F4 perform as labeled—invoking the UNDO, CUT, COPY, and PASTE commands, respectively. (These did not work before System Software 6.0.)

Function keys are very useful when used in conjunction with one of the macro programs described in the Macros entry in Section 1. The cursor-control keys (INSERT/HELP, DELETE/FORWARD DELETE, HOME, END, PAGE UP, and PAGE DOWN) are functional in many applications that require navigation around the screen, including many word processors, spreadsheets, and page-composition programs. These keys can be implemented from macro utilities in most other applications. The arrow keys on the extended keyboard are not really any different from those on the standard keyboard, but their placement is much more logical, and we find that as a result they are used much more frequently on the extended keyboard than on the standard keyboard. Additionally, the extended keyboard offers three status lights, which (theoretically at least—they are not fully implemented in the current System Software) denote the position of the NUMBER LOCK, CAPS LOCK, and SCROLL LOCK keys.

The retail price difference between Apple's standard and extended keyboards is $100. This may be a lot to pay for 21 new keys and the redistribution of some others, but if you have the desk space, we heartily recommend the extended keyboard.

Mouse

The standard ADB mouse included with SE's and later-model Macs has changed very little since the first mouse offered with the Lisa in 1983. A partially exposed ball rolling about in a chamber against three tracking wheels remains the most popular internal mechanism for mice, whether created by Apple, Microsoft, or MSC.

But there is an inherent problem with mechanical mice. Over time, dust and dirt collect on the surface of the tracking wheels inside the mouse. Due to the constant rubbing of ball against wheel, this dirt becomes worn to a smooth finish, causing the wheels to slip occasionally.

Other forms of mice exist. **Trackballs**, for example, are sort of like mice on their backs. The ball is exposed upward so you can swivel it around with your fingers. The advantage to trackballs is that you can make large cursor movements without a lot of desk space and without having to repeatedly lift your mouse and set it down. You can also send the cursor flying by scooting the ball quickly and letting it roll. However, the ball still uses the same mechanical means of conveyance as the traditional mouse, and we find it more difficult to use for detailed work.

If you hate cleaning mice but have gotten used to the way they feel in your hand, we recommend an optical mouse such as the A+ Mouse ADB from Mouse Systems. An optical light sensor and infrared red sensor work together to read movement off the matrix of a special mouse pad. The main advantage is that there are no moving parts to wear out. Also, your cursor always moves smoothly as long as you keep your pad clean of dirt and smudges, which involves a few wipes with some window cleaner and a paper towel. The only disadvantage is that you must keep the mouse as close as possible to perpendicular to the surface of the mouse pad at all times. This involves some wrist contortions at first, but we found it easy to get used to in the long run.

Mouse Cleaning

Apple's mechanical mouse rolls its small rubber ball across your desk or mouse pad as it's used, invariably picking up dirt from these surfaces. Inside the mouse, this dirt is transferred to the rotating sensors that convert the ball's movement into commands delivered to the Mac itself. When the ball and sensors get too dirty, mouse movements are not accurately transferred to the Mac, and your mouse appears sluggish and jumpy.

Cleaning the mouse is easy. Turn the mouse over, unscrew the cover on the ball, take the ball out, and rub it with a towel, or against your jeans, or in your hand. It is probably not the best idea to use any solutions that may eat into the rubber; this is usually not necessary anyway. To clean the sensors, use a cotton swab moistened with water or alcohol.

Mouse Pads

Although the plastic pads on the bottom of Apple's mouse allow it to move smoothly across most surfaces, the ball inside the mouse rolls more smoothly on a slightly rough service. Mouse pads give your mouse the surface they prefer, and you will notice the difference in smoother and more accurate mouse performance. At five to ten dollars, a mouse pad is the cheapest improvement you can make to your Macintosh.

Tablets

Many Mac-compatible tablets are now available, including those from SumaGraphics and Kurta. Numerous shapes and sizes are available, from as small as a foot square to as large as a freestanding card table. We generally recommend that you get the smallest tablet you think you can stand. It has to fit on your desk, after all, and you don't want to be three feet from your monitor using a freestanding device. In addition, most tablets allow you to magnify the movements of your pen.

The best tablets offer function-key buttons and other templates. It can be extremely difficult, not to mention hard on the neck, to try to use a pad and keyboard simultaneously. Most tablets provide a layer of acetate under which line art or photographs may be placed for tracing. But if you think tracing in real life is problematic, you should try this! We have yet to trace anything and have it come out looking even remotely like what we wanted. We highly recommend that if you intend to trace a lot of artwork, you buy a scanner instead.

Tablets are most useful with painting programs. They can also be used with drawing programs that provide freehand tools, but in general we find that a mouse gives you more control in less space.

 Modems

For standard personal or business use, modems for the Macintosh are available in 300, 1200, 2400, and 9600 baud models. Currently, 2400 baud is surpassing 1200 baud as the standard for most communications, and the price difference between a 2400-baud modems and a 1200-baud modem is very slight. Since the faster transmission rates result in lower phone and on-line charges in almost every case, even users on a tight budget should opt for a 2400-baud model. The 9600-baud models are much more expensive, usually demand a premium charge for connect times (although they will save on phone tolls), and can often be operated more cheaply than slower modems. But the communications protocol for 9600-baud modems is still not standardized, few people have them, and not all on-line services support them.

Many brands of modems are available, but we particularly like the Practical Peripherals modems, which include a 5-year warranty. One of our Practical Peripheral modems did break after about a year of use, but for just seven dollars postage it was promptly repaired, no questions asked. (Another of these modems has been operating constantly on our bulletin board for about 2 years without any problems.)

Fax

The rapid explosion of facsimile transmissions (fax) in the world of business and personal communications is a true phenomenon. Using your Macintosh, you can participate in this exciting turn of events, although the benefits of "Mac as fax" are not universal. The basic problem with using the Mac to fax is that the process of sending or receiving a fax transmission requires the integrated use of a scanner, a telecommunications device, and a printer. Dedicated fax machines integrate these devices, making them vastly easier to use than a combination of Mac, scanner, fax modem, and printer, which are totally separate devices never really intended to work together as a single unit.

With a fax modem connected to your Macintosh, sending a fax of computer documents is easy, but sending a fax from a hard-copy document, or receiving a fax, requires enough extra steps that it can be considered prohibitive. Future software products will probably allow for a computer-based fax to compete with dedicated fax machines in terms of features and convenience, but for now only certain requirements are best served by Mac-based fax.

If you have a modem, you can already send faxes via most major telecommunications services, including CompuServe, MCI Mail, AT&T Mail, and Connect (which uses MCI Mail). This is perfect for sending faxes from your computer-based documents; normally you would have to print them and then use a dedicated fax machine. Faxing via these services obviously incurs an extra charge, but for the occasional user these options are well worth taking advantage of—especially for those who are currently paying several dollars per transmission to use the fax machine at a local copy shop or service bureau.

Monitors

An important decision facing all Mac users, both those who've had their Macs for a while and those just purchasing a new Mac system, is deciding which type and brand of monitor to purchase for use with their system. Monitors for Macintoshes are available in sizes ranging from the 9-inch display included in the compact Macs to a 56-inch Mitsubishi presentation system. Some monitors are black and white only, some offer gray-scale support, and color is available in 4-bit, 8-bit, 24-bit, and 32-bit varieties.

Selecting a Monitor Size

Four basic monitor sizes are available on the Macintosh: the 9-inch monitor built into the compact Macintoshes, 12-inch monitors, 8.5-by-11-inch "full-page display" monitors, and 24-inch "two-page display" monitors. Obviously, with the compact Macs the monitor is not optional, and so the choice becomes whether to add an additional external monitor. We can tell you from our own personal experience that not only is it a pleasure to work on a larger monitor, but it also has an incredible effect on your productivity. When we added a Radius Full Page Display to one of our Mac SE's, we found that not only could we work faster, but we did more work because we no longer avoided tasks that we subconsciously found inconvenient on the smaller screen.

Each of the modular Macs allows you to choose your own display at the time of original purchase, although if you are currently working with an Apple 12-inch monitor you may also want to consider adding an additional display to your System. Any of the Mac II models can support up to six concurrent displays, and although six would be an extreme, two or even three monitors can be quite useful. Particularly when working in MultiFinder, the ability to keep open DA's or secondary applications fully visible while another application consumes your main display is really terrific. Users of Apple's 12-inch monochrome display will find that the resale value of their current monitor is very low, so keeping this as a second display when upgrading to a large-screen or color display is often realistic.

Apple's 12-inch monitors, available in black-and-white and color versions, are very high-quality displays and although they cannot vertically display a complete 8.5-by-11-inch page, we believe that their size is adequate for most tasks, including graphic design and page composition. The price at which the monochrome display is offered makes it an excellent value, and a good choice for Mac users without extraordinary needs or budgets. As mentioned above, an additional benefit of the monitor's low cost is that if and when you decide to obtain a larger or color monitor, the 12-inch monochrome becomes an excellent second monitor.

The full-page display size is great for almost any use, and is probably our favorite monitor size. The amount of scrolling eliminated by these monitors during word processing is incredible, and looking at such a long section of text rather than just a few paragraphs at a time allows you to get a better sense of your document on screen, making it less necessary to print repeatedly. Even for page-composition and drawing packages, we find that the full-page display size is more than adequate.

Black and White, Gray-Scale, or Color?

There are two reasons to consider making the jump from a black-and-white monitor to a color monitor. The first is that color is now almost fully supported in the user interface and by most software, so color becomes part of the computing experience. The second is that if you actually create documents, graphics, or pages that will be reproduced in color, you can see them that way on screen; or you can create multimedia presentations whose on-screen color images will be the final product.

Color monitors are distinguished by their size and by the number of colors that they can display simultaneously. Color monitors are available in 12-inch, 19-inch, and 24-inch models. The number of colors a monitor can display is determined by the amount of video memory provided by the video adaptor card that drives the monitor, and the software being used. Apple's basic video card offers 4 bits of memory per screen pixel, meaning that any pixel can display 2^4 different colors—16 different colors are then available on screen. Apple's video card can be upgraded to support 8 bits per pixel, and third-party video cards offer up to 32 bits of memory per pixel. (An 8-bit video card supports 256 different colors on screen, 16-bit video supports 65,000 colors, 24-bit offers 16 million colors, and 32-bit offers over 4 billion colors!) Not all software can support such large color palettes, and Apple has only recently begun supporting 32-bit color in its operating system.

Gray-scale monitors represent the different colors the software is expressing as shades of gray, providing an on-screen representation that is more realistic than a simple black-and-white rendering. Gray-scale monitors are much less expensive than color monitors, but they still cost significantly more than monochrome monitors. We don't think these are adequate replacements for color monitors, and can only recommend them for situations in which actual gray-scale editing will be performed, such as in photographic retouching.

Many monochrome monitors can display several gray shades. You can use the Monitors cdev to turn on 4 or 16 colors. If you choose colors carefully, you can then use many of the color utilities described in the Customization entry in Section 1 and spice up your Mac a little with these gray shades. The use of gray values does consume more of your RAM, however, so it is not advised unless you have at least 2 megabytes of RAM—4 megabytes or more when using MultiFinder.

 # RAM

Random-access memory (RAM) is a set of chips, attached to the Mac's logic board, that electronically store information in a form accessible by the computer's CPU. As your Macintosh is used, information stored on disk is moved into RAM, manipulated by the CPU, and then written back to disk for long-term storage.

Unlike most other chips on the logic board, memory chips are blank every time the Macintosh is turned on, and data is then written and rewritten to these chips repeatedly during the computer's operation. Software on the Macintosh ROM chips controls the management of memory, deciding what information is stored at which location in memory. This ROM software keeps track of what areas of RAM are available for use, and which areas are currently in use.

RAM Uses

RAM in the Macintosh has many uses, more than in most other personal computers; this partially explains why the machine is so RAM-hungry. RAM is used to hold portions of the ROM software, portions of the System Software, inits, information for the video display, open desk accessories, directories of mounted disks and volumes, the Clipboard, portions of open applications, and the data being used by current application programs.

The System Heap

The section of RAM that holds parts of the System Software, inits, and DA's is called the **system heap**. (Note: DA's are kept in the application heap and not in the system heap when you are using MultiFinder.) The size of the system heap is determined at startup, based on a value in the boot blocks of the disk used to start up the Macintosh. When using many inits and memory-intensive DA's, you may "run out" of system heap, causing system crashes and other strange behavior. As inits and DA's are loaded, the system heap should be automatically enlarged (providing that enough RAM is available), but this automatic enlargement does not always work properly, and in some cases, it provides enough space for the init or DA to load but not enough for it to operate properly.

☐ ▭▭▭▭ **About the Macintosh™ Finder** ▭▭▭▭

Finder : 6.1		**Elvis, Steve, Pete & Bruce**	
System: 6.0.2		**©Apple Computer, Inc. 1983–88**	
Total Memory :	5,120K	**Largest Unused Block :**	3,261K
◆ Word 4.0	750K	▓▓▓▓▓▓▓▓▓▓ ▒	
▤ Finder	160K	▓▒	
▤ System	949K	▓▓▓▓▓▓▓▓▓▓▓ ▒	

The A BOUT THE F INDER dialog box can help you to correctly reset the size of your system heap.

You can check the status of your system heap by choosing the ABOUT THE FINDER command in the APPLE Menu. In the ABOUT THE FINDER dialog box, the system heap's size and utilization is represented by the bar shown next to the small Mac icon and the word *System*. The bar itself represents the entire system heap, and the darkened area represents the portion of the system heap that is currently being used. The light area represents free memory in the system heap. If there is little or no free space in your system heap, you may be able to reduce the number of system crashes and overall software problems you experience by enlarging your system heap.

You can enlarge the system heap by changing the systems-heap specification contained in the boot blocks of your startup disk so that a larger-than-normal system heap is created at startup. This can be done with either of two utilities from CE Software, Heapfix or Widgets.

CE Software recommends that your system heap be large enough so that between 25 and 50 percent of it is free after all of your inits have been loaded. This means that the light area of the system heap bar in the ABOUT THE FINDER dialog box should represent 25 to 50 percent of the length of the bar. To achieve this, you must first determine the amount of system heap that you are currently using, and then calculate how much larger your system heap would have to be in order for 25 to 50 percent of it to be free. Check the ABOUT THE FINDER dialog box after restarting your Mac and allowing all the inits you normally use to be loaded, and then make your calculations. This value could be anywhere between 30K and 500K.

Both Heapfix and Widgets present you with a simple dialog box in which you specify how much larger than normal you want your system heap to be. Enter the value you have determined. After rebooting your Mac, check the ABOUT THE FINDER dialog box again. Your system heap should now contain a satisfactory amount of free space. If the system heap is still not correct, recalculate your requirements and modify the heap again. In general you may have to try several heap settings to find one that works best for your combination of software and utilities.

Of course, increasing the size of your system heap decreases the amount of RAM available for your application heap, so you can only increase your system heap if you have enough RAM available in your Mac—at least 2 megabytes in most cases. Also remember that since you edit the size of the system heap by resetting a value in the boot blocks of your startup disk, the new heap size does not take effect until the Mac is rebooted. And any time the Mac is started with another boot disk, the system-heap size specified by that disk is used.

Heapfix

This utility from CE Software offers the simplest and most direct method of increasing (or decreasing) the size of your system heap. Upon launching, Heapfix tells you how much larger than normal your system heap is currently, and allows you to alter this value as you wish.

Widgets

One of the many features of CE Software's Widgets utility is the ability to reset the size of the system heap. Widgets system heap-feature operates just like that of Heapfix, telling you the current size of the system heap relative to the normal system heap, and allowing you to edit this value as you see fit.

Spy

This init adds an extra line to the top of your display, which constantly shows the amount of free space in your system heap, application heap, and stack. If you are having problems that you believe are memory-related, Spy is a good way to keep track of the RAM in your Mac as it is used.

The Application Heap

The section of RAM that holds your application software and the data it uses is called the **application heap**. When a Macintosh application is launched, a large portion of the application is transferred into RAM (although in most cases, the entire application does not move entirely into RAM). This is why the drive is accessed so heavily when you launch an application, and why launching an application is relatively time-consuming.

The entire application is not initially loaded into RAM for two reasons. First, the entire application may not fit into the available RAM, and second it would waste time to load portions that may not be used. As an application is used, portions of the program not already in RAM are moved into RAM on a demand basis. In most cases, only a certain percentage of the application is ever kept in RAM at one time, and the rest is transferred in and then overwritten as needed.

The data files used by Mac software may also be transferred in and out of RAM. This transfer, which is controlled by the application, is dependent upon the amount of data being used and the amount of available RAM. Because data files are manipulated almost constantly during the execution of most applications, the more of a data file kept in memory, the better—although, as with applications, there is a cost in the time necessary to load the data into RAM.

Since the data file that is kept in RAM and manipulated by the application is actually a copy of the data file—the original data file still resides on disk—all changes made during the execution of an application are in danger of being lost until the SAVE command is executed. The SAVE command updates the on-disk copy of the data file to include all changes made since the file was read into RAM.

Applications that cannot fit their entire altered data files in RAM often create **temporary files** on disk to hold the file data until it is written to a permanent file with the SAVE command. Most applications automatically delete these temporary files when the data is saved, when the file is closed, or when the application is quit, although some applications tend to leave them littering your disks. (Microsoft Word is especially guilty on this charge. An init called Temperament automatically deletes all the temporary files that Word has left on your hard drive each time you restart your Mac.)

In most cases, these files can be deleted without worry, but it is very important to never delete temporary files while still running the application! This may seem obvious, but it can happen while running MultiFinder or using a desk accessory like DiskTop to delete in the interest of freeing some disk space. If you delete a temporary file being used by an open file, chances are good that you will not be able to save your work to a normal disk file. Temporary files can also be used to recover data that was not properly saved if your system crashes or if an application quits unexpectedly. See the Files entry in Section 1 for more information about recovering data from temporary files.

Some of today's Macintosh software has enormous RAM requirements, seemingly exceeding the requirements of the software application itself and its data files. Programs with large RAM requirements usually perform complex tasks involving large amounts of intermediate data. For example, the highly acclaimed OmniPage character-recognition application requires 4 megabytes of RAM, which it uses to recognize virtually any character on a page scanned into the Macintosh. Once the recognition is complete, the text file that OmniPage creates may take up only a few bytes of disk space, but the recognition process itself may have used the entire 4 megabytes.

Of course, programming prowess still affects the memory requirements that software imposes; Aldus FreeHand provides the same feature set as Adobe Illustrator, but requires only half the RAM without sacrificing execution speed. It is often said that the large amounts of RAM that are common today allow (and perhaps encourage) programmers to be much "sloppier" than they would be if memory was not so plentiful and they had to figure out ways to make their programs run in less RAM.

RAM Drawbacks

For all of its virtues, RAM also carries two serious drawbacks: It is volatile and it is expensive.

RAM is volatile because its storage is maintained by the flow of electricity to the RAM chips; any loss or fluctuation in the electric current causes an immediate loss of the data stored in RAM. When your computer is turned off, or when you experience a power loss or brown-out, all data in RAM that has not been transferred to disk storage is lost—permanently. When your Macintosh crashes or locks up (those rare occasions!) and you are forced to reboot in order to restart the Mac, RAM is initialized as if it were empty during the startup, also resulting in a total loss of the data in RAM.

As mentioned, all changes made to any data file from the time an application is opened, or from the time the SAVE command was last executed, are stored primarily in RAM and are therefore in constant danger of being lost due to any power loss or system crash. This is why computer users are constantly being told to save their work frequently; saving transfers data from RAM (and temporary files) to permanent disk files.

Although the cost of RAM chips can fluctuate dramatically, RAM remains relatively expensive. Nevertheless, application-software developers and Apple itself continue to produce software that demands more and more RAM. Although 1 megabyte remains the current average for Macintosh RAM, MultiFinder is virtually useless without 4Mb of RAM—but fantastic when 4Mb is available—and System Software 7.0 will require 2Mb of RAM in order to operate. (4 megabytes will probably be a more practical requirement, since MultiFinder is "always on" in System Software 7.0.)

The high cost of RAM leaves most Mac users wondering whether a RAM upgrade is worth the money. Here are our thoughts.

- **If you are operating a Mac with 128K or 512K**. The only way you could be running such a system is if you already have software that suits your needs; most new Mac software requires at least 1 megabyte. If you are entirely happy with the service your Macintosh is performing, and do not want to either update or expand those uses, more power to you. Of course, this also means that you cannot even take advantage of Apple's latest System Software. If you do want to upgrade, there are lots of memory upgrades that will bring your system up to the 1 megabyte standard. Only some of these upgrades allow you to later go to 2 or 4 megabytes, so keep in mind your long-term goals—and the realities of the Macintosh world—when shopping for your memory upgrade.

- **If you are operating on a 1 megabyte system**. There are always problems with being average. And in memory as in life, being slightly above average doesn't really do you much good either. This is why the move from 1Mb to 2 is of dubious value. Two megabytes is not really enough to use MultiFinder, so all you are able to do is set a larger RAM cache (which does help performance) and use a few programs that often don't run well in a single megabyte (like Illustrator 88 and sometimes HyperCard).

  At 4 megabytes, you know you've spent your money well. Suddenly MultiFinder is available to you, and you can run three to five applications without any problems. And you no longer have to worry about the RAM consumed by inits and DA's. RAM beyond 4Mb, for the time being, is purely the domain of special applications and users with heavy MultiFinder requirements. Of course, the way RAM is added to some Macintoshes allows 5 megabytes for the same price as 4, and extra memory never hurts.

- **If you already have 2 megabytes**. You can easily find yourself feeling content with 2 megabytes of RAM; after all, you have a good-sized RAM cache running, and almost never have memory-related problems. Unless you develop the need for a specific application that requires 4Mb or more, you may think that adding more RAM really isn't important. The only flaw in this thinking is that no matter how satisfied you are with your 2Mb Mac, you will know you have spent your money well when you move to 4Mb and really start using MultiFinder.

- **If you already have 4 or 5 megabytes**. The move past here can only be justified for special applications or MultiFinder freaks! We know lots of 8 megabyte users who swear that they just couldn't get along with less, but frankly, we have a hard time believing them.

A RAM Substitute: Virtual Memory

Virtual memory is a hardware/software trick that allows hard-drive storage space to be used in place of RAM. You can use 8 megabytes of hard-drive space as if it were 8 megabytes of RAM. This works because the CPU never knows that it is using disk-based data—requests for data that lies on disk cause the virtual-memory software to bring the requested data into RAM. Of course, virtual memory cannot perform as quickly as true RAM, because there is a time delay associated with the process of transferring data from disk into RAM when it is needed. But virtual memory allows access to a full "8 megabytes of RAM" at a cost of only 2Mb.

Virtual memory requires a **Paged Memory Management Unit (PMMU)**, which can be installed as a separate chip into the Mac II, and is built into the 68030 central processing unit of the Mac IIx, IIcx, and SE/30. Currently, a software product called Virtual, which is sold with the PMMU chip required for the Mac II or alone as a software-only product for Mac IIx, IIcx, and SE/30, is the only way to add virtual memory to your Macintosh. System Software 7.0 will also provide virtual-memory support.

We have used Virtual successfully on a Mac SE/30 with only 1Mb of actual RAM, and found that we could successfully run MultiFinder and most applications that demand large amounts of RAM. The performance of the virtual memory improves as the amount of actual RAM increases; with 2Mb of actual RAM, virtual memory is noticeable but not too slow, and when you have 4Mb of actual RAM, the performance degradation of the virtual memory is practically undetectable.

RAM Versus Storage

Although memory and storage operate in different ways and serve different purposes, the fact that they both serve as data repositories (and are both measured in kilobytes) causes people to confuse them quite regularly. If we compare the way memory and storage are used in the computer to the way we use them as humans, perhaps the difference will become more apparent and easier to remember. In this analogy, the CPU plays the part of the human brain, computer memory (RAM) is equated with our own memory, and floppy and hard disk storage is equated with written or typed notes.

As you know, no information can gain access to your brain without first entering your memory; regardless of whether information originates from your eyes, ears, or other senses, it is immediately put into memory (RAM) so that the brain (CPU) can access it. But what do we do with information that we want to use in the future? We transfer it to some storage medium, like paper (disk). This way we know that when this information is needed in the future we can transfer it back into memory by reading it. Of course, the fact that humans have both short-term and long-term memory weakens this analogy, but it is generally a useful way to make the distinction between RAM and storage.

Looking at it another way, here are some common situations and how they relate to memory and storage.

- Application software requires some amount of disk space (storage) in order to fit on your hard drive, and some amount of memory (RAM) in order to run. While occasionally these amounts may be approximately the same, there is no correlation between the amount of disk space an application file consumes and the amount of memory required in order for it to operate. For example, PageMaker requires over 800K of disk space just to hold its application file, but only 700K of RAM in order to operate, while OmniPage consumes only 640K of disk space but requires 4 megabytes of RAM to run.

- If you cannot save another file or copy a new program onto your hard disk, you are out of disk space (storage). Having lots of RAM won't help another file fit onto a full disk.

- If you cannot run an application because you don't have enough memory, you are out of RAM. Having plenty of available disk space won't allow you to open an application that needs more memory.

Parameter RAM

In order to maintain a few user-definable parameters that are not lost each time the machine is turned off, each Macintosh contains a small amount of RAM (256K) that is powered by the Mac's internal battery when the machine is turned off, thus preventing it from losing its contents. This RAM, called the **parameter RAM** (**PRAM**, pronounced "pea ram"), holds a number of settings that are customized by the user.

Most of the entries in the PRAM are set in the General cdev in the Control Panel. Items held in the PRAM include modem-port configuration (baud, data, parity, etc.), printer-port configuration (baud, data, parity, etc.), time/date setting, default application font, keyboard repeat threshold, keyboard repeat rate, printer port, speaker volume, mouse double-click time, mouse scaling, pointer blink, menu blink, and startup disk drive.

PRAM is read into regular RAM during the Mac's startup sequence. If the information in the PRAM ever becomes damaged, you can reset it either by removing the battery in the Mac for 5 minutes (Mac Plus only) or by holding down COMMAND-OPTION-CONTROL when choosing the Control Panel from the APPLE menu. This technique, known as "zapping the PRAM," completely erases the PRAM and restores its original values from ROM. Incidentally, the time is not zapped by this method, so you will not have to reset your clock after a PRAM zap. See the Control Panel entry in Section 1 for more information on zapping the PRAM.

Section Four

Resources

📖 Books

Although documentation has certainly improved since the old days, there are still times when you may not find all of the information you're looking for provided along with your software. Other times, a piece of software doesn't come with a manual, as was the case with the first release of HyperCard. Or perhaps you aren't looking for information on a specific piece of software, but rather on the Mac in general.

In any of these cases, you will find an inexhaustible supply of Mac-related books at your disposal. To make your shopping list more complete, we provide a list of every Macintosh book currently available (or at least, every book we know of).

Books are listed alphabetically and divided into nine categories. These categories include:

- **Communications and networks**. These books deal with telecommunications, including electronic mail, as well as establishing and organizing networks.

- **Database management**. Both relational database managers and flat file applications are covered by these books.

- **Desktop publishing and graphics**. Any books regarding page-layout or graphics applications, as well as general design and typography titles, are covered here.

- **General or introductory**. Books in this category range from John Sculley's autobiography to introductory or all-encompassing Mac titles along the lines of our *Encyclopedia Macintosh*.

- **HyperCard**. These books cover HyperCard and the HyperTalk programming language.

- **Miscellaneous applications**. If you're looking for a book about a piece of software that isn't HyperCard or a database manager, nor is it a spreadsheet or a word processor, and it isn't used for desktop publishing, it may be covered in this section. Books on Microsoft Works, for example, fall into this category.

- **Programming/technical**. Books about programming languages, such as Basic, Pascal, and C, as well as those covering technical hardware information, are included here.

- **Spreadsheets**. Microsoft Excel, Full Impact, and Wingz books dominate this category.

- **Word processing**. If you're having problems using MacWrite, Microsoft Word, or some other word processor, consult this list.

All list entries include the book's title, author, publisher, year of publication, ISBN number (often useful for ordering), and list price. You will probably be able to find cheaper prices through a discount reseller.

Thanks to David Angell at MacBooks, a mail-order Macintosh bookseller located in Palo Alto, California, for his help in compiling this list. Information about his service is provided at the end of this entry.

Communications and Networks

AppleTalk Network System Overview
Apple Computer
Addison-Wesley, 1989
0-20151-760-4
$14.95

Complete MCI Mail Handbook
Manes, S.
Bantam Books, 1988
0-55334-587-7
$22.95

Hands-On AppleTalk
Rogers/Bare
A Brady Book, 1990
0-13039-678-8
$21.95

IBM PC and Macintosh Networking
Michel, Stephen
Howard W. Sams & Co., 1990
0-67248-451-X
$22.95

Inside AppleTalk
Apple Computer
Addison-Wesley, 1989
0-20119-257-8
$34.95

Inside TOPS
New Riders
New Riders, 1990
0-93403-572-5
$21.95

Microsoft DOS-Mac Connection
Harriman, C.
A Brady Book, 1988
0-13449-448-2
$21.95

Mac To Vax
Sandler/Badgett
Scott, Foresman, & Co., 1990
0-67338-578-7
$24.95

MacAccess: Information in Motion
Gengle/Smith
Howard W. Sams & Co., 1987
0-67246-567-1
$21.95

MacLANs: Local Area Networking
Veljkov, Mark
Scott, Foresman, & Co., 1988
0-67318-732-2
$21.95

Networking Personal Computers
Durr, M.
Que Corp., 1990
0-88022-417-7
$22.95

Speaking of Networks: A Glossary
Apple Computer
Addison-Wesley, 1990
0-20151-761-2
$14.95

TOPS: The IBM/Macintosh Connection
Cobb/Jost
TAB Books, 1990
0-83063-210-7
$21.95

Understanding Computer Networks
Apple Computer
Addison-Wesley, 1989
0-20119-773-1
$9.95

Well-Connected Macintosh
Bove/Rhodes
Harcourt Brace Jovanovich, 1987
0-15695-666-7
$11.95

Database Management

Complete Guide to dBASE Mac
Shafer, Dan
Scott, Foresman, & Co., 1988
0-67318-732-2
$21.95

Complete Guide to Omnis 3
Mosich, Donna
Scott, Foresman, & Co., 1987
0-67318-595-8
$22.95

*Database Management
with Double Helix*
Harrington, Jan
A Brady Book, 1988
0-13560-053-7
$24.95

dBASE Mac: Advanced Techniques
Loggins, R.
Bantam Books, 1988
0-55334-392-0
$21.95

dBASE Mac in Business
Heid, Jim
Ashton-Tate, 1987
0-91267-790-2
$19.95

dBASE Mac Programmer's Reference
Jones, Edward
Howard W. Sams & Co., 1988
0-67248-416-1
$19.95

Dynamics of FoxBASE+ Programming
Goley, G.
Dow Jones-Irwin, 1990
1-55623-159-8
$21.95

4th Dimension: A Complete Guide
Knight, Tim
Scott, Foresman, & Co., 1988
0-67338-172-2
$21.95

FoxBASE+ Simplified: Mac Edition
Masterson, M.
TAB Books, 1990
0-83063-187-9
$24.95

Programming with dBASE Mac
Prague, Cary
TAB Books, 1990
0-83062-166-0
$26.95

S. Cobb User's Guide to FileMaker
Cobb, S.
TAB Books, 1990
0-83063-411-8
$24.95

Using ORACLE with HyperCard
Shafer, D.
Howard W. Sams & Co., 1990
0-67248-443-9
$24.95

Using dBASE Mac
Springer, Paul
Que Corp., 1988
0-88022-337-5
$19.95

Working with dBASE Mac
DeMaria, R.
A Brady Book, 1988
0-13939-760-4
$24.95

Desktop Publishing and Graphics

Adobe Illustrator 88
Bove, Tony
Bantam Books, 1988
0-55334-629-6
$24.95

Adobe Illustrator Expert Advisor
Burns/Venit
Addison-Wesley, 1989
0-20114-397-6
$22.95

Advanced PageMaker for the Mac
Kahn, Stephen
MIS: Press, 1990
0-94351-898-9
$19.95

Aldus Persuasion
Brown/Stielstra
John Wiley & Sons, 1990
0-47151-412-8
$22.95

Becoming a MacArtist
Guzelimian, V.
Compute Publications, 1985
0-94238-680-9
$17.95

Business Graphics for the Macintosh
Glau, G.
Dow Jones-Irwin, 1985
0-87094-693-5
$19.95

Desktop Publisher's Legal Handbook
Sitarz, D.
Nova Publishing, 1989
0-93575-502-0
$19.95

Desktop Publishing Bible
Waite Group
Howard W. Sams & Co., 1987
0-67222-524-7
$24.95

Desktop Publishing by Design
Shushan/Wright
Microsoft Press, 1989
1-55615-134-9
$19.95

Desktop Publishing: Macintosh Edition
Davis/Barry
Dow Jones-Irwin, 1987
1-55623-062-1
$24.95

Desktop Publishing Skills
Nace/Felici
Addison-Wesley, 1987
0-20111-537-9
$19.95

Desktop Publishing Type & Graphics
McClelland/Danuloff
Harcourt Brace Jovanovich, 1987
0-15625-298-8
$29.95

Desktop Publishing Using Pagemaker
Lucas, A.
HSTD, 1987
0-47020-819-8
$21.95

Desktop Publishing with Microsoft Word
Ericson, Tim
SYBEX, 1988
0-89588-447-X
$22.95

Desktop Publishing with PageMaker 3.0
Bove/Rhodes
John Wiley & Sons, 1990
0-47151-526-4
$21.95

Desktop Typography with QuarkXPress
Romano, F.
TAB Books, 1988
0-83069-323-8
$19.95

Dynamics of Desktop Publishing Design
Webster, T.
MacTutor, 1990
1-55851-051-6
$22.95

Dynamics of Presentation Graphics
Meilach, D.
Dow Jones-Irwin, 1990
1-55623-229-2
$24.95

Electronic Publisher
Burns/Venit
A Brady Book, 1988
0-13251-877-5
$24.95

Graphic Design with PostScript
Kunkel, G.
Scott, Foresman, & Co., 1990
0-67338-794-1
$24.95

Hands-on Mac PageMaker 3.0
Wallia, C.
Prentice Hall Press, 1990
0-13202-292-3
$21.95

Illustrated Ready,Set,Go!
Wang/Mueller
Wordware Publishing, 1989
1-55622-103-7
$21.95

Inside PostScript
Braswell, Frank
Peachpit Press, 1989
0-93811-511-0
$37.50

Introducing PageMaker 3, Mac Version
Webster, D.
Weber Systems, 1988
0-94730-200-X
$21.95

Laser Print It
Cavuto, James
Addison-Wesley, 1986
0-20111-349-X
$16.95

Laser Printer Handbook
Myers, D.
Dow Jones-Irwin, 1989
1-55623-133-4
$21.95

Looking Good in Print
Parker, Roger
Ventana Press, 1988
0-94008-705-7
$23.95

Macintosh Desktop Design
Baxter, John
The Baxter Group, 1986
0-93894-902-0
$15.95

Macintosh Desktop Products
Baxter, John
The Baxter Group, 1987
0-93894-903-9
$15.95

Macintosh Desktop Typography
Baxter, John
The Baxter Group, 1986
0-93894-904-7
$16.95

Macintosh Font Book
Fenton, E.
Peachpit Press, 1989
0-93815-105-3
$23.95

MakeOver Book 101 Design Solutions
Parker, Roger
Ventana Press, 1989
0-94008-720-0
$17.95

Making Art on the Macintosh II
Gosney/Dayton
Scott, Foresman, & Co., 1989
0-67338-159-5
$22.95

Managing Desktop Publishing
Berst, J.
New Riders, 1989
0-93403-527-X
$9.95

Mastering Adobe Illustrator
Holzgang, David
SYBEX, 1988
0-89588-463-1
$22.95

Mastering Adobe Illustrator 88
McClelland/Danuloff
Dow Jones-Irwin, 1988
1-55623-157-1
$24.95

Mastering Aldus Freehand, v2.0
McClelland/Danuloff
Dow Jones-Irwin, 1989
1-55623-288-8
$24.95

Mastering Graphics on the Macintosh
McNeill, D.
Compute Publications, 1990
0-87455-165-X
$19.95

Mastering MacDraw
McComb, G.
Compute Publications, 1987
0-87455-102-1
$19.95

Mastering Pagemaker: Mac Version 3.0
Gurganus, G.
TAB Books, 1990
0-83063-186-0
$17.95

Mastering Ready,Set,Go!
Kater, David
SYBEX, 1988
0-89588-536-0
$22.95

Mastering the Power of Persuasion
Parker, R.
Dow Jones-Irwin, 1990
1-55623-243-8
$24.95

Newsletter Publishing with PageMaker
Davis/Barry
Dow Jones-Irwin, 1988
1-55623-064-8
$24.95

PageMaker by Example 3.0
Webster, T & D
MacTutor, 1989
1-55851-049-4
$22.95

The PageMaker Companion
McClelland/Danuloff
Dow Jones-Irwin, 1989
1-55623-190-3
$29.95

PageMaker: Desktop Publishing
Strehlo, Kevin
Scott, Foresman, & Co., 1988
0-67318-764-0
$21.95

Painting on the Macintosh
McClelland, Deke
Dow Jones-Irwin, 1989
1-55623-265-9
$24.95

Personal Publishing with the Mac
Ulick, Terry
Howard W. Sams & Co., 1987
0-67248-406-4
$19.95

PostScript Language Program Design
Adobe Systems
Addison-Wesley, 1988
0-20114-396-8
$22.95

PostScript Language Reference
Adobe Systems
Addison-Wesley, 1987
0-20110-174-2
$22.95

PostScript Language Tutorial
Adobe Systems
Addison-Wesley, 1987
0-20110-179-3
$16.95

Presentation Design Book
Mathews, E.
PGW, 1990
0-94008-737-5
$24.95

QuarkXPress Companion
Hewson, D.
Hayden Book Co., 1988
0-86344-001-0
$15.95

Real World PostScript
Roth, Stephen
Addison-Wesley, 1988
0-20106-663-7
$22.95

ScanJet Unlimited
Roth, S.
PGW, 1990
0-93815-109-6
$24.95

SuperPaint Secrets
Rozells/Ennis
Scott, Foresman, & Co., 1990
0-67338-190-0
$22.95

Understanding PostScript Programming
Holzgang, David
SYBEX, 1988
0-89588-566-2
$24.95

Using Aldus Pagemaker 3.0
Kramer/Parker
Bantam Books, 1988
0-55334-624-5
$22.95

Zen & the Art of Macintosh
Green, M.
Running Press, 1986
0-89471-347-7
$16.95

General or Introductory

Apple Macintosh Book
Lu, Carry
Microsoft Press, 1988
1-55615-110-1
$21.95

Approaching Macintosh
Tchao, Michael
Addison-Wesley, 1986
0-02011-649-7
$29.95

Best Mac Deal, New Edition
Kueter/Cruz
Public Domain Exchange, 1989
0-96147-313-4
$9.95

Big Book of Amazing Mac Facts
Poole, L.
Microsoft Press, 1990
1-55615-252-3
$24.95

The Big Mac Book
Salkind, N.
Que Corp., 1990
0-88022-456-8
$27.95

CD-ROM: The New Papyrus
Lambert, S.
Microsoft Press, 1990
0-91484-574-8
$21.95

CD-ROM2: Optical Publishing
Ropiequet, S.
Microsoft Press, 1990
1-55615-000-8
$22.95

Complete Macintosh Sourcebook
Clapp, D.
InfoBooks, 1985
0-93113-703-9
$24.95

Computer Industry Almanac 1989
Juliussen, E.
A Brady Book, 1988
0-13167-537-0
$29.95

Computer Lib/Dream Machines
Nelson, T.
Microsoft Press, 1987
0-91484-549-7
$18.95

Computer Viruses
Roberts, R.
Compute Publications, 1988
0-87455-178-1
$14.95

Dr. Macintosh
LeVitus, B.
Addison-Wesley, 1989
0-20151-733-7
$19.95

Encyclopedia Macintosh
Danuloff/McClelland
SYBEX, 1989
0-89588-628-6
$24.95

Exploring Macintosh
Abernethy
John Wiley & Sons, 1989
0-47161-772-5
$36.00

Free & Almost Free Software
Eckhardt, R.
dilithium Press, 1987
0-51756-585-4
$19.95

*Hard Disk Management
for the Macintosh*
Andrews, Nancy
Bantam Books, 1987
0-55334-398-X
$34.95

Inside the Macintosh
Held/Norton
A Brady Book, 1990
0-13467-622-X
$22.95

Interactive Multimedia
Ambron (editor)
Microsoft Press, 1988
1-55615-124-1
$24.95

Lon Poole's Mac Insights
Poole, Lon
Microsoft Press, 1986
0-91484-573-X
$18.95

Mac Small Business Companion
Harriman, C.
A Brady Book, 1990
0-13542-721-5
$24.95

Macintosh Advisor
Harriman, C.
Howard W. Sams & Co., 1986
0-81046-569-8
$19.95

Macintosh Bible
Naiman, Arthur
Goldstein & Blair, 1988
0-94023-501-3
$38.00

Macintosh Hard Disk Management
Rubin/Calica
Howard W. Sams & Co., 1990
0-67248-457-9
$21.95

Macintosh Hypermedia, Volume I
Fraase, M.
Scott, Foresman, & Co., 1990
0-67338-791-7
$24.95

The Macintosh Way
Kawasaki, G.
Scott, Foresman, & Co., 1990
0-67346-175-0
$19.95

Odyssey: Pepsi to Apple
Sculley, John
Harper & Rowe, 1987
0-06091-527-7
$10.95

2500 Tips & Tricks for the Mac
Curtis, A.
ARCS, 1990
0-86668-066-7
$24.95

*Understanding Hard Disk Management
on the Macintosh*
Roberts, J.
SYBEX, 1989
0-89588-579-4
$22.95

West of Eden
Rose, Frank
Viking Press, 1989
0-67081-278-1
$19.95

HyperCard

Applied HyperTalk: Scripting Process
Daniels/Mara
A Brady Book, 1989
0-13040-882-4
$49.95

Applied HyperCard
Daniels/Mara
A Brady Book, 1988
0-13040-866-2
$39.95

Complete HyperCard Handbook
Goodman, Danny
Bantam Books, 1988
0-55334-577-X
$29.95

Complete SuperCard Handbook
Gookin, D.
Compute Publications, 1989
0-87455-198-6
$23.95

Concise Guide to HyperTalk
Shell, Barry
MIS: Press, 1988
0-94351-884-9
$9.95

Cooking with HyperTalk
Winkler/Knaster
Bantam Books, 1990
0-55334-738-1
$39.95

*Danny Goodman's
HyperCard Developer's Guide*
Goodman, Danny
Bantam Books, 1988
0-55334-576-1
$24.95

Dr. Dobb's Essential HyperTalk
Swaine, Michael
MacTutor, 1988
0-93437-598-4
$24.95

Exploring HyperCard
Anzovin, S.
Compute Publications, 1988
0-87455-152-8
$19.95

Hands-on HyperCard
Jones/Myers
John Wiley & Sons, 1988
0-47161-513-7
$22.95

HyperCard Handbook 1.2 Upgrade
Goodman, D.
Bantam Books, 1988
0-55334-684-9
$19.95

HyperCard Made Easy
Sanders, W.
Scott, Foresman, & Co., 1988
0-67338-358-X
$19.95

*HyperCard Power:
Technique and Scripts*
Kaehler, Carol
Addison-Wesley, 1988
0-20106-701-3
$17.95

HyperCard Quickstart
Maran, R.
Que Corp., 1988
0-88022-350-2
$21.95

HyperCard Script Language Guide
Apple Computer
Addison-Wesley, 1988
0-20117-632-7
$22.95

HyperCard Scripting, v. 1.2
Stoddard, J.
Computer Co-op Books, 1988
0-94521-701-3
$19.95

HyperCard Stack Design Guidelines
Apple Computer
Addison-Wesley, 1990
0-20151-784-1
$16.95

HyperCard: The Complete Reference
Michel, Stephen
Osborne McGraw-Hill, 1988
0-07881-430-8
$24.95

HyperDictionary
Brown, Phillip
Van Nostrand Reinhold, 1989
0-42230-329-7
$19.95

HyperTalk and the XCMDs
Gewirtz, David
PGW, 1988
0-94526-600-6
$11.95

HyperTalk Bible
Waite Group
Howard W. Sams & Co., 1989
0-67248-430-7
$24.95

HyperTalk Instant Reference
Harvey, Greg
SYBEX, 1988
0-89588-530-1
$10.95

HyperTalk Programming, v. 1.2
Shafer, Dan
Howard W. Sams & Co., 1988
0-67248-439-0
$24.95

HyperTalk Quick Reference
Poole, Lon
Microsoft Press, 1988
1-55615-137-3
$5.95

HyperTalk: The Book
Winkler/Kamins
Bantam Books, 1990
0-55334-737-3
$24.95

Mastering HyperTalk
Weiskamp, K.
John Wiley & Sons, 1988
0-47161-593-5
$22.95

Power User's HyperTalk Handbook
Goodman, P.
TAB Books, 1989
0-83069-143-X
$19.95

Quick and Easy HyperCard
Anzovin, Steven
Compute Publications, 1988
0-87455-145-5
$12.95

Running HyperCard with HyperTalk
Shell, Barry
MIS: Press, 1988
0-93518-792-X
$19.95

Steve Michel's SuperCard Handbook
Michel, S.
Osborne McGraw-Hill, 1990
0-07881-540-1
$24.95

Tricks of the HyperTalk Masters
Waite Group
Howard W. Sams & Co., 1989
0-67248-431-5
$24.95

Understanding HyperCard, v. 1.2
Harvey, Greg
SYBEX, 1989
0-89588-607-3
$24.95

Understanding HyperTalk (Series)
Shafer, Dan
Howard W. Sams & Co., 1988
0-67227-283-0
$17.95

Using HyperCard: Home to HyperTalk
Vaughan, W.
Que Corp., 1988
0-88022-384-7
$29.95

XCMD's for HyperCard
Bond, Gary
MIS: Press, 1988
0-94351-885-7
$24.95

Miscellaneous Applications

Advanced Microsoft Works Applications
Freeman/Holtz
Compute Publications, 1989
0-87455-143-9
$24.95

Balance of Power
Crawford, C.
Microsoft Press, 1986
0-91484-597-7
$10.95

Computer Aided Design on the Mac
Hastings
Prentice Hall Press, 1986
0-83590-992-1
$34.50

Essential GT to Mac Computers
Macek, R.
MECK, 1987
0-88736-078-5
$29.95

Fully Powered Mac
Eckhardt, R.
A Brady Book, 1988
0-13332-230-0
$39.95

Games and Utilities for the Mac
Shafer, Dan
New American Library, 1985
0-45225-641-0
$18.95

*Inside Microsoft Works
for the Macintosh*
McComb, G.
Bantam Books, 1990
0-55334-722-5
$24.95

MIDI Programming for the Macintosh
DeFuria, S.
MacTutor, 1988
1-55851-021-4
$22.95

Mac Bible Guide to Microsoft Works
Aker, S.
PGW, 1990
0-94023-530-7
$20.00

Macintosh CAD/CAM Book
Greco/Anders
Scott, Foresman, & Co., 1989
0-67338-446-2
$21.95

Mastering Dollars and Sense
Richardson, J.
Scott, Foresman, & Co., 1990
0-67338-557-4
$21.95

Mastering Microsoft Works
Aker, S.
Compute Publications, 1988
0-87455-042-4
$18.95

Mathematica
Wolfram, S.
Addison-Wesley, 1988
0-20119-330-2
$31.50

*Microsoft Works
on the Apple Macintosh*
Rubin, C.
Microsoft Press, 1989
1-55615-202-7
$19.95

Microsoft Works on the Macintosh
Freeman, T.
Compute Publications, 1988
0-87455-143-9
$21.95

Music through MIDI
Bloom
Microsoft Press, 1988
1-55615-026-1
$19.95

Power of Eureka: 125 Applications
Salkind, N.
Scott, Foresman, & Co., 1988
0-67338-592-2
$19.95

SmartForm Series Handbook
Shafer, D.
Compute Publications, 1990
0-87455-207-9
$26.95

Under the Apple
Bornstein, H.
InfoBooks, 1987
0-93113-706-3
$15.95

Using Dollars and Sense
Hannah, John
Que Corp., 1986
0-88022-164-X
$19.95

Using Microsoft Works
Mansfield, M.
Que Corp., 1988
0-88022-296-4
$19.95

Using Microsoft Works: Mac v. 2.0
Mansfield
Que Corp., 1990
0-88022-461-4
$21.95

Working with Microsoft Works
Campbell, John
TAB Books, 1988
0-83063-119-4
$21.95

Working with Works
Sloan, M.
Scott, Foresman, & Co., 1988
0-67318-359-9
$18.95

Programming/Technical

Advanced Mac Basic Programming
Calippe, P.
Compute Publications, 1988
0-87455-030-0
$18.95

Advanced Macintosh Pascal
Goodman, Paul
Howard W. Sams & Co., 1987
0-67246-570-1
$19.95

Apple Numerics Manual
Apple Computer
Addison-Wesley, 1988
0-20117-738-2
$29.95

Assembly Language for the Mac
Harrington, J.
Holt, Rinehart, & Winston, 1986
0-03000-833-6
$26.95

Assembly Language Primer for the Mac
Mathews, K.
New American Library, 1985
0-45225-642-9
$24.95

Assembly Language Programming on the Macintosh
Shafer, Dan
Howard W. Sams & Co., 1986
0-67222-447-X
$24.95

BASIC for the Mac
Finkel, L.
John Wiley & Sons, 1986
0-47181-152-1
$16.95

BASIC Primer for the Macintosh
Flock, E.
New American Library, 1985
0-45225-639-9
$17.95

C Programming Techniques
Mednieks/Schike
Howard W. Sams & Co., 1989
0-67222-461-5
$22.95

Chilton's Guide to Macintosh Repair
William, Gene
Chilton Book Co., 1986
0-80197-639-1
$13.95

*Complete Book of Mac
Assembly Programming*
Weston, Dan
Scott, Foresman, & Co., 1986
0-67318-379-3
$25.95

Complete Macintosh Turbo Pascal
Kelly, J.
Scott, Foresman, & Co., 1989
0-67338-456-1
$21.95

Designing Cards & Drivers
Apple Computer
Addison-Wesley, 1987
0-20119-256-X
$24.95

*Dr. Dobb's Toolbox
of 68000 Programming*
Dr. Dobb's Journal
A Brady Book, 1986
0-13216-557-0
$19.95

Encyclopedia Mac ROM
Mathews, K.
A Brady Book, 1988
0-13541-509-8
$29.95

*First Steps in Assembly
Language for 68000*
Erskine, R.
Bantam Books, 1986
0-55334-323-8
$19.95

Hidden Powers of the Macintosh
Morgan, C.
New American Library, 1985
0-45225-643-7
$24.95

How to Write Macintosh Software
Knaster, Scott
Howard W. Sams & Co., 1988
0-67248-429-3
$27.95

Human Interface Guidelines
Apple Computer
Addison-Wesley, 1988
0-20117-753-6
$14.95

ImageWriter II Reference Manual
Apple Computer
Addison-Wesley, 1987
0-20117-766-8
$19.95

ImageWriter LQ Reference
Apple Computer
Addison-Wesley, 1988
0-20117-775-1
$22.95

Inside Macintosh, V. I–V
Apple Computer
Addison-Wesley, 1986
0-20117-731-5
$24.95 each

Inside Macintosh Reference
Apple Computer
Addison-Wesley, 1988
0-20119-265-9
$9.95

Inside the Apple LaserWriter
Hart, Roger
Scott, Foresman, & Co., 1988
0-67338-064-5
$21.95

*Introductory Programming
with Macintosh Pascal*
Pritchard
Addison-Wesley, 1988
0-20117-539-8
$30.50

Introduction to Macintosh Pascal
Simonoff, J.
Howard W. Sams & Co., 1988
0-81046-562-0
$19.95

LaserWriter Reference
Apple Computer
Addison-Wesley, 1988
0-20119-258-6
$19.95

Learning Macintosh Pascal
Wikert/Davis
Scott, Foresman, & Co., 1986
0-67318-333-5
$19.95

Macalgebra: BASIC Algebra on the Mac
Marcus, M.
Computer Science Press, 1986
0-88175-135-9
$27.95

Mac Assembly Language
Little, Gary
A Brady Book, 1988
0-13541-434-2
$24.95

MacBits: Utilities and Routines
Aker, S.
Compute Publications, 1989
0-87455-076-9
$29.95

Macintosh AU/X Handbook
Harrington, J.
A Brady Book, 1990
0-13054-826-x
$29.95

Macintosh BASIC for Business
Bitter, G.
Prentice Hall Press, 1987
0-13542-390-2
$16.95

Macintosh Family Hardware Reference
Apple Computer
Addison-Wesley, 1987
0-20119-255-1
$26.95

Macintosh Graphics in MODULA-2
Schnapp, R.
Prentice Hall Press, 1986
0-13542-309-0
$19.95

Macintosh II Reference Guide
Veljkov, Mark
Scott, Foresman, & Co., 1989
0-67338-227-3
$21.95

Macintosh Midnight Madness
Waite Group
Microsoft Press, 1985
0-91484-530-6
$18.95

Macintosh Pascal
Moll, R.
Houghton Mifflin Co., 1987
0-39537-574-6
$34.95

Macintosh Pascal Illustrated
Kronick, Scott
Addison-Wesley, 1985
0-20111-675-8
$16.95

Macintosh Programming Primer
LightSpeedC
Mark, D.
Addison-Wesley, 1989
0-20115-662-8
$24.95

Macintosh Programming Secrets
Knaster, Scott
Addison-Wesley, 1987
0-20106-661-0
$24.95

Macintosh Revealed, V. I–III
Chernicoff, S.
Howard W. Sams & Co., 1987
0-67248-400-5
$26.95 each

Macintosh Technical Guide
Smith, D.
Prentice Hall Press, 1986
0-13542-341-X
$14.95

MacPascal
Goodman, P.
A Brady Book, 1988
0-89303-644-7
$19.95

Magic of Macintosh
Twitty, W.
Scott, Foresman, & Co., 1986
0-67318-253-3
$19.95

MC68000 8-/16-/32-Bit Microprocessor
Programming Reference
Motorola
Prentice Hall Press, 1989
0-13541-475-X
$19.95

MC68000 8-/16-/32-Bit Microprocessor
User's Manual
Motorola
Prentice Hall Press, 1989
0-13609-249-7
$22.95

MC68020 32-Bit Microprocessor
User's Manual
Prentice Hall Press, 1989
0-13567-017-9
$22.95

MC68030 32-Bit Microprocessor
User's Manual
Motorola
Prentice Hall Press, 1989
0-13566-951-0
$22.95

Microsoft Basic for Macintosh
Goldstein, L.
A Brady Book, 1986
0-13581-828-1
$23.95

MPW and Assembly
Language Programming
Kronick, S.
Howard W. Sams & Co., 1987
0-67248-409-0
$24.95

Object Oriented Programming
for the Mac
Schmucker, Kurt
Howard W. Sams & Co., 1988
0-81046-565-5
$34.95

Oh! Macintosh Pascal!
Beekman/Johnson
W. W. Norton & Co., 1986
0-39395-598-2
$7.95

Oh! Think's Lightspeed Pascal!
Johnson/Beekman
W. W. Norton & Co., 1988
0-39395-817-5
$7.95

On Macintosh Programming:
Advanced Techniques
Allen, D.
Addison-Wesley, 1990
0-20151-737-X
$24.95

Operating System Design
Comer, D.
Prentice Hall Press, 1989
0-13638-529-X
$44.00

Pascal on the Mac
Niguidula
Addison-Wesley, 1989
0-20116-588-0
$34.65

Pascal Primer for the Mac
Shafer, Dan
New American Library, 1985
0-45225-640-2
$19.95

Programmer's Apple Mac Sourcebook
Hogan, Thom
Microsoft Press, 1989
1-55615-168-3
$22.95

Programmer's Introduction
to the Mac Family
Apple Computer
Addison-Wesley, 1987
0-20119-254-3
$24.95

Programming C on the Macintosh
Ward, Terry
Scott, Foresman, & Co., 1986
0-67318-274-6
$21.95

Programming the Macintosh
in Assembly Language
Williams, S.
SYBEX, 1986
0-89588-263-9
$24.95

Programming the Macintosh in C
Cummings, B.
SYBEX, 1986
0-89588-328-7
$19.95

Programming the Macintosh,
Advanced Guide
Twitty, William
Scott, Foresman, & Co., 1985
0-67318-250-9
$19.95

Programming the Mac User Interface
Simpson, H.
McGraw-Hill Book Co., 1986
0-07057-320-4
$21.95

Programming the 68000
King/Knight
Addison-Wesley, 1988
0-80535-550-2
$15.95

Programming the 68000
Williams, S.
SYBEX, 1986
0-89588-133-0
$24.95

*Programming with Macintosh
Programming Workshop*
West, Joel
Bantam Books, 1987
0-55334-436-6
$29.95

Programming with Mac Turbo Pascal
Swan, Tom
John Wiley & Sons, 1987
0-47162-417-9
$22.95

*Scientific Programming
with Mac Pascal*
Crandall, R.
John Wiley & Sons, 1988
0-47182-176-4
$18.95

Short, Simple, and BASIC on the Mac
Robinson, M.
Scott, Foresman, & Co., 1986
0-67318-284-3
$18.95

68000 Assembly Language
Krantz/Stanley
Addison-Wesley, 1988
0-20111-659-6
$24.95

68000, 68010, 68020 Primer
Kelly-Bootle
Howard W. Sams & Co., 1985
0-67222-405-4
$21.95

68030 Assembly Language Reference
Williams, S.
Addison-Wesley, 1990
0-20108-876-2
$29.95

680X0 Programming by Example
Kelly-Bootle
Howard W. Sams & Co., 1988
0-67222-544-1
$17.95

*Technical Introduction
to the Macintosh Family*
Apple Computer
Addison-Wesley, 1987
0-20117-765-X
$19.95

Turbo Pascal for the Mac
Goodman, P.
A Brady Book, 1988
0-13933-011-9
$19.95

Turbo Pascal for the Mac
Wortman, L.
TAB Books, 1987
0-83062-927-0
$17.95

Using the Macintosh Toolbox with C
Takatsuka, J.
SYBEX, 1990
0-89588-572-7
$29.95

Spreadsheets

The ABC's of Excel on the Macintosh
Hergert, D.
SYBEX, 1988
0-89588-562-X
$18.95

The ABC's of Excel
on the Macintosh, v. 2.2
Hergert, D.
SYBEX, 1990
0-89588-634-0
$19.95

Bar Coding with Excel
Galter, I.
TAB Books, 1990
0-83063-302-2
$34.95

Beginner's Guide to MultiPlan
Sutphin, Susan
Prentice Hall Press, 1986
0-13071-697-9
$22.95

Business Problem Solving with Excel
Molloy, J.
Osborne McGraw-Hill, 1986
0-07881-224-0
$17.95

Command Performance Microsoft Excel
Hergert, D.
Microsoft Press, 1986
0-91484-578-0
$24.95

Complete Guide
to Microsoft Excel Macros
Kyd, C.
Microsoft Press, 1990
1-55615-250-7
$24.95

Dynamics of Macintosh Excel
Adler, John
Dow Jones-Irwin, 1986
0-87094-907-1
$19.95

Excel: A Business User's Guide
Salkind, N.
John Wiley & Sons, 1990
0-47150-878-0
$21.95

Excel Advanced User's Guide
Loggins, R.
Howard W. Sams & Co., 1987
0-67246-626-0
$19.95

Excel in Business, v. 2.2
Cobb, D.
Microsoft Press, 1990
1-55615-238-8
$24.95

Excel in Business (Updated to 1.5)
Cobb, Douglas
Microsoft Press, 1988
0-91484-561-6
$24.95

Excel Instant Reference
Orvis, William
SYBEX, 1989
0-89588-577-8
$12.95

Excel Macros for the Macintosh
Annaloro, J.
Scott, Foresman, & Co., 1989
0-67338-452-7
$21.95

Excel Made Easy for the Mac
Jones, Edward
Osborne McGraw-Hill, 1989
0-07881-523-1
$19.95

Excel Tips, Tricks, and Traps
Person, R.
Que Corp., 1990
0-88022-421-5
$22.95

Full Impact: A User's Guide
Thompson, K.
A Brady Book, 1990
0-13943-358-9
$21.95

*Full Impact Macros:
Programming with Full Talk*
Ashe, Dylan
A Brady Book, 1990
0-13329-426-9
$24.95

Hands-On Excel
Goodman/McComb
Scott, Foresman, & Co., 1989
0-67338-479-9
$22.95

Illustrated Excel 1.5
Schlieve/Young
Wordware Publishing, 1989
1-55622-110-X
$21.95

Making Your Macintosh Excel
O'Brien, B
Scott, Foresman, & Co., 1986
0-67318-370-X
$19.95

Mastering Excel on the Macintosh
Townsend, Carl
SYBEX, 1989
0-89588-622-7
$24.95

Mastering Macintosh Excel 2
Hoffman, Paul
Bantam Books, 1990
0-55334-709-8
$24.95

Mastering Wingz
Davis/Tymes
Bantam Books, 1989
0-55334-706-3
$24.95

Microsoft Excel Business Sourcebook
Kyd, C.
Microsoft Press, 1990
1-55615-206-X
$24.95

Microsoft Excel Money Manager
Nelson, S.
Microsoft Press, 1990
1-55615-241-8
$34.95

Power of Wingz
Salkind, N.
Scott, Foresman, & Co., 1990
0-67338-603-1
$21.95

Quick and Easy Excel on the Mac
Adler, John
Compute Publications, 1988
0-87455-131-5
$10.95

Stephen Cobb User's Guide to Wingz
Cobb, S.
TAB Books, 1990
0-83063-150-X
$22.95

Understanding Overvue
Cobb, S.
The Cobb Group, 1985
0-93676-701-4
$22.95

Using Excel: Macintosh Version
Campbell, Mary
Que Corp., 1987
0-88022-209-3
$21.95

Using Wingz
Prael, C.
Howard W. Sams & Co., 1990
0-67248-458-7
$21.95

Working with Full Impact
Campbell, J.
TAB Books, 1990
0-83062-919-X
$17.95

Word Processing

Best Book of Microsoft Word for the Mac
Krumm, R.
Howard W. Sams & Co., 1990
0-67248-445-5
$22.95

Dynamics of Microsoft Word
Pfaffenberger
Dow Jones-Irwin, 1986
0-87094-768-0
$19.95

Expert Advisor: Microsoft Word
Hoffman, P.
Addison-Wesley, 1989
0-20114-699-1
$19.95

FullWrite Professional: A User's Guide
Thompson, K.
A Brady Book, 1988
0-13331-712-9
$24.95

FullWrite Professional:
Advanced Techniques
Leban/Morrish
A Brady Book, 1990
0-13331-919-9
$24.95

FullWrite Professional
Business Handbook
Eckhardt, R.
A Brady Book, 1989
0-13331-729-3
$29.95

FullWrite Professional Complete
Salkind, N.
Scott, Foresman, & Co., 1989
0-67338-562-0
$21.95

Illustrated WordPerfect
Gold, J.
Wordware Publishing, 1989
1-55622-105-3
$21.95

Macintosh WordPerfect Guide
Read, D.
Compute Publications, 1988
0-87455-150-1
$24.95

Mastering Microsoft Word 4.0
Beason, P.
Bantam Books, 1989
0-55334-672-5
$21.95

Mastering Microsoft Word on the Mac
Aker, S.
Compute Publications, 1987
0-87455-118-8
$18.95

Mastering Microsoft Word
on the Macintosh
Young, M.
SYBEX, 1989
0-89588-541-7
$22.95

Mastering WordPerfect
on the Macintosh
Nelson, Kay
SYBEX, 1988
0-89588-515-8
$21.95

Microsoft Word 3.0/3.01 for the Mac
Salkind, N.
TAB Books, 1987
0-83062-955-3
$15.95

Microsoft Word 4.0 for the Macintosh
Salkind, N.
TAB Books, 1990
0-83067-400-4
$19.95

Microsoft Word:
A Power User's Companion
Jackel, J.
TAB Books, 1990
0-83063-215-8
$22.95

Microsoft Word for the Macintosh
Made Easy
Hoffman, P.
Osborne McGraw-Hill, 1989
0-07881-478-2
$19.95

Microsoft Word for the Macintosh
Quick Reference
Hoffman, Paul
Osborne McGraw-Hill, 1988
0-07881-403-0
$5.95

Microsoft Word Power Pack for the Mac
Eckhardt, R.
A Brady Book, 1990
0-13964-578-0
$39.95

The Official MacWrite II
Applications Library
Price/Korman
Bantam Books, 1990
0-55334-801-9
$39.95

Quick and Easy Microsoft Word Mac
Cady/Chapman
Compute Publications, 1988
0-87455-135-8
$12.95

Quick Reference Guide to
Microsoft Word for the Macintosh
Jacobs, L.
Microsoft Press, 1989
1-55615-209-4
$5.95

Understanding Microsoft Word
Swadley
Howard W. Sams & Co., 1990
0-67227-289-4
$19.95

Using FullWrite
Merriman, Greg
Osborne McGraw-Hill, 1989
0-07881-465-0
$22.95

Using FullWrite Professional
Bixby, R.
Compute Publications, 1990
0-87455-180-3
$21.95

Using FullWrite Professional
Kenyon, B.
Que Corp., 1989
0-88022-398-7
$21.95

Using Microsoft Word:
Macintosh Version
Lambert, S.
Que Corp., 1988
0-88022-333-2
$21.95

Using Microsoft Word 4:
Macintosh Version
Pfaffenberger, B.
Que Corp., 1989
0-88022-451-7
$21.95

Using WordPerfect for the Macintosh
Rosenbaum, D.
Osborne McGraw-Hill, 1988
0-07881-353-0
$21.95

Using WordPerfect: Mac Version
Blodgett, R.
Que Corp., 1988
0-88022-342-1
$19.95

Word 3.0 Companion
Mynhier/Cobb
The Cobb Group, 1987
0-93676-705-7
$19.95

Word 3.0 on the Mac
Knight, Tim
A Brady Book, 1988
0-13964-255-2
$19.95

Word 4.0 Companion
Cobb/McGuffey
The Cobb Group, 1989
0-93676-714-6
$22.95

Word Power: The Complete Guide
Sloan, Michael
Scott, Foresman, & Co., 1988
0-67338-059-9
$19.95

WordPerfect for the Mac
Salkind, N.
TAB Books, 1988
0-83062-963-7
$14.95

Working with Word
Kinata/McComb
Microsoft Press, 1988
1-55615-032-6
$21.95

Write Companion
Mynhier/Cobb
The Cobb Group, 1988
0-93676-709-X
$24.95

Working with WordPerfect on the Mac
Zimmerman, B.
Scott, Foresman, & Co., 1989
0-67338-091-2
$19.95

WriteNow—Right Now
Tymes/Prael
Scott, Foresman, & Co., 1990
0-67338-239-7
$19.95

Most of this list was provided by MacBooks, a mail-order bookshop devoted exclusively to Macintosh computing books. MacBooks offers discount prices on over 375 Macintosh-related titles, all of which are listed in a HyperCard stack, available by calling (415) 494-2154; BBS: (415) 969-9337.

Bulletin Boards

Bulletin boards offer you abilities that no other source of Macintosh information can match:

- You can read and participate in hundreds of public discussions and debates on every conceivable Macintosh topic.

- You can ask a question that hundreds or thousands of people will read, and in almost every case you will quickly get a complete answer.

- You can download any one of thousands of public-domain, freeware, and shareware programs. Your only cost is the call toll (if any) and the bulletin board's connect-time fee (if any).

There are local bulletin boards sponsored by user groups, individuals, and Mac-related businesses, most of which are available without charge, as well as national bulletin boards, which are commercial enterprises that sell their services for per-minute connect-time fees.

What You Need

Besides your Mac, all you need to access most bulletin boards is a modem. Anyone can call most local bulletin boards; the first time you connect, you will register as a bulletin-board user, providing the bulletin-board manager (Sysop or System Operator) with your name, address, and a password you would like to use. In some cases your access to the board's information will be limited until the SYSOP verifies the information that you provided and adds your name and password to the system. Usually this takes only one or two days.

To use one of the national bulletin-board services, you must first purchase a startup kit. (Startup kits are sometimes included along with modems or telecommunication software packages.) This startup kit provides you with the local telephone number used to access the bulletin board, along with a temporary account number and password. When you first log on using this temporary number, you register on-line, providing your name, address, billing information, and password preference. Subsequently, you are provided with your own account name or number, and can log in on your own permanent account using your own password. At this point you will have full access to the board's services.

Connecting to a Bulletin Board

The exact sequence required to log on to a bulletin board varies depending on the software that is controlling the board itself, but the following steps specify the general procedure used for most systems. In most telecommunications software you can record your log-on procedure for each bulletin board you use and assign it to a script or macro that can be replayed each time you wish to connect to a particular board again.

1.   **Load your telecommunications software and set the communications options.** In your telecommunications software you must specify the telephone number (usually preceded by the letters *ATDT*), baud rate (300/1200/2400/9600), parity (even/odd/none), number of data bits and stop bits (8/7 1/2), and duplex (full/half/echo). All Macintosh telecommunication uses no parity, 8 data bits, and 1 stop bit. Usually, full duplex is used. If you have Call Waiting, you may be able to temporarily disable it by adding *70 to the beginning of the phone number. (Check with your local phone company for details.)

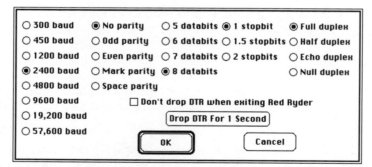

The Red Ryder Host communications options dialog box displaying the correct settings for communicating with a bulletin board on the Mac.

2.   **Execute the DIAL command.** Once the software is configured properly, executing the DIAL command (or equivalent) will instruct your modem to phone the number entered and attempt to connect to the computer that answers the line. When the bulletin board answers,

you will hear a high-pitched squealing sound as the modems attempt to establish communication. This should give way to a static sound within a few seconds.

3. **Connect to the bulletin board**. After your modem has connected to the bulletin-board modem, you must establish a connection with the bulletin-board software. To do this, you usually press the RETURN key once or twice. This should elicit the bulletin board's greeting message and initial prompt. If the RETURN key is unsuccessful, try pressing CONTROL-C. If you do not see a greeting message, your connection is unsuccessful. This is usually caused by improper communication-option settings. (Double-check the baud rate, parity, and duplex settings in your telecommunications software.)

4. **Follow the on-screen prompts**. Once you are connected to a bulletin board, its prompts and menus should allow you to easily navigate the board and utilize its services. Many boards have on-line help systems or special messages that are presented to first-time callers.

Downloading a File

The process of transferring a file from the bulletin board to your computer is called **downloading**. Most bulletin boards offer a wide range of software utilities that you will want to download, including many of those discussed in Section 1. The process of downloading varies on each bulletin board, but the general procedure is described here.

1. **Select the file you wish to download.** Before beginning to download a file, you must know the code name used to specify the file on the bulletin board. Most bulletin boards allow you to search for a particular file, view a list of all available files, or browse through the file descriptions.

2. **Select the bulletin board's download command.** Using the board's on-screen prompts, you should be able to select a download command, either from a menu or from a prompt that appears when you are browsing files. After selecting this command, you will have to respond to a few questions about how you want the file to be transferred. Usually you must select the transfer protocol that you will be using. In order for you to use a transfer protocol, it must be supported by both your telecommunications software and the bulletin board

from which you are downloading the file. There are several popular transfer protocols supported by most telecommunications software and Mac bulletin boards, including Xmodem and Ymodem. After you respond to the bulletin board's queries, the board will appear stagnant; it is waiting for you to begin receiving the file.

3. **Initiate the reception of the file.** You must select the RECEIVE FILE command (or equivalent) in your telecommunications software. Usually this will require you to name the incoming file and select the drive and folder you want the file put in. As soon as this command is executed, the file transfer will begin, and you should see a progress indicator within 30 seconds of executing the RECEIVE FILE command.

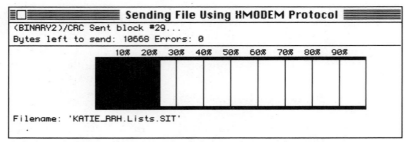

When transferring electronic files from a bulletin board to your computer, Red Ryder displays how much longer the file transfer will take to complete.

4. **Complete the transfer.** When the file has been successfully transferred, you will be notified that the transfer is complete, and you can then continue using the bulletin board. After you log off the bulletin board and quit your telecommunications software you will find your downloaded files stored in the drive and folder you specified with the RECEIVE FILE command.

CompuServe

CompuServe is the largest and most complete bulletin-board service available to Mac users. Seven different CompuServe sections (called *forums*) are dedicated to Macintosh topics, and many other forums service specific

Macintosh software products. Each forum contains ten or more general message topics, and file libraries relating to these topics. The Macintosh forums are:

- **MacPro**. The Macintosh Productivity Forum is the most general-interest Mac forum, covering topics such as DA's/inits/Fkeys, utilities, programming, software, hardware, and telecommunications.

- **MacDev**. The Macintosh Developers Forum supports programmers and developers with technical information and software.

- **AppHyper**. The Apple HyperCard Forum is dedicated to the use of HyperCard. Both stack programmers and stack users meet in this forum.

- **AppVen**. The Apple Vendors Forum provides support for software products from a number of Macintosh software vendors. This support is provided by the software vendors themselves. Data libraries here include product upgrades, technical notes, and tip sheets.

- **MacFun**. The Macintosh Fun Forum is the home to information about games for the Macintosh, plus sounds, artwork, and other "fun" stuff.

- **MacBiz**. The Macintosh Business Forum covers topics like databases, spreadsheets, and networking. Many specific applications such as 4th Dimension and Excel are heavily discussed in this forum.

- **AppUg**. The Apple User Group Forum provides a central meeting place for leaders and members of user groups to discuss all aspects of the Macintosh and swap public-domain and shareware software.

Other CompuServe forums of particular interest to Macintosh users include the Adobe Forum, the Aldus Forum, and the Microsoft Forum.

Using CompuServe

There are two ways to use CompuServe. You can log on with any telecommunications package and interact with CompuServe's menu and command system, or you can purchase a software package called Navigator and use it to interact with CompuServe.

CompuServe's menu and command system is much like that of any local bulletin board; it is slow, confusing, and ultimately frustrating. You can learn to really control CompuServe using this system, but you'll have to buy a book or two, and spend many (expensive) hours on-line practicing.

Navigator turns CompuServe from an unfriendly and unmanageable beast into the slickest and easiest telecommunications service available. Navigator acts as a liaison between you and the CompuServe menu and command system; you interact with Navigator's friendly menus and dialog boxes, and Navigator translates your settings into CompuServe menu commands and executes them. We hardly ever used CompuServe before we got Navigator. Now we log on several times each week. Navigator makes using CompuServe productive and cost-effective; you will save the cost of Navigator itself in reduced connect-time charges after just a few hours use.

The Navigator forum setup window provides CompuServe subscribers on the Macintosh with a friendly and familiar interface.

Using Navigator requires only familiarity with your mouse. You can tell Navigator the message topics in any forum you want to read or see summaries of, and the file libraries from which you want to see file listings or file summaries. After configuring Navigator, you tell it to run your CompuServe session, and it logs on and performs all of the tasks you have specified in the fastest manner possible. It can even perform all tasks in the background under MultiFinder. After Navigator has logged off, you can browse through the information that it has gathered; and you can browse at your leisure because you are no longer connected to the network or paying any connect charges.

Working in this "off-line" mode, you can reply to messages, write your own new messages, specify "message thread" to be read the next time you connect to the network, and specify files to be downloaded the next time you connect. Navigator can even run unattended at a specified time, and shut down your Mac when it has finished. We can't recommend Navigator highly enough. If you use CompuServe, don't even think about using it without Navigator.

Navigator Utilities

 Navigator Libarian
This HyperCard stack, written by Navigator's author Michael O'Conner, lets you archive all of the file listings collected in Navigator session files into a HyperCard stack. This stack then serves as your own reference to all the files available in CompuServe's libraries.

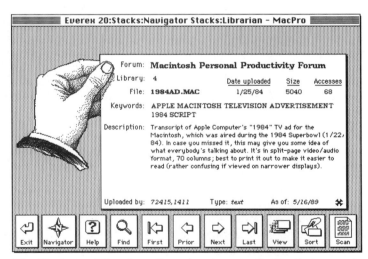

The Navigator Librarian allows you to compile Navigator session files into HyperCard stacks.

Message Browser

Although Navigator is a great way of gathering and reviewing messages from any CompuServe forum, it doesn't really do a very good job of letting you browse and manipulate the messages that you collect over long periods of time. Message Browser is an indispensable HyperCard stack that transfers messages collected in Navigator session files into a HyperCard stack, with each message on its own card. You can then browse the messages anytime, or search for an old message containing a particular discussion or topic.

Message Browser allows you to go directly to any reply messages that exist for any particular message; delete any message, thread, or duplicate messages; or mark important messages for later retrieval. The stack's search facility lets you search by message content, sender, recipient, date, or subject. If you take the time to collect CompuServe messages with Navigator, you should definitely be using Message Browser.

Connect Information Service

Connect, formerly known as MacNET, is a bulletin-board service that uses a purely graphic interface, which provides many of the productivity and economic benefits of CompuServe and Navigator. Connect's Macintosh section, called the Mac Symposium, is not as large or active as CompuServe's forums, but it is steadily improving, and surprisingly it contains discussions and files not found on CompuServe. Many Mac software vendors, including Affinity, Aldus, Symantec, Magnus, and Zedcor, provide direct support over Connect.

Finding and downloading files on Connect is much easier than it is on CompuServe; however, it is impossible to create a file directory that can be browsed off-line, you cannot download in the background in MultiFinder, and downloading is significantly slower than downloading with Navigator. Connect's graphics also benefit its E-mail and message system, although the lack of message subtopics (known as "message threads" on CompuServe) does make message browsing more difficult.

Local Bulletin Boards

Local bulletin boards, which are usually operated by individuals, small groups, or small companies, vary dramatically in terms of their software quality and the services they offer. Many specialize in one narrow topic; these bulletin boards often provide the best information available within their area of specialization. Some boards require a nominal membership fee, which may be required for download privileges or for access to all of the board's functions, but you can log onto any of these boards without any initial charge.

Below is a list of bulletin boards located throughout the United States and Canada. This list is by no means complete. It is provided just to give you an idea of the variety of boards in existence, and to allow you to try some out. Usually by logging onto a few boards in your area you can find out about many others. This list was compiled by Dennis Runkle.

Most of these boards probably operate at 2400 baud (bd). They are marked if 2400 bd is definitely supported, or if only slower rates are supported. Bulletin boards that participate in either the Opus or FidoNet BBS message exchange system are noted. Most boards run 24 hours a day, 7 days a week. All boards are listed in order according to phone number, including area code. N/A indicates a board for which a name is not available.

BBS at the End of the Universe	201-236-7401	
NJ Mac BBS	201-256-2067	
Power Surge	201-263-8167	2400 bd
Dragon's Cave BBS	201-299-1445	2400 bd
EEE's BBS	201-340-3531	Opus 7:520/563, 1:107/563
MacApple Peel	201-340-9792	
Rock Pile	201-387-9232	Opus 1:107/554, 7:520/554
White House/NJMUG BBS	201-388-1676	Opus 1:107/347, 7:520/347
MAC BBS	201-446-1421	
Big Mac BBS	201-531-3519	2400 bd; 9–3 M–F, 24 hr S–S
Mac Atlantic BBS	201-543-6950	
Adam's BBS	201-548-5107	
Macintosh NJMUG BBS	201-666-2013	2400 bd

ApplePeel	201-684-0931	
Mac Developers BBS	201-747-8814	2400 bd
Finishing Technology Hotline	201-838-0113	2400 bd
NJMUG BBS	201-839-7802	
Palace BBS	201-840-4463	2400 bd
Da Cave AE/Mac BBS	201-863-5422	2400 bd
Wizards Den	201-922-6943	
MacNet	201-968-1074	2400 bd; 6 P.M.–6 A.M. M–F, 24 hr S–S
Castle Tabby	201-988-0706	2400 bd
Golden Apple BBS	201-989-0545	300 bd
Swizzle Stick	202-234-3521	2400 bd; FidoNet 109/776
Quick Facts	202-289-4112	2400 bd
Eyrie/Falcon	202-341-9070	
Twilight Clone	202-471-0610	
N/A	202-846-5032	
Firesign Theatre	203-234-0742	
Lost Horizon BBS	203-259-2292	2400 bd
Country Club BBS	203-270-1739	2400 bd
Computer Lab	203-442-2411	
MacBBS	203-453-4114	
Mouse Hole	203-453-5317	
MacHeaven	203-637-3611	2400 bd
Unnamed Connecticut BBS	203-739-5411	300 bd
Silver Screen System	203-748-5146	
SmartMac BBS	203-762-1249	8 P.M.–3 A.M.
Ghost Ship East	203-775-6392	
AppleBamians	205-236-7262	7:30 P.M.–7 A.M.
MacTown	205-284-8484	
Joe's Board	205-288-1100	
FISHNET (ATF Forum)	205-767-7484	
Huntsville MUG BBS	205-881-8380	7 P.M.–7 A.M. M–Sat., 24 hr Sun.

(TBD) BBS	205-882-2995	2400 bd
MacUs Revenge	206-272-6343	2400 bd
dBBS	206-281-7338	
SeaSoftNet	206-453-1948	FidoNet 1:343/8.9
Dr. Radium's Lab	206-483-5308	
Mac Venture	206-487-2823	
South Puget Sound MUG	206-495-9595	evenings only
Mac Cavern	206-525-5194	
MacStuart	206-543-5350	5:30 P.M.–8:30 A.M. M–Thu.
dBBS	206-624-8783	
Mac Castle	206-630-4728	
Atlantis	206-634-1539	
'Belle	206-641-6892	
Library	206-641-7978	2400 bd
N/A	206-694-1833	
Sea/Mac	206-725-6629	2400 bd; FidoNet 343/31
Polynet	206-783-9798	
Information Station	206-852-7874	
Mac's Bar and Grill	206-859-4662	
Homework Hotline	206-859-7271	
N/A	206-872-2245	
Bumbershoot BBS	206-938-4463	2400 bd; Opus 1:343/43
CFWP Assoc	207-443-4657	FidoNet
Black Bear's Den	207-827-7517	
JJHS-BBS	208-455-3312	
MacStudio California	209-333-8143	2400 bd
Bitz 'n' Bytes	212-222-9536	
Machine	212-340-9666	2400 bd
LaserBoard	212-348-5714	2400 bd
LaserBoard New York	212-397-0729	2400 bd
New York News (aka NYMUG)	212-534-3716	2400 bd
Metro Area Mac Users Group	212-597-9083	2400 bd

CitiMac	212-627-4647	
New York Mac	212-643-1965	
Zap's Corner	212-645-0640	
NYMUG BBS	212-645-9484	2400 bd
Apl Pi	212-753-0888	2400 bd; FidoNet 107/103
Aztec Empire	212-769-8014	
Ellena Caverns	212-861-5484	
Links_II Midi_Inn	212-877-7703	FidoNet 107/111
Super 68 BBS	212-927-6919	FidoNet 107/108
Forge	212-989-0037	
Dark Side of the Mac	213-204-2459	2400 bd
Glassell Park BBS	213-258-7649	2400 bd; Opus 1:102/863
Ye Olde Pawn Shoppe	213-273-1158	
St. Elsewhere	213-273-8489	
Manhattan Transfer	213-372-4800	2400 bd
Keyboard Zone BBS	213-394-6929	
LA MUG BBS	213-397-8966	
Programmer's Paradise	213-454-7746	2400 bd
NewMac BBS	213-459-2083	
Showcase	213-470-0297	evenings only
Troll	213-477-2188	Mondays 8 A.M.–5 P.M.
Manhattan Transfer	213-516-7739	2400 bd; 6 P.M.–7 A.M. M–F, 24 hr S–S
Byte BBS	213-536-2651	
MachineDo	213-548-3546	2400 bd
Mac-HACers	213-549-9640	
LAMG	213-559-6227	2400 bd
Reality BBS/ Small Press BBS	213-666-6639	
DigiVision	213-732-6935	
MacBBS	213-732-9131	
Palantir	213-839-9271	
ROME BBS	213-858-3037	2400 bd
Computer Church	213-946-5923	

Maclectic BBS	213-947-4402	2400 bd
Rising Star	214-231-1372	2400 bd
HardWired	214-380-9063	2400 bd; FidoNet 124/210
Inside Track	214-442-4772	2400 bd; FidoNet 124/210
Board Europa	214-564-6282	
Mac Shack	214-644-4781	2400 bd
Ground Zero	214-892-1476	2400 bd; after 9 P.M.
Garden State Macintosh	215-222-2743	2400 bd
Kiss of Death	215-293-9703	
Stonewall BBS	215-367-8206	
Dragon's Land	215-387-1962	
Electric Holt	215-387-4326	
PennMug	215-387-6725	2400 bd
Lord's Keep	215-387-8442	
Bob's Mac	215-446-7670	2400 bd
Typesetters' BBS	215-626-4812	
Big Board	215-643-7711	2400 bd; FidoNet 150/621
Rydal Board	215-884-6122	2400 bd; FidoNet 150/602
Drexel University Library	215-895-1698	
Dragon Keep III	215-895-2579	
Omnicom Mac BBS	215-896-9020	
King's Realm	216-228-2702	11 P.M.–7 A.M.
Appleholic's BBS	216-273-1340	2400 bd; FidoNet 157/511
NE Ohio IBM BBS	216-331-4241	2400 bd; FidoNet 157/502
Cleveland FreeNet	216-368-3888	
Steel Valley BBS	216-545-0093	2400 bd; Opus 1:237/505
TARDIS BBS	216-671-2173	FidoNet 22/002; new users enter NEW; 11 P.M.–11 A.M.
North Coast MUG BBS	216-777-4944	2400 bd
Pipeline BBS	216-836-0990	
PMS BBS	216-867-7463	2400 bd; FidoNet 157/500
Fireside BBS	216-884-9728	
Mouse House	216-965-7233	9 P.M.–6 A.M.

Champaign-Urbana Mac Users	217-344-5204	
Tales of the Mouse BBS	217-367-1451	
CAMS Host	217-875-7114	
Mac Blade	219-264-5273	7 A.M.–7 P.M.
Connection BBS	219-277-5825	
MacCHEG	219-283-4714	2400 bd; 6 P.M.–8A.M. M–F
LINDA RBBS	301-340-1376	2400 bd
Boys from DOS	301-381-2257	FidoNet 261/1011
Time Machine	301-477-1624	
Mouse Event BBS	301-547-1381	2400 bd
System Error	301-547-2410	2400 bd
Nightclub BBS	301-564-9221	
Overflow Valve	301-572-2360	2400 bd
Mac USA	301-587-2132	
Overflow Valve	301-654-5812	2400 bd
Mouse Event BBS	301-752-7391	
Clinton Computer	301-856-2365	
Yucca's Domain BBS	301-869-1365	
Midnight MUG	301-871-9637	midnight–6 A.M.
Twilight Clone BBS	301-946-5032	2400 bd; FidoNet 109/205
Mac Files BBS (East)	301-946-8838	2400 bd
SMUG	301-963-5249	
Baltimore BBS	301-964-3397	
BABBS	301-974-0221	2400 bd
Double Nut BBS	301-997-7204	2400 bd; FidoNet 261/627
Chemist's Compor	302-479-0302	2400 bd; FidoNet 150/190
Starfleet Command	302-654-2900	FidoNet 150/130
Original Mousetrap	302-731-1583	
Mousetrap	302-737-7788	2400 bd
Mac Computer Works	303-444-2318	
STS Leisure Time BBS	303-444-5175	2400 bd
Boulder Mac Management	303-449-0917	

On-Line Consulting BBS	303-449-5251	2400 bd; Opus 1:104/45
N/A	303-469-7541	
CSU	303-491-5946	
TELETECH SERVICES BBS	303-493-8261	2400 bd; 4 P.M.–9 A.M. M–F
Boulder Mac Maniacs	303-530-9544	2400 bd; FidoNet 104/49
!Macintosh	303-665-0709	2400 bd
InaNet	303-665-4472	
Zoo	303-756-1627	
Fishery	303-756-3818	
N.O.R.A.D.	303-756-8789	
Mile High Mac Meet BBS	303-758-9159	2400 bd
N/A	303-770-7069	
MAGIC	303-791-8732	2400 bd
National DeskTop Publishing Board	303-972-1875	
Atlantis BBS	303-973-0369	2400 bd
Manville	303-978-3946	
Check-In	305-232-0393	2400 bd; Opus 7:43/11
Mac BBS 1	305-344-0533	
MacBBS	305-444-7088	
CSbbs Link	305-445-6481	
Apple Tree	305-472-1900	
SHAPE (1)	305-589-5422	evenings M–F
SHAPE (2)	305-589-8950	weekends
Winter Springs BBS	305-699-1741	
NatMAC BBS	305-748-7993	
Regina Fido	306-347-2351	2400 bd
Sask Echo Hub	306-347-4493	2400 bd; FidoNet 140/19
North Village	306-665-6633	2400 bd; FidoNet 140/26
Black Diamond Express	307-682-7987	
WYNET (Wyoming (Department of Education)	307-777-6200	2400 bd
Barney's BBS	308-345-3845	2400 bd
N/A	309-348-3498	

N/A	309-348-3684	
Mackey Mouse BBS	309-454-5477	9 P.M.–10 A.M. M–F, 24 hr S–S
The Electronic Post Office	309-682-4465	2400 bd
Working With Works	312-260-9660	2400 bd
Nexus	312-274-1677	
MACropedia	312-295-6926	2400 bd
Desktoppers I BBS	312-356-3776	2400 bd; FidoNet 115/622
Desktoppers II BBS	312-356-6420	2400 bd; FidoNet 115/622
Northern Illinois	312-392-6232	
UCC Comm Center	312-433-4563	
N/A	312-452-0333	
Consult-Net	312-475-5442	
Photos and Fun BBS	312-636-9612	
Spectrum MacInfo	312-657-1113	2400 bd; FidoNet 115/729
Rest of Us (TRoU) BBS	312-787-3008	2400 bd; Opus 115/400
Shangri-La	312-798-7634	2400 bd
MacPyramid	312-837-8996	2400 bd; Opus 1:115/837
Lost Horizon	312-898-4505	2400 bd
Spine Fido BBS	312-908-2583	FidoNet 115/444; 6–8 P.M. M–F, 24 hr S–S
Data-Mania	312-923-1932	2400 bd
Pete's Place	312-941-3179	
HyperCap+	312-969-7810	2400 bd
N/A	312-980-1613	
Mac Trade Center	313-259-2115	2400 bd; 11 P.M.–4 P.M.
Great Lakes BBS	313-360-0106	2400 bd
Michigan Connection	313-398-9359	2400 bd
Damn Yankee BBS	313-733-3695	2400 bd
Crystal Castle	313-856-3804	
AM Cross General	314-658-5866	2400 bd
Control Panel	314-867-3939	2400 bd; Opus 1:100/545
COM1: Communications Center	314-997-1605	2400 bd

Show Me More Stacks BBS	314-997-6912	2400 bd; FidoNet 100/255
Salt City BBS	315-451-7790	
Shockwave Rider	315-673-4894	2400 bd; FidoNet 260/330
Galaxia	315-695-4436	2400 bd
Lower & Sons BBS	316-442-7026	2400 bd
MSG Board	317-457-5576	evenings and weekends
Lake Charles Overboard	318-478-8109	7 P.M.–7 A.M.
MAClan Host	318-742-8520	
Mouse College	319-365-4775	2400 bd
Mac BBS	319-381-4761	
MiC MAC BBS	336-754-3542	2400 bd
Lands of Adventure	401-351-1465	
Lands of Adventure	401-351-5211	
MacLink	401-521-2626	
Omega System Electronic BBS	401-785-0998	2400 bd
Wind Dragon	402-291-8053	2400 bd; FidoNet 14/614
DungeonNet BBS	402-455-2788	2400 bd
Callisto BBS (Calgary)	403-264-0996	6 P.M.–8 A.M. M–F, 24 hr S–S
EurythMACs BBS	403-277-4139	
Info Shop	404-288-7535	2400 bd
Mind Machine	404-431-9384	300 bd
Atlanta Crackers	404-449-5986	
N/A	404-457-2417	
HAF/MD BBS	404-633-2602	
AMUG BBS	404-972-3389	2400 bd
Mac Multiboard	405-325-7516	8 P.M.–7 A.M.
N/A	405-355-3103	evenings only
Plasmatic Info Exchange	405-624-0006	2400 bd; Opus 1:19/41
BIKENET	406-549-1318	2400 bd; Opus 1:17/45
Abacus Information Center	407-774-3355	Opus 1:363/7
BBS Classified Ads	408-225-8623	
Backboard	408-226-3780	2400 bd

Bottom Line	408-226-6779	
Crumal's Dimension	408-246-7854	2400 bd
MacScience BBS	408-247-8307	2400 bd
Phoenix 2 BBS	408-253-3926	2400 bd; FidoNet 143/33
Phoenix 1 BBS	408-255-7208	2400 bd
A32 User's Group	408-263-0299	2400 bd
DWB's BBS	408-293-0752	2400 bd; 4 A.M.– 8 P.M. M–F
Laser Optical Technology	408-426-7292	2400 bd
Portal BBS	408-725-0561	
Mousehole	408-738-5791	2400 bd
SuperMac BBS	408-773-4500	
Entertainment Connection	408-978-9784	2400 bd
Jesus Freak BBS	409-265-3504	
Mountain View Electronic Mall	412-221-3564	FidoNet 129/42
PA-Bug Mac BB	412-241-4374	
Pittsburgh Link	412-243-5465	
Maltese Alien	412-279-7011	2400 bd; FidoNet 129/41
Cascade	412-362-2277	
PA BugBoard	412-373-2315	
LaserBoard Pittsburgh	412-521-8646	2400 bd
Enigma BBS	412-661-5425	Opus 1:129/27
Second Option	412-826-0822	
MacBBS	413-243-2217	
MacSheep BBS	413-283-3554	
Digital Bimmers	414-264-6789	
GENERIC BBS	414-282-4181	2400 bd; OPUS 1:154/5
Racine Area Mac (RAM) BBS	414-632-3983	2400 bd; FidoNet 154/122
Milwaukee Metro Mac BBS	414-682-7427	2400 bd; FidoNet 154/154
MacHeaven	415-258-9348	
Laserwriter BBS	415-261-4813	2400 bd
WELL	415-332-6106	
Records Department TBBS	415-426-0470	FidoNet 161/42

TIEnet (Teacher Information Exchange)	415-426-4265	
MacCircles	415-484-4412	2400 bd
TopsTalk BBS	415-549-5955	2400 bd
Harry's BBS / T39 BBS	415-563-2491	2400 bd
On Broadway	415-571-7056	
Dream Machine	415-581-3019	2400 bd
Jasmine BBS	415-648-1269	2400 bd
MacQueue I	415-661-7374	2400 bd; FidoNet 125/2
Billboard	415-686-4338	
Stanford MUG BBS	415-723-7685	2400 bd
Mac Exchange BBS	415-731-1037	
Micahlink BBS	415-771-1119	2400 bd
Bay	415-775-2384	
MACINFO BBS	415-795-8862	2400 bd; FidoNet 1:204/555
EBMUG BBS	415-848-2609	noon–8 A.M. M–F, 24 hr S–S
Berkeley Mac Users Group	415-849-2684	2400 bd; FidoNet 161/444
MailCom BBS	415-855-9548	2400 bd; FidoNet 143/444
ET3 Network	415-864-2037	
Mac Connection	415-864-3365	
HayMUG BBS	415-881-2629	
Macintosh Tribune	415-923-1235	2400 bd; FidoNet 125/444
Computer Language BBS	415-957-9370	
SuperMac BBS	415-962-1618	2400 bd
Zone BBS	415-965-3556	2400 bd
T-Room BBS	415-993-5410	
FidoNet (Canada 1)	416-226-9260	
Macintosh Information Exchange	416-270-0533	2400 bd
Ontario Science Centre	416-429-1700	2400 bd
Digital Dimensions Dataline	416-471-2343	
Dialog Box	416-485-3670	2400 bd
InfoSource	416-574-1313	2400 bd; FidoNet 148/264

Club Mac	416-591-7952	2400 bd
Arkon InfoSystem	416-593-7460	2400 bd
Real Mac, Eh?	416-620-4938	2400 bd
Far Jewel BBS	416-690-2464	2400 bd
Fireside	416-878-1248	
Macintosh Palace BBS	416-967-4500	7 P.M.–8 A.M. M–Sat., 24 hr Sun.
Computer Matrix	417-869-5294	2400 bd; FidoNet 14/630
Oasis	418-543-9121	
Synapse (Quebec Mac Club)	418-658-6955	2400 bd
L'Echangeur	418-696-3536	2400 bd
College Crier	419-537-4110	
Cavern	419-986-5806	
UBBS	501-568-9464	To log on: press RETURN twice, type BBS
Mac Programmers West	503-222-4258	2400 bd
Stax Express	503-228-7323	
MacSystem/NW	503-245-2222	2400 bd; FidoNet 105/349
PSG Coos Bay (Fido 122)	503-269-5202	
Frontier Station BBS	503-345-3108	2400 bd
MacSystem/NW	503-357-9329	2400 bd; FidoNet 105/349
PC Technics	503-393-0998	6:30 P.M.–8:30 A.M. M–Sat.
UCSD Pascal Programmer BBS	503-581-1791	10 P.M.–5 A.M. Sun.–Thu.
MacSystem/NW	503-648-5235	2400 bd; FidoNet 105/349
MacSystem/NW	503-667-5711	2400 bd; FidoNet 105/349
Corntown Connection	503-753-7250	2400 bd; Opus 1:152/203
Cajun Bytes	504-291-6339	
New Orleans MUG BBS	504-467-3339	2400 bd; FidoNet 396/13
Health Ed Electronic Forum BBS	504-588-5743	2400 bd
Pitstop	504-774-7126	
Connection BBS/ New Orleans	504-831-7541	

Connection of New Orleans	504-836-5932	
Computer People	504-851-1236	
Nexus 6	504-928-3372	2400 bd
Applequerque BBS	505-265-7357	
Drawing Board	505-525-0844	Opus 1:15/2
Macintosh^2	505-678-1318	2400 bd; FidoNet 381/401
Miscellaneous Mac	505-898-3609	2400 bd
Hummingbird BBS	505-984-1363	2400 bd
Back to the Future BBS	507-377-2316	
Cougar Connection	509-334-3652	
Annex	512-328-2015	
Pirates Ship	512-328-4353	
Megafone	512-331-1662	
Bull Creek BBS	512-343-1612	2400 bd; Opus 1:382/54
Diner	512-443-3084	2400 bd
Restaurant at the End of the Universe	512-451-9590	
Arcane Dimensions	512-832-1680	
Diner	512-836-1420	2400 bd
Reaper's Domain	512-852-6710	2400 bd
Lifeboat	512-926-9582	
Apple-Dayton BBS	513-429-2232	
Mac Exchange	513-435-8381	
Mac Cincinnatus	513-572-5375	
Riverfront Mac	513-677-9131	2400 bd
Connection BBS	513-874-3270	2400 bd
Users Connection BBS	514-354-2219	
MacLink	514-398-9089	2400 bd
N/A	514-636-9042	
Mac to Mac	514-766-3653	2400 bd
Dessie BBS	514-842-1094	6 P.M.–9 A.M. M–F, 24 hr S–S
Mousehole	515-224-1334	
Rod's BBS	515-232-0547	2400 bd

Computerland Des Moines	515-270-8942	7 P.M.–8 A.M. M–Sat.
Zoo System	515-279-3073	password: PLEASE
Mansion BBS	515-279-6769	
Micro Mack BBS	515-294-3977	2400 bd
Apple Corp Elite	515-989-4514	
Mac's Delight	516-499-8471	2400 bd
MacsHeadroom BBS	516-678-0423	2400 bd
NY Mac BBS/ Bread Board	516-868-8326	
Circus BBS	516-872-3430	
Impending Void	517-351-4194	2400 bd
NEUMac BBS	518-237-2720	
Teachers BBS	518-370-6007	
MECCA/Environus	518-381-4430	2400 bd; Opus 7:526/305
Mac BBS	518-489-2615	
U-Compute	518-563-1679	
Wonderland Regional Mac BBS	519-672-7661	2400 bd
Mac*Ontario BBS	519-673-4181	
Mac*Ontario	519-679-0980	2400 bd
MacHaven BBS	601-992-9459	2400 bd; Opus 1:361/106
STMUG-BBS	602-230-9549	2400 bd
Stacks R Us	602-252-7928	2400 bd
KroyKolor Support System	602-266-4043	
Phoenix Red Ryder Host #1	602-285-0361	2400 bd
Marquis' BBS	602-458-8083	
Arizona Macintosh User's BBS	602-495-1713	2400 bd
Mactivities	602-722-2924	2400 bd
Computer Room	602-774-5105	
Prof. Data Management	602-881-0473	2400 bd
Geoff's Board	602-887-8848	
EyeNet *HST*	602-941-3747	2400 bd; OPUS 1:114/14
Tiger's Den	602-951-4214	2400 bd
Crossroads	602-971-2240	

Monadnock Micro BBS	603-357-2756	2400 bd
Mac Snac	603-429-0263	2400 bd
Power Mac	603-429-1309	2400 bd
XLisp BBS	603-623-1711	
Hot Air Ballooner BBS	603-886-8712	8 P.M.–7 A.M. M–F, 24 hr S–S
Mac BBS B.C., Canada	604-362-1898	
NEON Light BBS	604-368-5931	300 bd
Simran MUBBS	604-688-0049	
Sunshine BBS	604-943-1612	2400 bd
Sunshine BBS	604-943-6540	2400 bd
Manzana BBS	605-665-5179	2400 bd; 5 P.M.–8 A.M. M–F
N/A	605-665-9221	
MacCincinnati BBS	606-572-5375	
Mutual Net *QNX*	607-533-7540	2400 bd; Opus 1:260/405
Mad Mac BBS	608-256-6227	2400 bd
Mies BBS	609-228-1149	2400 bd
Mies -	609-228-7325	2400 bd
Pinelands BBS	609-354-9259	FidoNet 107/414
Hands-On Communications	609-597-0653	2400 bd
Iconoclast BBS	612-332-4005	2400 bd
Time Machine HBBS	612-427-7487	
Fifth Dimension	612-440-5731	2400 bd
Nick's Nest	612-490-1187	Opus 1:282/3
TC Midi BBS	612-588-0410	
Conus BBS	612-642-4629	evenings and weekends
Sawbones BBS	612-822-1196	2400 bd
Mac Skyline	612-824-0333	2400 bd
SmorgasBoard	612-888-3712	2400 bd; Opus 7:44/513
Mac Programmer's North BBS	612-942-0134	
Whole BIT News	613-521-3690	2400 bd; Opus 1:163/206
MacOttawa	613-729-2763	2400 bd
Second Self BBS	614-291-1816	

Columbus Multi-Board	614-436-6284	2400 bd
Aurora Borealis	614-471-6209	2400 bd
Pandora	614-471-9209	
No Change	614-764-7674	
16th Dimension BBS	614-864-3156	
NoName BBS	614-875-7399	
Syrill BBS	615-483-3325	
Muon BBS	616-534-7149	2400 bd; Opus 1:228/23
Mac BBS	617-231-2810	
Tao of Telecommunications	617-244-4642	2400 bd
Softline	617-245-4909	2400 bd
Starbase BBS	617-264-0263	2400 bd
Mac BBS	617-279-0354	2400 bd
Dog House	617-334-2448	
Mac Boston	617-350-0263	
MacApple	617-369-1717	after noon
Nibble Mac Hot Line	617-369-8920	
Ed McGee Music BBS	617-374-6168	11 P.M.– 4 P.M.
Multinet BBS	617-395-6702	
Multinet BBS	617-395-9065	
Sears BBS	617-423-0847	
Mac Stoneham	617-438-3763	
Dungeon	617-456-3890	2400 bd
PhotoTalk	617-472-8612	2400 bd; Opus 1:101/206
4th Dimension BBS	617-497-6166	FidoNet 7:46/7, 1:101/450
Tao of Telecommunications	617-527-5677	2400 bd; Opus 1:101/470
F/X BBS	617-567-8993	
NPI	617-593-0081	2400 bd
NewWorld Magic	617-595-5626	
IComm	617-598-5616	
Stack Exchange	617-628-1741	2400 bd
Mac's Diner	617-643-2882	
Athex BBS	617-662-4840	

Wonderland BBS	617-665-3796	
Macro Exchange AMIS	617-667-7388	
Finance is Fun BBS	617-682-5982	9 A.M.–5 P.M. M–F
NEC Printer BBS	617-735-4461	
Mac Users at Berkley (MUB) BBS	617-739-2366	2400 bd; 7 P.M.–7 A.M.
Buzzard's Gulch BBS	617-759-8749	2400 bd
Microcom	617-769-9358	2400 bd
MacEast	617-776-7232	2400 bd
BCS Telecomm	617-786-9788	2400 bd; Opus 1:101/122
Raceway	617-788-0038	
Sears BBS	617-843-6743	
Graphics Factory	617-849-0347	2400 bd
ByteNet (BYTE Magazine)	617-861-9767	
Termexec	617-863-0282	300 bd
Third Dimension	617-876-4361	
BCS Mac BBS	617-876-4835	
Chest./ Infinity 2001	617-891-1349	
Moon Mist BBS	617-897-9422	
Blue Sands	617-899-5579	
S'Ware BBS	617-938-3505	2400 bd
Howlers Haven	617-963-3242	2400 bd
Newton's Corner	617-964-6088	2400 bd
BOARDWALK	617-964-6866	2400 bd
Bionic Dog	617-964-8069	Opus 101/138
Prism	617-965-7816	
Phoenix BBS (RBBS)	618-233-2315	
Systems Support Group BBS	618-549-1129	2400 bd
MacConnection	619-259-8735	2400 bd
Super Messenger	619-268-3636	2400 bd
Dirk Gently's Holistic Computer	619-286-2552	
People Net BBS	619-444-7006	2400 bd

San Diego MUG	619-462-6236	
Guardians Cavern	619-563-9004	2400 bd
Cabbie BBS	619-565-1634	
Macfanatic	619-574-6480	2400 bd
Telemac BBS	619-576-1820	2400 bd
Tele-Mac BBS (SDMUG)	619-582-7572	
Computer Merchant	619-582-9557	
Mystic Passage	619-726-1591	2400 bd
Zoo BBS	619-741-1962	
Sharkey's MAChine	619-747-8719	
Mac InfoNet	619-944-3646	
N/A	703-471-0610	
TMMABBS	703-471-1378	
Washington Networks	703-560-7803	
HOLE	703-642-1429	
Master Link	703-663-2613	
Electronic Guide	703-790-5934	
Macintosh Network	703-860-1427	
Access BBS	704-255-0032	2400 bd; FidoNet 151/601
RBBS Charlotte, NC	704-332-5439	
PC-BBS	704-537-1304	
PiVot Point	707-255-7628	
Human Interface BBS	707-444-0484	6 P.M.–9 A.M. M–F, 24 hr S–S
Redwood BBS	707-444-9203	
BBS	707-964-7114	
Montgomery County BBS/MCBBS	713-353-9391	7 P.M.–6 A.M.
WCC-Beta/Texas Talker #1	713-367-8206	
Loft	713-367-9726	2400 bd
Texas Mac BBS	713-386-1683	
Humble Mac	713-441-7278	2400 bd
Market	713-461-7170	2400 bd
DOC Board	713-471-4131	300 bd

Brain in a Pan	713-480-7422	Opus 1:106/260
Applesauce	713-492-8700	
Digital Dimension	713-497-4633	
Data Mac BBS	713-523-7249	
Stellar Empire	713-527-9161	
Arturus	713-550-4202	
Computer Country	713-580-3286	
HAAUG Heaven BBS	713-664-9873	2400 bd
Oceania	713-778-9356	
Club Mac BBS	713-778-9419	
Mr. Quigman's	713-863-1683	
Mines of Moria	713-871-8577	
Zachary*Net	713-933-7353	
SynTAX BBS	713-995-0537	
Cheese Factory	714-351-9104	
Desktop	714-491-1003	2400 bd
Roadhouse	714-533-6967	
Mac Exchange	714-594-0290	2400 bd
Blues Alley	714-633-2716	
VAXHOLM	714-681-0106	
Macroscopic	714-689-8683	2400 bd
O. C. Network	714-722-8383	
Unnamed BBS	714-731-1039	6 P.M.–8 A.M. M–F, 24 hr S–S
Electric Warehouse	714-775-2560	
Secret Service	714-776-7223	
Desktop Downloads	714-826-9232	
Consultants' Exchange (Unix)	714-842-5851	2400 bd; Login: guest
Consultants' Exchange BBS	714-842-6348	2400 bd; Login: BBS
Computrends Fido BBS	714-856-1029	6 P.M.–9 A.M. M–F, 24 hr S–S
MacVille USA	714-859-5857	
Mac Exchange	714-860-1805	2400 bd
Cactus BBS	714-861-2594	

BBS FreedomLine 86	714-924-1189	
Grandpa's	714-952-2312	2400 bd
New BBS	714-966-5371	2400 bd; 9 A.M.–midnight M–F
Mac BBS	714-970-0632	
La Habra Connection	714-992-0716	2400 bd
MacCursor	716-225-5189	
Blumenthal's	716-375-4617	
N/A	716-381-9524	2400 bd
Aardvark Burrow	716-461-4223	2400 bd
N/A	716-586-8616	
MacSpence	716-594-1344	
Apple Manor	716-654-7663	
ChalkBoard	716-689-1107	
MacHonorSystem BBS	717-464-0518	
Hackers Corner	717-597-7105	
MacBBS	717-766-2539	
Microvilla	718-237-2734	2400 bd
Wall	718-278-2120	
New York On-Line	718-852-2662	2400 bd
Broadway and 68th	718-852-2823	
Eagles' Nest	719-598-8413	2400 bd; Opus 1:128/18
Scorpion	719-637-1458	2400 bd
N/A	800-634-1105	
Night Flight BBS	801-224-9112	
MacBBS	801-378-4991	
Transporter	801-379-5239	2400 bd
Master's Castle	801-575-8542	
Underworld	801-581-1823	10 P.M.–7 A.M.
Iomega BBS	801-778-4400	2400 bd
N6KSZ's BBS	801-785-3172	
Mousetrapp	801-967-8967	
Grand Strand BBS	803-293-5676	2400 bd

Fort Mill BBS	803-548-0900	2400 bd; FidoNet 151/30
MacMoore	803-576-5710	2400 bd
Causeway	803-656-5244	6 P.M.–7 A.M. M–F, 24 hr S–S
Macintosh Stop	803-776-0163	2400 bd
CSC BBS	803-786-6120	evenings only except Sun.
Macinternational	803-957-6870	2400 bd
Roundtable BBS	804-276-7368	2400 bd; Opus 1:264/263
N/A	804-740-5389	
Desktop Exchange BBS	804-784-4324	
N/A	805-388-1445	2400 bd
CamMac BBS	805-482-3573	
Fido BBS	805-522-4211	
Apple Slug BBS	805-528-4958	2400 bd
Mac Board	805-656-3746	
N/A	805-659-1243	2400 bd
J. C. International	805-688-6276	
SpacePort BBS	805-734-3330	
Gold Coast Mac	805-984-9961	2400 bd
MacBoard	806-358-0406	6 P.M.–8 A.M.
Micro-Tech Net	806-742-2917	
D.A.C.-II BBS	806-791-1147	2400 bd
Hawaii BBS	808-456-1610	
MacBBS	808-456-8498	FidoNet 1:345/21
Restaurant	808-499-1101	FidoNet 345/12
Midnight Magic	808-623-1085	2400 bd
Caribbean Breeze	809-773-0195	2400 bd
Meganet BBS	813-545-8050	2400 bd
N/A	813-955-6181	
Five Points BBS	813-957-3349	7 P.M.–8 A.M.
Little Mac BBS	814-238-4276	2400 bd
Magical Mystery Tour BBS	814-337-2021	2400 bd
TimeMachine!	815-962-7677	
Primetime BBS	815-965-5606	2400 bd

MACapsara	816-356-6738	
SpaceNet	816-363-5199	
WilloughbyWare MEBBS	816-474-1052	
DAMUG BBS	817-383-3286	2400 bd
Computer Emporium	817-540-4894	
Crystal Rose	817-547-1851	
Baseboard	817-547-5634	
Apple Cart	817-634-7727	
San Angelo Apple User's BBS	817-683-2429	
Bear Pit BBS	817-755-3891	2400 bd
MUG BBS	817-766-0510	2400 bd
Mac BBS	818-355-7872	
SGVMUG BBS	818-444-9850	2400 bd; 4 P.M.–7 A.M. M–F
Smoothtalker BBS	818-716-0817	
Programmer's Haven	818-798-6819	
Computer Connexion	818-810-7464	
Apple Bus	818-919-5459	
Mac Lodge BBS	818-962-1324	2400 bd
Oasis BBS	818-964-2621	2400 bd
House Atreides	818-965-7220	2400 bd; FidoNet 103/602
Magic Slate	818-967-5534	
Bear's Lair	818-988-6694	2400 bd
MacASM BBS	818-991-5037	
Babil-Art	819-564-2907	
MacMemphis	901-756-6867	
Macky BBS	902-466-6903	
Gulf Coast BBS	904-244-8675	
N/A	904-371-2842	7 P.M.– 8 A.M.
Traders Tavern	904-434-8679	2400 bd
BBS Central	904-725-8925	
Telebit BBS	904-736-6430	2400 bd
Micro Midget	904-994-0255	

Graveyard	907-258-3912	
Mac BBS	907-272-0550	
Front Page	907-279-9263	10 P.M.–noon M–F, 24 hr S–S
Apple Diggins (line 1)	907-333-4090	
Apple Diggins BBS (line 2)	907-338-4373	
Pentagon	907-349-6540	2400 bd
KWHL BBS	907-349-8435	
Dark Side of the Moon BBS	907-479-4816	5 P.M.–9 A.M. M–Sat.
The Board	907-488-9327	
Orpheus	907-694-0963	
BST&L BBS	912-355-9014	
CannonBall House	912-477-9232	
Computer Patch	913-233-5554	
Dog Head	913-287-2184	2400 bd
Prairie Goat	913-299-8597	6 P.M.–8 A.M. M–F, 24 hr S–S
Hacker's Nest	913-462-8285	
MacCentral BBS	913-682-1254	2400 bd
Lawrence BBS	913-841-4612	
Timescape	914-356-1643	
Mid-Hudson Mac	914-562-8528	2400 bd
Info-Center BBS	914-565-6696	2400 bd
N/A	914-578-7917	
Hackers' Hideout	914-666-3360	2400 bd; 6:30 A.M.–11 P.M.
Apple Core BBS/ Cutthroats	914-737-6770	300 bd
M-bbs	914-967-8162	
Mouse Exchange	914-967-9560	
Symbiotic	914-986-7905	
Ed's Bar & Grill	915-593-8981	6:30 P.M.–8 A.M. M–Sat.
Pass	915-821-3638	2400 bd; FidoNet 381/30
Texas Cider	915-949-8447	
Footrot Flats	916-343-3554	
Ka Leo BBS	916-372-6457	

Teacher/Student Computer Information	916-457-8270	2400 bd
Davis MUG BBS	916-758-0269	2400 bd
AVES (Mac Section)	916-758-2314	
Grand Experiment	916-891-1631	6 P.M.– 8 A.M. M–Sat.
Sacramento MUG/MacNexus	916-924-9747	2400 bd
Phoenix Landing	916-966-8243	FidoNet 203/27
TUMS BBS	918-234-5000	2400 bd
Heaven & Hell BBS	918-299-8795	
Palindrome	918-743-8347	2400 bd
Solutions! BBS	919-392-5829	
Micro Message Service	919-779-6674	2400 bd; FidoNet 151/102
AppleSeeds/Raleigh Mac User's	919-828-9619	9 P.M.–9 A.M. M–Sat.
Moonlight Mac BBS	919-852-6427	11 P.M.–8 A.M.
Moonlight Mac BBS	919-929-0943	2400 bd; 11 P.M.– 8 A.M.

Magazines

Like any other popular topic, Macintosh computing is covered by dozens of magazines. Some publications concentrate specifically on the Macintosh and report on virtually every Mac-related topic, while others focus on one specific use of the Mac or one specific group of Mac users. A third category of magazines is actually dedicated to other topics, but frequently covers the Mac as it relates to their specialty.

There is no better way to keep up with the world of Macintosh hardware and software than to read a few of these magazines, but choosing among them and finding time to read them all can be a challenge. On the following pages, we have tried to compile a comprehensive list of all magazines that cover Macintosh news on a fairly regular basis. We include dedicated Macintosh periodicals in both the United States and international versions. We also list magazines that cover general computing topics, desktop publishing, CAD and engineering, computers in education, and computers in government. A few noteworthy publications are discussed at the beginning of each category.

If possible, you should read at least one general Macintosh magazine regularly, as well as any magazines that focus on the specific ways you use your Mac. If you're serious about the Mac, you'll probably find yourself subscribing to a wide variety of publications. Although this may make you unpopular with your mail carrier, it will allow you to keep abreast of today's ever-changing personal-computer trends.

Macintosh-Specific

The most popular magazines dedicated exclusively to the Macintosh are *MacWorld* published by IDG Communications and *MacUser* from Ziff-Davis. *MacWorld* and *MacUser* have been around for several years—*MacWorld*'s first issue coincided with the Mac's January 1984 introduction—and have come a long way recently in communicating essential Macintosh information more effectively and more accurately.

- **MacWorld** has historically been our favorite Mac monthly, though there have been periods of time when we let our subscription lapse, unable to bear up against yet another article on the Scrapbook. But in the past two years, *MacWorld* has steadfastly remained a magazine we enjoy reading every month. Of the regular sections, we recommend reading the "Features" and "How to" articles. Our particular favorites are Lon Poole's "Quick Tips" column, chock-full of very specific tips to solve all sorts of hardware and software problems, and Jim Heid's "Getting Started" articles, which provide consistently excellent introductory-level explanations of various Macintosh hardware components and software categories.

  MacWorld does an excellent job of reporting on entire software or hardware categories (comparing all tape backups or all word processors, for example), usually creating useful charts that allow you to quickly compare the specific features of each product reviewed. They tend to pull their punches on weaker products, however, so we recommend that unless *MacWorld* emphatically supports a product, you try to get a second opinion before rushing out to purchase it.

- **MacUser** has had its ups and downs, but lately it has been getting so good we actually look forward to it. In particular, the *MacUser* Labs testing department has proven itself capable of providing comprehensive, unbiased reviews that don't spare the more advanced technical information. Several excellent regular features have recently been added as well, including "Power Tools," which offers insightful how-it-works information, and "Bridges," which offers the most complete and technically detailed coverage of Mac networking issues found anywhere.

  MacUser's general product reviews and evaluations are good, but we give no credence whatsoever to their mouse rating system. In *MacUser*, products are rated by receiving from one to five mice, five being the best. As far as we can tell, an application gets one mouse for being on a disk, another for having a disk label, and a third for having a name. If the program boots, it gets mouse number four, and any redeeming feature earns another half a mouse. We've yet to determine the subtlety that elevates a product to a full five-mouse rating, but it seems to have no connection with software excellence.

Most Mac users would benefit from subscriptions to both of these publications; but if you have to choose, we'd advise more beginning or casual users to select *MacWorld*, and more experienced and frequent users to sign up for *MacUser*. In addition to their editorial content, both magazines are full of the latest advertisements, which provide almost as much information as the articles.

• **MacWeek** is without a doubt the information source for power-users, decision makers, and insiders of the Macintosh community. Recently purchased by Ziff-Davis, publishers of *MacUser*, *MacWeek* includes product announcements, reviews, and columns that provide a level of detail only possible with weekly frequency. Except for an occasional tendency to take its tabloid format too much to heart (offering headlines and articles like "Elvis's ashes used in prototype for future Macintosh"), the only negative aspect of *MacWeek* is that it provides so much good information, and comes so frequently, that you will find yourself either skipping meals or not getting your normal work done while you try to read it all.

Here are the phone numbers and addresses for these and other Macintosh publications.

Apple's On-Line
34 Spencer Dr.
Bethpage, NY 11714
(516) 735-6924

MacApple
290 SW 43rd St.
Renton, WA 98055
(206) 251-5222

MacBriefs
18421 Beach Blvd., PO Box 2178
Huntington Beach, CA 92647
(714) 842-0518

MacGuide Magazine
550 S. Wadsworth Blvd., #500
Lakewood, CO 80226
(303) 935-8100

Macintosh Buyer's Guide
660 Beachland Blvd.
Vero Beach, FL 32963-1794
(417) 231-6904

Macintosh Hands On
52 Domino Dr.
Concord, MA 01742
(508) 371-1660

Macintosh News
600 Community Dr.
Manhasset, NY 11030
(516) 562-5000

MacTutor
117 Primrose Ave.
Placentia, CA 92670
(714) 993-1701

MacUser
950 Tower Lane, 18th Floor
Foster City, CA 94404
(415) 578-9770

MacWeek
525 Brannan St.
San Francisco, CA 94107
(415) 882-7370

Macworld
501 Second St., #500
San Francisco, CA 94107
(415) 243-0505

Washington Apple Pi
8227 Woodmont Ave., #201
Bethesda, MD 20814
(301) 654-8060

Wheels for the Mind
P.O. Box 1834
Escondido, CA 92025
(800) 354-8400

International

These magazines appear outside of the United States. Some are simply for-eign-language versions of American-made magazines, while others are unique entities.

ACTA Informática
C/Mare de Deu del Carmel
08022 Barcelona
Spain SPA0010

Australian Macworld
IDG Communications
37-43 Alexander St.
Crow's Nest 2065
Australia

Macintosh
Neue Winterthurerstrasse 20
8305 Dietikon
Switzerland

MacUp Verlag Gmbh
Große Elbstraße 277
2000 Hamburg
Germany

Macworld
Sodra Hamnvagen 22
S-115 41 Stockholm
Sweden

Open Apple
103, rue Colonel Bourgstraat
1140 Brussels
Belgium WUYTS1

Toolbox
C/Doctor Fleming 54
28036 Madrid
Spain SPA0036

Wheels for Business
Apple Latin America
20525 Mariani Ave., M/S 29F
Cupertino, CA 95014
(408) 974-6366

General Computing

We consider one magazine in this list, *InfoWorld,* a must-buy for Macintosh owners. This weekly publication is well-known for its superb delivery of both intermediate and highly technical information. Although *InfoWorld* primarily covers the DOS-based environment, Macintosh news is always provided, and supplemental Macintosh editions occasionally appear.

Phone numbers and addresses for this and other Mac publications are included below.

Business Software
501 Galvaston Dr.
Redwood City, CA 94063
(415) 366-3600

Byte
One Phoenix Mill Lane
Peterborough, NH 03458
(603) 924-9281

Computer and Software News
425 Park Ave.
New York, NY 10022
(212) 371-9400 x480

Computer Currents
5720 Hollis St.
Emeryville, CA 94608
(415) 547-6800

Computer Dealer
PO Box 1952
Dover, NJ 07801
(201) 361-9060

Computer Dealer Monthly
3550 Wilshire Blvd., #660
Los Angeles, CA 90010
(201) 361-9060

Computer Decisions Magazine
Glenpoint Centre East
Degraw Ave.
Teaneck, NJ 07666
(201) 487-8200

Computer Language
500 Howard St.
San Francisco, CA 94105
(415) 397-1881

Computer Reseller News
600 Community Dr.
Manhassett, NY 11030
(516) 365-4600 x5939

Computer Systems News
600 Community Dr.
Manhassett, NY 11030
(516) 562-5929

Computers in Accounting
1 Penn Plaza, 40th Floor
New York, NY 10119
(212) 971-5557

ComputerWorld
PO Box 9171
Framingham, MA 01701
(617) 879-0700

ComputerWorld Focus
PO Box 9171
Framingham, MA 01701
(617) 879-0700

Database Management System
501 Galvaston Dr.
Redwood City, CA 94063
(415) 366-3600

Data-Based Advisor
4010 Morana Blvd., #200
San Diego, CA 92117
(619) 483-6400

Datamation
249 W. 17th St.
New York, NY 10011
(212) 645-0067

Electronic Business
275 Washington St.
Newton, MA 02158
(617) 964-3030

Electronic News
2479 E. Bayshore
Palo Alto, CA 94303
(415) 496-4001

High Technology Business
214 Lewis Wharf
Boston, MA 02110
(617) 723-6611

Home Office Computing
730 Broadway
New York, NY 10003
(212) 505-3575

InfoWorld
1060 Marsh Road, #C-200
Menlo Park, CA 94025
(415) 328-4602

Micro Times
1118 Fresno Ave.
Berkeley, CA 94707
(415) 527-2829

Mini-Micro Systems
275 Washington
Newton, MA 02158
(617) 964-3030

Modern Office Technology
1100 Superior Ave.
Cleveland, OH 44114
(216) 696-7000

PC Vendors Electronic Buyers Guide
17155 Newhope, Suite B
Fountain Valley, CA 92708
(714) 540-6744

PC Week
110 Marsh Dr., #103
Foster City, CA 94404
(415) 378-5520

PC World
501 Second St., #600
San Francisco, CA 94107
(415) 546-7722

Personal Computing
10 Mulholland Dr.
Hasbrouck Heights, NJ 07604
(201) 393-6143

International

These magazines appear outside of the United States. Some are simply for-eign-language versions of American-made magazines, while others are unique entities.

Asia Computer Weekly
100 Beach Road
#26-00 Shaw Towers
Singapore 0718

Computer Sweden
Sodra Hamnvagen 24
S-115 41 Stockholm
Sweden

ComputerWorld
701-4, Kam Chung Building
54 Jaffe Road
Wanchai, Hong Kong

Computerworld Schweiz
Witikonerstrasse 15
Postfach
8030 Zurich
Switzerland

Data News
Hulstlaan 42
1170 Brussels
Belgium

Datavarlden
Box 3188
S-103 63 Stockholm
Sweden

Datornytt
Box 200
S-172 25 Sundbyberg
Sweden

Dragens Industri
Box 3177
S-103 60 Stockholm
Sweden

Industriell Datateknik
Box 27315
S-102 Stockholm
Sweden

Informatikaweek
Rose Hoevellaan 3
1180 Brussels
Belgium

Línea Directa
Apple Latin America
20525 Mariani Ave., M/S 29F
Cupertino, CA 95014
(408) 974-6366

Markt und Technik
Hans-Pinsel-Straße
8013 Haar
Germany

Semaine Informatique
Rose Hoevellaan 3
1180 Brussels
Belgium

Veckans Affarer
Box 3188
S-103 63 Stockholm
Sweden

Desktop Publishing

Probably the most most popular magazine devoted strictly to desktop publishing is *Publish!* from PCW Communications. Although a strong magazine, it has become increasingly trivialized since its inception, often devoting more effort to its newest layout than to its content. The magazine always contains at least one purposeless real-life desktop publishing drama, and the "Page Makeover" section remains one of our least favorite columns in any magazine. Our favorite column, "About Faces," contains general typeface and design information you're not likely to find elsewhere.

Our preferred desktop publishing magazine is *Personal Publishing*. Although its format changes frequently, the magazine always contains very useful information about creating documents and having them output at service bureaus; the latter topic receives very little coverage in other publications. (It just goes to show you that a magazine can improve from its humble beginnings of lambasting well-intentioned, hard-working authors.)

Advertising Age
740 N. Rush St.
Chicago, IL 60611
(312) 649-5200

Association Management
1575 Eye St. NW
Washington, DC 20005
(202) 626-2711

Business Marketing
740 N. Rush St.
Chicago, IL 60611
(312) 649-5260

Communication World
870 Market St., #940
San Francisco, CA 94102
(415) 433-3400

Desktop Publishing
363 Ridge Road
PO Box 620025
Woodside, CA 94062
(415) 363-7757

Editor & Publisher
11 W. 19th St.
New York, NY 10011
(212) 675-4380

Electronic Publishing & Printing
29 N. Wacker Dr.
Chicago, IL 60606
(312) 726-2802

Folio
Six River Bend, PO Box 4949
Stamford, CT 06907
(203) 358-9900

Graphic Design
120 E. 56th St.
New York, NY 10022
(212) 759-8813

HOW
104 Fifth Ave.
New York, NY 10011
(212) 463-0600

ITC Desktop
2 Hammarskjold Plaza
New York, NY 10017
(212) 371-0699

Magazine Design & Production
8340 Mission Rd., Suite 106
Prairie Village, KS 66206
(913) 642-6611

Marketing & Media Decisions
1140 Avenue of the Americas
New York, NY 10036
(212) 391-2155

Personal Publishing
191 S. Gary Ave.
Carol Stream, IL 60188
(312) 665-1000

Print
104 Fifth Ave.
New York, NY 10011
(212) 463-0600

Printing Impressions
401 N. Broad St.
Philadelphia, PA 19108
(213) 238-5300

Public Relations Journal
33 Irving Pl.
New York, NY 10003
(212) 995-2230

Publish!
501 Second St.
San Francisco, CA 94107
(415) 243-0600

Quick Printing
1680 SW Bayshore Blvd.
Port St. Lucie, FL 34984
(407) 879-6666

Sales & Marketing Management
633 Third Ave.
New York, NY 10017
(212) 986-4800

The Seybold Report
6922 Wildlife Road
Malibu, CA 90265
(213) 457-5850

Step by Step Graphics
600 North Forest Park Dr.
Peoria, IL 61614
(309) 688-2300

Technical Communication
428 E. Preston St.
Baltimore, MD 21202
(301) 528-4000

Training
50 S. 9th St.
Minneapolis, MN 55402
(612) 333-0471

Typeworld
PO Box 170, 35 Pelham Rd.
Salem, NH 03079
(603) 898-2822

The Typographer
Typographer's International Association
2262 Hall Place NW
Washington, DC 20007

Verbum
PO Box 15439
San Diego, CA 92115
(619) 463-9977

Computer-Aided Design and Engineering

Architectural Record
1221 Avenue of the Americas
New York, NY 10020
(212) 512-3603

Architecture
1735 New York Ave. NW
Washington, DC 20007
(202) 626-7451

CAD/CAM Journal
16 Beaver St., #400
New York, NY 10004
(212) 425-4441

Chemical Engineering
1221 Avenue of the Americas
New York, NY 10020
(212) 512-3626

Civil Engineering
345 E. 47th St.
New York, NY 10017
(212) 705-7514

Computer Design
119 Russell St., PO Box 417
Littleton, MA 01460
(617) 486-9501

Computer Graphics Review
881 Dover Dr., #14
Newport Beach, CA 92663
(714) 641-1988

Computer Graphics Today
228 E. 45th St.
New York, NY 10017
(212) 983-5888

Computer Graphics World
119 Russell St., PO Box 417
Littleton, MA 01460
(617) 486-9601

Design Graphics World
6255 Barfield Rd.
Atlanta, GA 30328
(404) 256-9800

Design News
275 Washington St.
Newton, MA 02158
(617) 964-3030

Electronic Design
10 Holland Dr.
Hasbrouck Heights, NJ 07604
(201) 393-6000

Electronic Engineering Times
600 Community Dr.
Manhasset, NY 11030
(516) 562-5000

Electronics
10 Holland Dr.
Hasbrouck Heights, NJ 07604
(201) 393-6000

Industrial Engineering
25 Technology Park/Atlanta
Norcross, GA 30092
(404) 449-0460

Machine Design
1100 Superior Ave.
Cleveland, OH 44114
(216) 696-7000

Mechanical Engineering
345 E. 47th St.
New York, NY 10017
(212) 705-7345

Plan & Print
611 E. Butterfield Road, Suite 104
Lombard, IL 60148
(312) 852-3055

Plant Engineering
1350 E. Touchy Ave., PO Box 5080
Des Plaines, IL 60017
(312) 635-8800

Progressive Architecture
600 Sumner St., PO Box 1361
Stamford, CT 06904
(203) 348-7531

Educational Computing

Academic Computing
350 Sansome St., Suite 750
San Francisco, CA 94104
(415) 421-7330

Academic Technology
1311 Executive Center Dr., #220
Tallahassee, FL 32301
(904) 878-4178

Classroom Computer Learning
2451 East River Road
Dayton, OH 45439
(415) 457-4333

*College & University
Computer Directory*
PO Box 47667
Phoenix, AZ 85068
(602) 863-2212

Collegiate Microcomputer
Rose-Hulman Institute of Technology
Terre Haute, IN 47803
(812) 877-1511

Computing Teacher Journal
ICCE University of Oregon
1787 Agate St.
Eugene, OR 97403
(503) 686-4414

Curriculum Product Review
6 River Bend
Stamford, CT 06907
(203) 358-9900

Electronic Education
1311 Executive Center Dr.
Tallahassee, FL 32301
(904) 878-4178

Electronic Learning
730 Broadway
New York, NY 10003
(212) 505-3478

*National Collegiate
Software Clearinghouse*
NCSU Box 8101
Raleigh, NC 27695
(919) 737-3067

School & College Product News
1100 Superior Ave.
Cleveland, OH 44114
(216) 696-7000

Social Science Microcomputer
Duke University Press
PO Box 6697, College Station
Durham, NC 27708
(919) 684-2173

Teaching and Computers
730 Broadway
New York, NY 10003
(212) 505-3578

T.H.E. Journal
2626 S. Pullman, Suite 250
Santa Ana, CA 92705
(714) 261-0366

Governmental Computing

Federal Computer Week
3110 Fairview Park Dr., #1040
Falls Church, VA 22042
(703) 876-5108

Government Product News
1100 Superior Ave.
Cleveland, OH 44114
(216) 696-7000

Government Computer News
8601 Georgia Ave., #300
Silver Spring, MD 20910
(301) 650-2000

Government Technology
1831 V St.
Sacramento, CA 95818
(916) 443-7133

Government Data Systems
50 W. 23rd St.
New York, NY 10010
(212) 645-1000

URISA News
319 C St. SE
Washington, DC 20003
(202) 543-7141

Government Microcomputer Letter
PO Box 16645
Tampa, FL 33687
(813) 622-8484

Washington Apple PI Journal
8227 Woodmont Ave., #201
Bethesda, MD 20814
(301) 654-8060

Music and Entertainment

The Computer Show
1118 Fresno Ave.
Berkeley, CA 94707
(415) 527-2829

Music, Computers & Software
10 E. Main St.
Huntington, NY 11743
(516) 673-3243

Electronic Musician
19725 Sherman Way, Suite 160
Canoga Park, CA 91306
(818) 709-4662

Music Technology
22024 Lassen St., Suite 118
Chatsworth, CA 91311
(818) 704-8777

User Groups

User groups are organizations that provide facilities for Macintosh users to exchange information among themselves, and for hardware and software vendors (including Apple Computer) to disseminate information to them. Under this broad definition, all kinds of user groups exist, ranging from small special-interest user groups formed within a single company to huge national groups covering every aspect of Macintosh computing. The services user groups offer also vary widely. User groups hold meetings, write newsletters, manage bulletin boards, offer telephone support, sponsor exhibitions, distribute public-domain and shareware software, and more.

Meetings are the most distinctive service most groups sponsor, and the best reason for joining a user group. General meetings usually include announcements of important Macintosh-related news, question-and-answer sessions, in addition to presentations by hardware or software vendors. Special-interest group (SIG) meetings allow those Macintosh users who are particularly interested in some topic—desktop publishing or database programming, for example—to meet with others sharing the same interest in a smaller, less formal setting (if it's possible for anything to be less formal than a user-group meeting).

Who Should Join a User Group?

If you want or need to keep up to date on information about the Macintosh, you should definitely join a local user group. User groups provide a source of information that cannot be replaced no matter how many magazines or books you read: personal interaction with other people who use the Macintosh. Even if you're too shy to speak up at your first couple of meetings, the chance to see new products demonstrated and to hear others comment on their Macintosh experiences will clearly impress upon you the user group's value. And when you do bring a few questions to a meeting, the fast, friendly, and complete replies you receive will convince you that you've really found an important resource.

If you can't find a user group in your area—this should only occur in fairly rural areas—then you'll have to consider joining one of the national user groups, relying on printed materials and bulletin boards for your Mac information and support, or starting your own user group. The first two options, unfortunately, lose the personal interaction that user-group meetings provide. We believe this makes them rather inadequate substitutes. Starting your own user group requires both dedication and lots of hard work, but if you are interested you can probably find other local Mac users who are willing to help. Apple can provide you with information about forming a user group—specifically, a book called *Just Add Water*. Contact the Apple User Group Connection at the address listed later in this entry.

Selecting a User Group

Before selecting a user group, locate all of the groups in your area. To find the Macintosh user groups that have registered with the Apple User Group Connection, call 1-800-538-9696. This will provide you with a very complete list of local user groups. You might also want to ask your local Apple dealer if they know of any groups in your area.

In many areas, a number of local user groups will be available for you to choose from. Since user groups are such informal organizations, the best way to decide is to attend a few meetings and find the one that best matches your technical level and interest. User-group meetings are almost always open to the public, and many groups never actually require that you "join" (although newsletters and bulletin-board access are usually only provided to paying members). You might find that more than one user group seems right, perphaps one large general-interest group and a smaller group with a more direct focus. Once you've selected a user group, attend the meetings regularly and try to take advantage of the group's many services. Get involved by lending your expertise or volunteering to help out.

National User Groups

Two Macintosh user groups have grown so large that they can be considered national (or even international) user groups: the Boston Computer

Society (BCS) and the Berkeley Macintosh User Group (BMUG). If you live near the headquarters of one of these groups (Boston, MA, and Berkeley, CA, respectively), consider yourself very lucky, and sign right up. Both groups offer hundreds of meetings each year covering the complete range of Macintosh topics, and the chance to meet with the most knowledgeable Mac users and the most supportive Mac vendors.

If you aren't lucky enough to live near the headquarters of either of these groups, we recommend that you consider them in addition to, not in place of, membership in your local user group. Both offer excellent newsletters (each alone worth the price of membership), complete and well-organized public-domain and shareware libraries, extensive bulletin boards, and telephone support lines.

- **BMUG** (Berkeley Macintosh User Group) is the biggest independent user group in the world, with members numbering well into the thousands. Based at the University of California at Berkeley, the club began as a student organization in 1984. Since then, their services have grown to include local meetings, an extensive bulletin-board system (BMUGBBS), a special help line, a vast public-domain and shareware software library, a CD ROM of public-domain utilities (BMUG PD ROM), and a semiannual newsletter (the last issue of which hit 400 pages), which served as one of the many source materials for this book.

  The BMUG newsletter is reason enough for joining BMUG. Each issue is filled with straight-shooting articles about Macintosh hardware, software, and events. We especially like the "Choice Products" section, in which select hardware and software products in every category are recommended. Two issues of the newsletter, which is really more of a book, are included with each one-year membership.

  BMUG
  1442A Walnut St.
  Berkeley, CA 94709
  (415) 549-2684
  BBS: (415) 849-2684

- ***BCS•Mac*** (Macintosh Users Group of the Boston Computer Society) also grew out of a university student organization, this time at the Massachusetts Institute of Technology. The Macintosh group is just one of BCS's many user groups, but it operates fairly independently, with its own newsletter, *The Active Window,* public-domain and shareware library, bulletin boards, meetings, and help lines. *The Active Window,* like the BMUG newsletter, provides the type of no-nonsense reviews and tips that cannot be found in any of the national Macintosh publications.

  BCS•Mac Office
  48 Grove St.
  Somerville, MA 02144
  (617) 625-7080
  BBS: (617) 876-4835

Apple's Role

Just in case you're one of those people who finds solace in endorsements, Apple provides a user-group authorization service called the User Group Connection. User groups around the country are encouraged to register with Apple, which in turn provides club access to AppleLink, as well as product news and a ton of third-party developer mailings. Apple also conducts a national meeting annually so various groups can share ideas with each other.

For more information about creating or joining a local user group, write to the address below or call 1-800-538-9696. When you call, you will be provided with numbers for the five nearest local user groups (according to your zip code) as well as those of the Berkeley-based and Boston-based nationals.

  User Group Connection
  Apple Computer, Inc.
  M/S 36AA
  20525 Mariani Avenue
  Cupertino, CA 95014

Vendors/Products

Throughout this book we have mentioned a wide range of hardware and software products. The list below is designed to let you know which version of each product we reviewed, who markets the product, and how much it costs (if it costs anything).

Because much of the software we've discussed is public-domain, freeware, and shareware, we could not always find complete information on every product. We were amazed to discover how many programmers create truly useful software and then don't even stick their name on it. If any information about any of these products was missing or not applicable to the specific product, our listing includes N/A, meaning not available, or not applicable. Products for which we couldn't find any information at all have been omitted from this list.

There are four classifications of software: commercial, public-domain, shareware, and freeware. Commercial software can be purchased from local computer stores or from mail-order software dealers. For your convenience we have included a brief listing of popular Macintosh mail-order software vendors at the end of this listing. All prices quoted here are retail, so you will usually find that you can buy commercial products for somewhat less than the prices listed here.

Public-Domain, Freeware, and Shareware

Public-domain software is software that is given away by its author, and may be freely distributed without restriction. Freeware is software that is also given away by its author, but the author retains the copyright in order to control the methods by which it is distributed and protect their software from being modified by others without permission. Shareware is a program that is given away under the condition that anyone who keeps the software for longer than a specified trial period agrees to send a specified payment for the software to its author. Shareware is sometimes called *honorware* because it is up to the honor of the user to send in their payment, usually called a registration fee, if they keep the software. Often public-domain, freeware, and shareware software is lumped together and called simply public-domain software, but it is important to understand the distinction between these three formats.

Public-domain, shareware, and freeware products are not available in computer stores or from the mail-order software vendors, but instead are distributed via bulletin-board services, user groups, and the so-called "public-domain software vendors." You never pay for public-domain, freeware, or shareware, except when you send in your shareware fees, but sometimes you will have to pay a downloading charge or on-line fee to download this software from a bulletin board, or pay a disk duplication fee (somewhere between $2.00 and $8.00 per disk) to the user group or service that copies the software for you. Since one disk can contain a large number of programs—most public-domain, freeware, and shareware programs are quite small—buying them on disk is the most cost-effective way to obtain them. (Even if you pay a fee to obtain shareware, you still are obligated to pay the requested shareware fee if you keep this software.)

If you do not use any bulletin boards that offer large software libraries, and you don't belong to a user group with a complete software library, you can get disks full of this type of software from a number of services that charge a few dollars per disk (which they call a disk duplication fee) for disks full of public-domain, freeware, and shareware software. Unfortunately, some freeware and shareware developers specifically prohibit their software from being distributed by these services. They feel that since these companies are profiting by distributing their software, it is somehow a violation of the freeware or shareware concept. We disagree; the service these companies provide is legitimate, making the wide range of public-domain, freeware, and shareware software available to people who don't want to spend hours on-line or otherwise hunting for this relatively hard-to-find software. And these companies do not charge more for their service than the services themselves justify. For your convenience, a listing of some of these services is also included at the end of this entry.

Alphabetical Product Listing

Aask 1.0
CE Software
1854 Fuller Rd., Box 65580
W. Des Moines, IA 50265
(515) 224-1995
$49.95, included with
MockPackage Plus Utilities

Acta Advantage 3.01
Symmetry Corp.
761 E. University Dr.
Mesa, AZ 85203
(602) 844-2199
$129.00

*Adobe Collector's Edition I
Symbols, Borders,
and Letterforms*
Adobe Systems, Inc.
1585 Charleston Rd.
Mountain View, CA 94039
(415) 961-4400
$125.00

*Adobe Collector's Edition II
Patterns and Textures*
Adobe Systems, Inc.
1585 Charleston Rd.
Mountain View, CA 94039
(415) 961-4400
$225.00

Adobe Illustrator 88 1.8.3
Adobe Systems, Inc.
1585 Charleston Rd.
Mountain View, CA 94039
(415) 961-4400
$495.00

Adobe Streamline 1.0
Adobe Systems, Inc.
1585 Charleston Rd.
Mountain View, CA 94039
(415) 961-4400
$395.00

Aldus FreeHand 2.02
Aldus Corp.
411 First Ave. S., Suite 200
Seattle, WA 98104
(206) 622-5500
$495.00

Aldus PageMaker 3.02
Aldus Corp.
411 First Ave. S., Suite 200
Seattle, WA 98104
(206) 622-5500
$595.00

AltWDEF
public domain

Analyze 2.1
Micro-Systems Software
12798 W. Forest Hill Blvd., #202
West Palm Beach, FL 33414
(407) 790-0770
$149.00

Anonymity 1.0
public domain

Apple File Exchange 1.1
Apple Computer, Inc.
20525 Mariani Ave.
Cupertino, CA 95014
(408) 996-1010
N/A

ArchiText 2.03
BrainPower, Inc.
30497 Canwood, #201
Agoura Hills, CA 91301
(818) 884-6911
$349.95

Arc.pop 1.3
dogStar Software
PO Box 302
Bloomington, IN 47402
N/A
$25.00, shareware

Art Importer 1.0
Altsys
720 Avenue F, Suite 109
Plano, TX 75074
(214) 424-4888
$99.95

ArtRoundUp 2.0
Dubl-Click Software
9316 Dearing Ave.
Chatsworth, CA 91311
(818) 349-2758
$49.95, included with *MacTut/ ProGlyph*

Backdrop
N/A

Big Ben
N/A

Big Pat/Pic-a-Pat
Charles Dunn
Physics Dept., Cornell Universtiy
Ithaca, NY 14853
freeware

Big Thesaurus 1.0
Deneba Software
3305 NW 74th Ave.
Miami, FL 33122
(305) 594-6965
$99.95

BigCaps 3.2
Dubl-Click Software
9316 Dearing Ave.
Chatsworth, CA 91311
(818) 349-2758
$49.95, included with *MacTut/ ProGlyph*

BigZoomIdle
public domain

Blesser 1.0
freeware

Bomber 1.0
VNH
public domain

Boomerang 2.0
Hiro Yamamoto
UCLA
freeware

bootDiskIcon 1.0
David Dunham
freeware

Bugs Bunny
public domain

CanOpener 1.00
Abbott Systems
62 Mountain Rd.
Pleasantville, NY 10570
(800) 522-9157
$125.00

Canvas 2.0
Deneba Software
3305 NW 74th Ave.
Miami, FL 33122
(305) 594-6965
$299.00

cdev Shrinker
John Rotenstein
PO Box 165
Double Bay, NSW 2028
freeware

Clipboard Magician 0.50
Apple Computer, Inc.
20525 Mariani Ave.
Cupertino, CA 95014
(408) 996-1010
freeware

The Clipper 2.0
Solutions International
30 Commerce St.
Williston, VT 05495
(808) 658-5506
$89.95

ClipShare
Olduvai
7520 Red Rd., Suite A
South Miami, FL 33143
(305) 665-4665
$295.00

Clock
N/A

Clock 4.2
Green Mountain Software
9404 Valley Lane
Huntsville, AL 35803
freeware

Clock Adjust
James Nitchal
CompuServe 71001,2232
freeware

Color 3.3
Apple Computer, Inc.
20525 Mariani Ave.
Cupertino, CA 95014
(408) 996-1010
Included with *System Software 6.0*

Color Cursor
Mathias Urlichs
CompuServe 72437,1357
public domain

Color Finder
Chris Derossi/Apple
20525 Mariani Ave.
Cupertino, CA 95014
(408) 996-1010
freeware

ColorDesk 1.0
Microseeds Publishing, Inc.
7030-B W. Hillsborough Ave.
Tampa, FL 33615
(813) 882-8635
$79.00, included with
Dimmer and *Switch-A-Roo*

Complete Delete
Watercoarse Software
public domain

Control-1 1.10
CE Software
1854 Fuller Rd., Box 65580
W. Des Moines, Iowa 50265
(515) 224-1995
freeware

Copy II Mac 7.2
Central Point Software
15220 NW Greenbrier Pkwy., #200
Beaverton, OR 97006
(503) 690-8090
$39.95

Cricket ColorPaint 1.0
Computer Associates
40 Valley Stream Pkwy.
Malvern, PA 19355
(215) 251-9890
$295.00

Cricket Draw 1.1.1
Computer Associates
40 Valley Stream Pkwy.
Malvern, PA 19355
(215) 251-9890
$295.00

Cricket Paint 1.0
Computer Associates
40 Valley Stream Pkwy.
Malvern, PA 19355
(215) 251-9890
$195.00

The Curator 1.05
Solutions International
30 Commerce St.
Williston, VT 05495
(802) 658-5506
$139.95

DA menuz 1.0
jbx
111 Silver Hill Rd.
Concord, MA 01742
freeware

DAs Key 2.02
Loftus E. Becker
41 Whitney St.
Hartford, CT 06105
$5.00, shareware

DAtabase 1.12
Preferred Publishers, Inc.
5100 Poplar Ave., Suite 706
Memphis, TN 38137
(901) 683-3383
$129.95

Date Key 2.05
Loftus E. Becker
41 Whitney St.
Hartford, CT 06105
$5.00, shareware

Dawn 2.0.1
Frank Price, AOC Software
612 Doheny Rd.
Beverly Hills, CA 90210
$20.00, shareware

DaynaFile
Dayna Communications
50 South Main St., 5th Fl.
Salt Lake City, UT 84144
(801) 531-0600
$650.00

Deluxe Option Board
Central Point Software
15220 NW Greenbrier Pkwy., #200
Beaverton, OR 97006
(503) 690-8090
N/A

DeskDraw 1.3
Zedcor, Inc.
4500 E. Speedway, Suite 22
Tucson, AZ 85712
(602) 881-8101
$129.95, included with *DeskPaint*

DeskPaint 2.0
Zedcor, Inc.
4500 E. Speedway, Suite 22
Tucson, AZ 85712
(602) 881-8101
$129.95, included with *DeskDraw*

DeskScene 1.0
PBI Software
freeware

DeskZap 1.32
Bruce Tomlin
15801 Chase Hill, Apt. 109
San Antonio, TX 78256
$15.00, shareware

Dialog Keys 1.2
CE Software
1854 Fuller Rd., Box 65580
W. Des Moines, Iowa 50265
(515) 224-1995
$99.95, included with *QuicKeys*

Dimmer
Microseeds Publishing Inc.
7030-B W. Hillsborough Ave.
Tampa, FL 33615
(813) 882-8635
$79.00, included with
ColorDesk and *Switch-A-Roo*

Disk Dup+ 1.0
Rodger Bases
Route 1, Box 865
Hillsboro, OR 97124
$10.00, shareware

Disk Express 1.50
Alsoft, Inc.
PO Box 927
Spring, TX 77383
$69.95

Disk Imager 1.0
John Raymonds
freeware

Disk Ranger 4.0
Graham Software
8609 Ingalls Circle
Arvada, CO 80003
(303) 422-0757
$59.95

Disk-File Fkey 1.0
John Holder
7365 El Tomaso Way
Buena Park, CA 90620
$3.00, shareware

DiskFit 1.4
Super Mac Technology
295 N. Bernado Ave.
Mountview, CA 94043
(408) 245-2222
$99.95

DiskLibrarian 1.7
Little Bit
469 Edgewood Ave.
New Haven, CT 06511
$20.00, shareware

DiskQuick 2.1
IdeaForm
PO Box 1540
Fairfield, IA 52566
(515) 472-7256
$49.95

DiskTools 1.01
Electronic Arts
1820 Gateway Dr.
San Mateo, CA 94404
(415) 571-7171
$49.95

DiskTop 3.0.4
CE Software
1854 Fuller Rd., Box 65580
W. Des Moines, IA 50265
(515) 224-1995
$49.95

Drawing Table 1.0
Brøderbund Software
17 Paul Dr.
San Rafael, CA 94903
(415) 492-3200
$129.95

DRIVE 2.4
Kennect Technology
120-A Albright Way
Los Gatos, CA 95030
(800) 522-1232
N/A

Earth 1.0
Stefan Bilaniuk
Dartmouth College
Hanover, NH 03755
freeware

Easy Icon 1.5
Rolf Rando
13838 Templeton Pl.
Los Angeles, CA 94022
public domain

Elapse 2.0
Jim Hamilton
2914 Aftonshire Way, #13102
Austin, TX 78748
$1.00, shareware

Empower 2.05
Magna
2540 N. First St., Suite 302
San Jose, CA 95131
(408) 433-5467
$395.00

Eraser 1.0
Solar Systems
freeware

ExpressWrite 1.01
Exodus Software
8620 Winton Rd., Suite 304
Cincinnati, OH 45231
(513) 522-0011
$99.95

Facade 1.06
Greg Marriot
freeware

Fade Key
public domain

Fast Formatter 2.2
Beyond
3865 N. Oracle Blvd.
Tucson, AZ 85705
(602) 323-4547
public domain

FastCopy 1.0
Central Point Software
15220 NW Greenbrier Pkwy., #200
Beaverton, OR 97006
(503) 690-8090
$79.00, included with
PC Tools Deluxe

Fedit Plus 1.07
John Mitchel
108 E. Fremont Ave., #37
Sunnyvale, CA 94087
$40.00, shareware

File Minder 1.1
Seanook Software
CompuServe 75366,1233
public domain

FileMaker II 1.0
Claris Corp.
440 Clyde Ave.
Mountain View, CA 94043
(408) 987-7000
$299.00

FileMaster 2.30
Alexander Falk
Freistadterstr. 150/5/13 A-4040
Linz, Austria
$25.00, shareware

FileStar 1.0
Scott Searle
PO Box 87
Mukilteo, WA 98275
$15.00, shareware

FileZero 1.0
OITC, Inc.
PO Box 73
Melbourne Beach, FL 32951
(305) 984-3714
$15.00, shareware

FileZero Init 1.0
OITC, Inc.
P.O. Box 73
Melbourne Beach, FL 32951
(305) 984-3714
$49.95

Find File 1.3
Apple Computer, Inc.
20525 Mariani Ave.
Cupertino, CA 95014
(408) 996-1010
Included with *System Software 6.0*

Finder Colors 1.0
Jan Linder
Flensburger StR 5 1000
Berlin21 W. Germany
freeware

Findswell 2.0
Working Software
PO Box 1844
Santa Cruz, CA 950614
(408) 423-5696
$59.95

Fkey... DA 2.02
Loftus E. Becker
41 Whitney St.
Hartford, CT 06105
N/A
$10.00, shareware

Fkey Installer
Dreams of the Pheonix
PO Box 10273
Jacksonville, FL 32247
(404) 356-6452
$39.95

Fkey Manager 2.50
Carlos Webber
250 Douglas St., #12
San Francisco, CA 94114
(415) 861-8956
freeware

Fkey Sampler 3.14
Dave Kaun
2214 ½ Wiocean Front
Newport Beach, CA 92663
chocolate, shareware

Fkey View 2.5
John Holder
7365 El Tomaso Way
Buena Park, CA 90620
public domain

Fkey/Sound Mover 1.11
Alsoft, Inc.
PO Box 927
Spring, TX 77383
(713) 353-4090
$89.95, included with *MasterJuggler*

Font Downloader 3.1
Adobe Systems, Inc.
1585 Charleston Rd.
Mountain View, CA 94039
(415) 961-4400
freeware

Font Harmony 1.2
Fifth Generation Systems
11200 Industriplex Blvd.
Baton Rouge, LA 70809
(800) 873-4384
$59.95, included with *Suitcase II*

FONTastic Plus, 2.01
Altsys
720 Avenue F, Suite 109
Plano, TX 75074
(214) 424-4888
$99.95

Font/DA Juggler Plus
Alsoft, Inc.
PO Box 927
Spring, TX 77383
(713) 353-4090
$59.95

Font/DA Mover 3.8
Apple Computer, Inc.
20525 Mariani Ave.
Cupertino, CA 95014
(408) 996-1010
Included with *System Software 6.0*

Font/DA Utility 1.11
Alsoft, Inc.
PO Box 927
Spring, TX 77383
(713) 353-4090
$89.95, included with *MasterJuggler*

FONT-FKEY-DA Sampler
Dave Kalin
501 Larsson St.
Manhattan Beach, CA 92663
freeware

FontLiner 1.0
Taylored Graphics
PO Box 1900
Freedom, CA 95019
(408) 761-2481
$129.95

Fontographer 2.4.1
Altsys
720 Avenue F, Suite 109
Plano, TX 75074
(214) 424-4888
$395.00

FontSizer 1.7
U.S. MicroLabs, Inc.
1611 Headway Circle, Bldg. 3
Austin, TX 78754
$99.95

Formatter Deluxe 1.0
Jan Eugenides
Route 1, Box 9463
Waterbury Center, VT 05677
(617) 371-1660
freeware

Full Impact 1.1
Ashton-Tate
6411 Guadalupe Mines Rd.
San Jose, CA 95120
(408) 268-2300
$395.00

FullPaint 1.0SE
Ashton-Tate
6411 Guadalupe Mines Rd.
San Jose, CA 95120
(408) 268-2300
$99.95

FullWrite Professional 1.1
Ashton-Tate
6411 Guadalupe Mines Rd.
San Jose, CA 95120
(408) 268-2300
$395.00

GOfer 1.1.8
Microytics, Inc.
1 Tobey Village Office Park
Pittsford, NY 14534
(800) 828-6293
$79.95

Guard Dog 2.3
Nemesis Systems
PO Box 29263
Minneapolis, MN 55429
$20.00, shareware

Guide 2.0
Owl International, Inc.
28000 156th Ave. SE
Bellevue, WA 98007
(206) 747-3203
$199.95

Gumby Clock
public domain

Hard Disk Deadbolt 1.0
FWB, Inc.
2040 Polk St., Suite 215
San Francisco, CA 94109
(415) 474-8055
$89.95

Hard Disk Partition 2.0
FWB, Inc.
2040 Polk St., Suite 215
San Francisco, CA 94109
(415) 474-8055
$69.95

HD Backup
PBI Software
1163 Triton Dr.
Foster, CA
(415) 349-8765
$49.95

HD Partition 1.11
Symantec Corp.
10201 Torre Ave.
Cupertino, CA 95014
(408) 253-9600, (800) 441-7234
$149.95, included with
Symantec Utilities

HD TuneUp 1.11
Symantec Corp.
10201 Torre Ave.
Cupertino, CA 95014
(408) 253-9600, (800) 441-7234
$149.95, included with
Symantec Utilities

HyperDA 1.1.1
Symmetry Corp.
761 E. University Dr.
Mesa, AZ 85203
(602) 844-2199
$69.00

HyperSound 2.0
Farallon Computing
2150 Kitteredge St.
Berkeley, CA 94704
(415) 849-2331
$199.00, included with *MacRecorder*

Icon Colorizer 1.0
Robert Manafo
freeware

Icon Designer 3.0
John Nairin
7108 South Pine St.
Salt Lake City, UT 84121
(801) 942-7768
$10.00, shareware

Icon Wrap 1.2
Ken McLeod
freeware

Icon-It
Olduvai
7520 Red Rd., Suite A
South Miami, FL 33143
(305) 665-4665
$79.95

Idle
public domain

Init 1.0
John Rotenstein
public domain

Init Manager
Steve Byran
529 7th St., #625
Minneapolis, MN 55415
freeware

Init Picker 1.0
Microseeds Publishing Inc.
7030-B W. Hillsborough Ave.
Tampa, FL 33615
(813) 882-8635
$39.95

Inix 1.1
Natural Intelligence, Inc.
86 Richdale Ave.
Cambridge, MA 02140
(617) 266-7858, (800) 999-4649
$49.95

International Time
freeware

*Keynotes Associated
Press Stylebook*
Digital Learning Systems
4 Century Dr.
Parsippany, NJ 07054
(800) 992-0264
$59.95

Kolor 1.0
Apple Computer, Inc.
20525 Mariani Ave.
Cupertino, CA 95014
(408) 996-1010
freeware

LapLink
Traveling Software
18702 N. Creek Pkwy.
Bothell, WA 98011
(800) 343-8080
$139.95

LaserFX 1.6
Postcraft International, Inc.
27811 Avenue Hopkins, Suite 6
Valencia, CA 91355
(800) 257-1797
$195.00

LaserStatus 3.0.4
CE Software
1854 Fuller Rd., Box 65580
W. Des Moines, IA 50265
(515) 224-1995
$49.95, included with
MockPackage Plus Utilities

Launcher 3.3
Bill Steinberg
freeware

Layout 1.7
Michael O'Conner
freeware

LetraStudio 1.0
Letraset USA
40 Eisenhower Dr.
Paramus, NJ 07653
(201) 845-6100
$495.00

LetrTuck 1.05
EDCO Services, Inc.
12410 W. Dale Mabry Hwy.
Tampa, FL 33618
(813) 962-7800
$149.00

Locare 1.8
Raymond Lau
100-04 70 Ave.
Forest Hills, NY 11375
$10.00, shareware

Locate 2.0
Central Point Software, Inc.
15220 NW Greenbrier Pkwy., #200
Beaverton, OR 97006
(503) 690-8090
$79.00, included with
PC Tools Deluxe

LockOut 2.0
Beyond, Inc.
PO Box 31990
Tucson, AZ 85712
freeware

MacCalc 1.2
Bravo Technologies, Inc.
PO Box 10078
Berkeley, CA 94709
(415) 841-8552
$139.95

MacChuck 1.5
Vano Associates
PO Box 12730
New Brighton, MN 55418
(612) 788-9547
$99.95

MacDraw II 1.1
Claris Corp.
440 Clyde Ave.
Mountain View, CA 94043
(408) 987-7000
$395.00

MacInTalk 1.31
Apple Computer, Inc.
20525 Mariani Ave.
Cupertino, CA 95014
(408) 996-1010
freeware

MacLink Plus 3.0
DataViz
35 Corporate Dr.
Trumbull, CT 06611
(203) 268-0030
$195.00

*MacLink Plus
Translators 3.0*
DataViz
35 Corporate Dr.
Trumbull, CT 06611
(203) 268-0030
$159.00

MacPaint 2.0
Claris Corp.
440 Clyde Ave.
Mountain View, CA 94043
(408) 987-7000
$125.00

MacPassword 3.0
Art Schumer
13814 176th Place NE
Redmond, WA 98052
$35.00

MacRecorder
Farallon Computing
2150 Kitteredge St.
Berkeley, CA 94704
(415) 849-2331
$199.00

MacroMaker
Apple Computer, Inc.
20525 Mariani Ave.
Cupertino, CA 95014
(408) 996-1010
Included with *System Software 6.0*

MacSnoop 1.5.4
Art Schumer
13814 176th Place NE
Redmond, WA 98052
$25.00, shareware

MacTools 7.2
Central Point Software
15220 NW Greenbrier Pkwy., #200
Beaverton, OR 97006
(503) 690-8090
$79.00, included with
PC Tools Deluxe

MacTree Plus 2.0
Go Technologies
PO Box 4535
Incline Village, NV 89450
$69.95

MacWelcome 1.3
Chris Klugewiez
2704 East Towers Dr. #508
Cincinnati, OH 45238
freeware

MacWrite II 1.0v2
Claris Corp.
440 Clyde Ave.
Mountain View, CA 94043
(408) 987-7000
$249.00

MainWDEF
public domain

Mass Init 1.01
Fredric Anderson
freeware

MasterJuggler 1.50
Alsoft, Inc.
PO Box 927
Spring, TX 77383
(713) 353-4090
$89.95

Message Browser
Brad Doster
Heizer Software
1941 Oak Park Bldg., #30
Pleasant Hill, CA 94523
(800) 888-7667
$20.00

MFDetective
Richard Guerra Jr.
public domain

Mickey Mouse
public domain

Microsoft Excel 2.2
Microsoft Corp.
16011 NE 36th Way, Box 97017
Redmond, WA 98073
(206) 882-8080
$395.00

Microsoft File 2.00a
Microsoft Corp.
16011 NE 36th Way, Box 97017
Redmond, WA 98073
(206) 882-8080
$195.00

Microsoft Word 4.0
Microsoft Corp.
16011 NE 36th Way, Box 97017
Redmond, WA 98073
(206) 882-8080
$395.00

Microsoft Write 1.0
Microsoft Corp.
16011 NE 36th Way, Box 97017
Redmond, WA 98073
(206) 882-8080
$175.00

MindWrite Express 2.1
DeltaPoint, Inc.
200 Heritage Harbor, Suite G
Monterey, CA 93940
(408) 648-4000
$250.00

Moiré 1.41c
John Lim
18 Nottingwood St.
Doncaster East 3109, Victoria Australia
shareware

Moving Lines
Data Magic
public domain

MultiClip 1.01
Olduvai
7520 Red Rd., Suite A
South Miami, FL 33143
(305) 665-4665
$99.00

MultiDisk 1.11
Alsoft, Inc.
PO Box 927
Spring, TX 77383
(713) 353-4090
$69.95

Multi-Launch 1.0
James Stout
CompuServe 73240,2052
freeware

MultiLaunch 1.1
Jan Eugenides
Route 1, Box 9463
Waterbury Center, VT 05677
(617) 371-1660
freeware

Multi-Scrap
N/A

MultiSet 1.0
Donald Neff
32 Knightsbridge Way
San Jose, CA 95148
$15.00, shareware

Navigator 2.1
CompuServe
5000 Arlington Centre Blvd.
Columbus, OH 43220,
(614) 457-8600, (800) 848-8199
$49.95

Network DiskFit 1.41
SuperMac Technology
295 Bernardo Ave.
Mountain View, CA 94043
(415) 964-8884
$395.00

NEVR
jbx
111 Silver Hill Rd.
Concord, MA 01742
public domain

News Clock 3.0
Ethereal Dreams
freeware

Nisus 1.01
Paragon Concepts, Inc.
4954 Sun Valley Rd.
Del Mar, CA 92014
(619) 481-1477
$395.00

NuPaint 1.0.3
NuEquation, Inc.
1701 N. Greenville Ave., Suite 703
Richardson, TX 75081
(214) 699-7477
$139.95

On Cue 1.3
Icon Simulations
648 S. Wheeling Rd.
Wheeling, IL 60090
(312) 520-4440
$59.95

oops Clock
N/A

Optimizer 1.0
Central Point Software
15220 NW Greenbrier Pkwy., #200
Beaverton, OR 97006
(503) 690-8090
$79.00, included with *PC Tools Deluxe*

Other...
Loftus E. Becker
41 Whitney St.
Hartford, CT 06105
$10.00, shareware

Packit 3.2
Harry Chesley
1850 Union St., #360
San Francisco, CA 94123
$20.00, shareware

Panorama 1.1
Provue Development Corp.
15180 Transistor Ln.
Huntington Beach, CA 92649
(714) 892-8199
$395.00

PC Secure
Central Point Software
15220 NW Greenbrier Pkwy., #200
Beaverton, OR 97006
(503) 690-8090
$295.00

PC Tools Deluxe
for the Macintosh
Central Point Software
15220 NW Greenbrier Pkwy., #200
Beaverton, OR 97006
(503) 690-8090
$79.00

Photon Paint 1.1
MicroIllusions
17408 Chatsworth
Granada Hills, CA 91344
(818) 360-3715
$299.95

PictureBase 1.2.3
Symmetry Corp.
761 E. University Dr.
Mesa, AZ 85203
(602) 844-2199
$99.00

PixelPaint 2.0
SuperMac Software
295 Bernardo Ave.
Mountain View, CA 94043
(408) 245-2202
$595.00

PixelPaint Professional 1.0
SuperMac Software
295 Bernardo Ave.
Mountain View, CA 94043
(408) 245-2202
$699.00

Plus 1.1
Olduvai
7520 Red Rd., Suite A
South Miami, FL 33143
(305) 665-4665
$199.00

Pop-it! 1.3
Pete Helme, Eel Pont Software
1939 Marshal Ave., H25
St. Paul, MN 55104
$10.00, shareware

Pop-up 2.0
Robert Stromberg
PO Box 1788
Sandy, UT 84091
$10.00, shareware

PopWMenu 1.0
Douglas Wyatt
freeware

PowerStation 2.5
Fifth Generation Systems
11200 Industriplex Blvd.
Baton Rouge, LA 70809
(504) 291-7221
$59.95

PS Download
Altsys
720 Avenue F, Suite 109
Plano, TX 75074
(214) 424-4888
freeware

Pyro 3.3.1
Fifth Generation Systems
11200 Industriplex Blvd.
Baton Rouge, LA 70809
(504) 291-7221
$24.95

QuarkXPress 2.11
Quark, Inc.
300 S. Jackson St., Suite 100
Denver, CO 80209
(303) 934-2211
$795.00

QuickCopy 1.11
Symantec Corp.
10201 Torre Ave.
Cupertino, CA 95014
(408) 253-9600, , (800) 441-7234
$149.95, included with
Symantec Utilities

QuicKeys 1.2
CE Software
1854 Fuller Rd., Box 65580
W. Des Moines, IA 50265
(515) 224-1995
$99.95

QuickLetter 1.01
Working Software, Inc.
PO Box 1844
Santa Cruz, CA 95061
(408) 423-5696
$124.95

QuickShare
Compatible Systems
PO Drawer 17220
Boulder, CO 80302
(800) 356-0283
$465.00

Ragtime 2.1
Migrant Software
313 Iona Ave.
Narberth, PA 19072
(215) 667-9781
$395.00

Ragtime 3
Migrant Software
313 Iona Ave.
Narberth, PA 19072
(215) 667-9781
$595.00

Ready,Set,Go! 4.5
Letraset USA
40 Eisenhower Dr.
Paramus, NJ 07653
(201) 845-6100
$495.00

Rebound 0.95
Fred Reed
freeware

Redux 1.5
Microseeds Publishing, Inc.
7030-B W. Hillsborough Ave.
Tampa, FL 33615
(813) 882-8635
$99.00

ResEdit 1.3
Apple Computer, Inc.
20525 Mariani Ave.
Cupertino, CA 95014
(408) 996-1010
freeware

Resource Resolver 1.11
Alsoft, Inc.
PO Box 927
Spring, TX 77383
(713) 353-4090
$79.95, included with
MasterJuggler

Retriever 1.01
Exodus Software
8620 Winton Rd., Suite 304
Cincinnati, OH 45231
(513) 522-0011
$89.95

Retrospect 1.0
Dantz Development Corp.
1510 Walnut St.
Berkeley, CA 94709
(415) 849-0293
$249.00

ScrapMaker 2.0
Solutions International
30 Commerce St.
Williston, VT 05495
(802) 658-5506
$89.95, included with *SmartScrap*

ScreenMaker 1.0
Bill Atkinson
20525 Mariani Ave.
Cupertino, CA 95014
(408) 996-1010
freeware

Scroll 2 1.1
Mason Lancastor
1492 W. Colorado Blvd.
Pasadena, CA 91105
$15.00, shareware

Sentinel 1.0
SuperMac Technology
295 Bernado Ave.
Mountain View, CA 94043
(408) 245-2202
$295.00

Set Clock
public domain

Set Paths 1.3
Paul Snively
3519 Park Lodge Ct., Apt. E
Indianapolis, IN 46205
$20.00, shareware

SFScroll 3.00
Andy Hertzfeld
freeware

SFVol 1.5
Raymond Lau
100-04 70 Ave.
Forest Hills, NY 11375
$20.00, shareware

Show Key 1.0a
Loftus E. Becker
41 Whitney St.
Hartford, CT 06105
N/A
freeware

SilverLining 4.0
La Cié
16285 SW 85th, Bldg. 306
Tigard, OR 97224
(503) 684-0143
$69.95

Sleep
public domain

Slicer 1.0
John Bradley
freeware

Small Icon Editor 1.00
Paul DuBois
freeware

SmartArt 1.0.1
Emerald City Software
800 Menlo Ave., Suite 102
Menlo Park, CA 94026
(415) 324-8080
$149.95

SmartScrap 2.0
Solutions International
30 Commerce St.
Williston, VT 05495
(802) 658-5506
$89.95

SNSay 1.0
PEEK [65]
PO Box 586
Pacifica, CA 94044
freeware

SoftPC 1.3
Insignia Solutions
787 Lucerne Dr.
Sunnyvale, CA 94086
(408) 446-2228
$595.00

Sound 3.3.1
Apple Computer, Inc.
20525 Mariani Ave.
Cupertino, CA 95014
(408) 996-1010
N/A

Sound Converter 1.0
Kelly E. Major
freeware

SoundEdit 2.01
Farallon Computing
2150 Kitteredge St.
Berkeley, CA 94704
(415) 849-2331
$199.00, included with *MacRecorder*

SoundMaster
Bruce Tomlin
15801 Chase Hill, Apt. 109
San Antonio, TX 78256
shareware

SoundMover 1.4
Richard Ettore
67 Rue de la Limite
1970 W. Oppen
Belgium
$20, shareware

SoundPlay 1.0
Bruce Tomlin
15801 Chase Hill, Apt. 109
San Antonio, TX 78256
public domain

Space Warp
public domain

*Spelling Coach
Professional 3.1*
Deneba Software
3305 NW 74th Ave.
Miami, FL 33122
(305) 594-6965
$195.00

Spellswell 2.1
Working Software, Inc.
PO Box 1844
Santa Cruz, CA 95061
(408) 423-5696
$74.95

Splitt
public domain

Stars
public domain

StrongBox 1.0
Mark 3 Software
29 Grey Rocks Rd.
Wilton, CT 06897
$10.00, shareware

Studio/1 1.0
Electronic Arts
1820 Gateway Dr.
San Mateo, CA 94404
(415) 571-7171
$149.95

Studio/8 1.0
Electronic Arts
1820 Gateway Dr.
San Mateo, CA 94404
(415) 571-7171
$494.95

Stuffit 1.51
Raymond Lau
100-04 70 Ave.
Forest Hills, NY 11375
$20.00, shareware

Suitcase II 1.2
Fifth Generation Systems
11200 Industriplex Blvd.
Baton Rouge, LA 70809
(800) 873-4384
$79.00

SuperCard 1.0
Silicon Beach Software
9770 Carroll Center Rd., Suite J
San Diego, CA 92126
(619) 695-6956
$199.00

SuperClock 3.3
Steve Christensen
freeware

SuperDrive
Apple Computer Inc.
20525 Mariani Ave.
Cupertino, CA 95014
(408) 996-1010
$629.00

SuperGlue II 1.05
Solutions International
30 Commerce St.
Williston, VT 05495
(802) 658-5506
$89.95

SuperPaint 2.0
Silicon Beach Software
9770 Carroll Center Rd., Suite J
San Diego, CA 92126
(619) 695-6956
$199.00

SuperPlay 4.0
John Raymounds
21738 Barbara St.
Torrance, CA 90503
shareware

Symantec Tools 1.11
Symantec Corp.
10201 Torre Ave.
Cupertino, CA 95014
(408) 253-9600, (800) 441-7234
$149.95, included with
Symantec Utilities

Symantec Utilities 1.11
Symantec Corp.
10201 Torre Ave.
Cupertino, CA 95014
(408) 253-9600, (800) 441-7234
$149.95

SysErrors 2.0
Bill Steinberg
freeware

System Switcher 1.0
public domain

TakeOff 3.0
Jim Richardson
10623 Canyon Crest Lane
Houston, TX 77086
$5.00, shareware

Talking Mouse
shareware

TattleTale 1.01
Wildwood Software
freeware

Tempo II 1.02
Affinity Microsystems, Inc.
1050 Walnut St., Suite 425
Boulder, CO 80302
(303) 442-4840
$149.95

Thunder II 1.01
Electronic Arts
1820 Gateway Dr.
San Mateo, CA 94404
(415) 571-7171
$49.95

Tops/Macintosh 2.1
Tops, division of Sun Microsystems
950 Marina Village Pkwy.
Alameda, CA 94501
(415) 769-8700
$249.00

Trapeze 2.1
DeltaPoint, Inc.
200 Heritage Harbor, Suite G
Monterey, CA 93940
(408) 648-4000
$295.00

TurboCache 2.0
Peripheral Land, Inc.
47800 Westinghouse Dr.
Fremont, CA 94539
(800) 288-8754
$129.00

TurboFloppy
Peripheral Land, Inc.
47800 Westinghouse Dr.
Fremont, CA 94539
(800) 288-8754
$499.00

TurboOptimizer 2.0
Peripheral Land, Inc.
47800 Westinghouse Dr.
Fremont, CA 94539
(800) 288-8754
$79.00

Vaccine
CE Software
1854 Fuller Rd., Box 65580
W. Des Moines, IA 50265
(515) 224-1995
$49.95, included with
MockPackage Plus Utilities

Vantage 1.1
Preferred Publishers, Inc.
5100 Poplar Ave., Suite 706
Memphis, TN 38137
(901) 683-3383
$99.95

Vol Fkey
Bryan Ressler
14461 Galy St.
Tustin, CA 92680
N/A
$5.00, shareware

Watch
public domain

Widgets 3.0.4
CE Software
1854 Fuller Rd., Box 65580
W. Des Moines, IA 50265
(515) 224-1995
$49.95, included with
MockPackage Plus Utilities

Wingz 1.0
Informix Software
16011 College Blvd.
Lenexa, KS 66219
(913) 599-7100
$495.00

WordPerfect
for the Macintosh 1.0.2
WordPerfect Corp.
1555 N. Technology Way
Orem, UT 84057
(801) 225-5000
$395.00

World Time
public domain

WriteNow 2.0
T/Maker Co.
1390 Villa St.
Mountain View, CA 94041
(415) 962-0195
$195.00

xFer 3.0
Messenger Software, Inc.
20202 Center Ridge Rd., Suite 5
Rocky River, OH 44116
(216) 333-9936
$129.00

XTreeMac 1.02
XTree Company
4330 Santa Fe Rd.
San Luis Obispo, CA 93401
(805) 541-0604
$99.00

Zippy 1.0
Chuck Shotton
PO Box 580622
Houston, TX 77258
freeware

Public-Domain, Freeware, and Shareware Software Distributors

BCS•Mac
48 Grove St.
Somerville, MA 02144
(617) 876-4835

BMUG
1442A Walnut St., #62
Berkeley, CA 94709
(415) 849-9114

Budgetbytes
1647 SW 41st St.
Topeka, KS 66609
(800) 356-3551

EduComp Computer Services
742 Genevieve, Suite D
Solana Beach, CA 92075
(800) 843-9497, (619) 259-0255

P.D.E.
2074C Walsh Ave., #122
Santa Clara, CA 95050
(800) 331-8125

Quantum Leap Technology
The Right Stuffed CD-ROM
(800) 762-2877

Software Excitement
PO Box 3097
Central Point, OR 97502
(800) 444-5457

Somak Software
535 Encinitas Blvd., Suite 113
Encinitas, CA 92024
(619) 942-2556

Section Five

Glossary

Glossary

Accelerator. An add-on board that allows your computer to operate more quickly. Accelerators may use faster CPU chips, math coprocessors, and high clock speeds to provide performance improvements.

Active window. The window that is currently selected. The active window is distinguished from other windows by the highlighting in its title bar. *See also* Window.

ADB. *See* Apple Desktop Bus.

Add-on board. *See* Expansion card.

Address lines. The paths on a CPU chip or bus that are used to carry data addresses. The more address lines are available, the larger the number of different addresses that can be specified, and therefore the larger the amount of memory that can be used simultaneously. *See also* Bus; Central processing unit; Data lines.

Alert box. A message box that the Mac displays to pass along information. Alert boxes include only an OK button that you click to indicate that you have read the message.

Apple Desktop Bus (ADB). A communications path provided on the SE, II, IIx, IIcx, and SE/30. The ADB is used to connect the mouse and keyboard to these computers. Two ADB ports are provided on the Macintosh, and most ADB devices allow you to daisy-chain one device to the next. In addition to keyboards and mice, trackballs and drawing tablets often connect via the ADB.

Apple key. Another name for the COMMAND key. *See also* COMMAND key.

APPLE menu. The leftmost menu in almost every menu bar, containing all desk accessories currently loaded on your Macintosh. Some other programs, such as Suitcase II and MasterJuggler, also put their commands in the APPLE menu.

AppleShare. Software from Apple that provides centralized hard-disk storage to users of an AppleTalk network. The Macintosh running AppleShare becomes a dedicated server while AppleShare is running, and cannot be used for any other purpose.

AppleTalk. Apple's local area network, which includes a chip and connector built into every Mac. Apple's LocalTalk cabling and LocalTalk connectors can be used to link the Macintoshes and other computers together.

Application. A program that creates, manages, or manipulates data. Software that is not an application is either part of the operating system or a utility program.

Application heap. An area of RAM set aside for use by software applications. The size of the application heap is determined by a value in the *boot blocks* of the disk used to start-up the Macintosh.

Archival backup. *See* Incremental backup.

Arrow keys. The keys on the keyboard, labeled with arrows, that move the cursor or insertion point on the screen. A few very old programs may not support the arrow keys.

ASCII (American Standard Code for Information Interchange). A standard by which the Mac and most other computers assign binary definitions to letters and numbers. A data file using only these standard definitions is called an ASCII file, and can be used by almost any computer and many software applications. Files that are saved in Text or Text-Only format are ASCII files.

Asynchronous communication. A communications protocol in which a start and stop signal is sent before each character. *See also* Synchronous communications.

Audio port. The Macintosh port that provides sound output. Connecting a speaker to this port allows you to augment or replace the internal speaker. The audio port on the Mac II, IIx, IIcx, and SE/30 supports stereo sound.

Automatic font downloading. The process by which PostScript fonts are automatically transferred to a PostScript printer. When PostScript fonts are used, a corresponding printer-font file must be available to the printer. The font is available if it is in ROM chips built into the printer, loaded on the printer's hard disk, manually downloaded into the printer's memory, or downloaded automatically by the printer driver when it is needed. The automatic downloading reads the printer-font file from the hard disk of the printing computer, stores it in the printer while it is needed, and then removes it from the printer's memory. *See also* Laser font; Manual downloading; Printer font.

A/UX (Apple/UNIX). Apple's version of AT&T's V2.2 UNIX Operating System, available for all 68020- and 68030-based Macs. A/UX requires 4 megabytes of RAM and an 80-megabyte hard drive.

Background printing (spooling). Printing that takes place while you are free to use your Mac simultaneously for another purpose. Background printing can be accomplished in MultiFinder using the Chooser's "Background Printing" option, or using a third-party print-spooling utility.

Background processing. The ability of a computer to run one program while another program is in the foreground. When a program is running in MultiFinder but is not the current foreground application, it is in the background. If the program can do something while it is in the background without interfering with the operation of the foreground software, it is capable of background processing. Most Mac software that runs in Multi-Finder is capable of background processing. Background processing is sometimes called multitasking, because the computer appears to be doing two things at once, although really it is just switching back and forth very rapidly between the foreground and background tasks. *See also* Foreground application.

Baud. A unit of measure that describes the communication speed of modems and network data transfer. The baud rate reflects the number of signal events ocurring per second on the communication channel. In some cases only one bit of data is transferred during a single event, but other times two or more bits of data can be transferred in a single event (so baud cannot be universally equated with bits per second).

BBS. *See* Bulletin board.

Bézier control handles. The handles, associated with curve points in high-end drawing applications, that allow you to manipulate the curvature of the segments between points. A Bézier control handle forces a line segment exiting or entering a point to curve. If you drag a handle away from its point, the curvature of a segment becomes more pronounced; if you drag a handle toward its point, a segment becomes less curved.

Binary. A numbering system that uses 2 as its base, expressing all numbers as strings of 0s and 1s.

Bit (contraction of *binary digit*). The smallest unit of digital information, equal to a single 0 or 1.

Bit map. An image that is defined as a fixed number of colored or monochrome pixels, so that it appears the same on screen as when printed. A bit map may be an image produced by a painting program like MacPaint or PixelPaint, or a screen font. Bit-mapped images are typically stored in MacPaint format, PICT, or TIFF.

Blessed folder. *See* System folder.

Block. Another name for *sector*, used in reference to a numbering scheme that does not restart at 0 for each cylinder but instead numbers all sectors on an entire platter. *See also* Platter; Sector.

Bomb. *See* Crash.

Boot blocks. Specific sectors on a disk that contain information used to start up the Macintosh. On most Mac disks, these are blocks 0 and 1 on the disk; they contain information such as the name of the System file that will be used, the amount of RAM to allocate to the application heap, and the first application to be run. Boot blocks are written when the disk is formatted, or when System Software is installed with the Installer application. *See also* Application heap; System file.

Boot disk. *See* Startup disk.

Booting. The process of starting up the Macintosh or a specific application, often called "booting up." This phrase evolved because the computer, or the application, is "pulling itself up by its bootstraps."

Bridge. A hardware and software system that joins similar computer networks (one AppleTalk network to another AppleTalk network, or one Ethernet network to another Ethernet network). Each network user can access all network devices. *See also* Gateway.

Bug. A programming error that causes a software package to operate erratically or incorrectly.

Bulletin board. A computer-operated communications center that you communicate with using a modem. Bulletin boards usually allow you to leave messages or read existing messages, and send ("upload") or receive ("download") files and software. Commercial bulletin boards charge by the minute for their use, while many private bulletin boards are operated as a free service.

Bus. A series of wires or electronic connections that link various computer hardware components.

Byte. The amount of storage space or memory required to hold a single alphanumeric character; equal to 8 bits. 1024 bytes is 1K of storage space or memory.

Cache. *See* RAM cache.

Card. *See* Expansion card.

Cdev (pronounced *see dev*, contraction of *Control Device*, or *Control Panel Device*). Software program with the file type cdev that when placed in the System folder appears in the Control Panel desk accessory. Selecting the cdev's icon in the Control Panel gives you access to its options.

Central processing unit (CPU). The chip, or set of chips, that performs most of the information processing in a computer. The CPU handles program control and arithmetic manipulation, and provides centralized timing signals to the computer's other hardware components.

Character width. *See* Data bits.

Check box. A type of dialog-box option that presents a square box that can be set on or off. Check boxes are often presented in sets, and each option in the set can be turned off and on independently. *See also* Dialog box; Options; Radio buttons.

Chooser. An Apple-supplied desk accessory that is used to select among printers and other network devices. The Chooser displays the icons for printer drivers and network drivers available in the System folder (file types rdev or PRER). Selecting one of these icons activates that driver, and makes it possible to further configure the driver, if necessary.

Click. To press and release the mouse button.

Clipboard. A utility function of the System Software, supported by almost every Macintosh application, that holds text or graphic elements temporarily. Elements are moved to the Clipboard with the CUT or COPY command, and transferred from the Clipboard with the PASTE command. The contents of the Clipboard are usually maintained in RAM, but sometimes the contents are written to a Clipboard file in the System folder.

Clock speed. The number of instructions per second that can be processed by a CPU chip. Clock speed is regulated by the CPU chip itself and by a clock crystal included on the logic board. *See also* Central processing unit.

Close box. The small white box, located on the far left side of the title bar of an active window, that closes the window when it is clicked. In most applications, clicking the Close box will bring up a SAVE CHANGES? dialog box.

Cold boot. The process of restarting a computer by turning its power on, or by turning its power off and then on again. A warm boot is preferable to a cold boot because it puts less strain on the electronic circuitry. *See also* Warm boot.

Command. A menu item that, when chosen, either performs some action, brings up a dialog box, or toggles a setting. Commands appear dimmed (gray) when they cannot be chosen.

COMMAND key. The key on the Macintosh keyboard with the ⌘ and/or symbol on it, used in conjunction with other keys to execute commands from the keyboard. Sometimes referred to as the APPLE key.

Command key equivalent. *See* Keyboard equivalent.

Compact Mac. A Macintosh using the original-style casing with the monitor built into the main unit, such as the Macintosh 128, 512, Plus, SE, and SE/30.

Control Device. *See* Cdev.

Control Panel. An Apple-supplied desk accessory that is used to access software released in cdev format. A list of all cdevs in the current System folder appears on the left side of the Control Panel window, and the options from the currently selected cdev appear on the right side of the window.

Coprocessor. *See* Numeric coprocessor; PC coprocessor.

COPY. A command in the EDIT menu that creates a copy of the selected elements on the Clipboard without disturbing the elements themselves. Once on the Clipboard, elements can be pasted to another part of the current application, or to another application or desk accessory.

Copy protection. A method of making it difficult or impossible to produce or distribute unauthorized copies of software. Copy protection is rarely used on current applications, except in the form of *personalization*, which encodes your name into the application so that if unauthorized copies are distributed, their owner will be easy to detect.

CPU. *See* Central processing unit.

Crash. An error that prevents any software from continuing to operate. When an error is encountered that makes it impossible for an application, or the System Software, to continue operating, an Alert dialog box appears, containing the bomb icon, an error code number, and the RESTART and CONTINUE buttons. This even is described as a bomb or a crash.

Creator signature string. A file resource used by System Software 6.0 and later to provide information to the Get Info comments window that is not lost when the Desktop file is rebuilt. *See also* Get Info comment.

Creator type. A four-letter code that identifies the application that was used to create a document. Creator codes are assigned by the software programmer, and registered with Apple Computer so that no two applications use the same creator code. Many utilities allow you to view and edit a file's creator type.

Cursor. An on-screen icon that the user manipulates by moving the mouse, or in some cases, by using the arrow keys from the keyboard. The arrow, watch, and I-beam are common Macintosh cursors. *See also* I-beam.

Cut. A command in the EDIT menu that moves the selected elements to the Clipboard and removes them from their current location. Once on the Clipboard, elements can be pasted to another part of the current application, or to another application or desk accessory.

Cylinder. All of the tracks on all platters in a disk that can be accessed from a single position of the drive's read/write heads. For double-sided floppy disks, a cylinder consists of two tracks. For hard drives, which use many platters, a cylinder may consist of four tracks or more.

Daisy-chaining. A method of connecting multiple devices to the Macintosh in which the first device is connected directly to the Macintosh, the second device is connected to the first device, the third is connected to the second, and so on. Daisy-chain connections are used on the Macintosh to connect SCSI devices and ADB devices. *See also* SCSI; SCSI ID number; SCSI terminators.

Daisy wheel. The printing element in many letter-quality printers, consisting of a wheel with each character embossed on one of the spokes. As a character is printed, the spoke is bent to strike a ribbon and mark the page.

DA suitcase. A file that holds one or more desk accessories. A suitcase icon is used by these files, and they can be manipulated with the Font/DA Mover. *See also* Font/DA Mover.

Data bits. A telecommunications term for the bits that contain data. (Other bits are used to control the telecommunication itself.) Apple sometimes uses the term *character width* to mean data bits.

Data fork. The part of a Macintosh file that holds traditional data—text, numbers, and graphics—rather than program code. The information in a file's data fork can be viewed and edited with a number of utilities. A Macintosh file does not have to have a data fork. *See also* Resource fork.

Data lines. The paths on a CPU chip or bus that carry information from one location to the other. The more data lines that are available, the more information can be moved at one time and hence the faster a specific amount of information can be transferred. *See also* Address lines; Bus; Central processing unit.

Data transfer loops. The protocol used by a SCSI drive and the CPU to coordinate data transfer. Different data transfer loops allow different amounts of data to be transferred per second. Data transfer loops are set during hard-drive formatting, but many utilities set the data transfer loops automatically.

DB-9. The semirectangular 9-pin connector used for the modem and printer port of the Macintosh 128, 512k, and older versions of the Macintosh Plus.

Decryption. The process of decoding a document that has been encrypted. Decryption removes the document's protection, making it available for use. Files must be decrypted using the same software that was used to encrypt them, and if a password was assigned during encryption, the password will be required for decryption. *See also* Encryption.

Defragment. To move files on a disk so that they are written in sequential sectors. *See also* File fragmentation; Disk fragmentation.

Desk Accessory (DA). Software that can be loaded into the System file or attached using a utility like Suitcase or MasterJuggler, and then accessed from the APPLE menu at any time, even when another application is running. Apple provides several DA's with its System Software, including the Alarm Clock, Control Panel, Chooser, and Find File. Many other DA's are available commercially and as freeware or shareware programs.

Desktop. The gray area displayed when an application is opened but no data file is being used. Under MultiFinder, application desktops are not used, but the Finder desktop can be seen when no data window is open or the data window does not cover the entire display. *See also* Finder Desktop.

Desktop file. An invisible data file created and maintained by the Finder to hold information about the files and folders on a disk.

Dialog box. A box that appears on the screen when you need to supply information or specify options for an application or for the System Software. Dialog boxes contain several types of options, along with buttons that are used to execute the options selected or to escape the dialog box. Dialog boxes usually appear when a command followed by an ellipsis (three dots) is chosen. *See also*: Alert box; Modial dialog box; Options.

Dialog-box options. *See* Options.

Dimmed command. A command that appears in gray rather than black, indicating that it is currently inappropriate and cannot be executed.

DIN-8. The round 8-pin connector used for the modem and printer port of all Macs since the Mac Plus.

Directory. A catalog of information about the files on a disk or volume. Mac disks have a volume directory that contains general information about the disk and its files, and a file directory that contains specific information about each file, such as its name and the disk sectors in which the file can be found.

Disk. A magnetic storage medium that holds information when it is not being used by the CPU. *See also* Floppy disk; Hard disk.

Disk buffer. An area of RAM that holds frequently used information from a disk. A disk buffer is similar to a RAM cache, except that it usually holds specific data, such as the disk directory. By maintaining the data in a disk buffer, the Mac avoids constantly rereading information from disk.

Disk controller. The hardware components that transfer the electronic signals from the bus into instructions that the disk drive can use to read and write data.

Disk directory. *See* Directory.

Disk drive. The hardware component that reads and write information to disks. *See also* Floppy disk; Hard disk.

Disk-drive port. The external connector on most Macs that is used to connect an external floppy disk drive.

Disk fragmentation. The result of repeated addition and deletion of files to a disk, characterized by files written across nonconsecutive disk sectors, and empty sectors that are scattered throughout the disk rather than being all aligned at the end of the disk.

Disk partitioning. The process of dividing one physical volume into two or more logical volumes. There are two types of partitions, *SCSI* partitions and *File System partitions*, each of which can be created using one of several utilities including MultiDisk and SUM Partition.

Diskette. *See* Floppy disk.

Dot-matrix printer. A printer that creates characters and graphics by applying patterns of dots to the paper. Most dot-matrix printers use the impact of pins against a ribbon to create their dots—these printers are often called impact printers—but ink-jet and even laser printers can be dot-matrix printers.

Dots per inch (dpi). A unit of measure reflecting the maximum number of dots a device is capable of placing in a linear inch. Dots per inch determines the quality of screens and printers; the more dots per inch, the higher the quality. The Mac screen is 72 dpi, and the LaserWriter printer is 300 dpi.

Double-click. To press and release the mouse button twice in rapid succession. Many actions are initiated when the user double-clicks on a specific icon or location in a window.

Download. To transfer a file from another computer to your own computer. Downloading requires that you have a modem connected to your computer and the proper telecommunications software to communicate with the other computer.

Downloadable font. A PostScript font that consists of two parts: a screen font used by the System file, and a printer font that must be downloaded into the RAM of the PostScript printer in order for the font to be imaged correctly. This term is sometimes used to refer to the whole font, and other times to mean just the printer-font portion. The printer-font portion of a downloadable font may be built into the ROM chips in the printer, or stored on the printer's hard disk, making it unnecessary to download them manually or automatically. *See also* Automatic font downloading; Laser font; Manual font downloading; Printer font.

Dpi. *See* Dots per inch.

Dragging. The process of positioning the mouse cursor on some object, pressing and holding down the mouse button, and moving the mouse. This action is performed to move items on the screen, or to use tools in various software and utilities.

Driver. Software that handles the interaction between a hardware peripheral and the Macintosh or its System Software or applications. Examples include the LaserWriter and ImageWriter printer drivers, SCSI drivers that are included with hard disks, and keyboard and disk-drive drivers that are an internal part of the System Software.

Dvorak keyboard. An alternative key arrangement that puts the most frequently typed letters under the most powerful fingers. This is preferred by some to the so called QWERTY key arrangement used on all Macintosh keyboards.

E-mail. *See* Electronic mail.

Echo. A telecommunications setting that causes the receiving communications software to return the characters received back to the sender so that they may be verified for accuracy; also used to specify whether the characters sent via telecommunication software should be displayed on the screen of the computer that is sending them.

Electronic mail (E-mail). The electronic transmission of a communication between computers. E-mail can be sent directly from one computer to another, but it is more often sent to a central computer, which holds the message until its recipient collects it electronically.

Em dash. The correct name for a long dash (—). The length of an em dash is equal to the typeface's size in points. (A 12-point em dash would be 12 points long.) In most fonts, you can create an em dash by pressing SHIFT-OPTION-HYPHEN. *See also* Em space.

Em space. A space as wide as the point size in which it is set. A 12-point em space is 12 points wide. Not all Mac software or all fonts support the creation of em spaces. *See also* Em dash.

Emulation. A software simulation that makes one type of hardware or software appear to be another. Emulation can make incompatible devices compatible with other software or hardware.

En dash. A dash half as long as an em dash, equal to half the point size in which it is set. (A 12-point en dash would be 6 points long.) In most fonts, you can create an en dash by pressing OPTION-HYPHEN.

En space. A space as wide as half the point size in which it is set. A 12-point en space is 6 points wide. Not all Mac software or all fonts support the creation of en spaces. *See also* En dash.

Encryption. The process of scrambling data so that it is unusable unless *decrypted*. Encrypted files are usually assigned a password that must be used in order to decrypt them. *See also* Decryption.

ENTER key. The key used to confirm an entry or a command. In most but not all cases, the RETURN key can be used in place of the ENTER key.

EPS (EPSF, Encapsulated PostScript). A file format containing a complete PostScript definition of the file, and in some cases a PICT image for use on the screen.

Erase. Informally, to either initialize or format a disk. Since initializing and formatting have distinctly different meanings, the word *erase* is best left unused, as its meaning is unclear. *See also* Formatting; Initialize.

Ethernet. A network communications protocol that offers very high-speed data transfer. Ethernet requires special cabling and expansion cards in each computer connected to the network.

Event. An occurrence that triggers some response by the Macintosh operating system or a specific software application. Events include disk insertions, mouse clicks, and communications from peripherals via any port.

Expansion card. A circuit board that attaches to a computer, usually via the expansion slot, adding features or abilities to the computer. Examples include video-display adaptors and modems. *See also* Expansion slot.

Expansion slot. A port that allows additional circuit boards to be easily added to the computer to give it new features or abilities. The Macintosh SE and SE/30 have one expansion slot, the Macintosh II and IIx have six, and the Macintosh IIcx has three. Earlier Macintosh models do not have expansion slots. *See also* Expansion card.

Facsimile (fax). A method of sending documents to remote locations via telephone lines. Adding a fax board or fax modem to the Macintosh allows it to send almost any Macintosh file, or any document scanned in with a scanner, to any fax machine in the world.

Fax. *See* Facsimile.

Field. A container that can hold editable text or a formula in a flat-file database manager as well as in other applications such as HyperCard. Often, information in one field can be referenced or interpreted by another.

File. A generic term referring to information stored on disk as a discrete element, such as a document or application. On the Macintosh, each file has its own file name, icon, and file attributes.

File-by-file backup. *See* Incremental backup.

File creator. *See* Creator type.

File directory. *See* Directory.

File format. The special manner in which an application stores textual or graphic information. Most programs can read (open or import) and write (save or export) in multiple file formats. For example, Microsoft Word reads and writes its text files in RTF (Rich Text Format), ASCII (text-only), and MacWrite file formats, in addition to its own custom format. SuperPaint reads and writes graphics in the MacPaint, PICT, TIFF, and startup-screen formats.

File fragmentation. The storage of files on disk in noncontiguous sectors. File fragmentation occurs when contiguous sectors are not available as the file is written on the disk. A fragmented file requires more time and effort on the part of the disk drive each time it is read and rewritten than it would if saved in sequential sectors. Several utilities move files so that they are stored in sequential sectors. *See also* Disk fragmentation.

File server. A hard disk that can be accessed by most or all Macintoshes connected to the same network. A computer becomes a file server when special network software such as TOPS, AppleShare, or MacServe is run on it.

File System partitions. Hard-drive partitions that are created using software that tricks the System Software into thinking that the hard drive is partitioned. Each partition is maintained as one single large file, with the partitioning software maintaining a directory for the partition. Only one entry in the real directory represents the entire partition. *See also* Partition; SCSI partition.

File tag. A small amount of information written along with each sector on any Mac disk, containing information about the data in the sector.

File type. A four-letter code that is assigned to each Macintosh file to identify the file format. The file type can be viewed and manipulated in many utilities. Text files have the file type TEXT, Microsoft Word files have the file type WDBN, MacPaint files have the file type MPNT, and applications have the file type APPL. *See also* Creator type; File format.

Finder. A Macintosh software application that provides file and disk management and the ability to launch applications. The Finder is a part of the System Software, and is run automatically when the Macintosh is started up and each time an application is quit (unless another application has been specifically selected to run at these times). *See also* Finder desktop; MultiFinder; System Software.

Finder desktop. The visual display shown when the Finder is the current application. The Finder desktop includes the Finder's menu bar, and icons for all disks and volumes (and any files or folders that have been opened or dragged out of their disk icons). When MultiFinder is on, the Finder desktop is almost always at least partially visible, even when the Finder is not the foreground application. *See also* Desktop

Finder flags. A set of attributes maintained for each file stored on a Macintosh disk. These include Locked, Invisible, Busy, Bundle, System, Changed, Bozo, and other attributes. These attributes can be seen and modified with many utilities.

Fkey (function key). A small program, usually providing utility functions, that is normally accessed when the user presses COMMAND-SHIFT and a number between 0 and 9. Fkeys can be added to the System file, much like fonts or DA's, or accessed with utilities like Suitcase or MasterJuggler. Several macro programs allow you to execute Fkeys using keyboard equivalents.

Flat file manager. A database-management application that uses a single data file for all of its information. Typically, information cannot be accessed from other files, although recently the term has broadened with increasing software sophistication to include programs that will look up information in a single foreign field or record.

Flatness. The distance from the farthest point on any side of a printed polygon rendering of a curve to the same point on the mathematical curve. When a curved line is printed to a PostScript printer, the printer actually draws the curve as a series of tiny straight lines. Usually, all lines are so short that they appear to form a smooth curve. Some applications, like Adobe Illustrator and Aldus FreeHand, allow you to increase or decrease the number of lines used—thereby making the appearance of the printed curve more smooth or more jagged—by respectively decreasing or increasing a flatness value.

Floppy disk. A small, magnetically coated piece of plastic, used to hold electronic information. Macs use 3.5-inch floppy disks, which are built into a rigid plastic case with a small metal door that opens to allow the disk drive to read from or write to the disk. There are three kinds of floppy disks used on the Macintosh, 400K single-sided floppies, 800K double-sided floppies, and 1.2Mb high-density floppies. *See also* Hard disk.

Folder. The electronic equivalent of a paper folder, used to organize files and other folders, stored on computer disk. Folders inside of other folders are said to be *nested*.

Folder bar. A pop-up menu that appears above the scrolling file listing in Standard File dialog boxes when the current disk uses the HFS filing system. Holding down the mouse button while pointing to the folder bar displays a list of the folder hierarchy, allowing you to move directly up to any other level. *See also* HFS; Standard File Open.

Font. A collection of letters, numbers, and symbols executed in a recognizable and consistent style. In the old days of handset type, a font was a holding receptacle that included a set of characters in the same typeface, style, and size. But in modern usage, the term has become synonymous with *typeface*. A PostScript typeface is divided into two fonts: a bit-mapped screen font for viewing characters on screen and a mathematically defined printer font that is translated by a laser printer or other output device.

Font substitution. A feature of the LaserWriter printer driver that substitutes laser fonts for the Geneva, Monaco, and New York bit-mapped fonts if they are used in a document being printed to a PostScript printer. Font substitution improves the quality of these fonts, but often results in poor character spacing.

Font suitcase. A file that holds one or more fonts. A suitcase icon represents these files, and they can be manipulated using the Font/DA Mover. *See also* Font; Font/DA Mover.

Font/DA Mover. A utility program that moves or deletes screen fonts and desk accessories from font or DA suitcases or System files. *See also* Font, Desk Accessory.

Foreground application. Under MultiFinder, the application that is currently selected, as indicated by the presence of its menu bar and activation of one or more of its windows. *See also* Background processing; Multitasking.

Format. To electronically create sectors and empty directory entries on a disk. This is done both to prepare a disk for its first use and to empty a previously used disk. *See also* Initialize.

Fragmentation. *See* Disk fragmentation; File fragmentation.

Freeware. Software that is freely distributed, but to which the author has retained a copyright. Freeware is widely available on bulletin boards and through user groups. Many freeware programs are mistakenly termed public-domain. *See also* Public-domain software; Shareware.

Function key. *See* Fkey.

Gateway. A hardware and software system that joins dissimilar computer networks—one AppleTalk network and one Ethernet network, for example—so that all users on the networks can communicate and share peripheral devices. *See also* Bridge.

Get Info comment. A small block of text provided in the Get Info dialog box to hold information about a file. This text can be edited at any time, but unfortunately is lost when the Desktop file on the disk holding the file is rebuilt. If the file has a creator signature string, that text is automatically reset in the Get Info comment even after the Desktop file has been rebuilt. *See also* Creator signature string.

Gigabyte (Gb). A unit of measure equal to 1024 megabytes; sometimes used to express the rounded-off figure of 1000 megabytes.

Glossary. A dictionary of abbreviations offered by many high-end word processors. For example, you might specify that the abbreviation *DOI* stands for *The Declaration of Independence*. Then whenever you type *DOI*, the words *The Declaration of Independence* appear on your page, eliminating the drudgery of entering lengthy phrases repeatedly and eliminating the possibility of making a mistake.

Go Away box. *See* Close box.

Gray-scale monitor. A monitor which displays true grays, as opposed to monochrome monitors that display grays as clusters of black and white pixels. Only the Mac II series and the SE/30 are capable of driving gray-scale monitors.

Hanging indent. A text-formatting device that allows a number or symbol to call attention to a paragraph by hanging out in the left margin. The first-line indent marker for the paragraph is positioned roughly ¼ inch to the left of the left indent marker, and a tab stop is positioned coincident with the left indent marker.

Hard disk. A device containing several magnetically coated platters used to hold electronic information. Hard disks generally store larger quantitie of information than floppy disks because they contain multiple platters and use more exacting storage media and mechanics. Most Mac hard disks connect to the Macintosh via an SCSI interface. *See also* Floppy disk; SCSI.

Hardware. The physical part of a computer system, including the computer, monitor, modem, etc. Software, in contrast, is the electronic part of a computer system.

Header. *See* PostScript dictionary.

HFS (Hierarchical Filing System). A method of storing files on disk that allows folder boundaries to be recognized by all software; any file or folder can be inside of another folder. Two files with the same name can be on the same disk as long as they are not in the same folder, and folders appear in all Standard File dialog boxes. HFS is used by default on all current disks. *See also* MFS.

Hierarchical Filing System. *See* HFS.

High-level formatting. *See* Initialize.

High-profile SIMM. A type of SIMM that uses larger chips, which make the SIMM board taller than normal. These SIMMs can be used in the Mac II, IIx, and IIcx without any problems, but may make it impossible to use other internal add-ons when used in a compact Mac. *See also* SIMM.

Highlight. To select an object or element, usually by clicking or dragging it with the mouse. The highlighted object or element is visually distinguished; usually, the color of its pixels is reversed (black becomes white, white becomes black).

HyperCard. A popular application created by Apple that allows storage, retrieval, and organization of text and bit-mapped graphics. Editable text is stored in fields. Fields are combined with graphics on individual *cards*, like cards in a deck or pages in a book. Buttons are also included with cards, allowing a user to perform certain actions, such as going to a different card or displaying a field. Using buttons, a programmer can link any piece of information to another. And finally, cards are collected into files called *stacks*. HyperCard has been bundled with every Macintosh since August, 1987.

Hypertext. A term coined by Ted Nelson in his visionary 1973 title *Computer Lib,* representing his idea of a new form of communication exclusive to computers. Theoretically, any word of text appearing on a screen can be linked to thousands of words in other volumes of text in an intuitive and editable structure, as if each word were its own living card catalog. Although no application running on a personal computer provides even a fraction of the features or power required to embody hypertext in its fullest sense, Guide and ArchiText come closest on the Mac, with HyperCard running a distant third. In Guide, for example, you may identify a single word as one of four kinds of buttons, each of which access related information in a different manner when double-clicked by the user.

I-beam. The text-editing cursor that consists of a vertical bar with a small horizontal bar crossing it in its lower half. The I-beam is used to set the insertion point or to highlight text for editing. *See also* Insertion point.

Icon. Originally a graphic representation of a document, application, folder directory, or disk at the Finder level. Icons now also serve as graphic representations of tools, functions, commands, and even ideas. Icons are generally activated when the user clicks on them. Clicking on a Finder icon selects it, allowing you to move the icon to a new location or to open the file, folder, or disk that the icon represents. Clicking on a tool icon in an application changes your cursor to that tool, allowing you to perform manipulations or create new elements with the tool.

Icon mask. A bit-mapped image that distinguishes an icon from its background. Usually an icon mask is either a solid outline of the icon or a reverse image of the icon.

Image backup. *See* Mirror-image backup.

ImageWriter font. A font consisting of only a screen-font file (without a corresponding printer-font file). These fonts are always printed at a resolution of 72 dots per inch, regardless of the printer used to print them. *See also* Font; Laser font; Printer font; Screen font.

Impact printer. *See* Dot-matrix printer.

Incremental backup. A method of backing up data in which only those files that have been modified since the last time the drive was backed up are copied to the backup medium. Files that are backed up are never erased, and the size of the backup medium must continue to grow each time a backup is performed.

Information service. A larger commercial bulletin-board system that offers a wide range of on-line data. Examples include CompuServe and Genie, which provide information on hundreds of different topics. *See also* Bulletin board.

Init (abbreviation of *initialization program*). A small utility software program that is run automatically on startup if it is in the System folder. Inits almost always add basic features to the System Software. Many inits are also cdevs, and their options can be accessed in the Control Panel. *See also* Cdev; Init manager.

Init manager. A software utility, usually itself an init, that controls the operation of all inits in the System folder. Most init managers allow the user to select which inits will be run, and sometimes the order in which they are loaded.

Initialize. To clear the directory on a floppy or hard disk so that files can be written in any sector on the disk (except those used by the directory itself). New disks must be both formatted and initialized before they can be used, and any disk can be reinitialized at any time. When a hard drive is initialized, the data on the disk before the initialization is not erased, but the directory is cleared so the disk appears to contain no information. Special utilities can retrieve files from hard disks that have been initialized. On floppy disks, initialization also formats the disk, so existing information is actually erased and cannot be retrieved. *See also* Formatting.

Ink-jet printer. A type of printer that creates characters or images by squirting tiny drops of ink onto paper. *See also* Dot-matrix printer.

Insertion point. The location at which text will be added when entered from the keyboard, marked by a flashing vertical bar. The insertion point can be reset using the mouse and the I-beam cursor, or using the keyboard's arrow keys. *See also* I-beam.

Internal modem. A modem that is installed inside the computer, usually as an add-on board inserted in an expansion slot. *See also* Expansion slot.

Invisible file. A file whose icon does not appear at the Finder, and whose name does not appear in most scrolling file listings. The user can make files invisible, or visible again, by setting a special file attribute using a utility like Symantec Tools or Disktop.

Kerning. The process of adjusting the space between two characters of type to enhance its visual effect. Characters are generally set apart by a standard letter spacing defined by the screen font. If two letters are jammed too close together or, more commonly, spread too far apart, you may kern them to a more suitable spacing. A pair of letters for which special kerning information is included in the screen font is known as a *kerning pair*. Kerning is usually measured in fractions of an em space (a character that is as wide as the current type size is tall).

Keyboard equivalent. A combination of keys that, when pressed, causes some command to be executed as though it were selected from a menu or a dialog box.

Keyboard macro. *See* Macro.

Kilobyte (kbyte, Kbyte, or K). A unit of measure equal to 1,024 bytes, often used as the standard unit of measure for disk space or RAM. 1K can hold slightly less than one typewritten page of data.

Laser font. A Macintosh font that consists of a screen font and a corresponding printer font containing a PostScript-language definition for each character in the font. These fonts can be printed on any PostScript printer at any resolution. *See also* Font; Printer font; Screen font.

Laser printer. A printer that creates images by using a laser beam to initiate a xerographic printing process.

Launch. To start a software application, by double-clicking on it, using an application-launching utility, or highlighting and opening it via the OPEN command in the Finder.

Leading. The amount of space between the baseline of one line of type and the baseline of the next, normally measured in points; also known as *line spacing*. Solid leading is line spacing identical to the current type size. Auto-leading is the "ideal" line spacing, typically 120 percent of the current type size.

Lisa. An Apple Computer product that preceded the Macintosh and introduced the Mac's graphic interface. Lisas used different operating-system software than the Macintosh, but with software called MacWorks, it is possible to run Macintosh software on Lisa computers.

Local area network (LAN). A hardware and software connection among computers and some peripherals that allows these devices to communicate. Usually LANs are set up so that computer users can access a centralized hard disk, share each other's hard disks, and/or share printers and modems. Most Mac LANs use AppleTalk and LocalTalk hardware, along with software like TOPS or AppleShare.

LocalTalk. The cables and connectors sold by Apple for connecting Macintoshes using the AppleTalk network hardware built into each Macintosh. These used to be called AppleTalk cables and connectors, but now *AppleTalk* refers only to the network protocol and the built-in connectors.

Logic board. The primary circuit board in a computer, holding most of the chips responsible for the computer's computing power, and connectors for all other hardware and peripherals.

Logical volume. A volume that is software-defined, such as one created by disk-partitioning software. Logical volumes contrast with physical volumes, which are hard drives or floppy disks. Logical volumes are treated just like physical volumes by most (but not all) software. *See also* Disk partitioning; Volume.

Lookup field. A database field that is programmed to display the same information contained in a specified field in another database file.

Low-level formatting. *See* Formatting.

Low-profile SIMM. A type of SIMM that uses small chips so that it is not very tall. Low-profile SIMMs must be used in most Mac Plus, SE, and SE/30 RAM upgrades. *See also* High-profile SIMM; RAM; SIMM.

MacBinary. A file-transfer protocol, used along with another transfer protocol such as XMODEM, that ensures the proper transfer of Macintosh files. MacBinary is often not supported by non-Macintosh computers.

Macintosh Filing System. *See* MFS.

Macintosh XL. *See* Lisa.

Macro. A user-defined shortcut that allows you to record one or more actions (pressed keys, chosen commands, mouse clicks, etc.) and assign them to any keyboard equivalent you choose.

Manual font downloading. The process of transferring a printer-font file into the RAM of a PostScript printer so that the characters of the font can be printed at maximum resolution. Printer fonts can be downloaded with a number of utilities, including Adobe Font Downloader and Send PS. *See also* Automatic font downloading; Printer font; Screen font.

Marquee. A box formed by moving lines, created by clicking and dragging the mouse in certain situations. Items enclosed in the marquee usually become selected when the mouse button is released.

Master directory block. Block number 2 on an HFS floppy disk, containing basic information about the files on the disk. This block is read into RAM when the disk is first inserted.

Math coprocessor. *See* Numeric coprocessor.

MAUG (Micronetworked Apple User's Group). A set of forums on the CompuServe information service that offer information and files for Apple computers.

Mbps. *See* Megabits per second.

Megabits per second (Mbps). Millions of bits per second—a measure of data-transfer speed.

Megabyte (Mb). A unit of measure equal to 1,024 kilobytes.

Memory. *See* RAM.

Menu. A list of commands that appear when the mouse cursor is positioned on the menu title and the mouse button is held down. You choose a command in the menu by dragging down until the command is highlighted and then releasing the mouse button.

Menu Bar. The strip across the top of the screen that contains the menu titles.

MFS (Macintosh Filing System). A method of storing files on disk in which folder boundaries are only recognized by the Finder. Using MFS, two files with the same name cannot be on the same disk, even in different folders, because all files are treated as one group. Under MFS, folders are not seen in Standard File dialog boxes. MFS was used primarily before System Software 4.1, and is now used only in special cases. *See also* HFS.

Microfloppy. A 3.5" floppy disk. This name distinguishes 3.5" floppy disks from 5.25" floppy disks. *See also* Floppy disk; Minifloppy.

Minifloppy. A 5.25" floppy disk. This name distinguishes 5.25" floppy disks from 3.5" floppy disks. *See also* Floppy disk; Microfloppy.

Mirror-image backup. A method of backing up data in which the backup medium becomes an exact duplicate of the source disk—every file is backed up. Files that were on the backup medium before the image backup are completely replaced by the newer files.

Modem. A device that converts outgoing digital signals into sound frequencies, and incoming sound frequencies into digital signals. With a modem attached to your computer, you can connect to almost any other computer that is also equipped with a modem and transfer files between them, provided that compatible telecommunications software is used on both machines.

Modial dialog box. A dialog box that makes it impossible to click anywhere else on the screen except in it or on its buttons. DA's are inaccessible when a modial dialog box is being displayed. Modial dialog boxes must be closed before any other action can occur. *See also* Dialog box.

Modular Mac. A Macintosh using the larger case that is separate from the monitor, such as the Mac II, IIx, and IIcx.

Moiré pattern. The pattern created by the juxtaposition of two repetitive graphic structures, such as overlaying halftone screens or different resolutions. This unfortunate effect generally occurs when printing a bit map whose resolution conflicts with that of the printer, or when printing color separations that conflict with each other.

Motherboard. *See* Logic board.

Mount. To establish a logical connection between a disk or drive and the computer. When a disk or drive is mounted, the computer can access it. A disk can be mounted but physically disconnected from the computer, or physically connected but not logically mounted.

Mouse. A hand-operated pointing device that translates its movement along a flat surface into corresponding movement on the computer screen. The effect of the movement on the screen is determined by the software that is currently being run. *See also* Mouse button.

Mouse button. A button on the mouse that is pressed to initiate some action. The action initiated by the mouse is controlled by the software currently being run.

MUG (Macintosh User Group). *See* User group.

MultiFinder. A System Software file that makes it possible to run multiple applications simultaneously. The number of separate applications that can be run depends on the amount of RAM installed in the computer. If multiple applications are being run, the one that is currently active is called the foreground application, and the others are called background applications. *See also* Background processing; Foreground processing.

Multitasking. The process by which a computer performs several tasks at one time, usually by switching between discrete tasks very quickly, giving the appearance of continuously working on each one. *See also* Background application; Foreground application.

Nanosecond (ns). One billionth of a second (0.000000001 second).

Native file format. The file format in which an application normally stores its data files. Some native file formats are common to applications, but others are unique to a single one. *See also* File formats; File type.

Nesting. The layering that occurs when folders are placed inside of other folders, usually further defined by the number of levels deep that the folders are placed. (A folder inside of a folder inside of another folder is nested three levels deep.)

Network. A hardware and software connection between multiple computers and peripherals. Usually, any device on a network can communicate with any other device on the network. *See also* Bridge; Gateway; Local area network.

Node. A device on a network. *See also* Network.

NuBus. The bus used in the Mac II, IIx, and IIcx. NuBus allows expansion cards to communicate at very high speeds. *See also* Bus; Expansion card.

Null-modem cable. A cable that links two computers in place of a modem connection.

Numeric coprocessor. A chip that specializes in very fast mathematical calculations, increasing the speed of these calculations, which are normally handled by the CPU. A numeric coprocessor is included on the Macintosh II, IIx, IIcx, and SE/30, and can be added to older Macs on accelerator boards.

Object-oriented graphic. A graphic made up of mathematically defined lines and shapes. An object-oriented graphics application allows you to select and manipulate elements within your drawing as though they were loose materials in a collage. MacDraw and Adobe Illustrator are examples of applications that produce object-oriented graphics.

On-line service. *See* Information service.

Open. To launch an application, to display a window that makes a folder's contents visible, or to access a document so that it can be used or edited in an application. *See also* Launching.

Open architecture. A computer design that allows for the easy expansion of the system with add-on cards.

Operating system. The software that manages the interaction of the computer hardware with other computer software, hardware peripherals, and the computer user. The Macintosh also has a specific software component called the Operating System, which resides on ROM chips on the logic board and provides basic features that interface the Mac hardware with other software.

Optical disc. A storage medium that digitally represents information using laser beams to read or write surface deformations. Optical disks can hold large quantities of information, and are available in read-only or read/write format.

Option box. A type of dialog-box option, visible as a small box, in which characters are entered from the keyboard. A flashing insertion point appears inside the box when the option is selected for text entry. *See also* Dialog box; Options.

OPTION key. A special Macintosh key that, like the SHIFT key, provides access to alternate keyboard combinations, usually to produce nonstandard characters or invoke software commands.

Options. Commands found in dialog boxes that present the user some alternatives to choose between. Radio buttons, check boxes, option boxes, and pop-up menus are all types of options. *See also* Check box; Dialog box; Option box; Radio button.

Outline font. A new type of font to be released after System Software 7.0, including both a screen-font file and an outline-font file. The outline-font file will contain mathematical definitions of each character in the font and allow printers that can understand outline fonts to print them at high resolution. Sometimes this term is used as a synonym for laser font. *See also* Font; Laser Font; Screen font.

Parallel port. An electrical connection found on many computers, but not on the Macintosh, that transmits eight or more bits of information simultaneously in one direction. Also know as a Centronics parallel port or Centronics port.

Parity bit. An extra bit tagged onto the end of a character or other unit of data, whose value is used to check for errors in the data. In computer communication, for example, "even parity" means that if the total number of ls in a byte is even, then the parity bit is set to l; if the number is odd, the bit is set to 0. If both sending and receiving devices come up with the same value after independently computing parity, the character is correct.

Partition. A logical subdivision of a hard disk. Partitions act as separate disks, providing an additional tool for hard-drive organization. Some partitioning software offers password protection for partitions. There are two types of partitions, SCSI partitions and File System partitions. *See also* File System partition; SCSI partition.

Paste. To add a copy of the Clipboard's contents to the current document or file. Text is usually pasted at the location of the insertion point.

PD software. *See* Public-domain software.

PDS. *See* Processor Direct Slot.

Phosphor. The material that coats the inside of a computer screen, emitting visible light when struck by the monitor's electron beam.

Pica. A unit of measurement equal to almost exactly ⅙ inch.

PICT. Apple's preferred saving format for bit-mapped and object-oriented images. The PICT format is supported by most desktop publishing and graphics applications on the Mac, but the method of support is open to wide interpretation. The standard PICT format supports eight colors: black, white, blue, red, green, cyan, magenta, and yellow. An upgraded PICT format, known widely as PICT2, supports as many colors as your monitor will display.

Pixel. The smallest element in a computer-produced image. Text and pictures created on a monitor or printed by a laser printer or modern typesetter (which uses a laser to develop film) are the result of thousands or even millions of tiny square dots packed together. The smaller and more abundant these dots, or pixels, the better the dots blend together, fooling your eye into perceiving freehand lines and smooth type. Depending on the sophistication of your monitor, a screen pixel can display a wide array of shades and colors, though Macintosh monitors only support 72 pixels per linear inch. Pixels on a printed page, while generally more numerous and densely packed than those of a monitor, can only display a single color—usually black. Even high-end color printers must separate colors into their cyan, magenta, yellow, and black components, adding each layer of color in a separate pass.

Platter. A disk used in a floppy disk or hard drive. Each side of a platter is called a cylinder. *See also* Cylinder; Sector; Track.

Point. A unit of measurement equal to ¹⁄₁₂ pica or almost exactly ¹⁄₇₂ inch. The screen pixel of a Macintosh monitor measures 1 point square.

Pointer. A generic name referring to either the current cursor, or the arrow cursor used in many Mac applications and the Finder. The arrow cursor is used to select menu commands, icons, and other objects.

Pop-up menu. A menu that appears in any place other than a menu bar. Usually pop-up menus are used in dialog boxes and indicated by titles contained in drop-shadow boxes. Microsoft software that contains pop-up menus in dialog boxes sometimes includes a downward-pointing arrowhead to indicate pop-up menu titles.

Port. A connection through which data is exported and imported. The specifications of the port determine what type of information it can carry. Each Macintosh includes a number of different ports, including the modem, printer, and ADB ports; in addition, every model after and including the Plus includes a SCSI port.

Portrait mode. A printing option that orients a page so that it is taller than it is wide, usually found as an option in the Page Setup dialog box.

PostScript. A computer language that was developed specifically to allow elements on printed pages to be described easily and efficiently. Using the LaserWriter driver, Macintosh software creates PostScript-language descriptions of pages; the pages can then be sent to a printer containing a PostScript-language interpreter, which executes the PostScript commands and prints the page.

PostScript dictionary. A file containing definitions of terms that are used in other PostScript files. A PostScript dictionary is sent to the PostScript printer before all files using terms contained in the dictionary so that they will be understood when included as part of the file. The LaserPrep file and the Aldus Prep file are PostScript dictionaries.

PostScript font. A special type of font that includes a printer-font file allowing the font to be printed on PostScript printers at their maximum resolution. *See also* Printer font; Screen font.

PRAM (contraction of *parameter RAM*). A small portion of the MAC's RAM that stores user-defined preferences like the startup volume and RAM cache setting.

Print spooling. *See* Background printing.

Printer driver. A file that enables an application to convert a document so that it can be printed on a specific type of printer. Printer drivers must be kept in the System folder, and are selected using the Chooser DA.

Printer font. A file that provides a PostScript printer with the mathematical definitions of each character used in the corresponding screen-font file of a PostScript font. Printer-font files can be manually or automatically downloaded to PostScript printers. *See also* Automatic font downloading; Manual font downloading; Screen font.

Printer port. The port that connects the Macintosh to a printer or to an AppleTalk network. The Mac's printer port uses the RS-422 serial communications protocol.

Printer resource. *See* Printer driver.

Processor Direct Slot (PDS). The expansion slot included on the SE and SE/30. These two slots are not compatible however, and add-on cards must be designed specifically for one or the other. *See also* Expansion card; Expansion slot.

Program. *See* Application.

Programmer's switch. A plastic part included with every Macintosh. The programmer's switch has two buttons; the front button is the Reset button, which restarts the Mac, and the rear button is the Interrupt button, which is used along with various programming utilities.

Public-domain software (PD software). Software to which the author retains no rights. Public-domain software can be exchanged freely, and is available through bulletin boards and user groups. *See also* Freeware; Shareware.

Pull-down menu. A command menu that appears only when the mouse button is held down while the cursor is positioned over the menu title. Menus contain commands. *See also* Command; Menu.

QuickDraw. The part of the Macintosh operating-system software that defines graphic images so that they can be displayed on screen or printed on non-PostScript printers.

Radio button. A small round button, usually found in dialog boxes, that is used to turn an option on or off, and to indicate the current status of that option. Radio buttons appear empty when turned off, and filled when turned on. Radio buttons usually appear in sets, and only one radio button in a set can be turned on at one time.

RAM (random-access memory). The chips that electronically store information that is being used by the CPU; also known as *memory*. Both software and data files are transferred from disk into RAM when they are being used. Information in RAM must be written back to disk or it will be lost when the computer is restarted or the power is turned off. The more RAM installed in a computer, the more information can be manipulated at one time. *See also* SIMM.

RAM cache (pronounced *cash*). An area of RAM that holds recently accessed data so that it is readily available should it be needed again. The larger the RAM cache, the better the chance that it will contain data that is needed. If the required data is not available from the RAM cache, it must be read from the disk.

RAM disk. A disk created in RAM that acts like a normal floppy or hard disk, except for its extremely fast operation, which is due to the complete lack of moving parts. RAM disks are created with special utility software.

Read Me file. A file of documents packaged with some software and hardware to provide information that was not included in the product manual. Sometimes these files are in the format of a popular word processor, like MacWrite or Microsoft Word, and other times they require a specific application like TeachText to be read and printed.

Read-only memory (ROM). Chips containing information that cannot be changed. The information from these chips is read by the computer, but new information cannot be stored on these chips. Large portions of the Mac's operating system are stored on ROM chips in the Mac, and the term "Mac ROM" is often used to refer to these specific ROM chips.

Reboot. To restart the computer, either by using the Finder's RESTART command, pressing the Reset button on the programmer's switch, or turning the power off and then on again. The Finder's RESTART command should be used in most cases; turning the power off and then on again should be avoided when possible.

ResEdit (Resource Editor). An application that is used to modify parts of other Macintosh applications. ResEdit is a freeware program from Apple Computer that can be obtained on many bulletin boards, from user groups, or from the Apple Programmers and Developers Association.

Resolution. The number of pixels in a linear inch on a computer screen or on a page produced by a printer. Macintosh-compatible monitors display 72 pixels in an inch. Most laser printers, including Apple's LaserWriter, print 300 pixels per inch. Therefore, the two devices have resolutions of 72 dpi (dots per inch) and 300 dpi, respectively.

Resource fork. A portion of Macintosh files that contains parts of applications, such as menus, fonts, and icons. Not every Macintosh file has a resource fork, and no non-Macintosh computer file has a resource fork. *See also* Data fork; ResEdit.

Restore. To return backup copies of files to their source. Usually files are restored only when the original copies have been lost or damaged.

ROM. *See* Read-only memory.

Root directory. The top level of the folder hierarchy on any disk. Files and folders are in the root directory if they are not inside any other folders.

RS-422. The Electronic Industries Association specification that defines the serial ports (modem port and printer port) on the Macintosh.

Run. *See* Launch.

Sampling rate. The number of times per second that a sound is tested when being digitized. The higher the sampling rate, the more accurate the digitization. Common sampling rates are 22 kHz (22,000 times per second), 11 kHz, 7 kHz, and 5 kHz.

Scrapbook. An Apple-supplied DA that can hold text or graphic images. The Scrapbook can have any number of pages, each of which contains one text block or image. Elements are moved to and from the Scrapbook via the Clipboard and the CUT, COPY, and PASTE commands. *See also* Clipboard.

Screen capture. *See* Screen dump.

Screen dump. A picture of the current screen image, captured to a disk file or printed on paper. You can create a Macintosh screen dump by pressing COMMAND-SHIFT-3 or by using one of several screen-dump utilities like Capture or SnapJot.

Screen font. A font file that provides Macintosh applications and the System Software with the characters in one typeface for use on the screen and with dot-matrix printers. Screen-font files are manipulated with the Font/ DA Mover, and may be loaded into the System file directly or used with utilities including Suitcase and MasterJuggler. *See also* Font; Printer font.

Scroll. To move through a window or listing so that new sections of the file or list become visible. On the Mac, scrolling is almost always controlled by a scroll bar, which presents a scroll box and up and down arrows that are used to determine the position of the scrolling field. *See also* Scroll bar.

Scroll arrow. *See* Scroll bar.

Scroll bar. A horizontal or vertical bar used to control the scrolling of a window or listing. A *scroll box* marks the relative position of the current display in the entire file or list, and you can reset the display by clicking on one of the scroll arrows, by dragging the scroll box, or by clicking in the dimmed area to either side of the scroll box.

Scroll box. *See* Scroll Bar.

SCSI (Small Computer System Interface). A high-speed communications port and protocol supported by the Mac Plus, II, IIx, IIcx, SE, and SE/30. Up to six SCSI (pronounced "scuzzy") devices can be attached to the Mac via its SCSI port by means of daisy-chaining. *See also* Daisy chain; SCSI ID number.

SCSI bus. Another name for the SCSI port and communications protocol. *See also* SCSI.

SCSI ID number. The ID number assigned to a SCSI device for purposes of electronic identification. SCSI ID numbers range from 0 to 7, with 7 always taken by the Macintosh itself. SCSI ID numbers are preset by the manufacturer of a SCSI device, but they can usually be changed by a hardware switch or, sometimes, a software utility. Each SCSI device connected to a Macintosh must have a unique SCSI ID number.

SCSI partition. A hard-drive partition that is defined in the SCSI partition table on a SCSI hard drive. Each partition maintains its own directory acting as a totally independent drive. *See also* Partition.

SCSI terminators. Electronic devices that are placed at each end of a SCSI daisy-chain to prevent electronic signals from echoing at the end of the chain. Some SCSI devices have built-in SCSI terminators that engage automatically when they are needed, but other devices require external SCSI terminators that plug into the device's SCSI connector.

Sector. A subdivision of a single track on a floppy or hard disk. Sectors are the smallest unit of disk space that can be used, representing 512 bytes (0.5K).

Sector interleave factor. The order in which sectors on one track of a hard disk are read and written. A 1:1 interleave reads every sector, 2:1 reads every other sector, 3:1 reads every third sector. In most cases the Mac II, IIx, IIcx, and SE/30 use a 1:1 interleave, the Mac SE uses a 2:1 interleave, and older Macs use a 3:1 interleave. The interleave factor is determined when the drive is formatted.

Select. To choose an icon, tool, or some amount of text, usually to designate what will be affected by the next command chosen. When selected, text or graphic elements become highlighted. *See also* Highlight.

Selection. The currently highlighted text or graphic elements, which will be affected by the next command chosen.

Selection rectangle. *See* Marquee.

Serial port. A generic name for the modem and printer ports on the Macintosh. Mac serial ports follow the RS-422 specifications, transferring data one bit at a time. *See also* Modem port; Printer port; RS-422.

Server. A device that can be shared by all network users. Examples include printer servers and file servers.

Shareware. Software that is freely distributed under the condition that if you keep it for longer than some specified period of time, a fee will be paid to its author. *See also* Freeware; Public-domain software.

SHIFT key. A key on all Mac keyboards that is pressed to generate uppercase letters and special symbols from the standard alphanumeric keys, and used in conjunction with other special keys to invoke commands from the keyboard.

Side bearings. The amount of letter spacing assigned to the left and right sides of a character of type. This information is contained in the screen font of a PostScript typeface; the user may override it for any two letters by kerning them closer together or farther apart.

SIMM (Single In-line Memory Module). A small board containing RAM chips used to add RAM to your Mac. SIMMs usually contain either 256K or 1Mb of RAM. Some SIMMs are high-profile, using larger RAM chips, and others are low-profile, using smaller RAM chips.

68000 family. The group of CPU chips used in Macintosh computers. The chips in the family share a number of characteristics; chips with higher numbers generally include a superset of the commands supported by chips with lower numbers, allowing them to run all software written for the lower-numbered chips.

Size box. A box in the bottom-right corner of many windows that resizes the window when dragged.

Slot. *See* Expansion slot.

Software. Instructions that control the operation of the CPU and thereby all other hardware components of a computer. Software programs generally fall into one of three categories: operating-system software that serves to control the computer or help it utilize other software; applications that create, manage, or manipulate data; or utility programs that perform housekeeping or other miscellaneous functions.

Spooling. *See* Background printing.

Standard File Close. A dialog box commonly presented when a SAVE AS command is chosen. Provided by the System Software, a Standard File Close dialog presents a scrolling file listing, a file-name option box, and OPEN, DRIVE, and CANCEL buttons.

Standard File Open. A dialog box commonly presented when an OPEN command is chosen. Provided by the System Software, a Standard File Open dialog presents a scrolling file listing and OPEN, DRIVE, and CANCEL buttons.

Startup disk. A disk containing any matching System file, Finder, and boot blocks that can be used to start up the Macintosh and run an initial application (usually the Finder). The System file on the startup disk provides the Macintosh with its fonts and DA's. Via a process known as switch-launching, another disk can become the current startup disk while the Macintosh is running. *See also* Switch-launching.

Startup document. *See* Init.

Startup-screen format. A file format used by the Macintosh to display a graphic at startup. A file named StartupScreen must be in this format and in the System folder in order to be displayed.

Stop bit. A bit that is added to the end of each character in asynchronous communications.

Storage. *See* Disk.

Style. *See* Style sheet; Type style.

Style sheet. A system of assigning formatting commands to an entire paragraph at once. Generally, one style sheet is defined for headlines, another for body copy, and so on. Any paragraph formatted using a style sheet is linked to that style sheet, so you can achieve global style changes by editing a style sheet rather than editing individual blocks of text.

Suitcase. An icon used by font and desk-accessory files. These files can be manipulated with the Font/DA Mover. *See also* DA suitcase; Font/DA Mover; Font suitcase.

Switcher. An old Apple utility that allowed multiple programs to run simultaneously. Switcher is incompatible with current versions of the System Software, but its features are superseded by MultiFinder.

Switch-launching. The process of making a System file and Finder the currently used System file and Finder. In order to switch-launch, the user must double-click the Finder icon while holding down the COMMAND and OPTION keys, hold down the OPTION key while running an application on the disk containing the System file and Finder to be made current, or run an application that has its Switchlaunch bit set on.

Synchronous communication. A communications protocol in which large numbers of characters are sent between timing signals. This is in contrast to the single character sent between stop and start signals in asynchronous communication. *See also* Asynchronous communication.

Sysop. *See* System Operator.

System disk. *See* Startup disk.

System error. *See* Crash.

System file. A Mac file that is a central part of the System Software, providing many often-used features to other software applications that run on the Macintosh. The System file is loaded when the Mac is started, and used almost constantly as the Mac is operating. *See also* Switch-launching; System Software.

System folder. A folder that contains the Finder and the System file, as well as many other files that must be in the same folder as the System file. Technically known as the *blessed folder*, this folder does not have to be named "System folder".

System heap. A part of RAM that holds portions of the System file and inits. The size of the system heap is determined by a setting in the boot blocks of the startup disk, and can be modified using disk editors or a system-heap utility. *See also* Application heap.

System Operator. A person who administers a bulletin-board system. *See also* Bulletin board.

System Software. The collection of operating-system and utility software provided by Apple Computer to operate the Macintosh. A number of different versions of the System Software have been released, and new releases are usually made every 18 months.

Telecommunications. The process of transferring information from one computer to another via a connection made over telephone lines. Modems are needed on both computers to enable them to communicate over the telephone lines. *See also* Modem.

Temporary files. Files created by applications to hold data needed only until the file being used is saved to disk. These files are usually deleted automatically by the application that created them.

Terminating resistors. *See* SCSI terminators.

Terminators. *See* SCSI terminators.

Text file. A file containing only ASCII-defined characters. The text-file format is the most generic file format; files in this format can be used by many applications on many different kinds of computers. *See also* ASCII.

Text runaround. A feature common to most page-layout programs, allowing text to run around an intruding graphic.

Text wrapping. *See* Text runaround.

TIFF (Tagged Image File Format). A high-resolution bit-map file format that can store gray-scale and color information, designed by Aldus Corporation especially for storing scanned images. When printed, the shaded or colored pixels in a TIFF image are halftoned to create an effect similar to a photograph printed in a newspaper.

Title bar. The top frame of any window, usually containing the window's title, and in some cases a Zoom box and Close box. When the window is selected, the title bar contains horizontal lines.

Toolbox. A portion of the software on the Macintosh ROM chips, containing routines by which other software applications communicate with the Macintosh user. Toolbox routines include dialog-box management, font management, and window management. Some software applications also have toolboxes, which are palettes of tools selected with the mouse. *See also* Operating system; Read-only memory.

Track. One of the concentric circles into which each side of a disk is logically divided. Each track is further divided into *sectors*, which are used to hold data. *See also* Platter; Sector.

Trackball. An input device, used in place of a mouse, that controls the cursor with a hand-operated ball that rotates within its base unit. Because the base unit remains stationary, trackballs require less desk space than mice, while offering similar cursor control.

Tracking. A form of letter spacing that varies depending on the current type size. Typically, large type such as a headline looks better when spaced closer together than normal; small type such as body copy is more legible when spread farther apart. Tracking allows you to specify size-dependent letter spacing, increasing the spacing of small type, decreasing that of large type, and leaving moderately sized type unchanged.

Trash can. The Finder icon that looks like a garbage can and is used to hold files that are to be deleted. Files remain in the trash can until the EMPTY TRASH command is executed, the disk containing the files is dismounted, or an application is run.

Type. *See* File type.

Type style. A stylistic variation of a typeface. Some type styles—such as plain, bold, italic, and bold-italic—must be defined as separate printer fonts. These type styles together make up a typeface family. Other type styles—such as underline, outline, shadow, and strikethru—are effects created by software.

Upload. To transfer a file from one's own computer to another computer. Uploading requires that you have a modem connected to your computer and the proper telecommunications software to communicate with the other computer.

User group. A group of people who join together to exchange information about using computers, usually one specific type of computer. Macintosh user groups hold meetings where speakers present new products and other information, maintain bulletin boards, offer access to public-domain and shareware software libraries, and publish printed information. Apple Computer will refer you to a user group in your area if you call 1-800-538-9696, extension 500.

Utility software. Software that provides housekeeping features or assists in the use of computer hardware or other software applications, rather than actually creating or manipulating data. Examples of utility software include file-compression utilities, disk editors, and hard-drive backup programs. *See also* Application; Software.

Video card. An add-on board that is used to interface a particular computer monitor to the computer hardware. The video board determines many of the attributes of the monitor, including the number of colors or gray-scales the monitor can display. *See also* Expansion card.

Video RAM. The section of RAM that holds the image being displayed on the computer display.

Volume. Any physical or logical drive. A volume can be a floppy disk, a hard drive, or a hard-drive partition.

Volume bitmap. A record of all used blocks on a disk. Each block is represented by a bit, which is set on if the block is in use, or off if it is currently unused. The volume bitmap is used to quickly determine which sectors are available for use. *See also* Block; Sector.

Volume directory. *See* Directory.

Volume partition. *See* Partition.

Warm boot. The process of restarting a computer without turning its power off. On the Mac, a warm boot is performed with the Finder's RESTART command or with the Reset button on the programmer's switch. A warm boot is preferable to a cold boot because it puts less strain on the electronic circuitry. *See also* Cold boot.

Window. An area on the screen, defined by distinct borders, that displays information from a file or application. Most windows can be opened, closed, repositioned, and resized.

Worksheet. A spreadsheet document or template. Many independent programmers provide predefined worksheets containing cell relationships and sample data designed to help in the management of a moderate budget or in the accounting for a small business.

WORM (Write Once, Read Many). A type of optical drive to which data can be saved but never erased. Any data written on the drive remains there permanently, and can be read from the drive any number of times. WORM drives usually have very large storage capacity, over 300Mb.

Write-protect tab. The small plastic tab located in the upper-right corner of 3.5" floppy disks. Sliding the tab so that you can see through the hole in the disk locks the disk so that data cannot be written to it, and files cannot be erased from it. Sliding the tab to cover the hole unlocks the disk so that data can be written to it and files can be erased from it.

Zone. An individual AppleTalk network that is connected to other AppleTalk networks via bridges. Each zone has a name that distinguishes it from the other AppleTalk networks that are connected. *See also* Bridge.

Zoom box. A box in the upper-right corner of a window, in the title bar, that toggles the size of a window between its maximum size and its last non-maximum size. *See also* Title bar; Window.

Index

M

The Encyclopedia Macintosh Disks

Two Great Offers!

- ◆ Encyclopedia Macintosh: The Stack
- ◆ The Utility Disk Set

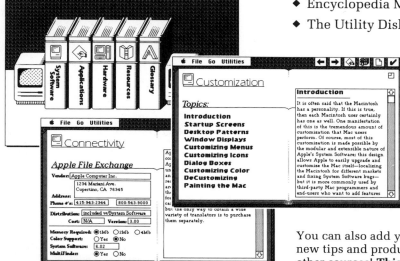

The Stack

The complete text of *Encyclopedia Macintosh*, including all graphics, menus, and keyboard charts in an easy-to-use HyperCard stack! **Almost 5 megabytes of information.** Quickly find the exact information you need by browsing the stack or by using one of the custom search commands.

You can also add your own information, including new tips and product reviews that you gather from other sources! **This stack will become your own custom database of Macintosh information!** And our periodic stack updates will keep you informed of the latest tips, tricks, and important software.

The Utility Disk Set

A 4-disk set containing the best noncommercial software available. These disks include most of the utilities discussed in *Encyclopedia Macintosh!*

Contains **more than 50 great programs and utilities**, including: Color Finder, Earth, Layout, Locate, Lockout, Moiré, MultiSet, SoundPlay, Stuffit!, Init Manager, Fkey Manager, Virus Rx, and the EncloMac font used for special characters (⌘, ⌥, ⇧, ⋀, ⌁, ⌫, etc.) throughout this book.

To order stack or utility disks, fill out this coupon and mail it to:

Heizer Software, PO Box 232019, Dept. 210, Pleasant Hill, CA 94523

☐ **Encyclopedia Macintosh: The Stack**
  product no. 30320—$50.00

☐ **The Utility Disk Set**
  product no. 30321—$20.00

Name _____

Address _____

_____

Phone _____

Method of payment:

☐ Check *(payable in US dollars to Heizer Software)*

☐ Credit card *(Visa, MasterCard, & American Express accepted)*

_____ _____
Card number   Expiration date

_____
Signature (orders cannot be processed without a valid signature)

CA residents add 7% sales tax; all customers add $3.00 shipping and handling.

Or save 25¢ and call Heizer Software toll-free at **1-800-888-7667,** EXT **210**

To ensure accurate and prompt delivery, be sure to request items by both name and product number.

This offer is made by PRI, Inc. in cooperation with Heizer Software. Heizer Software warrants all disks for 90 days. SYBEX is not affiliated with Heizer Software and assumes no responsibility for any defect in the disks or programs.

SYBEX ®

TO JOIN THE SYBEX MAILING LIST OR ORDER BOOKS
PLEASE COMPLETE THIS FORM

NAME _____ COMPANY _____

STREET _____ CITY _____

STATE _____ ZIP _____

☐ PLEASE MAIL ME MORE INFORMATION ABOUT **SYBEX** TITLES

ORDER FORM (There is no obligation to order)

PLEASE SEND ME THE FOLLOWING:

TITLE	QTY	PRICE
_____	____	____
_____	____	____
_____	____	____
_____	____	____

TOTAL BOOK ORDER ____ $____

CUSTOMER SIGNATURE _____

SHIPPING AND HANDLING PLEASE ADD $2.00 PER BOOK VIA UPS ____

FOR OVERSEAS SURFACE ADD $5.25 PER BOOK PLUS $4.40 REGISTRATION FEE ____

FOR OVERSEAS AIRMAIL ADD $18.25 PER BOOK PLUS $4.40 REGISTRATION FEE ____

CALIFORNIA RESIDENTS PLEASE ADD APPLICABLE SALES TAX ____

TOTAL AMOUNT PAYABLE ____

☐ CHECK ENCLOSED   ☐ VISA
☐ MASTERCARD   ☐ AMERICAN EXPRESS

ACCOUNT NUMBER _____

EXPIR. DATE _____ DAYTIME PHONE _____

CHECK AREA OF COMPUTER INTEREST:

☐ BUSINESS SOFTWARE

☐ TECHNICAL PROGRAMMING

☐ OTHER: _____

THE FACTOR THAT WAS MOST IMPORTANT IN YOUR SELECTION:

☐ THE SYBEX NAME

☐ QUALITY

☐ PRICE

☐ EXTRA FEATURES

☐ COMPREHENSIVENESS

☐ CLEAR WRITING

☐ OTHER _____

OTHER COMPUTER TITLES YOU WOULD LIKE TO SEE IN PRINT:

_____

_____

OCCUPATION

☐ PROGRAMMER   ☐ TEACHER

☐ SENIOR EXECUTIVE   ☐ HOMEMAKER

☐ COMPUTER CONSULTANT   ☐ RETIRED

☐ SUPERVISOR   ☐ STUDENT

☐ MIDDLE MANAGEMENT   ☐ OTHER:

☐ ENGINEER/TECHNICAL

☐ CLERICAL/SERVICE   _____

☐ BUSINESS OWNER/SELF EMPLOYED

CHECK YOUR LEVEL OF COMPUTER USE

☐ NEW TO COMPUTERS

☐ INFREQUENT COMPUTER USER

☐ FREQUENT USER OF ONE SOFTWARE

   PACKAGE:

   NAME _____

☐ FREQUENT USER OF MANY SOFTWARE

   PACKAGES

☐ PROFESSIONAL PROGRAMMER

OTHER COMMENTS:

_____

_____

_____

_____

_____

_____

_____

PLEASE FOLD, SEAL, AND MAIL TO SYBEX

- - - - - - - - - - - - - - - - - - -

SYBEX, INC.
2021 CHALLENGER DR. #100
ALAMEDA, CALIFORNIA USA
                     94501

SEAL

SYBEX Computer Books are different.

Here is why . . .

At SYBEX, each book is designed with you in mind. Every manuscript is carefully selected and supervised by our editors, who are themselves computer experts. We publish the best authors, whose technical expertise is matched by an ability to write clearly and to communicate effectively. Programs are thoroughly tested for accuracy by our technical staff. Our computerized production department goes to great lengths to make sure that each book is well-designed.

In the pursuit of timeliness, SYBEX has achieved many publishing firsts. SYBEX was among the first to integrate personal computers used by authors and staff into the publishing process. SYBEX was the first to publish books on the CP/M operating system, microprocessor interfacing techniques, word processing, and many more topics.

Expertise in computers and dedication to the highest quality product have made SYBEX a world leader in computer book publishing. Translated into fourteen languages, SYBEX books have helped millions of people around the world to get the most from their computers. We hope we have helped you, too.

For a complete catalog of our publications:

SYBEX, Inc. 2021 Challenger Drive, #100, Alameda, CA 94501
Tel: (415) 523-8233/(800) 227-2346   Telex: 336311
Fax: (415) 523-2373

Keyboard Quick Reference

The Mac allows you to access many characters that are not shown on the keyboard. The following list shows the key combination and font required to create some of the most popular of these characters. In this chart, ⇧ represents the SHIFT key and ⬎ represents OPTION. *Standard Character Set* indicates any font that uses Apple's standard keyboard layout, including Times and Helvetica. Keep in mind that this is only a partial listing; see pages 174–184 for a complete alphabetical character list.

A with ring accent	å	Standard Character Set	⬎A
Acute accent	´	Standard Character Set	⬎E*
Apostrophe	'	Standard Character Set	⇧⬎]
Arrow, bidirectional	↔	Symbol Font	⬎E, ⎵
Arrow, down	↓	Symbol Font	⇧⬎0
Arrow, left	←	Symbol Font	⬎U, ⎵
Arrow, right	→	Symbol Font	⇧⬎'
Arrow, up	↑	Symbol Font	⬎=
Box with drop shadow	❏	Zapf Dingbats	0
Bullet	•	Standard Character Set	⬎8
C with cedilla	ç	Standard Character Set	⬎C
Cent	¢	Standard Character Set	⬎4
Check mark	✔	Zapf Dingbats	4
Circumflex diacritic	^	Standard Character Set	⬎I*
Copyright	©	Standard Character Set	⬎G
Dagger	†	Standard Character Set	⬎T
Degree	°	Standard Character Set	⇧⬎8
Diaeresis or umlaut	¨	Standard Character Set	⬎U*
Diesis	‡	Standard Character Set	⇧⬎7
Divide	÷	Standard Character Set	⬎/